VAN GOGH IN
AUVERS-SUR-OISE

Van Gogh in AUVERS-SUR-OISE

HIS FINAL MONTHS

Nienke Bakker, Emmanuel Coquery, Teio Meedendorp and Louis van Tilborgh (eds.)
with essays by Bregje Gerritse, Sara Tas and Wouter van der Veen

CONTENTS

Here we're far enough from Paris for it to be the real countryside, but nevertheless, how changed since Daubigny. But not changed in an unpleasant way, there are many villas and various modern and middle-class dwellings, very jolly, sunny and covered with flowers. That in an almost lush countryside, just at this moment of the development of a new society in the old one, has nothing disagreeable about it; there's a lot of well-being in the air. I see or think I see a calm there à la Puvis de Chavannes, no factories, but beautiful greenery in abundance and in good order.

Letter from Vincent to Theo and Jo,
Auvers-sur-Oise, 25 May 1890

FOREWORD

Vincent van Gogh spent his final two months in Auvers-sur-Oise, near Paris (May–July 1890). The artist's output in this brief period – seventy-four paintings and over fifty drawings – is almost unfathomable, and includes some of his greatest masterpieces. Strangely, the work that Van Gogh produced in Auvers is less well known to the broad public than the sunny landscapes he painted in Arles and Saint-Rémy-de-Provence. The exhibition *Van Gogh in Auvers-sur-Oise. His Final Months*, jointly organized by the Van Gogh Museum and the Musée d'Orsay, aims to right that wrong. And it does so on the occasion of the Van Gogh Museum's fiftieth anniversary.

Van Gogh in Auvers-sur-Oise. His Final Months can be rightly called a 'once in a lifetime' exhibition. It explores the artist's entire time in Auvers, from his arrival in the village, when he set to work in his new environment full of hope and with fresh enthusiasm, through to the last weeks of his life, when he increasingly struggled with his feelings of failure, loneliness and melancholy, yet nevertheless continued to produce powerful and passionate art.

No previous exhibitions about this period have had the scope and aspiration that this one does. In 1954–55, the Musée de l'Orangerie in Paris presented *Van Gogh et les peintres d'Auvers-sur-Oise*. Roughly thirty works from the Auvers period were included in *Van Gogh in Saint-Rémy and Auvers* at the Metropolitan Museum of Art in New York in 1986. The Musée d'Orsay, together with the Metropolitan Museum of Art and the Van Gogh Museum, devoted an extensive exhibition to the collection of Dr Paul Gachet in 1999, which included works by Van Gogh as well as by other artists such as Camille Pissarro and Paul Cézanne. The current exhibition is, however, unprecedented.

An exhibition with the ambition of *Van Gogh in Auvers-sur-Oise. His Final Months* could only have been organized by the Van Gogh Museum and the Musée d'Orsay working together. The collection of the Van Gogh Museum contains nine paintings and over forty drawings from the Auvers period, all of which originate from the estate of the artist and his brother Theo. The Musée d'Orsay houses eight paintings and five drawings, which are part of the collection of Dr Paul Gachet, Van Gogh's physician in Auvers, and which were donated by his children. The remaining works from this period are scattered across museums and private collections all over the world. Remarkably, this exhibition reunites fifty paintings and over thirty works on paper from the Auvers period. Not only will it introduce visitors to this relatively unknown period, it will also provide new insights into the development Van Gogh underwent as an artist during those intensive final two months.

The idea for the exhibition originated at the Van Gogh Museum, where scholars have spent the last ten years conducting extensive research into this ultimate and prolific phase of Vincent van Gogh's career, in which the painter experimented with new directions in colour, brushstrokes, formats and subjects, with a renewed vision. This research, which will be published in the museum's forthcoming collection catalogue of paintings by Van Gogh from Arles, Saint-Rémy-de-Provence and Auvers-sur-Oise, has already informed major exhibitions focusing on his time in Arles and Saint-Rémy: *Van Gogh & Japan* (2017–18), *Van Gogh and the Sunflowers* (2019) and *Van Gogh and the Olive Groves* (2021–22). It was a long-cherished wish of Senior Researchers Louis van Tilborgh and Teio Meedendorp to devote an exhibition to the works created in Auvers. They, together with Senior Curator Nienke Bakker, developed the exhibition concept, which is based on their research undertaken for the earlier projects and for the exhibition and publication *On the Verge of Insanity. Van Gogh and his Illness* (2016). When the partnership with the Musée d'Orsay was embarked upon, Emmanuel Coquery joined the team. The present publication is the result of their exemplary collaboration, and we congratulate them for this important accomplishment. The exhibition was curated by Nienke and Emmanuel, whose immense enthusiasm and effort have made it possible to assemble an exceptional group of works. Bregje Gerritse, Sara Tas and Wouter van der Veen contributed insightful essays to the catalogue.

We are deeply grateful for the immense generosity of the many museums and collectors who have lent their precious works of art to the exhibition. Our particular thanks are due to the Vincent van Gogh Foundation, which owns the vast majority of the Van Gogh Museum's collection and has wholeheartedly supported this ambitious project. The exhibition has received special support from Rosaline Wong and HomeArt. Thanks are also due to the exhibition designers Agence NC and Studio Berry Slok for the Van Gogh Museum and L'Atelier Maciej Fiszer for the Musée d'Orsay, and to Barbara Costermans and Ronny Gobyn at Tijdsbeeld who coordinated and produced this catalogue, designed by Janpieter Chielens and published by Tijdsbeeld, Hazan and Thames & Hudson. This exhibition and publication are the result of the enthusiastic collaboration of many colleagues at our museums, and we thank them for their hard work and unflagging support.

A research project and exhibition such as this is an expensive endeavour, and a special word of thanks should go to the many institutions that made this exhibition and catalogue possible. The Van Gogh Museum owes a particular debt of gratitude to our main partners the Ministry of Education, Culture and Science, VriendenLoterij, ASML and DHL. We are further indebted to our exhibition partners Mondriaan Fund, Blockbusterfonds, Prins Bernhard Cultuurfonds, Zabawas, Van Lanschot Kempen and Hyundai for their generous contributions. Sincere acknowledgement is also due to the Gerda Henkel Stiftung for providing a grant to Associate Curator Sara Tas to research the collection of prints and letters by Dr Gachet at the Van Gogh Museum. The exhibition has been supported by the Dutch government: an indemnity grant has been provided by the Cultural Heritage Agency of the Netherlands on behalf of the Minister of Education, Culture and Science. At the Musée d'Orsay, we extend our warmest thanks to Mazars, Société Générale and UGGC Avocats, whose decisive support has enabled this landmark exhibition.

Emilie E.S. Gordenker
Director of the Van Gogh Museum, Amsterdam

Christophe Leribault
President of the Musée d'Orsay and
the Musée de l'Orangerie, Paris

LIST OF LENDERS

AUSTRIA

Vienna, Belvedere Museum

FINLAND

Helsinki, Finnish National Gallery, Ateneum Art Museum

FRANCE

Lille, Palais des Beaux-Arts
Paris, Bibliothèque Nationale de France
Paris, Musée d'art et d'histoire de l'Hôpital Sainte-Anne
Paris, Musée d'histoire de la médecine
Paris, Musée d'Orsay
Pontoise, Archives départementales du Val-d'Oise

NETHERLANDS

Amsterdam, Van Gogh Museum (Vincent van Gogh Foundation)
Otterlo, Kröller-Müller Museum
The Hague, Kunstmuseum Den Haag

SWEDEN

Stockholm, Nationalmuseum

SWITZERLAND

Geneva, Musée d'art et d'histoire
Riehen/Basel, Fondation Beyeler
Rudolf Staechelin Collection
Zurich, Stiftung Sammlung E.G. Bührle

UNITED KINGDOM

Cardiff, Amgueddfa Cymru – National Museum Wales
London, Tate

UNITED STATES

Boston, Museum of Fine Arts
The Art Institute of Chicago
Cincinnati Art Museum
The Cleveland Museum of Art
Dallas Museum of Art
Detroit Institute of Arts
Providence, Museum of Art, Rhode Island School of Design
Saint Louis Art Museum
San Antonio, McNay Art Museum
Toledo Museum of Art
Washington, The Phillips Collection

PRIVATE COLLECTIONS

Private collection, Larry Ellison
Collection of David and Heidi Freilich
Private collection – courtesy of HomeArt
The Levett Collection
and those who wish to remain anonymous.

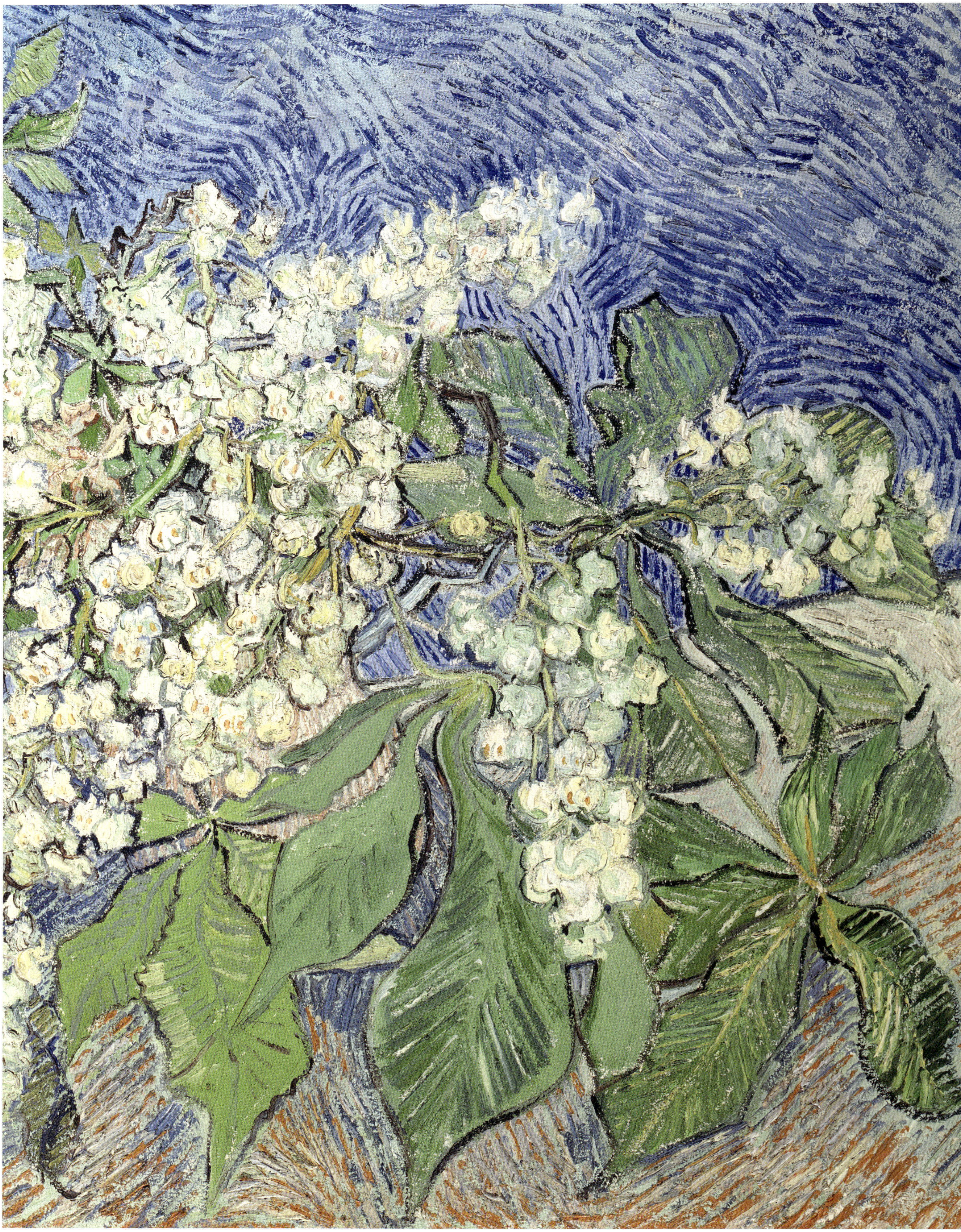

NOTE TO THE READER

For the purposes of this publication, the seventy-four paintings that Vincent van Gogh produced in Auvers-sur-Oise are identified by two numbers: one for the illustrations in this book and another preceded by a # sign referring to the same works in the 'Catalogue of Paintings from Auvers-sur-Oise' (pp. 202–19).

The reproduced works and documents from the Van Gogh Museum collection belong to the Vincent van Gogh Foundation and are on permanent loan to the museum.

Letter or RM (related manuscript) followed by a number refer to the scholarly online edition of Van Gogh's complete correspondence: Vincent van Gogh: The Letters, ed. Leo Jansen, Hans Luijten and Nienke Bakker, 2009 (www.vangoghletters.org).

B numbers indicate letters and documents kept at the Van Gogh Museum in Amsterdam.

When referring to the letters, we identify members of the Van Gogh family by their first name alone: Theo for Theo van Gogh, Vincent's brother; Jo for Jo van Gogh-Bonger, Theo's wife; and Willemien for Willemien van Gogh, Vincent and Theo's sister. Unless stated otherwise, Vincent van Gogh was the author of the letters.

F numbers accompanying Van Gogh's works refer to De la Faille 1970 and JH numbers to Hulsker 1996a.

'Gachet Papers' refers to the archive 'Paul Ferdinand Gachet and Paul Louis Gachet Papers, Wildenstein Plattner Institute, New York'.

Use was made for the 'Catalogue of Paintings from Auvers-sur-Oise' (pp. 202–19) of data from the Automated Canvas Analysis Project led by Prof. Don H. Johnson of Rice University in Houston, Prof. William A. Sethares of the University of Wisconsin, and Bregje Gerritse, Teio Meedendorp, Kathrin Pilz and Louis van Tilborgh of the Van Gogh Museum. Additional information regarding the priming of Van Gogh's paintings was provided by Muriel Geldof, Conservation Scientist at the Cultural Heritage Agency of the Netherlands, Amsterdam.

PREFACE

Vincent van Gogh arrived in the artists' village of Auvers-sur-Oise, near Paris, on 20 May 1890. Having spent a year at an asylum in the south of France, he hoped that being back in society and in a more northerly region would help him cope more effectively with his mental suffering. His new surroundings offered him inspiration, yet within little more than two months he decided to end his own life. Van Gogh died on 29 July. The following day, he was accompanied to his final resting place in Auvers cemetery by his brother Theo, Dr Paul Ferdinand Gachet and a handful of friends and acquaintances.

His reputation as a painter might still have been limited at the time, but he left behind a magnificent body of work. In the last few months of his life, he threw himself into his art, treating it as a lifeline, much more than he had in the past. The result was a fairly substantial output within a short space of time. The paintings and drawings he created in Auvers are the focus of this publication and the exhibition of the same name at the Van Gogh Museum and Musée d'Orsay.

Views on the artistic value of what Van Gogh produced in his final period varied in the course of the past century. All the same, the exhibitions *Van Gogh in Saint-Rémy and Auvers* at New York's Metropolitan Museum of Art in 1986 and *Los últimos paisajes* at the Museo Thyssen-Bornemisza in Madrid in 2007 clearly demonstrated the degree to which much of this work speaks directly to our imagination. *Wheatfield with Crows* **(137)** and *Doctor Paul Gachet* **(159)** have enjoyed considerable public recognition from an early stage, but there is much more besides to impress us. To do justice to the variety of work he produced there, this publication pays attention both to his larger paintings and to smaller, lesser-known works, such as *Glass with Carnations* **(69)** and *House at Auvers-sur-Oise* **(54)**, which stand out in all their simplicity. A large number of drawings are also examined – some of them casual pencil scribbles that are quite unusual in his late oeuvre – in order to bring us as close to his artistic practice as possible.

Artists and collectors were not slow to appreciate the work Van Gogh produced in Auvers. The Danish artist Alice Ruben-Faber bought the first version of Dr Gachet's portrait **(159)** in 1897, while the better-known German Neo-Impressionist Curt Herrmann was won over seven years later by *Green Wheatfields* **(11)**. The colourful and inventive *Farmhouses in Auvers-sur-Oise* **(46)** was one of Van Gogh's first paintings to enter a public collection in 1903, and although Max Liebermann, leader of the German Realists, did not rate the new generation of artists very highly, he nevertheless acquired *Wheatfield with Cornflowers* **(144)**, a masterpiece of wet-on-wet painting, in 1907. Shortly afterwards, Van Gogh's most exuberant bouquet of flowers from this period **(84)** came into the possession of the young Hungarian painter Gyula Andorkó while roughly around the same time the eye of the Russian-born artist Alexej von Jawlensky was caught by the serene image of cottages along a country road with a blossoming chestnut tree set against a dark sky **(61)**.

From a scholarly point of view, there was something of a gap in our knowledge of Van Gogh's work from Auvers. A great deal of work has thus been devoted in this publication to presenting a firmly grounded proposal regarding the order in which the paintings were executed. Considerable effort has likewise gone into identifying all of the depicted locations. While his works of art have a complexity 'that bear[s] as much relationship to a surveyor's record as a poem bears to a police report', to quote the art historian Ernst Gombrich,[1] when we look over the painter's shoulder, as it were, it becomes even clearer how he took reality and bent it to his own ends, drawing on his surroundings as material for his art. Or, as Van Gogh himself so aptly wrote: 'I don't invent the whole of the painting; on the contrary, I find it ready-made – but to be untangled – in the real world.'[2]

This book aims to do justice to both the factual context of the works of art and the magic of Van Gogh's artistry. Readers will therefore find an introductory survey of the Auvers work together with separate essays on the still lifes, portraits and landscapes that he painted there as well as on his drawings. In the final weeks of his life, meanwhile, the artist produced panoramic landscapes with an unusual 'double-square' format, and so a specific essay has been devoted to these works too. When great artists die, we comfort ourselves with the notion that they live on through their art. The essay section of the book closes with an article that attempts to map Van Gogh's burgeoning reputation, while also paying attention to the role played in this regard by Dr Gachet.

Nor do we shy away from the process leading up to Van Gogh's self-chosen death – a sensitive subject on many levels. It hardly needs to be said that a variety of myths arose in the twentieth century concerning Van Gogh's work and life. It was nevertheless startling in 2011 when it was suddenly trumpeted that he did *not* actually take his own life at all.[3] This entirely unfounded suggestion denied Van Gogh's suffering and shone a strange, retrospective light on how those closest to him had dealt with it. When a person feels compelled to end their own life, the least they deserve is to be heard with empathy. Recognizing signals and acknowledging pain always matters, also in the case of a historical figure.

Nienke Bakker, Emmanuel Coquery,
Teio Meedendorp and Louis van Tilborgh

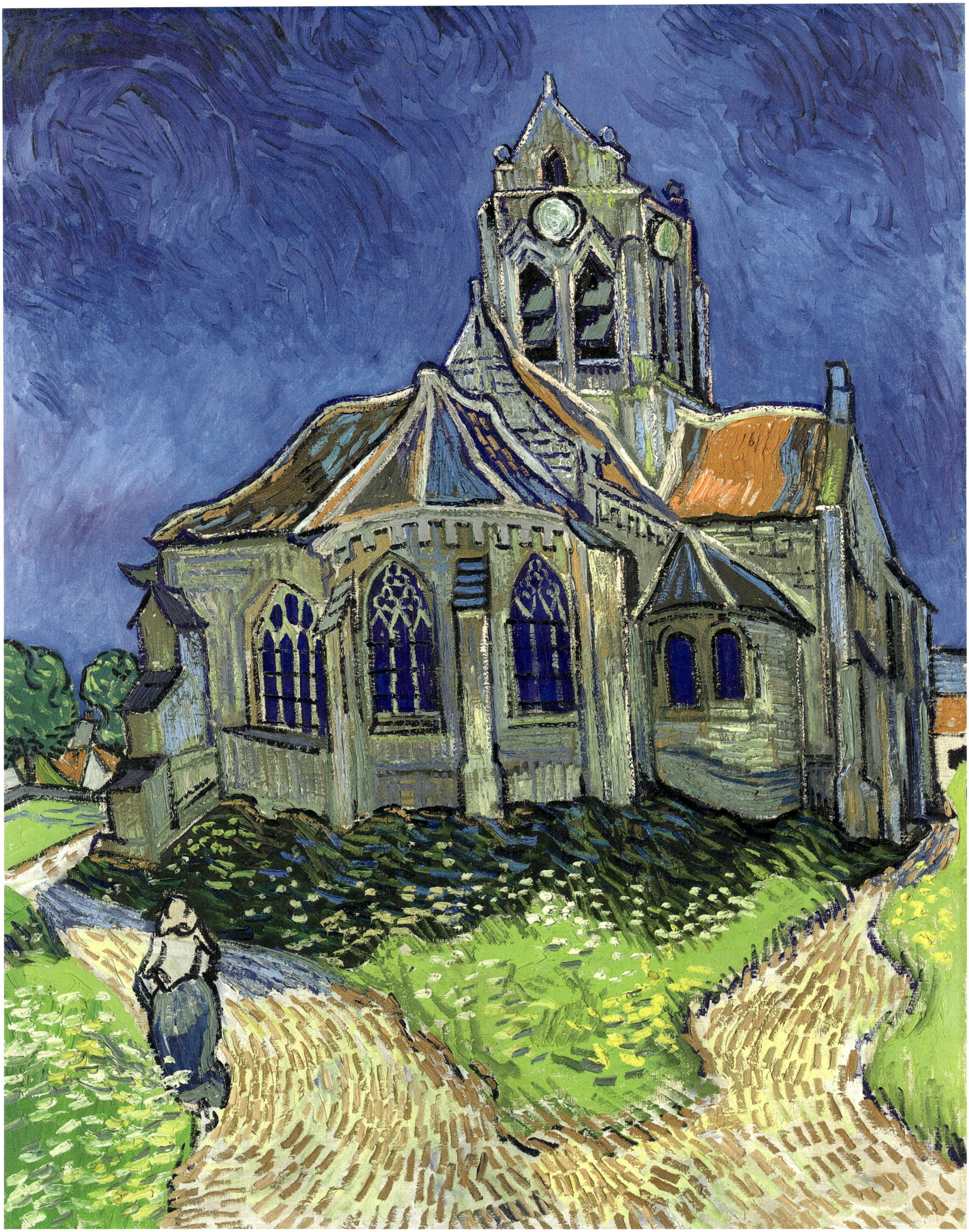

VINCENT VAN GOGH'S FINAL MONTHS

LOUIS VAN TILBORGH

The pace of Van Gogh's artistic development within a relatively short space of time is one of the great marvels of his career. He took up drawing when he was twenty-seven and only began to paint seriously at thirty. But by the age of thirty-seven, he left behind a body of work that was both substantial and unusual for his era, and the stylistic variety of which was recognized immediately after his death as highly distinctive and remarkable. To quote the art historian Julius S. Held, his rapid intellectual and technical growth was comparable to that of other figures who died prematurely, such as Caravaggio, Mozart and Schubert. Like Van Gogh, it was if they 'had been programmed by a benevolent nature to run an accelerated course, encompassing stylistic phases that in luckier individuals were spread out comfortably over many decades'.[1]

This book focuses entirely on the final stage in Van Gogh's rapid development, the time he spent in Auvers-sur-Oise. It is a somewhat less examined period in his artistic life, and one that might, if anything, raise even more questions than all that preceded it. The concluding phases of great artists exert an exceptional attraction on us.[2] We feel a pressing need to know not only which was an artist's last work, but also how the art produced at the end of a life compares with earlier, so much more youthful achievements. There has even been a (baseless) feeling since the beginning of the twentieth century that despite the accumulation of physical and mental ailments at this stage of life – or, perhaps, precisely because of them – the works that artists produce in it have a special, almost existential significance. All outward display has supposedly been shed as they now concentrate on the essence of their talent, enabling them to transcend themselves.[3]

But we are talking in such instances of elderly artists like Rembrandt or Claude Monet, whereas Van Gogh had yet to reach his thirty-seventh birthday. All the same, you can also feel old before your time, which is what happened in his case. Life had not exactly smiled on Vincent since his teenage years and the young artist actively assumed that he was not destined to live a long life. Brief and intense: that was his expectation. 'My plan is *not* to spare myself', he wrote in 1883, 'not to avoid a lot of emotions or difficulties. It's a matter of relative indifference to me whether I live a long or a short time. Moreover, I'm not competent to manage myself in physical matters the way a doctor can in

1 (#21)
Vincent van Gogh
The Church at Auvers-sur-Oise, 1890
Oil on canvas, 93 × 74.5 cm
Musée d'Orsay, Paris

this respect.'[4] He did not expect his life as an artist to last more than ten years or so, and it would depend on the intensity whether this could be prolonged: 'If one goes into a serious decline in those years, one won't get past 40.'

In retrospect, such thoughts are very striking. Van Gogh suffered from what psychologists now term a negative self-image. Yet he learned to cope with it, as he did the other kinds of difficulty he faced in his life, and his immense willpower and resilience will certainly have helped him in this respect. Towards the end of his two-year stay in Paris, however, he increasingly concluded that his existence on the fringes of society might prove permanent, an idea that left him feeling 'old and broken' at the age of thirty-five.[5] At the same time, though, he was firmly convinced that he could withstand his multiplying physical and mental difficulties by continuing to create in his art the more 'humane' and meaningful world that was so sorely needed.[6] In the hopes of achieving it, he departed for Provence, where a rich, exuberant and colourful nature would help him keep his art youthful and optimistic 'by doing brilliant colour, well arranged, resplendent'.[7]

He ended up walking a tightrope and would ultimately prove unequal to the mounting stress of the ambitious, drink-fuelled life of the artist abroad. After developing a psychiatric condition in late 1888, his voluntary admission to the Saint-Rémy clinic and the deterioration in his mental condition, Van Gogh found it increasingly difficult to hold things together. He struggled with his identity, feeling more like a patient at times than an artist, and also began to question whether art offered a sufficient remedy for his mental ailments. After more than eight months in the asylum, he found 'the day more difficult to do and the future more mysterious, and my word a little more gloomy too'.[8]

After his final, severe attack of depression in the spring of 1890, he bet everything on *leaving*, and doing so as soon as possible. Even so, he did not view the move to Auvers as a solution, but as a relief, a final straw for him to clutch. While the danger of fresh breakdowns was as acute as ever and he was likely to remain every bit as much a patient as he was in the asylum, Van Gogh insisted on leaving it. He did not want to fall into the torpor of his fellow inmates and was eager to become part of free society once more, regardless of the consequences.[9]

His caregivers acquiesced and, following a three-day visit to his brother Theo and sister-in-law Jo in Paris, he arrived on 20 May 1890 at the popular painting village on the river Oise, recommended by Camille Pissarro. Auvers had attracted a multitude of artists since the painter Charles-François Daubigny had settled there, making Van Gogh just one of many. He took up residence at an inn that had a small workplace for its artist-guests and began to paint one canvas after another, raising his output to a higher level than ever before.

By the end of six weeks, the total stood at roughly sixty paintings, an unprecedented number. His weekly visits to Paul Ferdinand Gachet – the doctor Theo had asked to keep an eye on his brother – came to an end around that time and his output declined somewhat. By 29 July, when he died from a self-inflicted gunshot wound, he had produced at least seventy-four paintings, averaging more than one per day.[10] As far as we know, he had given eight of them away.[11] The others – with the exception of what were probably his last, not yet fully dried canvases – were stowed away in his small room at the inn. They had been removed from their stretchers and 'spread out under his bed to take up less space'.[12]

GROWING APPRECIATION

As discussed below, Van Gogh's artistic achievement in Auvers assumed somewhat negative connotations in the course of the twentieth century, but things were very different in 1890. He had barely any reputation at that point and the paintings from his very last months would actually play a substantial role in cultivating appreciation for him as a painter of unusual talent who had died too young.[13] While at least sixteen paintings remained in Auvers after the funeral,[14] Theo had the other works transferred to his stockpile at the premises of the Paris paint seller Julien Tanguy. He then selected a large number of those works for the retrospective of Vincent's oeuvre, which he ended up holding in his new apartment in Paris. He did not have a catalogue made, but we know from reviews that the exhibition included the first version of *Two Girls* **(133)**, 'everything flat, in a single fresco tone';[15] *Rain – Auvers-sur-Oise* **(145)**;

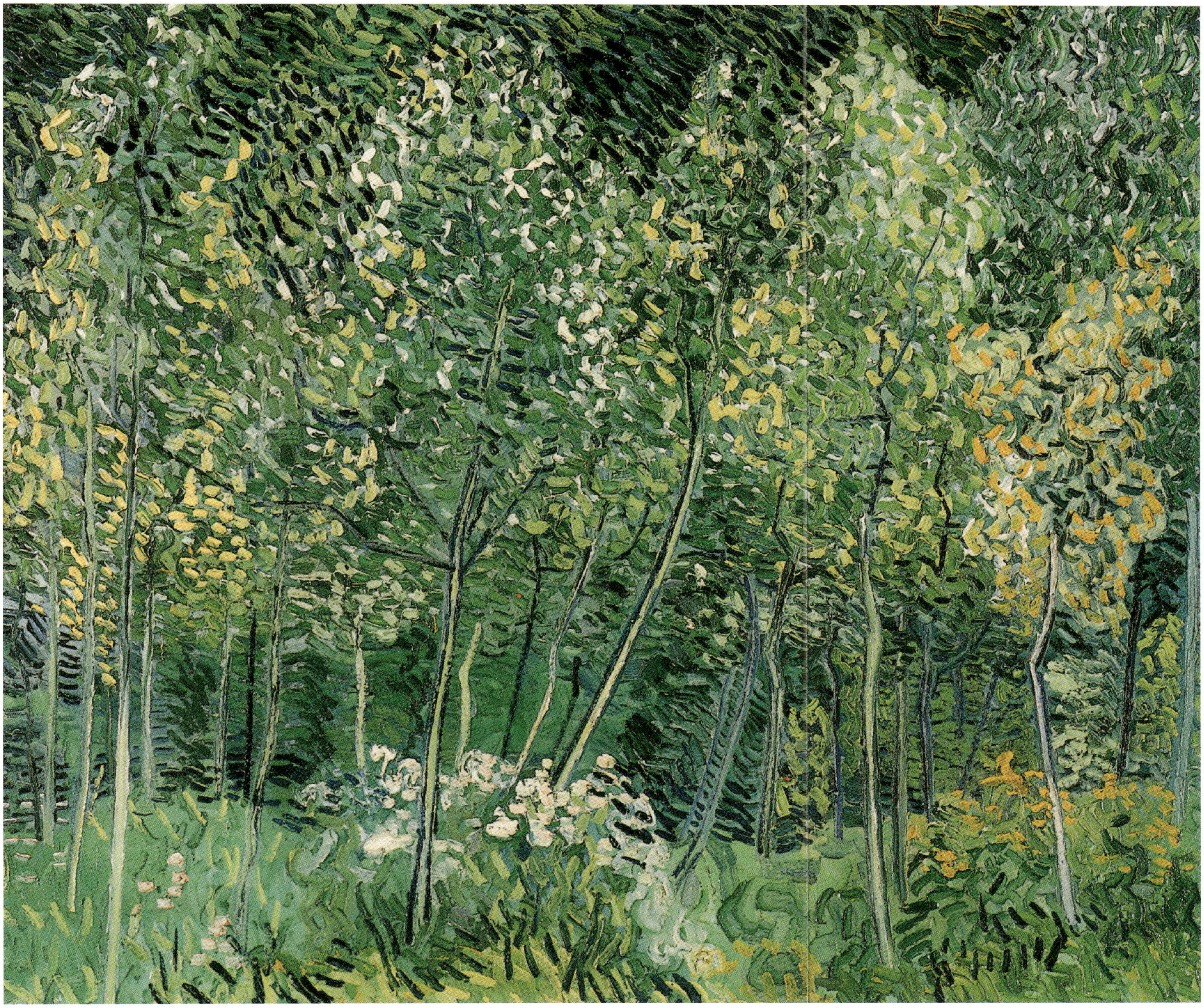

2 (#44)
Vincent van Gogh
Undergrowth, 1890
Oil on canvas, 73 × 90 cm
Private collection

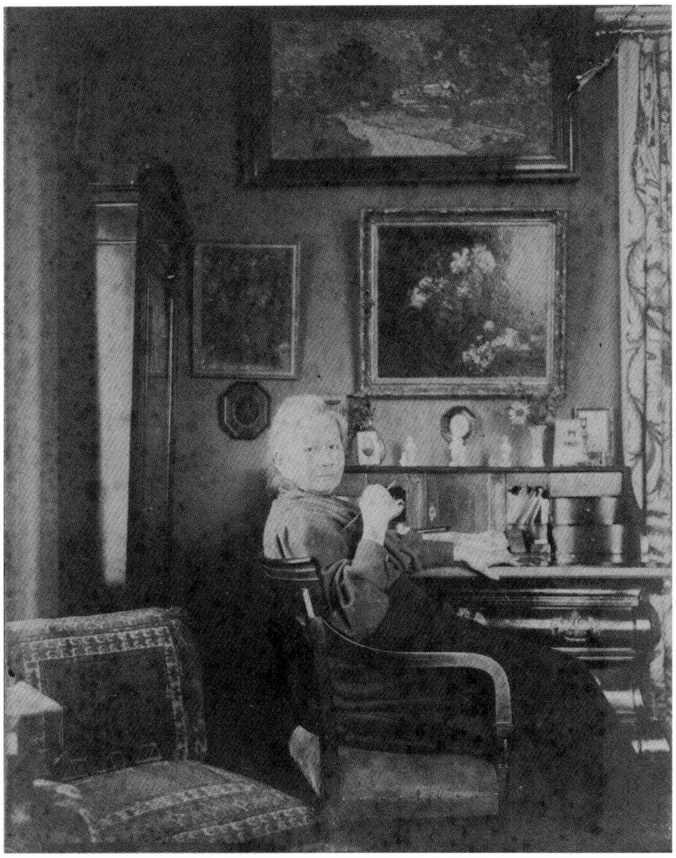

3
Jo van Gogh-Bonger in the living room of her home at 77 Koninginneweg, Amsterdam, 1909 or later
Van Gogh Museum, Amsterdam

Wheatfield with Crows **(137)**; *Sheaves of Wheat* **(146)**; the first version of *Daubigny's Garden* **(139)**; and, 'a very beautiful green-on-green undergrowth' **(2)**.[16] There is a good chance that *Landscape at Twilight* **(138)** was also selected, as the work became one of Jo van Gogh-Bonger's favourites, whether or not following her husband's lead. She gave the beautiful, atmospheric painting pride of place above her desk in her later home in Amsterdam **(3)**.

It was an open secret in Theo and Vincent's circle of acquaintances that Van Gogh had died by his own hand. Two of the works at the exhibition were suggestively linked with this fact, one of them being *Rain – Auvers-sur-Oise*, which the Dutch writer and psychiatrist Frederik van Eeden described as a landscape 'oppressive in its dismal anguish. A dreary violet landscape of hills [...], empty, infinitely sinister in its bare, deadly lines, [...] and over which is laid streaming rain [...], everything killed in despair.'[17] The other was *Wheatfield with Crows*, which the same author called 'a violent expression of the utmost desperation', painted most notably in 'a terribly, deathly blackish blue'. Possibly inspired by Van Eeden's description, Johan de Meester called it '*La désolation des champs*'.[18] Three months or so later, the Dutch critic was still impressed by the work: 'Tremendous feelings must have coursed and howled within him [Van Gogh], and it is still very much in question whether painting was sufficient to express them.'[19]

Rather surprisingly, Theo's exhibition did not include the canvas that his brother-in-law, Andries Bonger, described in a newspaper article in 1892 as Vincent's very last.[20] The painting – *Tree Roots* **(157)** – had evidently become a taboo subject: Andries did not include it in the inventory of Theo's collection that he drew up at the end of 1890 and, like *Gauguin's Chair* (Van Gogh Museum, Amsterdam), Jo never loaned the work, no doubt reflecting the fact that Theo had ignored it. Andries did, however, show the painting to De Meester in 1891, prompting the Dutch critic to confess that he struggled to detect Van Gogh's imminent death in it. Unlike *Wheatfield with Crows*, this *sous-bois* was 'full of sun and life'.[21] De Meester considered it 'a splendidly sumptuous piece drawn from a rich, joyous nature – a very good painting [...] but it was impossible for me to see in it the supreme expression, the final adieu of Vincent's temperament. That temperament was more abundantly tempestuous, as it was more powerful with every complete revelation.'

Although the first painting from this period, *Daubigny's Garden* **(139)**, was sold as early as 1894, sales of Auvers works from Jo's collection did not really take off until the early twentieth century.[22] Van Gogh's reputation was burgeoning at the time and it is noteworthy that several of these paintings were among the first works of his to be included in museum collections.[23] The widow of the critic and dealer Julien Leclercq donated *Farmhouses in Auvers-sur-Oise* through the Antell fund to the Ateneum in Helsinki in 1903 **(46)**, while Jo sold *Fields near Auvers-sur-Oise* in the same year to the Vienna Secession **(135)**, which then donated it to the Moderne Galerie, now the Belvedere Museum. In 1905 Hugo von Tschudi acquired two superb landscapes from Auvers **(55, 68)**, possibly with a view to giving at least one of them to the Nationalgalerie in Berlin, of which he was the director. Nothing ultimately came of the plan, however. While progressive museum directors like him were chiefly enthused at first by Van Gogh's landscapes, his portraits later caught on with them too. One of the first to enter a public collection was *Doctor Paul Gachet* **(159)** from Jo's collection, which the Städtische Galerie in Frankfurt acquired in 1911.

A growing need was felt in the meantime to interpret Van Gogh's paintings as a kind of autobiography. *Wheatfield with Crows*, for instance, became much more strongly linked than before with his suicide. In 1905, Jo's then husband Johan Cohen Gosschalk believed that Vincent had been struck in this work by 'the paroxysm of fear', which 'drove him into death'.[24] He also stated that it was 'one of his last paintings', fuelling the notion that this was actually his final work. The first time such a claim was made explicitly was at a 1908 exhibition in Munich.[25] Once created, the myth did not diminish the work's popularity: its insurance value, for instance, was a good deal higher in 1924 than that of *Sunflowers*, one of the other highlights of Van Gogh's oeuvre.[26]

CHANGING OPINIONS

The biographical interpretation of Van Gogh's work took a new and much more far-reaching turn in the 1920s, when the German psychiatrist and philosopher Karl Jaspers was the first to make a detailed study of the relationship between the artist's mental illness and his art. That he was suffering from 'the possible collapse of delicacy of feeling, and even more, of discipline' was supposedly visible in his work.[27] When psychiatric ideas became more firmly established in the public mind after the Second World War, what had been a cautiously expressed comment in the increasingly popular genre of Van Gogh biographies now turned almost into a concrete fact. According to the French critic Frank Elgar in 1958, for instance, the artist's style in Auvers 'was getting slack, his line hardening, his touch going astray and his colour dimming'. As a result, 'clumsily sketched forms, dissonant tones, smeared paint, irresolute composition and a dry, mechanical, devitalized handling all attested to irremediable decline.'[28]

Not everyone was quite so outspoken, however, and the weight placed on such opinions gradually diminished. The subsequent rehabilitation of the artist's later work led in part to the 1986 exhibition *Van Gogh in Saint-Rémy and Auvers* at the Metropolitan Museum of Art in New York. In contrast to the critics of the 1950s and 1960s in particular, Ronald Pickvance now argued firmly that Van Gogh's paintings from these periods were 'neither graphs of this so-called madness nor primarily indicators of his mental state'.[29] While the latter is certainly true, it does not alter the fact that changes in the artist's mental condition influenced what he made. But we are not talking in this instance of his periods of bewilderment but what that condition meant to his emotional world in the times in between, when he was in his right mind.

Appreciation of Van Gogh's work from Auvers peaked again in 1990. In spite of the New York exhibition, many still considered his time in Arles to be 'the zenith, the climax' of his ten-year career as an artist.[30] Rudi Fuchs, then director of the Gemeentemuseum in The Hague, judged otherwise after seeing the major retrospective at the Van Gogh Museum. To his mind, it was precisely in Auvers that Van Gogh achieved the pinnacle of his art. 'Perhaps he was driven by an inimitable ecstasy, perhaps by a feeling of great haste', in response to which the artist 'freed himself of the last impressionistic conventions' during this period.[31] He no longer strove to achieve harmony in style, but showed that individual parts of the picture 'can acquire an autonomous beauty'.[32] Such fragments escaped 'the bonds of the whole', allowing 'new possibilities for the twentieth century' to emerge.

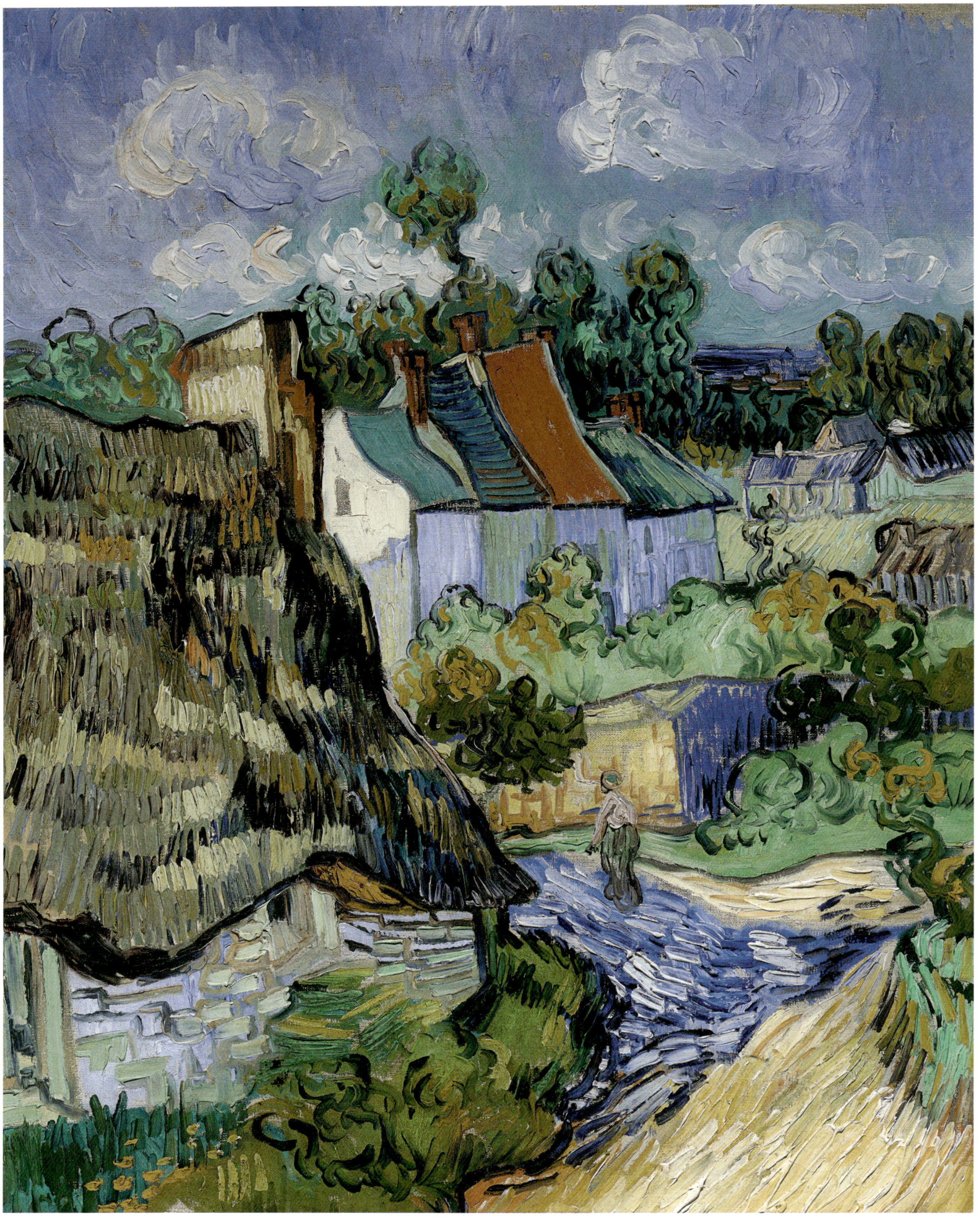

4 (#27)
Vincent van Gogh
Houses at Auvers-sur-Oise, 1890
Oil on canvas, 75.6 × 61.9 cm
Museum of Fine Arts, Boston,
Bequest of John T. Spaulding

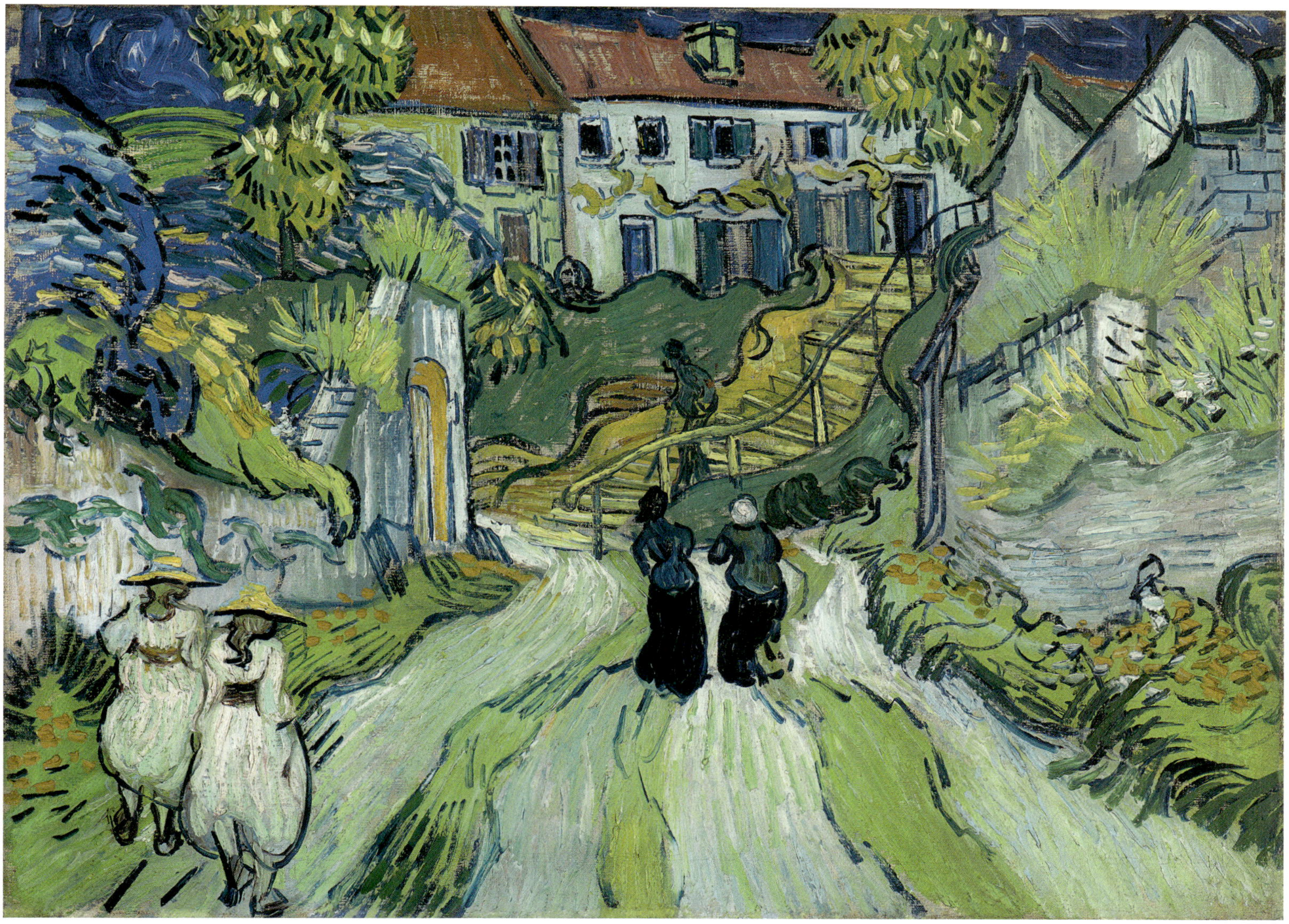

5 (#7)
Vincent van Gogh
Stairway at Auvers-sur-Oise, 1890
Oil on canvas, 50 × 70.5 cm
Saint Louis Art Museum, purchased 1935

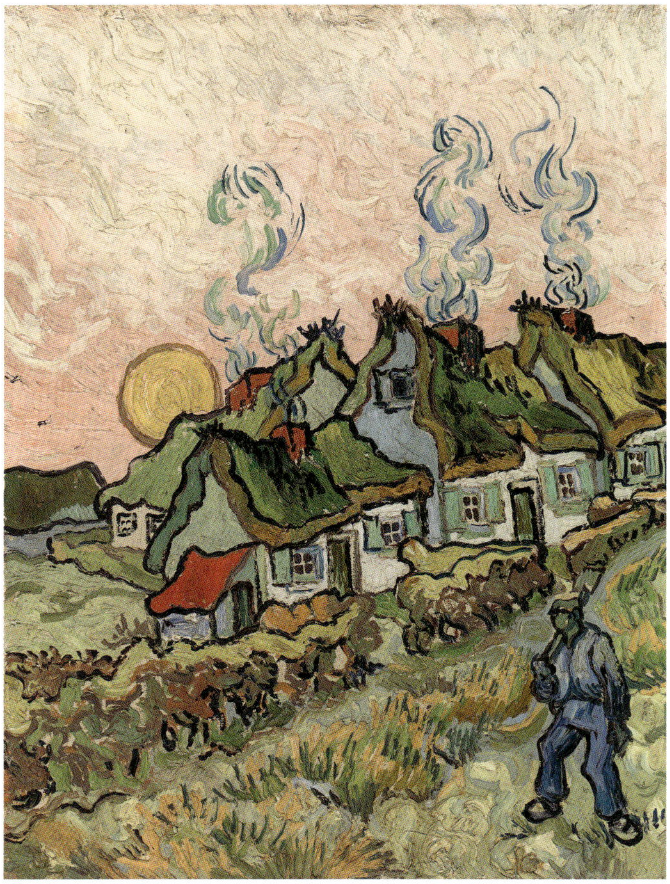

6
Vincent van Gogh
Cottages at Sunset
('Reminiscence of Brabant'), 1890
Oil on canvas, 52 × 40.5 cm
The Barnes Foundation, Philadelphia

YEARNING FOR BRABANT

Fuchs openly advocated an ahistorical appreciation of Van Gogh's work, but it is perhaps more logical and intellectually more challenging to look at what the artist himself had in mind. One thing we know for certain is that he arrived in Auvers with a pronounced nostalgia for the art of his Brabant years. His yearning for that earlier time and for an unspoilt, 'primitive' life in the north came on him strongly in the late summer of 1889, during his first attack in the asylum. Van Gogh was overcome by 'an over-melancholy nostalgia', during which his mind turned to the 1850 novel *Le conscrit* (The conscript) by Hendrik Conscience, in which the Flemish author sings the praises of the Kempen region – the sandy heathland straddling the border between the south-east Netherlands and north-east Belgium.[33]

Van Gogh interpreted Conscience's introduction to the book as indicating that 'he'd been very ill' and that 'in his illness, despite all his efforts, he had felt his affection for mankind withering away'.[34] During a stay in the moors, however, 'long walks out in the open fields brought his feelings of love back to him'. To quote Conscience directly, this was thanks to the salutary effect of the Kempen: 'where the soul [...] forgets society and frees itself from its bonds with the vigour of returning youth; where every thought takes on the form of prayer; [...] there, the exhausted man regains a youthful strength. [...] this is human life: to be born, to work, to love, to grow up, and to die.'[35]

Thinking of this kind would take on obsessive forms during Van Gogh's very last, severely depressed episode in the spring of 1890.[36] Towards the end of it, he was given permission to draw and also eventually to paint, and while he did include gloomy rain showers and agitated, stormy skies in his work – entirely in keeping with his profound despondency – the principal motif was provided by his memories of Brabant rural life **(6)**. He painted or drew from memory 'those *human* nests, those cottages on the heath and their inhabitants'; their shared, tough rural labour; the security of family life; the unifying churchgoing, and along the same lines, *la foi du charbonnier* ('collier's faith') – the honest, naive faith of those whom the Bible calls 'the poor in spirit', because in their quest for a better life, they had supposedly stripped themselves of all spiritual and social hindrances.[37]

When Van Gogh saw Pierre Puvis de Chavannes's *Inter artes et naturam* (*Between Art and Nature*)

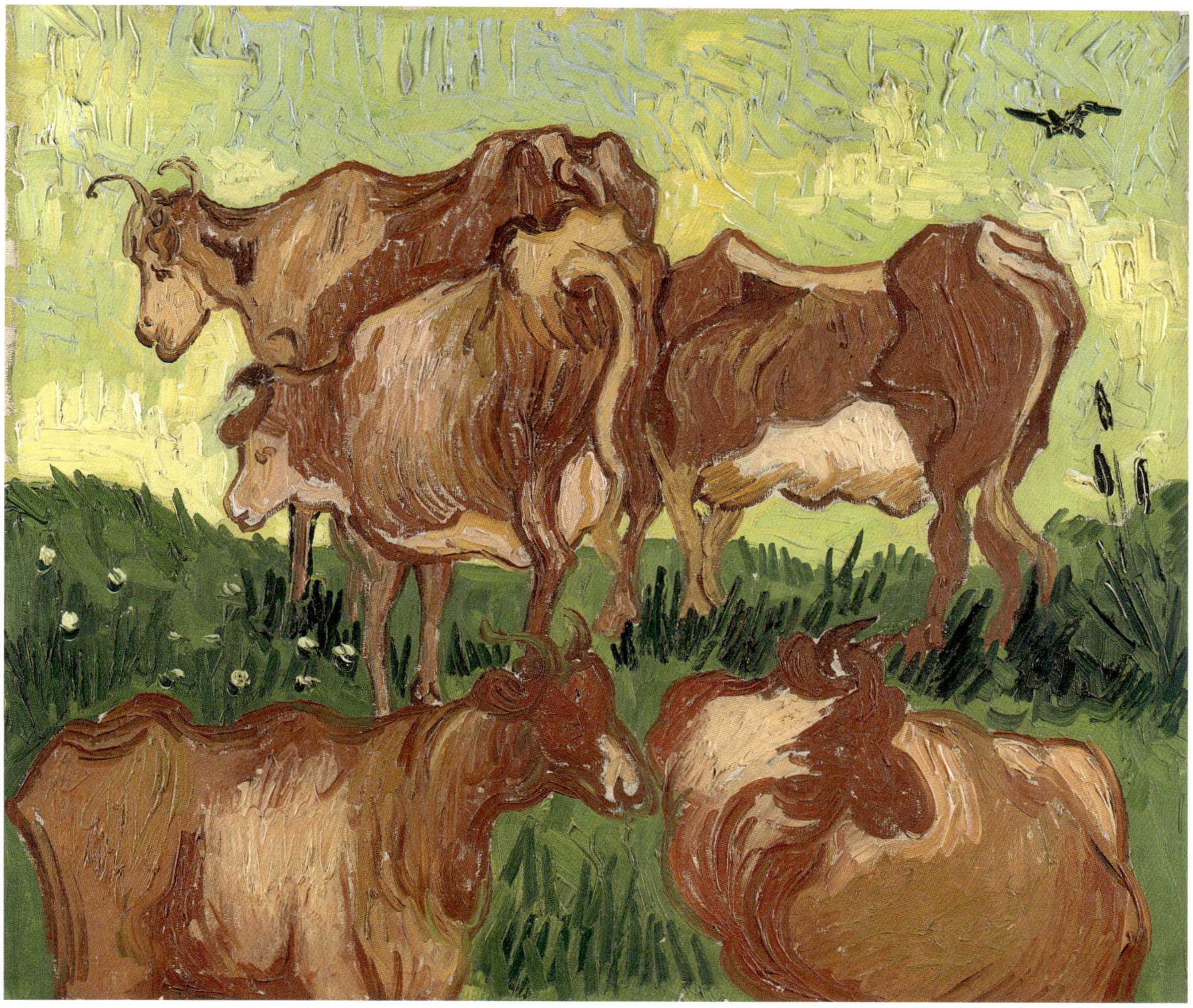

7 (#36)
Vincent van Gogh
Cows (after Gachet, after Jordaens), 1890
Oil on canvas, 55 × 65 cm
Palais des Beaux-Arts, Lille

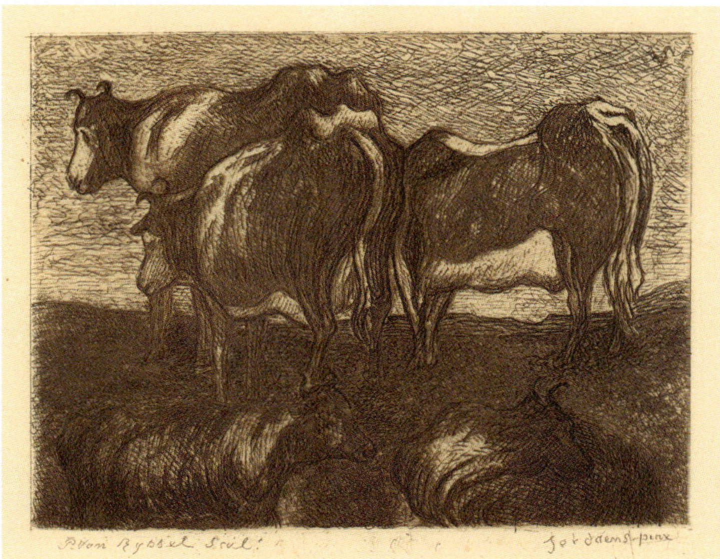

8
Paul van Ryssel (Paul Ferdinand Gachet)
Cows (after Jordaens), 1873
Etching and roulette on paper, 22.5 × 27.7 cm
Van Gogh Museum, Amsterdam

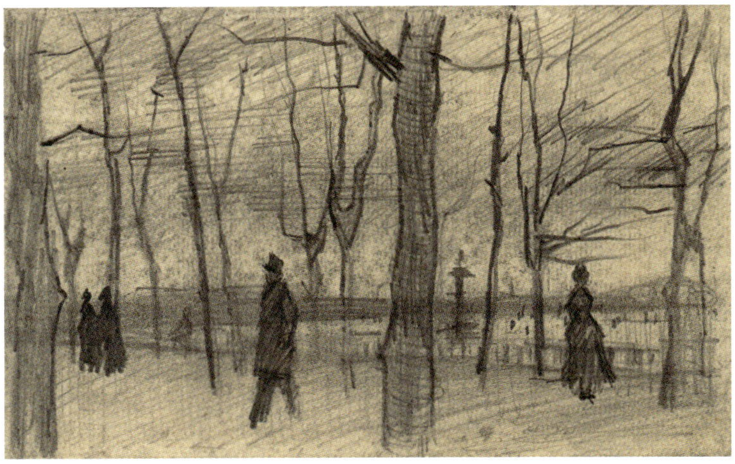

9
Vincent van Gogh
Jardin du Luxembourg,
from sketchbook Paris, 1886
Pencil on paper, 9.7 × 15.8 cm
Van Gogh Museum, Amsterdam

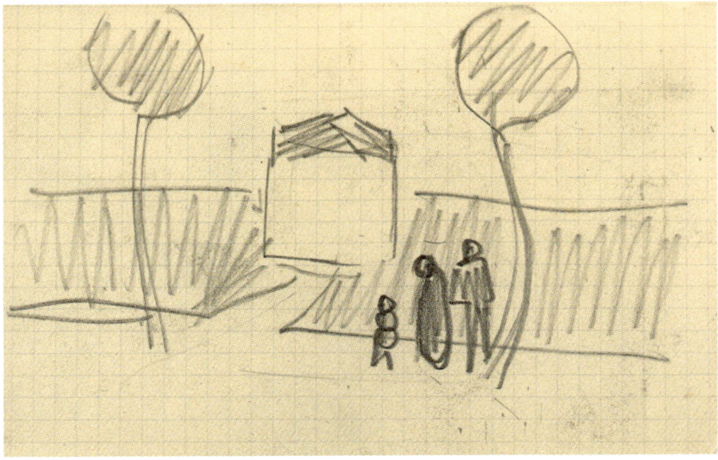

10
Vincent van Gogh
Town Hall with Figures,
from sketchbook Paris-Auvers-sur-Oise, 1890
Pencil on paper, 8.5 × 13.4 cm
Van Gogh Museum, Amsterdam

during his stopover in Paris in May 1890 **(153)**, he immediately recognized that his fellow artist had been mesmerized, as was he, by this search for a utopian idyllic place. He saw in the painting 'an inevitable but benevolent rebirth of all things that one might have believed in, that one might have desired, a strange and happy meeting of the very distant days of antiquity with raw modernity'.[38] Only in this way could art offer hope. Yet in Auvers, Van Gogh's nostalgia for a lost past proved stronger than the desire or imperative to reflect also on his own time and surroundings and on his own needs.

Although his letters still testified to his keen eye for the beauty of newly built villas and for all that he did not neglect to include factories in his works (in which they symbolize the advance of modern civilization), he continued to focus on those '*human* nests' **(4)**.[39] They were the subject of his very first painting **(33)** and ultimately became his favourite motif in Auvers **(4, 29, 30, 40, 41, 43, 44, 46, 55, 66, 147)**. He set out in this way to praise the sense of security offered by country life, which was inextricably linked with an institutional practice of religion that he viewed as in decay. All the same, he certainly continued to respect its underlying moral values, prompting him to paint the local church too **(1)**. It was a relatively small building, but the composition for which he opted makes it seem positively monumental. Van Gogh believed that with paintings like this he was perpetuating the achievement of Charles-François Daubigny in Auvers, and his two versions of *Daubigny's Garden* – 'a painting I'd been thinking about ever since I've been here' and 'one of my most deliberate canvases' **(139, 140)** – can best be interpreted as odes to his sheltered, familiar life as an artist in the French countryside.[40] He wanted to live that way, ideally with a pet cat, but it was not to be.

AMBITION

While Van Gogh had painted almost exclusively on large canvases in his final weeks in Provence, it was not until the third week of June that he found himself in anything like a comparably, ambitious flow of work in Auvers. Up to then, he was living more day by day in artistic terms, with several of those smaller works apparently little more than attempts to pass the time pleasantly. They included the cheerful still lifes and garden views he made during his weekly visits to his doctor **(34, 35, 76, 77)**.[41] Van Gogh's

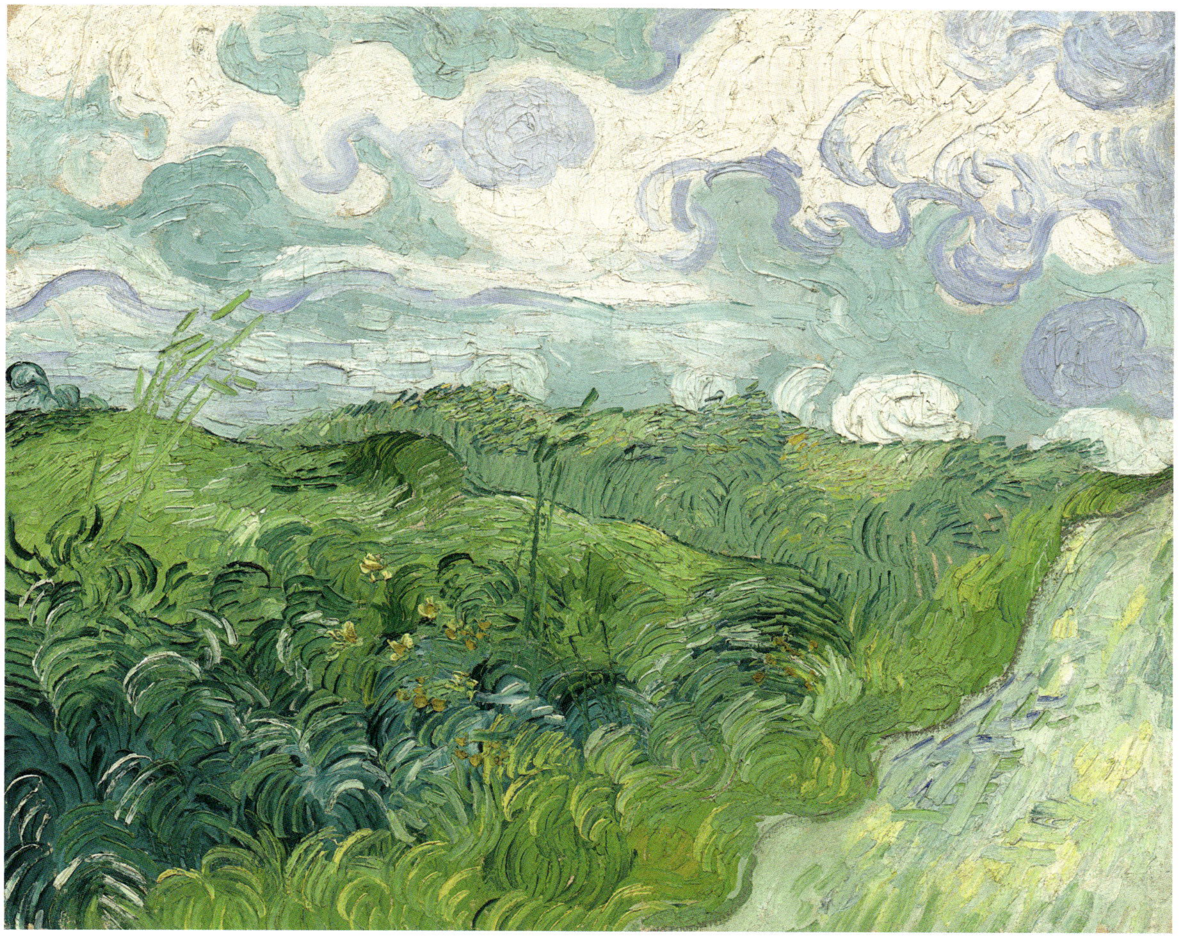

11 (#26)
Vincent van Gogh
Green Wheatfields, 1890
Oil on canvas, 72.4 × 91.4 cm
National Gallery of Art, Washington, Collection of Mr. and Mrs. Paul Mellon

amusing translation of Gachet's etching of *Cows* after the painting by Jacob Jordaens shows that he also produced studies from time to time with the aim of pleasing his host **(7, 8)**. During his stay in Antwerp, he had closely observed and admired Jordaens's lively touch and firm modelling of flesh. This, combined with the unusual subject of old, worn-out cattle, apparently tempted him to translate the black-and-white representation into his own colours.[42] Following the example of Paul Cézanne's *Crossroads at Rue Rémy* in Gachet's collection, he also applied himself briefly to working with a palette knife, but only kept it up for a couple of small studies **(43, 44)**.[43]

His choice to begin each painting afresh, with no preconceived plan, benefited his time-honoured pursuit of variety in technique. If we look at what he produced between around 9 and 14 June **(4, 13, 29, 40, 54, 55, 144)**, for instance, we can only admire the huge repertoire of means of expression that he had assembled by that point. The works testify to the immense pleasure with which he painted, although there had been something of a shift in emphasis. More so even than in Saint-Rémy, he opted for a graphic representation, determined by line, which is sometimes painterly, sometimes more drawing-like. While Van Gogh achieved the latter effect using short and straight brushstrokes, we also find a great many curved, almost meandering forms, which were based on the example of Paul Gauguin **(5)**. He could not refrain from giving bushes, country roads and even buildings certain curves, bringing an exceptional animation to the pictures. In doing so, he became highly skilled in the representation of something in nature that we feel rather than see, namely the wind. *Wheatfield with Crows* **(137)** illustrates this perfectly, but *Green Wheatfields* **(11)** comes very close too. It shows an intimate, empty landscape without figures, which speaks through its abundance of nimble brushstrokes. While everything obviously stands still, we still sense the wind blowing through the wheat, the stalks and the grass swaying and the clouds moving steadily along.

If we look for a common denominator in this diversity, it lies in Van Gogh's pursuit of a highly condensed, almost stenographic rendering of reality. His paintings look more concise and compact than before. Just how much he had learned to simplify in recent years is apparent if we compare a sketchbook

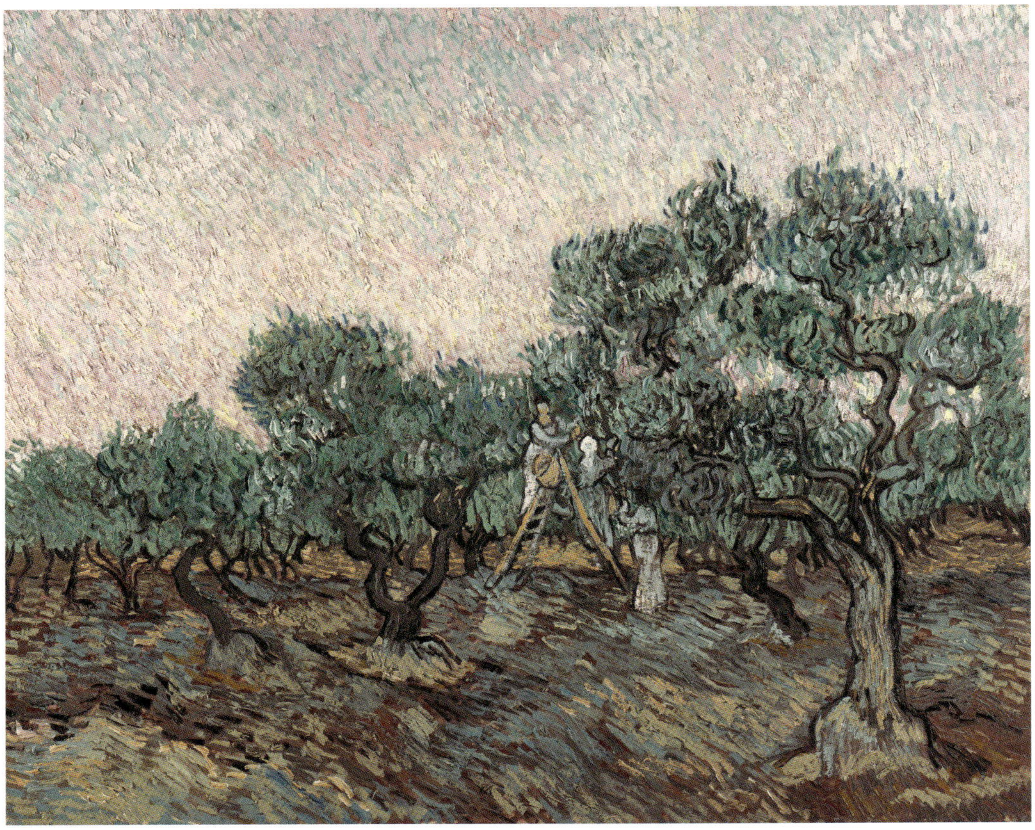

12
Vincent van Gogh
Women Picking Olives, 1889
Oil on canvas, 73.5 × 92.5 cm
Basil & Elise Goulandris Foundation, Athens

page from 1886 with one from Auvers **(9, 10)**. When setting out his paintings, he now thought much more than in the past of the example of Japanese printmaking, with its use of large planes. His dislike of the 'old tricks and *trompe l'oeil* of schemers' meant that the illusion of spatiality had to be curbed,[44] albeit in such a way as this was barely noticeable. It was not only his compositions that he simplified but his colours too. He sought to catch the viewer's attention much more frequently than before with a single dominant colour, mostly an arresting red **(13)** or a solid blue, such as the mesmerizing cobalt of the sky in *The Church at Auvers-sur-Oise* **(1)**. By the end of his time in the village, however, hard colour effects of this kind had disappeared from his palette, leaving a preference for gentle contrasts. Harmony became more important, with light green and pink taking precedence.

RENEWAL THROUGH NATURE

This general simplification was more than an autonomous development arising from his work. In the autumn of 1889, Van Gogh had been angered by what he viewed as affected biblical pictures painted by Emile Bernard and Gauguin. He decided in future to shun any particular any convention or style.[45] In practice, this meant opting for more simple, direct effects, 'rather harsh and coarse'.[46] Examples include *Poppy Field* **(13)**, which follows on in terms of its uncultivated, 'primitive' expression from *Women Picking Olives*, made in the autumn of 1889 **(12)**. He also began to make occasional use at this time of an almost clashing combination of different styles within his landscape works, and he took this further in Auvers **(46, 130)**. This was the fragmentation to which Fuchs referred, but contrary to what he thought, Van Gogh's pleasure lay precisely in the question of how far he could go in the application of such anti-illusionist elements without sacrificing mimetic credibility.[47]

Van Gogh's search for uncultivated rather than artificial expression had a spiritual component as well:[48] as far as he was concerned, traditional theology had run its course and he had long pinned his hopes on the emergence of a new moral – 'religious', if you prefer – stance that would draw on nature as a liberating, life-affirming force. The aim in Auvers too was 'to renew myself in nature',[49] but this only occurred from the final weeks of June onwards, when he showed much more ambition than

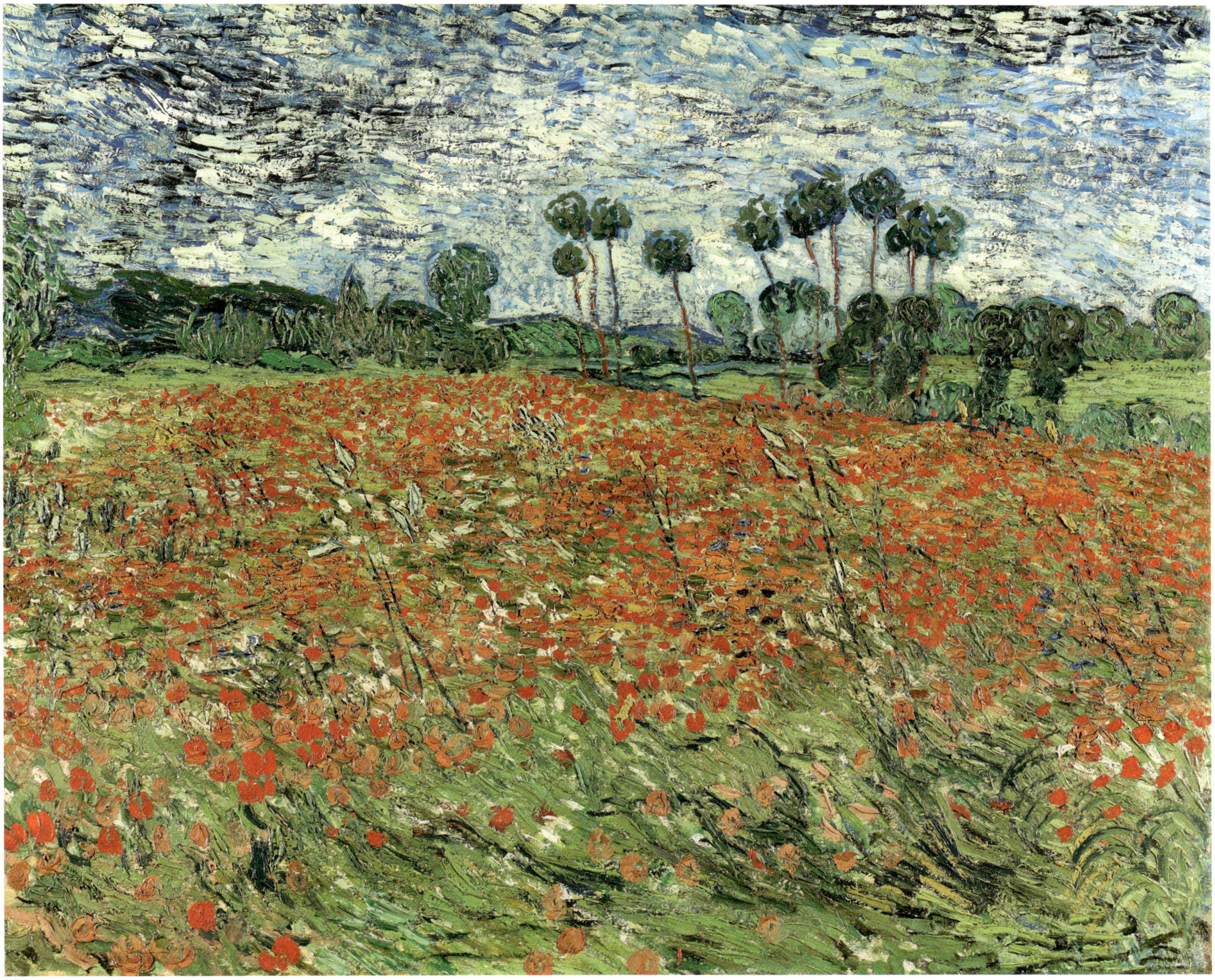

13 (#32)
Vincent van Gogh
Poppy Field, 1890
Oil on canvas, 73 × 91.5 cm
Kunstmuseum Den Haag, long-term loan
Cultural Heritage Agency of the Netherlands

at the beginning of his stay and switched to using a relatively new, panoramic-looking canvas – a format that enabled him to visualize the universal, all-encompassing aspect of nature even more emphatically than before.[50]

The example of the seventeenth-century Dutch painter Jacob van Ruisdael played a crucial part in this. In his publication *Les Maîtres d'autrefois*, of which Van Gogh was a great admirer, the writer and artist Eugène Fromentin had portrayed Van Ruisdael as a rather wistful artist, endowed with great, intuitive powers of thought. As a landscape painter, he was 'one of the solitary ramblers who fly from the town, frequent the outskirts, [...] who are made uneasy by distant horizons, charmed by large plains, affected by a shadow, and enchanted by a ray of sunshine'.[51] One perceived in his landscapes 'an air of plenitude, of conviction, of profound peace',[52] and Van Gogh sought a similarly reassuring effect in his panoramic works.

He hoped in this way to resist what life threw at him, and it also underpinned the portraits of girls and women.[53] While he was at the asylum, he became increasingly distraught at what his own failure had denied him: a wife, children and the security of a family life.[54] When Theo sent him a photograph of Jo with their new-born son towards the end of his stay in Saint-Rémy, he immediately expressed a desire to make a painting of it for himself **(185)**.[55] In the end he did not do so, but he did hang two Japanese prints of women – one with her child – on the wall of his room in Auvers **(126)**.[56]

The historian and author Jules Michelet, of whom Van Gogh was also an admirer, recommended that women be guided by a man from a young age to help them develop into ideal marriage partners – an attitude suggesting that the true subject of the portraits was the '*je ne sais quelle* surprising *youthfulness*' of the sitters.[57] Nature was traditionally seen as 'feminine',[58] and it is no coincidence that Van Gogh depicted one of his models against a background of ripened corn **(125)**. He also suggested that the portrait of Gachet's daughter Marguerite be placed among his series of elongated landscapes, to highlight the connection between 'one piece of nature and another', and looked for similarities in colour to lend weight to this idea **(130, 135)**.[59]

FINAL WORKS

Van Gogh made a study in which he attempted to take his portraits of women even further by transforming them into a more idyllic figure piece, drawing on the example of Puvis de Chavannes and incorporating a panoramic view of nature and a multitude of Gauguin-style undulating lines **(127)**. After he had visited Theo and Jo in Paris on 6 July, however, he exclusively produced landscapes and village scenes, albeit – with a single exception – on a large scale **(14, 17, 63, 67, 68, 136, 137, 139, 140, 143, 145, 146, 147, 157)**. The difference compared to his much less decisive attitude in the previous month is especially marked and is evidence that he had entirely regained his artistic confidence in the meantime.

Wheatfield with Crows **(137)**, produced two days after the eventful visit to Theo and Jo, played a crucial part in this.[60] Vincent had been caught in a summer storm on the rolling plains, and he sought emphatically in both that work and the following day's *Wheatfield under Thunderclouds* **(136)** 'to express sadness, extreme loneliness'.[61] At the same time, he believed that 'these canvases will tell you what I can't say in words, what I consider healthy and fortifying about the countryside'. This has often been characterized as contradictory, but it was not: Van Gogh's statement indicates only that after the first painting was finished, he had reconciled himself to his earlier view that, for him, 'the drama of a storm in nature, the drama of sorrow in life, is the best. A "paradou" is beautiful, but Gethsemane is more beautiful still.'[62]

Ever since his time in Paris, Van Gogh had wrestled with the question of whether there was a place in his art for the previously mentioned sorrow in life. The raging of the heart is impossible to suppress, yet this is at odds with the idea that he wanted to offer in his work a more 'humane', meaningful world. This could only be achieved if he accepted his suffering as part of it; but what if that pain were unbearable? For some time now, this had been the overriding issue.

In terms of its symbolism, *Wheatfield with Crows* follows on from the gloomy rain showers and agitated, stormy skies he painted in the spring of 1890 during a bout of depression. Since then – with the exception

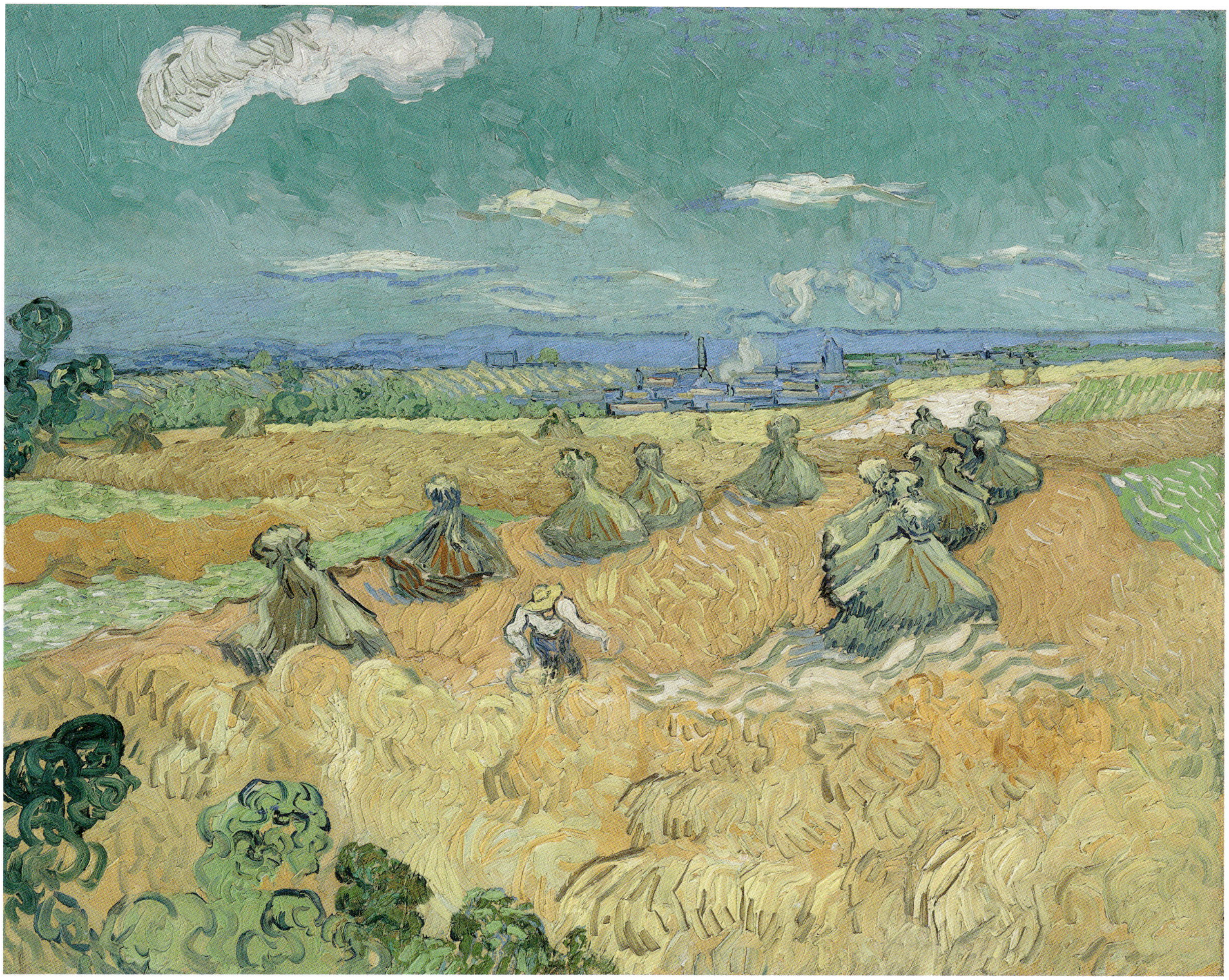

14 (#66)
Vincent van Gogh
Wheatfields with Reaper, Auvers-sur-Oise, 1890
Oil on canvas, 73.6 × 93 cm
Toledo Museum of Art, purchased with funds from the Libbey Endowment, Gift of Edward Drummond Libbey

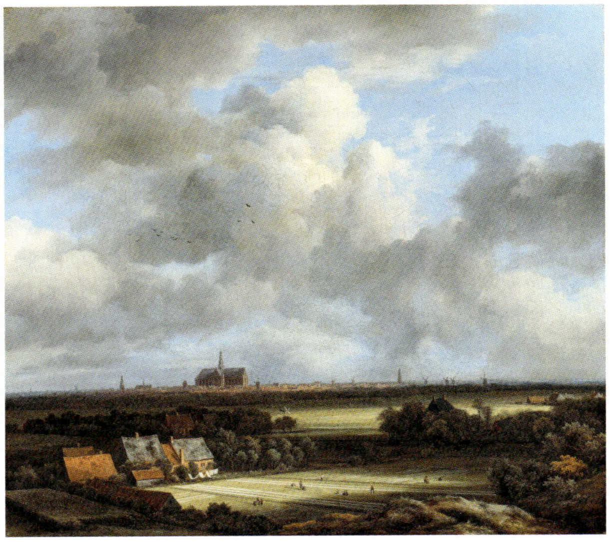

15
Jacob van Ruisdael
View of Haarlem with Bleaching Grounds, c. 1670–75
Oil on canvas, 55.5 × 62 cm
Mauritshuis, The Hague

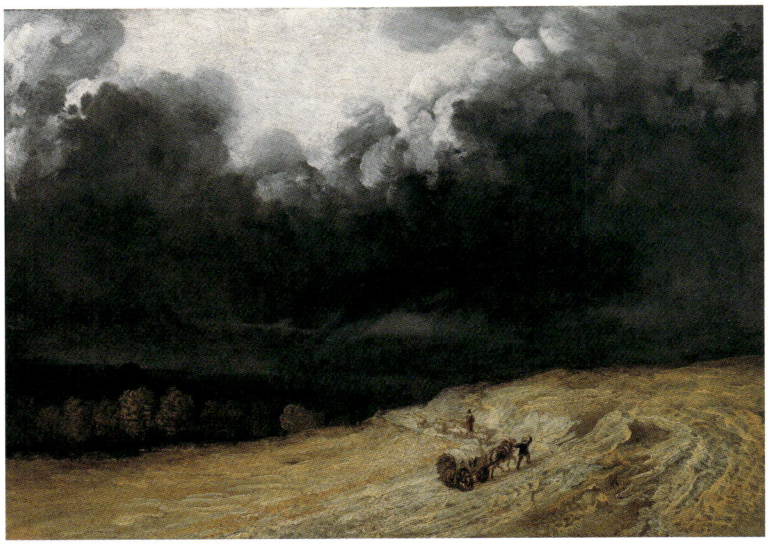

16
Georges Michel
Stormy Landscape, 1830–40
Oil on paper on panel, 51.5 × 73 cm
Belvedere Museum, Vienna

of *Sorrowing Old Man ('At Eternity's Gate')* **(167)** and his portrait of Dr Gachet **(159)** – he had managed to resist the urge to take suffering and existential exhaustion as his principal motif. In the early part of his stay in Auvers, he latched onto motifs that were more optimistic, youthful and redolent of security. This would change, however, after his visit to Paris on 6 July. The sense of despair that he had suppressed was now intensified, and when a storm broke out, he suddenly felt at one with a suffering nature.

Anyone who has experienced bad weather in the countryside knows how frightening it can be: thunderstorms can be accompanied by strong air currents, and this pronounced turbulence seems to have been particularly disconcerting to him. In his rendering of the scene, it is not only the wheat and the looming sky that taken on an agitated, wild expression, but the paths too: everything is in motion. This is the big difference compared to Georges Michel, his great example in the stormy landscape genre, who also excelled in the 'mode pathétique', but did so only by means of dramatic light-dark contrasts **(16)**.[63] Van Gogh went further, but – to quote De Meester again – it 'is very much the question whether painting was sufficient' truly to express what he felt. So strong were his emotions while painting, in fact, that he found it hard to stop the brush 'almost falling from my hands'.[64] To do justice to the gravity of the experience, he probably added the black shapes of the birds at the very end as a more literary symbol of impending doom.

It remains a sensitive subject even after so many years, but viewed in these terms, it would seem that it was after this that Van Gogh entered the final, 'intentional phase' of the suicide process.[65] Painting a scene of afflicted nature seems to have helped him accept the inner pain he had been building up for so long. Having suicide in mind as a potential solution, and even planning to go through with it in the near future, can actually be reassuring and it is telling that Vincent wrote to his mother and sister shortly afterwards that he was 'wholly in a mood of almost too much calm'.[66] What this 'too much calm' entailed is visible in several of the following paintings. *Wheatfields with Reaper, Auvers-sur-Oise* **(14)** and *Sheaves of Wheat* **(146)**, seem to have been painted – like the *Wheatfield with Reaper* of 1889 (Van Gogh Museum) – to express the idea that death is simply a part of life. The mown wheat represented 'humanity', but 'in this death nothing sad, it takes place in broad

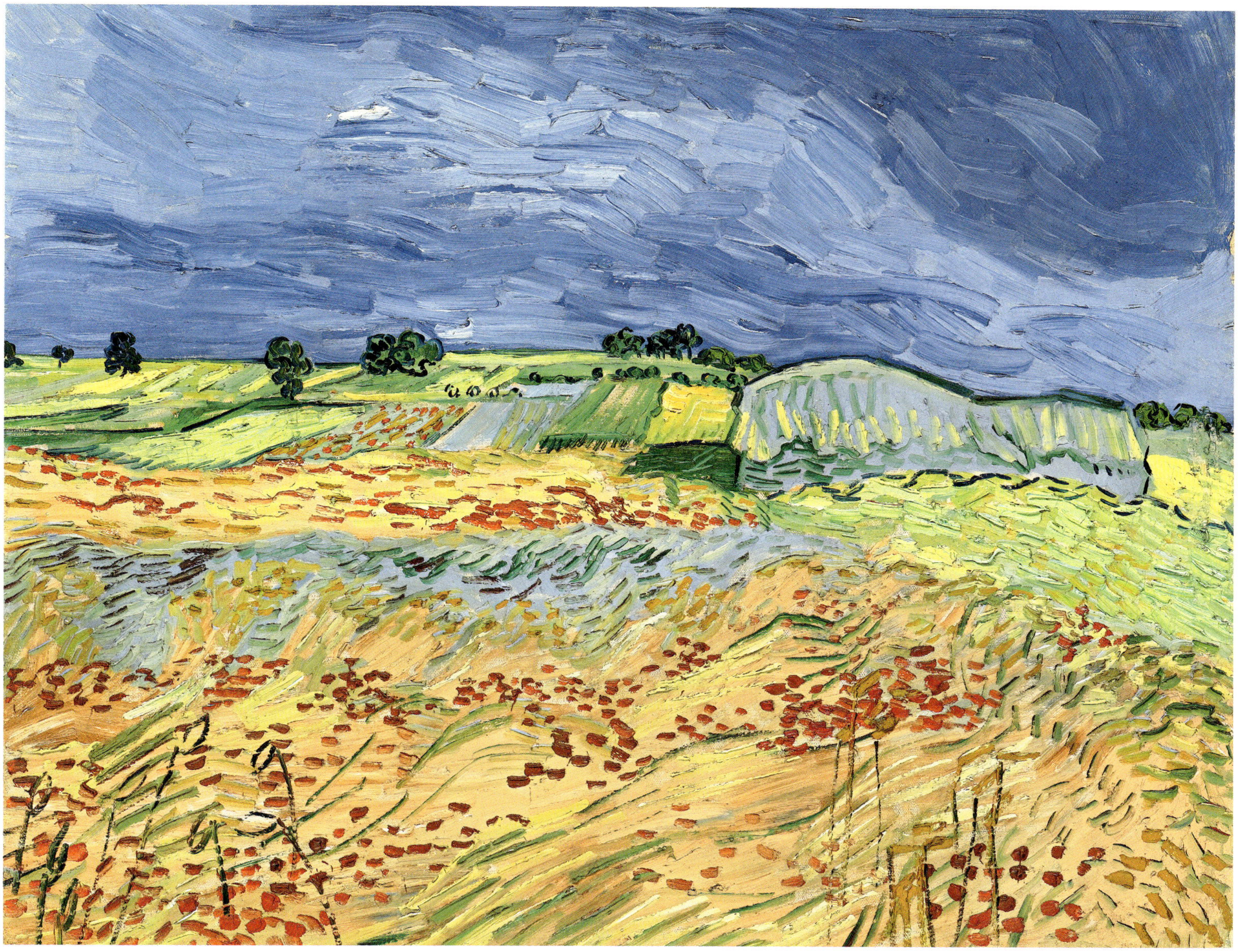

17 (#63)
Vincent van Gogh
The Fields, 1890
Oil on canvas, 50 × 65 cm
Private collection

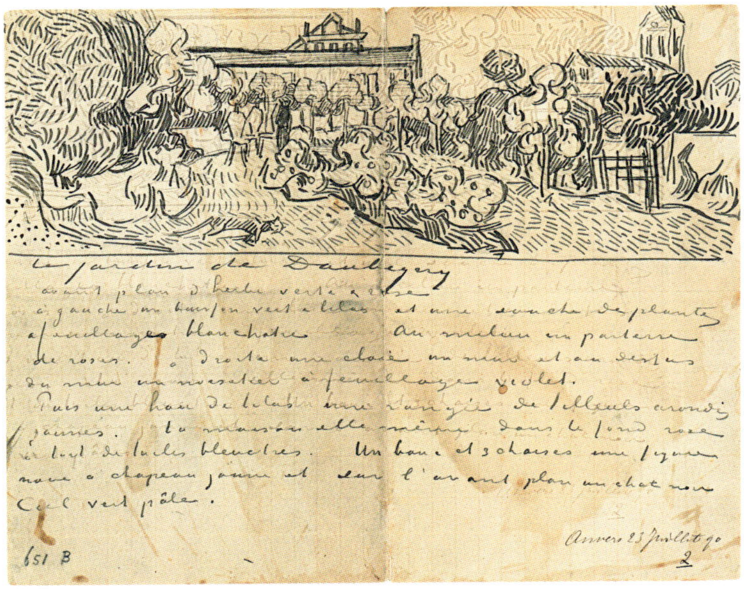

Le jardin de Daubigny
avant plan d'herbe verte et rose
à gauche un buisson vert et lilas et une souche de plante
à feuillage blanchâtre au milieu un parterre
de roses. à droite une claie un mur et au dessus
du mur un noisetier à feuillage violet.
Puis une haie de lilas une rangée de tilleuls arrondis
jaunes. la maison elle même dans le fond rose
le toit de tuiles bleuâtres. Un banc et 3 chaises une figure
noire à chapeau jaune et sur l'avant plan un chat noir
Ciel vert pâle.
651 B
Auvers 23 juillet 90
2

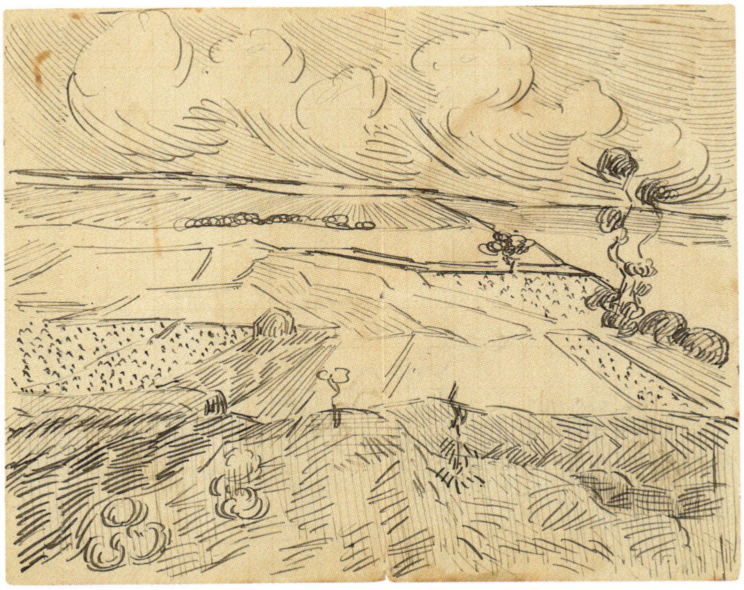

daylight with a sun that floods everything with a light of fine gold'.[67]

This is the same life lesson that *Tree Roots* **(157)**, his last painting, seems to convey. Echoing his description of a drawing in 1882, the roots stand for 'frantically and fervently rooting oneself, as it were, in the earth, and yet being half torn up by the storm';[68] yet all this plays out in a place that, as De Meester rightly observed, is 'full of sun and life'. A similar contradiction underlies *Auvers-sur-Oise Town Hall on 14 July 1890* **(63)**, which shows the joyful celebration of the French national day, yet curiously without people. Returning to Fromentin's book, we viewers might ask the same question that he posed about Ruisdael: 'What had life done to him that he should have so contemptuous or so bitter a feeling for it? What had men done to him that he should retire into solitude and should, to such a point, avoid having anything to do with them – even in his pictures?'[69]

A UNIVERSAL AND HUMAN MESSAGE

The biographical interpretations of the Van Gogh paintings described above are presented in the belief that changes in his frame of mind affected what he produced, in the same way that a change of surroundings results in different paintings. Yet art is never generated by a mindset alone: the influence of Van Gogh's mental state was limited to certain choices he made in the artistic process. It does not explain the magic of his artistry.[70]

Nor did Van Gogh view his paintings as reflections on his own mental state: the meaning he pursued was more universal, although this could only be achieved in his opinion if the expression was grounded in an authentic, personal experience. Despite the inevitable sadness in any individual existence, he was keen to sing the praises of life and nature too, and did so in those final panoramic landscapes above all, which seem so closely modelled on those of Ruisdael **(15, 17)**. But the way he worked them out was plainly not the same. We are struck by the light, blond tone, which the critic Maurice Beaubourg praised so effusively in *Sheaves of Wheat* in 1890. The 'pale golden sheaves', he wrote, 'cast shadows of an almost ravishing, silvery and soft colouring' **(146)**, and we find the same refined, more muted palette in many of the other paintings from the final weeks of his life **(67, 68, 143, 145, 146)**.[71]

Although their colour is likely to have shifted somewhat due to Van Gogh's use of red lakes, these works stand out for their lack of pronounced colours. As in his *Women Picking Olives* from the previous year **(12, 103)** – a work that was intended to be idyllic

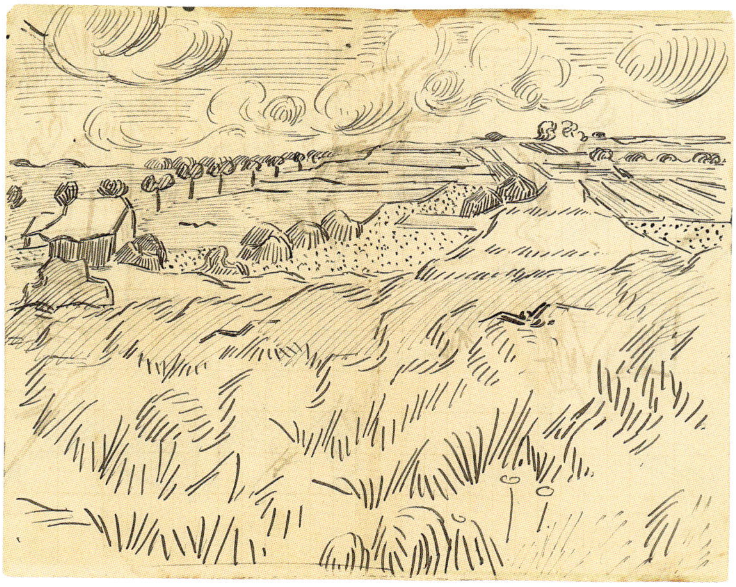

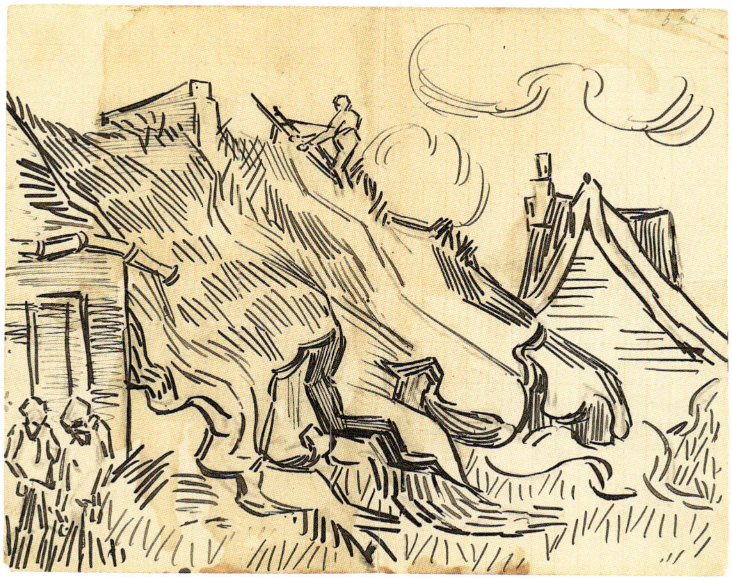

18
Letter from Vincent to Theo with sketches of *Daubigny's Garden*, *Wheatfields* and *Cottages in Chaponval*, 23 July 1890
Pen and ink on paper, 17 × 21.7 cm
Van Gogh Museum, Amsterdam

– soft greens and pinks dominate, and it is fair to assume that the artist had an elegiac effect in mind in the vein of Puvis de Chavannes's fresco-like approach in *Inter artes et naturam*. His *Rain – Auvers-sur-Oise* **(145)** is not in the least 'infinitely sinister in its bare, deadly lines' as Van Eeden had it in his 1890 review, but slightly wistful, a sense heightened by the way Van Gogh did not set down the rain as a heavy curtain of continuous streaks, but a gossamer fabric that links subtly and effortlessly with the landscape beyond.[72]

Van Gogh's magic as an artist also rested on this craftsmanship, which he valued as much as the universal, 'humane' message of his pictures. Which brings us back to the question with which this essay began. How does the work from his very last months compare with his earlier achievements? Did he transcend himself? No, in essence, he was unchanged – as inventive and experimental as he had been before. It is simply that different circumstances led him to make different choices. He might have been a little uncertain when he arrived as to which artistic course he would follow, but stylistic variety remained his highest goal. Although he felt old, he was still relatively young and was, moreover, an artist full of promise. It was his self-chosen end that nipped this artistry in the bud.

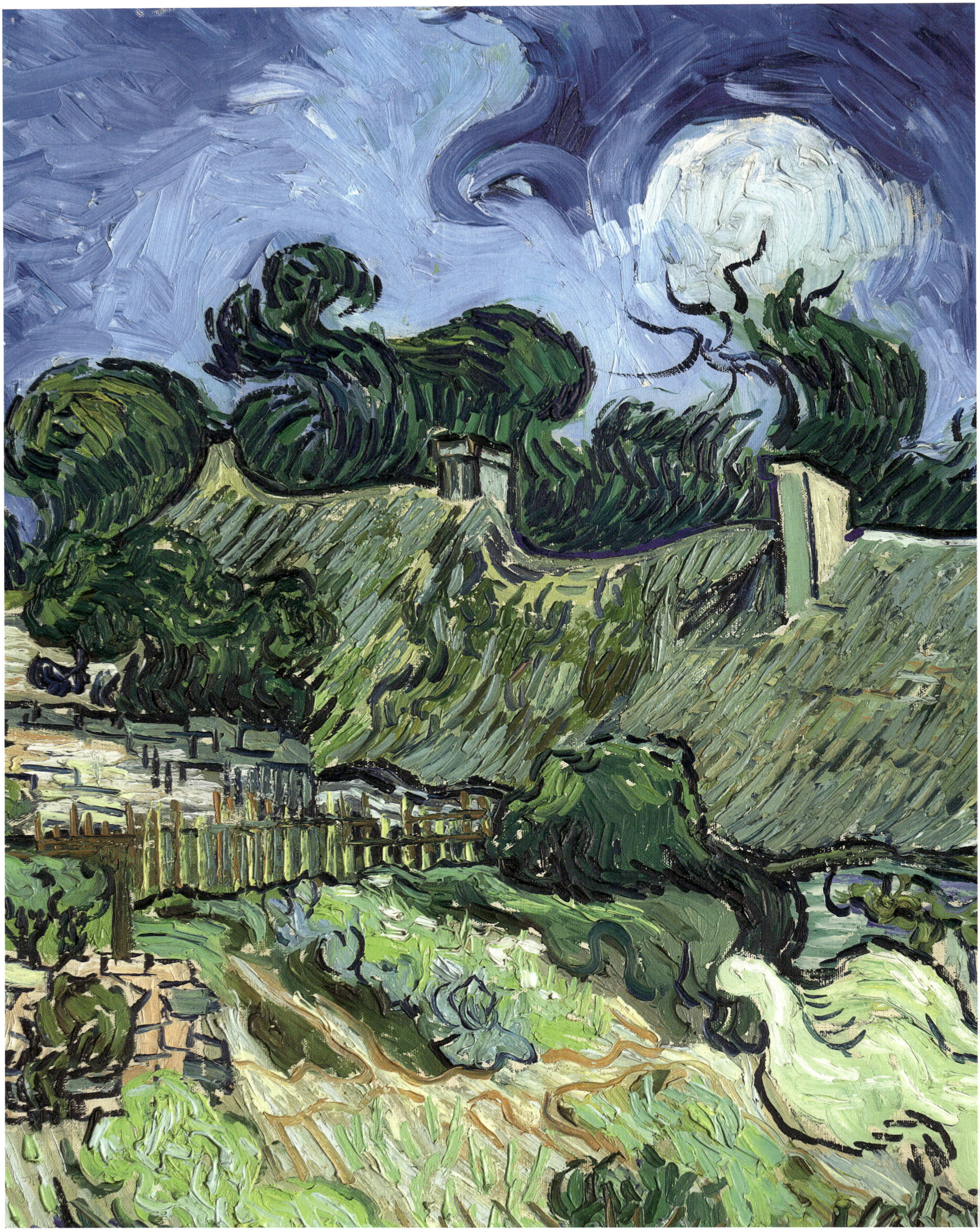

EXPLORING AUVERS-SUR-OISE

PEOPLE AND PLACES

WOUTER VAN DER VEEN

On 15 August 1887, while Vincent van Gogh was still living in Paris, the writer and journalist Paul Alexis, under the pseudonym Trublot, published a light-hearted article about Auvers-sur-Oise and its artists' colony in *Le Cri du peuple*.[1] In a few lines, he sketches the portrait of a 'large village' of about two thousand inhabitants, stretching for eight to ten kilometres between the river Oise and 'a long, rocky ridge eaten away by quarries'. Alexis recalls Paul Cézanne's stay in the village in the 1870s and his emblematic painting *The Hanged Man's House, Auvers-sur-Oise* **(27)**. He mentions the more and less well-known artists who have settled in or regularly visit this picturesque rural setting, including Pierre-Auguste Renoir and Camille Pissaro, and he writes of Eugène Murer and his renowned collection of Impressionist works. Murer's fellow villager, the 'sympathetically opinionated' doctor Paul Ferdinand Gachet **(182)** is also described as an allopath and homeopath, devoted to painting, fishing, literature, rowing and the education of his children, whom Alexis somewhat curiously but also lovingly refers to as 'Monsieur Coco' and 'the two know-it-alls'.

Alexis notes that he had travelled to the village by train, a detail that largely explains Auvers-sur-Oise's popularity with Parisians. There had been a railway connection to the village since 1846, making the journey from Paris less than an hour, and that made it a perfectly situated holiday destination for the capital's residents – for a day in the country or a longer stay **(25)**. Charles-François Daubigny, who had spent his early childhood not far from there in Valmondois and knew the area like the back of his hand, had a large studio house built in Auvers in 1861. There he welcomed painter friends, paving the way for numerous artists who, in turn, were inspired by the banks of the Oise, the picturesque village and the surrounding countryside.

When Van Gogh arrived in Auvers on 20 May 1890, he sensed immediately that it was a special place. That same day, he wrote to his brother Theo and his wife Jo: 'it's gravely beautiful, it's the heart of the countryside, distinctive and picturesque.'[2] The following day, he described how two intertwined worlds coexisted, with 'modern villas' in close proximity to 'the old thatched cottages that are falling into ruin'.[3] He was fascinated by 'the

Vincent van Gogh
Thatched Cottages in Cordeville, Auvers-sur-Oise, 1890
Detail of 41 (#14)

AUVERS-SUR-OISE

1890

19
Rue Daubigny, Auvers-sur-Oise, the location where Van Gogh painted *Tree Roots*, c. 1910

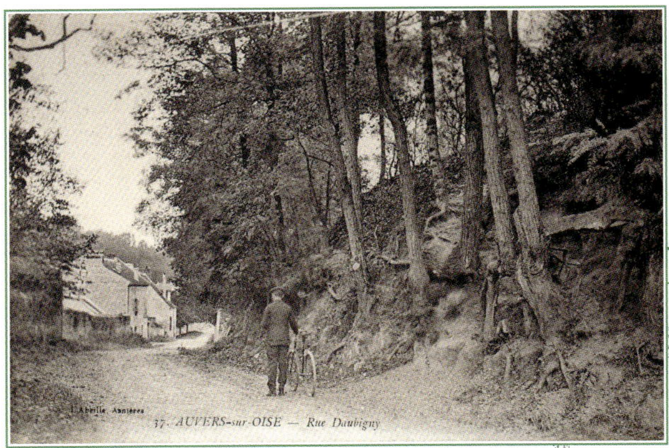

20
Rue Daubigny, painter at work, c. 1900–10

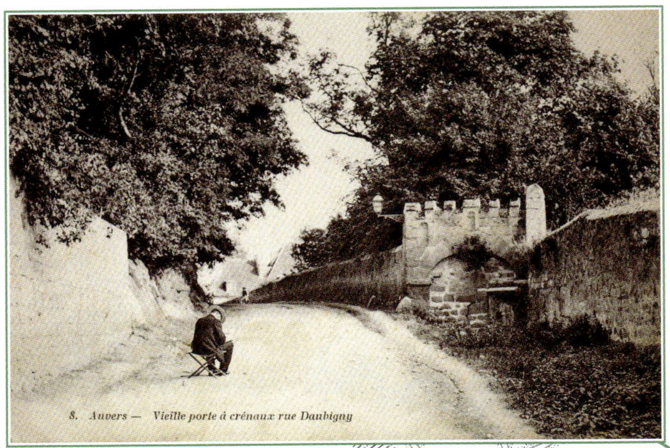

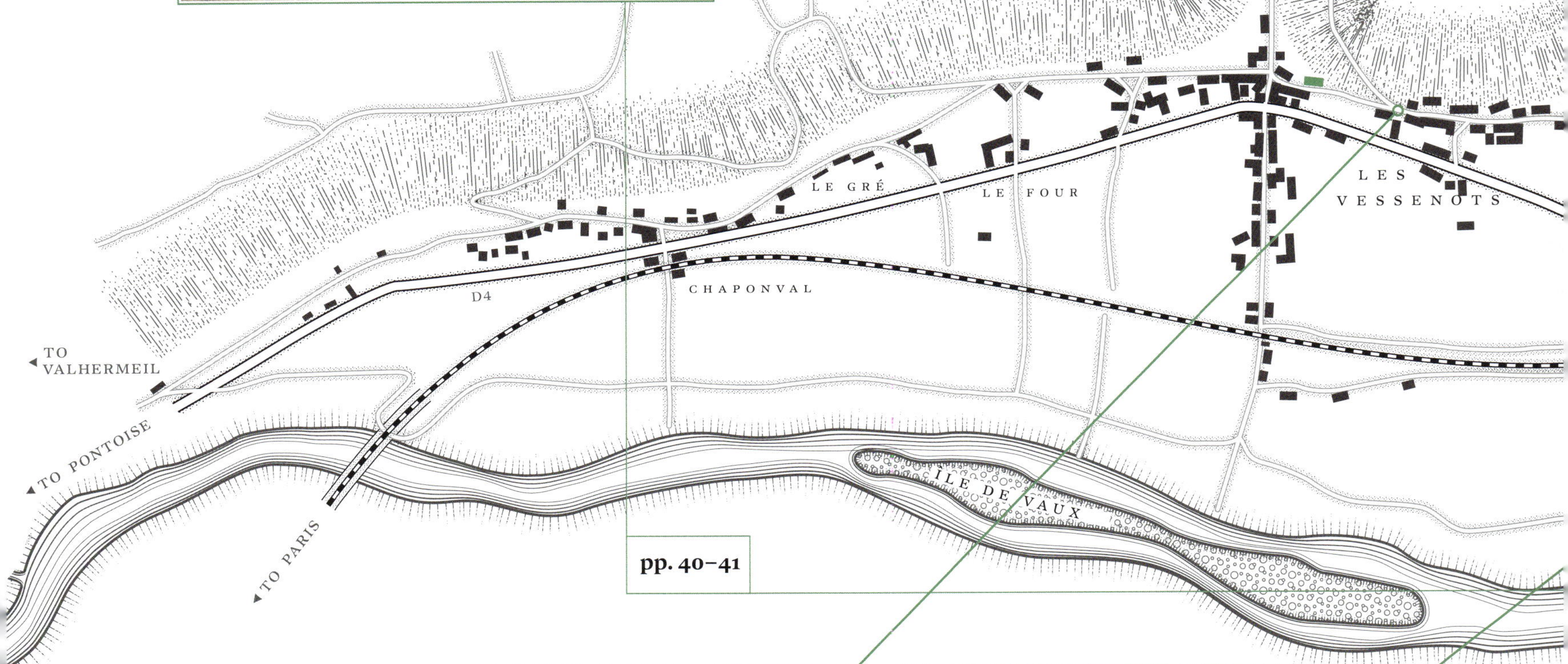

pp. 40–41

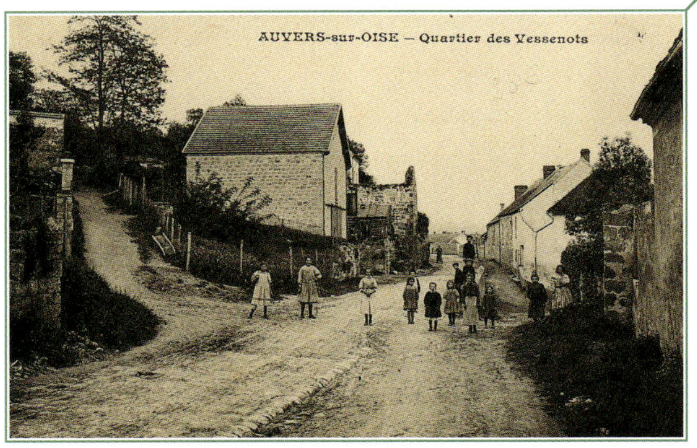

21
Rue des Vessenots, c. 1905

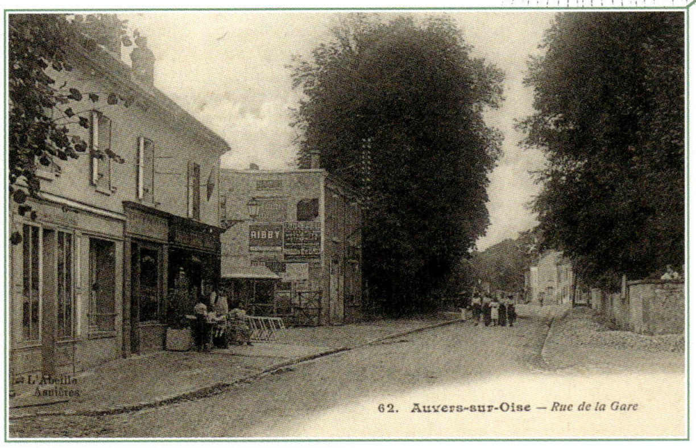

22
Rue de la Gare, c. 1905

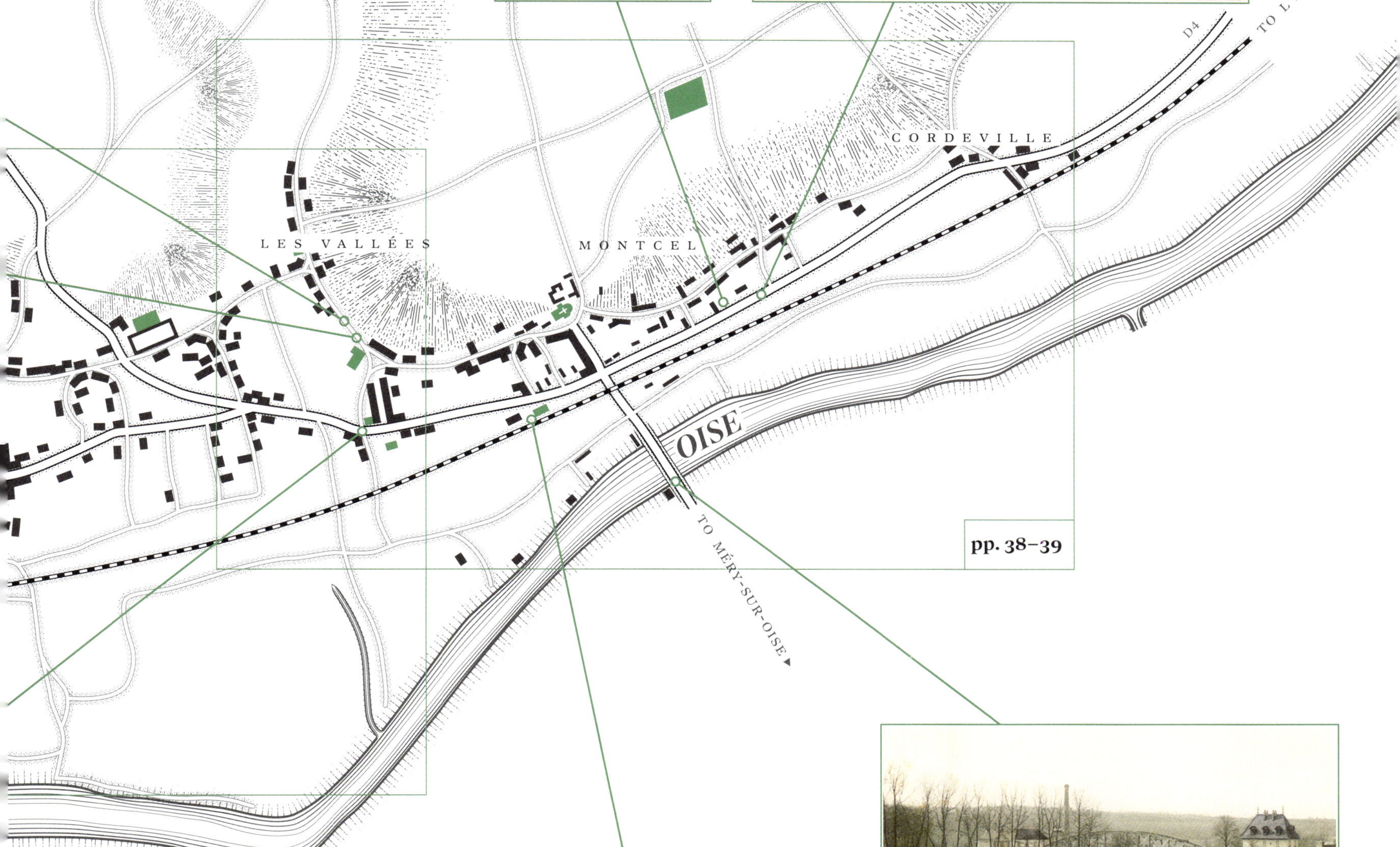

pp. 38–39

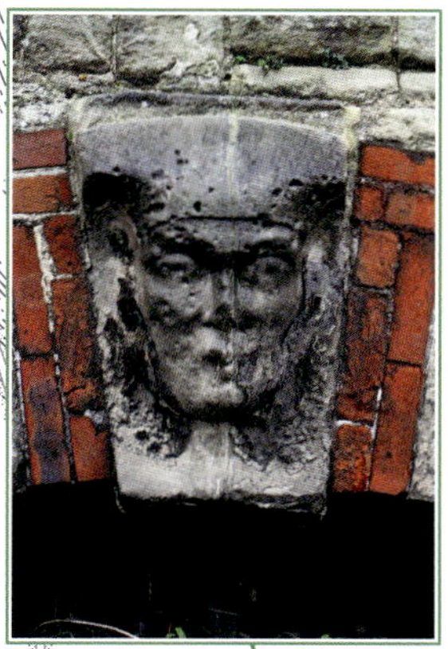

23
Rue Rajon, keystone with the head of a sphinx, c. 1870

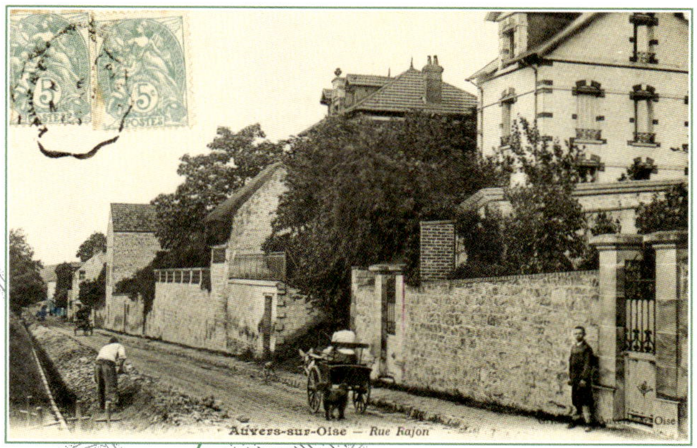

24
Rue Rajon, c. 1905

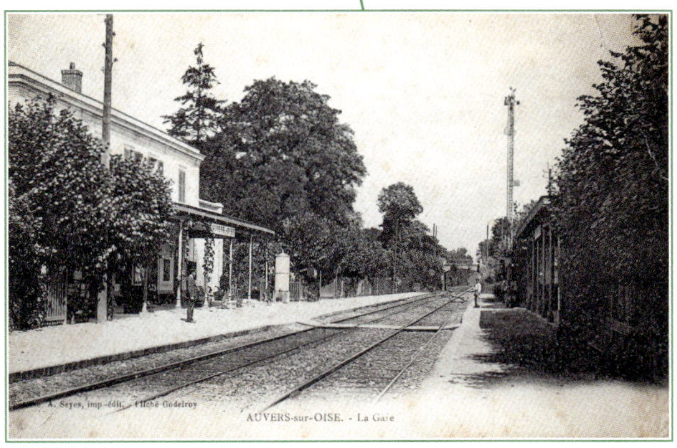

25
Station at Auvers-sur-Oise, c. 1900–10

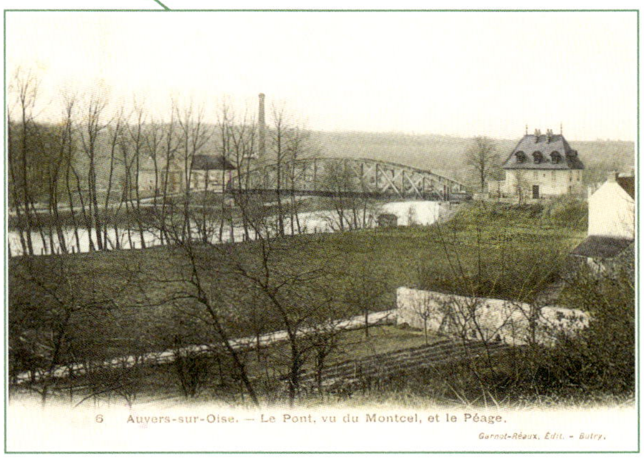

26
Bridge over the Oise viewed from Montcel, c. 1905

AUVERS-SUR-OISE

TOWN CENTRE

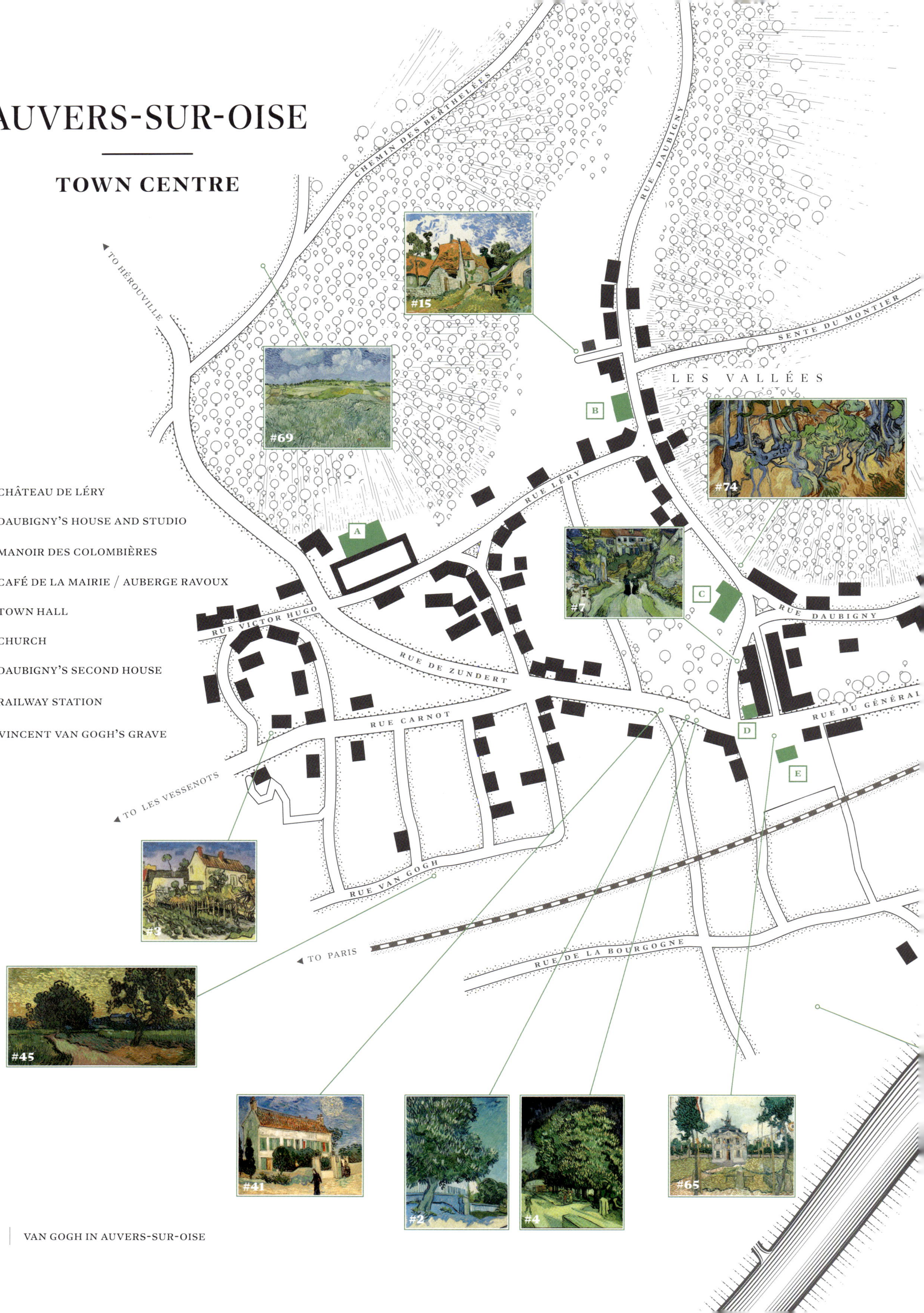

- A CHÂTEAU DE LÉRY
- B DAUBIGNY'S HOUSE AND STUDIO
- C MANOIR DES COLOMBIÈRES
- D CAFÉ DE LA MAIRIE / AUBERGE RAVOUX
- E TOWN HALL
- F CHURCH
- G DAUBIGNY'S SECOND HOUSE
- H RAILWAY STATION
- + VINCENT VAN GOGH'S GRAVE

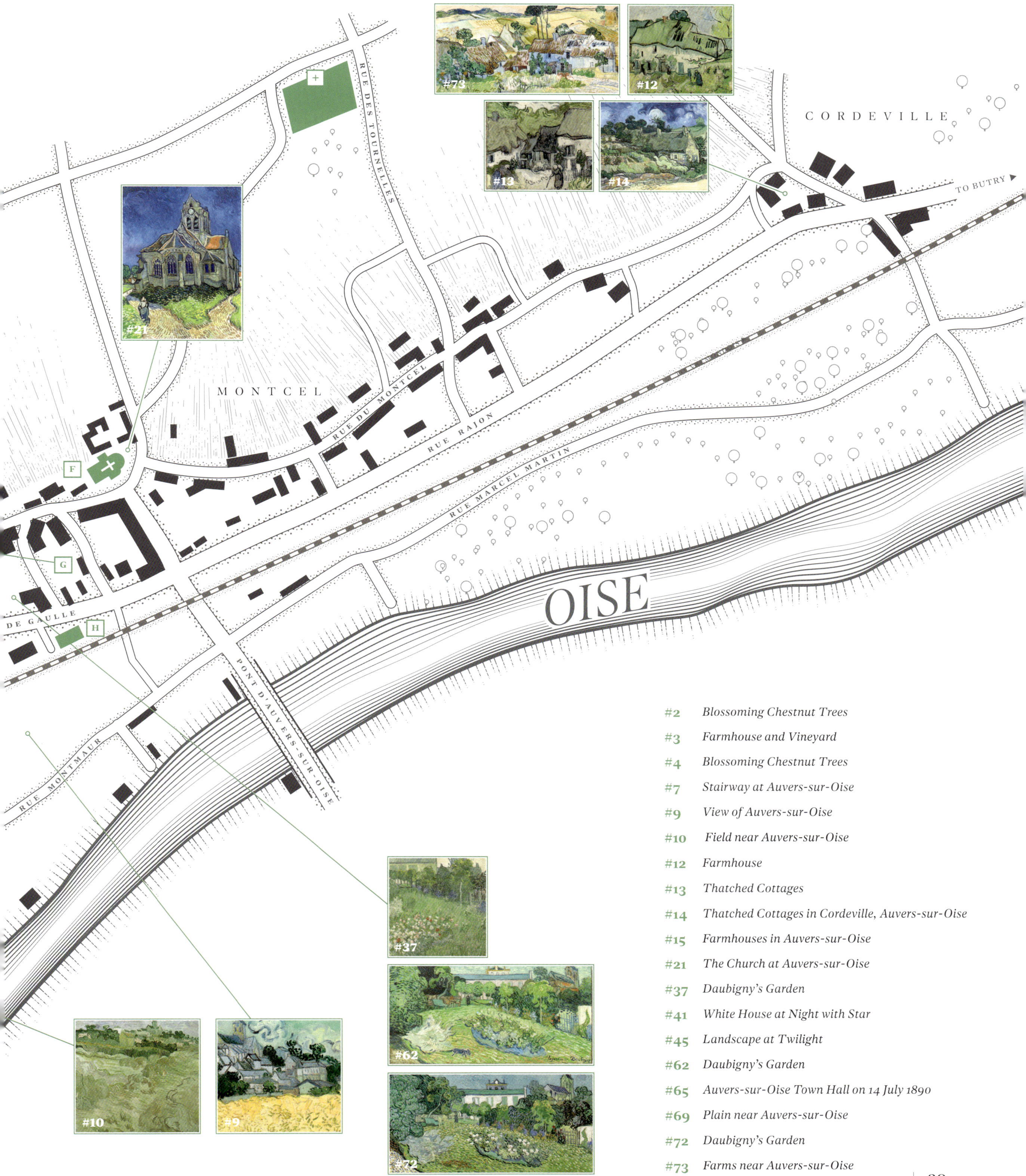

#2 *Blossoming Chestnut Trees*
#3 *Farmhouse and Vineyard*
#4 *Blossoming Chestnut Trees*
#7 *Stairway at Auvers-sur-Oise*
#9 *View of Auvers-sur-Oise*
#10 *Field near Auvers-sur-Oise*
#12 *Farmhouse*
#13 *Thatched Cottages*
#14 *Thatched Cottages in Cordeville, Auvers-sur-Oise*
#15 *Farmhouses in Auvers-sur-Oise*
#21 *The Church at Auvers-sur-Oise*
#37 *Daubigny's Garden*
#41 *White House at Night with Star*
#45 *Landscape at Twilight*
#62 *Daubigny's Garden*
#65 *Auvers-sur-Oise Town Hall on 14 July 1890*
#69 *Plain near Auvers-sur-Oise*
#72 *Daubigny's Garden*
#73 *Farms near Auvers-sur-Oise*
#74 *Tree Roots*

AUVERS-SUR-OISE

LES VESSENOTS

- **#1** *Thatched Cottages*
- **#5** *The House of Père Pilon*
- **#8** *Doctor Gachet's Garden*
- **#16** *Marguerite Gachet in the Garden*
- **#20** *Doctor Paul Gachet*
- **#23** *Blossoming Acacia*
- **#27** *Houses at Auvers-sur-Oise*
- **#28** *Houses at Auvers-sur-Oise*
- **#30** *Landscape with Carriage and Train*
- **#31** *Vineyards at Auvers-sur-Oise*
- **#52** *Marguerite Gachet at the Piano*
- **#71** *Cottages in Chaponval*

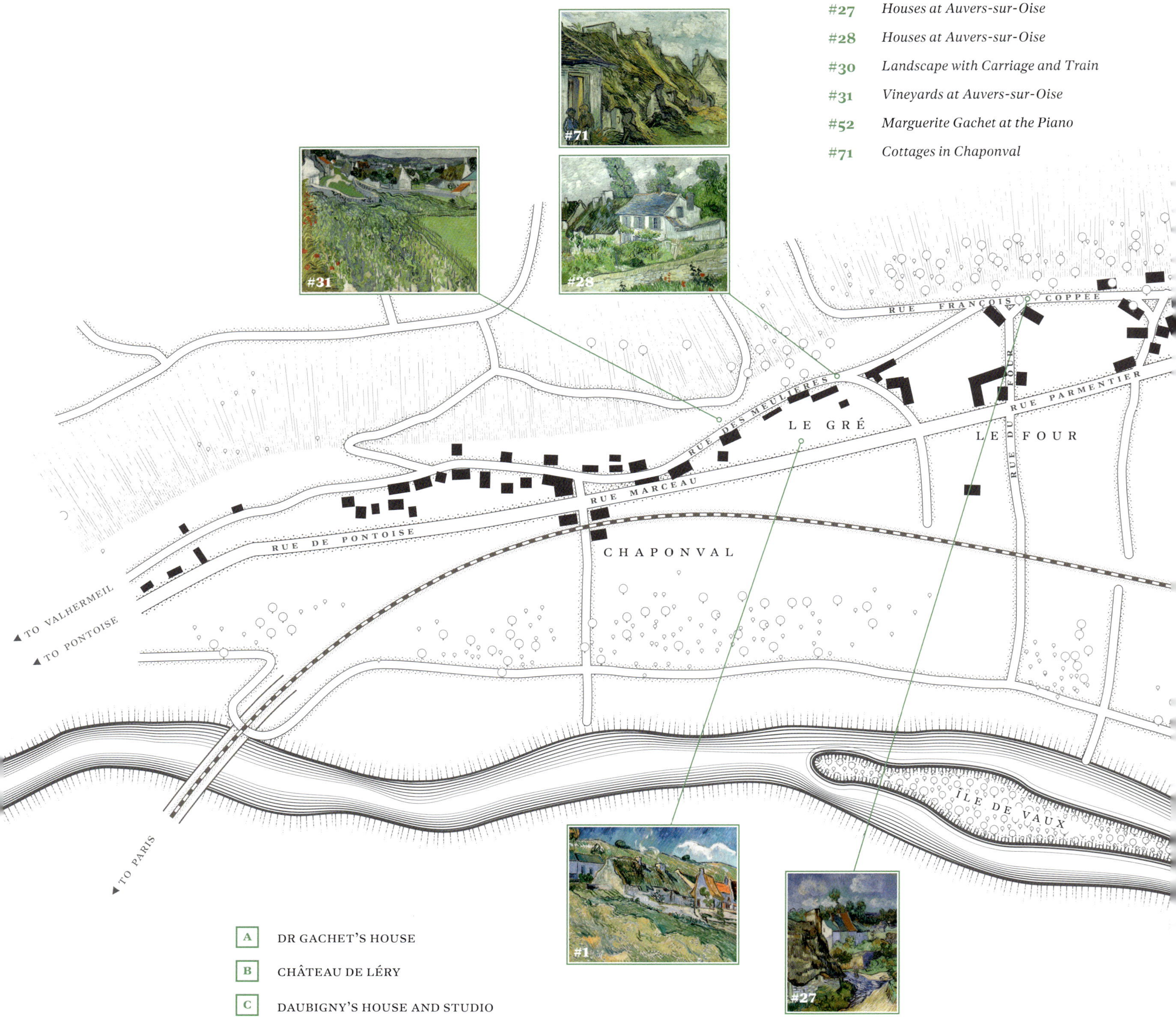

- A DR GACHET'S HOUSE
- B CHÂTEAU DE LÉRY
- C DAUBIGNY'S HOUSE AND STUDIO
- D MANOIR DES COLOMBIÈRES
- E CAFÉ DE LA MAIRIE / AUBERGE RAVOUX
- F TOWN HALL

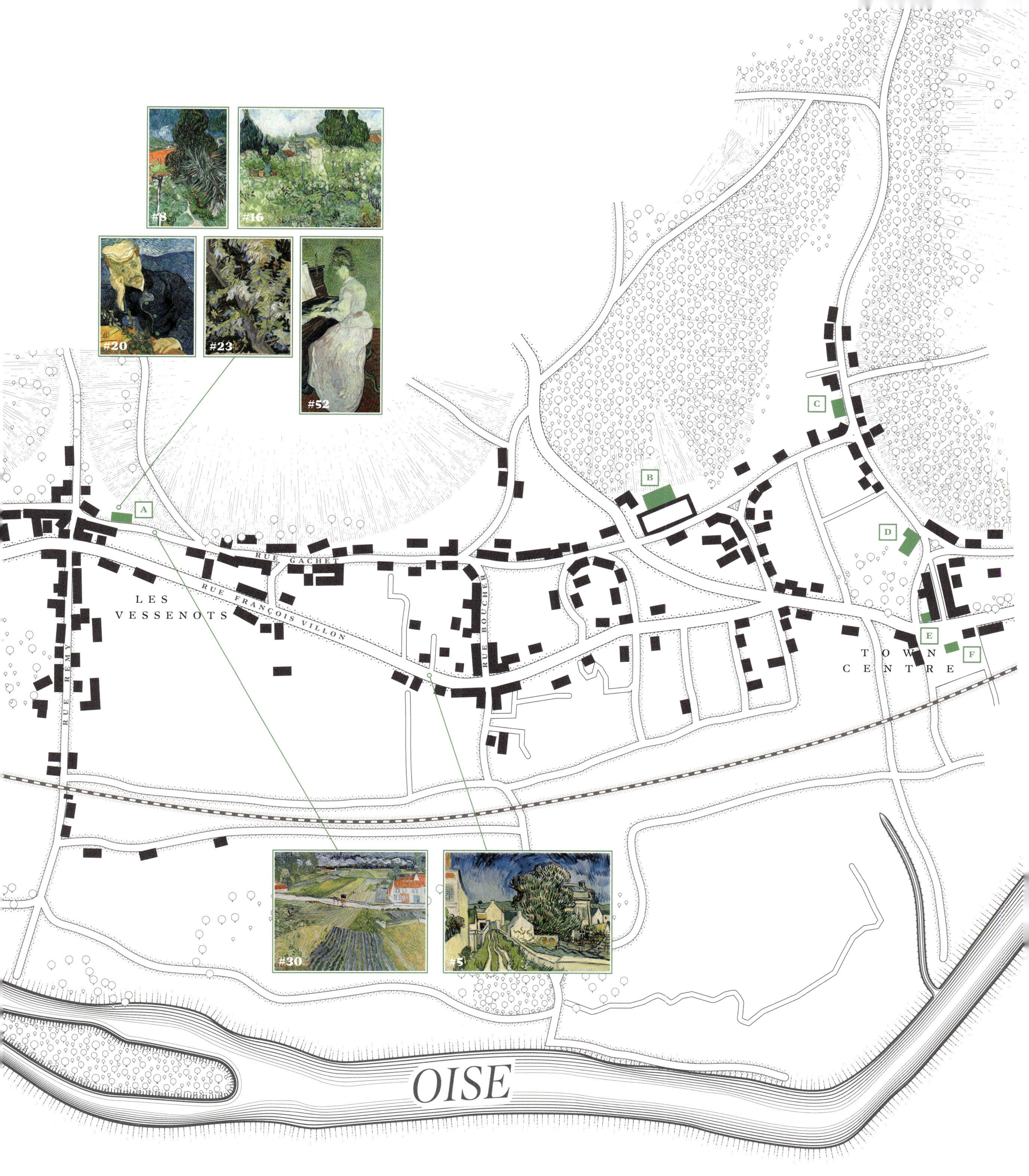
#8
#16
#20
#23
#52
A
B
C
D
E
F
RUE GACHET
RUE FRANÇOIS VILLON
RUE BOUCHER
RUE RÉMY
LES VESSENOTS
TOWN CENTRE
#30
#5
OISE

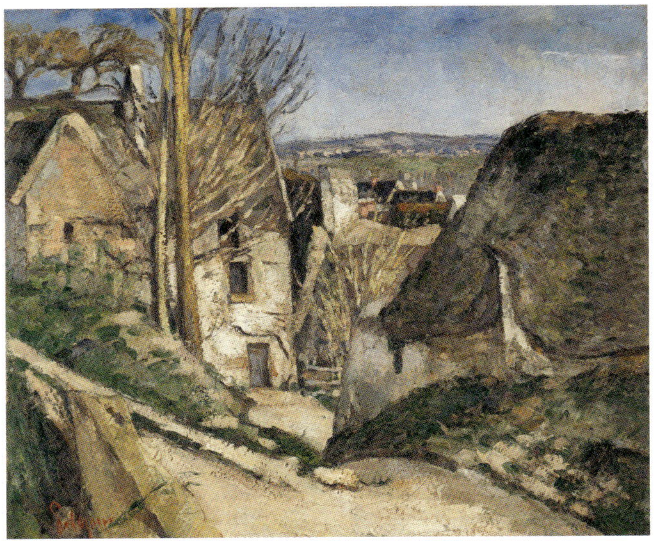

27
Paul Cézanne
The Hanged Man's House, Auvers-sur-Oise, 1873
Oil on canvas, 55.5 × 66.3 cm
Musée d'Orsay, Paris, bequest
of Comte Isaac de Camondo, 1911

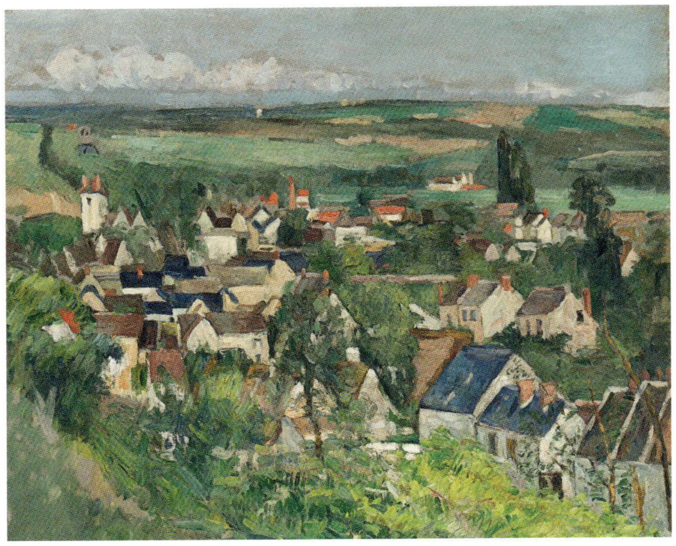

28
Paul Cézanne
View of Auvers-sur-Oise, 1873–75
Oil on canvas, 65.2 × 81.3 cm
The Art Institute of Chicago, Mr. and Mrs.
Larned Lewis Coburn Memorial Collection

development of a new society in the old one,' and resolved to express in his work 'the desperately swift passage of things in modern life.'[4]

For Van Gogh, who had left the institution in Saint-Rémy-de-Provence at his own request on 16 May 1890 after a stay of more than a year, Auvers-sur-Oise was the ideal destination. There he could count on the benevolent attention of Dr Gachet, who was known for his affinity with innovative artists,[5] thus ensuring a medically safe environment in a region frequented by numerous painters, draughtsmen, watercolourists and engravers **(20)**. Van Gogh wanted to paint and draw to his heart's content, and in picturesque Auvers he would surely be able to find the necessary motifs. He had brought a few frames, stretcher frames and his easel so that he could set to work immediately.[6]

The primary and least problematic sources for following Van Gogh's footsteps in Auvers-sur-Oise are his letters, drawings and canvases, most of whose motifs can be identified and located. A few secondary sources may supplement or clarify some of the details: a series of testimonies by Adeline Carrié-Ravoux from the mid-1950s,[7] an interview with René Secrétan,[8] several texts by Dr Gachet's son, Paul Louis Gachet **(184)**,[9] and the publications of Alain Mothe and Claude Millon,[10] both *Auversois* with an in-depth knowledge of the village.

This essay looks at Van Gogh's explorations in Auvers not chronologically, but from his two main vantage points: the home of Dr Gachet, which he visited about ten times times, and the Café de la Mairie, where he occupied a small attic room.

AROUND DR GACHET'S HOUSE

Van Gogh's first destination in Auvers-sur-Oise was Dr Gachet's house, which was located in the geographical centre of the village, equidistant from the hamlets of Butry and Valhermeil. The house was located on the old road from L'Ile-Adam to Pontoise and offered an unobstructed view of the Oise valley **(28)**. From the station,[11] Van Gogh passed numerous motifs that he would soon immortalize: the town hall, the Château de Léry, villas, scattered farms and finally the cultivated fields between rue Boucher and the hamlet of Les Vessenots. To the right rose the plateau of Vexin and to the left ran the railway line alongside the Oise to Chaponval, where it crossed the river.

From the rue des Vessenots (today's rue Gachet), a flight of steps led to the entrance of Gachet's house.

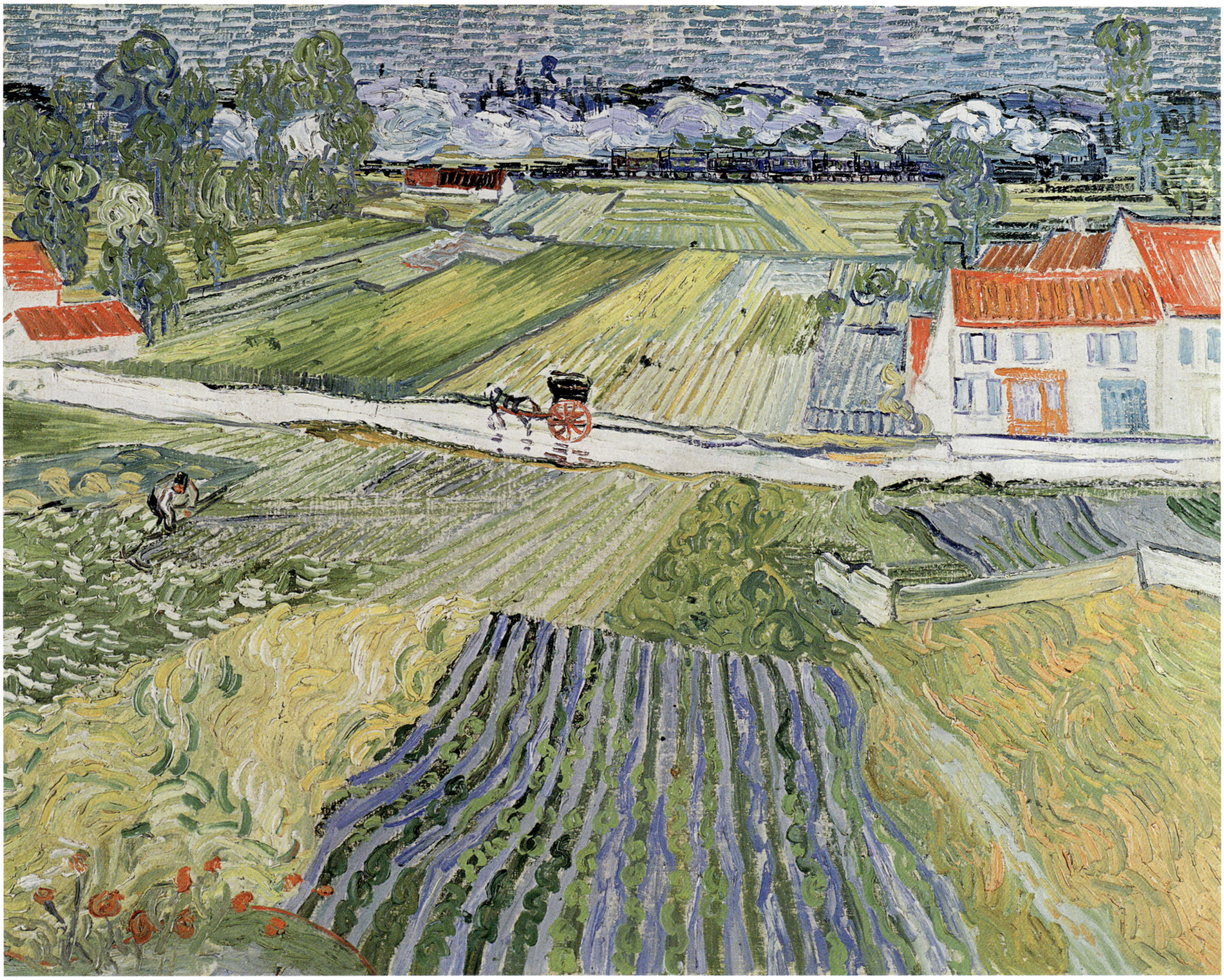

29 (#30)
Vincent van Gogh
Landscape with Carriage and Train, 1890
Oil on canvas, 72 × 90 cm
The Pushkin State Museum of Fine Arts, Moscow

According to Paul Gachet Jr, Van Gogh turned halfway up the stairs and uttered a drawn-out, admiring 'Oh ...' when he saw the landscape stretched out before him.[12] This seems a somewhat theatrical anecdote that served mainly to emphasize that the then sixteen-year-old young man was a privileged witness to all the important phases of Van Gogh's stay in Auvers, but it is consistent with the reaction visitors may have when they see that view for the first time. *Landscape with Carriage and Train* **(29)**, painted a few dozen metres from the doctor's house, gives a good impression of part of the panorama.

Van Gogh was less enthusiastic about the interior of the house. Apart from a few Impressionist paintings by Cézanne, Armand Guillaumin and Camille Pissarro, the doctor's furnishings found no mercy in his eyes. After his third visit, on Sunday, 1 June, he wrote to Theo: 'his house [...] is full, full like an antique dealer's, of things that aren't always interesting, it's terrible, even'. It did have the advantage that he could always find something there 'for arranging flowers or still lifes' **(190)**.[13]

After a brief examination on the day they met, the doctor reassured his patient. He advised him to stop thinking about his illness and to focus on his work. Van Gogh saw in this a further indication that his problems were primarily the result of an 'illness of the south'.[14] According to Paul Gachet Jr and biographer Gustave Coquiot, Van Gogh spent at least the first night after his arrival at the Saint-Aubin inn, near the doctor's house.[15] It is true that Gachet had recommended lodgings to him, but whether it was this inn is not certain. In any case, what is certain is that from the beginning, Van Gogh stayed only at Café de la Mairie.[16]

Dr Gachet, who occasionally painted and engraved, had set up a modest studio with a printing press in the attic of his large house. He used this press for his own creations, of course, but also made it available to the artists he hosted. Van Gogh made and printed an etching here, on 15 June, his only one – a portrait of Gachet that would be titled 'The Man with the Pipe' **(115, 116, 169)**.[17] Incidentally, on 3 and 4 June he had already painted a portrait of Dr Gachet **(159)**, a variation of which he made shortly thereafter and gave to his model **(112)**.

Gachet may have advised Van Gogh to look for motifs in the immediate vicinity of his home, for the first thing Van Gogh painted was *Thatched Cottages*, in the hamlet of Gré, a few hundred metres from the rue des Vessenots **(33, 37)**. These houses had long appealed to artists – Gachet, too, had painted and engraved them, as seen from the main road to Pontoise, in the 1870s. Van Gogh returned to the motif at least four more times. In *Houses at Auvers-sur-Oise*, he emphasized the contrast between the modern house with a slate roof – also called 'the house of père Lacroix', after the mason who lived there[18] – and the traditional cottages with thatched roofs leaning against it **(40)**. Later, towards the end of his stay, he focused on the same thatched cottages, now seen from the rue du Gré **(30, 36)**. This first subject immediately shows that the painter took liberties in the representation of what he observed, so that it is not always easy to identify the places depicted. Thus, among other things, he made changes to the perspective, dividing walls, buildings and vegetation.

Van Gogh did not venture much further west from the village, unlike Cézanne and Pissarro, who explored the area thoroughly, particularly around the hamlet of Valhermeil.[19] Unlike what he had been accustomed to in Provence, the painter did not travel great distances during the first weeks of his stay in Auvers. He frequently walked back and forth between the Café de la Mairie and Dr Gachet's house, thus being able to observe the heart of the village from all angles. The surroundings of Ferme du Four **(4)**, Les Vessenots **(50, 66)** and Gré offered him more than enough inspiration. There he saw women and children at work in the fields, busy harvesting mainly peas, broad beans and green beans, as well as carters, woodcutters, gardeners, reapers and haystack builders in and around the village.[20]

The 'modern portrait' was a second major theme for Van Gogh early on during his stay in Auvers-sur-Oise – by which he meant portraits 'which would look like apparitions to people a century later', as he wrote to his sister Willemien.[21] Gachet could perhaps 'give me a hand with the models'[22] and, Van Gogh hoped, find portrait-lovers. To begin with, the doctor's family was able to provide models. His twenty-year-old daughter Marguerite **(183)** posed for the ambitious canvas *Marguerite Gachet at the Piano* **(130)** and Louise ('Lisette') Joséphine Elisa Chevalier may have been the 'country girl'

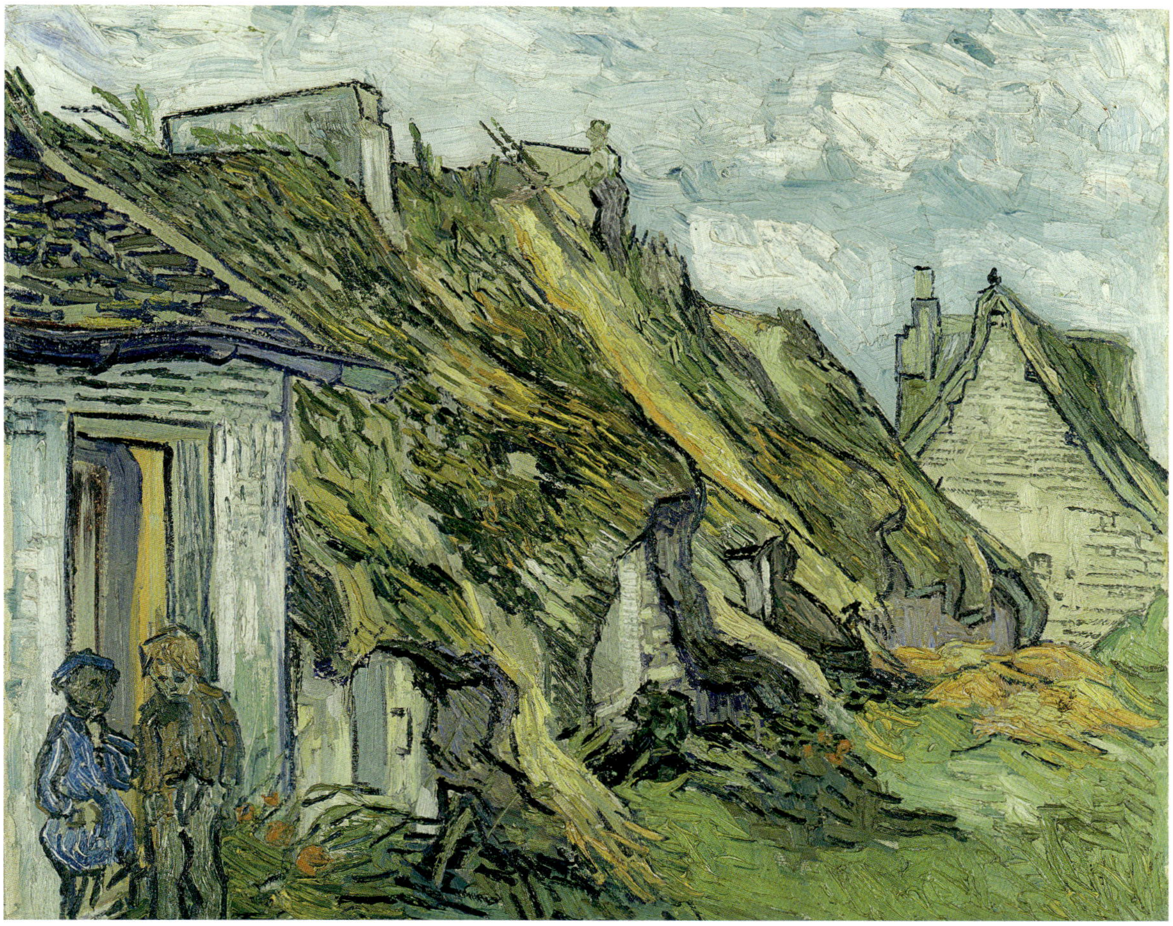

30 (#71)
Vincent van Gogh
Cottages in Chaponval, 1890
Oil on canvas, 65 × 81 cm
Kunsthaus Zürich, bequest of
Dr. Hans Schuler, 1920

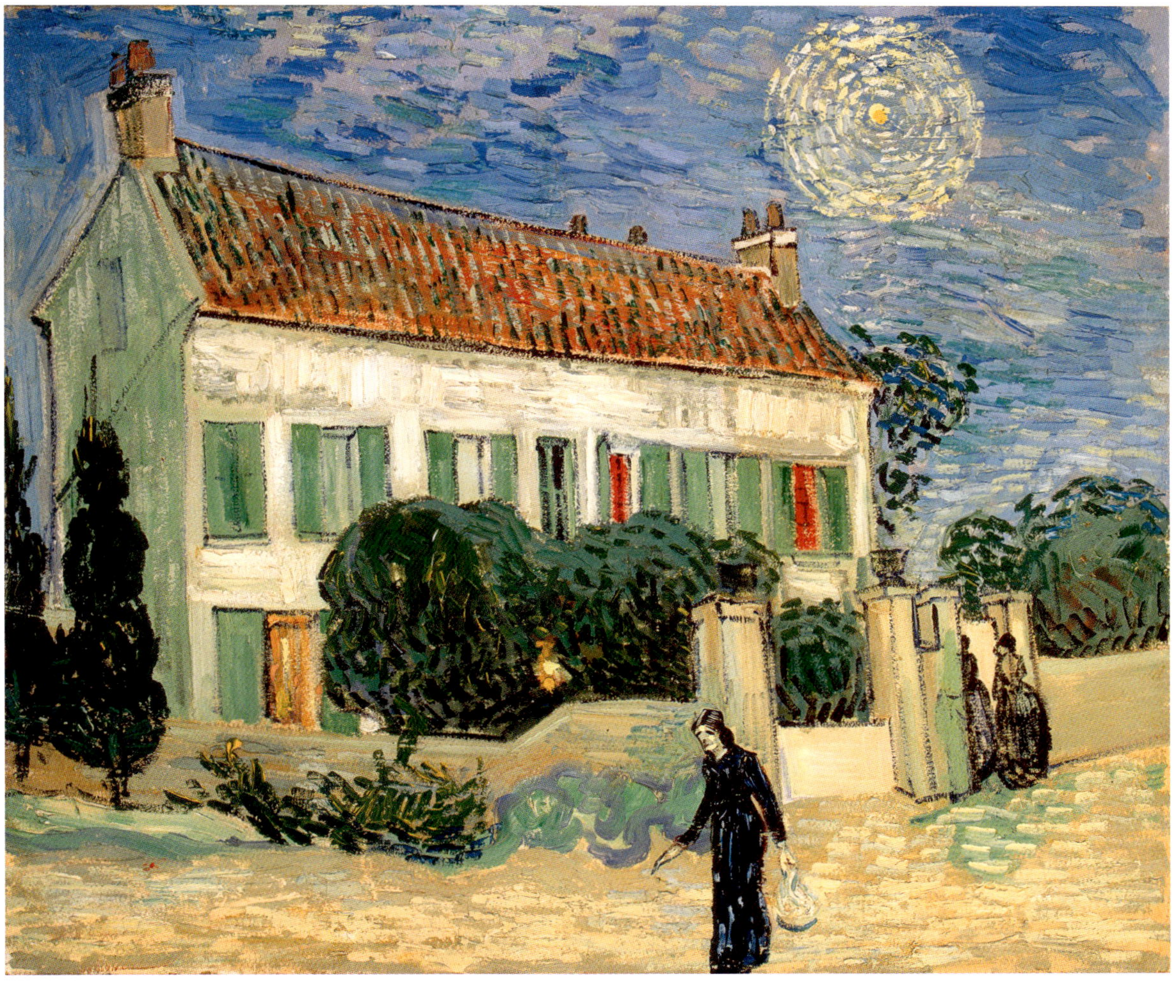

31 (#41)
Vincent van Gogh
White House at Night with Star, 1890
Oil on canvas, 59 × 72.5 cm
The State Hermitage Museum, Saint Petersburg

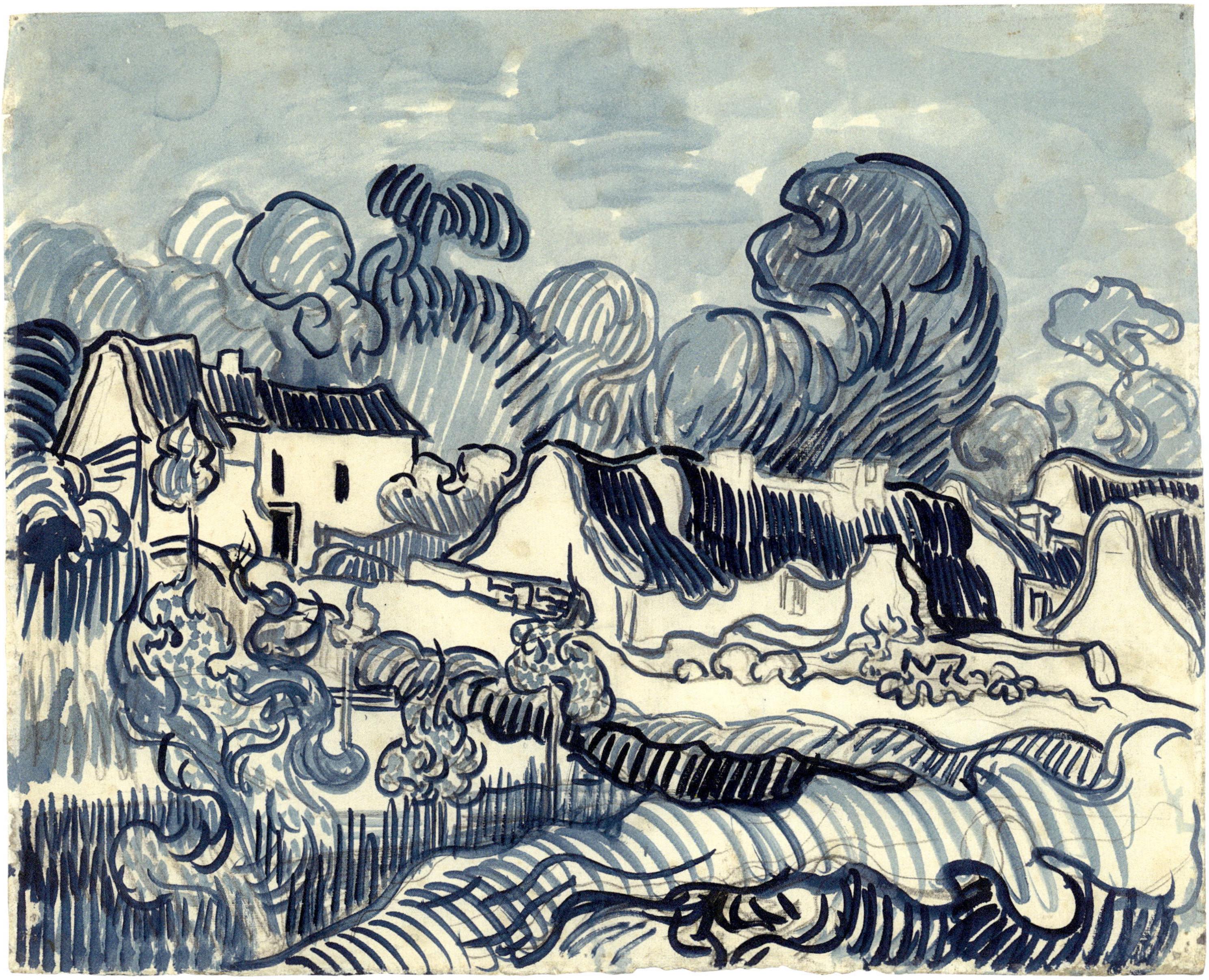

32
Vincent van Gogh
Landscape with Houses, 1890
Pencil, brush and oil paint and watercolour, on laid paper, 44 × 54.4 cm
Van Gogh Museum, Amsterdam

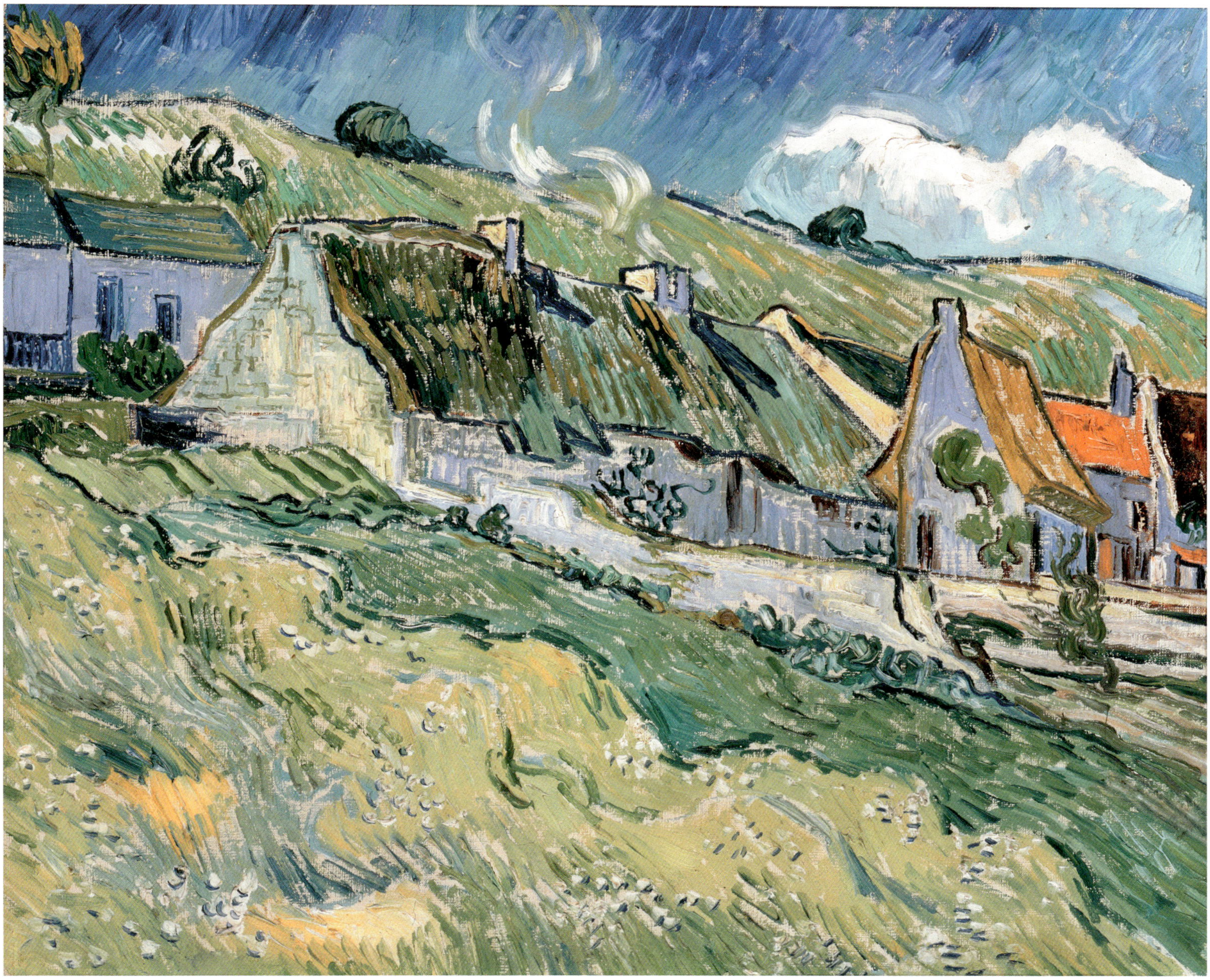

33 (#1)
Vincent van Gogh
Thatched Cottages, 1890
Oil on canvas, 59 × 72 cm
The State Hermitage Museum, Saint Petersburg

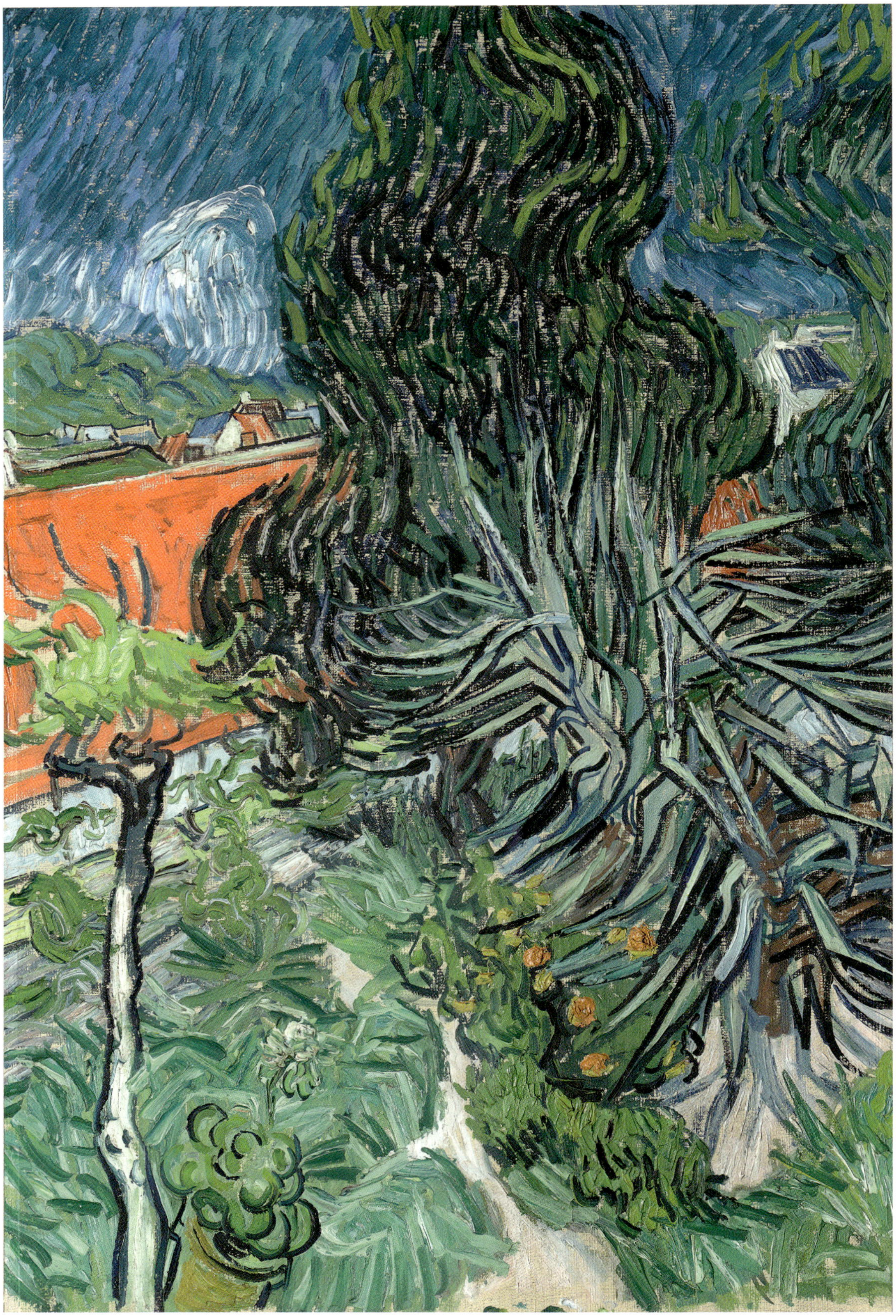

34 (#8)
Vincent van Gogh
Doctor Gachet's Garden, 1890
Oil on canvas, 73 × 52 cm
Musée d'Orsay, Paris

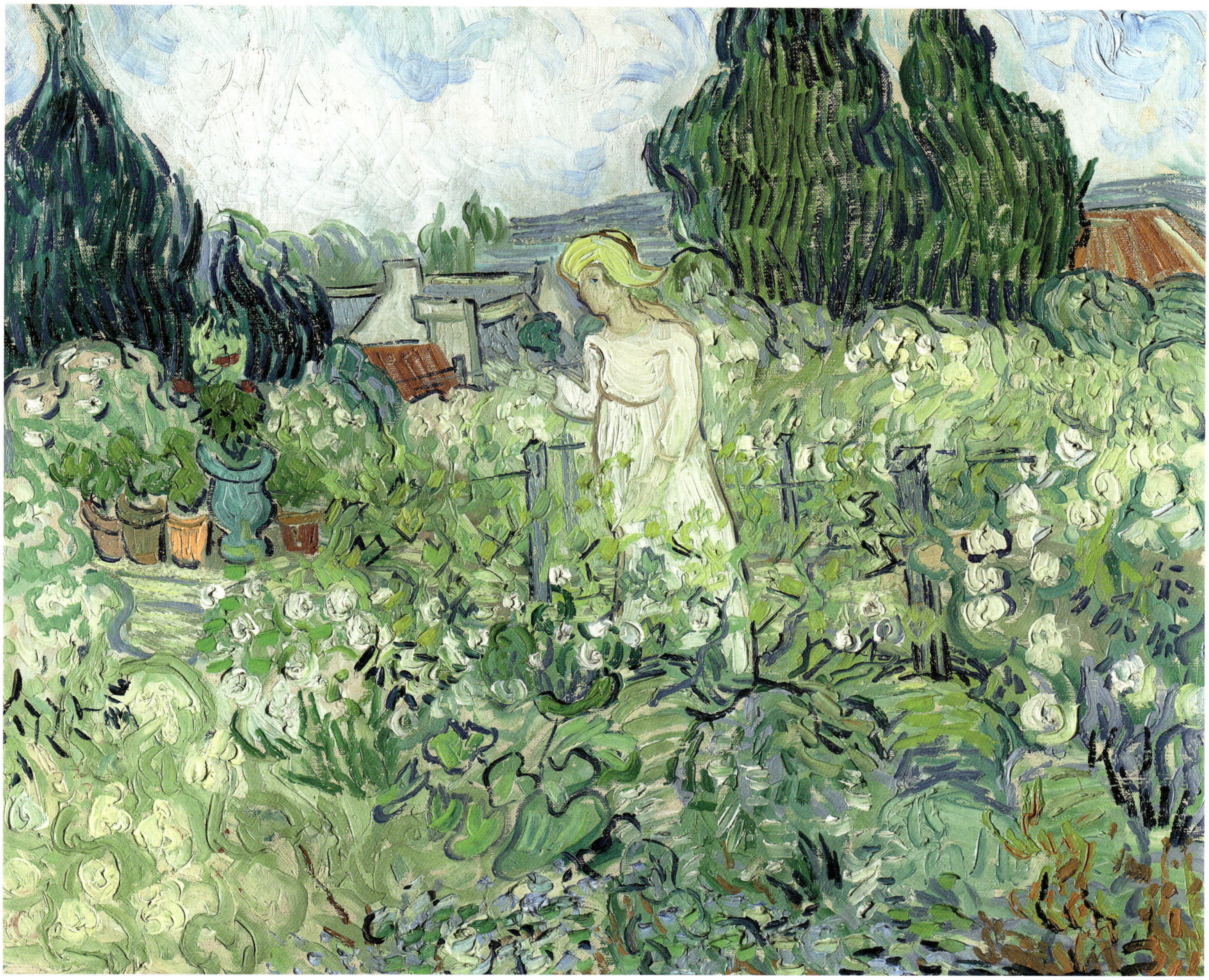

35 (#16)
Vincent van Gogh
Marguerite Gachet in the Garden, 1890
Oil on canvas, 46 × 55.5 cm
Musée d'Orsay, Paris

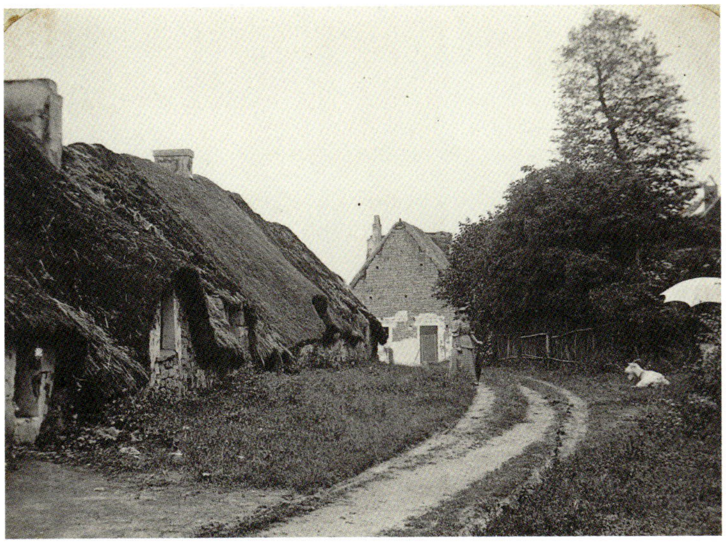

36
L. Lasnier (?)
Thatched cottages in rue du Gré, Auvers-sur-Oise
Photograph, c. 1887
Bibliothèque Nationale de France, Paris

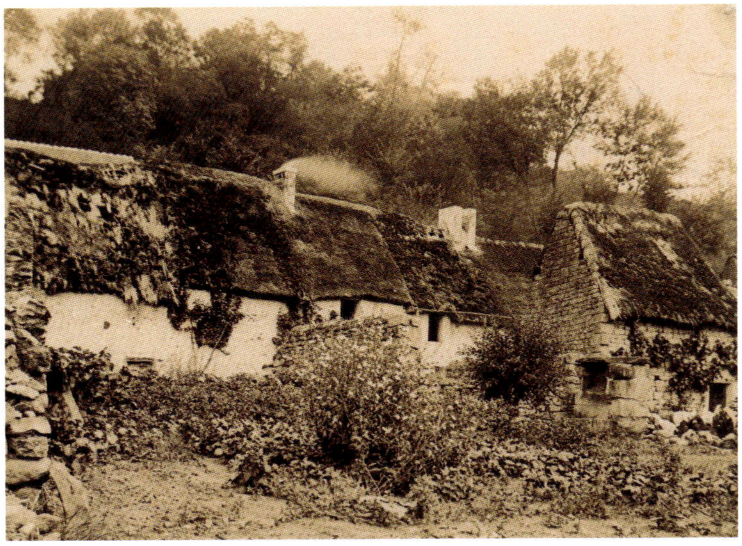

37
L. Lasnier (?)
Houses in Gré, Auvers-sur-Oise
Photograph, c. 1887
Archives départementales du Val-d'Oise, Pontoise

who modelled for *Country Girl with Straw Hat* **(125)**.[23] Lisette, twenty-three in 1890, was the illegitimate daughter of the governess of the Gachet home, Louise Anne Virginie Chevalier, and most likely Dr Gachet.[24] Her features bear some resemblance to an unidentified portrait in a photo album of the Gachet family in which only relatives and close friends are pictured **(39)**. It cannot be said with certainty who is depicted in *Marguerite Gachet in the Garden* **(35)**; both young women in the house could have been models.[25]

Van Gogh initially had no desire to seek contact with others in Auvers: 'relations with people [...] is very secondary, because I have no talent for that', he wrote to Theo and his wife Jo.[26] It seems he kept to his plan. Remarkably, although he visited Gachet, a sociable man, around a dozen times, no source mentions that he sought to associate with other visitors to the house. Eugène Murer, for instance, lived a few hundred metres from the doctor's house; it is hard to imagine that Van Gogh had no interest in his illustrious collection of Impressionist paintings. According to Murer himself, he did have contact with the artist, but his testimony is questionable and could not be verified.[27]

AROUND THE CAFÉ DE LA MAIRIE

The second base of operations for Van Gogh's exploration of the village was, of course, the inn where he had taken up residence, the Café de la Mairie, which was operated by Arthur Ravoux and therefore also called the 'auberge Ravoux' **(38)**. Van Gogh led a regular life, without drama or excess. He got up early and went to bed early. According to Adeline Carrié-Ravoux, the innkeeper's daughter, he was in the habit of working after nature in the morning and in the afternoon retouching his paintings in a room at the back of the inn, which Ravoux made available to the painters among his patrons.[28]

It seems that everything in the immediate vicinity of the inn inspired the artist: the town hall, which he painted on Bastille Day **(63)**, the chestnut trees near the dried-up stream Les Ponceaux **(59)**, the rue de la Sansonne **(5)**, the 'house of Victorine' **(31)**,[29] the Château de Léry **(138)**, the church and the railway station **(1, 52, 53)**, the Romaru's farm **(#3)**, the coppice on the slope of the Grande rue (today's rue Daubigny) **(157)**. Even if this list is supplemented by Père Pilon's house **(61)**, the thatched houses on the estate of Vallembourg **(46)**,[30] and the garden of Daubigny's widow **(139)**, it should be noted that Van Gogh did

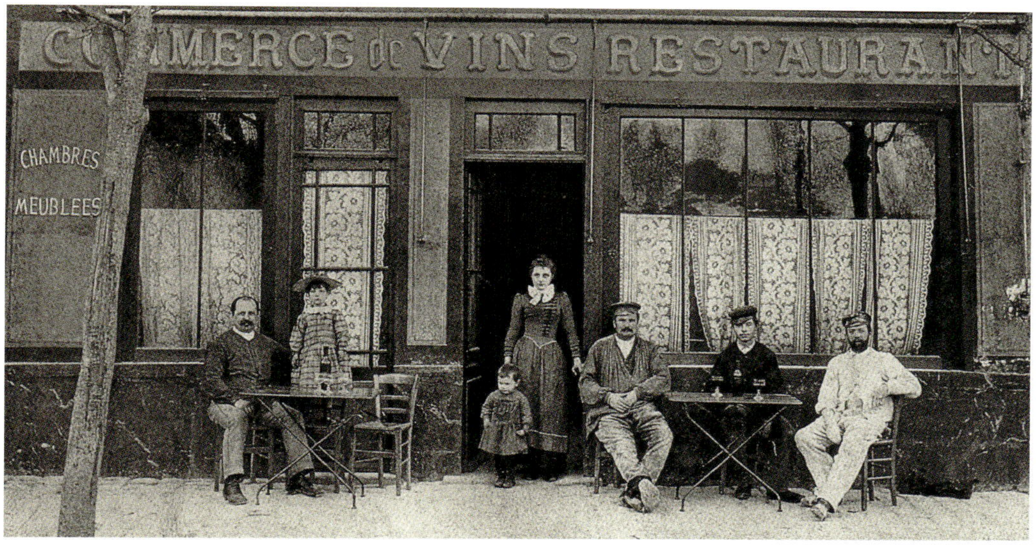

38
The inn at which Van Gogh stayed, with landlord Arthur Ravoux and his daughter Germaine on the left. His eldest daughter, Adeline, stands in the doorway, c. 1891
Auvers-sur-Oise, Institut Vincent van Gogh

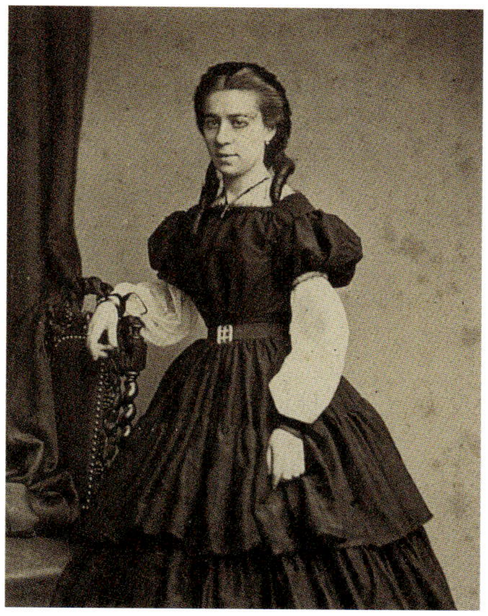

39
Photograph of an Unidentified Woman, undated
From: family album of Paul Ferdinand Gachet
Wildenstein Plattner Institute, New York

not often move more than 500 metres from the café where he resided – even when working in the fields on the plateau above the village, which he could reach via a steep path at the level of the western junction of rue de la Sansonne.

The Café de la Mairie's public character made it a suitable place for spontaneous new encounters, but the social life of 'Monsieur Vincent' at the inn seems to have been cursory and limited to the strictly necessary. Apart from the Dutch painter Anton Hirschig, who from 16 June moved into a room on the same landing as Van Gogh,[31] and the Spanish engraver Nicolas Martinez de Valdivielso, who was present at some of the meals,[32] no other patron, to judge from the sources, had any significant exchange with him.

Nor did Van Gogh apparently make any attempt to meet any of the numerous artists who resided in the village, and whom in other times he had wanted to get to know. Although he did so in Paris between 1886 and 1888, and in Arles in 1888, he did not seek an atmosphere of creative collaboration in Auvers-sur-Oise, did not undertake any joint projects and seemed to foster a certain solitude in order to devote himself wholeheartedly to his art. Yet there is nothing to suggest that he was asocial; he did not avoid contact, as evidenced by his sketchbooks, which contain not only many figure sketches of the inhabitants of Auvers, but also quick scribbles of works he had already made before he came there, presumably serving to show to an interlocutor and exchange ideas.[33] Still a newcomer to the village, he also managed to get permission from parents to have their children pose for him: twelve-year-old Adeline Ravoux, the toddler in *Child with Orange* **(132)** and the two girls he immortalized in two double portraits **(133, 134)**.

It is also well established that Van Gogh met the brothers Gaston and René Secrétan, two well-to-do, bored Parisians, aged nineteen and sixteen, who were on vacation; the youngest, René, told Victor Doiteau in an interview that, among other things, they met Van Gogh 'at Ravoux', where they 'bought him rounds', and also that the painter went regularly to the left bank of the Oise, the territory of Méry-sur-Oise.[34] Yet it seems unlikely that he spent much time there: *Bank of the Oise at Auvers* **(57)** is his only painting that has water recreation as its theme. This spectacular work contains no elements by which to locate it on one bank of the river or the

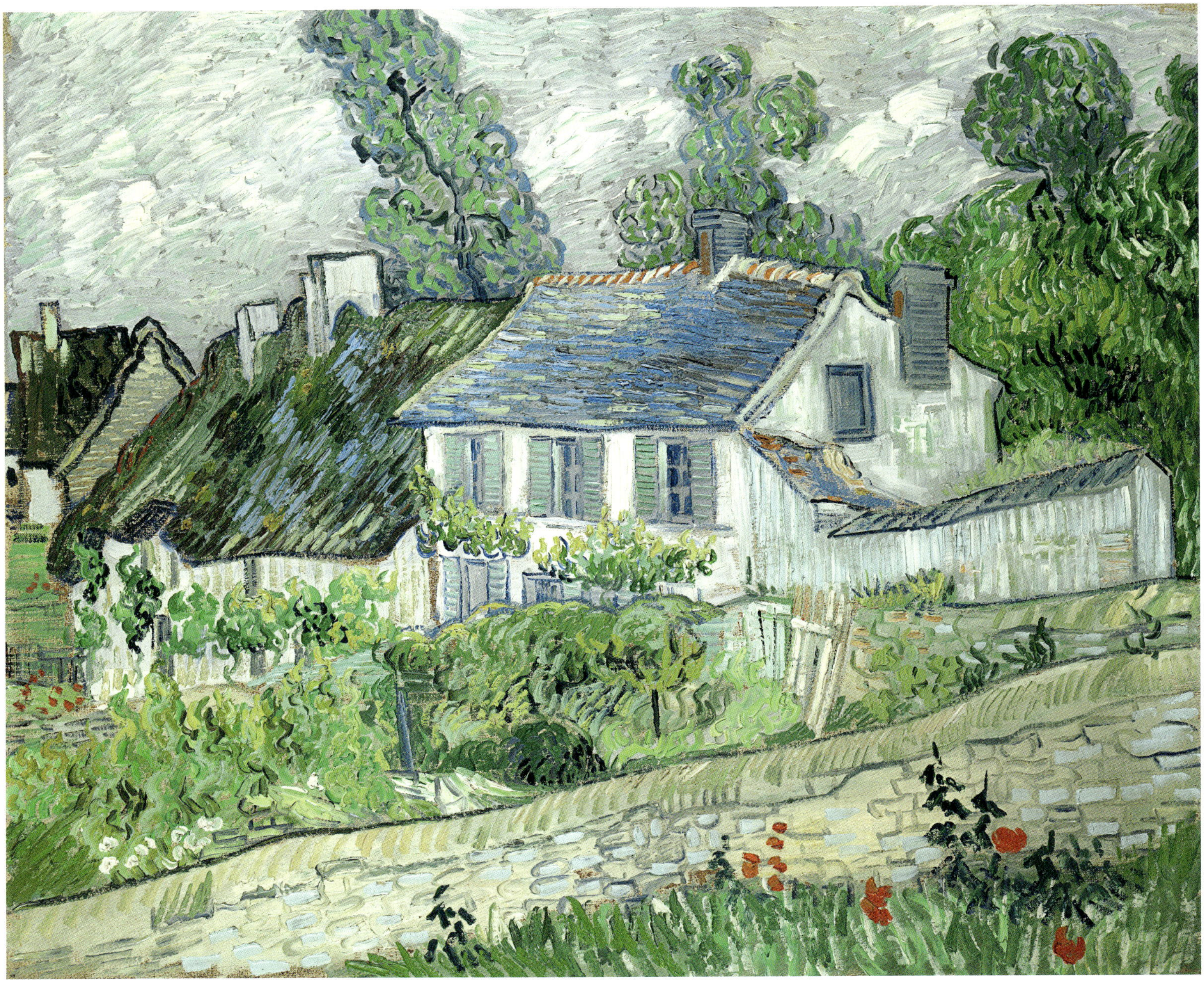

40 (#28)
Vincent van Gogh
Houses at Auvers-sur-Oise, 1890
Oil on canvas, 60 × 73 cm
Toledo Museum of Art, purchased with funds from the Libbey Endowment, Gift of Edward Drummond Libbey

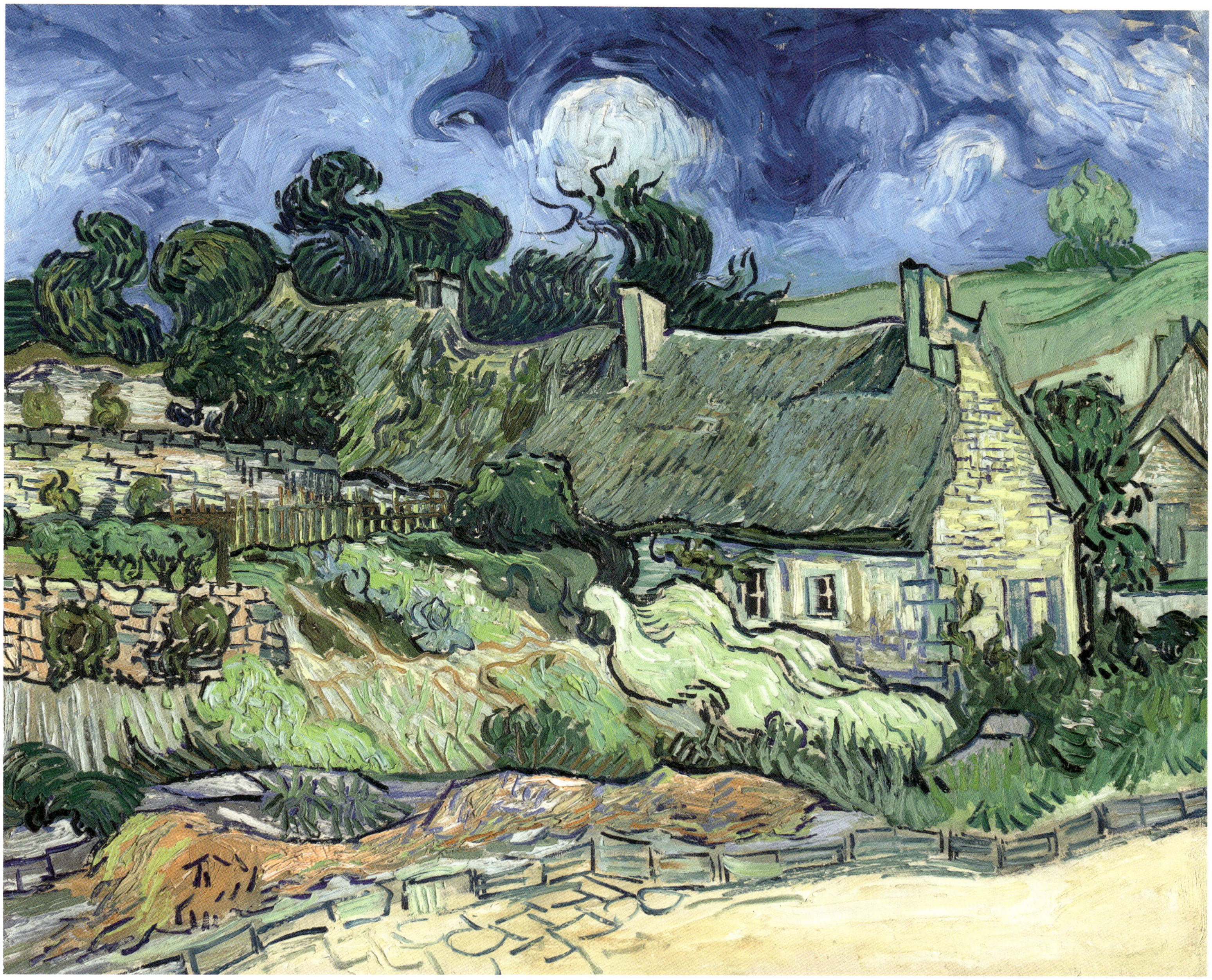

41 (#14)
Vincent van Gogh
Thatched Cottages in Cordeville, Auvers-sur-Oise, 1890
Oil on canvas, 73 × 92 cm
Musée d'Orsay, Paris

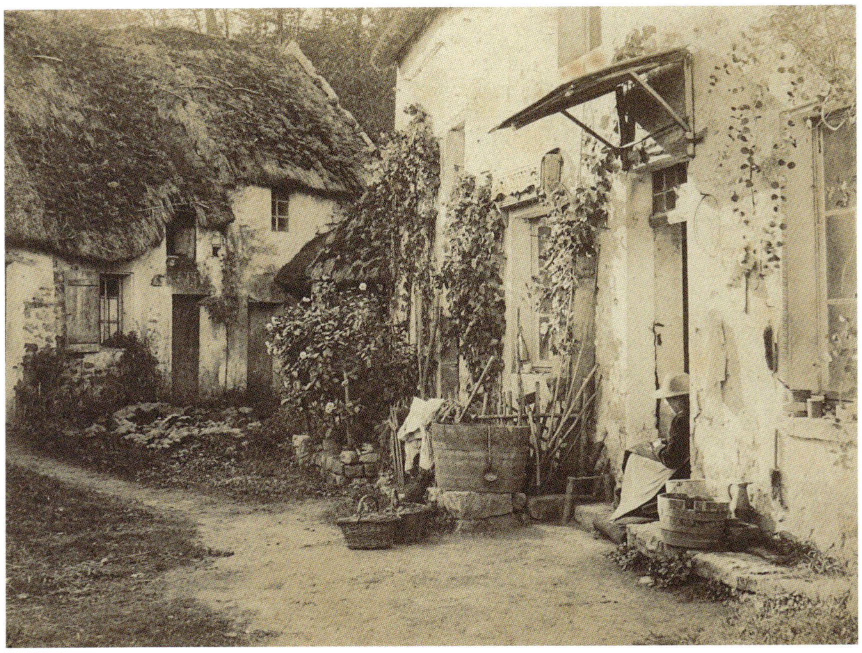

42
L. Lasnier (?)
Farmyard in Cordeville, Auvers-sur-Oise, c. 1887
Bibliothèque Nationale de France, Paris

other. An excursion to Méry-sur-Oise is nevertheless confirmed by the identification of the place where the artist set up his easel to paint *Rain – Auvers-sur-Oise* **(145)**: above a limestone quarry between today's rue Thérèse Lethias and rue de Pontoise, overlooking the church at Auvers, a row of houses along the road to the hamlet of Cordeville, the poplars along the Oise, and the factories on the left bank.

Those same poplars and one of the factories can be seen in the drawing *The Oise at Auvers* **(105)**. In nearly the same place – at the edge of the road – he found a very different motif: a sculpture of an Egyptian head, probably based on that of a sphinx, which had been placed as a keystone over the gate of a villa **(23)**. He used this keystone as the basis for five drawings in a homemade sketchbook.[35] Van Gogh continued his exploration of the village along that road, rue Rajon, arriving at the border of the hamlets of Montcel and Cordeville, where he painted *Thatched Cottages in Cordeville, Auvers-sur-Oise* **(41)**.[36] The fields that can be seen in the background, between the roofs, cover the plain where he painted *Wheatfields with Reaper, Auvers-sur-Oise* **(14)**, with Auvers church and a factory chimney in the distance on the left bank.

Cordeville, meanwhile, also appears to be the best candidate for the motif of five canvases that Alain Mothe still situated in Valhermeil: *Farmhouse* **(43)**, *Thatched Cottages* **(44)**, *Farms near Auvers-sur-Oise* **(147)** and the two versions of *Two Girls* **(133, 134)**. The map of the centre of Auvers-sur-Oise made by Samson Cazier in 1899 for his *Monographie communale* shows a rough indication of a farmhouse at the junction of rue du Montcel and rue de Cordeville: the roof of its western wing features an east-facing extension in the centre.[37] That extension appears not only in *Farms near Auvers-sur-Oise*, but also in the background of the two versions of *Two Girls*.[38] A late nineteenth-century photograph of this farmyard **(42)** also shows elements very similar to the farmhouses that Van Gogh painted. Yet the painter has changed the motif here and there, as he did in *Thatched Cottages* **(33)**. In *Farms near Auvers-sur-Oise*, for example, the large building with the double gable in the middle sprang from his imagination. In addition, farms in Auvers were very similar: they were often built on a square ground plan, with successive additions depending on the expansion of families or the development of activity. Thus, despite the numerous similar elements, the identification proposed here cannot be considered definitive.

Among Van Gogh's last masterpieces from Auvers-sur-Oise are the 'immense stretches of wheatfields under turbulent skies' he painted on

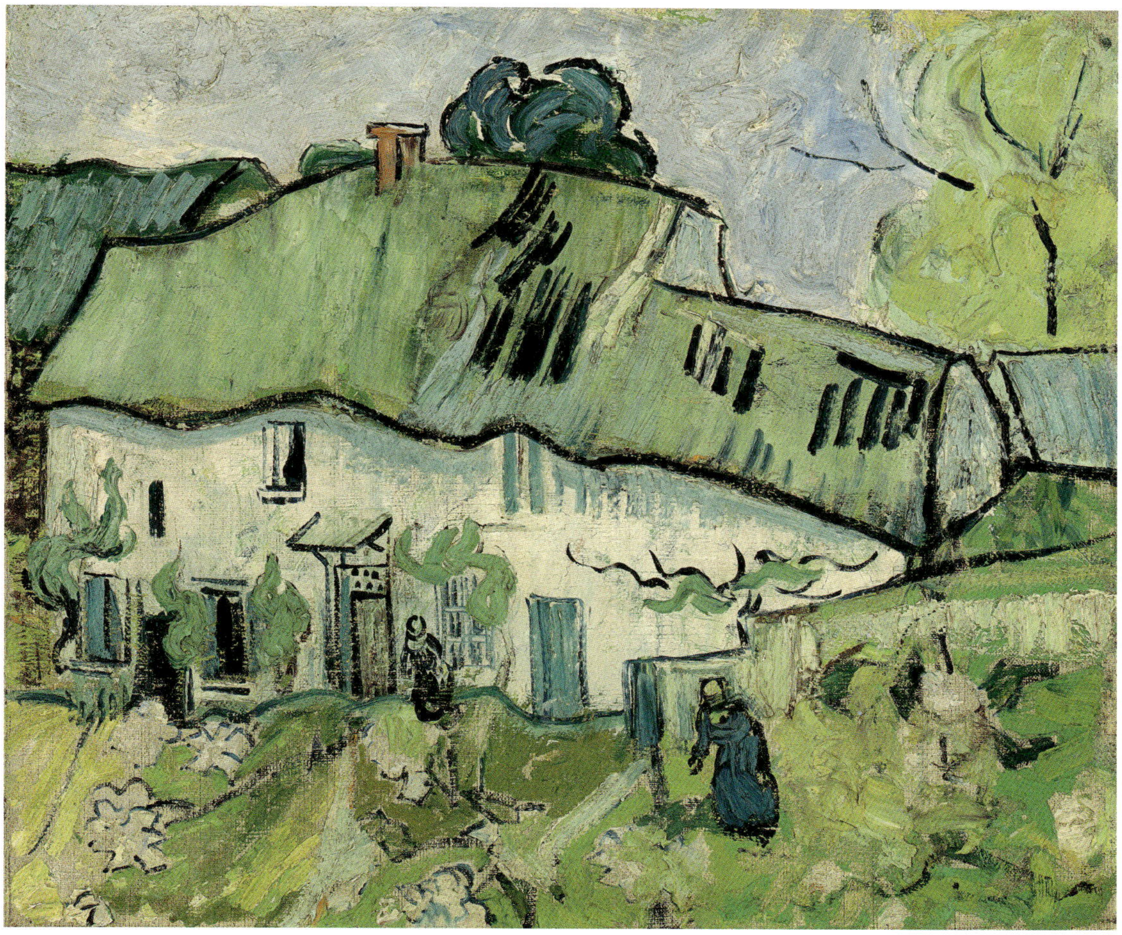

43 (#12)
Vincent van Gogh
Farmhouse, 1890
Oil on canvas, 38.9 × 46.4 cm
Van Gogh Museum, Amsterdam

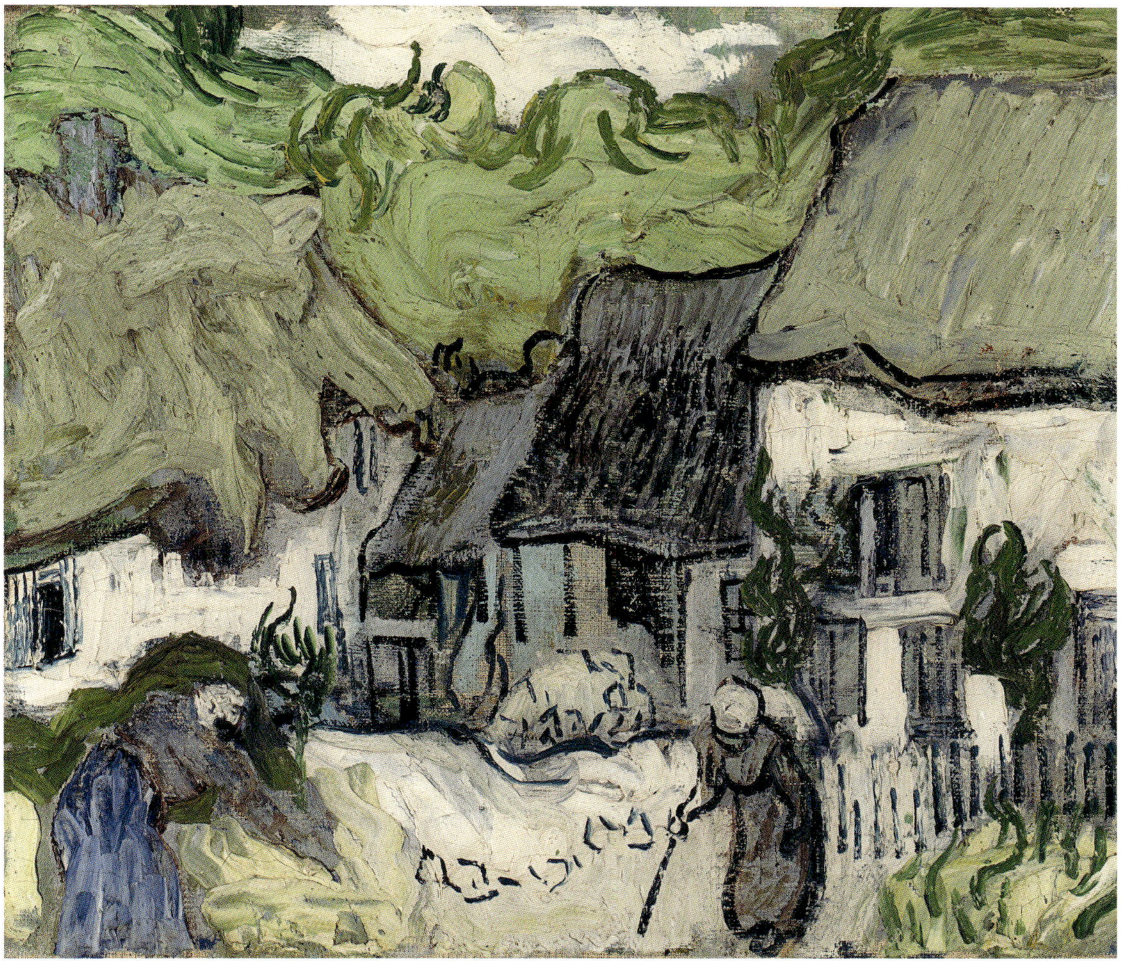

44 (#13)
Vincent van Gogh
Thatched Cottages, 1890
Oil on canvas, 33 × 40.5 cm
West Coast Masters

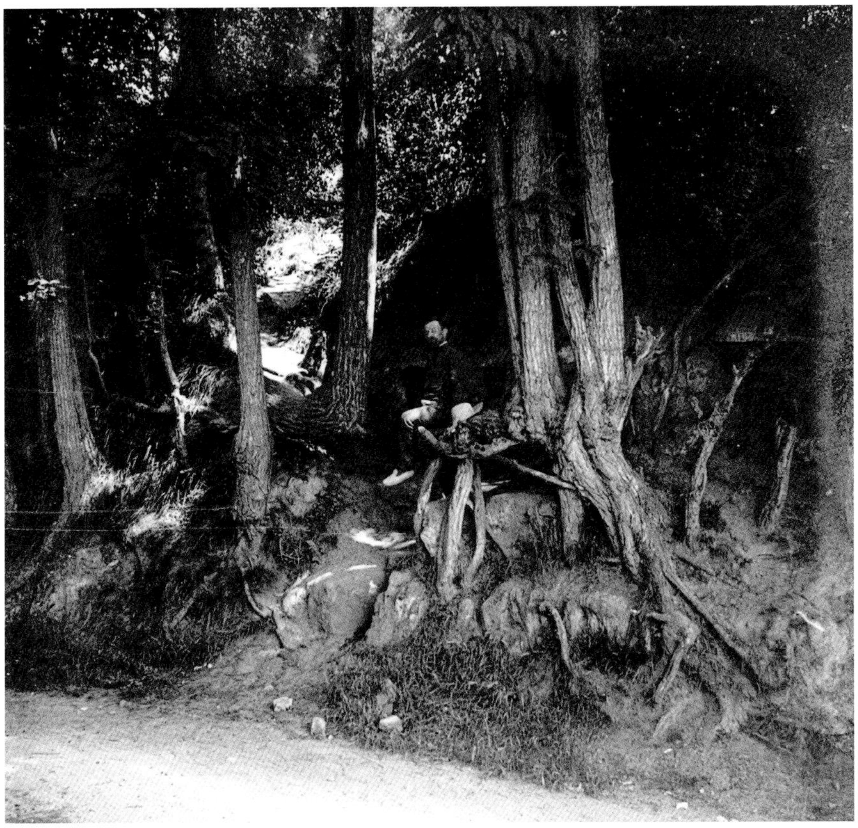

45
Rue Daubigny, Auvers-sur-Oise, the location where Van Gogh painted *Tree Roots*, c. 1906
Fabrice Dassé collection, Pontoise

the plain, which are conspicuous by a remarkable absence of people at work – July was, after all, a very labour-intensive time of the year in the fields.[39] But Van Gogh was not concerned with depicting this activity; in these canvases, he had 'made a point of trying to express sadness, extreme loneliness'. *Wheatfield with Crows* **(137)** is traditionally situated on the chemin du Montier, which leads through the fields of Les Vallées to the cemetery.[40] This location may correspond to Samson Cazier's 1899 map, assuming at least the premise that here – as in *Daubigny's Garden* **(139)** and *Tree Roots* **(157)** – the painter combined several points of view in a single plane, creating a panoramic view. In doing so, he applied a process that he had previously used on the vertical plane: merging the foreground and the vistas within a large, open angle. The deployment of this compositional method across the horizontal plane is specific to the period in Auvers.

FINAL STEPS

On the day that culminated in his fatal deed, Sunday, 27 July, Van Gogh painted his last masterpiece: *Tree Roots* **(157)**. The place where he made it was identified in 2020 from an old postcard: the western junction of the rue de la Sansonne – accessible from the back of the Café de la Mairie – and the Grande rue (today's rue Daubigny), about a hundred metres from the inn **(19)**.[41] Van Gogh could place an easel there on a strip of earth by the road without interfering with traffic, which may have been quiet on this Sunday in the heart of summer. Perhaps he saw parishioners passing on their way to Mass, or strollers taking a breath of fresh air along the slope of limestone rock at the edge of the road. But his attention was focused on the sinuous, interwoven forms of the coppice of false acacia trees that clung to the rock as best they could. Between the half-loose boulders and trunks, branches, undergrowth, roots and shoots, a path led before him straight to the plain with the fields that had inspired him for a dozen paintings the weeks before. He had walked regularly past the impressive coppice that provided him with his final motif. The resulting – unfinished – painting recalls a letter to Theo dated 29 July 1888, in which Van Gogh compared his work to a 'green shoot growing from the roots of the old felled trunk,' which contributed to a 'great revival of art', but at the expense of his mental and physical health.[42]

Since Van Gogh worked intensely and regularly, just as Gachet had advised him, and since he was a model customer at the Café de la Mairie who never caused trouble, his suicide attempt came as a complete surprise to the Gachet and Ravoux families.[43] According to Gachet Jr, 'Vincent shot himself with a revolver in the heart region, on the plain behind the park of the chateau' and went 'back to the inn, at Ravoux's, about 800 metres from there'.[44] To illustrate that location, he produced the small oil painting *The Spot where Vincent van Gogh Committed Suicide* under the pseudonym Louis van Ryssel in 1904.[45] It shows the wall of the park of the Château de Léry running along the chemin des Berthelées, as well as a few haystacks.

Among the last people to meet the painter were the two gendarmes who were investigating the circumstances of his self-inflicted injury.[46] No official report has been recovered – if one was ever made, as the facts did not warrant further inspection.[47] After death throes lasting around thirty hours, Van Gogh died in his modest attic room at 1.30 am on Tuesday, 29 July, while his brother, confidant and friend Theo watched over him **(186)**.

The funeral took place on 30 July. Theo, Dr Gachet and his son, Ravoux and a dozen friends from Paris, including Emile Bernard, brought him to his final resting place, and residents of Auvers also came to offer their condolences. Their presence showed the esteem in which they had held the painter of the fields, farms and gardens of their village, according to Bernard, who wrote a detailed account of the funeral.[48]

The multitude of motifs offered by Auvers-sur-Oise had limited the artist's radius of action, just as his social interactions had been limited by the intensity of his production. Working methodically and taking full advantage of the possibilities offered by the place and the circumstances, he was able to rapidly produce a coherent whole: an accurate and sensitive testimony to the social and physical reality of a commune in the Val-d'Oise at the end of the nineteenth century, which today owes its fame mainly to the ten weeks Vincent van Gogh spent there.

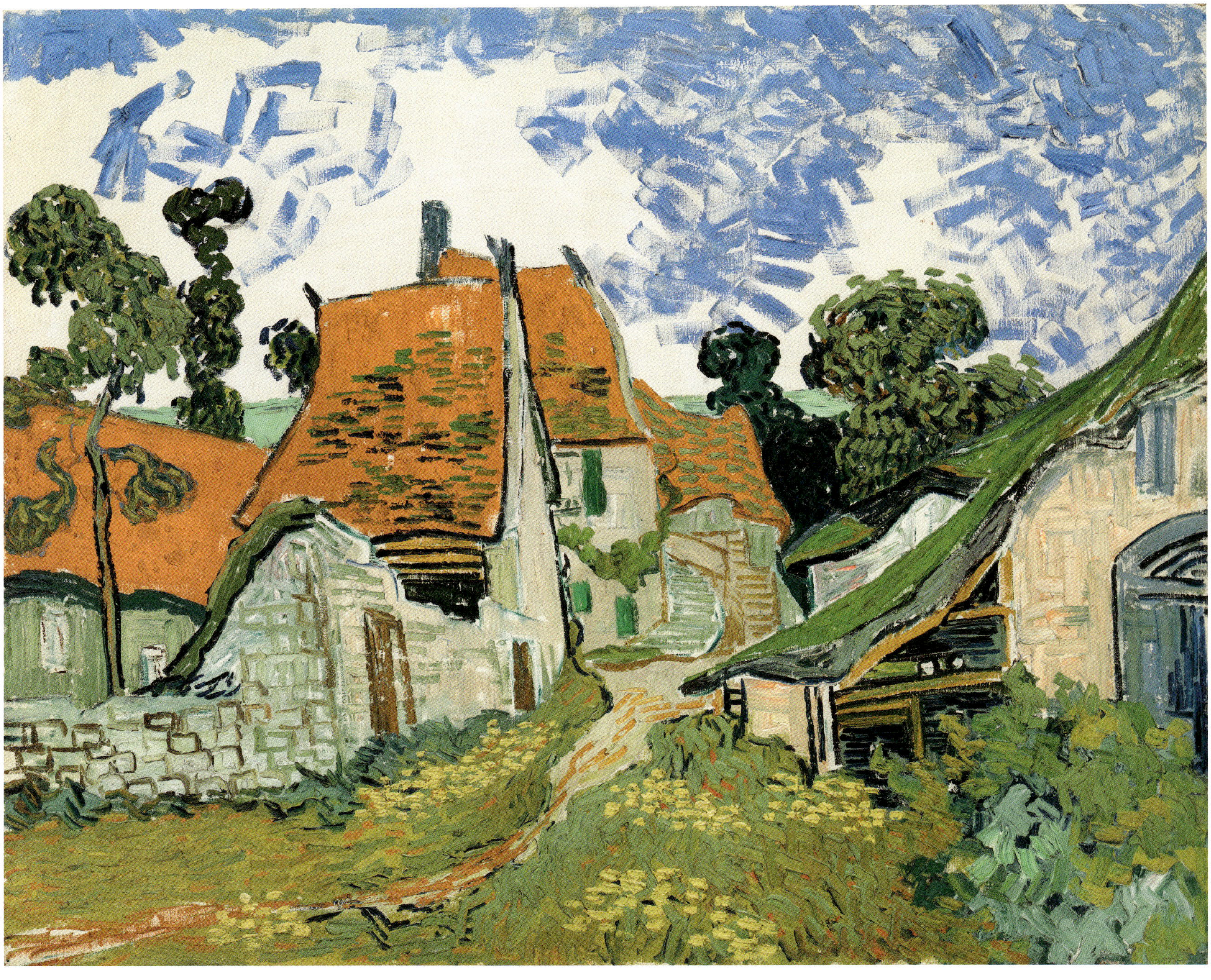

A RURAL VILLAGE IN ALL ITS ASPECTS

TEIO MEEDENDORP

At the end of his first day in Auvers-sur-Oise, Van Gogh wrote that his new surroundings were 'the heart of the countryside, distinctive and picturesque'.[1] The artist was delighted that old houses with thatched roofs could still be found there, but also considered 'modern villas and the middle-class country houses almost as pretty'.[2] He went on to paint old farmhouses and new second homes alike, albeit the former slightly more often than the latter. And it goes without saying that he took time to capture the landscape around Auvers, especially the expansive fields on the plateau north of the village.

There are some significant differences between the work Van Gogh produced in Auvers and that of other artists who painted there from the mid-nineteenth century onwards. His forthright use of colour and expressive application of paint are unique, but the motifs he chose were occasionally at variance with theirs too. Few of his fellows, for instance, painted the fine old church as a motif in its own right **(1)**, and we have yet to find another artist who bestowed a leading role on the town hall **(63)**.[3] Conversely, with a single exception Van Gogh ignored the river Oise and its banks, even though they were popular subjects for other painters. We explore some of his motifs in more detail below, but before that, we will briefly sketch how Auvers first caught the eye of artists around the middle of the nineteenth century.

PIONEER

'Of all Europe's capitals, it is Paris whose surroundings are both the most charming and most worthy of interest', Adolphe Joanne's 1856 travel guide, *Les Environs de Paris illustrés*, enthused.[4] The development of the French countryside was given a substantial boost in the nineteenth century as the rail network was steadily expanded. Joanne's guidebook meticulously followed each railway line connecting Paris to its immediate surroundings, and provided an entry for everywhere that the train stopped. Auvers, whose railway station opened in 1846, was granted a single paragraph plus illustration **(47)**.[5] Artists could now explore the landscape around Paris much more readily, and so the Oise river basin, with its picturesque villages and varied nature, swiftly caught their attention.[6]

Nowadays, Auvers-sur-Oise is chiefly linked with Vincent van Gogh. Until well into the twentieth century, however, the artist most associated with the village and the surrounding area was the landscape painter Charles-François Daubigny.[7] He was born in

46 (#15)
Vincent van Gogh
Farmhouses in Auvers-sur-Oise, 1890
Oil on canvas, 73.5 × 92.5 cm
Finnish National Gallery, Ateneum Art Museum, Helsinki, Antell Collections

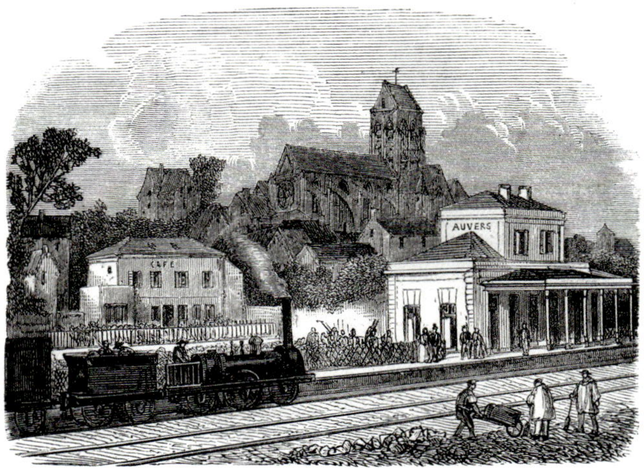

Auvers.

47
Auvers-sur-Oise
Illustration in Adolphe Joanne,
Les Environs de Paris illustrés, Paris 1856

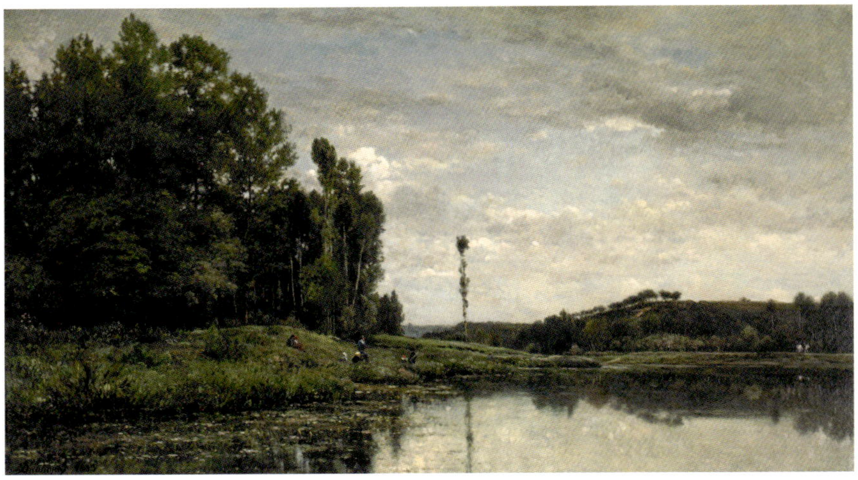

48
Charles-François Daubigny
Banks of the Oise at Auvers, 1863
Oil on canvas, 88.9 × 161.3 cm
Saint Louis Art Museum, Friends Fund Endowment, and Gift of Justina G. Catlin in memory of her husband, Daniel Catlin, 2007

Paris but due to poor health he lived until the age of nine with a wet nurse in the village of Valmondois, between Auvers and Isle-Adam. It was at this early age that he developed his love for the region. Daubigny's main base was always Paris, but Auvers-sur-Oise became his second home in 1861, after earlier periods spent working in Barbizon and elsewhere. He had a house and studio built in the district of Les Vallées.[8] Even before then, however, the pioneering artist was frequently found in Auvers in the summer, sailing up and down the river in search of motifs in *Le Botin*, his floating studio. The riverscape became his principal subject **(48)**, but Daubigny also painted the expansive fields above Auvers in varying weather conditions. He rarely painted in the village itself,[9] although at an exhibition in The Hague in 1882 Van Gogh did see a village scene by him 'that I couldn't get enough of', presumably without being aware that it had been painted in Auvers.[10]

ATTRACTION

The main stopping place for artists who came to Auvers in the early days was the Café de la Gare, directly opposite the railway station, which is clearly visible in the illustration in Joanne's guide. Daubigny's studio became an important artistic centre after he had set up there: students and admirers sought the master out and some moved to the village or nearby for varying periods of time.[11] Léonide Bourges, for instance, who settled in Auvers in 1874, mainly drew and painted in the village. Victor Vignon, meanwhile, regularly worked in Auvers during the 1870s and 1880s and also stayed in the area in 1890.[12]

Van Gogh had got to know Vignon in Paris, and when in the autumn of 1889 Theo started to look for a suitable place in the region for his brother should the need arise and Vincent decided he wanted to relocate as quickly as feasible, the possibility was actually broached of his moving in with Vignon.[13] Camille Pissarro, whose intercession eventually led to Van Gogh ending up in Auvers, lived – with intervals – in nearby Pontoise between 1866 and 1882. He had deliberately chosen the spot on the grounds that no landscape painter of any repute was working there at the time.[14]

Daubigny's admirers continued to visit even after his death in 1878. The arrival in Auvers of the collectors Paul Ferdinand Gachet and Eugène Murer in 1872 and 1880 respectively, both of whom moved in artistic circles and dabbled in painting themselves, only served to increase the attraction. Writing in 1886, the journalist Louis Barron reported that Auvers was gradually filling up: 'A colony of painters, small as yet in number but growing, brings this sweetly hued corner of nature to life during the summer season.'[15]

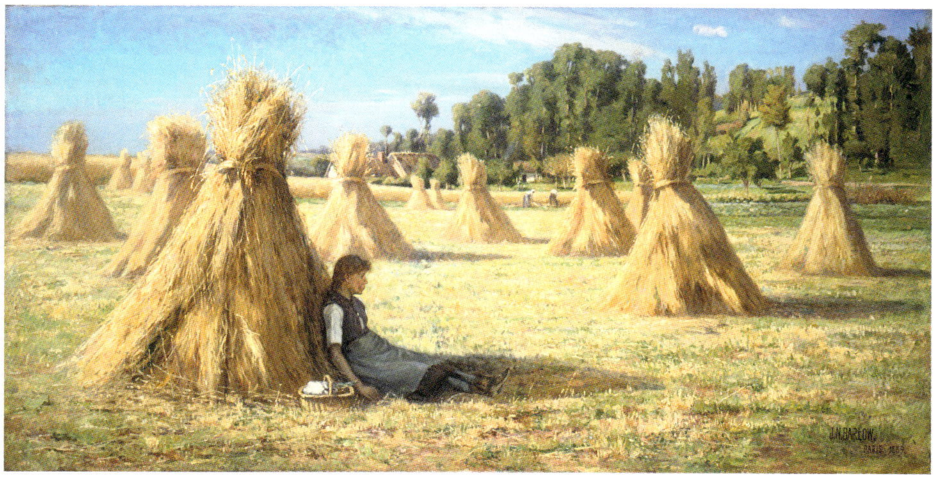

49
John Noble Barlow
Harvest, 1889
Oil on canvas, 99.7 × 198.1 cm
Museum of Art, Rhode Island School of Design, Providence

Van Gogh himself noted that plenty of other painters were also in Auvers. A group of Americans, for instance, 'who paint day in day out', had set up next to the Café de la Mairie, and while he had not seen any of their art, he concluded that 'it's usually just all too weak'.[16] His view might have reflected work he had seen by American artists like Charles Sprague Pearce, Robert Wickenden and John Noble Barlow who had lived in Auvers for some time.[17] These were figure and landscape painters, who worked in a strongly realist tradition. Barlow's *Harvest* of 1889 is a typical example of their abilities **(49)**. While the iconography is identical, it would be hard to imagine a sharper contrast with Van Gogh's *Sheaves of Wheat* **(146)**.

According to Wickenden's son, Van Gogh paid them a visit, accompanied by Anton Hirschig.[18] Wickenden rented various places that summer, including Daubigny's former house and studio, not far from the Café de la Mairie.[19] The building was beautifully decorated, and while Van Gogh himself did not mention it, he might have seen the interior of the house.[20] The murals there with landscape motifs such as ears of wheat with wild flowers, playful rabbits and various types of poultry, as well as the huge, wall-filling paintings that Camille Corot and Karl Daubigny had made in the large studio, might have given him ideas of an artist's dwelling of his own in the countryside.[21] He did not view his stay at the inn as permanent and began to look for a workspace of his own soon after his arrival. After two weeks, however, he wrote: 'I still haven't found anything interesting in the way of a possible studio.'[22] When Theo and Jo visited Auvers on 8 June, they actually viewed a property, following which Vincent told them that 'I'd very much like you to have a pied-à-terre in the country at the same time as myself'.[23] This was to remain a daydream, but later in June, when he began to paint wide-format landscapes, he also had it in mind that works like this could be useful as decorations for a home in the country.[24]

DISTINCTIVELY ORIGINAL

It was near to Daubigny's former home and studio that Van Gogh found the motif for *Farmhouses in Auvers-sur-Oise* **(46)**. If we compare this work with the similarly sized *Thatched Cottages in Cordeville, Auvers-sur-Oise* **(41)**, we are struck by the degree to which the artist was able by now to vary his style. *Thatched Cottages* displays a tight, compact structure in its brushwork, compared to the more irregular construction of *Farmhouses in Auvers-sur-Oise*. Van Gogh used harsh orange and green tones in the houses and a foreground delineated using a different colour and texture, to break the composition into sections.[25] The most striking of these is the sky, which was

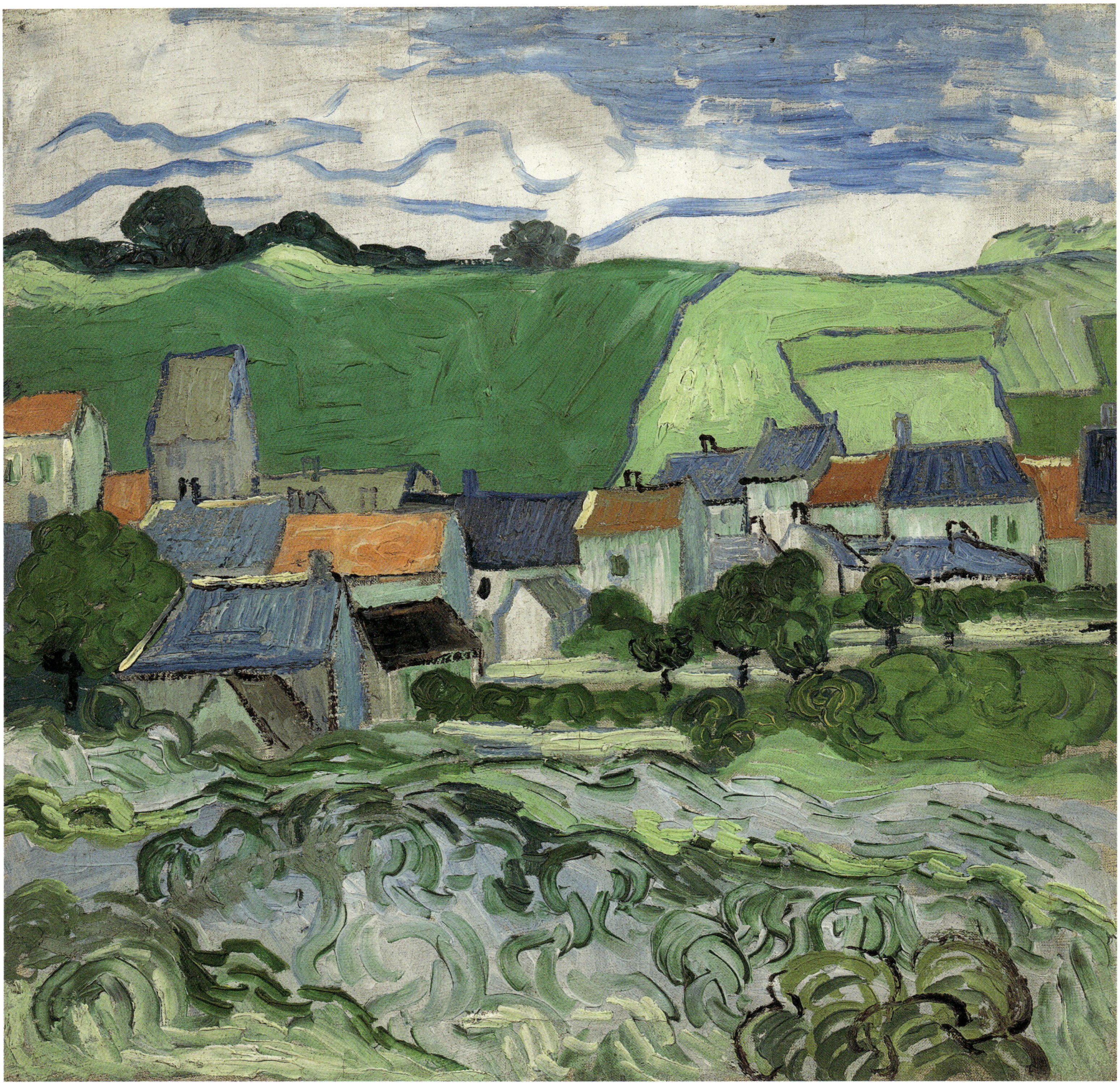

50 (#11)
Vincent van Gogh
View of Auvers-sur-Oise, 1890
Oil on canvas, 50.2 × 52.5 cm
Van Gogh Museum, Amsterdam

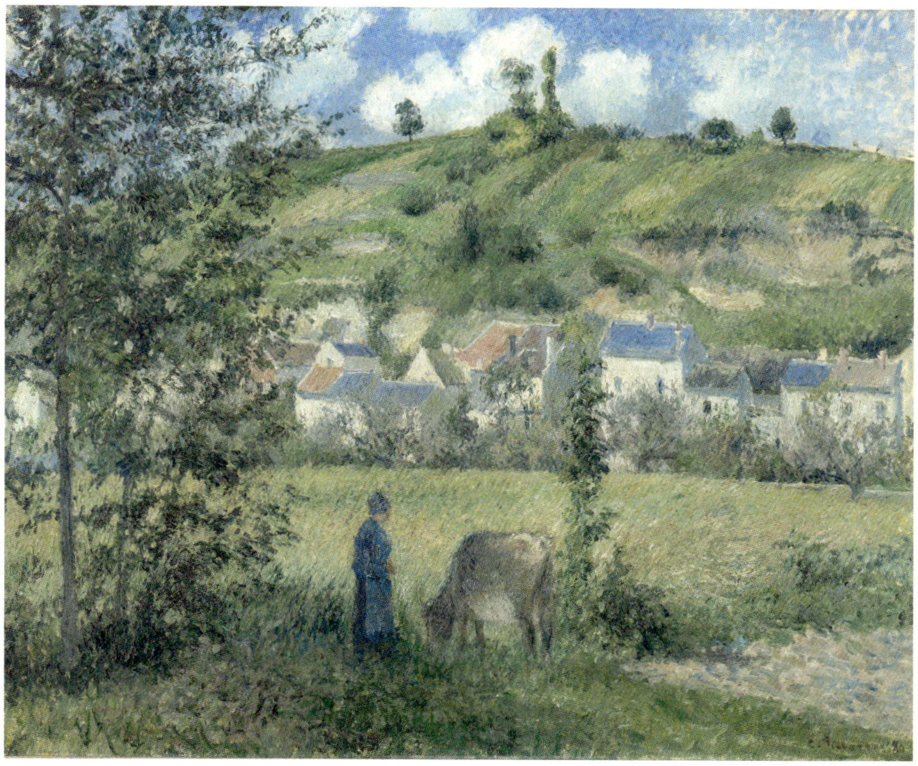

51
Camille Pissarro
Landscape at Chaponval, 1880
Oil on canvas, 54.5 × 65 cm
Musée d'Orsay, Paris, Bequest of Antonin Personnaz to the Louvre, 1937

given an appropriate, fragmentary treatment with broad, blocky strokes of blue paint against a bright white background. This loosely painted sky led to suggestions that the work was unfinished and hence his last work.[26]

Farmhouses in Auvers-sur-Oise is nevertheless a finished work. The white in the sky is not that of the primed canvas, but a white layer applied by the artist himself, over which he added the touches of blue. This creates a kind of reverse sky effect – a white sky with blue clouds, rather than the other way around.[27] The aim will have been to see how far he could go in his application of anti-illusionist elements – something he achieved here in a highly inventive way.

We find something similar in *View of Auvers-sur-Oise* **(50)**, although in this instance, the freely applied blue lines on the white ground are a touch more convincing as a blue sky with white clouds. This is another broadly conceived work, in which the variation in brushstrokes and the interacting expanses of colour are defining elements in the composition. The approach begins in the front with coarse, swirling touches of paint, which then become a little more subtle and suggestive of depth, before greenish-white toned houses with blue and orange roofs enliven the middle ground like a set of toy building blocks. Above these, Van Gogh uses flat, green tones to paint the fields on the steep slope that bounds Auvers to the north, with a few wooded areas on the horizon to the left and right – repeating shapes that are also found lower in the canvas.

It is remarkable how radically different his approach was here compared to a canvas that Camille Pissarro painted nearby ten years earlier **(51)**. Where Pissarro's forms flow harmoniously into one another and the even brushwork instils an overall unity, Van Gogh offers simplified contrasts in his paint strokes, colour and delineation of the different elements, including the contours of the houses, and also in the division of the fields in the background, the example for which was drawn from Japanese prints. Pissarro created depth in the traditional way, by placing a repoussoir consisting of a few trees and a figure in the foreground. Depth is actually negated in Van Gogh's painting by the flatly rendered slope in the background, and it is precisely the contrast between the different ways in which foreground, hillside and sky are painted that makes his composition so original.

Van Gogh produced two more views of Auvers closer to the centre of the village, in which the same concise brushwork can be detected and the colour and division of surfaces once again stand out. Both works are modest studies in which he used a restricted palette to pursue harmonies and contrasts. In the first

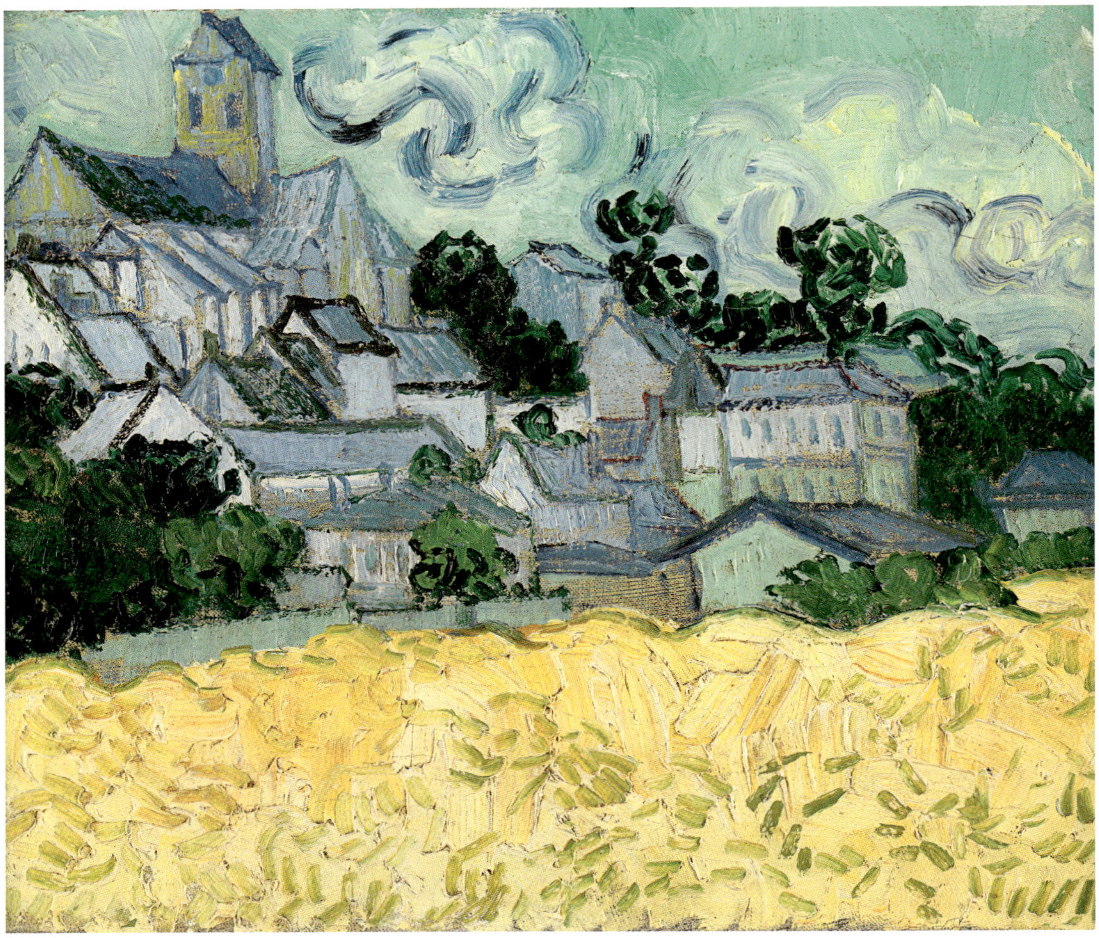

52 (#9)
Vincent van Gogh
View of Auvers-sur-Oise, 1890
Oil on canvas, 34 × 42.1 cm
Museum of Art, Rhode Island School of Design, Providence, given in memory of Miss Dorothy Sturges by a Friend

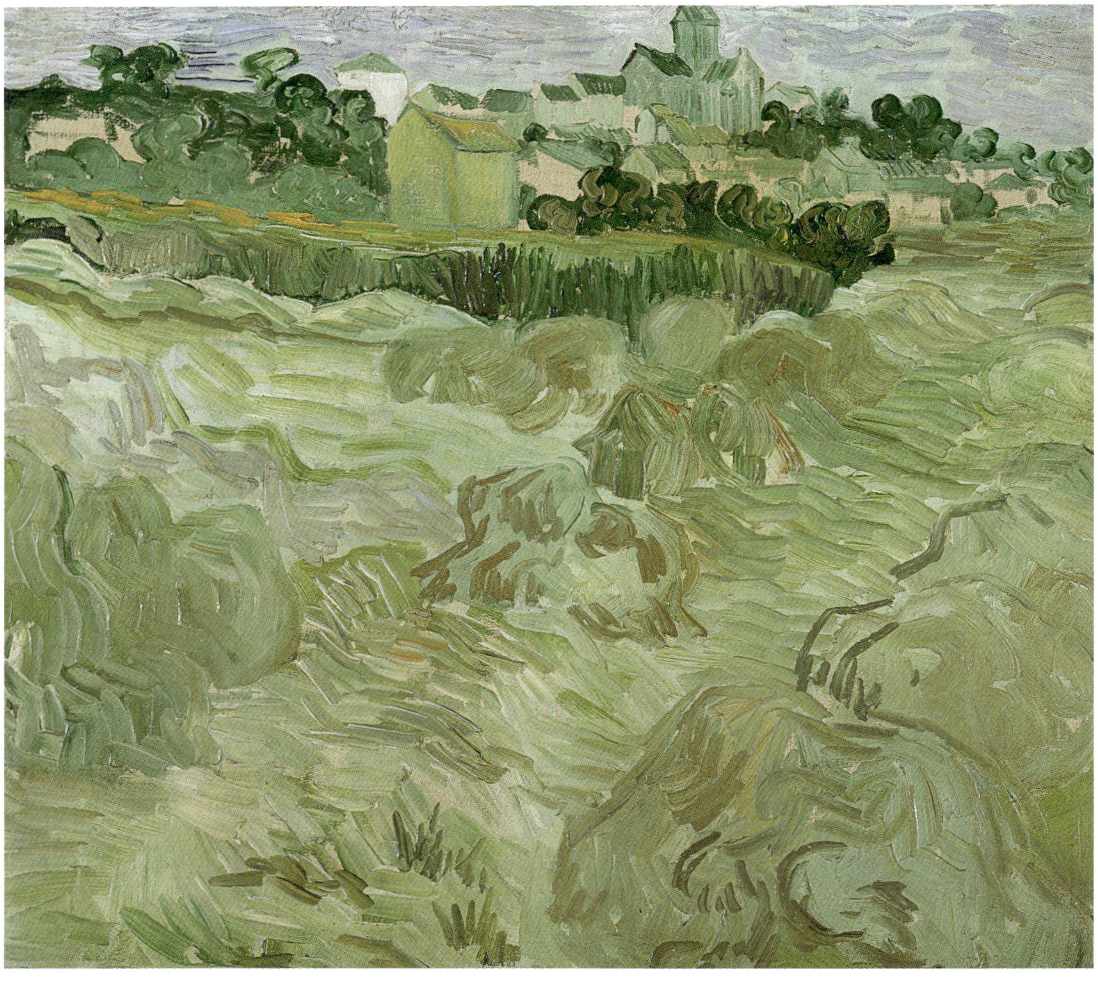

53 (#10)
Vincent van Gogh
Field near Auvers-sur-Oise, 1890
Oil on canvas, 44 × 51.5 cm
Musée d'art et d'histoire, Geneva, former loan of the Fondation Garengo, 1990

work, *View of Auvers-sur-Oise* **(52)**, a small painting the composition of which is remarkably similar to the illustration from *Les Environs de Paris* **(47)**, the foreground is occupied by a yellow wheatfield painted in a highly schematic way. Van Gogh invented this element, as there were no such fields at the location in question, immediately to the back of the station.[28] We are fairly sure, moreover, that he painted it at the beginning of his stay in Auvers, at which point the wheat would not have been ripe.[29] He most likely included the field to emphasize, on the one hand, that we are looking at a village in the countryside. It is tempting to link the scene, moreover, with Jacob Jan van der Maaten's print *The Funeral in the Wheatfield*, which Van Gogh admired **(110)**. On the other hand, the field creates a colour contrast when set against the dominantly blue buildings of the village.[30] The extremely compact execution of the canvas suggests that it might have been an exercise for a more ambitious piece.

He allowed himself more distance for the second view of the village with the church tower, firmly placing the emphasis on the foreground and the piles of mown grass, which demand all the viewer's attention **(53)**. It is hard to determine the extent to which the work has suffered from discolouration, but green was clearly always the dominant tone.[31] Even the village at the top is executed entirely in light and dark-green tones, beneath a pale lilac sky that probably turned a little bluer over the years. This exercise in colour, in which the artist sought to achieve a harmony in green, is in keeping, one might say, with his efforts in Auvers to work more simply, more primitively.[32] The two small, fluently painted studies of a farmhouse in Cordeville **(43, 44)** are another example of this – roughly elaborated sketches with an expressive touch and a limited palette of mainly green and yellow-brown tones.

STYLISTIC DIVERSITY

Just how much Van Gogh could vary his style in the space of a few days is clear from his next series of works. He painted three landscapes between around 11 and 13 June: *House at Auvers-sur-Oise* **(54)**, *Landscape with Carriage and Train* **(29)** and *Vineyards at Auvers-sur-Oise* **(55)**.[33] For the first of these works, he positioned himself in front of a green field with yellow ears of wheat, painted with a succession of rhythmic brushstrokes that result in a tight structure. A modern white villa is set against a purple-tinted row of trees in the background, which acts as another secondary colour along with the greenery in the foreground. Van Gogh placed the horizon extremely high, as he did in the other two paintings, but in those instances he viewed his motifs from above, creating a different type of vista.

Landscape with Carriage and Train, the largest of the three, leads the eye into the distance. Compared to *House at Auvers-sur-Oise*, it is painted in a much more open and slack manner with loose touches, while the patchwork of fields in the foreground and background looks as though the artist dragged a wide-toothed comb through the wet paint. *Vineyards at Auvers-sur-Oise*, lastly, is quite different in character. Once again, Van Gogh adopted a high vantage point, looking out over the western part of Auvers with Dr Gachet's house in the left background. The middle ground contains a group of old farmhouses, a winding wall and, at the very front, a vineyard painted in fluttering brushstrokes, with purple vines round which the green leaves curl loosely. It takes up almost a third of the composition. A roughly painted yellow-green verge with bright red poppies, which form a strong complementary colour contrast, is located along the edge of the picture on the left. Cézanne painted a similar view of the neighbourhood in 1873–75 but from an even higher vantage point **(28)**, which Van Gogh is highly likely to have seen at Gachet's and of which the tones of his own palette are somewhat reminiscent.

RIVER

As previously noted, Van Gogh was not really interested in the Oise and its banks, even though they had been favourite motifs for Daubigny and many of his followers. A drawing with a view of the bridge across the river **(105)** has survived, along with a few loose sketches featuring riverside vegetation, but Van Gogh mostly looked in the opposite direction – towards the village and the landscape beyond.[34] There was plenty of pleasure boating on the Oise in the summer, and the fishing was good too.[35] This did not hold much appeal for Van Gogh either, although he did paint a boat-hire firm on one occasion – a colourful bankside view, including a woman casting a line **(57)**.[36] It is a distinctly Impressionist theme of the kind with which Claude

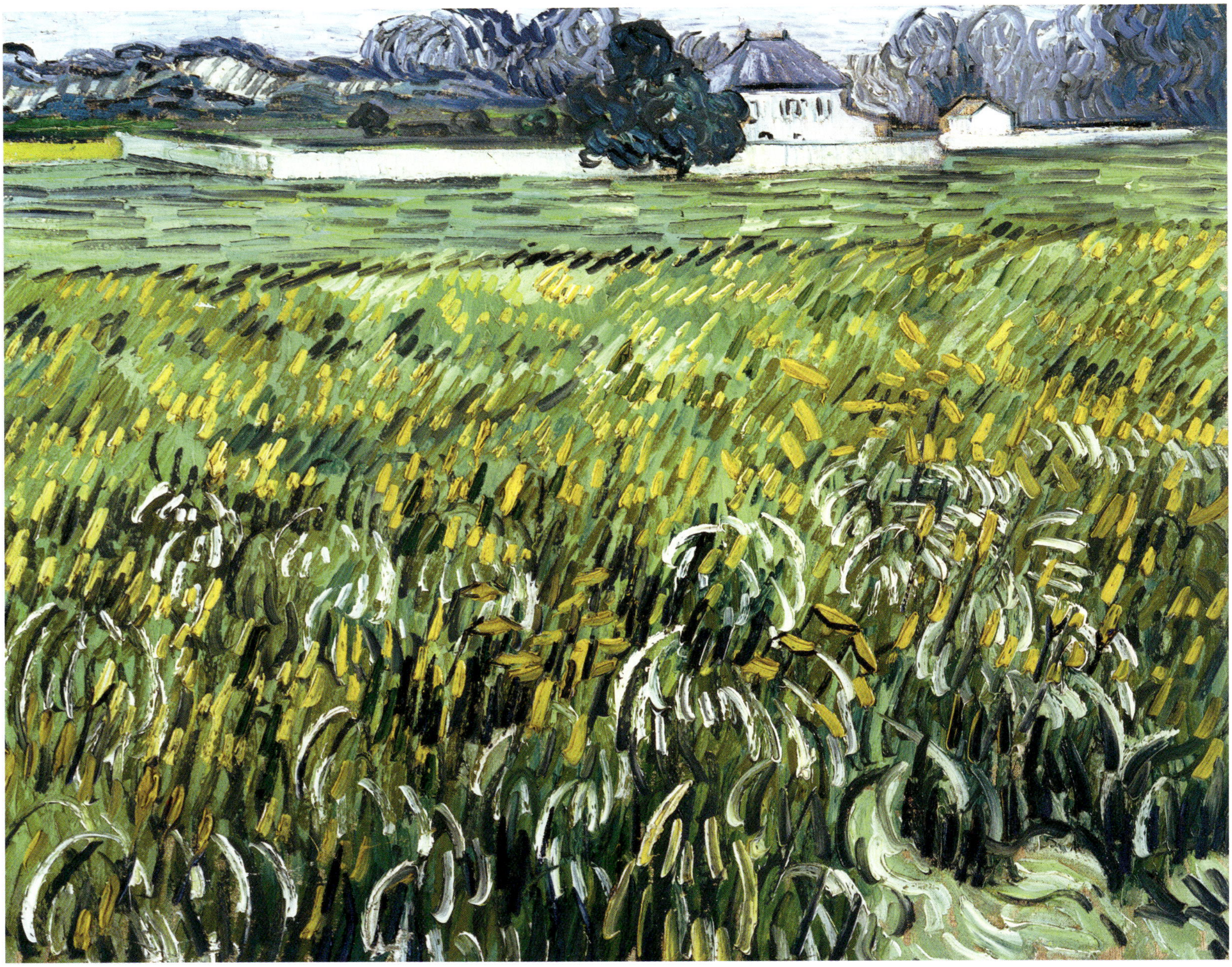

54 (#29)
Vincent van Gogh
House at Auvers-sur-Oise, 1890
Oil on canvas, 48.6 × 62.9 cm
The Phillips Collection, Washington, acquired 1952

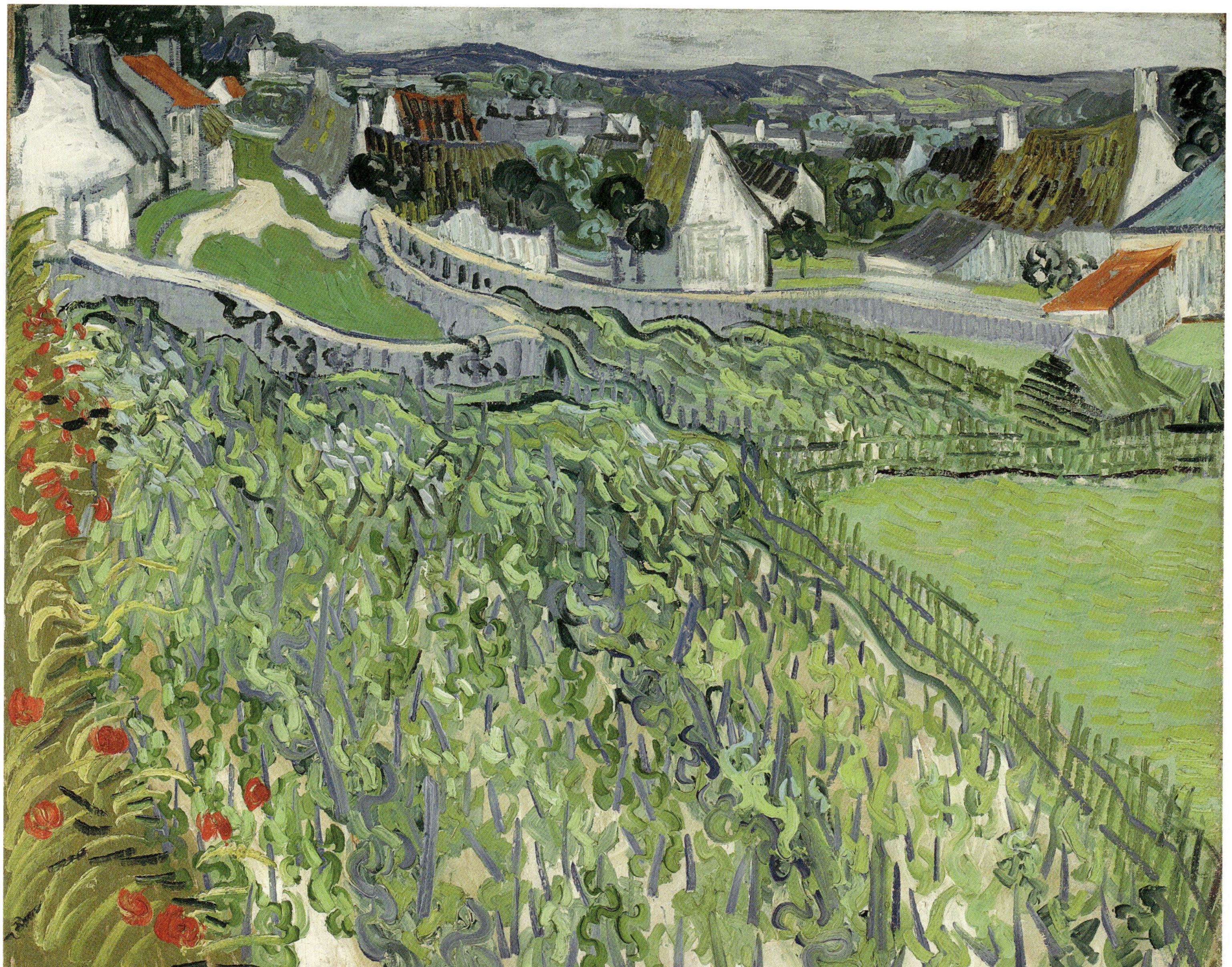

55 (#31)
Vincent van Gogh
Vineyards at Auvers-sur-Oise, 1890
Oil on canvas, 65.1 × 80.3 cm
Saint Louis Art Museum, Funds given by Mrs. Mark C. Steinberg

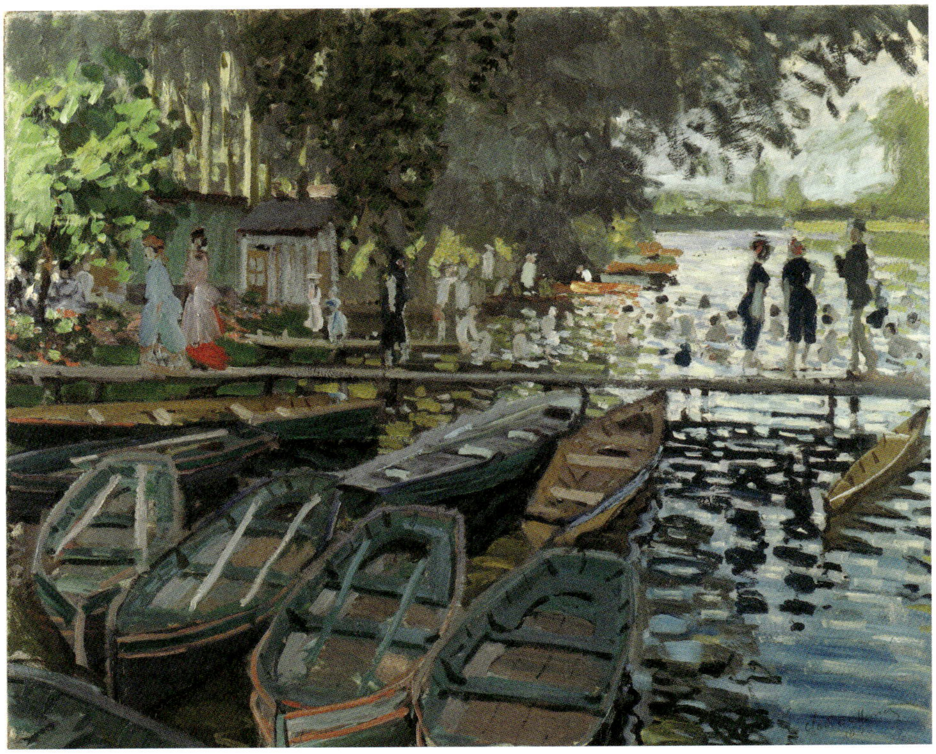

56
Claude Monet
Bathers at La Grenouillière, 1869
Oil on canvas, 73 × 92 cm
The National Gallery, London, bequeathed by Mrs M.S. Walzer as part of the Richard and Sophie Walzer Bequest

Monet and Pierre-Auguste Renoir in particular first made a name for themselves.[37]

Compared to Monet's *Bathers at La Grenouillière* **(56)**, for instance, Van Gogh worked with distinctly bright hues in *Bank of the Oise at Auvers* **(57)**. Where Monet painted from the shadows, Vincent did so in the full sunshine. The works are the same size, but Monet's is executed with broad, blocky strokes, setting down a figure in a few licks of paint and smearing out his brushes in the foliage. Van Gogh, by contrast, turns the vegetation on the riverbank into a feast of foliage, using short, angularly overlapping strokes of paint in numerous shades of green, and with dark graphic accents. His work also contains beautiful reflections in the water of both the multicoloured boats and the green of the leaves, done with somewhat longer but tightly horizontal strokes of paint. The composition terminates in the upper left with a pink (originally bright pink) sail.

What Van Gogh seems to have been aiming at with this cheerful, summery scene was primarily a saleable item for the art market, although he did not write to Theo about it. It is also notable that he included just three figures in the composition, two young women in matching summer outfits and a darkly dressed gentleman – the boat-hire operator, perhaps – turning grandly towards the painter.[38] In terms of motif, the painting is a little off his beaten path, but it is less unusual if we consider that the two women are more the subject than the boat-hire firm. It fits in well in this respect with other compositions in Auvers **(5, 35, 127)**, his portraits of young women and his street sketching.[39]

IN THE VILLAGE

Most artists working in Auvers ignored the contemporary buildings in the centre. A painter like Léonide Bourges did work a great deal in that part of the village, but she focused on the old buildings near the church and rue Daubigny, whereas Van Gogh also included the high street.[40] Close to the Café de la Mairie, for instance, he found the elongated white house that he used as the subject for a nocturnal scene, placing the planet Venus in the firmament as a reminder of his starry nights in Provence **(31)**.[41] He painted the work at a moment when Gauguin was in his thoughts once more. His former companion had written to him recently and Vincent wanted to tell him about the last painting he had made in Saint-Rémy – a cypress tree with a star, which he described in his reply as 'a night sky with a moon without brightness, [...] a star with exaggerated brightness'.[42] On that occasion too, he had painted a constellation in which Venus held a dominant place.

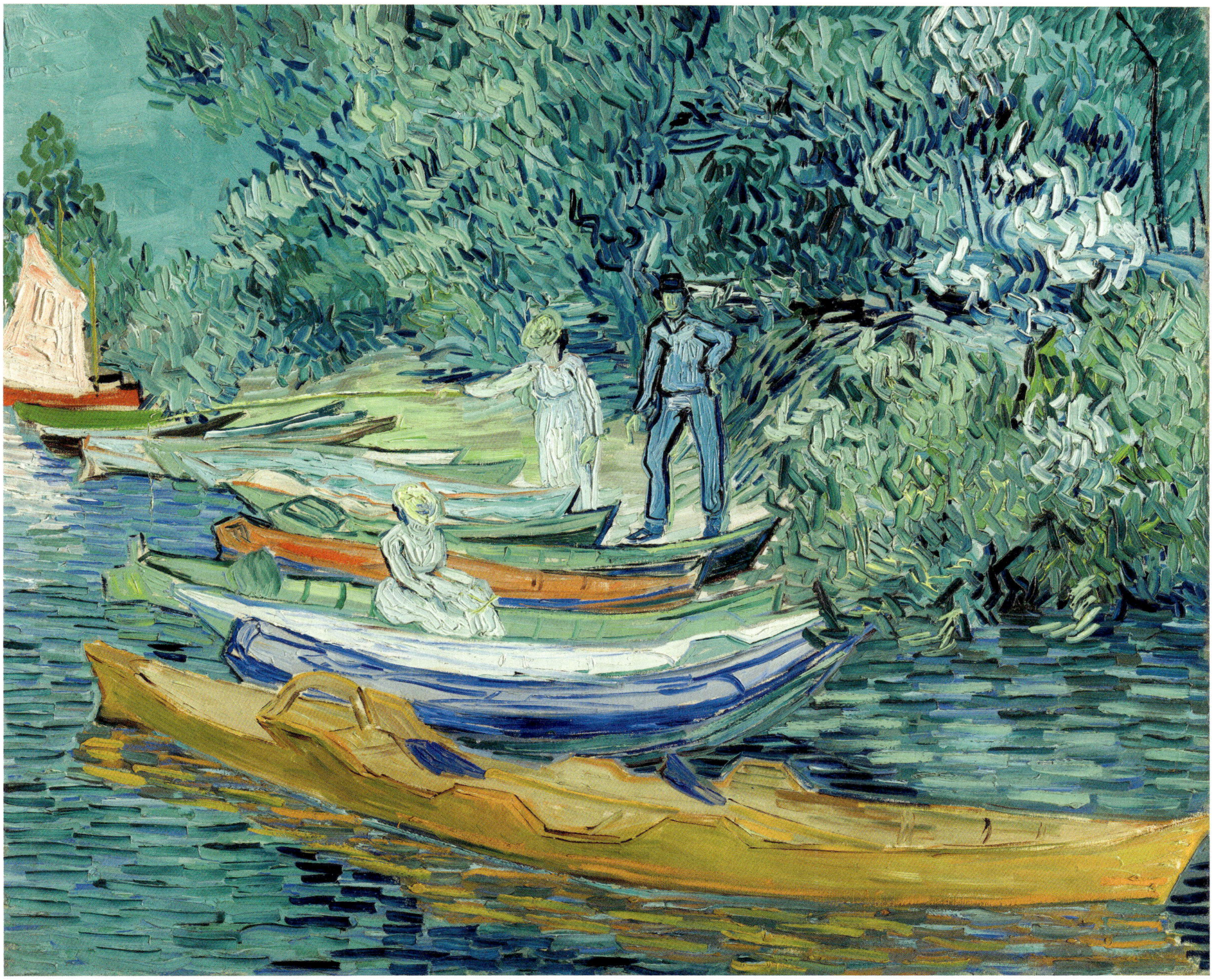

57 (#43)
Vincent van Gogh
Bank of the Oise at Auvers, 1890
Oil on canvas, 71.1 × 93.7 cm
Detroit Institute of Arts,
Bequest of Robert H. Tannahill

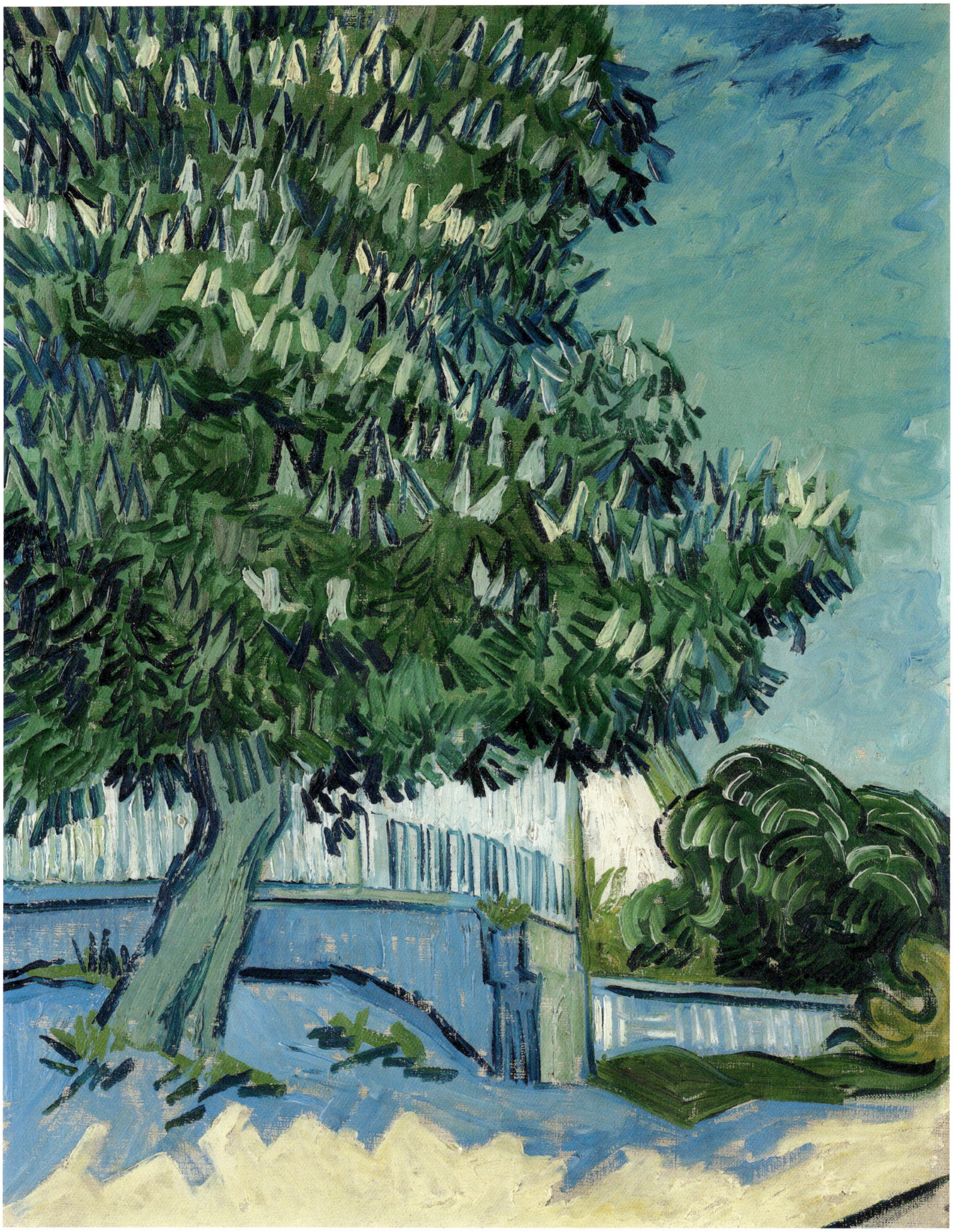

58 (#2)
Vincent van Gogh
Blossoming Chestnut Trees, 1890
Oil on canvas, 63.3 × 49.8 cm
Kröller-Müller Museum, Otterlo

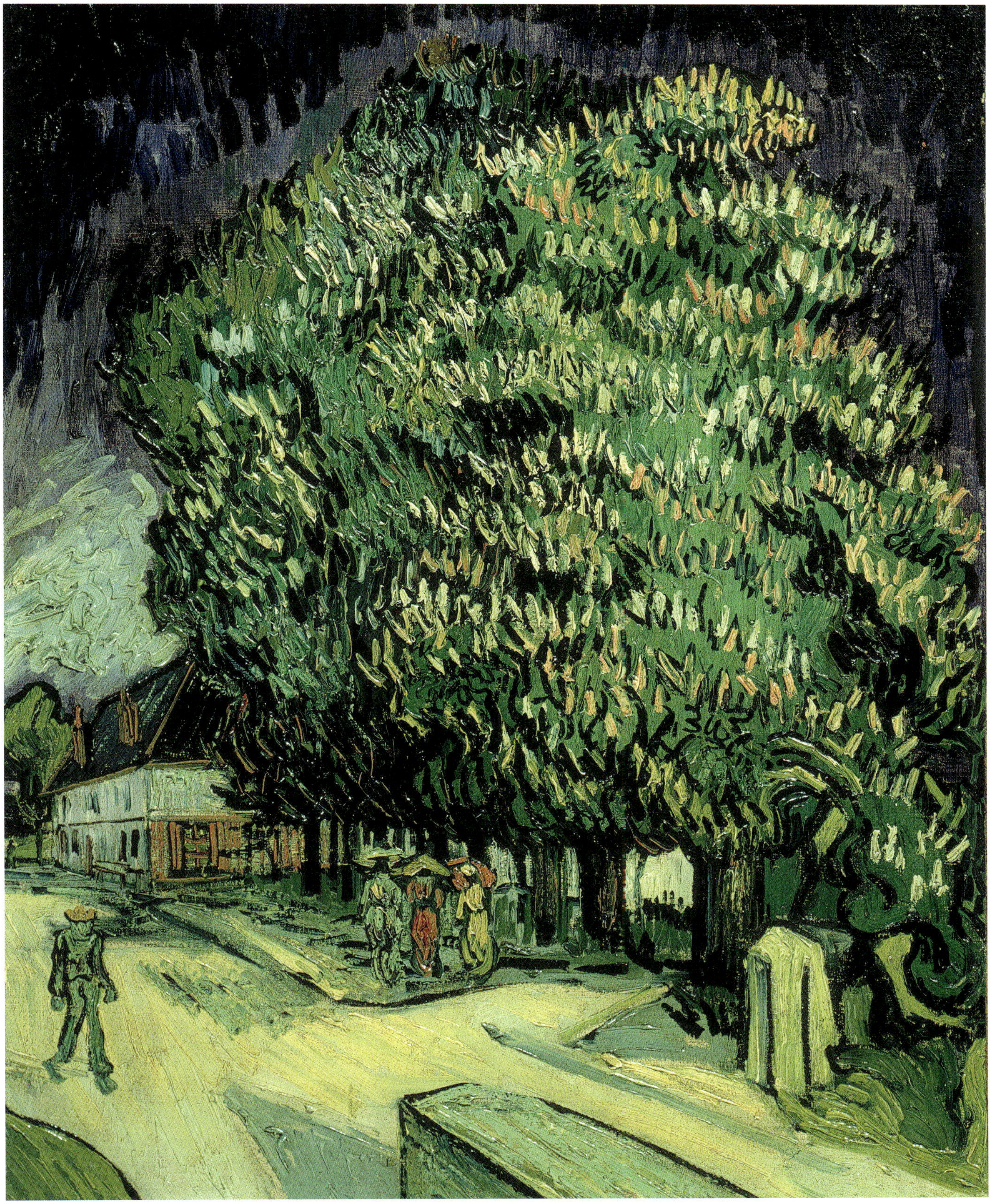

59 (#4)
Vincent van Gogh
Blossoming Chestnut Trees, 1890
Oil on canvas, 70 × 58 cm
Private collection

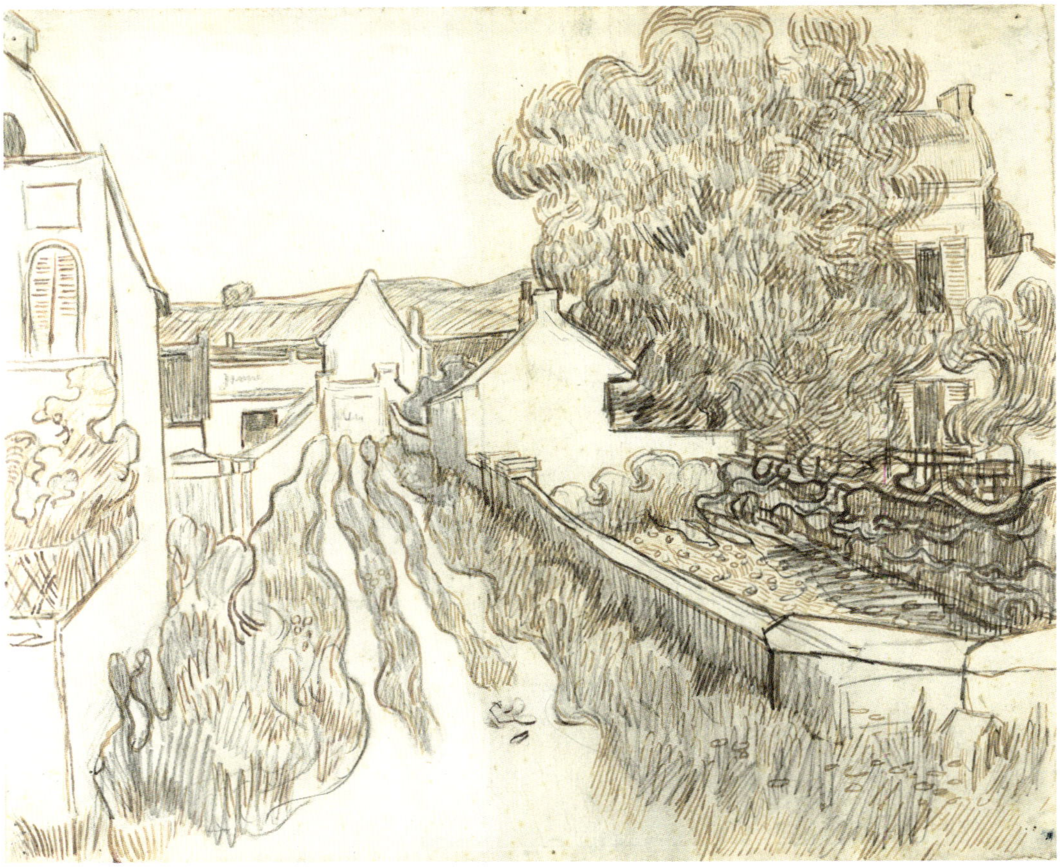

60
Vincent van Gogh
Dead-End Street with Houses, 1890
Pencil, pen and ink, on laid paper, 45 × 55.6 cm
Van Gogh Museum, Amsterdam

Van Gogh had been interested in trees in blossom since the spring of 1887, his second year in Paris. Henceforth, he tried to find time for the motif every spring and did so again in 1890. The same white house from the previous painting appears in *Blossoming Chestnut Trees* **(58)**, in which it is largely obscured by the white flowers. Another, somewhat larger work features a group of horse chestnut trees with pink blossoms next to the same building **(59)**.[43] The latter work is particularly intriguing: Van Gogh painted a powerful lighting effect, with an intense sun that brightly illuminates the street and trees from the right, while the sky behind the trees is a deep blue, almost black. He painted it at a time when the weather was rainy and stormy, 'but it isn't unpleasant to see these effects again', he wrote.[44] It was precisely the backlit effect caused by the weather conditions that interested him here. In the background, we make out the block of houses that stood diagonally opposite the inn; beyond it is the square with the town hall.

Further along the main road to Pontoise Van Gogh came across another house hidden from view by a chestnut tree, the house of Père Pilon. He presumably began with the drawing **(60)**, which contains a number of colour notes, before using it to help him work on the painting **(61)**. The question remains as to whether he was interested in the house as such, given that the title was coined later by Paul Gachet Jr.[45] It seems more likely that it was the splendid chestnut tree that caught his attention. He positioned himself directly in front of the path, which was given its own central perspective on the left side in the composition, with another fragment of a nearby house with a walled garden on the far left along the edge of the picture. The part on the right is open and shows a vegetable garden behind a low wall, and beyond this the chestnut tree, with just a fragment of the house behind it. Van Gogh painted a blue sky like a halo around it, which grows darker higher up. The intense colour recalls the dark sky in *Blossoming Chestnut Trees* **(59)**. This might be an indication that the sky was not so much observed as constructed, and that Van Gogh used the painting as a further example alongside the drawing. Recently built middle-class houses and villas, such as that of Père Pilon, were often set somewhat further back from the road and had 'a little garden with flower borders and small lawns separating them'.[46] Van Gogh painted a garden like this too **(142)**, although it is not entirely clear where it was located.

The most striking of the subjects he painted in the centre of Auvers was, perhaps, the town hall **(63)**. Adeline Ravoux, daughter of the innkeeper Arthur Ravoux, later recalled how Van Gogh worked on it 'from our pavement in front of the café' on 14 July.[47]

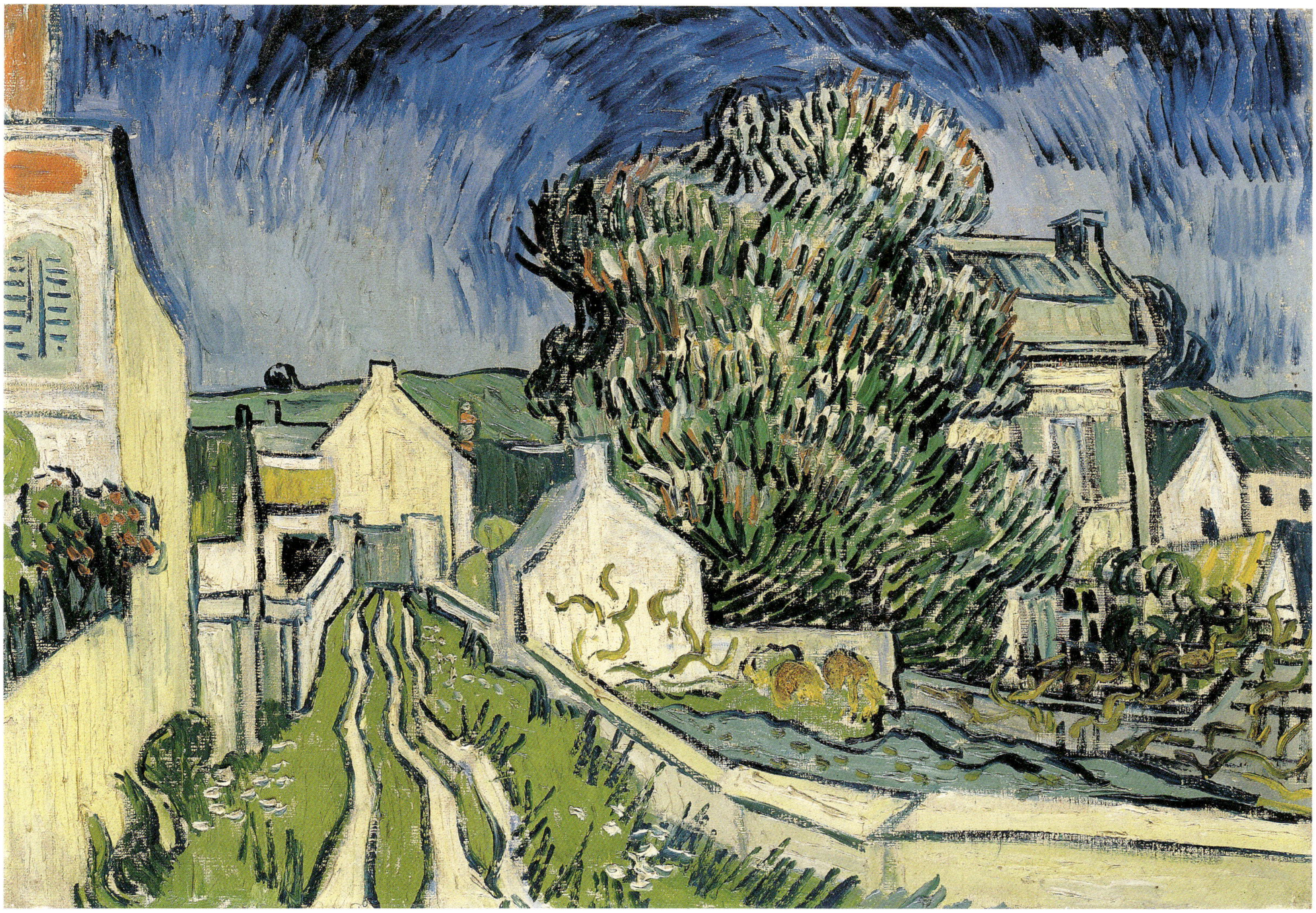

61 (#5)
Vincent van Gogh
The House of Père Pilon, 1890
Oil on canvas, 49 × 70 cm
Private collection

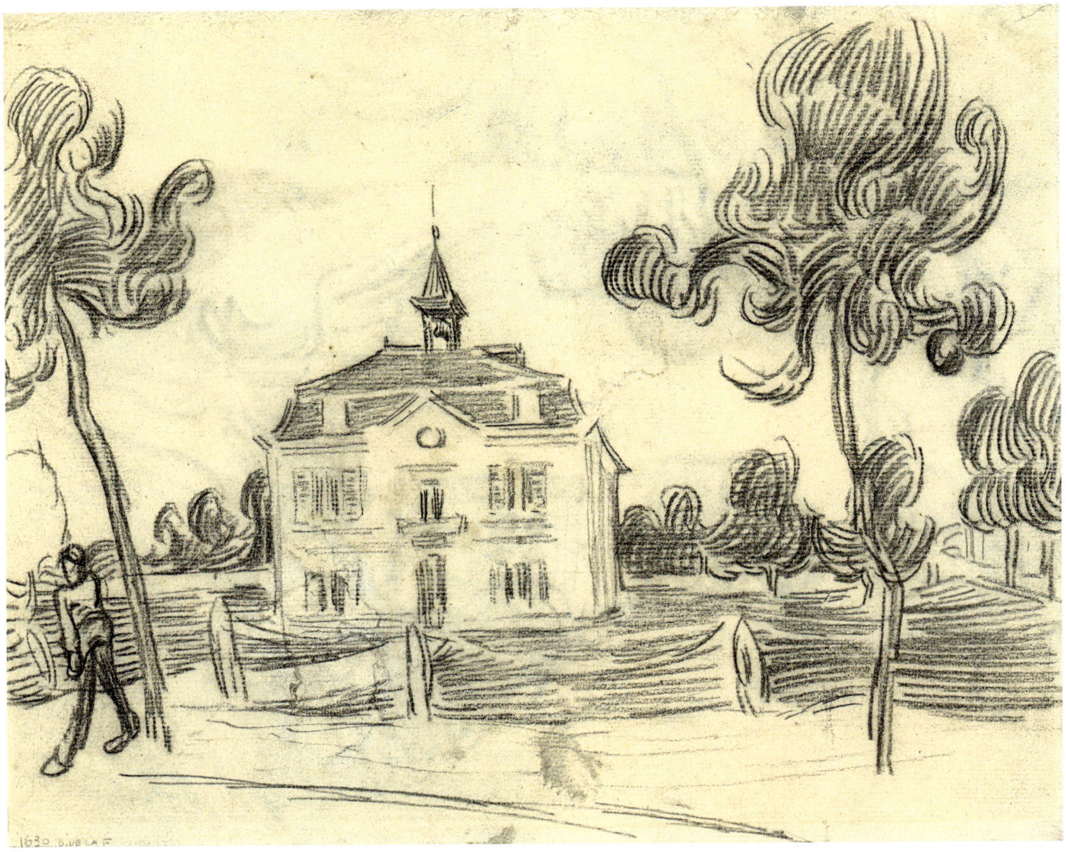

62
Vincent van Gogh
Auvers-sur-Oise Town Hall, 1890
Chalk, on laid paper, 24.2 × 31.2 cm
Van Gogh Museum, Amsterdam

The painting, done on a large, size 30 standard canvas, is somewhat curious when examined more closely. Albert Chatelet described its depiction of the town hall as a 'pathetic little building, thrown down in the middle of the empty square, it seems twisted by dancing brushstrokes'.[48] Compared to the drawing of the building, which Van Gogh probably made a little earlier **(62)**, it does indeed look rather diminutive – almost like a doll's house.[49] This is due to the hefty bollards and the tall, slender saplings in the foreground, and the small amount of intermediate space that the artist left for the building beyond them; in reality, the town hall stood much further back than is suggested here. The strokes of paint do indeed dance around it, as Chatelet observed, while the grassy square has been worked up dynamically with short, brownish touches into a continuous, graphic carpet. The only indication that this is a holiday is provided by the decorations – lanterns and flags – while a few scattered benches have been placed on the grass for visitors. But there are no people to be seen, which is what makes the scene so unsettling.

Le quatorze juillet (Bastille Day) was celebrated on a large scale in Auvers, beginning the previous evening. Houses were decorated with the French tricolour and on the day itself, there was a 'banquet' and a 'grand ball, open to the public and free of charge, on the brightly lit town hall square'.[50] Van Gogh mentioned neither the event nor the painting in his letters. His thoughts must chiefly have been with Theo, who left for the Netherlands the following day with Jo and their baby, just as he was yearning for them to come to Auvers more often.[51] So Vincent was not in the mood to celebrate and this empty work – the bunting has been hung out but no one has turned up – somehow reflects his own situation, a psychological emptiness. He gave it, appropriately enough, to his landlord at the inn. Perhaps it was a kind of adieu two weeks before his death, which might help explain his choice of this iconographically unusual subject in his oeuvre.

LANDSCAPE

Van Gogh's depiction of a quarry dwelling **(65)** is almost as unusual as that of the town hall.[52] Van Gogh found it by the steep slopes of the limestone plateau against which Auvers is situated. There were several abandoned quarries here of varying size, which were used for storage or mushroom-growing. For many years, people had also turned to them as a place to live **(64)**.[53] The drawing Van Gogh made of it is no more than a blue chalk sketch, but the sheet nevertheless offers a good impression of the living conditions of some of the poorer villagers. It might be

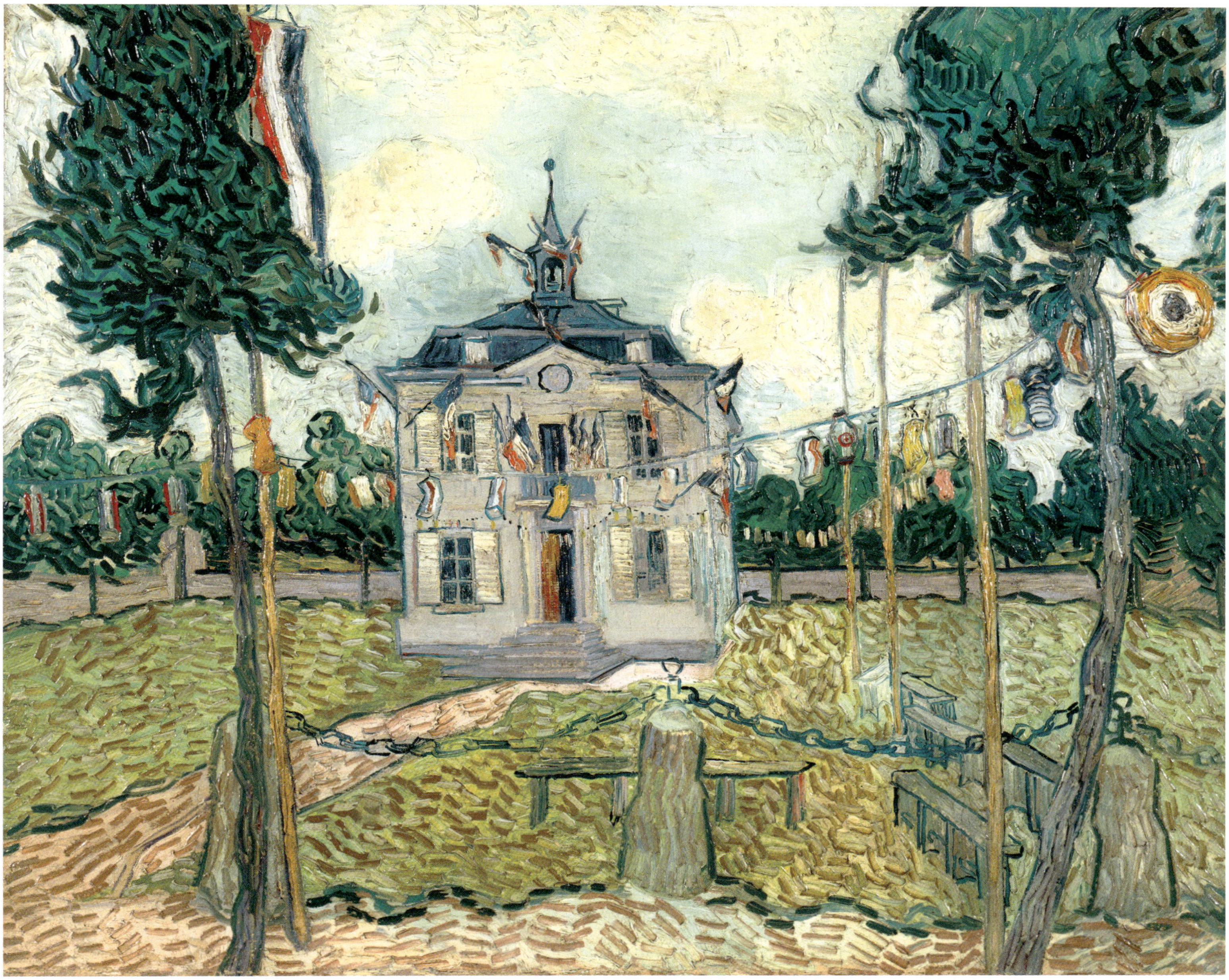

63 (#65)
Vincent van Gogh
Auvers-sur-Oise Town Hall on 14 July 1890, 1890
Oil on canvas, 72 × 93 cm
Private collection

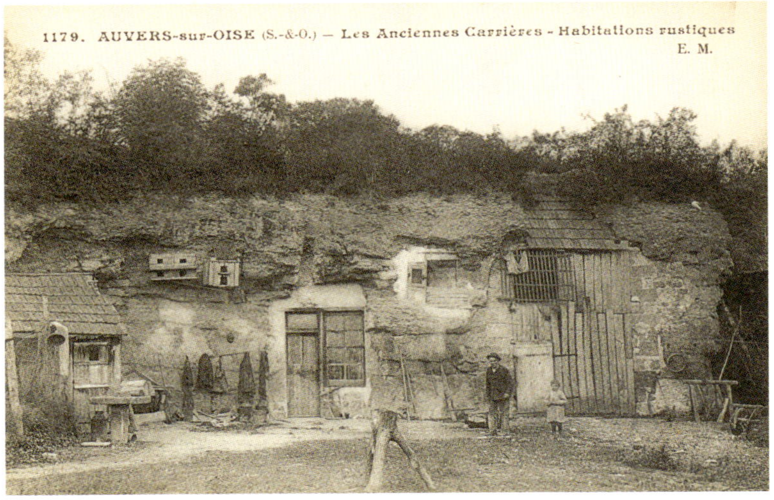

64
Auvers-sur-Oise, Dwelling in a Former Quarry
Postcard, c. 1910
Private collection

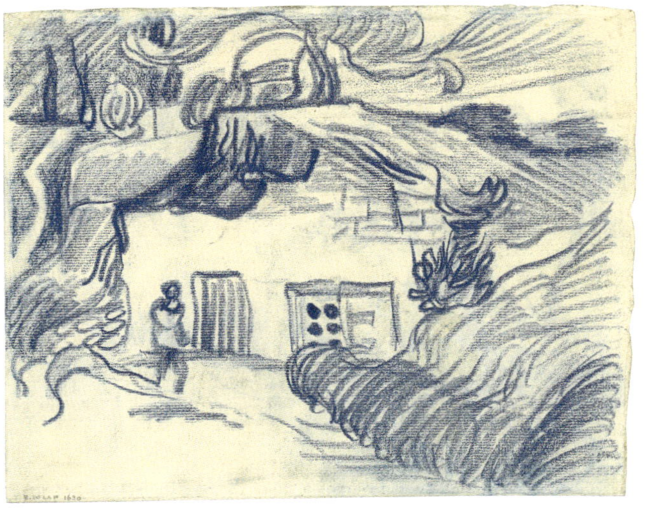

65
Vincent van Gogh
Landscape with House, 1890
Blue chalk on laid paper, 24.2 × 31.2 cm
Van Gogh Museum, Amsterdam

less picturesque than an old farmhouse with a mossy thatched roof, and hence not worthy of a painted version, but Van Gogh still drew an intimate view of the dwelling, with a figure in front of it and, on the left, a path leading up the slope and marked on the horizon by two tall trees, as if this were the entrance to an access road.

It was on the sweeping plateau above Auvers that Van Gogh painted his final landscapes, *Plain near Auvers-sur-Oise* **(68)** and *Wheatfields after the Rain (The Plain of Auvers-sur-Oise)* **(67)**, just over a week before his death. It is clearly visible in these works how the land was parcelled out into smaller fields. Strictly speaking, therefore, he did not only depict wheatfields as the traditional titles sometimes suggest:[54] there were very few large, contiguous fields of that type in the area. Crop rotation meant that other produce such as beets, potatoes and several types of cabbage were grown in addition to the different cereals.[55] A colour photograph by Antonin Personnaz, who took a great many pictures in Auvers in the early decades of the twentieth century, shows a cabbage field, for instance, located right next to a field of grain **(187)**. It is somewhat reminiscent of the green foliage found in the foreground of Van Gogh's *Field with Haystacks* **(143)**.

Van Gogh showed once again in these two large vistas how he could depict a similar motif in different ways in a short space of time. *Plain near Auvers-sur-Oise* is set out tone in tone, predominantly with pale greens, and worked up with graphic brushstrokes; *Wheatfields after the Rain* is painted more fluidly, with a larger number of brighter and stronger shades of green and yellow, and looks more realistic. Both works have a near foreground, across which the eye is led towards the slightly lower, seemingly endless fields beyond, and each painting is likewise closed off by a heavily cloudy sky. Van Gogh employed graphic brushstrokes in the sky of *Plain at Auvers-sur-Oise*, which link effectively with the foreground. The middle ground, painted with greater refinement and with a larger variety of yellow, brown and green tones, is somewhat sandwiched between the two.

Wheatfields after the Rain has a slightly paler-toned sky and is loosely painted with swirling movements that drive the white clouds towards the upper edge. The foreground occupies slightly less space in this instance, but is much more colourfully conceived, with a greater variety of vegetation. This left more space for the carpet of loose fields that zigzag towards the horizon. A dark yellow flower, probably an orange lily, stands out forlornly in the lower centre against the lower-lying fields.[56] Ever the descriptive realist, Van Gogh was not going to let an appealing detail like this elude him. It also illustrates the sensitivity with which he continued to respond to nature until the very end.

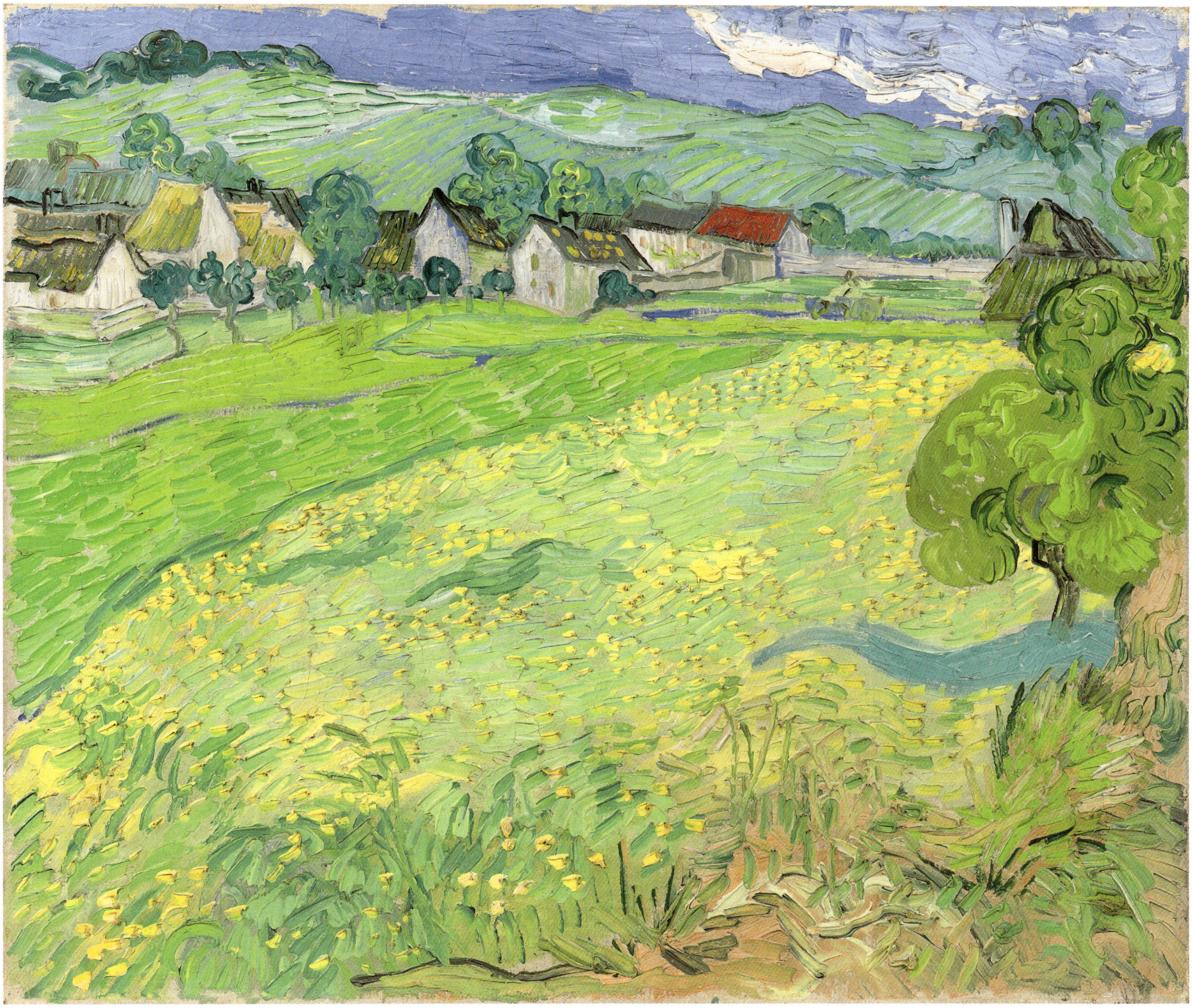

66 (#35)
Vincent van Gogh
Les Vessenots in Auvers-sur-Oise, 1890
Oil on canvas, 55 × 65 cm
Museo Nacional Thyssen-Bornemisza, Madrid

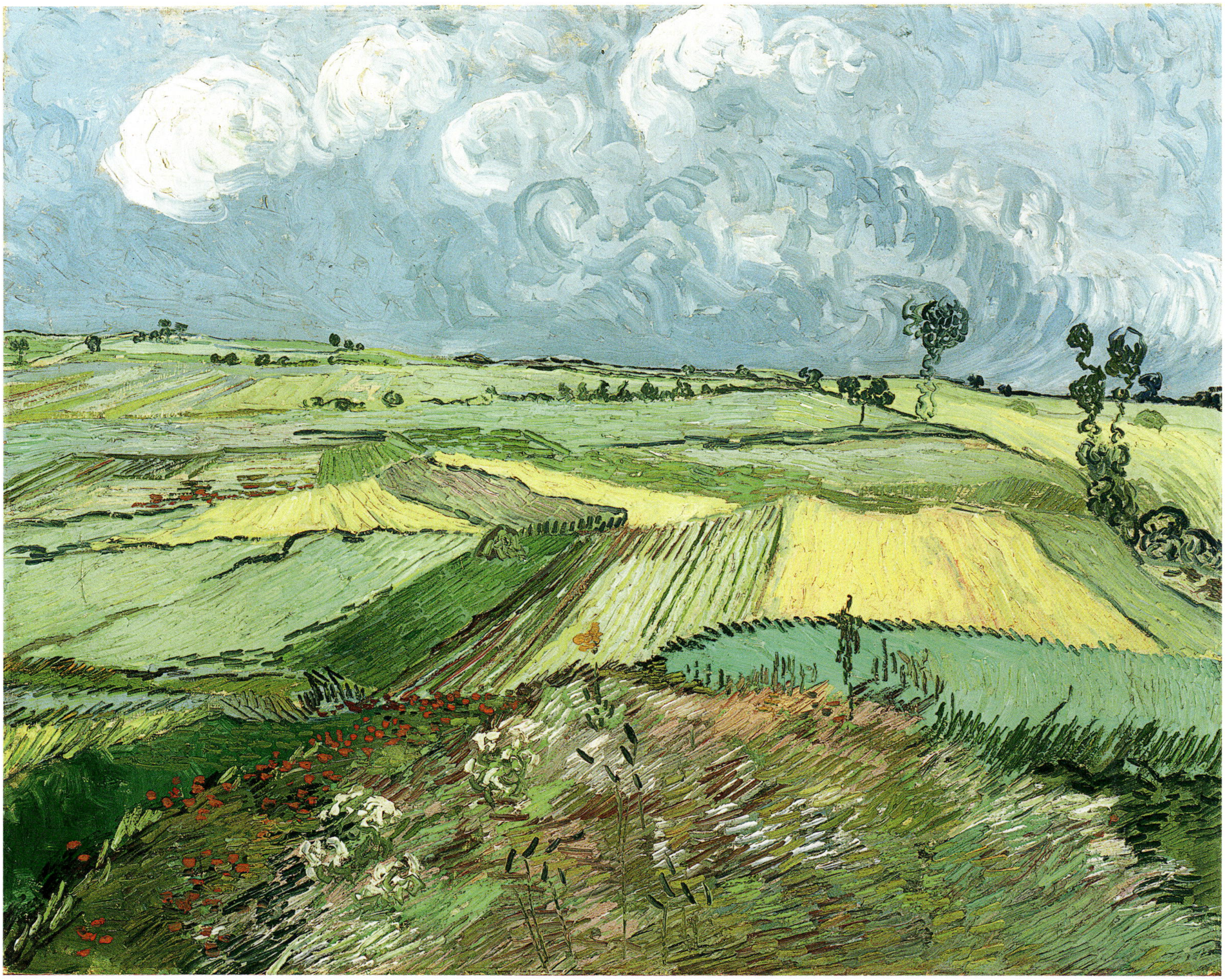

67 (#70)
Vincent van Gogh
Wheatfields after the Rain
(The Plain of Auvers-sur-Oise), 1890
Oil on canvas, 73.3 × 92.4 cm
Carnegie Museum of Art, Pittsburgh, acquired
through the generosity of the Sarah Mellon Scaife family

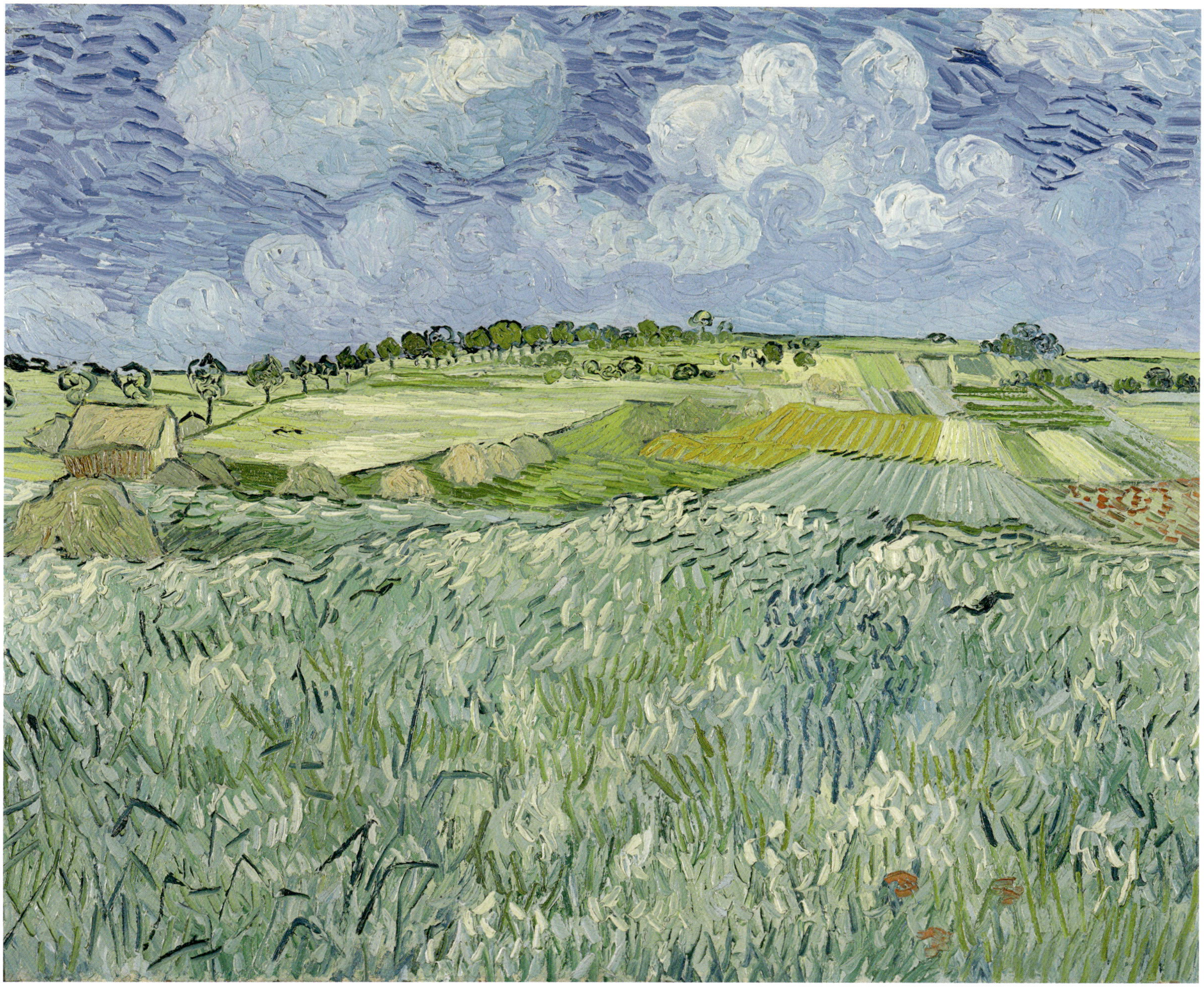

68 (#69)
Vincent van Gogh
Plain near Auvers-sur-Oise, 1890
Oil on canvas, 73.5 × 92 cm
Bayerische Staatsgemäldesammlungen –
Neue Pinakothek, Munich

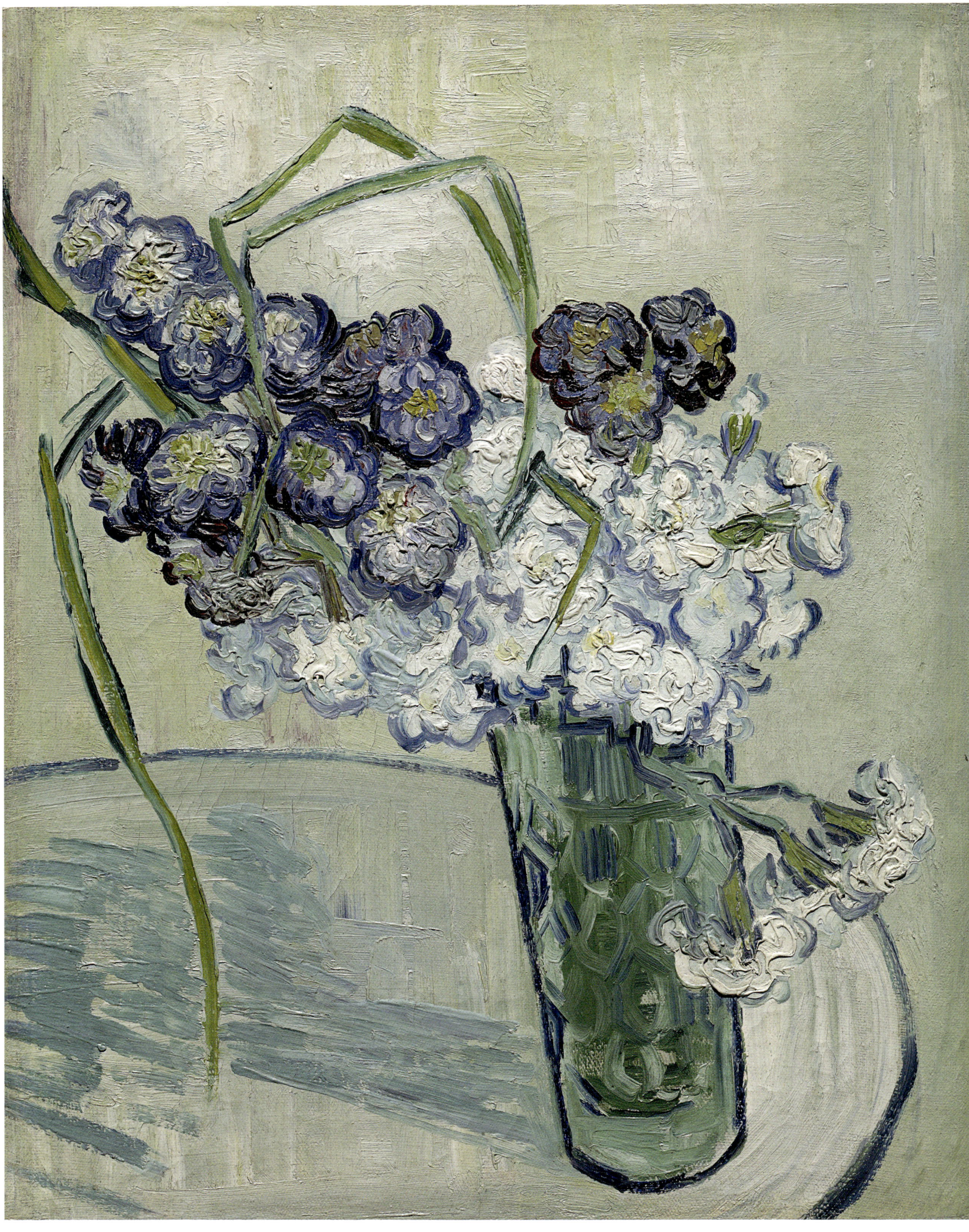

CHARMED BY FLOWERS

NIENKE BAKKER

Auvers-sur-Oise was at its loveliest when Van Gogh arrived there in the final days of May 1890. The fields and gardens were full of flowers and the chestnut trees were in blossom. He took to the village straight away – the old thatched roofs in particular – while the modern houses were 'very jolly, sunny and covered with flowers' and there was 'beautiful greenery in abundance'.[1] All this loveliness resulted primarily in a large number of landscapes, but Van Gogh also painted floral still lifes during his first weeks in Auvers: nine in all, which is more than he had produced in this genre in the whole of the preceding year.[2] They date from roughly late May to mid-June, after which he shifted his attention back to landscapes and portraits.[3] What prompted this brief focus on floral still lifes and what did these works mean to him?

RENEWED INTEREST

With a single exception, Van Gogh had not produced any floral still lifes since the final canvases with sunflowers made in Arles in January 1889.[4] His interest revived towards the end of his stay in Saint-Rémy when, 'with calm, unremitting ardour', he painted four bouquets on a large scale (92 × 73 cm), two with irises and two with roses **(72)**, 'with so much enthusiasm that packing my trunk seems more difficult to me than doing the paintings'.[5] Now that he was about to head back north and would be living near to Theo, his thoughts turned once again to sales, prompted chiefly by his obsession with repaying his brother for the selfless financial support he had provided since the very beginning of his career. Floral still lifes struck him as eminently saleable.[6] Moreover, he had already proved himself in that genre: it was for good reason that his canvases of irises and roses were a continuation, albeit less experimental and innovative, of his sunflower paintings in terms of the format and composition. The sunflower works had recently featured in exhibitions, and they had been admired not only by Theo, but also by artists like Paul Gauguin and Claude Monet, and the poet and critic Albert Aurier.[7]

Van Gogh continued to work 'in a frenzy' on his irises and roses right up to his departure from Saint-Rémy.[8] He expressed the hope in a letter that the still lifes would cover the cost of his travel – a sign that he saw commercial opportunities for them and that his confidence in his work, which had been badly shaken by his mental problems, had been somewhat restored by painting them.[9] His revived interest in cheerful spring motifs of this kind is also apparent from his curiosity about Ernest Quost's painting *Easter Flowers*, which was shown at the Paris Salon

69 (#24)
Vincent van Gogh
Glass with Carnations, 1890
Oil on canvas, 41 × 32 cm
Private collection

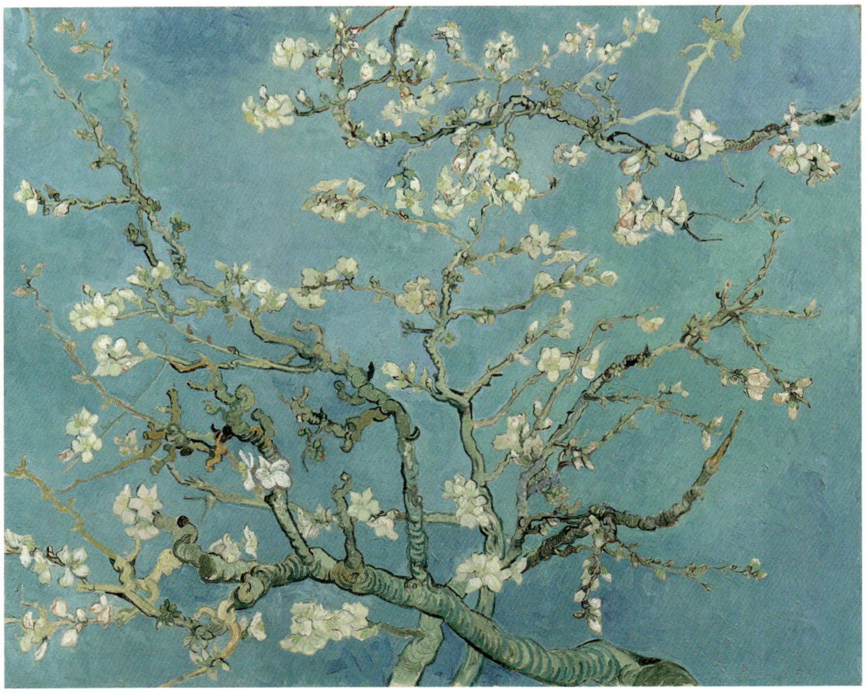

70
Vincent van Gogh
Almond Blossom, 1890
Oil on canvas, 73.3 × 92.4 cm
Van Gogh Museum, Amsterdam

and which he had read about **(73)**.[10] He went to see the work at the exhibition during his brief stay with his brother, and the large canvas of a garden full of colourful spring flowers, like one great decorative tapestry, must have affected him deeply so soon after painting his own *Irises* and *Roses*.[11] Quost – an acquaintance of Theo's and a successful painter of floral still lifes – had been a role model for Vincent since his time in Paris in 1886–87, as was Georges Jeannin, another artist with flower paintings at the 1890 Salon and by whom Theo owned two still lifes.[12] Vincent must also have been pleased to see Adolphe Monticelli's *Vase with Flowers* again at Theo's, as it was one of his favourites.[13] In addition, he now also had the chance to see his own paintings for the first time in a long while, both at his brother's home and in storage at the paint seller Julien 'Père' Tanguy. They included his Parisian floral still lifes, his canvases of flowering fruit trees and sunflowers from Arles, which Theo and Jo had hung in their flat, and the *Almond Blossom* he had painted in Saint-Rémy as a gift to mark his nephew's birth. The latter painting had been given pride of place above the piano in Theo and Jo's living room **(70)**.[14]

BLOSSOMING CHESTNUT BRANCHES

Van Gogh arrived in Auvers on 20 May with all these paintings fresh in his mind, but the ambition that had been awakened in Saint-Rémy to start producing still lifes for sale initially gave way to the need to record his new surroundings. Possibly prompted by the sight of his own pictures of blossoming trees at Theo's, he did however seize the opportunity to paint that same motif again: the chestnut trees near the Café de la Mairie, Arthur Ravoux's inn, where he was staying, were in blossom and he painted them twice during the first days after his arrival **(58, 59)**. His first still life in Auvers, the expressively painted *Blossoming Chestnut Branches* **(71)**, arose more or less by chance shortly afterwards when stormy weather on 24 and 25 May created an opportunity to capture the blossoms not only in street scenes, but in a still life too. The hefty branches in the painting must have blown down in the wind, instantly awakening the floral artist within him.[15] To do full justice to the monumentality of the chestnut's large leaves and clumps of blossom, Van Gogh opted for his largest canvas format (73 × 92 cm). Compared to the still lifes from his final days in Saint-Rémy, this was a much bolder piece, placing it closer to his large, truly innovative sunflower

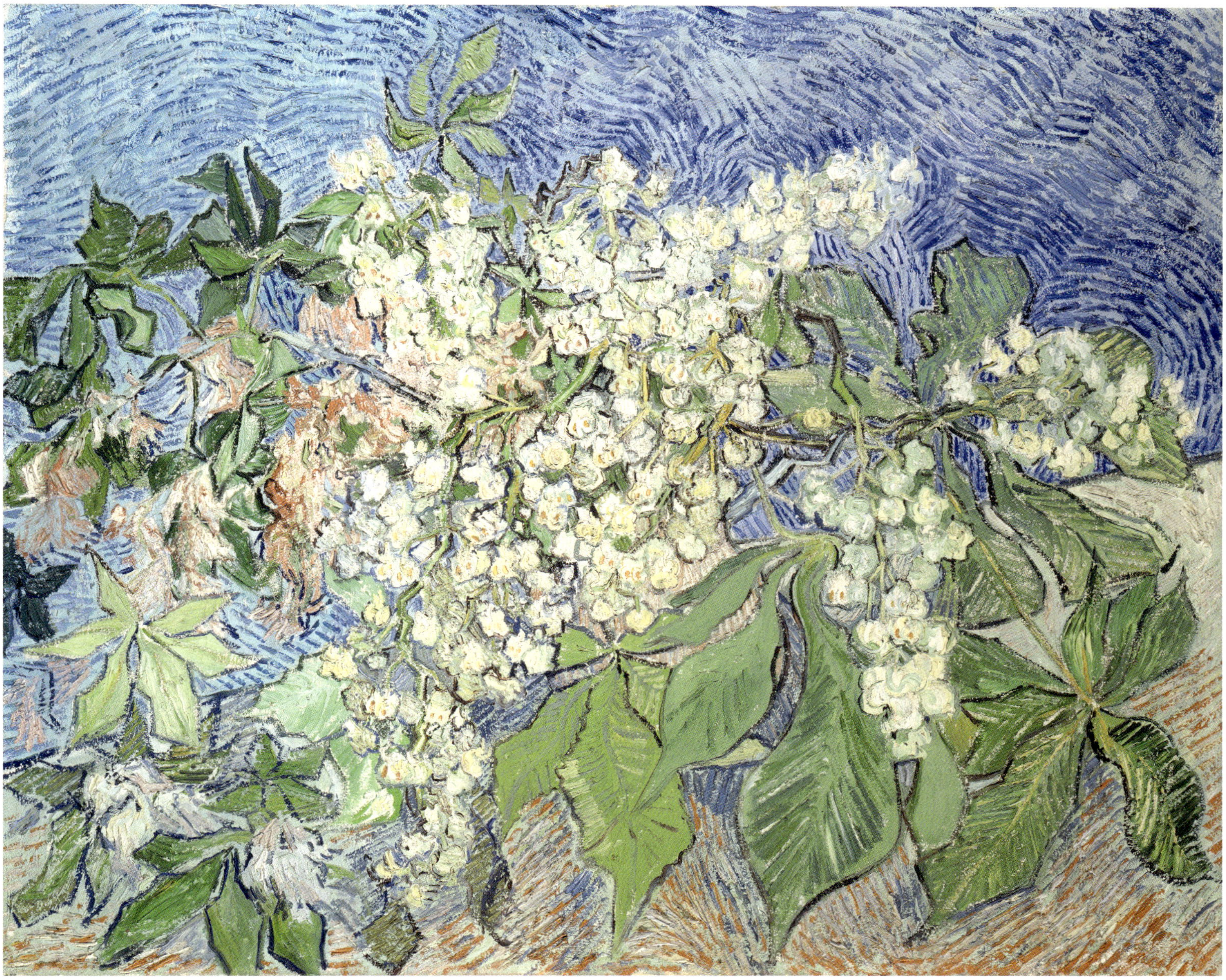

71 (#6)
Vincent van Gogh
Blossoming Chestnut Branches, 1890

Oil on canvas, 73 × 92 cm
Emil Bührle Collection, on long-term
loan to Kunsthaus Zürich

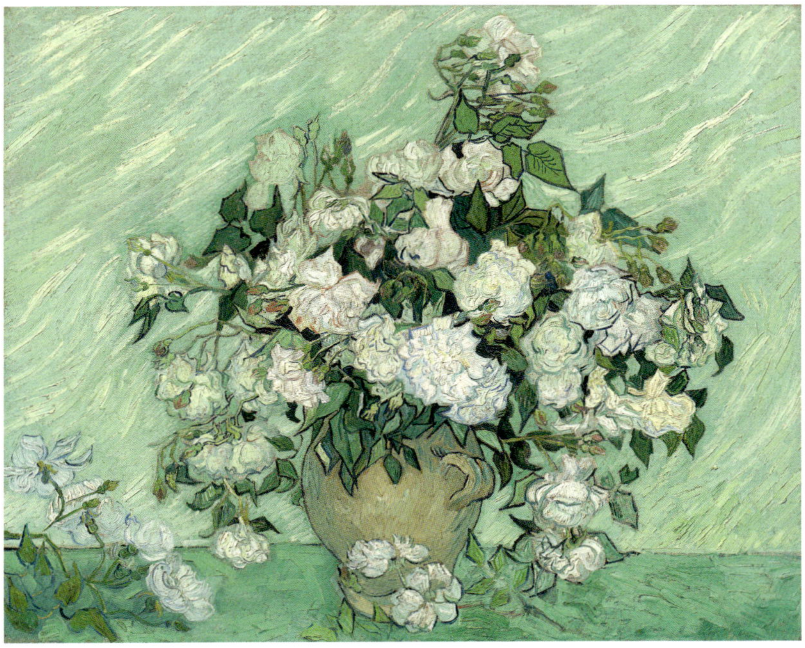

72
Vincent van Gogh
Roses, 1890
Oil on canvas, 71 × 90 cm
National Gallery of Art, Washington,
Gift of Pamela Harriman in memory
of W. Averell Harriman

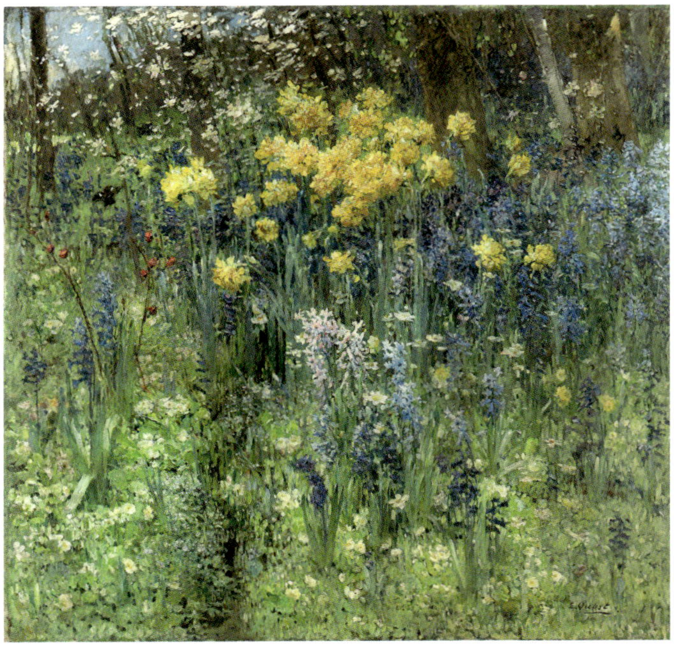

73
Ernest Quost
Easter Flowers, 1890
Oil on canvas, 140.6 × 146.2 cm
La Piscine – Musée d'art et d'industrie
André Diligent, Roubaix

paintings of 1888–89 than to those later, and by his standards somewhat more conventional, works.

Blossoming Chestnut Branches is an exceptional painting in Van Gogh's oeuvre because of the way he transformed the traditional subject of the floral still life into a spectacular, highly decorative image. Only on closer viewing do you spot the vase in which the branches stand and the sloping line of a table, hidden behind the blossom clumps and leaves of two varieties of horse chestnut tree: large white flowers at the front and smaller, pink ones at the back. The differences in the size of the leaves and the diagonally positioned table introduced perspective to the scene, but the fact that the vase is barely visible between the frame-filling chestnut branches actually creates a flat effect. The composition is reminiscent in this regard of Katsushika Hokusai's close-up prints of flowers, which Van Gogh saw at the exhibition of Japanese prints he had visited in Paris **(74)**.[16] His choice of a bright blue background is striking, suggesting as it does that the scene is set outdoors, as in *Almond Blossom*, although the effect is very different in this new work. The emphasis here is on the graphic lines, with the vein pattern in the leaves carried through into the rest of the picture, culminating in the stylized background of wavy brushstrokes – a rarity in his works from Auvers, with the exception of *Doctor Paul Gachet* **(159)** and *Poppy Field* **(13)**. The astonishing dynamism of the touch – impastoed and rounded for the blossoms, wider and flatter for the leaves, and parallel lines for the table and background – make this one of his best still lifes: a marvellous image of the vitality and energy exuded by nature in spring.

Van Gogh must have started to work on this painting on 26 May, the day after the storm, in the 'salle des peintres' behind Ravoux's café.[17] The first time he worked at Gachet's house was on 27 May when, according to the doctor's son, Van Gogh painted the garden in the morning **(34)**. After lunch, father and son accompanied the artist to see his canvases at Ravoux's, including *Blossoming Chestnut Branches*, which must thus have been largely if not entirely finished at that point.[18] The impressive work was undeniably a fresh achievement by Van Gogh as a painter of flowers, although we do not know whether he himself was satisfied with it. His next letter only dates from a week later, by which time he was working on other paintings and so did not mention it.[19] Having completed *Blossoming Chestnut Branches*, he did not use canvas size 30, which he reserved for ambitious works, for any further floral still lifes.[20]

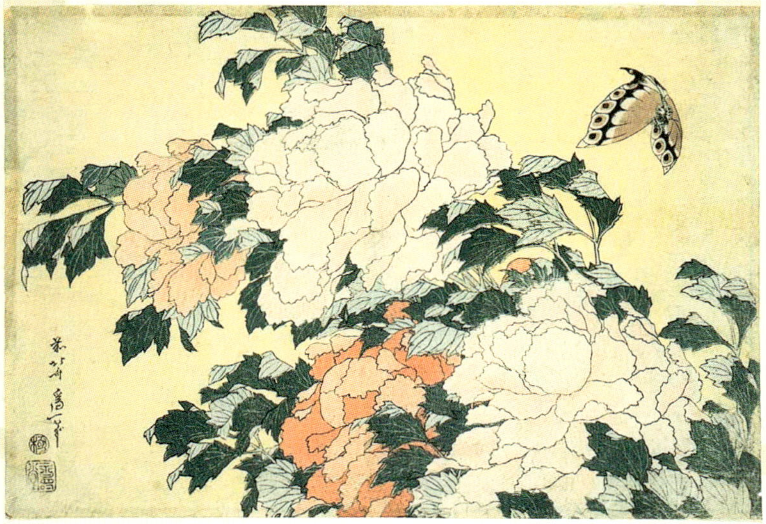

74
Katsushika Hokusai
Peonies and Butterfly, from an untitled series of large flowers, c. 1833–34
Colour woodblock print; *oban*, 25.4 × 37.7 cm
The Art Institute of Chicago,
Clarence Buckingham Collection

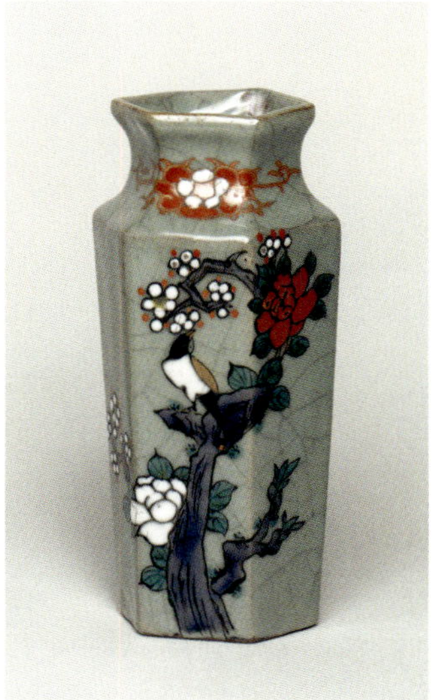

75
Vase, France, before 1890
Stoneware, 28.5 × 9 cm
Musée d'Orsay, Paris

PAINTING AT GACHET'S

The other floral still lifes from Auvers are smaller in format and their compositions simpler. There are eight of them in all: five studies and three larger, more advanced pieces. We date this group of still lifes to the first half of June, the period when Van Gogh began to paint several days a week at Gachet's home. As mentioned already, he first worked there on 27 May and continued to do so regularly in the weeks that followed. Van Gogh basically came whenever the doctor was at home, certainly on Sunday and Monday, and occasionally on Saturday and Tuesday too. He also joined the family for meals. 'I feel that at his place I can do not too bad a painting every time I go there, and he'll certainly continue to invite me to dinner each Sunday or Monday', he wrote on 3 June.[21] 'There would always be what I need [at the doctor's home] for arranging flowers or still lifes', and so he went on to paint eight still lifes there, featuring various glasses and vases belonging to Gachet, filled with flowers from his garden or the surrounding fields picked on the way. Only two of the pieces are mentioned in Van Gogh's letters: the 'bouquet of buttercups' in early June **(77)** and the 'bouquet of wild plants' on which he was working on 17 June **(82)**.[22]

Among the works Van Gogh brought to Auvers from Paris are also likely to have been two floral still lifes, which he may have taken with him to offer as gifts to the people he met in the village.[23] He had painted many flower arrangements of this type during his time in Paris in 1886–87. They served primarily as colour experiments, but were also intended to sell, exchange or give away.[24] While Van Gogh's decision to paint flower arrangements was also an obvious way of spending the days he worked at Gachet's, it was less the marketability of such pictures that played a role at this stage than the possibility of using them as gifts. Aware that his place in Theo's life had changed now that his brother had a family, Vincent's fear of being a burden had increased and with it the urgency of earning something back through his work. He hoped to use it to offset his accommodation costs and at least to reimburse Gachet for his support ('I can pay him in paintings') and perhaps others in the village too.[25] He began in Gachet's case with two paintings of the doctor's garden **(34, 35)** 'to show him that should he not be paid in money we'll nevertheless still compensate him for what he does for us'.[26]

His first still life comprised a 'bouquet of buttercups' **(77)**, which he mentioned in the same breath as the two garden studies.[27] The square format Van Gogh chose for this still life was not one he had used before and he might have been inspired to

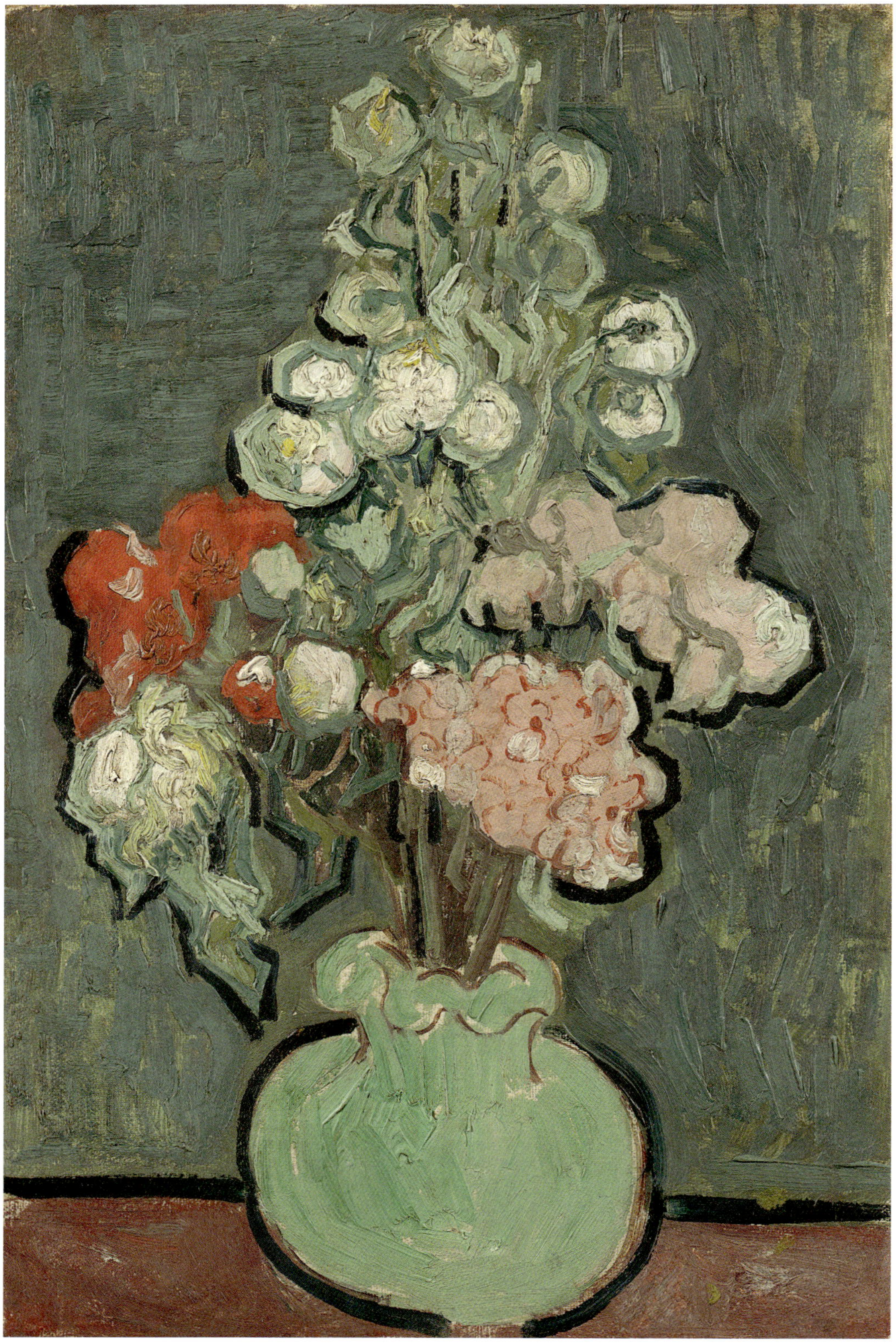

76 (#18)
Vincent van Gogh
Vase of Flowers, 1890
Oil on canvas, 42.2 × 29 cm
Van Gogh Museum, Amsterdam

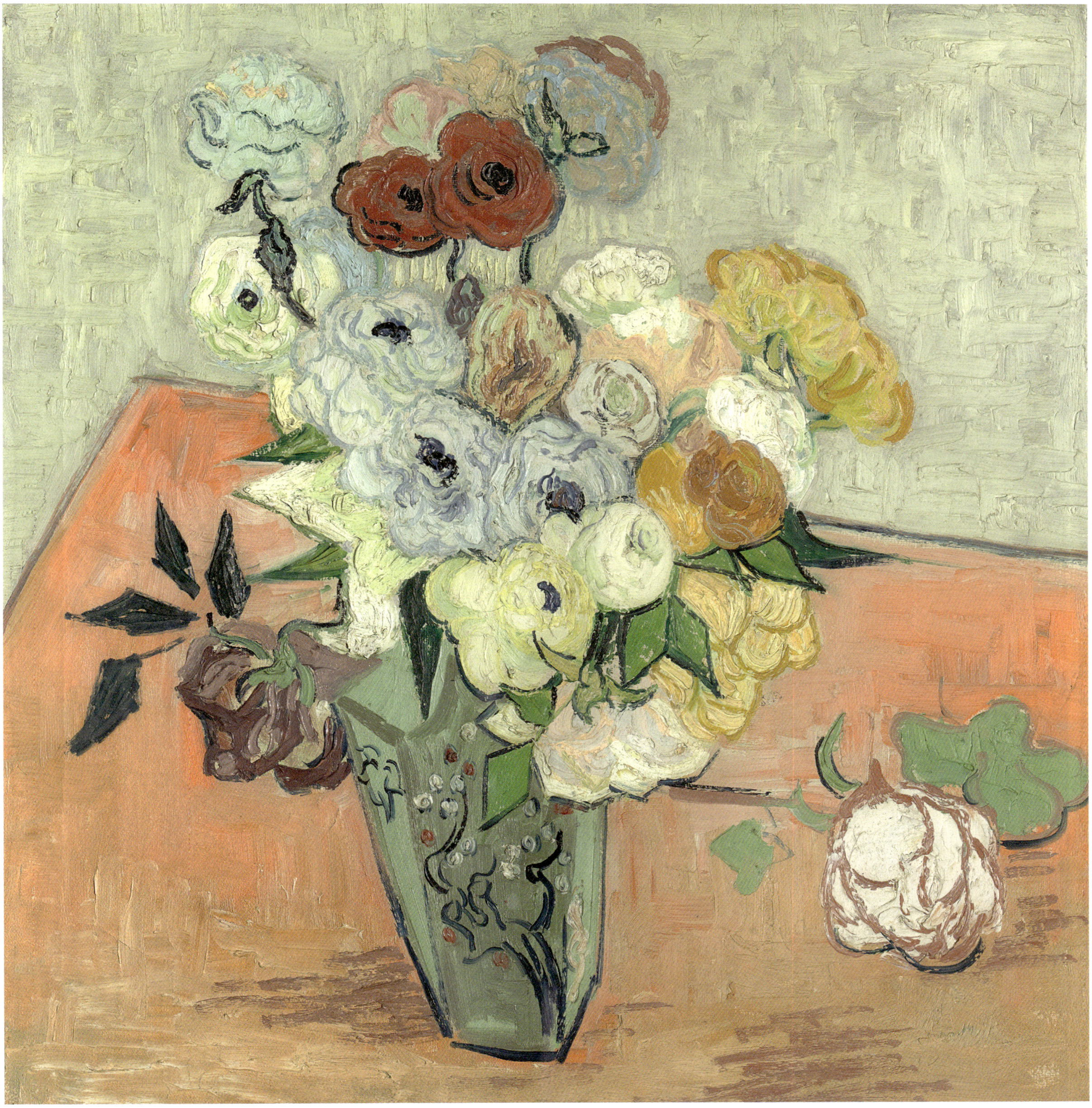

77 (#17)
Vincent van Gogh
Roses and Turban Buttercups, 1890
Oil on canvas, 51.7 × 52 cm
Musée d'Orsay, Paris

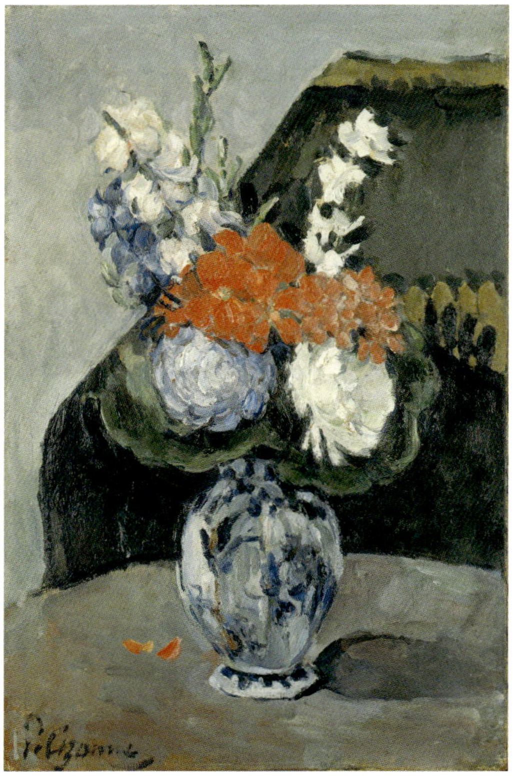

78
Paul Cézanne
Bouquet in a Delft Vase, 1873
Oil on canvas, 41 × 27 cm
Musée d'Orsay, Paris

do so by Quost's painting at the Salon (140 × 146 cm) or the surimono prints at the Paris exhibition (21 × 18.9 cm). These too were almost square – a format that enhances a picture's decorative effect.[28] The decorative element in Van Gogh's flower painting resides primarily in the symmetry of the bouquet, with a rose sticking out on either side of the buttercups, the contour lines around the flowers and the flat perspective. Gachet's son recalled that Van Gogh painted *Roses and Turban Buttercups* in a single session in the garden.[29] The vase in the picture – Japonist-inspired French earthenware[30] – belonged to Dr Gachet **(75)**; his son later donated it to the Louvre, followed by the painting. The vase stands on the 'red garden table' that Van Gogh also painted in his portraits of the doctor **(112, 159)**.[31]

DIALOGUE

For some of the floral still lifes he made at Gachet's place, Van Gogh entered into a dialogue with the 'two fine bouquets by Cézanne' in the doctor's collection, which had impressed him from his very first day in Auvers.[32] They comprised a large bouquet of dahlias **(174)** and a small study of geraniums **(78)**, which Paul Cézanne had painted in 1873 at Gachet's home, arranged in his Delftware vases. According to Gachet Jr, his father advised Cézanne to use a small canvas for the *Bouquet au petit Delft* 'to better "liven up" the piece'.[33] It is noteworthy that Van Gogh chose precisely the same size of canvas for his *Vase of Flowers* **(76)**, while the composition, with flowers projecting from the bouquet, is also somewhat similar to that of Cézanne's flower arrangement. Like *Roses and Turban Buttercups*, *Vase of Flowers* was painted in a single session, with coarse brushstrokes and an emphasis on planes and contours, as in Japanese prints. The flowers in the bouquet are hard to identify: what we see is probably two pink peonies on the right, a red poppy on the left and several stocks rising above the rest.

Van Gogh also produced three equally fluently brushed studies with more or less the same format as *Vase of Flowers*. The first, *Absinthe Glass with Wild Flowers* **(79)**, is a loosely set out, thinly painted study of an absinthe glass with an arrangement of ears of wheat, a few red vine leaves, white flowers and heart-shaped bindweed leaves, and a sprig of bluebells or harebells. *Glass with Carnations* **(69)** displays more verve in terms of touch and composition. Van Gogh positioned the glass some way from the centre of the table and neatly rebalanced the picture by having the bouquet lean over to the left with long stalks of grass poking out on that side and several hanging carnations on

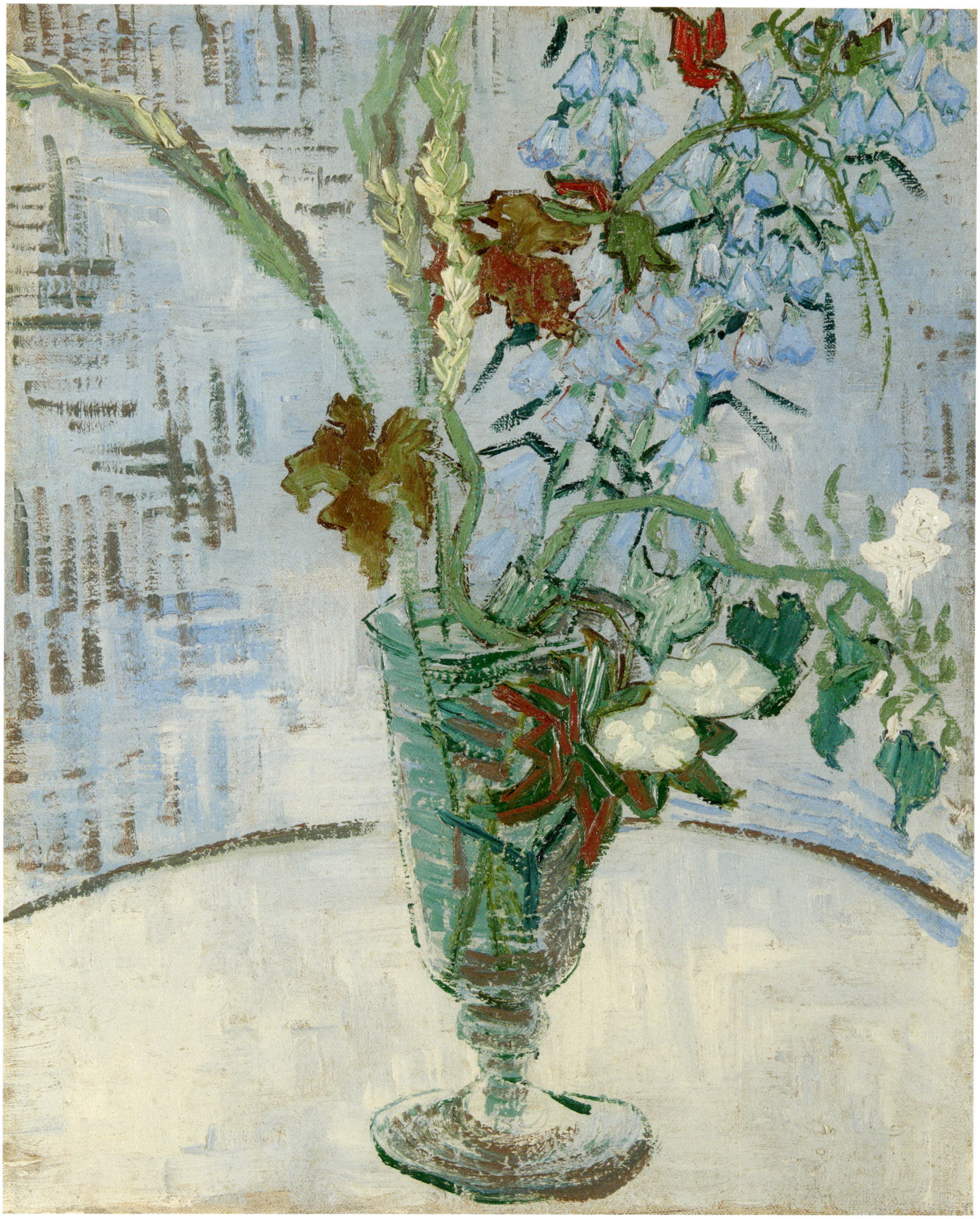

79 (#19)
Vincent van Gogh
Absinthe Glass with Wild Flowers, 1890
Oil on canvas, 41.3 × 33.3 cm
Private collection

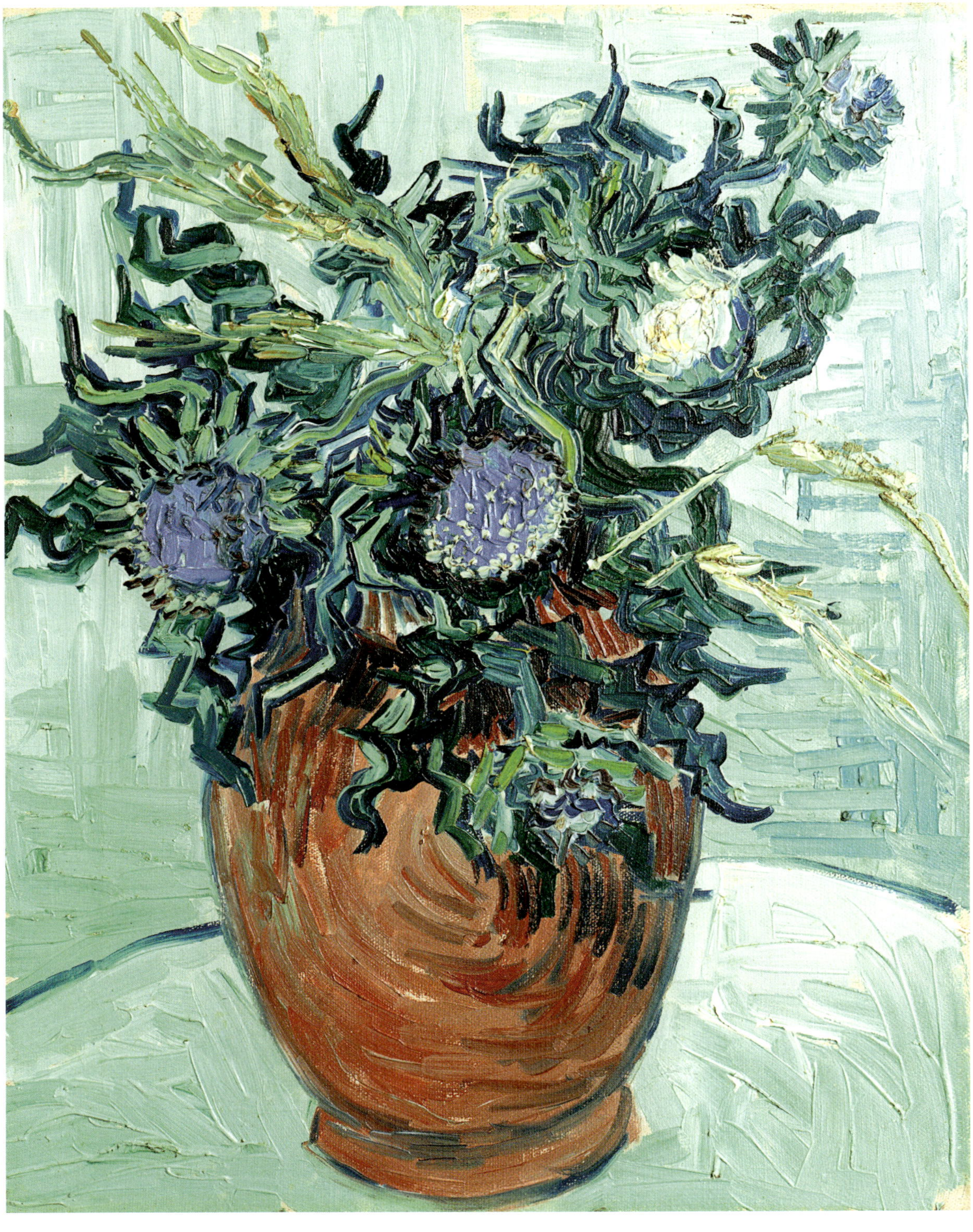

80 (#39)
Vincent van Gogh
Vase with Thistles, 1890
Oil on canvas, 40.8 × 33.6 cm
Pola Museum of Art, Hakone

the right. The artist's main concern in *Vase with Thistles* **(80)** was to convey different shades of blue (possibly more violet originally) and green. For contrast's sake, he heightened the brown of the earthenware pot with red. The depicted variety of thistle is an artichoke or cardoon, both of which have characteristic green sepals.

A new element in these three still lifes is the round shape of the table, which creates an interesting dynamic with the lines of the vase. Round, metal tables, painted white, were popular as garden furniture and this one might have been in Gachet's garden. It is always executed so sparsely, however, that it need not have been based on reality. The curved shape is what interested Van Gogh. After these three small works, he returned to it in two larger still lifes **(81, 82)**, possibly inspired by Cézanne's small still life at Gachet's, in which the roundness of the table is contrasted with the dark plane of the chair behind it **(78)**.

In these two canvases, Van Gogh depicted the bouquets as frontally and frame-filling as in Cézanne's large floral painting in Dr Gachet's collection. *Vase with Red Poppies, Cornflowers and Daisies* **(81)** is a kind of reinterpretation of the posy of wild flowers painted in Paris which he had taken with him to Auvers and which shows the same summer blooms **(175)**. *Bouquet of Flowers in a Vase* **(84)** is an atypical piece within his Auvers work because of the high degree of stylization that the artist applied. The graphic brushwork comes close to that of *Blossoming Chestnut Branches*, while the background is worked out with parallel brushstrokes over a deep dark blue, as in the portraits of Dr Gachet and Adeline Ravoux **(119, 159)**. The flowers – for the most part Chinese asters, carnations and marigolds – are rendered as a rhythmic pattern, raising the question of whether he observed them from nature or partly imagined them. He opted here for a dark background, unlike those of his other flower paintings from Auvers, as was common in traditional floral still lifes, ranging from seventeenth-century Dutch examples through to works by contemporaries such as Jeannin and Monticelli. What Van Gogh was seeking here might have been the 'orchestration of colours' that Monticelli had achieved in the *Vase of Flowers* in Theo's collection, by placing 'his richest and most balanced tones' against a dark ground. Or perhaps he was looking to continue his own Parisian still lifes.[34]

Most of the Auvers flower paintings cannot be dated more precisely than the first half of June, although it is safe to assume that Van Gogh moved from small canvases to large ones, in keeping with his normal working process. The final piece in the series is likely to have been *Vase with Wild Flowers* **(82)**, which he described on 17 June as a study he was working on at the time: 'a bouquet of wild plants, thistles, ears of wheat, leaves of different types of greenery. One almost red, the other very green, the other yellowing.'[35] The thistles in the bulbous earthenware pot from the small still life **(80)** are joined here by colourful leaves resembling those of the greater burdock, although in reality the colours of that plant do not vary as much as Van Gogh painted here. The schematically depicted white flowers with their cruciform structure might be damask, while in the upper centre, a few red poppies, blue cornflowers and ears of wheat stick out from the bouquet. Van Gogh was waiting for a shipment of canvas from Paris and apparently had nothing else available, so he painted this still life on a piece of *torchon* (household cloth).[36] The same unconventional support was used for *Vase with Red Poppies, Cornflowers and Daisies*, which must have been made shortly before *Vase with Wild Flowers*, around the same time as the field of poppies he painted on 14 June **(13)**, and in which the earthenware pot appears once again.[37] Van Gogh took a more experimental approach once more to *Vase with Wild Flowers*, with the frontally positioned vase and the range of irregular plant shapes with which he filled the canvas to the edges. He was interested in wild, uncultivated plants like the thistle for the same reason as the sunflower, because of their everyday simplicity and rugged, rustic appeal. He depicted them with a great deal of expression in this final flower painting, which follows on in that respect from *Blossoming Chestnut Branches*, the first and most innovative floral work he painted in Auvers.

FLORAL STILL LIFES AS GIFTS

Van Gogh's painting of a blossoming acacia, a close-up study of an experimental character, ought not to be overlooked here **(83)**. Gachet's son Paul described how Van Gogh made this small, swiftly executed

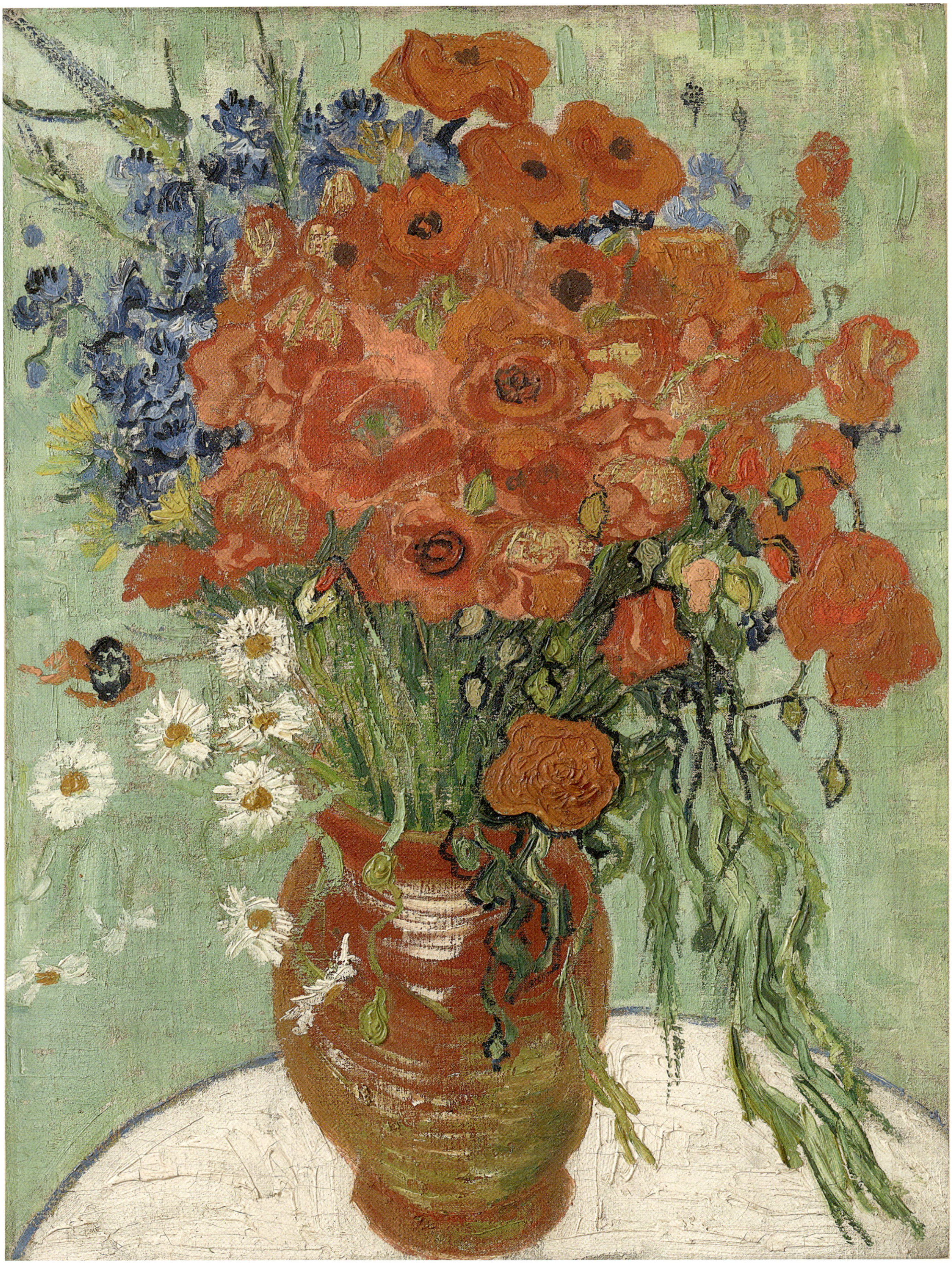

81 (#34)
Vincent van Gogh
Vase with Red Poppies, Cornflowers and Daisies, 1890
Oil on *torchon*, 65 × 50 cm
Private collection

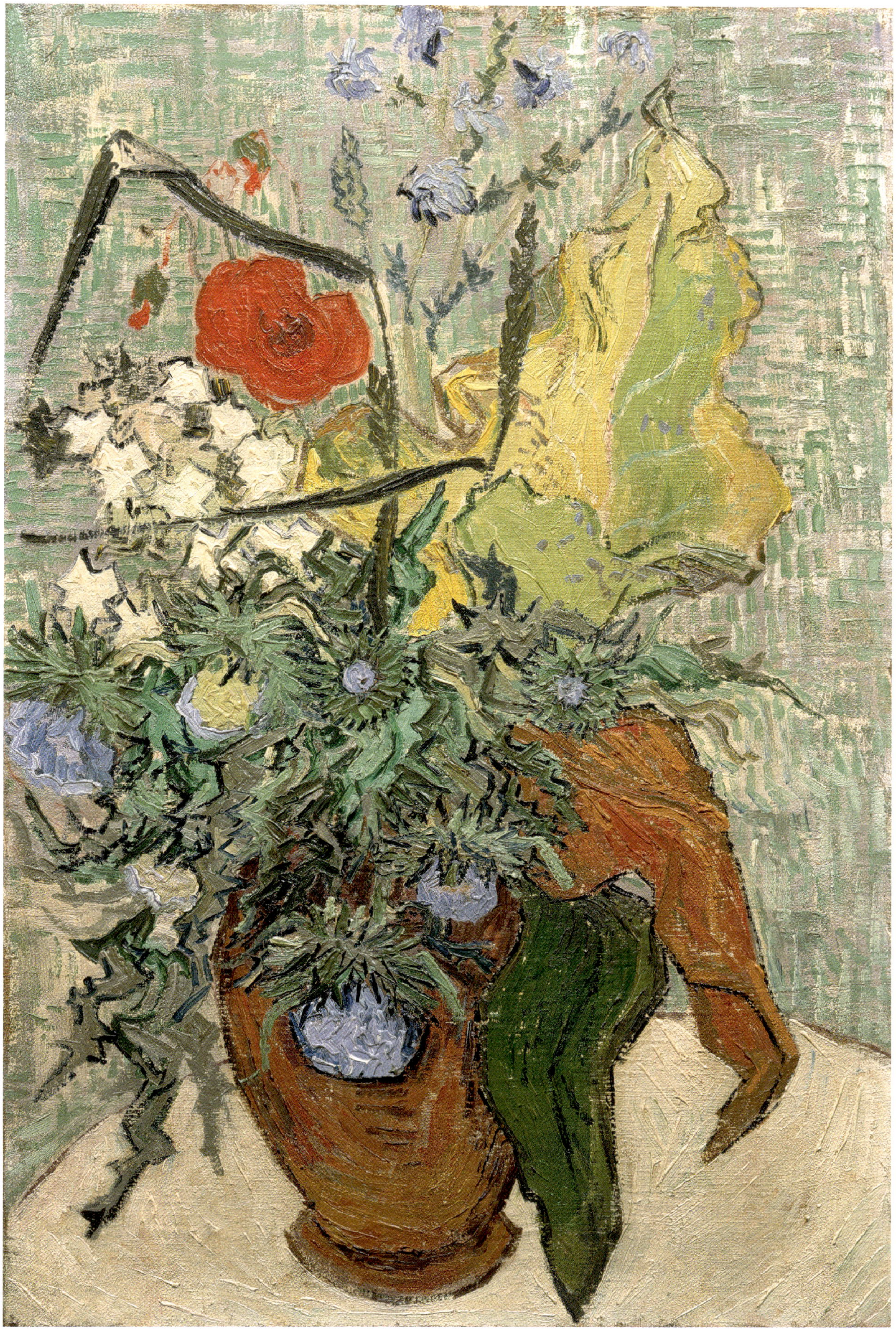

82 (#40)
Vincent van Gogh
Vase with Wild Flowers, 1890
Oil on *torchon*, 66 × 45 cm
Private collection

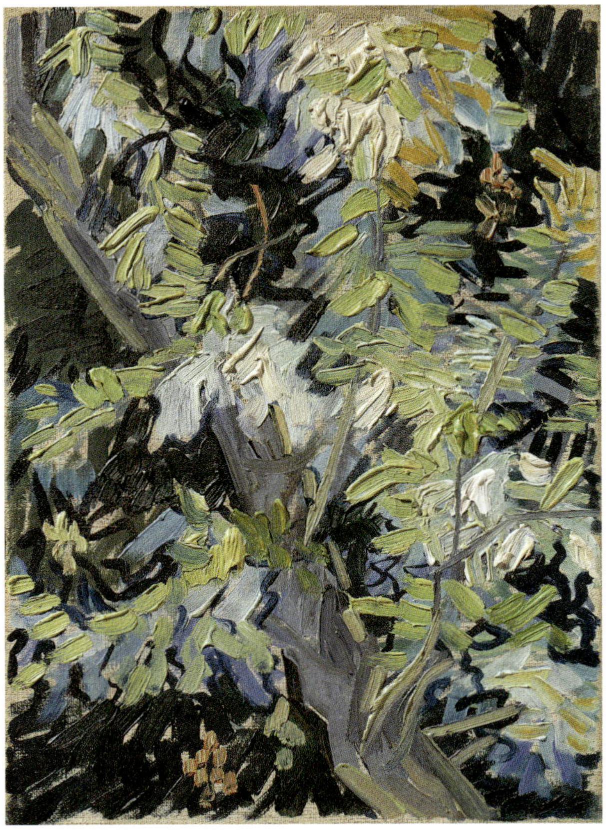

83 (#23)
Vincent van Gogh
Blossoming Acacia, 1890
Oil on canvas, 33 × 24 cm
Nationalmuseum, Stockholm

study in the doctor's garden on Saturday 7 June 1890, after first putting 'the finishing touches' to Gachet's portrait. 'Having noticed when he arrived that the acacias in the garden were suddenly in full blossom, he set up his easel [...] under the motif, rather than in front of it. So there was no distance. It was genuinely curious to observe. Before applying a few touches of colour to the little canvas, he threw his head back each time so that, with eyes half closed, he could view the flowers above him at the same time as the sky, which was barely visible on either side through the dense foliage.' Gachet Jr was surprised by this unusual approach and wondered whether it made Van Gogh's neck ache.[38] The depicted tree is a *Robinia pseudoacacia*, which blossoms with white hanging clusters of flowers, summarily indicated here by Van Gogh with a few broad, white strokes of paint.

Blossoming Acacia found its way into Dr Gachet's collection, as did *Vase with Wild Flowers* **(82)** and *Blossoming Chestnut Branches* **(71)**. He obtained them either from Vincent himself or from Theo after his brother's funeral, along with the other works he received in return for his assistance and support. The two floral still lifes from Paris also ended up in his collection.[39] Paul Gachet Jr, who was seventeen at the time, later recorded that Theo gave him *Roses and Turban Buttercups* **(77)** as a gift for keeping vigil over the deceased Vincent.[40] The other floral still lifes from Auvers were subsequently dispersed. *Vase of Flowers* **(76)** ended up in the Van Gogh family collection, as did *Glass with Carnations* **(69)**, but Jo van Gogh-Bonger sold the latter in 1905. The first owner of *Absinthe Glass with Wild Flowers* **(79)**, *Vase with Thistles* **(80)**, *Bouquet of Flowers in a Vase* **(84)** and *Vase with Red Poppies, Cornflowers and Daisies* **(81)** is not known. All these works turned up in French collections in the early years of the twentieth century. Vincent might have given them away to a person in Auvers other than Dr Gachet or the café-owner Ravoux, or else Theo might have offered them to someone at the funeral in gratitude for their support.

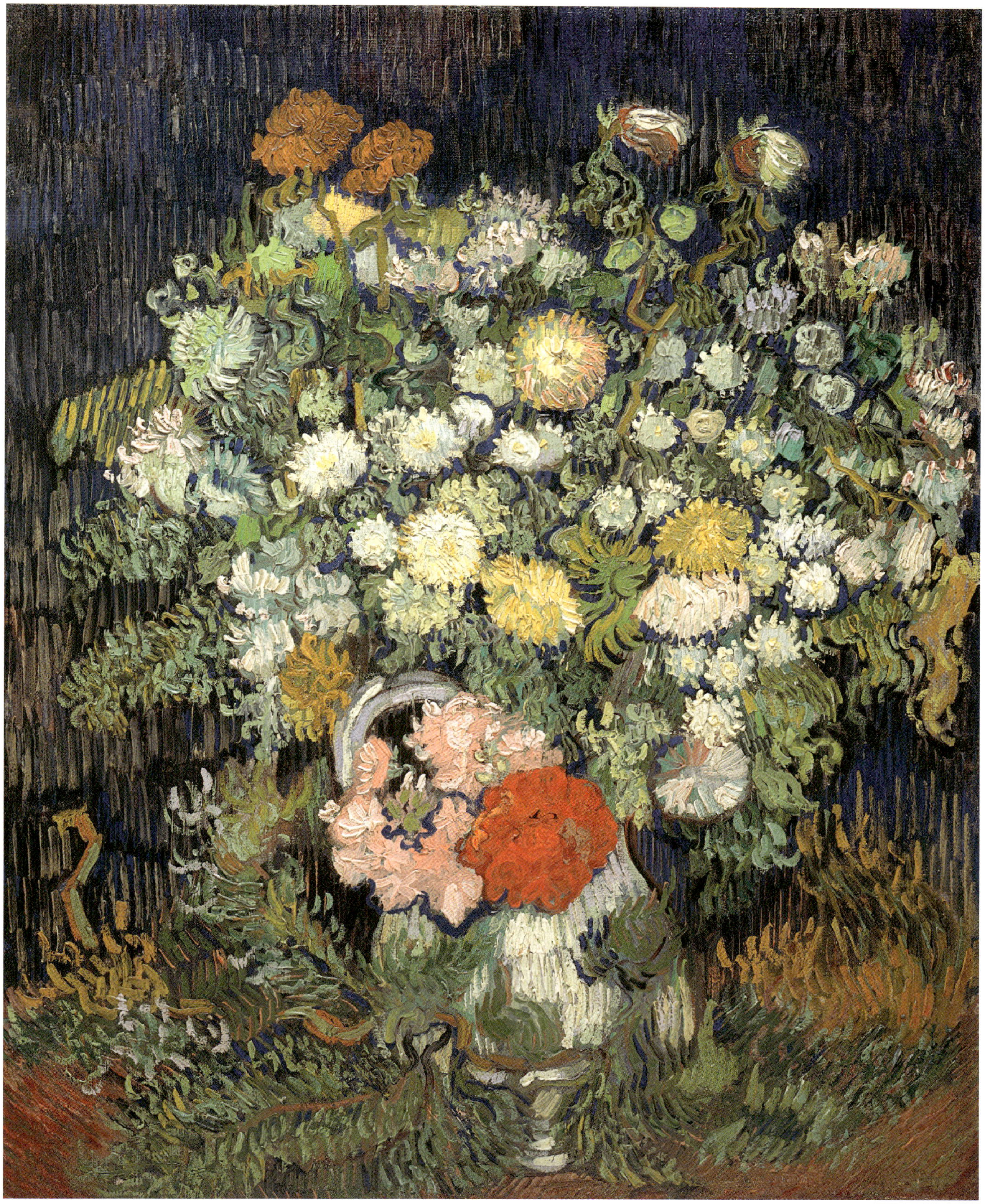

84 (#25)
Vincent van Gogh
Bouquet of Flowers in a Vase, 1890
Oil on canvas, 65.1 × 54 cm
The Metropolitan Museum of Art, New York,
The Walter H. and Leonore Annenberg Collection,
Gift of Walter H. and Leonore Annenberg, 1993,
bequest of Walter H. Annenberg, 2002

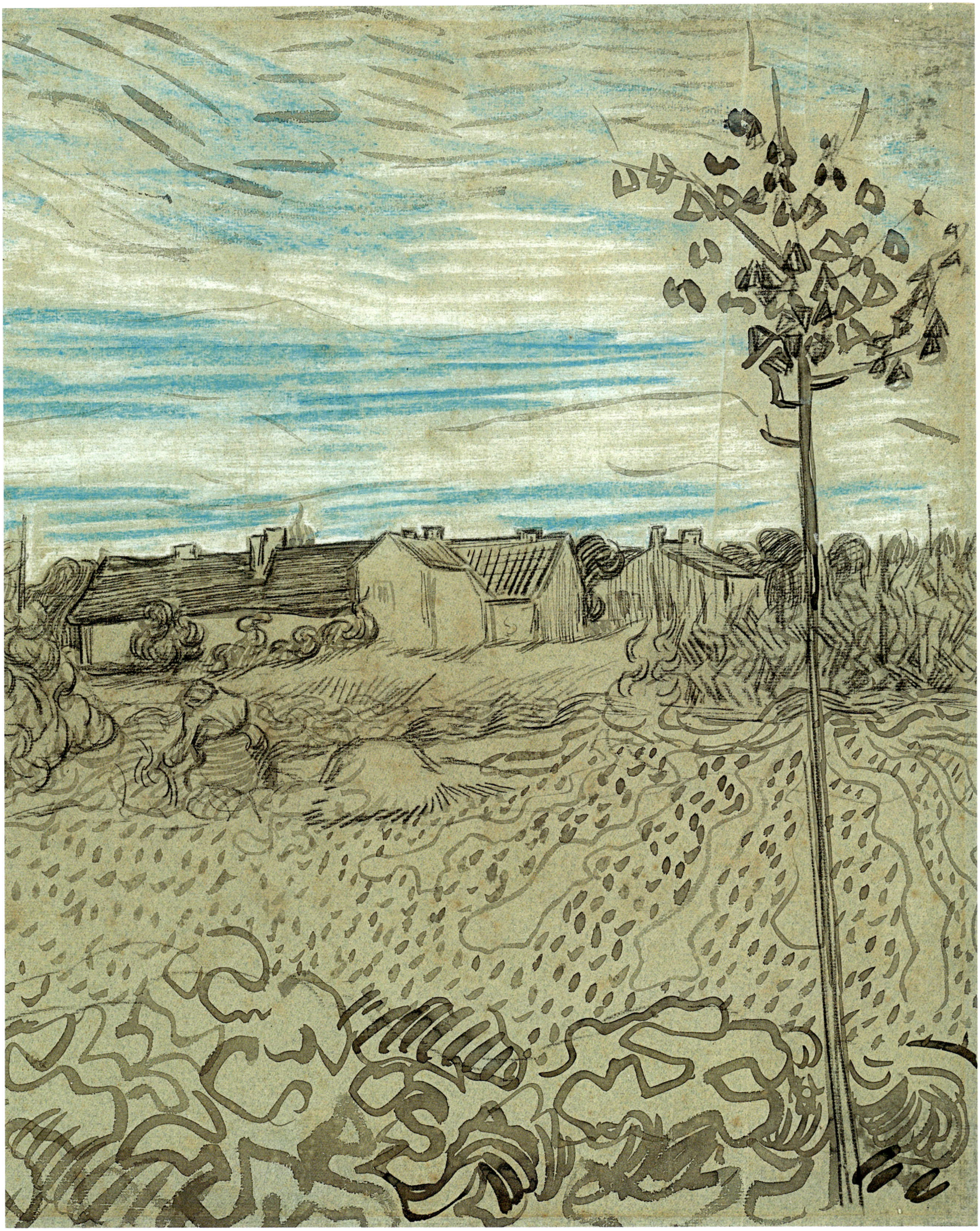

DRAWING IN AUVERS-SUR-OISE

TEIO MEEDENDORP

The fact that Van Gogh completed seventy-four paintings in Auvers in the space of seventy days might suggest he had little time for anything else. But that would be far from the truth: he also produced nine large, independent drawings and twenty-eight sheets with a total of forty-eight sides of drawings – mostly studies and sketches. In all, some fifty-seven surviving works on paper.[1] We also know of one etching, a portrait of Dr Gachet **(169)**, and a sketchbook has survived too. Or rather a notebook with squared paper, which he bought in Paris before setting off for Auvers, more than half filled with scribbles on a variety of subjects **(100)**.[2]

With the possible exception of the etching, none of these works is widely known to the public. The vast majority of the Auvers drawings, including the sketchbook and eight of the large drawings, came into Theo's possession after Vincent's death and are now in the Van Gogh Museum, apart from four drawings previously sold by the family.[3] The other group, comprising a large drawing, five double-sided drawn sheets and five pages from the sketchbook, remained in Auvers with Dr Gachet. The latter's son donated the large work **(101)** and four small sketchbook pages to the French state in 1954 and these are now in the Musée d'Orsay in Paris.[4] Three of the four drawings sold from the family collection also ended up in public collections: *Hayricks* was acquired by the Whitworth Art Gallery in Manchester in 1927, *The Oise at Auvers* **(105)** by the Tate Gallery in London in 1933 and *Cottages with a Woman Working in the Middle Ground* **(102)** in 1949 by the Art Institute of Chicago.[5]

'THERE'S A LOT TO DRAW HERE'

Van Gogh wrote this shortly after arriving in Auvers. All the same, he barely mentions drawing elsewhere in his correspondence,[6] which makes it tricky to identify and date the works on paper. We are not entirely bereft, though: the type of paper he used, the relationship with a painting and the subject matter all mean that the sheets can reveal more than one might expect. On the other hand, Van Gogh's love for drawing with a pen (the reed pen, particularly) and ink, with which he achieved such wonderful results in Arles and Saint-Rémy, noticeably faded into the background in Auvers. Pencil and especially chalk dominate most of the studies and sketches, and he tended to use a combination of materials for his large drawings, including oil paint, a single watercolour, and, a little more often, brush or pen and ink combined with black chalk or pencil. He worked not only on white or cream paper, but also on blue-grey and pink tinted sheets. Besides black chalk, moreover, we find blue and brown, although the latter is confined to the sketchbook.

Vincent van Gogh
Cottages with a Woman Working in the Middle Ground, 1890
Detail of 102

The drawings Van Gogh produced in Auvers have never been studied comprehensively, in detail.[7] In his book on Impressionist and Post-Impressionist drawing, Nicholas Wadley concluded somewhat harshly: 'The fact that he abandoned the developed discipline of the drawing practice used since Arles – pencil, reed pen, pen – for a new and erratic mixture of media suggests a less fixed focus on the art of drawing. It may also reflect the confused state of feeling and confidence that precipitated his suicide.'[8] Whether the latter is true is questionable, while a mixed technique – which, incidentally, can hardly be called 'erratic' – was used only for the large drawings that are among the better ones he produced in Auvers **(32, 85, 105)**. It is fair to say, on the other hand, that the Auvers drawings display a wider range of subjects and materials and that Van Gogh seems to have worked faster and hence more boldly, as witnessed by the generally freer lines, limited detail and simplification of compositions.

Another factor is the relatively large number of drawings that have survived from this short period, unlike the years in Paris or Arles, for instance. His time in Provence is almost entirely represented by a group of beautiful pen-and-ink drawings, with very little in the way of the rapid, simple sketches he must also have produced there. The strength of the Auvers survivals is precisely how many of them there are, especially when the sketchbook is included. Not only does this offer a more complete picture of Van Gogh's drawing activity, it also brings us closer to the artist and the spontaneity with which he explored his surroundings.

As for the range of subjects, there are sheets filled with small figure studies and copies after a drawing course, together with a few larger village scenes and landscapes, further preliminary studies or ideas for paintings, and also several remarkable sketches including some of an Egyptian head. With a single important exception, which we discuss in detail below, he did not really commit to a drawing campaign – a series of works in a single technique – in Auvers, the way he had in Arles and Saint-Rémy, and at earlier stages too. Drawing seems largely to have been a matter of filling time between painting, to clear his mind, to give him something to do or to come up with new ideas and try things out. This led to some brilliant results as well as curious scribbles and quick notes, the latter mostly in his sketchbook.

DOMINANT BLUE

There was much to draw and Van Gogh did not wish to waste time, so the moment he arrived he wrote to his brother to ask, in block capitals, for '20 SHEETS OF INGRES PAPER'.[9] These duly arrived at some point after 25 May, by which time he had already completed two drawings, presumably using paper he had brought with him from Paris.[10] He wrote in a letter on 24 May that he had not indeed been idle during those first few days, but had produced two drawings in addition to four painted studies, including 'a drawing of an old vineyard with a figure of a peasant woman'.[11] The work in question **(85)** is closely related in terms of style and dimensions to *Landscape with Houses* **(32)**, which must have been the other, unspecified drawing.

Both sheets are among the best and most striking works from Auvers and are fairly unique in his oeuvre because of their working out predominantly in blue.[12] These are large, experimental brush drawings, with dynamic, tightly curling lines in both oil and watercolour over a sketchy pencil drawing. Just a few days earlier, he had seen a substantial exhibition of over a thousand Japanese prints at the Ecole des Beaux-Arts in Paris, including several landscapes by Hokusai almost entirely in shades of blue. Van Gogh had long been interested in working with variations of a single colour, and the fact that he applied this drawing with blue in his very next works speaks to the pleasure with which he must have viewed the Japanese prints – his great passion – at the exhibition.[13]

Landscape with Houses features the same motif as his first painting in Auvers **(33)**, but where the latter shows a barren high ridge in the background, in the drawing we see a spiralling group of treetops above the thatched roofs, which reinforces the dynamic lines of the foreground. A wonderful photograph of this group of houses, taken a few years before Van Gogh drew the motif **(37)**, also shows trees in the background, suggesting that he based his drawing on the actual situation. The foregrounds of his drawing and his painting are likewise quite different. In the former, the fields of white pea blossoms, which Van Gogh also described in a letter, have given way to a tangle of vegetation.[14]

It seems very likely, therefore, that he set the drawing down in situ, before working it out back at the Ravoux inn, where he was staying. In the process, he reverted to the round, arabesque lines of the drawings

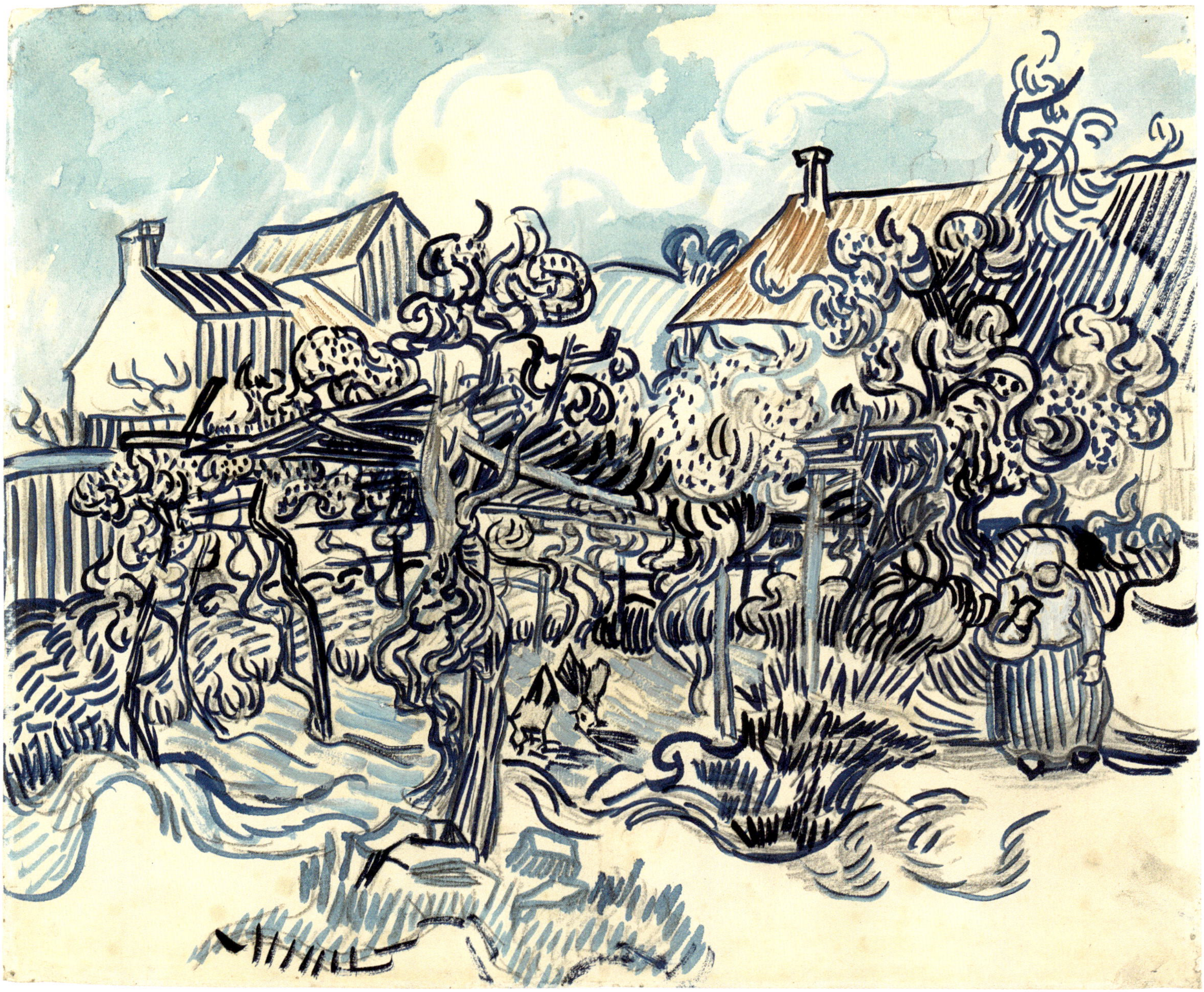

85
Vincent van Gogh
Old Vineyard with Peasant Woman, 1890
Pencil, brush and oil paint and watercolour, on laid paper, 44.3 × 54 cm
Van Gogh Museum, Amsterdam

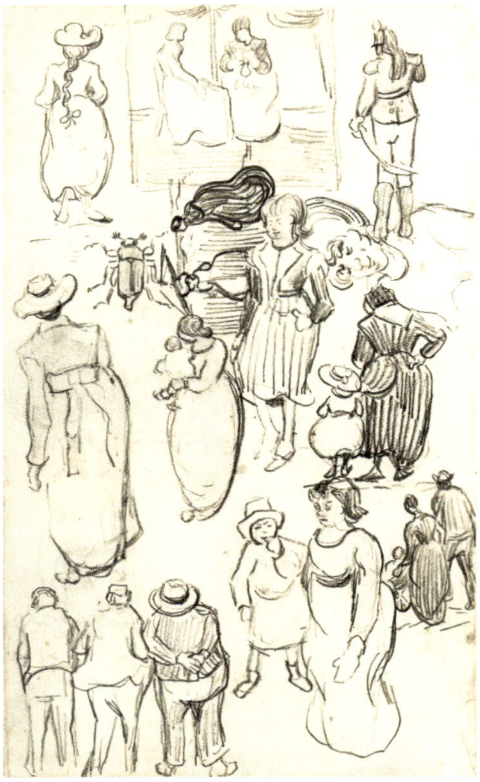

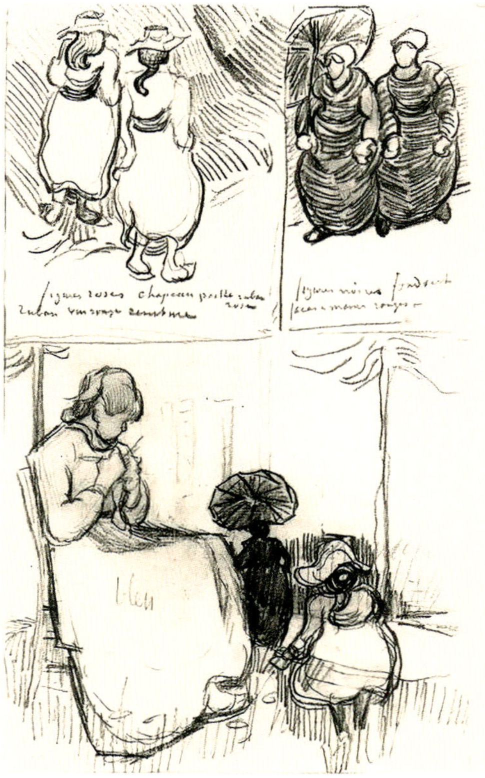

86
Vincent van Gogh
Sheet with Figure Sketches and a Maybug, 1890
Pencil on laid paper, 44.3 × 27.3 cm
Private collection

87
Vincent van Gogh
Sheet with Sketches of Women and Children, 1890
Pencil on laid paper, 44 × 27.5 cm
Private collection

he had done during his most recent major crisis at the asylum in Saint-Rémy **(99)**. He was yearning for the north at that point, which led him to idealize the peasant life he remembered from Brabant in a series of sketches. So it was with pleasure that during his first walk around the somewhat similar rural environment of Auvers, he saw 'among other things many old thatched roofs', which he immediately adopted as a subject **(41, 43, 44, 46)**.[15]

Van Gogh likewise began with a painting **(#3)** at the location of *Old Vineyard with Peasant Woman* **(85)**. It shows the vineyard from a different side to the drawing, so that the farmhouse of the Romaru family, who owned the plot, can also be seen. The grapes produced in vineyards as small as this were generally intended for the grower's own use. The distinctive, very old vines are supported by tall wooden frames.[16] The drawing is a touch more colourful than *Landscape with Houses*, as Van Gogh included a few orange-red tones alongside the blue and purple ones. The underdrawing in pencil is also more extensive, while varied use of dots and, in this instance, short dashes too, generally sharpens the graphic rendering of the scene.

Van Gogh was evidently satisfied with it and considered painting another 'No. 30 canvas' of the motif, but never got round to it,[17] making it unclear whether he was envisaging an image in dominant blue tones. It is noteworthy, though, that he painted two smaller views of Auvers shortly afterwards in which he experimented with dominant hues. The village buildings in one of them are rendered entirely in blue (and presumably some purple), contrasting with a yellow foreground **(52)**. Greens predominate in the other, contrasted this time with pink and originally purplish tones **(53)**.[18] These efforts were not followed up, however.

Both drawings were done on a full sheet (*carré* format) of cream-coloured laid paper, watermarked 'Hallines HP – Dambricourt Frères', which is not a paper type previously found in Van Gogh's oeuvre.[19] Judging from the other identified drawings on the same paper, we deduce that he probably picked up seven sheets of it. He used another two full sheets for *Dead-End Street with Houses* **(60)** and for copies he made after a drawing course by Charles Bargue **(89)**. He tore the remaining three sheets in half and used both sides for a variety of sketches, including more copies after Bargue, but mostly small figure studies **(86, 87, 88)**. A single half-sheet, lastly, was used for an atmospheric village view **(90)**.

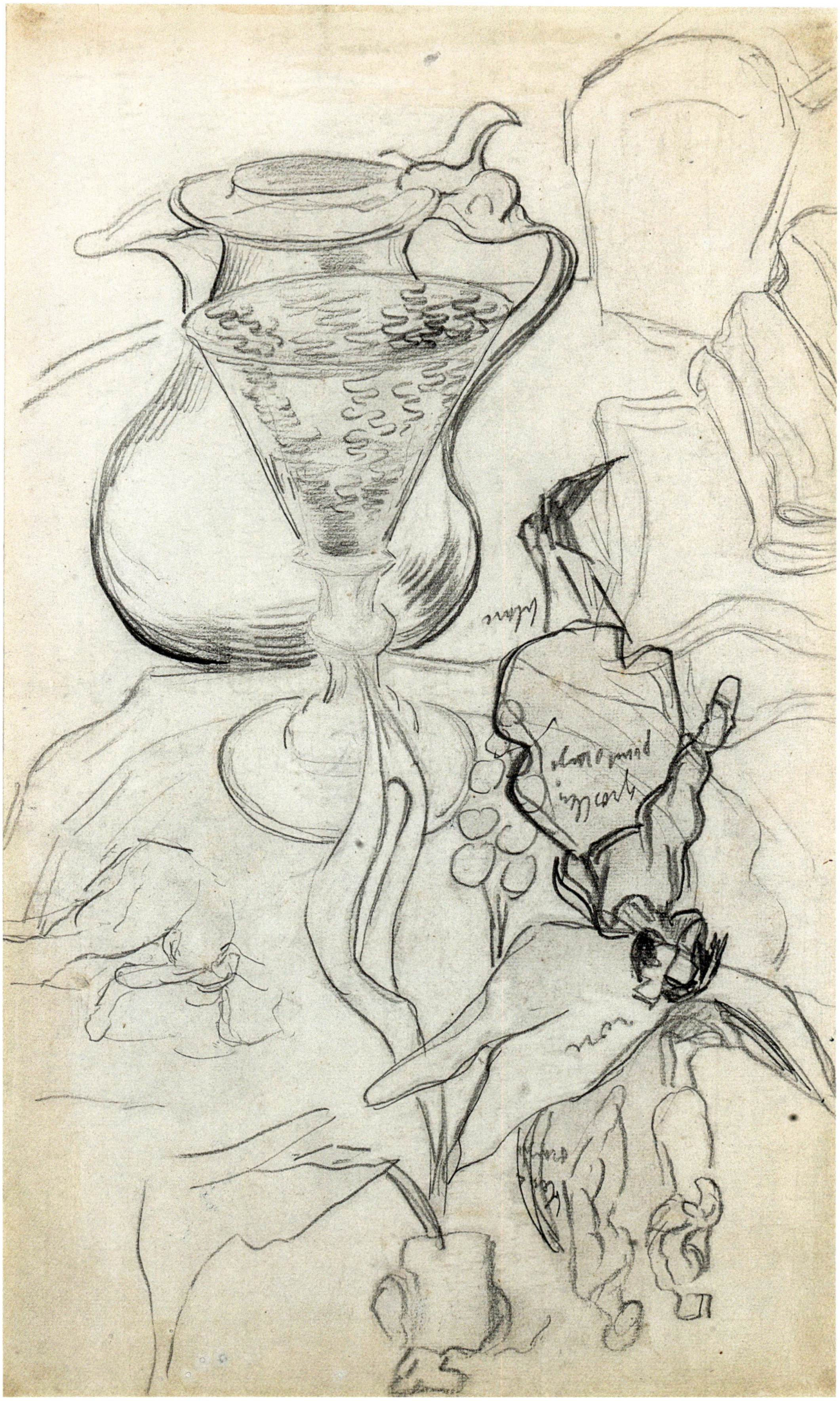

88
Vincent van Gogh
Glass, Pewter Jug, Arum Lily and other Sketches, 1890
Pencil on laid paper, 44.5 × 27.4 cm
The Levett Collection

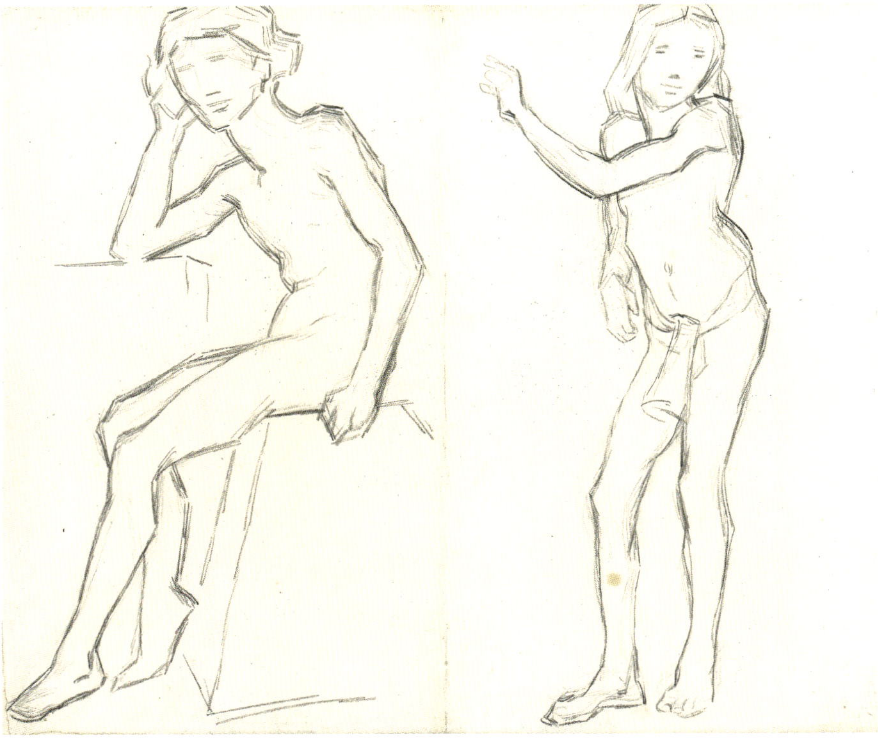

89
Vincent van Gogh
Sitting and Standing Male Nude (after Bargue, Cours de dessin, vol. III, plates 1 and 5), 1890
Pencil on laid paper, 44.6 × 54.6 cm
Van Gogh Museum, Amsterdam

FIGURE DRAWING

Van Gogh had ordered Bargue's course via Theo as soon as he arrived, but having not heard anything in the meantime, he wrote two weeks later: 'I'd be absolutely set upon copying all of Bargue's Etudes au fusain again, you know the nude figures. I can draw them quite quickly, let's say the 60 sheets that there are in a month [...]. If I neglected to keep on studying proportions and the nude I'd find myself in a bad position later on. Don't think this absurd or futile.'[20] He had copied out Bargue's entire three-volume course several times at the beginning of his career and his urgent wish to recopy the particular volume with the nudes speaks to his loss of self-confidence. The motivation will primarily have been to tackle the painting of models seriously too, now that he was back among people.[21] He is likely to have got straight down to it when the examples arrived a few days later, around 6 June, although all the surviving copies were made after the first five illustrations in the course **(89)**.[22] The sketchbook contains another six copies and there too he limited himself to the first examples, which very much suggests that the idea of recopying the 'Bargues' had only been a whim.[23] Another factor will have been how useful such exercises actually were to him by now. The figures in Van Gogh's work, both large and small, are highly distinctive due to the imperfection of their proportions. As such, they form an integral part of his style, which no amount of study is likely to have changed.[24]

The copies after Bargue were probably also the last works he drew on the paper he brought with him from Paris. Judging by a number of colour notes, *Dead-End Street with Houses* **(60)** was a preparatory study for the painting *The House of Père Pilon* done in late May **(61)**. Having served its purpose, however, it also made for a fine sheet in its own right.[25] The three half-sheets with drawings on both sides, mostly of small figures, were probably filled up with scribbled drawings in late May, early June, as the two girls in the upper left on *Sheet with Sketches of Women and Children* **(87)** also appear in *Stairway at Auvers-sur-Oise* **(5)**, which can be dated to that period. We know at any rate that Van Gogh worked at Gachet's house on the drawing that includes a pewter jug and an ornate glass **(88)**. Both objects were among the doctor's household effects, and according to his son, Van Gogh drew them during the time he was working on Gachet Sr's portrait around 3 June.[26]

The beautiful village view he drew on another of the half-sheets, lastly, is a vertically oriented composition of rue des Vessenots (now rue Gachet) **(90)**. Van Gogh might have drawn it on his way back

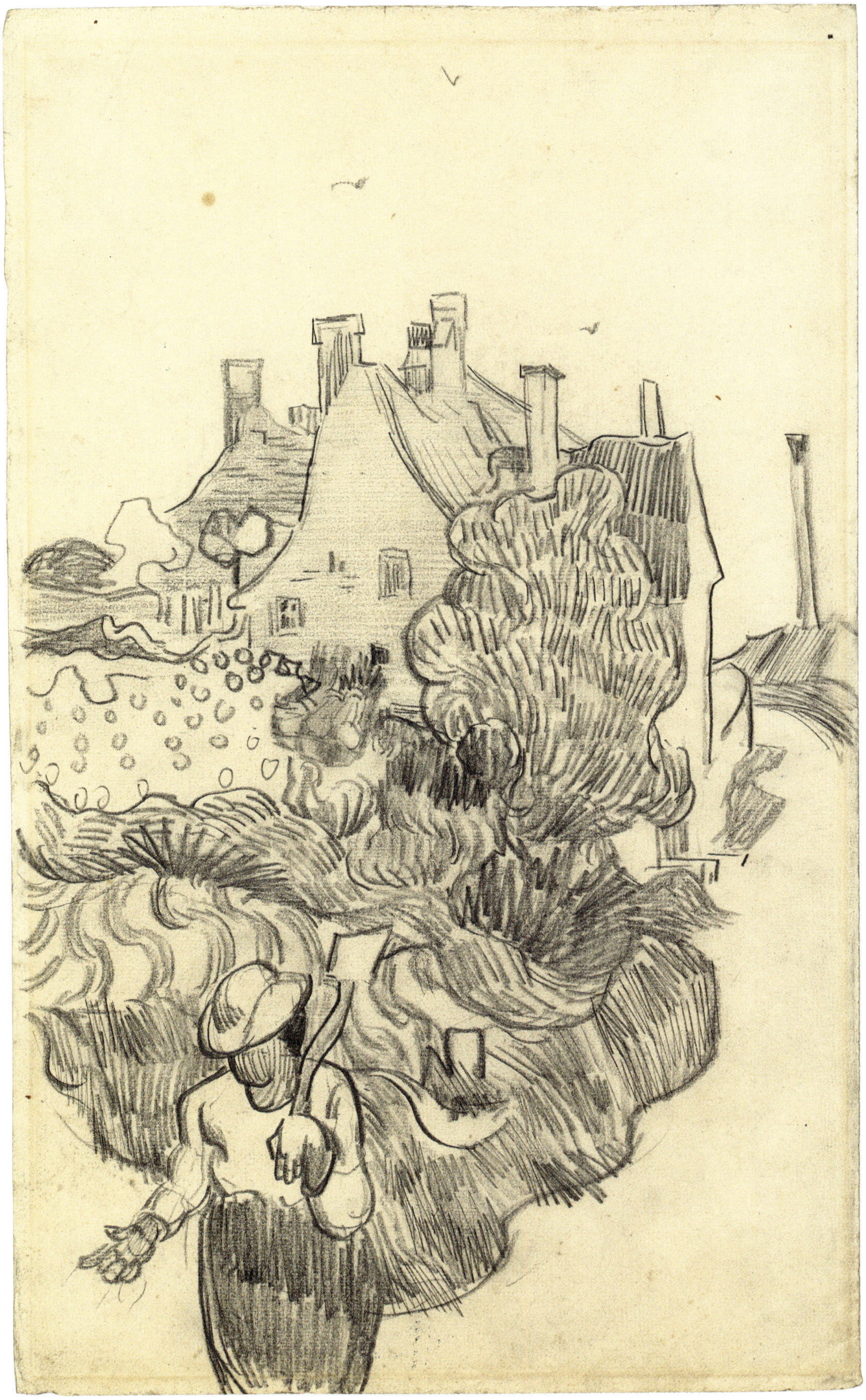

90
Vincent van Gogh
Village Street, 1890
Pencil on laid paper, 44.5 × 27.5 cm
Van Gogh Museum, Amsterdam

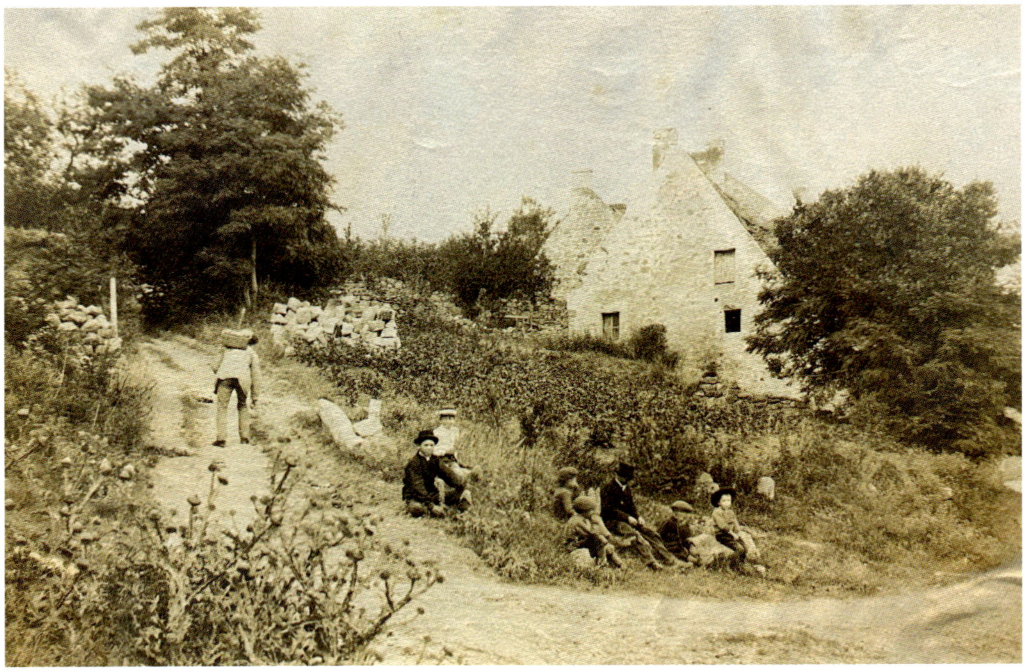

91
L. Lasnier (?)
Rue des Vessenots
Photograph, c. 1887
Archives départementales du Val-d'Oise, Pontoise

from visiting Gachet's house, as it was done nearby. He stood with his back to the doctor's home, where he had a view of a slight curve in the road. The ground rises in the left foreground, where steps lead up to a path ascending sharply to the left, but which the artist omitted from the drawing **(21, 91)**.[27] In the right background, we see the chimney of the local starch factory, which was no less than 33 metres high.[28] The person walking in the foreground (it is not clear whether it is a man or a woman) was drawn at the bottom of the sheet at an early stage, since the rest appears to have been laid down around it. We view the figure from an elevated, floating position, to which the sheet owes much of its appeal. It recalls the way Gauguin composed some of his work, while the example of Japanese printmaking is not far away either.

The walker seems to be a product of Van Gogh's imagination. It recalls the many rural labourers with a shovel in the previously mentioned sketches of peasant life, *Memories of the North*, which Van Gogh made a few months earlier in Saint-Rémy. There is one significant difference, however: he only worked on a small scale in the asylum and, lacking models, had done so entirely from his imagination. This resulted in template-like figures – dolls with, at times, curiously flailing limbs.[29] They chiefly consist of people working on the land, together with figures walking in the street or across the fields **(99)**. In Auvers, by contrast, for the first time in ages, Van Gogh found himself back among people he could observe outside on the street. Many such walking or working figures can be found in drawings and the sketchbook, frequently viewed from the back, suggesting that he drew them surreptitiously. Drawn from life, they no longer seem anywhere near as template-like **(86)**.

FAMILY LIFE

Van Gogh began to pay more attention to children, no doubt prompted by the birth of his nephew and the family life on which his brother Theo had embarked. This too was already apparent in sheets from Saint-Rémy, in which the youngsters are mostly shown walking while holding their parent's hand **(99)** and sometimes as babies sat on their mother's lap.[30] The sheet of figure sketches mentioned earlier **(86)** has a standing woman in the middle with a baby on her arm, a type that seems to be new. An example is also found in his sketchbook, next to a seated mother with child **(94)**. He lacked models in the asylum, but he had previously painted babies on laps.[31] Van Gogh is sure to have come across the standing variation

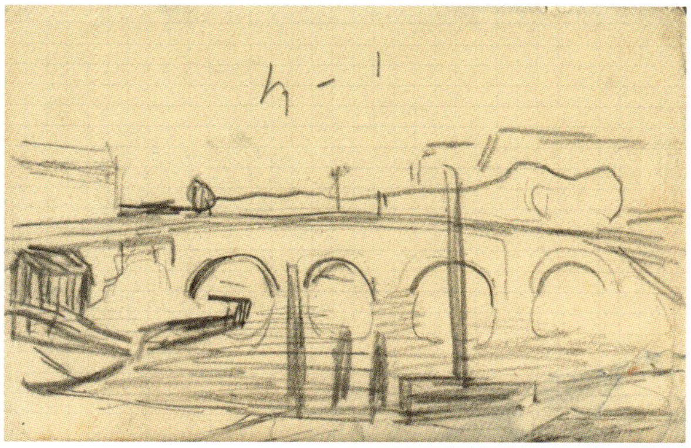

92
Vincent van Gogh
Town View with Bridge, from sketchbook
Paris-Auvers-sur-Oise, 1890
Chalk on paper, 8.5 × 13.4 cm
Van Gogh Museum, Amsterdam

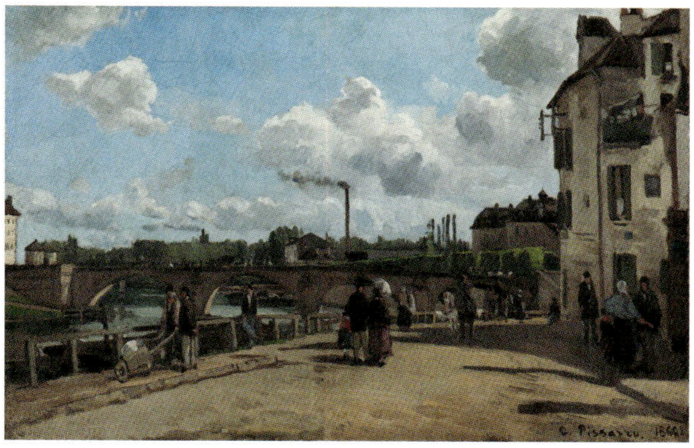

93
Camille Pissarro
Quai du Pothuis, Pontoise, 1868
Oil on canvas, 52 × 81 cm
Kunsthalle Mannheim

in Auvers, but he also found it in Pierre Puvis de Chavannes's painting *Inter artes et naturam (Between Art and Nature)*, which he had recently admired at an exhibition in Paris **(153)**. He included a small sketch of the work, done from memory, in a letter to his sister Willemien, in which the figure is granted an even more prominent place than in the painting **(155)**.

This focus on young children and familial contentment partially expresses Vincent's own lack of those things, with which his brother Theo was now blessed. 'For me life might well remain solitary', he wrote to his mother from Auvers. But he did have painting: 'Last year I read somewhere that writing a book or making a painting was the same as having a child. I don't dare claim that for myself, though; I've always thought the latter was the most natural and best thing – only *if* it were so and *if* it were the same.'[32] In this way, his work became 'the only tie that links the past and the present for me'.[33] The same busily drawn sheet **(86)** includes a young family in the bottom right, viewed from the back: a father and mother pushing a barely visible pram. A young family, now holding a child's hand can also be found in the sketchbook **(95)**, while the most touching scene in this context might be the extremely naively drawn family walking past the front of Auvers town hall, with the surroundings (street, trees, building and square) simplified in the extreme **(10)**. It is entirely possible, moreover, that Van Gogh immortalized his own baby nephew in the pram in Gachet's garden when Theo, Jo and little Vincent visited Auvers on 8 June **(98)**.

The sketchbook, mentioned above, also contains several drawings that were not done in Auvers but in Paris or elsewhere. They include a schematic scribble of the avenue des Champs-Elysées with people strolling and a little sketch of the bridge over the Oise in Pontoise **(92, 93)**. It has not been possible so far to identify the location from which Van Gogh viewed a two-page scene with a strongly foreshortened bridge with people walking and an incline with steps and houses in the background **(100)**. He also sketched a woman on a remarkable bicycle **(96)**, presumably using the vehicle to propel herself through fashionable Paris rather than rural Auvers. This is not just any old bike, but an 'Otto's bicycle' or 'dicycle', patented in Britain in 1880 by Edward Otto **(97)**.[34] The way Van Gogh placed the woman on, rather than between, the wheels, ignoring the intricate drive mechanism, suggests that he only glimpsed her gliding by and set the experience down in his notebook from memory.[35]

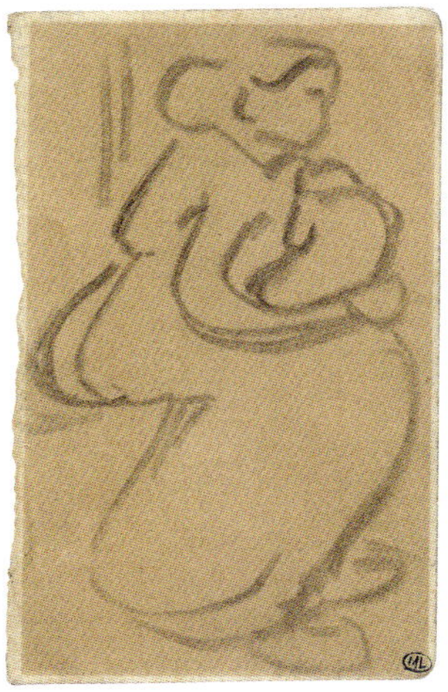

94
Vincent van Gogh
Sitting Woman with Child,
from sketchbook
Paris-Auvers-sur-Oise, 1890
Chalk on paper, 13.2 × 8.3 cm
Musée d'Orsay, Paris

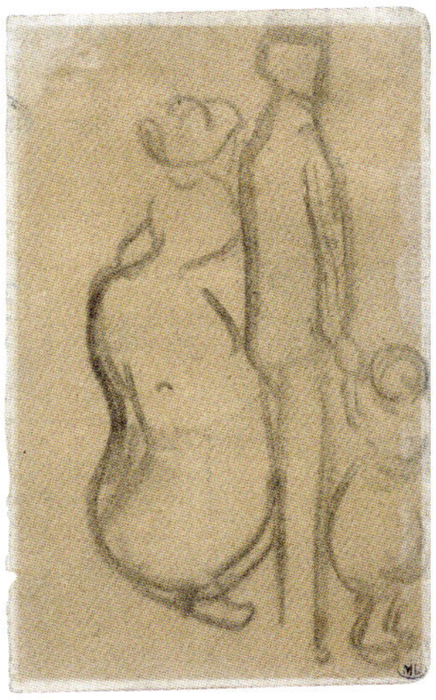

95
Vincent van Gogh
Couple with Child,
from sketchbook
Paris-Auvers-sur-Oise, 1890
Chalk on paper, 13.2 × 8.4 cm
Musée d'Orsay, Paris

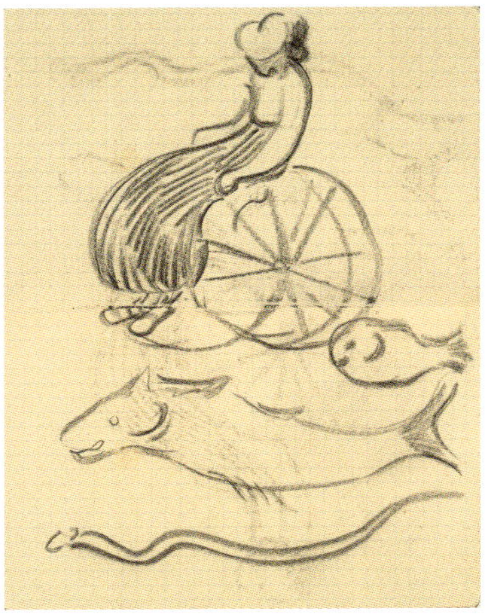

96
Vincent van Gogh
Woman on a Velocipede,
from sketchbook
Paris-Auvers-sur-Oise, 1890
Chalk on paper, two pages, each 8.5 × 13.5 cm
Van Gogh Museum, Amsterdam

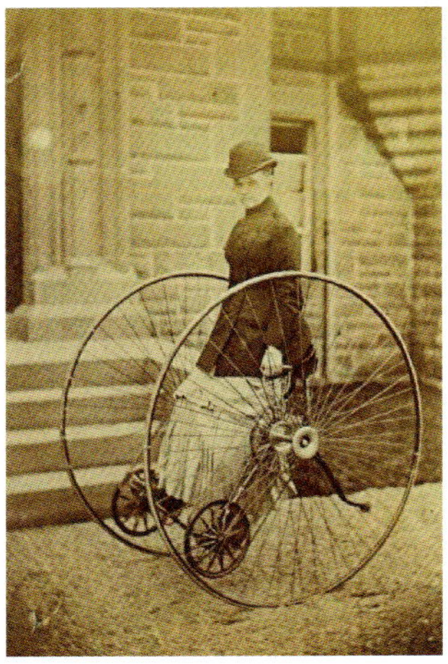

97
Otto dicycle
Photograph, c. 1900
Private collection

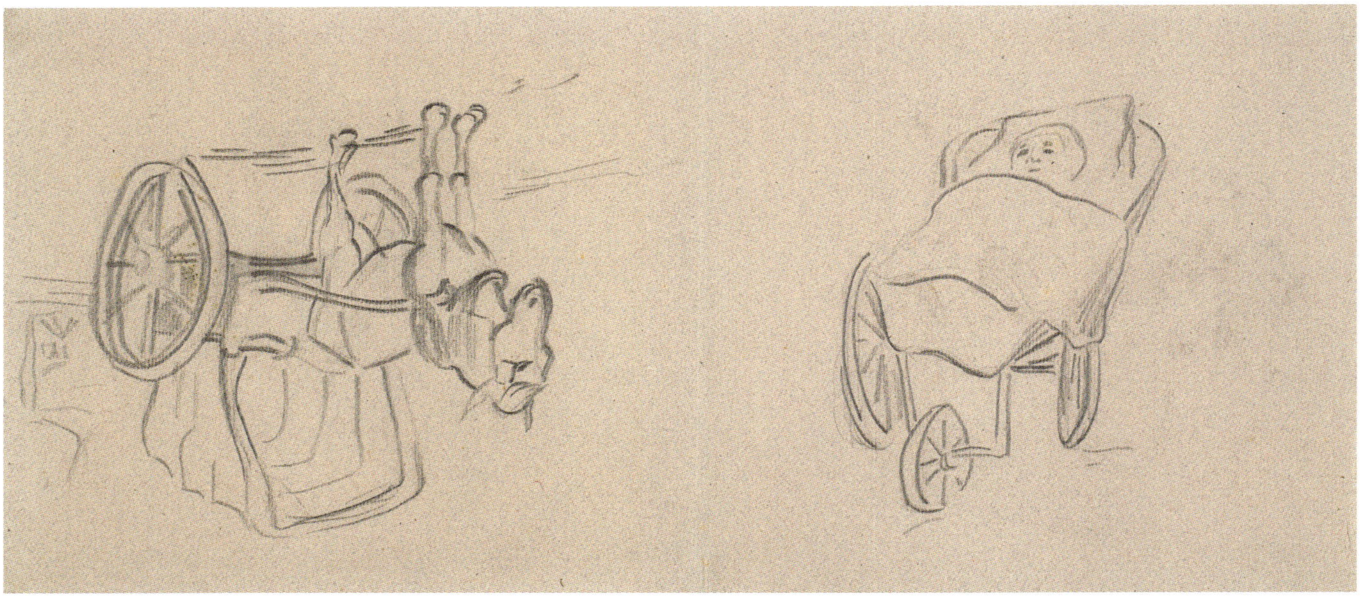

98
Vincent van Gogh
Sketches of Horse with Covered Wagon and Baby in a Pram, 1890
Pencil on pink laid paper, 21.3 × 47.3 cm
Van Gogh Museum, Amsterdam

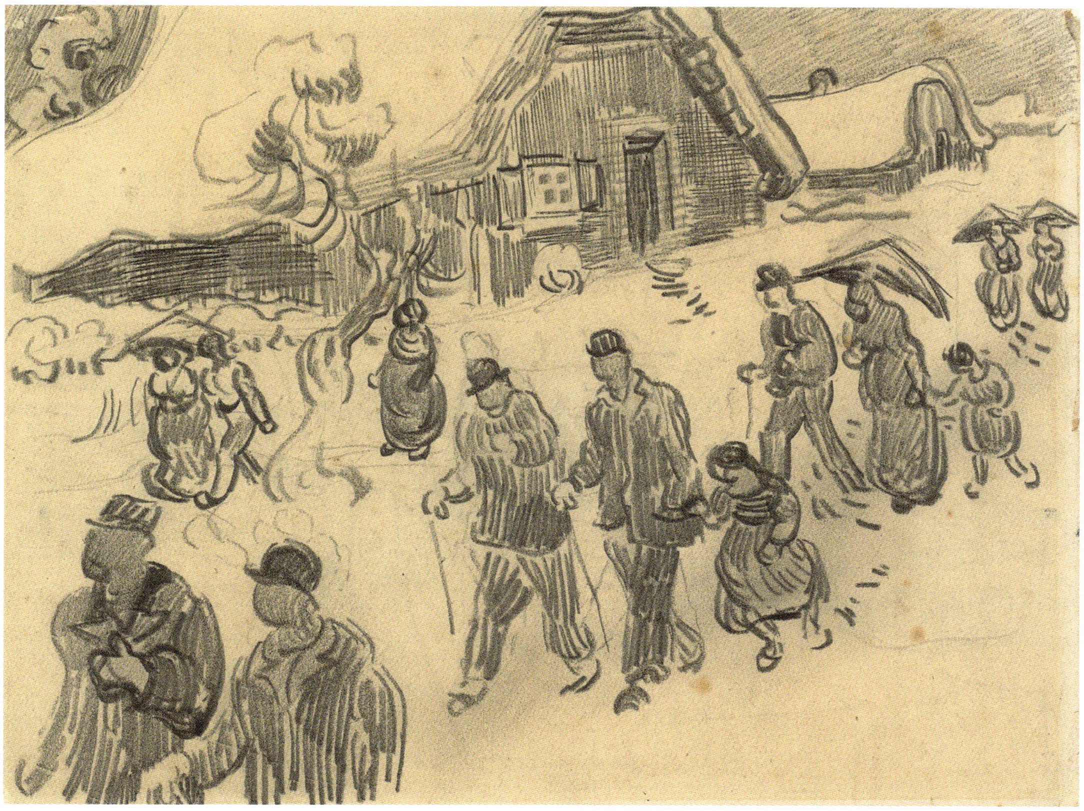

99
Vincent van Gogh
Winter Landscape with Figures Walking, 1890
Pencil on wove paper, 23.8 × 31.9 cm
Van Gogh Museum, Amsterdam

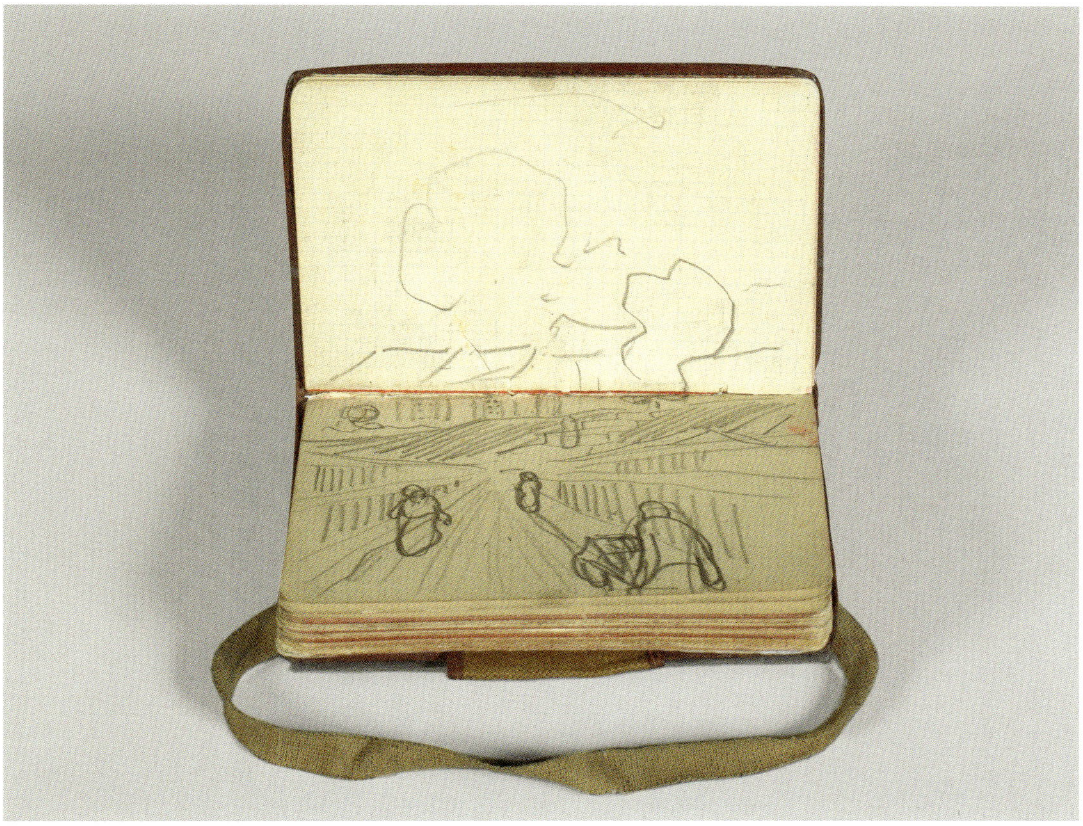

100
Sketchbook Paris-Auvers-sur-Oise, 1890
Van Gogh Museum, Amsterdam
142 pages, 84 of which contain sketches, notes, smudges or rub-offs, 13.5 × 8.5 cm

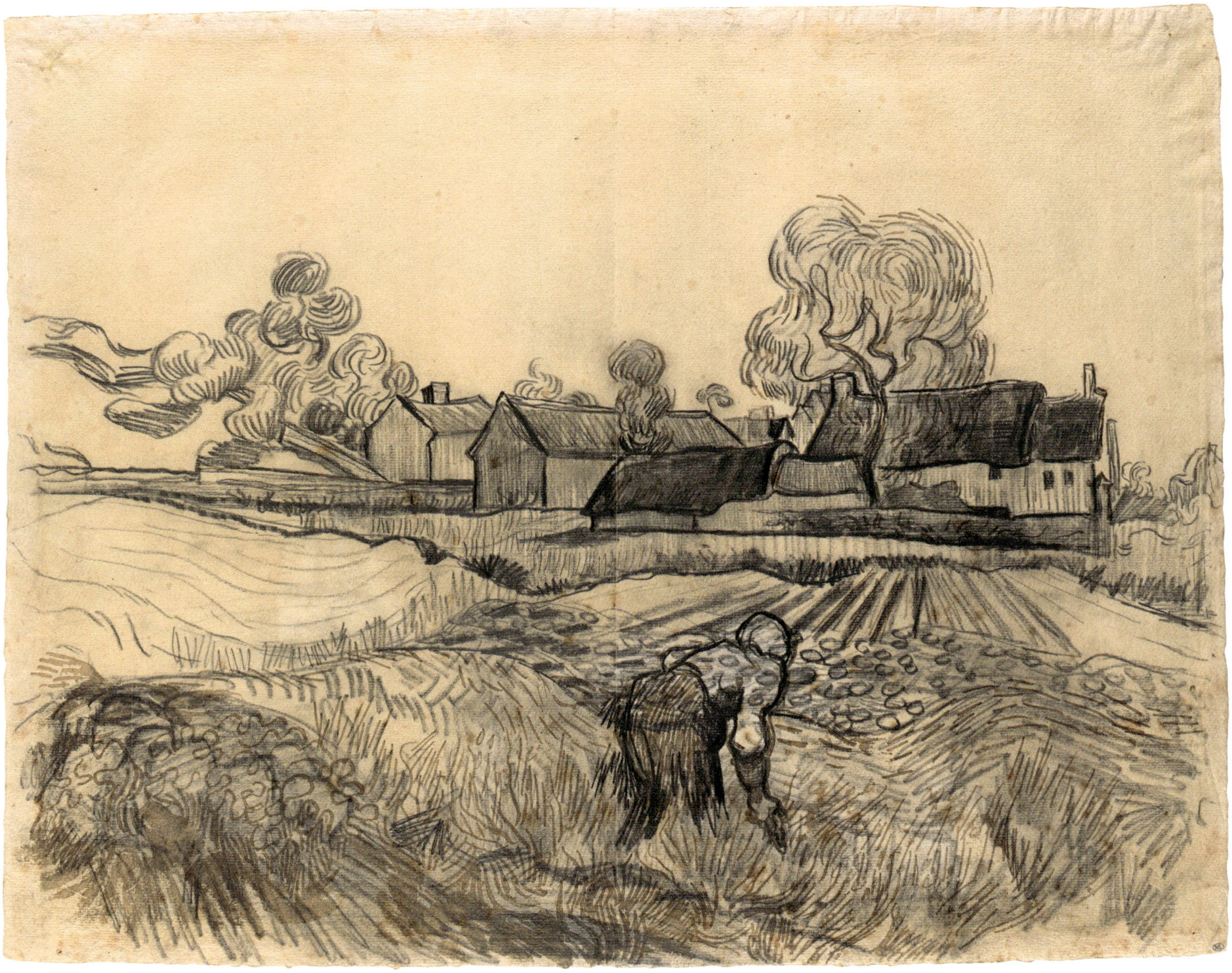

101
Vincent van Gogh
Père Eloi's Farm, 1890
Pencil, reed pen and brush in ink, on faded pink laid paper, 48 × 61.7 cm
Musée d'Orsay, Paris

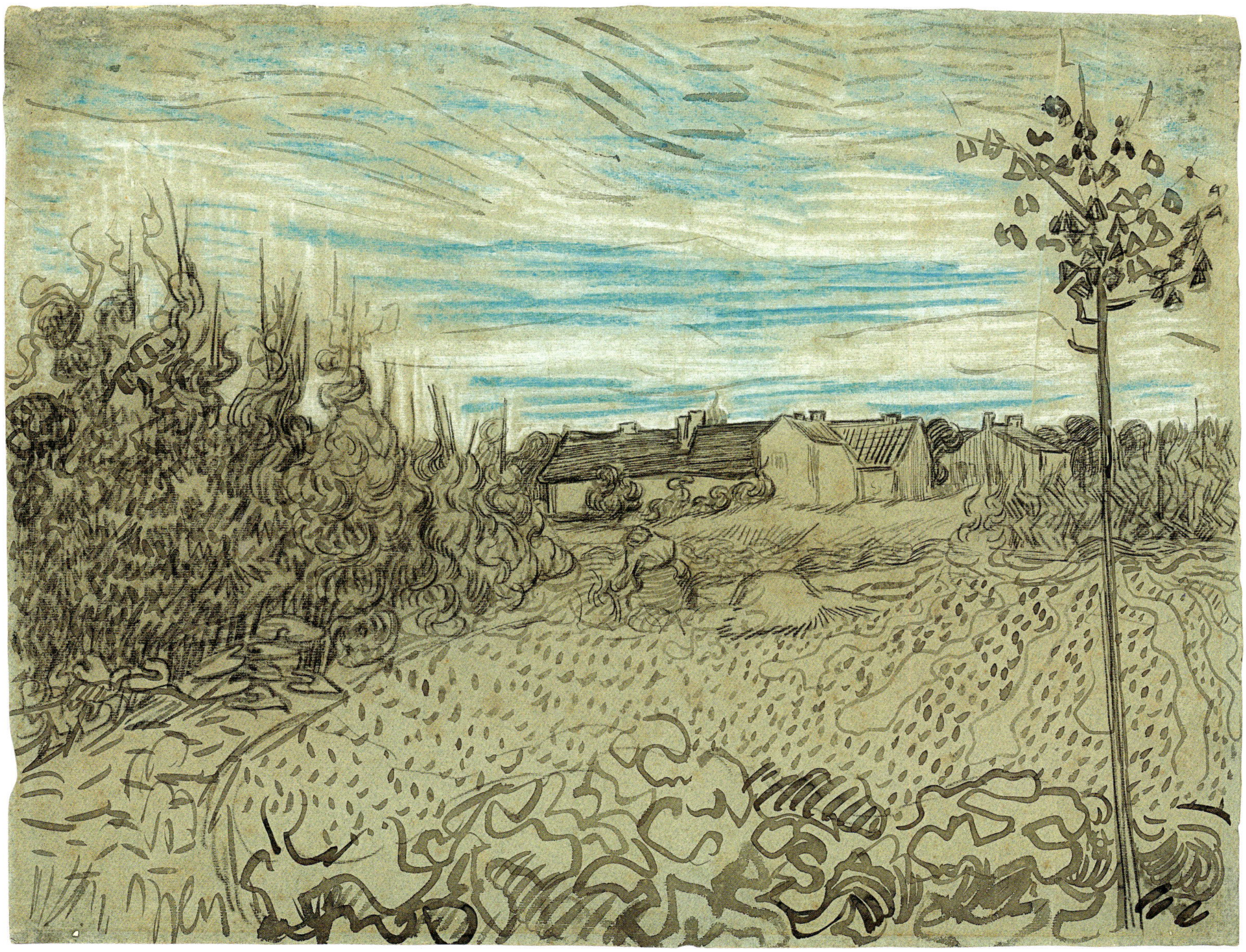

102
Vincent van Gogh
Cottages with a Woman Working in the Middle Ground, 1890
Black and white chalk, blue pastel, reed pen and brush in ink, on faded blue-grey laid paper, 47 × 62.5 cm
The Art Institute of Chicago, Bequest of Kate L. Brewster

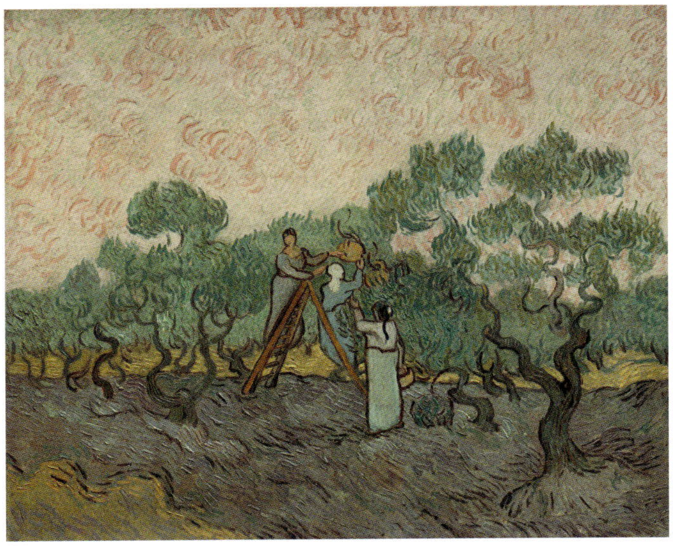

103
Vincent van Gogh
Women Picking Olives, 1889
Oil on canvas, 72.7 × 91.4 cm
The Metropolitan Museum of Art, New York,
The Walter H. and Leonore Annenberg Collection,
Gift of Walter H. and Leonore Annenberg, 1995,
Bequest of Walter H. Annenberg, 2002

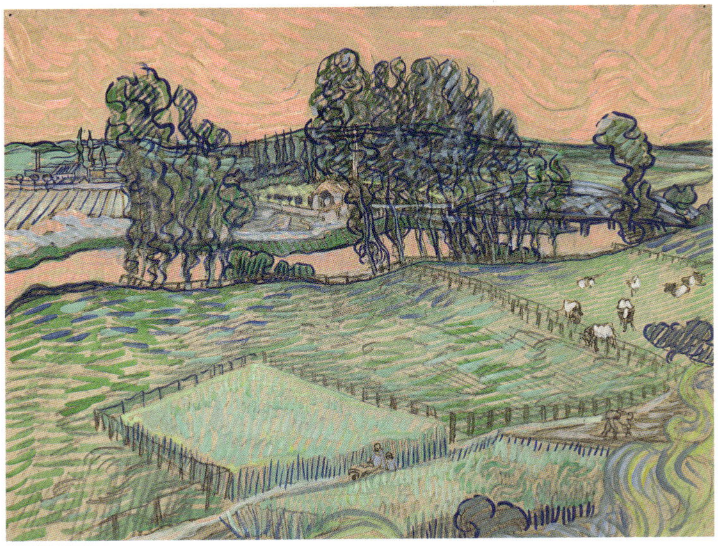

104
Colour reconstruction of *The Oise at Auvers*, based on surviving fragments of colour along the edges

TINTED PAPER

It is not known whether Van Gogh asked for it specifically, but the paper sent from Paris included pink and blue-grey sheets.[36] He made sketchbooks using both types, but also drew on full sheets or pieces of them.[37] He used the pink paper for two large sheets, *Père Eloi's Farm* **(101)** and *The Oise at Auvers* **(105)**, which was the only watercolour that Van Gogh made in Auvers, if we can call it that, given that it also contains a certain amount of oil paint. He used his familiar combination of pencil and pen (and brush) and ink for the former work – the motif of which was located in the district of Les Vessenots – albeit with a now more or less even distribution of materials. Ink is usually the dominant material, but the grey pencil plays at least as big a role here. The discolouration of both the ink, from black to shades of brown, and the paper, the pink of which has faded to beige, means that the balance between the materials has been somewhat lost. He drew in the figure later. The location was visible from Dr Gachet's elevated garden and can also be seen in the foreground of *Landscape with Carriage and Train* **(29)**, which was painted close to his house. We see a figure working in the field there too, but Père Eloi's farm, situated more to the left, remained out of view.[38] Dr Gachet's son later wrote to Jo that the drawing hung in his Paris apartment, along with others by Armand Guillaumin and Honoré Daumier. He knew the spot well, 'having drawn it myself. You can see the place where the motif was from my garden, but not from the angle that Vincent chose.'[39]

Van Gogh drew *The Oise at Auvers* **(105)** from a vantage point in the Montcel district. A photographer, who cannot have been aware of the Dutch artist's watercolour, took a postcard picture from the same spot just over a decade later **(26)**. While many of the artists – Charles-François Daubigny among them – looked to the Oise for their motifs, Van Gogh showed little interest in it. This is his only landscape in which the river features prominently.[40] The choice of pink paper appears to have been more deliberate in this instance, as it forms an attractive complementary colour contrast with the many shades of green. This effect will originally have been much stronger, as the sky and its reflection in the river will have had a deep pink hue **(104)**. Now that the pink has faded in the paint and the paper too has lost the full intensity of its colour, the intended contrast has been entirely lost, all the more so since Van Gogh left a particularly large amount of paper visible in the scene.[41]

As an artistic concept, however, it corresponds with the soft green olive groves with pink skies

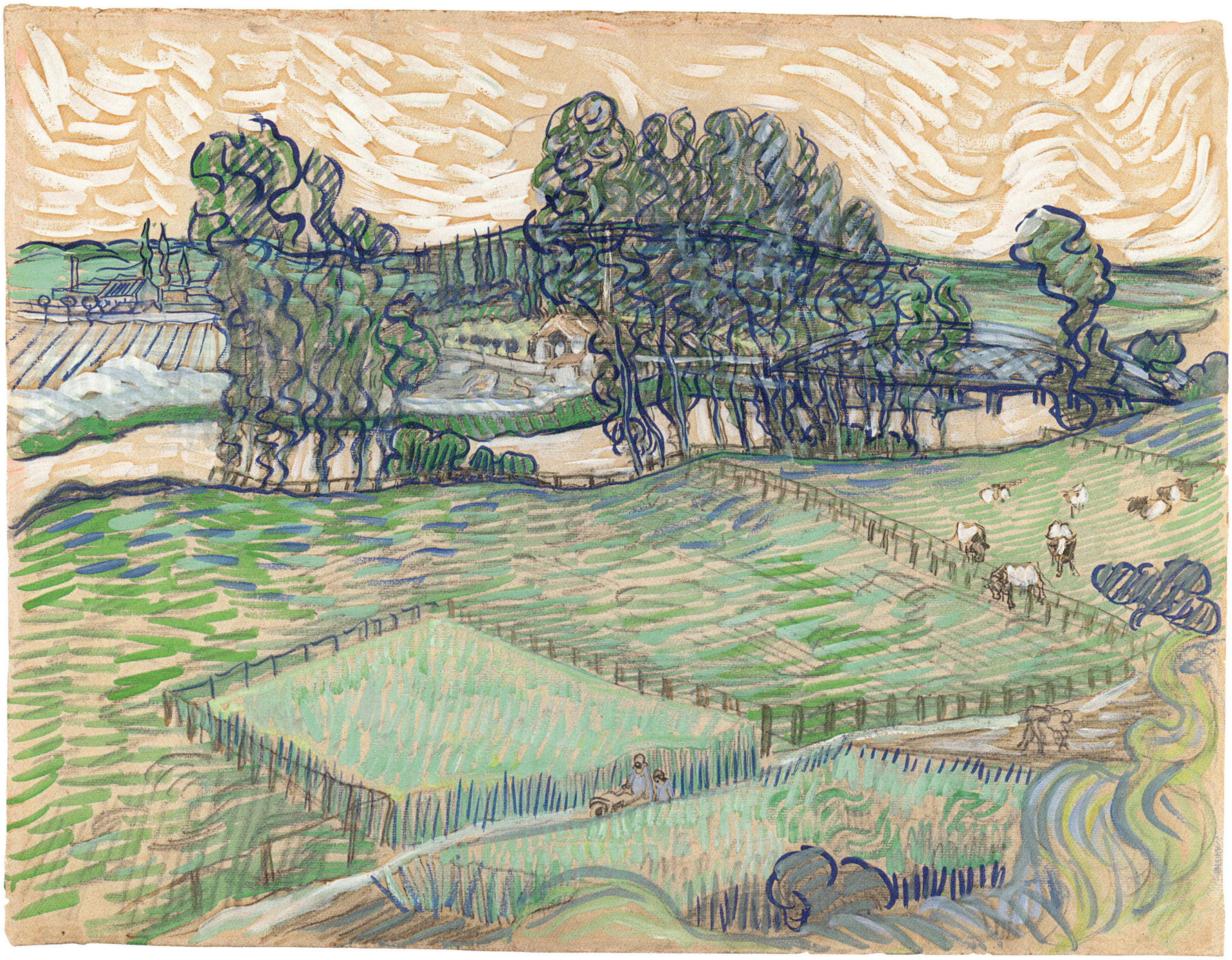

105
Vincent van Gogh
The Oise at Auvers, 1890
Pencil, pen and ink, watercolour and oil paint, on pink laid paper, 47.3 × 62.9 cm
Tate, London, bequeathed by C. Frank Stoop, 1933

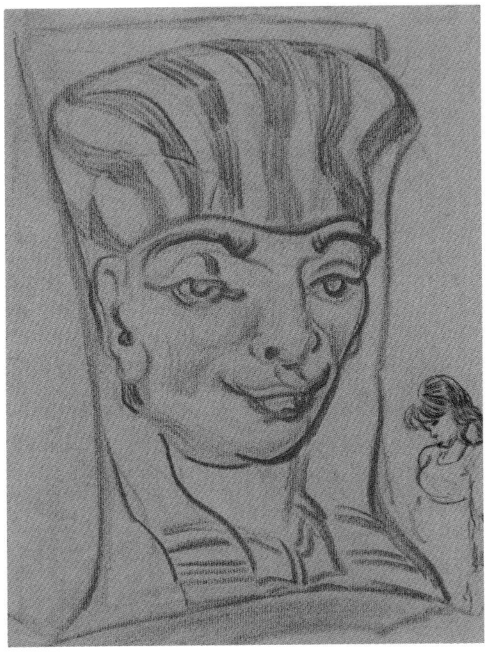

106
Vincent van Gogh
Egyptian Head and Figure Study, 1890
Chalk on blue-grey laid paper, 31.4 × 23.9 cm
Van Gogh Museum, Amsterdam

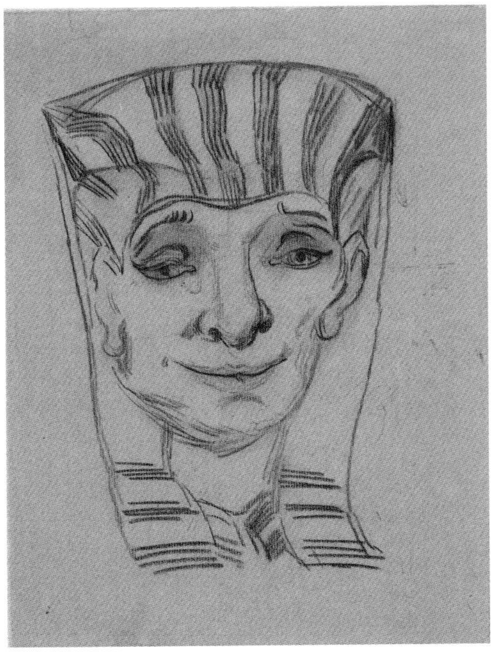

107
Vincent van Gogh
Egyptian Head, 1890
Chalk on blue-grey laid paper, 31.4 × 23.8 cm
Van Gogh Museum, Amsterdam

that he painted in late 1889 in Saint-Rémy, several versions of which he took with him to Auvers **(103)**.[42] In stylistic terms, it is a beautifully swirling drawing, with deep-blue, curling poplars, between which the chimney of a factory on the far bank of the Oise can just be made out. The foreground is rendered in variegated green tones with mosaic-like short and horizontal brushstrokes, which he interrupted with a small fenced-off field rendered with vertical strokes of light-green watercolour. Together with the cows in the background and a handful of human figures in the front, the result was an idyllic scene, in which modernity (a second factory visible on the left horizon and the iron bridge, installed less than a year earlier) was skilfully interwoven with the traditional beauty of nature and the historic countryside.

Van Gogh came across this view of the river along the road connecting Auvers to Cordeville (now rue Rajon). It was close to a spot where he also found an entirely different motif: a sculpture of an Egyptian head, more specifically that of a sphinx **(23)**, installed to ward off misfortune. It served as the keystone above a gateway that gave access to the grounds of a villa located higher up. Like the wall surrounding it, the house is decorated with banded brickwork that also has something of an Egyptian feel.[43] The sketchbook Van Gogh made for himself with the blue-grey paper contains five drawings based on the keystone, while not depicting it literally. Rather than faithfully capturing the sphinx's serene expression, he drew a more animated head, smiling and rather pharaonic in appearance.[44] The archaic smile, modest and enigmatic, associated with sphinxes of this type is barely recognizable nowadays due to damage to the head.

It will certainly have been the latter, however, that Van Gogh wished to emphasize.[45] He was fascinated by ancient Egypt and would have loved to have seen the Egyptian Pavilion at the Paris World Exhibition in 1889, had he not been in the asylum in Saint-Rémy at the time. 'Now Egyptian art, [...] what makes it extraordinary', he wrote to his brother, 'is it not that those calm, serene kings, wise and gentle, patient, good, seem unable to be other than they are; eternally farmers who worship the sun. How I'd have liked to see an Egyptian house in the exhibition [...]'.[46] The 'serene kings' to whom Van Gogh referred are clearly the pharaohs, suggesting that he did indeed interpret the keystone with the sphinx as representing one of them. He attempted to capture the noble character of these kings in different ways in his drawings, emphasizing their serenity and nobility in some instances **(106)**, while in others giving the large eyes a melancholy expression **(107)**, in keeping – consciously

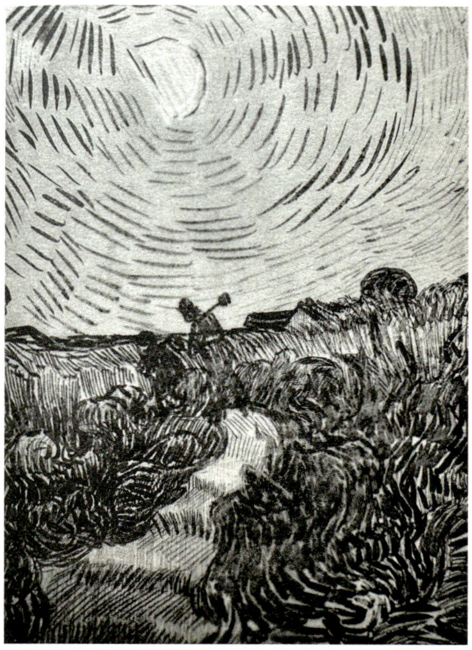

108
Vincent van Gogh
Reproduction of *Evening Landscape with Two Peasants* from J.-B. de la Faille's 1928 catalogue raisonné

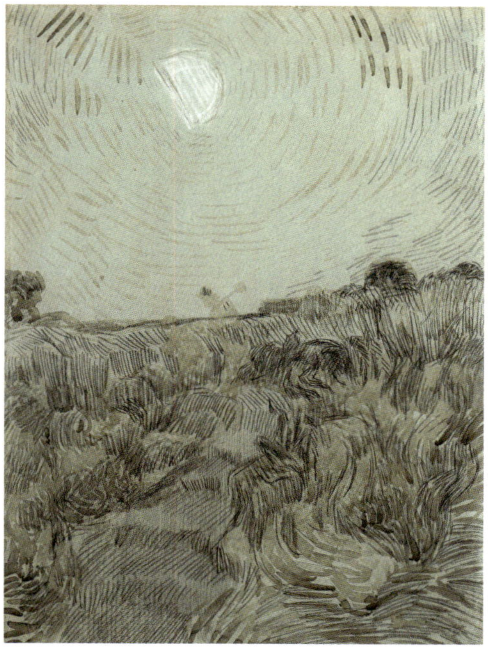

109
Vincent van Gogh
Evening Landscape with Two Peasants, 1890
Black and white chalk, brush and ink, on blue-green laid paper, 62.5 × 47.2 cm
Private collection

or otherwise – with his personal motto: 'sorrowful, yet always rejoicing'.[47] He seems to have used the studies as a source of inspiration for portraits too. One even wonders whether the portrait of a young man with a flower in his mouth **(131)** was not created entirely from those drawings. The similarities are even more striking if we reverse the version of the Egyptian head with the sorrowful expression **(107)** horizontally: not only the smiling mouth, but also the broad nose, the ear, the large eyelids and the curved eyebrows are very similar. The dancing locks of hair on the forehead actually correspond more or less with the edges of the *nemes* headdress.[48]

FINAL TRIBUTE TO THE COUNTRYSIDE

Van Gogh did not use all his blue-grey paper for the sketchbook: he reserved three full sheets for drawings that have not previously been associated explicitly, but which can nevertheless be interpreted as an artistically and substantively coherent group: *Cottages with a Woman Working in the Middle Ground* **(102)**, *Evening Landscape with Two Peasants* **(109)** and *Field with Sheaves of Wheat* **(111)**.[49] They form an atmospheric triptych of the countryside around Auvers, each with a different approach, and they are unlikely to date very far apart from each other. The drawing with sheaves of wheat suggests that this must have been around mid-July at the start of the grain harvest, which would probably place the drawings among the last – possibly the very last – that Van Gogh ever made. Not only are they linked by the choice of paper, they are also related in terms of their technical execution. Each one was laid down with black chalk and brush or reed pen in ink, with the chalk dominating here, the ink there. These were the only materials in the drawing with the sheaves of wheat, while the other two also contain coloured chalk: white for the half-moon in the evening landscape, and blue and white accents in the sky of the other work. Something else the compositions have in common is the way Van Gogh worked out the drawing over a light chalk sketch entirely in ink, before going over it again with chalk.[50]

Cottages with a Woman Working in the Middle Ground **(102)**, in which the blue-grey tone of the paper has faded slightly towards grey, has a woman working in a field at the centre of the composition. The row of what look like conifers on the left screens off the plot and recalls the rows of cypress trees that Van Gogh knew from Provence, making them a kind of memory of the South. In this case, the row looks a little ragged – a hurried mixture of short straight strokes and curved lines in both chalk and ink. The foreground is laid out very crudely, with broad, jagged ink lines reminiscent of *écriture automatique*, but

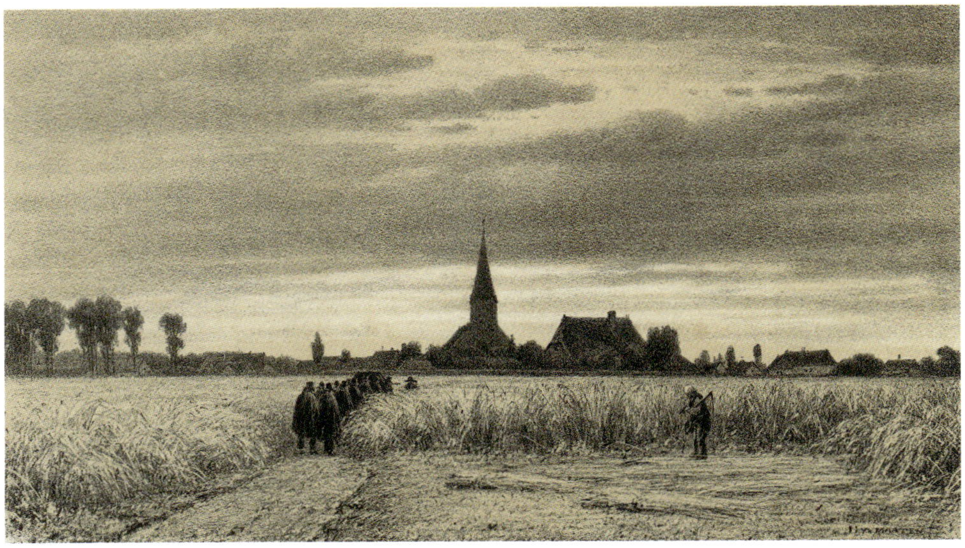

110
Jacob Jan van der Maaten
The Funeral in the Wheatfield, 1862
Lithograph, published in
Kunstkronijk 3 (1862), no. 20
Van Gogh Museum, Amsterdam

which still provide clear delineation.[51] Above it, the field is indicated with a little more restraint, with short dashes and curious lobe shapes that have been left blank on the right of the field. The houses on the horizon are really the only element that is crisply drawn, while the horizontal, alternatively blue and white bands in the sky instil a sense of tranquillity in the overall image. Depth is further emphasized by a scrawny tree that functions as a repoussoir on the right – a trick Van Gogh also used in *Field with Sheaves of Wheat*, where it consists of long stems and a fragment of a wheatsheaf. The irregular execution heightens our awareness that what we are looking at is a construct: a shorthand rendering of a landscape, in which the technique occasionally hinders legibility while simultaneously intriguing the viewer.

Something similar occurs in *Evening Landscape with Two Peasants* **(109)**, although it should be pointed out straight away that the work has been robbed of a great deal of its contrast by the heavily faded ink, as can be seen in an old photograph of the drawing **(108)**.[52] The black tone of the ink was originally deeper than that of the chalk, which means the balance has been lost, especially in the robust vegetation at the bottom. So much so, in fact, that the two peasants drawn in ink, each with a spade over his shoulder, have become almost invisible. They seem to have just climbed the steps in the foreground, before turning left to continue on their way along a wheatfield. The half-waxing moon, surrounded by an aureole of short lines, makes for an attractive contrast with the busy, scribbled lines in the foreground, even if a little more imagination is now required to appreciate the inherent poetry of the evening scene properly. Once again, the technique is distracting at times and we have to look a little past the swirling lines in the foreground. Whether knowingly or not, Van Gogh used the blue-grey paper here in a manner for which it was traditionally intended: its cool sombre tone lends itself perfectly to the depiction of evening and nocturnal effects.[53] The same hue has more of a general sobering effect in the other two sheets.

Field with Sheaves of Wheat **(111)**, lastly, is the 'calmest' of the three and was much less busily drawn. It is related to a painting with the same motif **(146)** and might have originated in the same place, as both works feature a long, light stone wall in the background. There are not so many of these in the large fields above Auvers, but it could be the wall marking the boundary between the fields and the

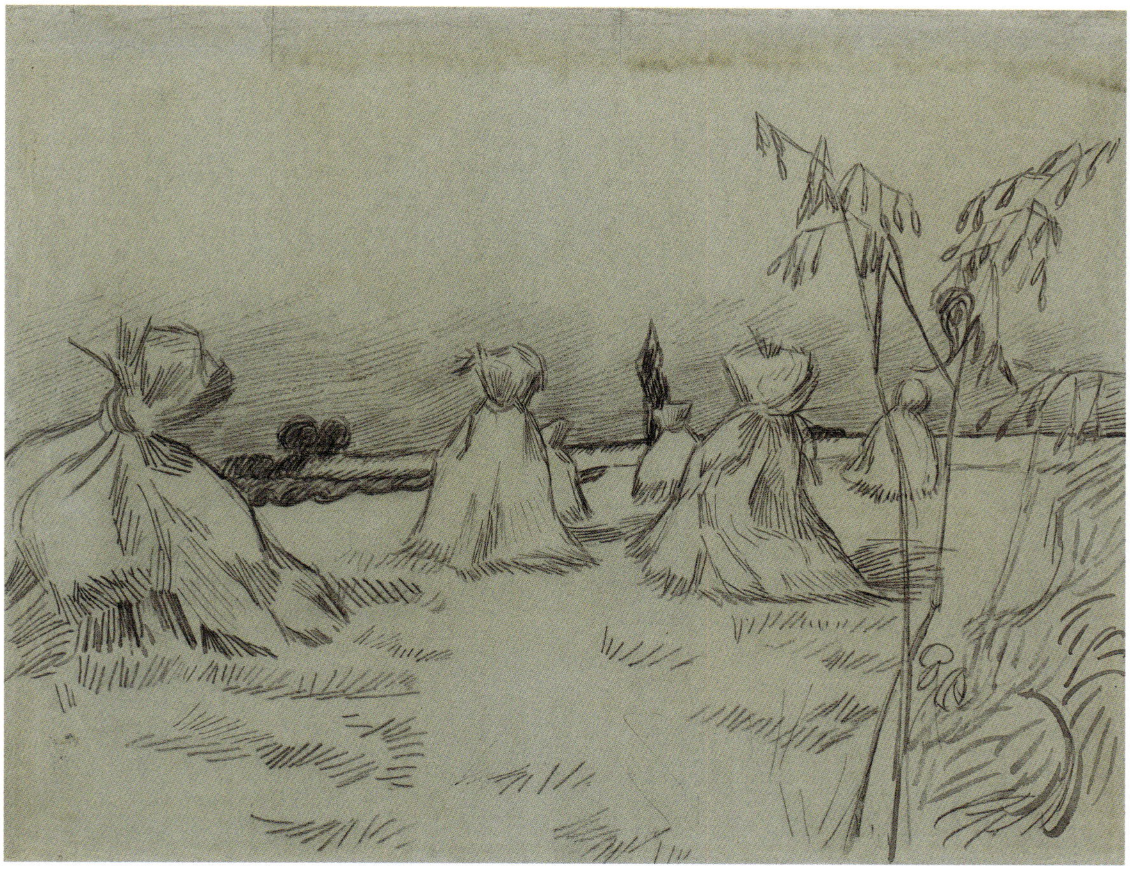

111
Vincent van Gogh
Field with Sheaves of Wheat, 1890
Black chalk and brush in ink,
on blue-grey laid paper, 47.5 × 62.8 cm
Van Gogh Museum, Amsterdam

private land beyond them near the church in Auvers **(188)**. Viewed from this angle, the church tower ought to have been visible, but Van Gogh might have left it out deliberately. The wall might also be the shorter one nearby around the cemetery in which the artist would be laid to rest not long afterwards. If so, the cypress-like tree looming behind it could hardly be anything but a reference to the graveyard. Its warm yellows and its shadow tones – originally purple but now light blue – make the painting a sunny and strongly contrasting scene, while the blue-grey paper of the drawing lends a cool character to the image. The further working out, which is sparse by Van Gogh's standards, adds to this. There are no swirling lines here, but simplified shapes and, above all, a lot of paper without any drawing.

The scene is even lent a sinister touch by the shadowy sky above the horizon. This, combined with the dark silhouette of the cypress, suggests that Van Gogh really did intend to suggest the presence of a graveyard immediately beyond the reaped field. The content of the drawing is thus related to that of another painting he was working on in this period **(14)**: an expansive view of fields with a solitary reaper at work, which was a variation on what he had previously painted in Saint-Rémy (*Wheatfield with a Reaper*, Van Gogh Museum, Amsterdam). The latter work contained 'the image of death', according to Van Gogh, but 'in this death nothing sad, it takes place in broad daylight'. He seems to have felt no differently in Auvers.[54] The reference to a cemetery in *Field with Sheaves of Wheat* is a similarly ominous note in an otherwise tranquil landscape, in which the wheat has just been reaped. In this way, it evokes the memory of a print that Van Gogh had admired early in his life, namely *The Funeral in the Wheatfield* by Jacob Jan van der Maaten **(110)**. A labourer in that scene pauses his reaping to pay his respects to a funeral procession making its way through the wheatfield towards the church on the horizon – an allusion to the fate that inevitably awaits every human being, but also to a certain acceptance of it.[55] In retrospect, the three drawings form a kind of final chord – a triptych celebrating the beauty and poetry of the countryside. One is more irregularly drawn than the other, but all three are made on cool blue paper, and ultimately share a lugubrious undertone, a genuine *et in arcadia ego*.[56]

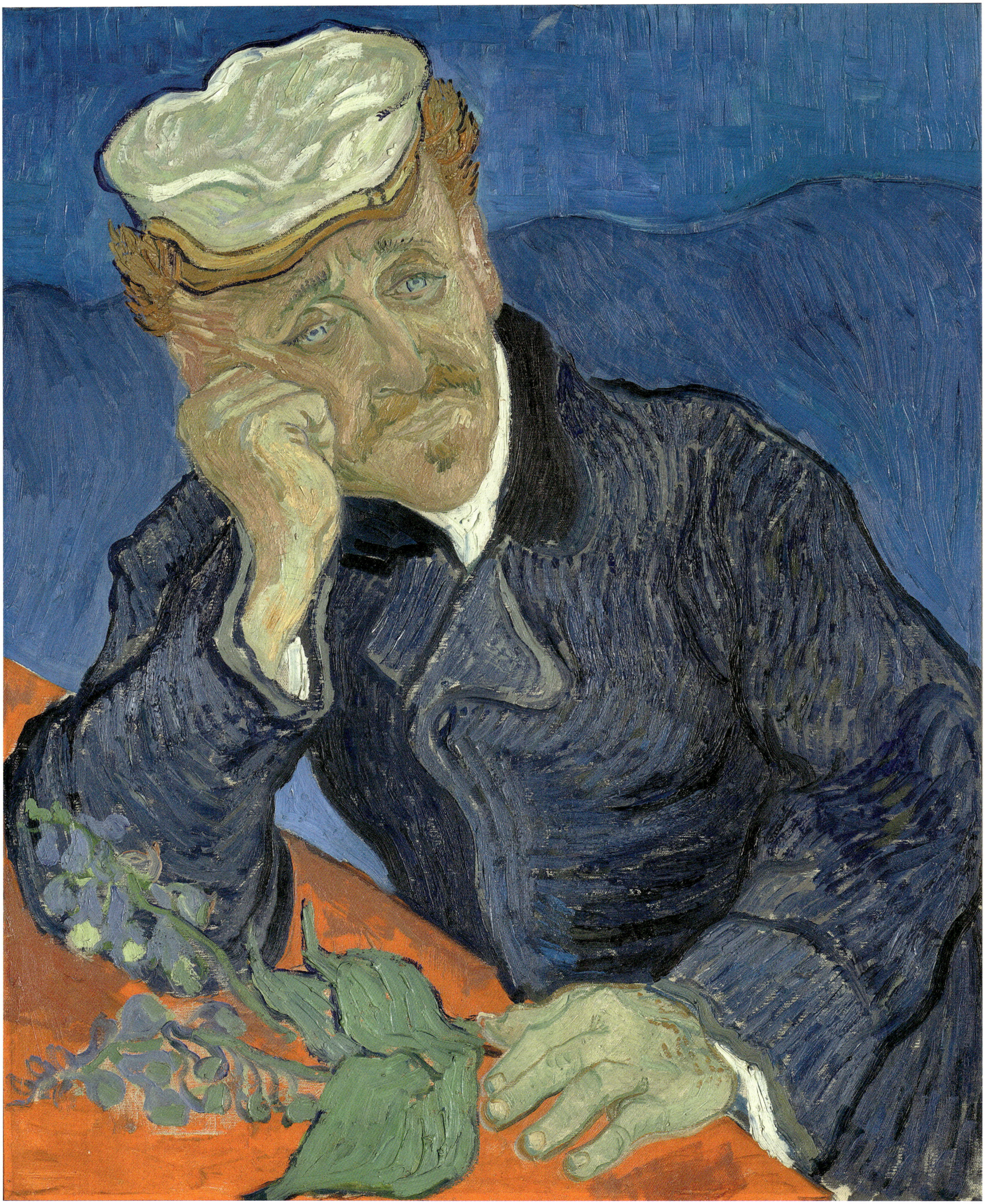

TIMELESS PORTRAITS

ON MELANCHOLY AND YOUTH

NIENKE BAKKER

Van Gogh wrote in Arles, after persuading several locals to sit for him in the summer of 1888, that making portraits was 'the only thing in painting that moves me deeply and that gives me a sense of the infinite. More than the rest'.[1] He had been convinced since leaving the Netherlands that the future of painting lay in the portrait, 'with the model's thoughts, his soul'.[2] A portrait painter could shine by focusing on style alone, yet the greatest honour, in Van Gogh's view, was to be had where the likeness offered a more universal meaning, lending the portrait 'something consoling'.[3] In Arles, for instance, he wanted to paint ordinary men and women 'with that *je ne sais quoi* of the eternal, of which the halo used to be the symbol, and which we try to achieve through the radiance itself, through the vibrancy of our colorations'. He succeeded brilliantly in this ambition with majestic portraits of local people as generic types such as the lover, the young woman, the peasant, the poet, the mother and the baby.

Van Gogh's portrait output had necessarily been limited at the asylum in Saint-Rémy, but something of his old passion for the genre flared up again in Auvers-sur-Oise, even if the number of portraits remained relatively small compared to the large volume of landscapes and village views he painted there. As soon as he arrived in Auvers he planned 'if circumstances permit [...] to do a little figure work'.[4] We know of thirteen portraits from this period, the first two of which were of Paul Ferdinand Gachet **(112, 159)**, the doctor whose presence in the village was what drew him there. They were painted in early June, with the remaining eleven following between roughly 22 June and the beginning of July.

Van Gogh had depicted numerous different types in Arles; but there would be less variety on this occasion. While Gachet was portrayed as a melancholic, seven of the other eleven works show young women or girls **(118, 119, 120, 121, 122, 125, 130)**. One portrait is a little hard to interpret **(131)**, and we also know of three works with small children, one of which is a 'repetition' **(132, 133, 134)**. The latter three were in the vein of the many portraits he had painted in Arles of Augustine and Joseph Roulin and their three children, while his depictions of young women and girls were in keeping with *La Mousmé* (National Gallery of Art, Washington) from that same period.

112 (#22)
Vincent van Gogh
Doctor Paul Gachet, 1890
Oil on canvas, 68.2 × 57 cm
Musée d'Orsay, Paris

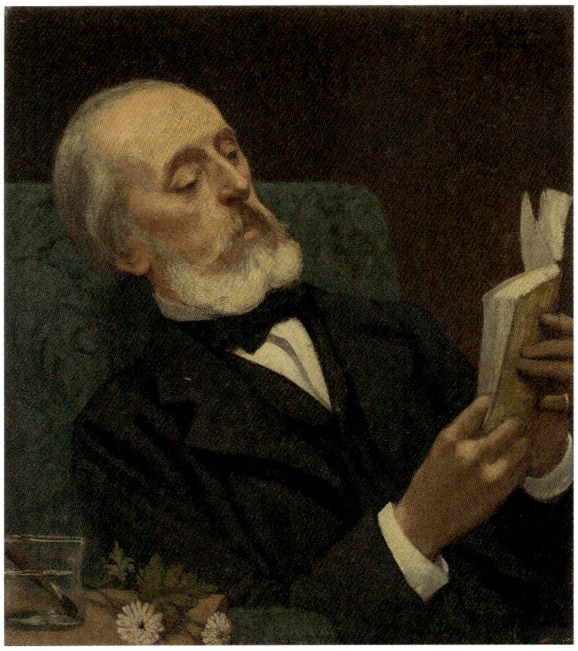

113
Pierre Puvis de Chavannes
Portrait of Eugène Benon, 1882
Oil on canvas, 60.5 × 54.5 cm
Van Gogh Museum, Amsterdam

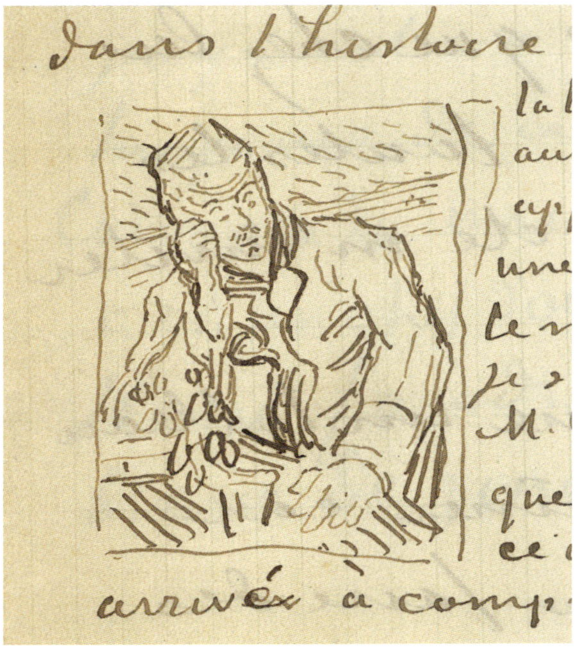

114
Sketch of *Doctor Paul Gachet*
in letter from Vincent to Theo, 3 June 1890
Van Gogh Museum, Amsterdam

GACHET, THE MELANCHOLIC

Van Gogh's portraits of Dr Gachet had their forerunners too. He presented his doctor as the victim of strained nerves, which he held to be the greatest malady of the age. The type flowed from his own ambitious self-portraits, particularly those from Saint-Rémy.[5] At that point, in the aftermath of his first and so far most intense crisis at the asylum, he explored his suffering in three successive self-portraits, the last of which he considered the most successful **(158)**.[6] In February 1890, he went on to paint five versions of the *Arlésienne*, a portrait of his friend Marie Ginoux from Arles, whose health problems led him to view her as a fellow sufferer. He hoped that portraits like this would offer solace in 'the struggle for life [...] our present weaknesses, our sicknesses, our confusions',[7] and he took one of the *Arlésiennes* with him to Auvers, together with the aforementioned self-portrait **(168)**.[8]

Van Gogh resolved to paint Gachet's portrait after their very first meeting, having immediately recognized the physician as a kindred spirit, in whom he detected a fellow victim of 'melancholia' (broadly what we nowadays call 'depression'). The eccentric doctor resembled him not only in terms of temperament but also, as a fair-skinned redhead, in appearance. Van Gogh viewed him as a kind of 'new brother' and one who specialized, moreover, in treating the ailment from which they both supposedly suffered.[9] When it came to a soulful portrait, the painter could not have wished for a better model than this widower with his grief-furrowed face.

Gachet was deeply impressed by the self-portrait and the *Arlésienne* that Van Gogh had brought with him and was happy to pose.[10] The artist painted the first portrait on 3 June with Gachet sitting for him **(159)**, followed three days later at the inn by a second version based on the first **(112)**, which he completed at Gachet's home.[11] Both works show the doctor sitting at the red table in his garden, dressed in the dark-blue overcoat from his days as an ambulance man and his white cap.[12] He leans on the table with his head resting on his hand – the classic pose of the melancholic and matching that of the *Arlésienne*, although now reversed.[13] The foxglove (*digitalis*) is an allusion to Gachet's profession as it was used in homeopathy, of which the doctor was a staunch advocate, to treat heart disease.[14] The flowers, the glass of water and the books on the table in the first version of the portrait echo Pierre Puvis de Chavannes's portrait of an elderly man reading a book **(113)**, which Van Gogh considered the perfect representation of the 'intimacy of our very own epoch'.[15]

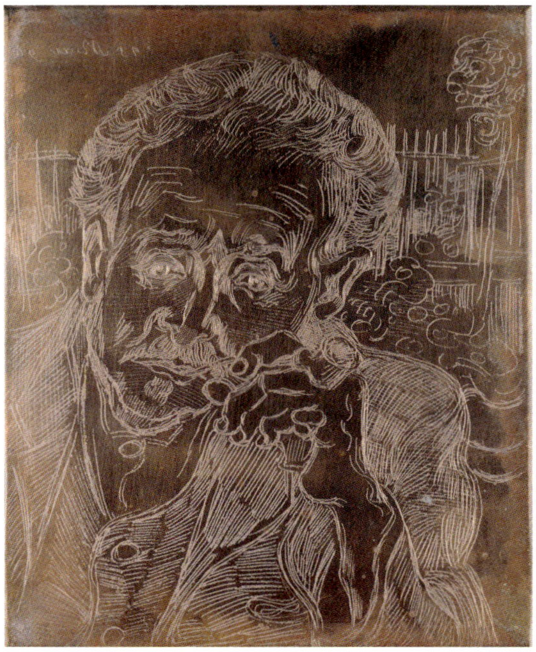

115
Vincent van Gogh
Portrait of Doctor Paul Gachet, 1890
Etched copper plate, 18.5 × 15.1 cm
Musée d'Orsay, Paris

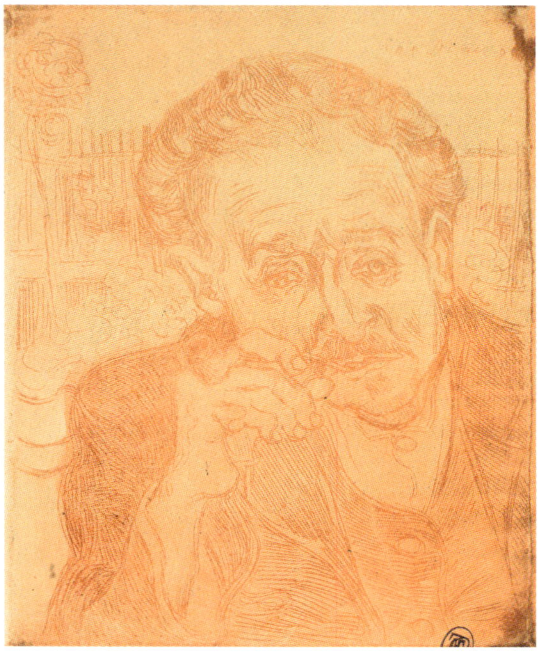

116
Vincent van Gogh
Portrait of Doctor Paul Gachet, 1890
Colour etching on paper, 18.3 × 15.1 cm
Van Gogh Museum, Amsterdam

Van Gogh viewed books as emblematic of the modern era and had also included two of them in his portraits of the Arlésienne: Charles Dickens's *Christmas Tales* and Harriet Beecher Stowe's *Uncle Tom's Cabin*, both of which highlight the importance of compassion in times of need. He selected two other personal favourites for Gachet's portrait: *Germinie Lacerteux* and *Manette Salomon* by Edmond and Jules de Goncourt. The first of these novels describes the emergence of neuroses and addresses the harshness of modern existence, while the second deals with the difficult Bohemian life led by painters in contemporary Paris. By including the latter novel, Van Gogh presented the doctor as someone who cared about artists in need, of whom Vincent himself was one.

According to Gachet's son, the first portrait was painted over five hours in the garden, interrupted only by a short lunch break.[16] Van Gogh was still working on the painting when he informed his brother Theo about it on 3 June and, judging by his description and the small sketch he included, it only featured one book at that point **(114)**.[17] While this first work was intended for the artist himself, the second version was for Gachet and does not include the books. The painter also gave greater prominence to the foxglove – emblem of the physician – which now lies on the table like the chrysanthemums in the portrait by Puvis. As in his self-portrait, which Gachet thought magnificent and later came to own, Van Gogh used animated brushstrokes to create his first likeness of the doctor. The second portrait, which lacks not only the books but also the glass and the buttons on the coat, is less worked out and flatter in colour, so that it seems inspired more by the example of Japanese woodcuts. This simpler, more sober version was more suitable as a gift for Gachet than the first version, which was so much more than merely a portrait of a doctor.

'What I'm most passionate about, much much more than all the rest in my profession – is the portrait, the modern portrait', Van Gogh wrote to his sister Willemien immediately after painting the first version. He described Gachet's portrait at greater length to her than he did to Theo and also explained what he had in mind: 'I *would like* to do portraits which would look like apparitions to people a century later. So I don't try to do us by photographic resemblance but by our passionate expressions, using as a means of expression and intensification of the character our science and modern taste for colour.'[18] The portrait was 'in the same sentiment'[19] as his self-portrait from Saint-Rémy, with similar contrasts between warm and cool tones. Gachet's face in 'the

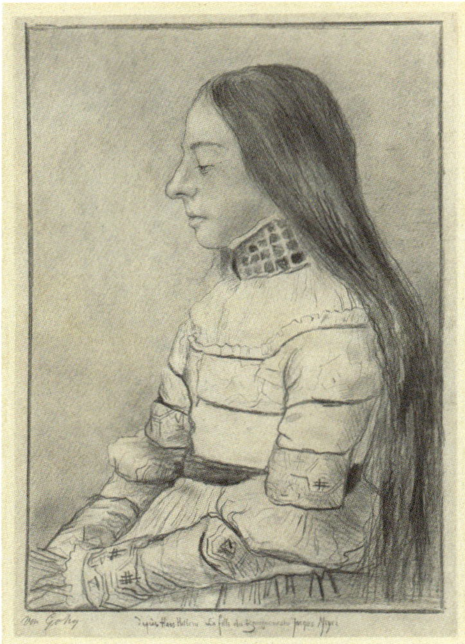

117
Vincent van Gogh
The Daughter of Jacob Meyer (after Bargue, after Holbein), 1890
Pencil on paper, 42.6 × 30.5 cm
Kröller-Müller Museum, Otterlo and Van Gogh Museum, Amsterdam

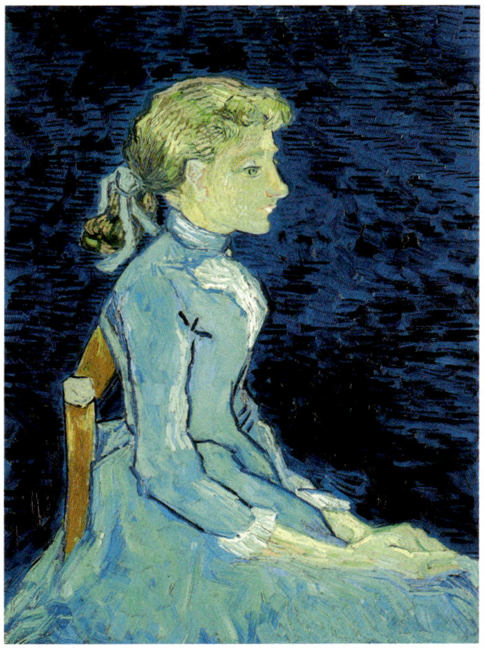

118 (#49)
Vincent van Gogh
Adeline Ravoux, 1890
Oil on canvas, 71.5 × 53 cm
Private collection

colour of an overheated and sun-scorched brick'[20] and his reddish hair stand out against the deep ultramarine of his clothes and the background of blue hills that suggest the rolling countryside of Auvers.

Gachet's portrait was the most personal that Van Gogh produced in Auvers – a worthy successor to his *Self-Portrait* and the *Arlésienne*, and, in a sense, a kind of self-portrait in itself. He saw his own existential pain and at the same time that of all humanity reflected in Gachet's 'deeply sad expression of our time'.[21] 'Sad but gentle but clear and intelligent', is how he summed up the work,[22] echoing what he had previously written about Puvis's portrait of a man: 'These are consolatory things, to see modern life as bright despite its inevitable sadnesses.'[23]

Gachet was also the subject of Van Gogh's only etching, which he made just over a week later at the doctor's home.[24] In this work, showing Gachet as 'the man with the pipe', as his son Paul later dubbed it, Van Gogh zoomed in more on the doctor's face with its furrowed brows and deep-set eyes, conveying the same pensive, sorrowful expression as in his painted portraits. Gachet had a press in his attic studio, which he used to print etchings made by himself and by others.[25] Paul, who was sixteen at the time, was present when Van Gogh made the etching and later described how it was done. Outside in the garden, while Van Gogh and Gachet were smoking their pipes after lunch, the artist drew the portrait 'very quickly' on the prepared copper plate **(115)**, following which they printed the etching together in the studio, as the artist – enthusiastic about what was a new process for him – tried out different colours **(116, 169)**.[26]

PORTRAITS OF YOUNG WOMEN

Painting Gachet's portrait renewed Van Gogh's captivation with figure pieces. His enthusiasm was also fired by what he saw in the doctor's collection: an etched portrait by Félix Bracquemond ('a masterpiece'), a 'dark but interesting' self-portrait by Armand Guillaumin, and in particular the latter's painting of a nude woman on a bed, which he found 'very beautiful'.[27] He had already asked his brother to send Charles Bargue's drawing course in his first letter from Auvers and he now wrote again to remind him. Copying the series of nudes would give him a chance to study their proportions.[28] Van Gogh was keen to do more portraits after having painted Gachet, because 'to have clients for portraits one must be able to show different ones that one has done. That's the only possibility I can see of placing something.'[29] Van Gogh already had his eye on a new model, namely Gachet's twenty-year-old daughter

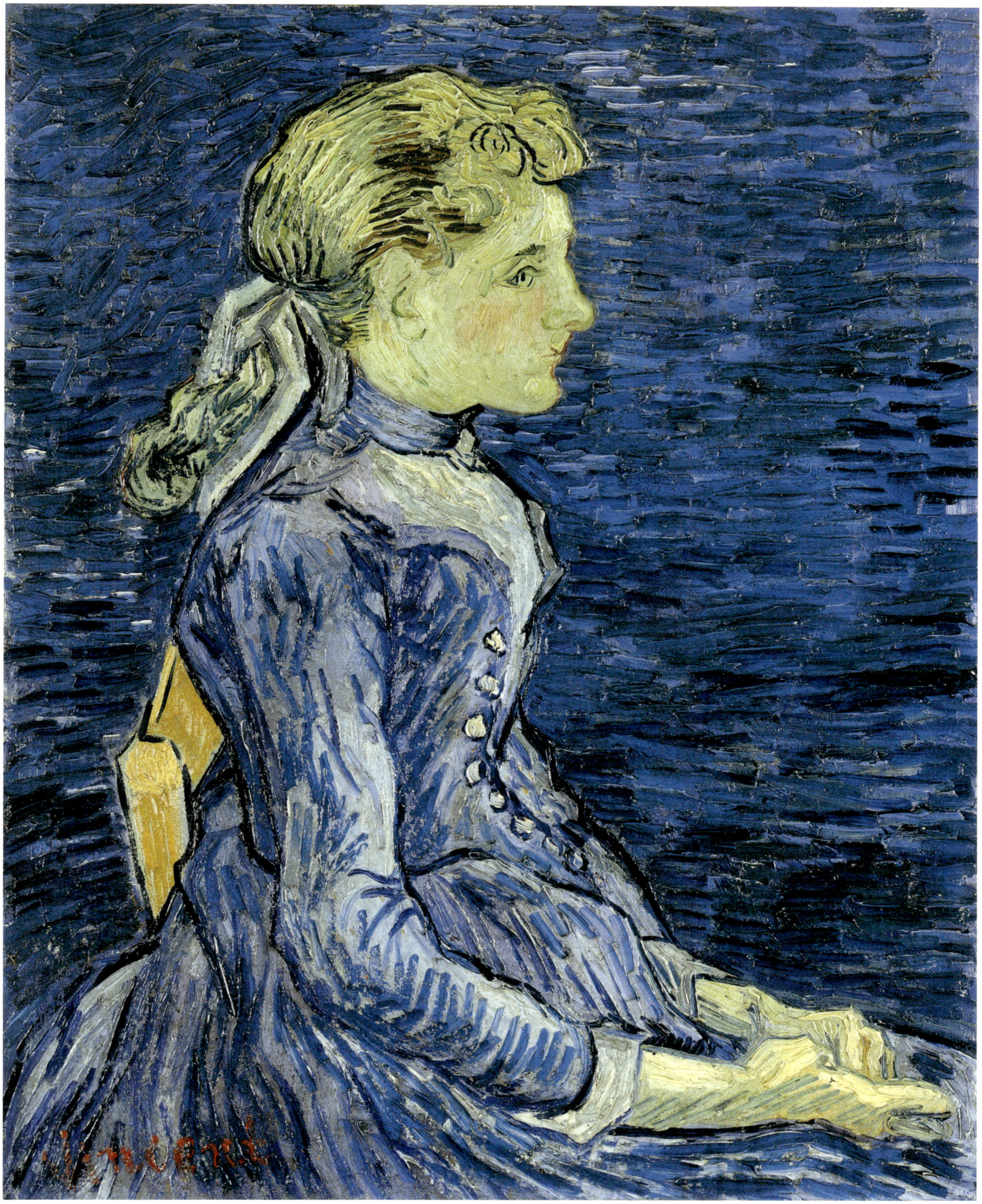

119 (#48)
Vincent van Gogh
Adeline Ravoux, 1890
Oil on canvas, 67 × 55 cm
Private collection – courtesy of HomeArt

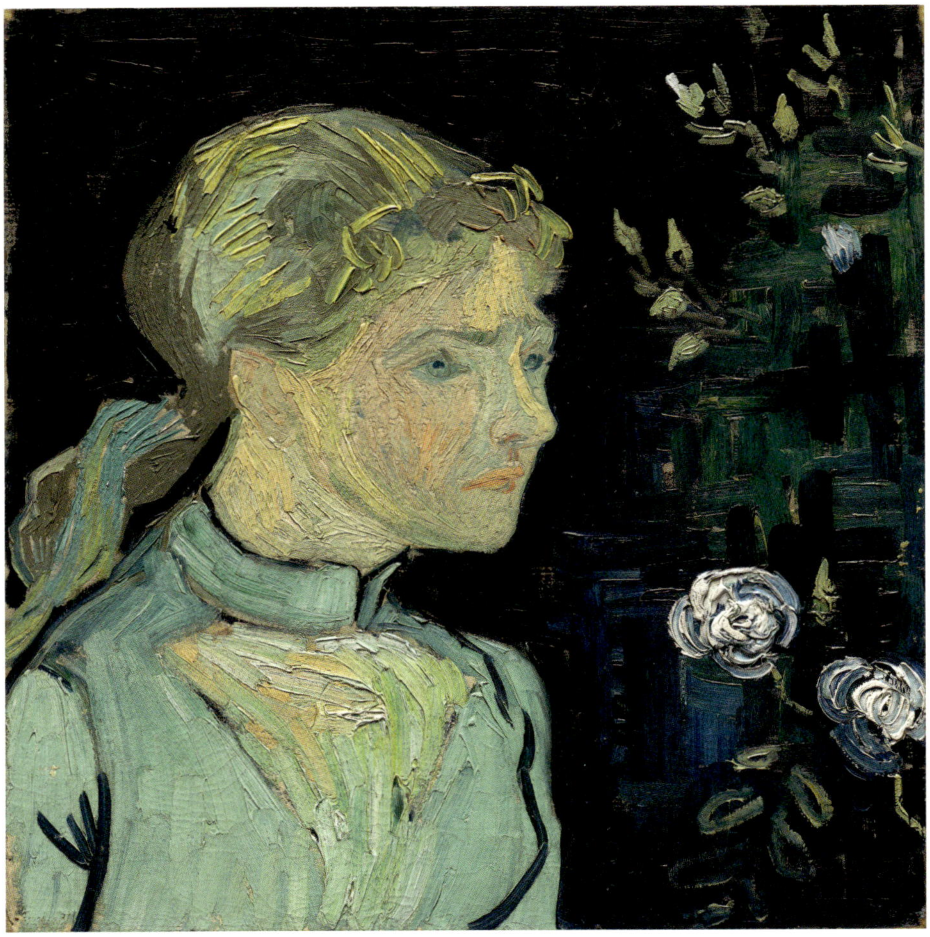

120 (#50)
Vincent van Gogh
Adeline Ravoux, 1890
Oil on canvas, 50.2 × 50.5 cm
The Cleveland Museum of Art, bequest of Leonard C. Hanna, Jr. 1958

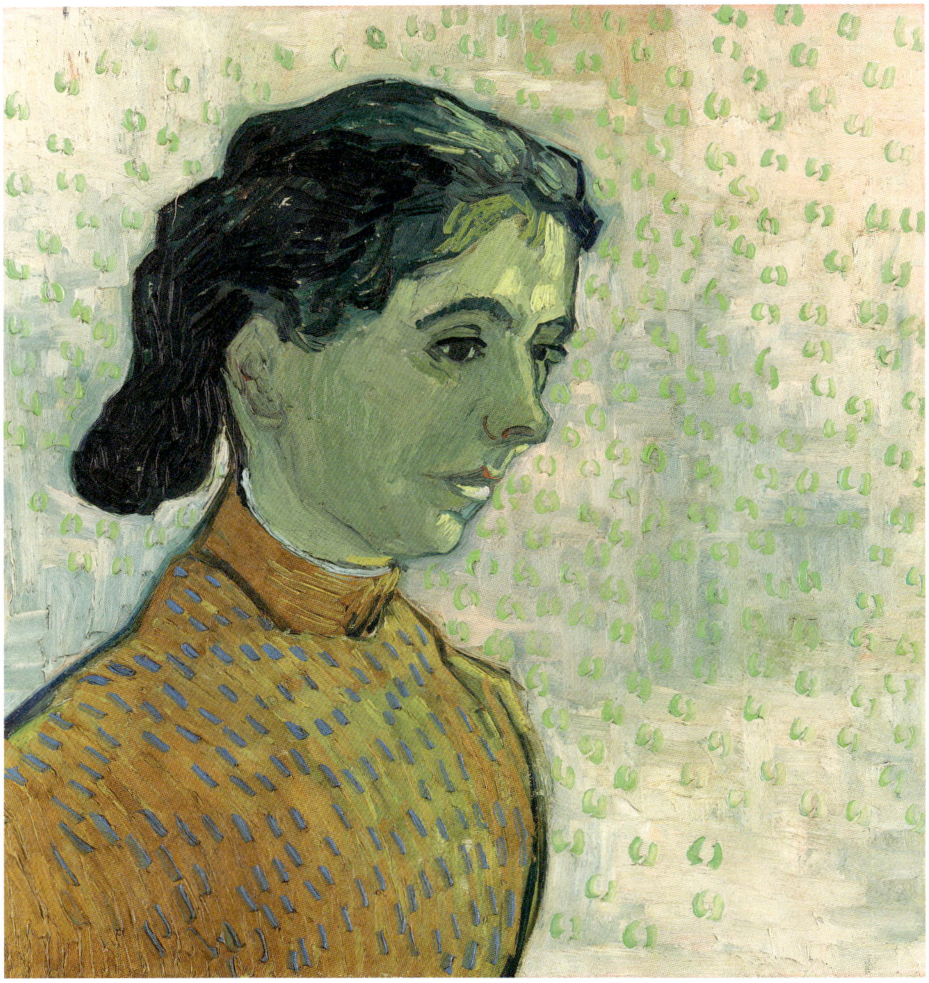

121 (#51)
Vincent van Gogh
Portrait of a Young Woman, 1890
Oil on canvas, 51.9 × 49.5 cm
Kröller-Müller Museum, Otterlo

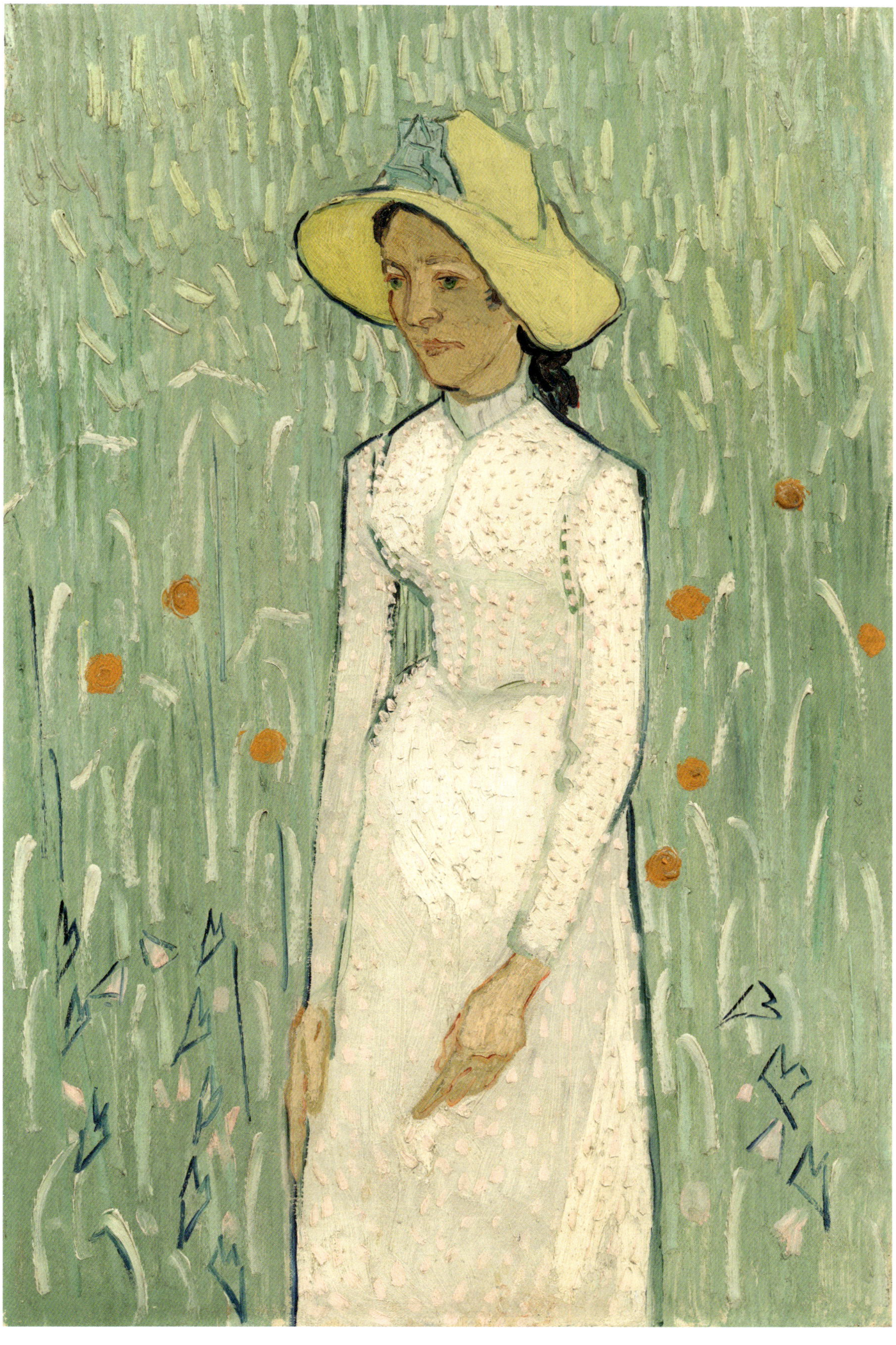

122 (#54)
Vincent van Gogh
Girl in White, 1890

Oil on canvas, 66.7 × 45.8 cm
National Gallery of Art, Washington,
Chester Dale Collection

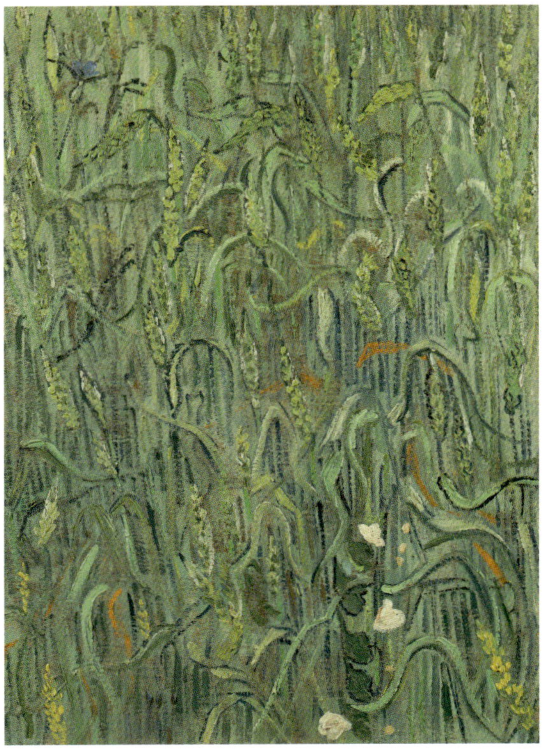

123 (#38)
Vincent van Gogh
Ears of Wheat, 1890
Oil on *torchon*, 64 × 48 cm
Van Gogh Museum, Amsterdam

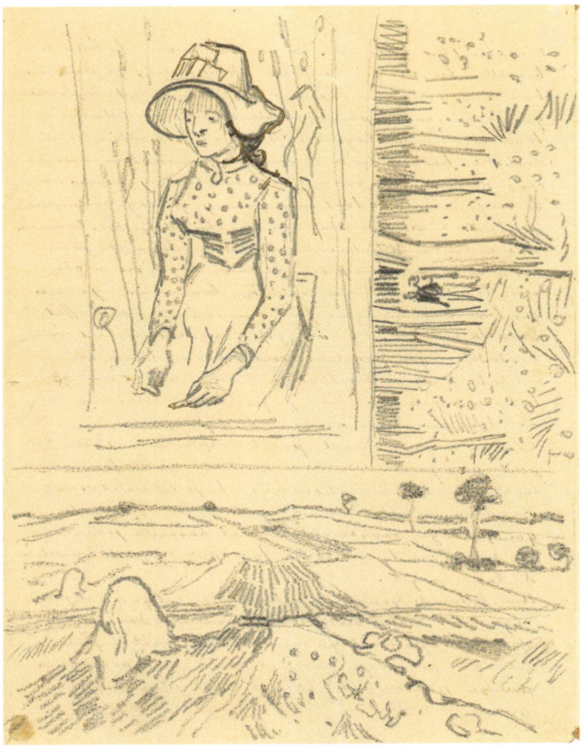

124
Letter from Vincent to Theo and Jo with sketches of *Country Girl with Straw Hat*, *Undergrowth with Two Figures* and *Fields near Auvers-sur-Oise*, 2 July 1890
Pencil, pen and ink, on paper, 27 × 21 cm
Van Gogh Museum, Amsterdam

Marguerite. He also informed Theo that he was 'looking forward to doing the portraits of all of you in the open air, yours, Jo's and the little one's'. Beyond a few sketches, however, nothing came of this on the Sunday that Theo and his family spent at Auvers on 8 June.[30]

Gachet's admiration for the *Arlésienne* and above all the praise that Gauguin lavished on the same work in a letter that Van Gogh received in mid-June strengthened his conviction that women's portraits would enable him to set out a new vision for the genre.[31] He soon got the chance to paint Marguerite Gachet, as he had been hoping, but only after discovering that the daughter of Mr and Mrs Ravoux, the landlords of the Café de la Mairie, was also willing to pose. 'This week I've done a portrait of a young girl of 16 or so, in blue against a blue background, the daughter of the people where I'm lodging', he wrote to Theo on 24 June. 'I gave her that portrait but I've done a variant for you, a no. 15 canvas.'[32] The first work is *Adeline Ravoux* **(119)**, which remained in the family's possession until 1908. The presentation *en profil*, which is unusual in Van Gogh's French work, lends Adeline the air of a Renaissance portrait. The memory might have resonated here of Hans Holbein the Younger's *Daughter of Jacob Meyer*, which was included in Bargue's drawing course; Vincent had copied the profile portrait of a sitting girl several times in his early days as an artist **(117)**.[33] As in his portraits of Gachet, he used a deep blue for the background of *Adeline Ravoux*. It harmonizes with the young woman's clothes and heightens the light tones of her face and blonde hair. Van Gogh had seen the effect of blue on blue in an *aizuri-e* colour woodcut by Katsushika Hokusai at the exhibition of Japanese prints in Paris, which might have given him the idea for his 'Symphonie en bleu', as Adeline later referred to her portrait.[34]

The eldest Ravoux daughter was not sixteen but twelve at the time and was posing in her 'first girl's dress' – a rite of passage for her.[35] Her memories of Van Gogh were chronicled in several interviews that were given over sixty years after the event and are occasionally contradictory; but she did state firmly that she only sat for one portrait.[36] The second one **(118)** was therefore based on the first, while the bust-length portrait of Adeline that he later painted on a smaller, square canvas was also done without the model, though more from memory in this instance **(120)**. The girl in the version he did for Theo is proportionately a little smaller and rendered more schematically, with

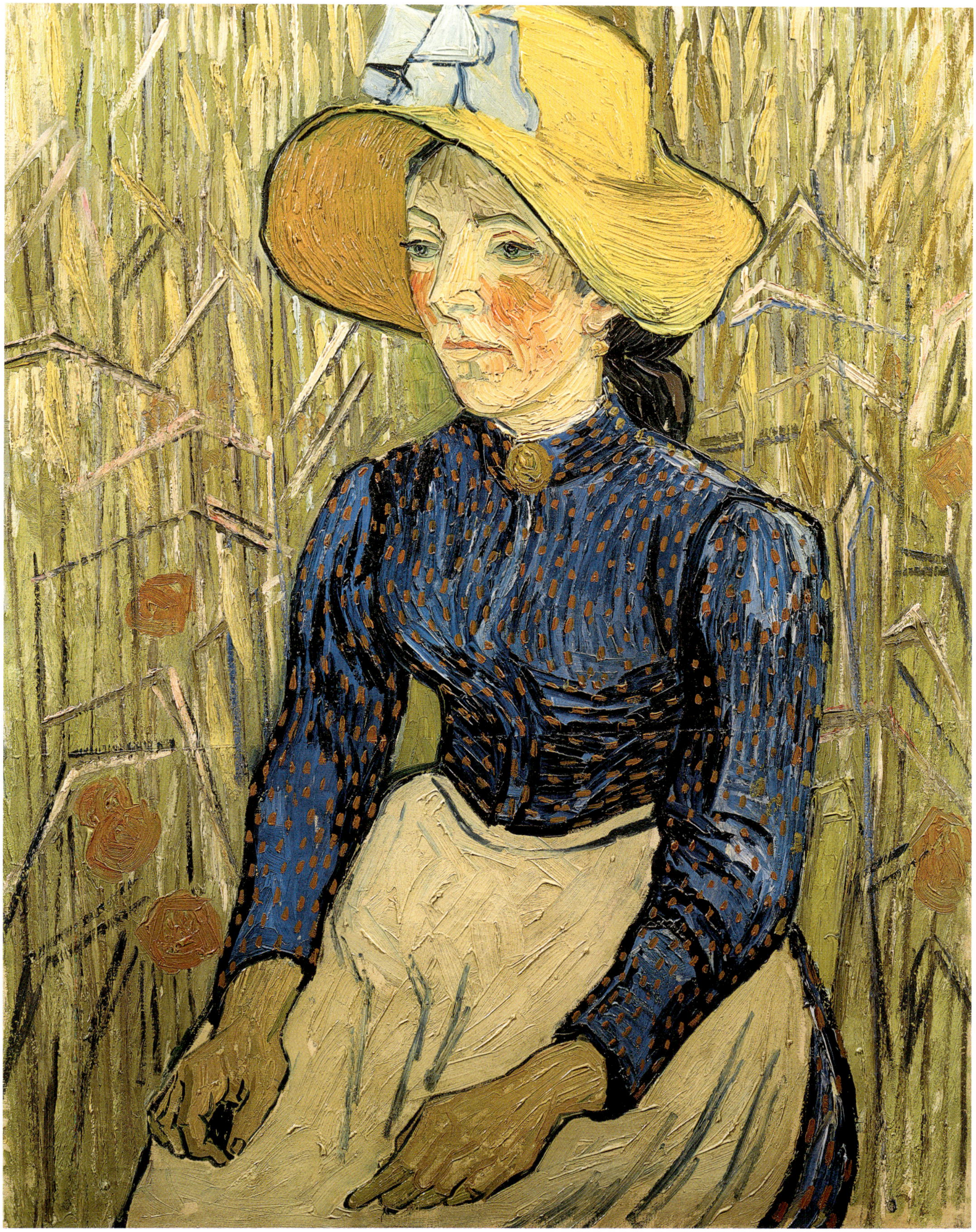

125 (#53)
Vincent van Gogh
Country Girl with Straw Hat, 1890
Oil on canvas, 92 × 73 cm
Private collection

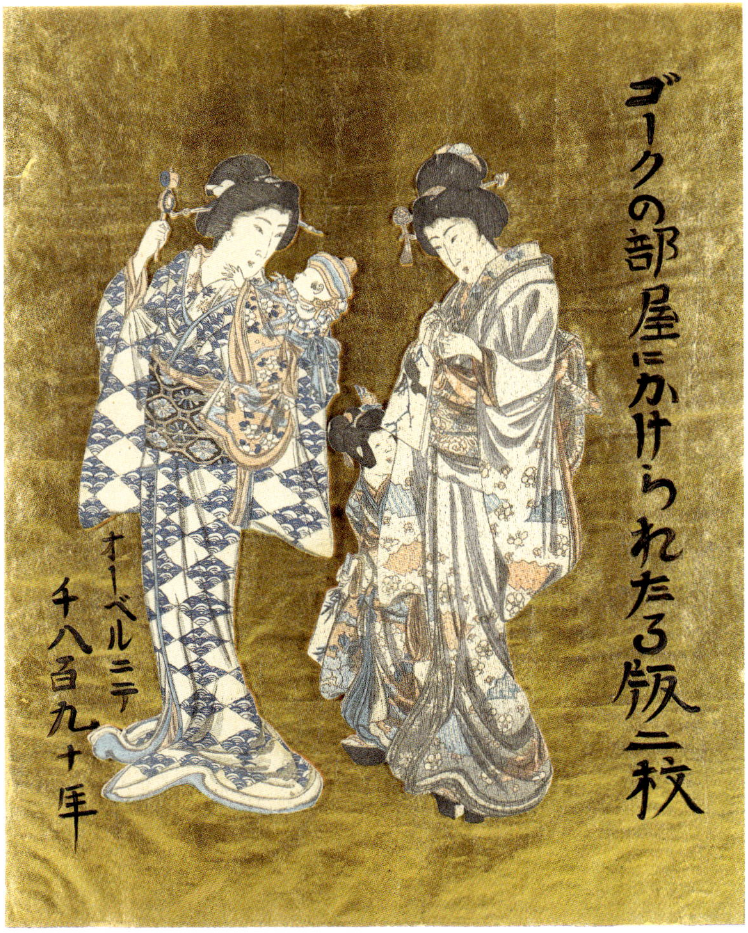

126
Anonymous
Two Female Figures Cut Out from Japanese Crêpons, c. 1860–70
Colour woodblock prints pasted onto paper, 56 × 46 cm
Inscribed: two prints that hung in Van Gogh's room / in Auvers 1890
Musée d'Orsay, Paris

fewer details. Especially so in her dress, which is also considerably lighter in colour, as is the ribbon in her hair. For the smaller, bust portrait, Van Gogh adopted the light colour from the 'variant' and darkened the background to create an even stronger contrast. He also added a rose motif in the background – a fitting emblem for the young girl, just as the foxglove had said something about Gachet.

The 50 × 50 cm format which Van Gogh used here for the first time to paint a portrait,[37] was derived from the formats twice as wide (50 × 100 cm) he had used that same week to paint the first three landscapes of what would become a series of thirteen.[38] A square format lends itself to a more decorative approach, which he continued to pursue in the portrait of a young woman against a dotted background, made shortly afterwards on a canvas with the same dimensions **(121)**.[39] A small drawing in Van Gogh's sketchbook of a woman with the same hairstyle shown in profile can be linked to this.[40]

The identity of the young woman who posed for the portrait and for the 'figure of a peasant woman' that Van Gogh painted soon after **(125)** remains a mystery.[41] He presented the girl here against a bright pink background (now faded to a greyish pink), over which he placed light-green, comma-shaped touches, while providing her orange dress with short, blue strokes of paint, in a play of complementary colour effects. The composition of this bust-length portrait and the one of Adeline strongly resembles Eugène Delacroix's portrait of the French writer George Sand, a wood engraving of which Van Gogh had seen in a magazine.[42] The identical dimensions and composition of his two square portraits, the different hair colour of the two girls and the green and pink contrasting with yellow and blue, make it easy to imagine that he intended them as a pair. These were canvases that he did not give away but painted for himself, for his room at the inn, just as he had hung portraits above his bed in Arles, or for a possible permanent residence or studio of his own in Auvers.[43]

The method of dots in complementary contrasts that he had introduced in the *Portrait of a Young Woman* was applied even more convincingly when painting his most ambitious figure piece from Auvers, *Marguerite Gachet at the Piano* **(130)**, for which he chose the exceptional, elongated canvas format that he otherwise used exclusively for landscapes. He took his inspiration for the subject from the etching Gachet had made of his wife,

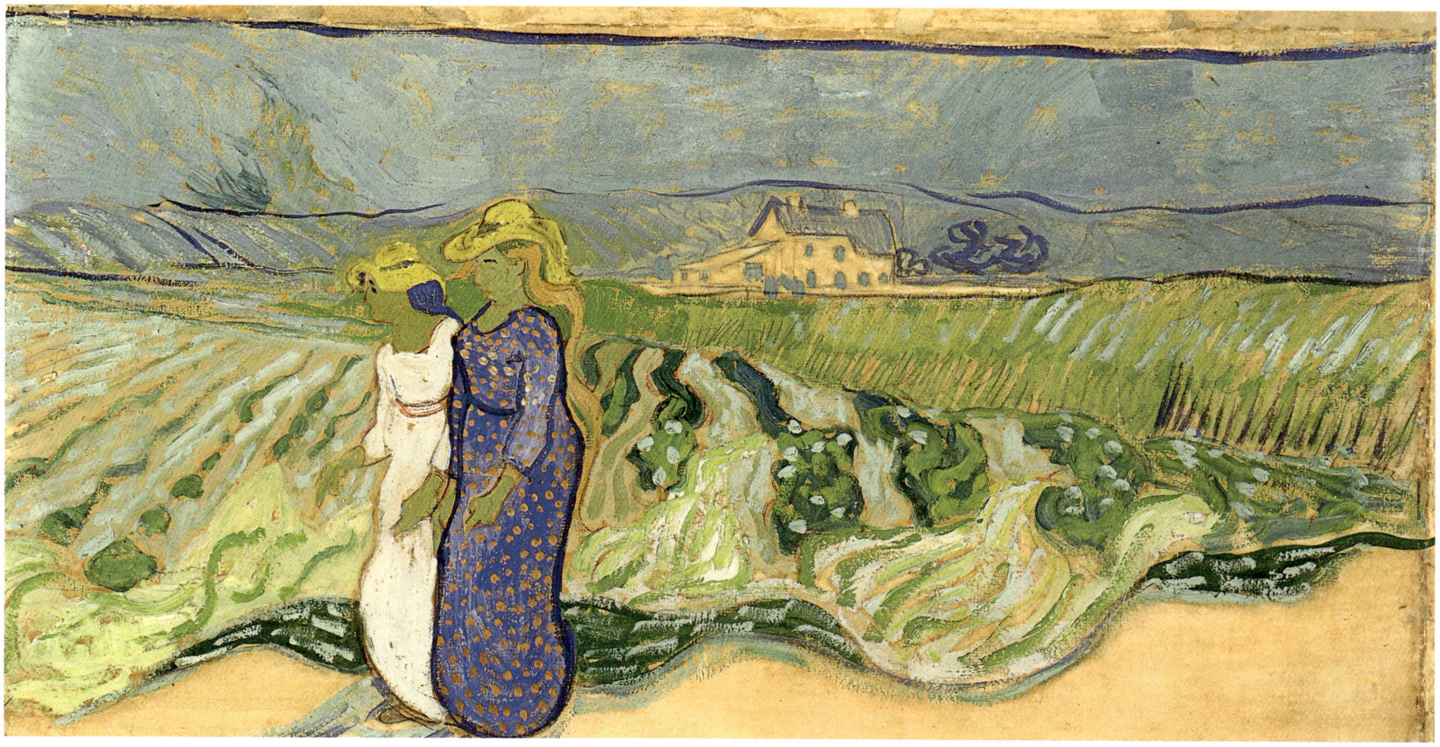

127
Vincent van Gogh
Women Crossing the Fields, 1890
Oil on paper, 30.3 × 59.7 cm
McNay Art Museum, San Antonio, bequest of Marion Koogler McNay

Marguerite's mother, at the piano. The thought of what Theo had written to him about an 'excellent portrait' by Henri de Toulouse-Lautrec of a woman playing the same instrument might also have contributed.[44] Van Gogh described his painting to his brother on 28 June, including a little sketch: 'Yesterday and the day before yesterday I painted Miss Gachet's portrait, which you'll see soon, I hope. The dress is pink. The wall in the background green with orange spots, the carpet red with green spots, the piano dark violet. It's 1 metre high and 50 cm wide. It's a figure I enjoyed painting – but it's difficult.'[45] The unusual composition and canvas format were 'deliberately chosen like a kakemono', according to Gachet's son Paul, and – 'like Utamaro' – Van Gogh elongated his model to make her taller and more elegant.[46] He followed the example of Japanese prints by keeping the image flat, without perspective, by stylizing Marguerite's portrait with broad, wavy brushstrokes, and through the graceful forms of her dress, which stand out against the decorative pattern of the floor and background.

Paul Gachet recorded in some detail how his sister's portrait was created at their father's home in two sittings.[47] According to his account, Van Gogh first made a drawing in chalk **(128)** as a preliminary study for the composition before starting to paint.[48] On the second day, the artist turned up without his palette so Dr Gachet lent him one to enable him to finish the portrait; Gachet Jr later donated the palette to the Louvre **(189)**. Van Gogh wrote to his brother that the doctor had promised to have Marguerite sit for him again at a small organ and that he planned to do a portrait for Theo as well, but nothing came of this. Regarding *Marguerite Gachet at the Piano*, he noted that it formed a good combination with a horizontal canvas of wheatfields **(135, 129)**, as these seemingly contrasting subjects with their complementary colours 'however explain and bring each other out'.[49] This might suggest that he took the portrait of Marguerite to the inn to compare it alongside *Fields near Auvers-sur-Oise*, but according to Gachet Jr, 'he did not take with him the canvas, which he presented the same day to Mademoiselle Gachet'.[50] The painting hung in Marguerite's bedroom for over forty years between the two Japanese prints Van Gogh had displayed on the wall in his room at the inn **(126)**. She and her brother eventually sold the portrait to the Kunstmuseum in Basel in 1934.[51]

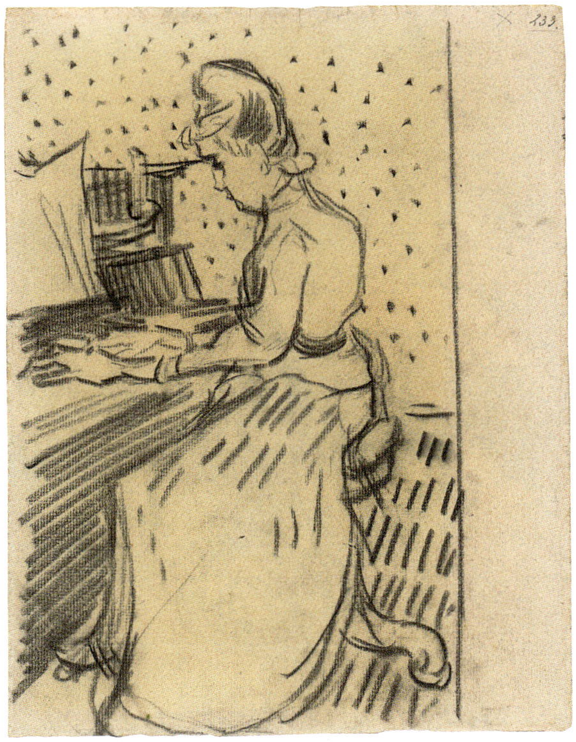

128
Vincent van Gogh
Marguerite Gachet at the Piano, 1890
Chalk on laid paper, 30.5 × 23.8 cm
Van Gogh Museum, Amsterdam

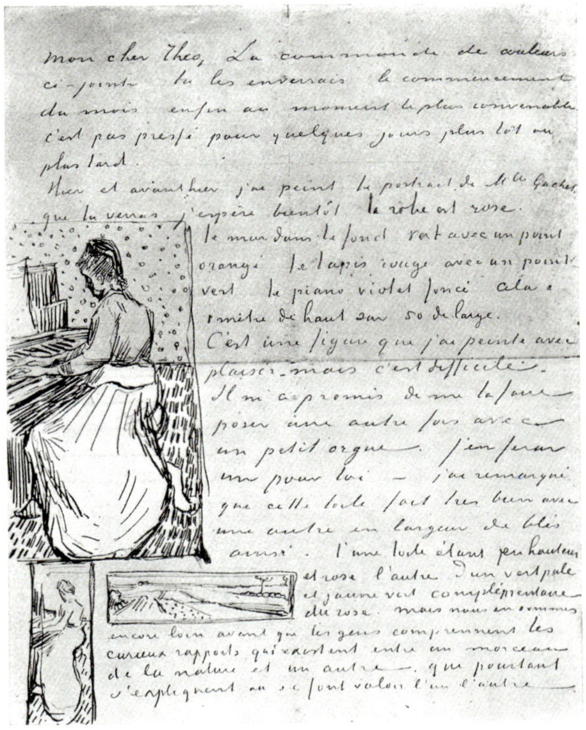

mon cher Theo, La commande de couleurs ci-jointe tu les enverrais le commencement du mois enfin au moment le plus convenable c'est pas pressé pour quelques jours plus tôt ou plus tard.
Hier et avant hier j'ai peint le portrait de Mlle Gachet que tu verras j'espère bientôt la robe est rose. le mur dans le fond vert avec un point orangé le tapis rouge avec un point vert le piano violet foncé. 1 mètre de haut sur 50 de large.
C'est une figure que j'ai peinte avec plaisir – mais c'est difficile.
Il m'a promis de me la faire poser une autre fois avec un petit orgue. j'en ferai un pour toi – j'ai remarqué que cette toile fait très bien avec une autre en largeur de blés ainsi. l'une toile étant en hauteur et rose l'autre d'un vert pâle et jaune vert complémentaire du rose. mais nous en sommes encore loin avant que les gens comprennent les curieux rapports qui existent entre un morceau de la nature et un autre – qui pourtant s'expliquent et se font valoir l'un l'autre

129
Letter from Vincent to Theo with sketches of *Marguerite Gachet at the Piano* and *Fields near Auvers-sur-Oise*, 28 June 1890, whereabouts unknown

THE HEALTHY COUNTRY LIFE

The 'curious relationships that exist between one piece of nature and another',[52] which a thoughtful viewer might discern between *Marguerite Gachet at the Piano* and *Fields near Auvers-sur-Oise*, tempted Van Gogh between late June and early July into creating an intriguing group of portraits of youthful types in the open air, especially women and children, in which he sang the praises of country life. 'If only one could have the individuals one sees pass by to do their portraits, it would be as pretty as any past era, and I even think that often in nature there is currently all the grace of Puvis's painting, Between art and nature', he wrote on 28 June, referring to Puvis de Chavannes's Arcadian landscape with figures, which had made such a powerful impression on him in Paris **(153)**. 'Thus yesterday I saw two figures, the mother in dark carmine dress, the daughter in pale pink with a yellow hat without any ornamentation, very healthy figures, rustic, well tanned by the open air, burned by the sun, the mother especially with a very, very red face and black hair and two diamonds in her ears.'[53] The observed motif inspired a landscape à la Puvis, which he painted on an elongated sheet of paper, the sketchy, unfinished character of which suggests that it might have been a study for a larger, unexecuted canvas in the series of panoramic landscapes **(127)**. Contrary to his description, he gave the mother orange rather than black hair and a deep-blue dress with orange dots rather than a carmine one. He used the same combination of colours in the portrait on a number 30 canvas – the largest portrait he would paint in Auvers – of a 'figure of a peasant woman' **(125)**, which he described and sketched in a letter dated 2 July: 'big yellow hat with a knot of sky-blue ribbons, very red face. Coarse blue blouse with orange spots, background of ears of wheat' **(124)**.[54]

The young woman, whose portrait he had already painted **(121)**, is depicted here as the type of the healthy peasant girl – a young, female counterpart to Patience Escalier, the sunburnt gardener, whose portrait Van Gogh had painted in Arles and titled 'The Peasant'. Although there is no suggestion of it in the sketch, in which she looks charming and shy, Van Gogh found his portrait of the girl 'a little coarse'. It is painted with a broad, impastoed touch in robust colours, while the background is filled with rough strokes of paint. This background – an invented setting, like that in his portraits of Gachet – was the implementation of an idea that he had expressed in a letter to Gauguin, where he wrote that he wanted to paint portraits 'on a very alive and yet tranquil background' of wheat, a single unity

130 (#52)
Vincent van Gogh
Marguerite Gachet at the Piano, 1890
Oil on canvas, 102.5 × 50 cm
Kunstmuseum Basel

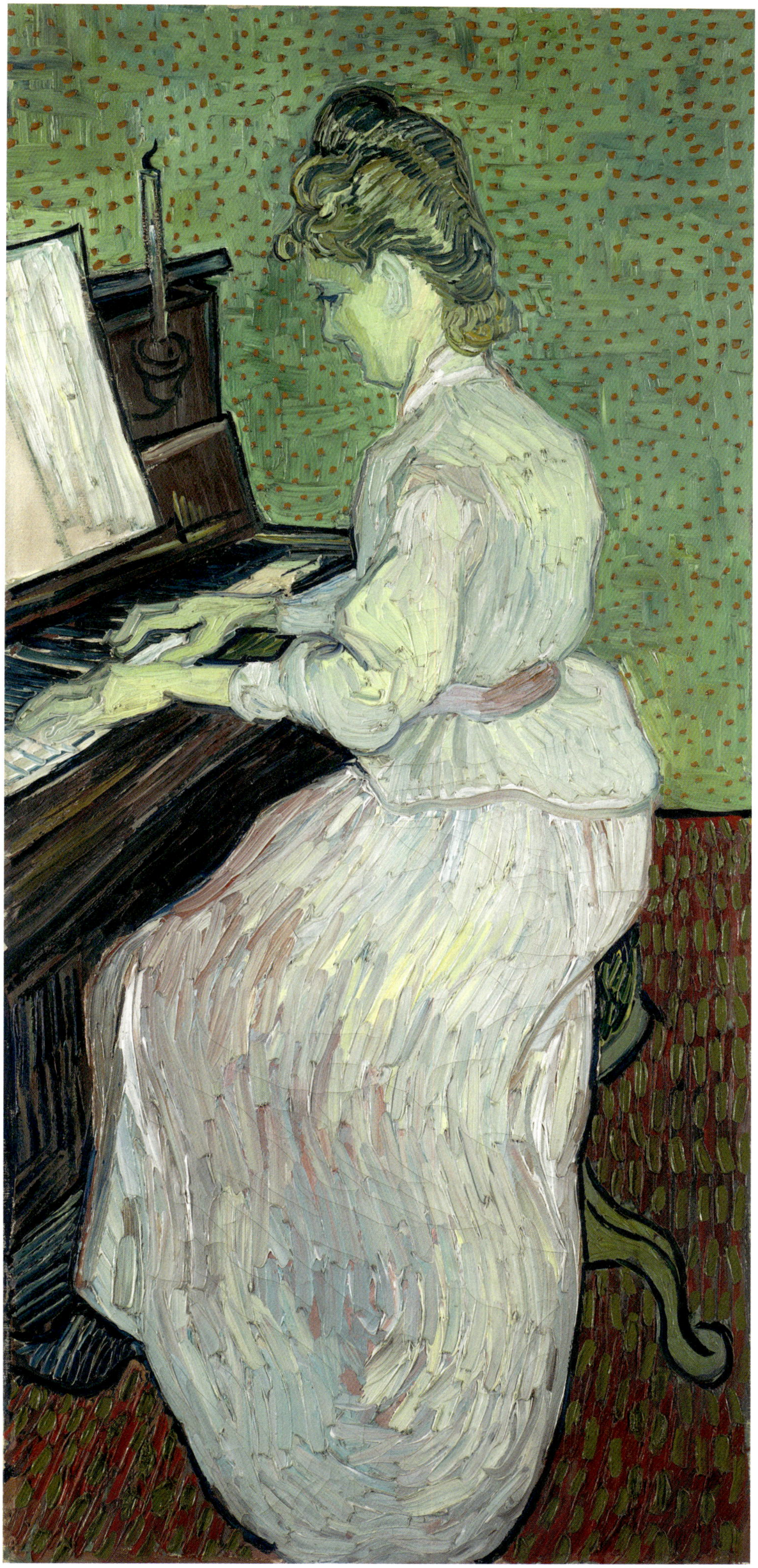

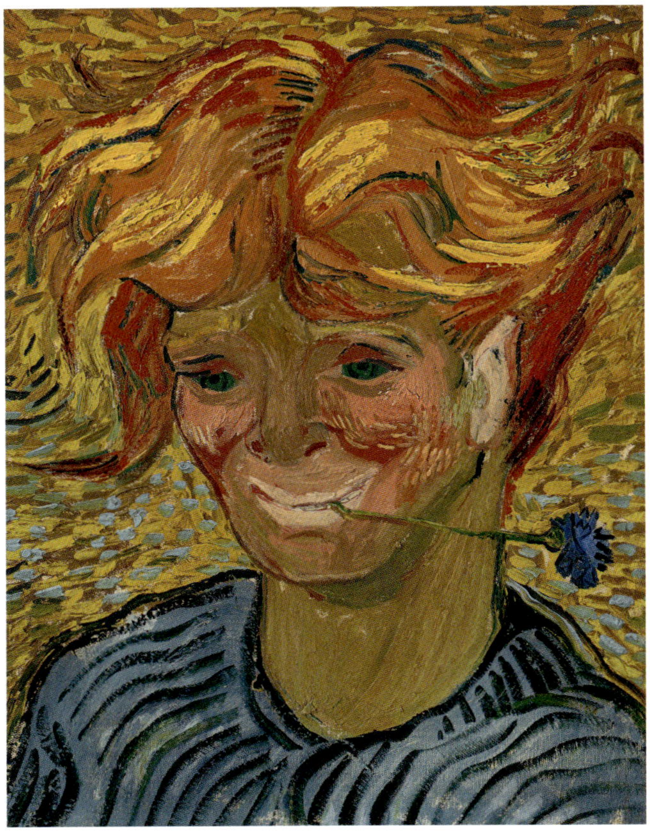

131 (#59)
Vincent van Gogh
Young Man with Cornflower, 1890
Oil on canvas, 39 × 30.5 cm
Private collection

of green tones, 'which would by its vibration make one think of the soft sound of the ears swaying in the breeze'.[55] The wheat in his portrait of the peasant girl is ripe and yellow, with a few cursorily indicated poppies in between, which did not result in a soft colour effect as in his study of ears of wheat **(123)** but in a strong yellow-blue contrast that evokes the summer heat. Having completed this large painting with the model in front of him, Van Gogh made a second, smaller portrait based on the first, where he reused the pose but lengthened the body and arms so that the girl is shown standing in front of the wheat, which is light green in this instance and forms a softer contrast with her white dress with pink dots **(122)**.

In addition to the two paintings of the peasant girl against decorative backdrops of wheat, Van Gogh produced several smaller portraits, presumably on the rainy days between 30 June and 5 July, including an intriguing caricature-like head of a young man with a cornflower in his grinning mouth and a wild mop of blond hair against a background the colour of ripe wheat **(131)**. With his sunburnt face, the boy stands for the glory of rural life, just as the peasant girl had done. The portrait does not appear to have been painted from a model and shows a curious resemblance to Van Gogh's drawings of the Egyptian-looking head he encountered on a gate in Auvers **(23, 106, 107)** – an image of times long past, which plainly fascinated him.[56]

There are three more portraits from this period, lastly, with small children painted in a square format: *Child with Orange* **(132)** and *Two Girls*, the latter in two versions **(133, 134)**. Van Gogh was convinced that children grew up much better in the countryside and ever since his arrival in Auvers he had been urging Theo and Jo to visit often, noting that 'the children here look well in the healthy fresh air' and that this environment with 'children, animals, flowers and good air' would benefit little Vincent.[57] He was keen to convey this idea in his portraits of happy, rosy-cheeked children against a background of rustic houses with thatched roofs and a meadow full of flowers. Adeline Ravoux stated that the toddler with an orange **(132)** was the two-year-old son of their neighbour Vincent Levert, the carpenter who, tragically, would be called on just a few weeks later to make Van Gogh's coffin.[58] According to Gustave Coquiot, who presumably had it from Gachet Jr, the two girls in the double portrait were the daughters of the signalman at a railway crossing.

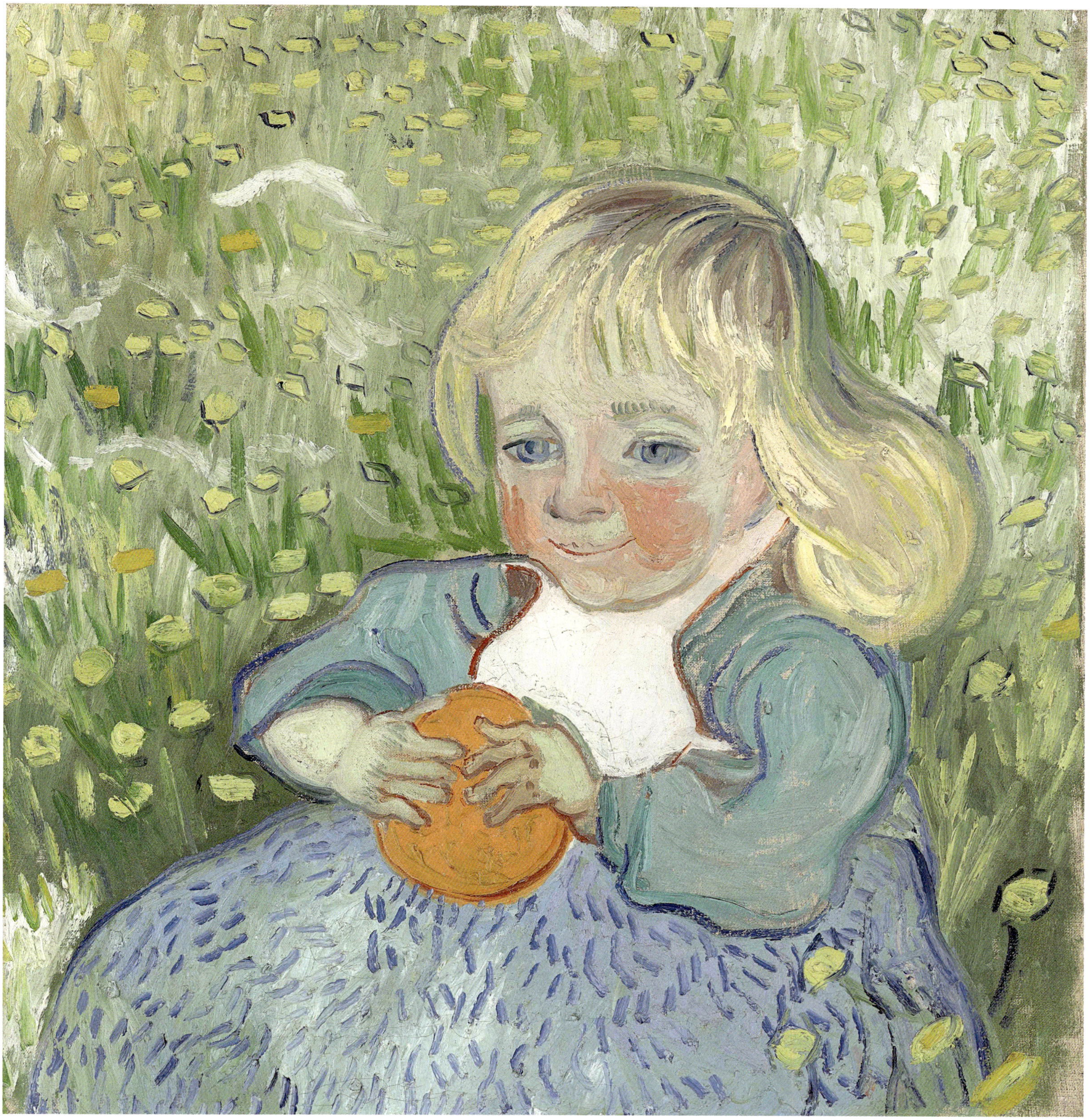

132 (#52)
Vincent van Gogh
Child with Orange, 1890
Oil on canvas, 50 × 51 cm
Private collection

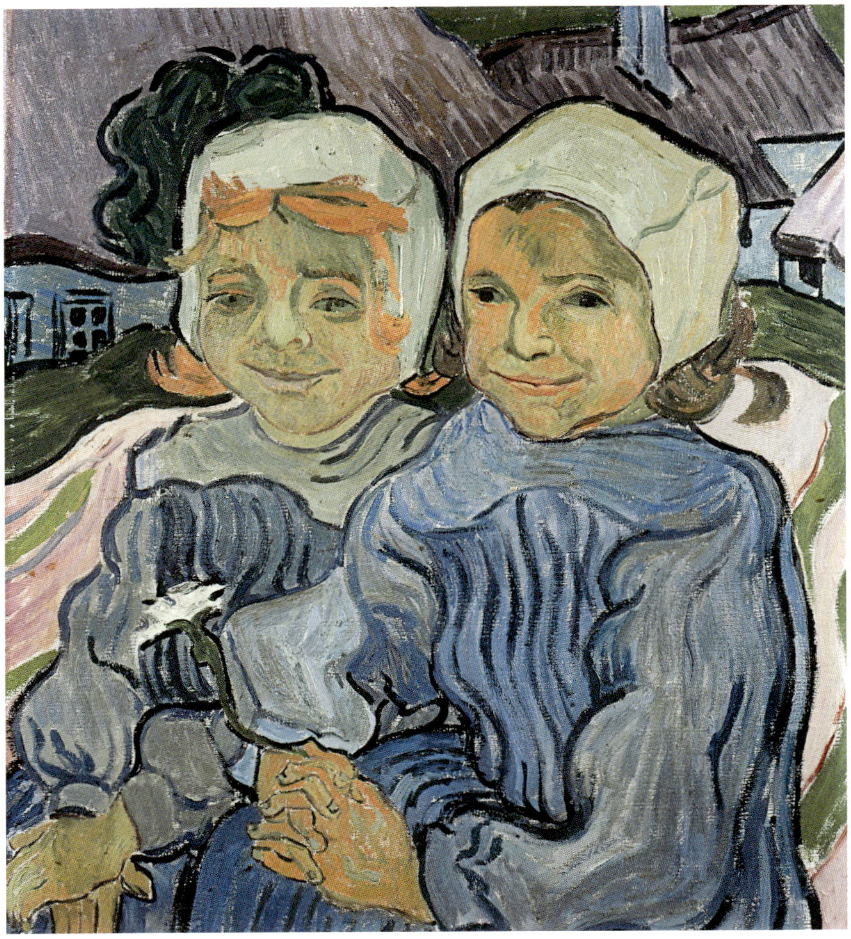

133 (#56)
Vincent van Gogh
Two Girls, 1890
Oil on canvas, 51.5 × 46.5 cm
Private collection

Further information regarding their identification is, however, lacking.[59]

The cosy cottages in the background, which Van Gogh based on studies he had made in situ **(43, 44)**, together with the flower held by the girl shown nearest the front, lends weight to the image of salutary country life, just as the orange and the richly flowering meadow did in the other portrait. Van Gogh painted *Child with Orange* and the first version of *Two Girls* **(133)** not to give away but to keep for himself and for Theo and Jo, in whose possession they ended up after his death. The second double portrait **(134)** found its way into Doctor Gachet's collection, where it was admired in 1894 by the artist Joseph Delattre: 'I saw quite a few very interesting Van Goghs at his home: I was particularly taken with several landscapes and two children in the open air. Because of the fine rendering of the expression.'[60]

With a few exceptions, Van Gogh only painted young women and children in Auvers, and there are many examples of them in his sketchbook too. They are an illustration of something he missed more than ever: the love of a wife, a family. Although he had long since resigned himself to this vacuum in his existence, it was still painful to him. What's more, he became acutely aware after moving to Auvers that there was now less room for him in his brother's life – a brother who possessed what he himself had been denied. 'For me, life might well remain solitary,' he wrote to his mother. Having children was 'the most natural and best thing', but, failing that, producing paintings was 'the only tie that links the past and the present for me'.[61] Regarding Theo and his family, he confided to his mother that it was 'a very reassuring feeling for me to be more in their vicinity again'. His yearning for connection and family had driven him back north, but he still saw very little of them even now he lived closer. Vincent continued to insist that they come to Auvers more often, while the house he wanted to rent as a home and studio also needed to be a place, above all, where they could all be together.

Viewed in this light, his paintings of happy, well-nourished children and young people glowing with health and zest for life, with tanned faces and rosy cheeks, were stand-ins for the outdoor portraits he wanted to make of Theo, Jo and little Vincent. Perhaps he painted these canvases in the hope of hanging them in the dreamed-for country house the young family would visit as respite from the hectic life of Paris. Like the magisterial, expansive landscapes he created in his final weeks, the portraits were intended to convey to Theo and Jo just how 'healthy and fortifying' he found the countryside.[62]

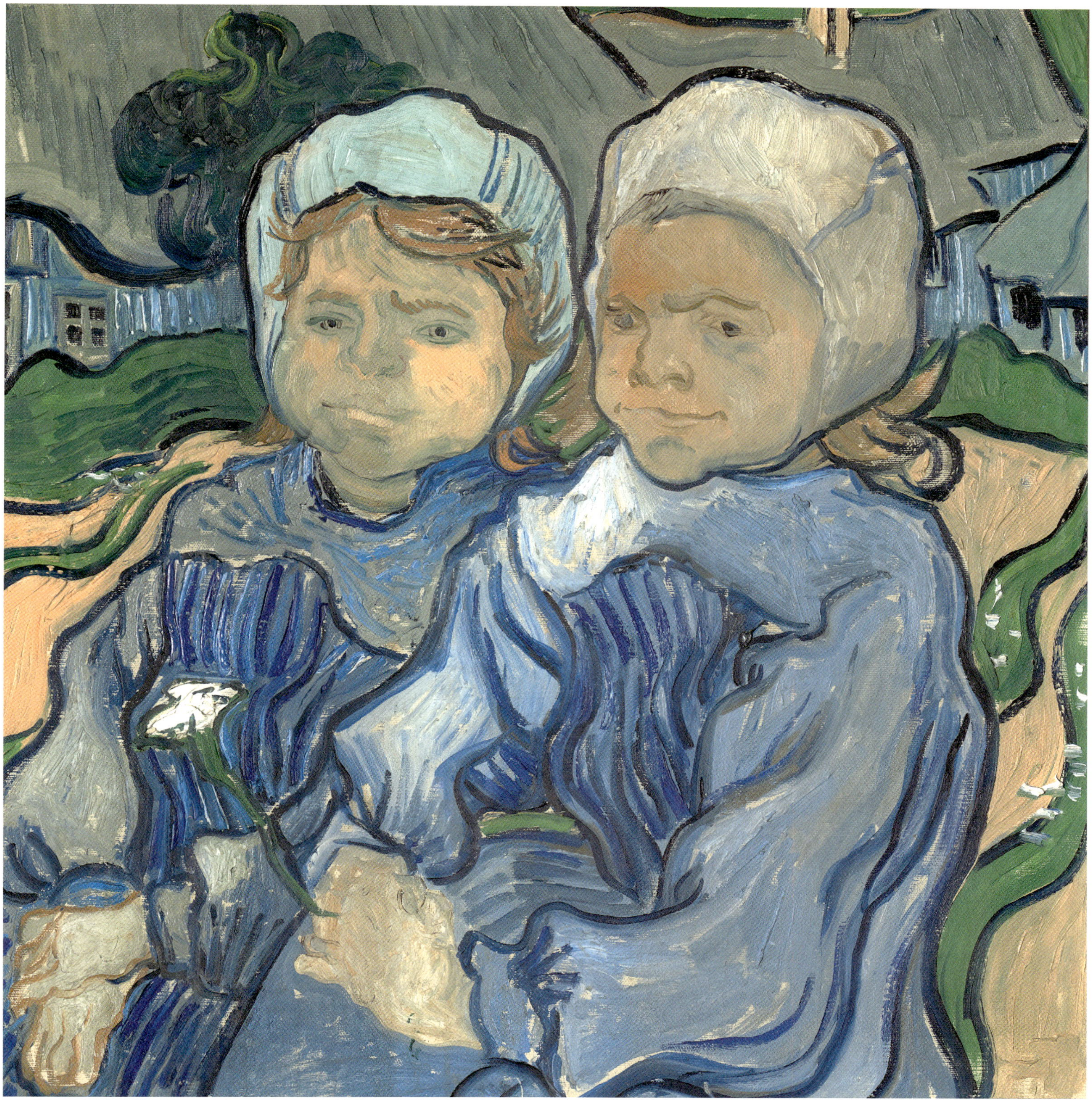

134 (#57)
Vincent van Gogh
Two Girls, 1890
Oil on canvas, 51.2 × 51 cm
Musée d'Orsay, Paris

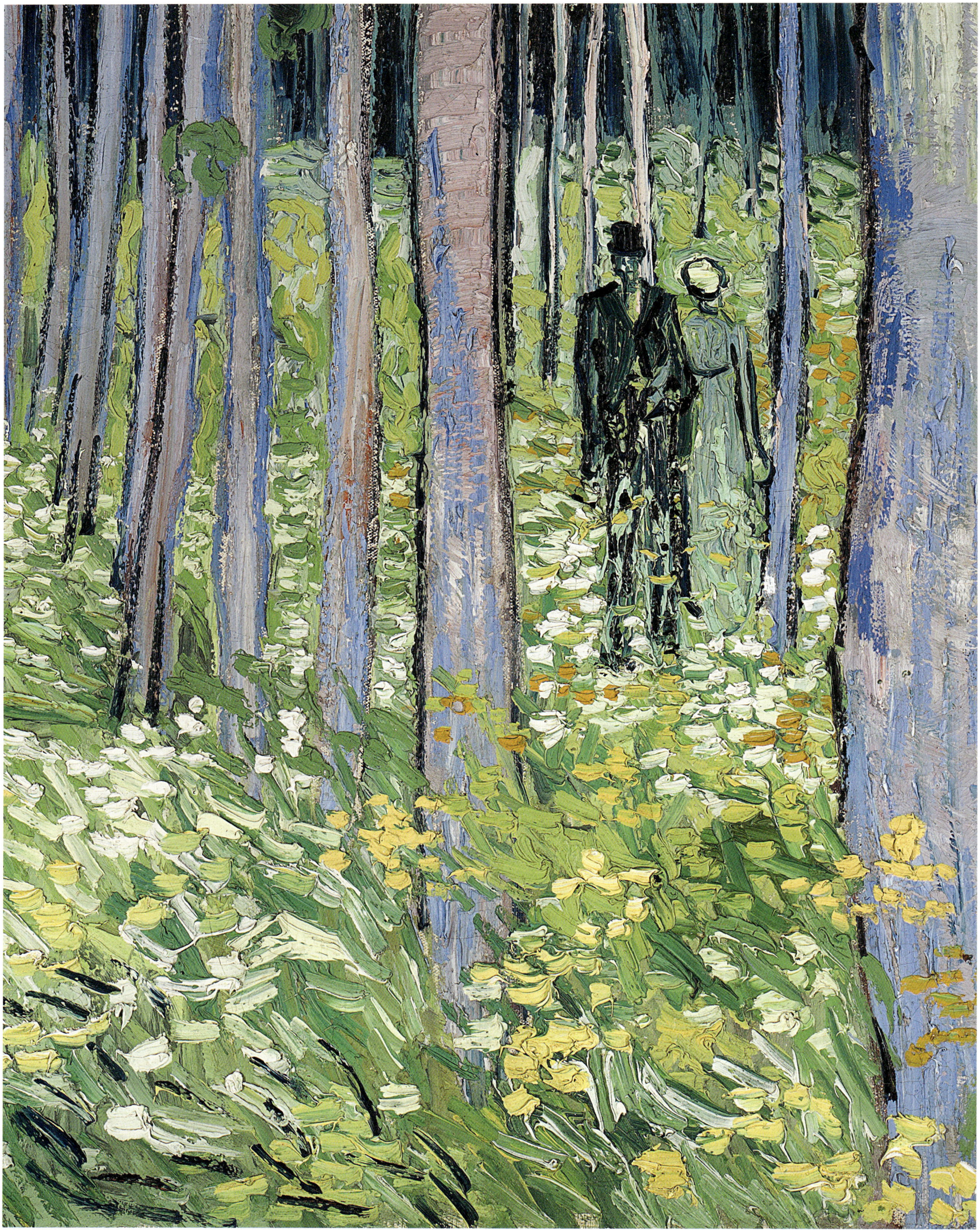

ON THE THRESHOLD OF A 'NEW PAINTING'

THE DOUBLE-SQUARE WORKS

EMMANUEL COQUERY

Among the seventy-four paintings from Auvers, thirteen stand out – twelve landscapes and one portrait – for their elongated double-square format and dimensions of 50 × 100 cm, unique in Van Gogh's work. The artist himself specifies the format twice: 'a canvas one metre long by only 50 centimetres high'; 'It's 1 metre high and 50 wide'.[1] This indication of numerical measurement, almost unique in the correspondence, is notable because of its round figures, unusual in canvas formats, and its display of geometrical intention. By emphasizing that it was 'only' 50 cm high, Van Gogh seems perfectly conscious, and even proud, of the audacious form that makes the painting a remarkable *object* in itself.

This was not a standard commercial format, but one chosen by the artist. Technical analysis has shown that the canvases of these double squares come from two different rolls, each with its own primer, received by Van Gogh in Auvers on 17 June.[2] From a roll about 210 cm wide, he cut his canvases to the desired height of half a metre, with the exception of *Fields near Auvers-sur-Oise* **(135)**, which is cut lengthwise along the roll, indicating a positive desire to keep to this format, rather than a simple practical contingency.

In his letters Van Gogh mentions no fewer than eight of the thirteen double squares, which makes it possible to follow their creation over more than a month, from 20 June to the last day of his life. This is not a continuous sequence, painted in a creative rush, but a special project, a carefully thought-out exploration interrupted, returned to, and progressively deepened.

These canvases with their identical format are striking for their variety of subjects, treatments and references, and this raises a question that has never really been resolved: what was the plan behind such an ensemble?[3] In particular, what interpretative weight should be attributed to biographical data, given that these paintings were created in the last month of his life, amid the acute anxieties he had in July, until his self-imposed death?

THE THIRTEEN PAINTINGS IN THE OEUVRE FROM AUVERS

When Van Gogh arrived in Auvers, he seemed more than ever driven by an artistic project. On 25 May he wrote to Theo: 'Paintings vaguely *present themselves to my sight* which it will take time to shape, but that will come little by little.'[4] The 'gravely beautiful'[5]

Vincent van Gogh
Undergrowth with Two Figures, 1890
Detail of 156 (#46)

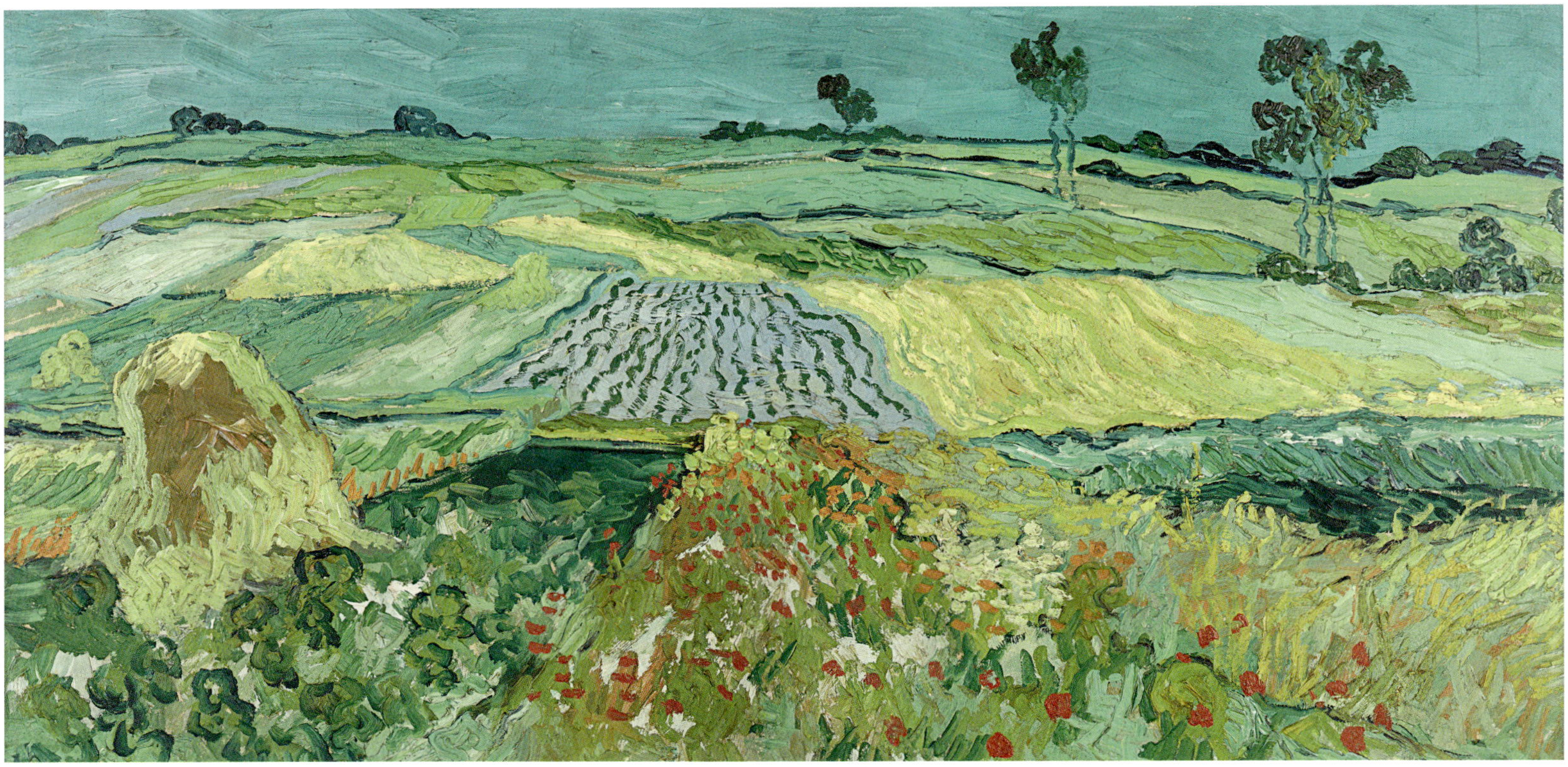

135 (#47)
Vincent van Gogh
Fields near Auvers-sur-Oise, 1890
Oil on canvas, 50 × 101 cm
Belvedere Museum, Vienna

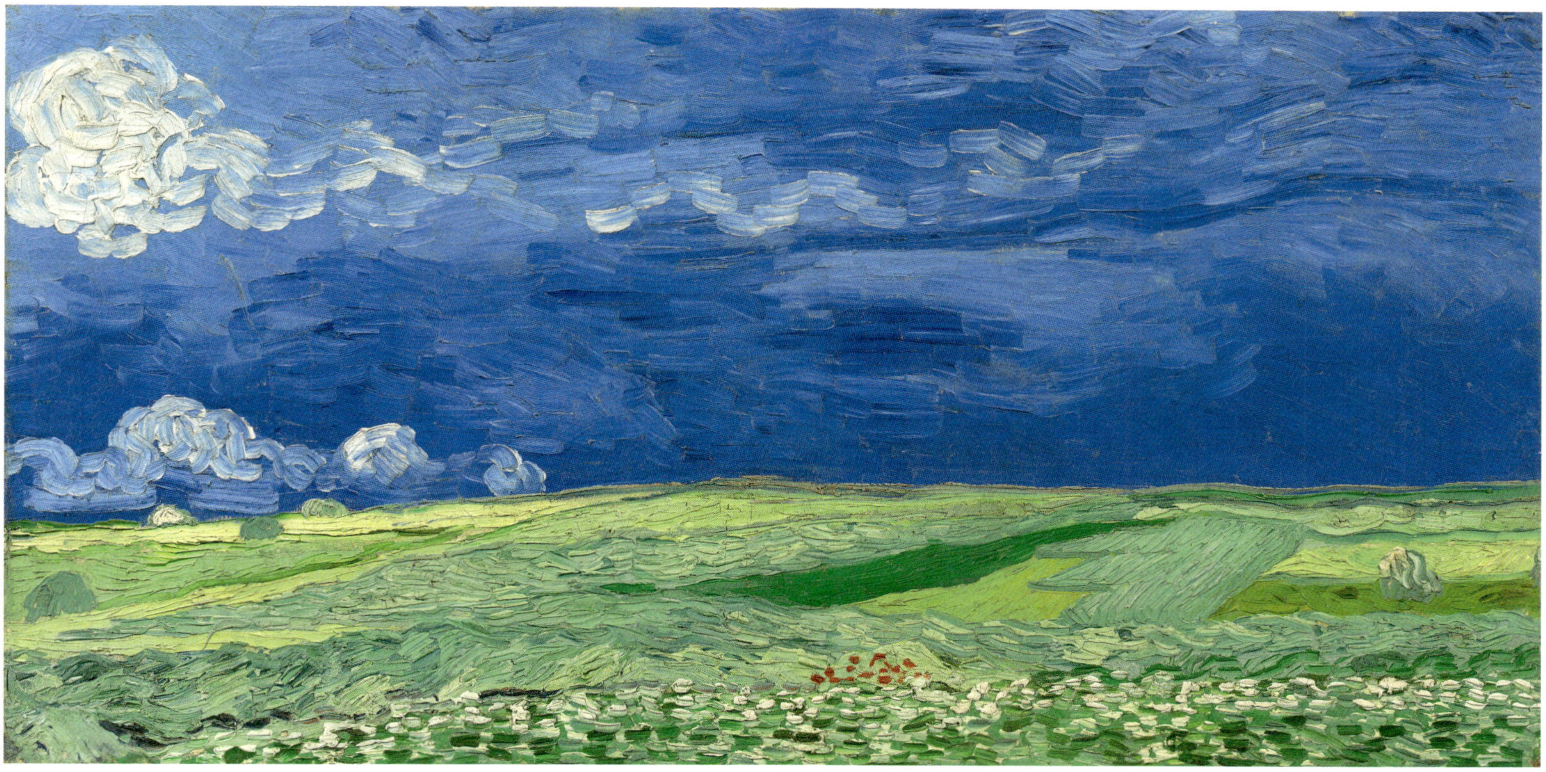

136 (#61)
Vincent van Gogh
Wheatfield under Thunderclouds, 1890
Oil on canvas, 50.4 × 101.3 cm
Van Gogh Museum, Amsterdam

village offered him many 'motifs' – subjects to paint. Van Gogh's usual way of working was to 'disentangle'[6] these motifs in nature, to bring out their 'intimate character' – for 'one can't paint as one sees'.[7]

Fields near Auvers-sur-Oise **(135)**, a landscape 'like one of [Georges] Michel's',[8] is striking for its spatial depth, with its artificially exaggerated perspective due to the receding, zigzag lines of the fields, but also because of the absence of any human figure. The high horizon is no more than a narrow strip of sky whose turquoise colour merges with that of the fields, reinforcing the illusion of an infinite space enlivened and further drawn out by the long, undulating, fluid and quivering brushstrokes. Aware of the flattening effect that accentuates this receding perspective, Van Gogh referred to the work as 'a canvas one metre long by *only* 50 centimetres high'.[9]

The squarer format of *Wheatfields after the Rain (The Plain of Auvers-sur-Oise)* **(67)**, painted a month later from the same spot, but with a much wider and bluer strip of sky, clearly shows the energizing effect of the elongated format in this quest for depth. In a comparison of the two paintings, the variations in the vanishing lines of the fields, as well as their visual implausibility, testify to Van Gogh's concern with animating that flat surface, at the expense of an exact depiction of reality.

Undergrowth with Two Figures **(156)** is one of the most unusual compositions in the series.[10] The artist describes it as 'undergrowth, lilac trunks of poplars, and underneath them some flower-dotted grass, pink, yellow, white and various greens'.[11] No horizon here, rather a closed space punctuated by the hypnotic rows of poplars with their uncertain vanishing lines; and in the foreground a trunk that is abnormally large compared to the others, designed to intensify the perspective. The geometry of the trunks, emphasized by strong black outlines, contrasts with the vigorous profusion of grasses and flowers, more thickly painted and hardly credible as undergrowth.

Strangely, Van Gogh does not mention the ghostly, frontally rendered couple, and the uncertainty of scale as they seem to float between the trunks and the waist-high grass that sprinkles their Sunday clothes. The pair – especially the man who wears a kind of top hat – resembles a bridal couple who have strayed too far from a church square. It represents the last instance of the loving-couple motif that pervades the artist's oeuvre like a poignant regret.

In its haunting geometry this painting can be read as a reinterpretation of the orchard in Pierre Puvis de Chavannes's great work, *Inter artes et naturam (Between Art and Nature)* **(153)**, but it also recalls Bernard's *Madeleine in the Bois d'Amour*, of which Van Gogh had made a highly interpretative sketch.[12]

The third elongated format is *Landscape at Twilight* **(138)**. Described as 'a night effect – two completely dark pear trees against yellowing sky with wheatfields, and in the violet background the castle encased in the dark greenery',[13] it has no more of an equivalent in Van Gogh's Auvers oeuvre than its predecessor. The unusual eye-level viewpoint divides earth and sky into two contrasting, but proportionately balanced, horizontal halves, 'dark against sky', making it the most stable composition of the series, with its volumes well-defined by dark contours. The short, homogeneous brushstrokes contribute to this 'effect' of quivering twilight, whose yellow sky, like the wheat, evokes memories of Saint-Rémy.[14]

Painted about a week later, *Marguerite Gachet at the Piano* **(130)** is sketched in a letter **(129)** in which the painter succinctly describes the canvas in terms of its elements and colours, emphasizing the format: 'The dress is pink. The wall in the background green with orange spots, the carpet red with green spots, the piano dark violet. It's 1 metre high and 50 [centimetres] wide.'[15] Here again, in this four-part invention (dress/wall/carpet/piano, each with its own specific brushwork), the space is imaginary, with a perspective that is reinforced by the piano, in contrast with the wall in the background, as well as the frontally rendered carpet and the skirt, which is generously spread across the picture surface. The variation in the brushstrokes, specific to each zone, contributes even more to the extraordinary animation of this rather static motif. The detail of the extinguished candle with its long black wick is a traditional symbol of mortality. As has often been noted, *Marguerite Gachet at the Piano* interacts at a distance with a painting made the same year by Van Gogh's friend Henri de Toulouse-Lautrec – *Mademoiselle Dihau au piano* (Musée Toulouse-

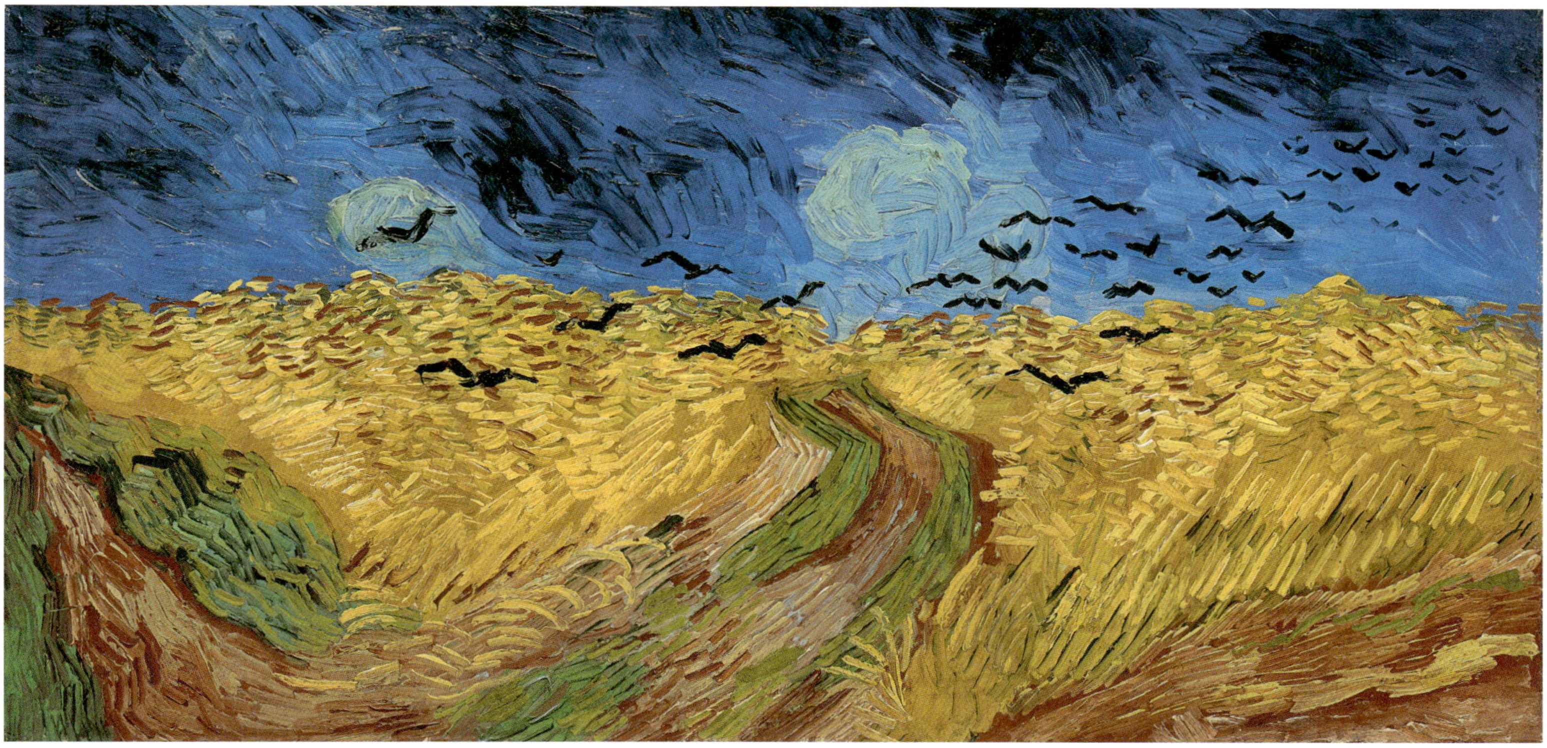

137 (#60)
Vincent van Gogh
Wheatfield with Crows, 1890
Oil on canvas, 50.5 × 103 cm
Van Gogh Museum, Amsterdam

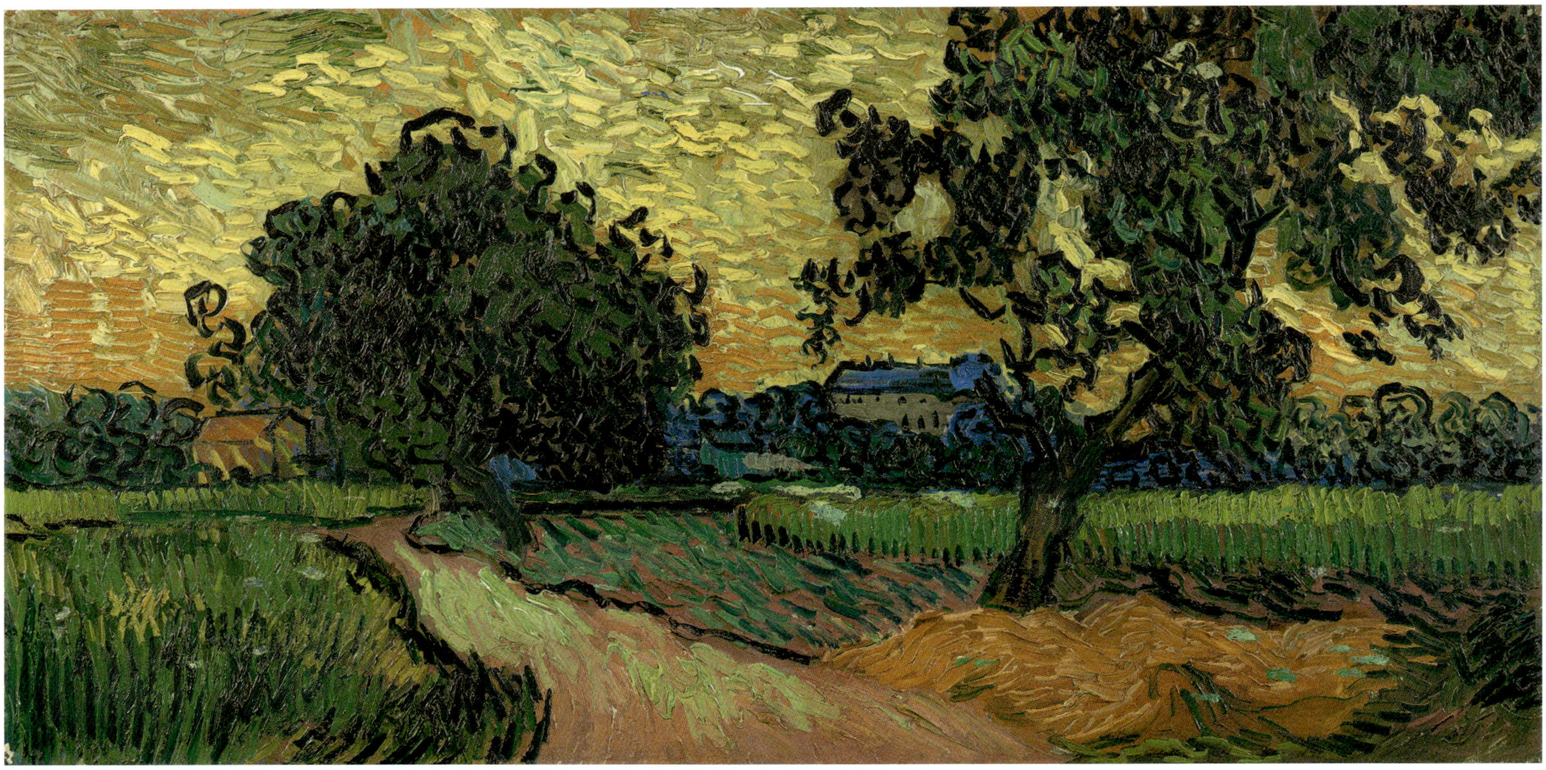

138 (#45)
Vincent van Gogh
Landscape at Twilight, 1890
Oil on canvas, 50.2 × 101 cm
Van Gogh Museum, Amsterdam

Lautrec, Albi) – which Theo had mentioned to Vincent in a letter.[16]

Around 10 July, Van Gogh wrote about a new series of three canvases, explaining their ambivalent emotional intent which sets them apart: 'knowing clearly what I wanted I've painted another three large canvases since then. They're immense stretches of wheatfields under turbulent skies, and I made a point of trying to express *sadness*, *extreme loneliness*. You'll see this soon, I hope – for I hope to bring them to you in Paris as soon as possible, since I'd almost believe that these canvases will tell you what I can't say in words, what I consider *healthy and fortifying* about the countryside.'[17]

The famous *Wheatfield with Crows* **(137)**, painted around 8 July, is the most eloquent example of this concern with sadness and loneliness, with its space reduced entirely to the picture plane and given depth only by the junction of three winding paths. This perspective with a double (or triple) vanishing point – pre-Renaissance, in the style of Giotto – gives a fragmented, 'primitive' character to the space, which is enlivened by the long brushstrokes, sometimes straight, sometimes broken, the double circumflexes of the crows merging with those of the sky and the wheat, but also that of the central path, in an interplay of multiple echoes and an effect of cosmic amplification, from earth to sky. The composition is tensioned by marked contrasts of yellow-dark blue and green-red, whose juxtaposition in homogeneous masses underpins the power of this turbulence, devoid of human presence.

The crows are drawn from works by Jean-François Millet and Charles-François Daubigny, as Van Gogh had already indicated long before: 'hosts of crows, famous from the paintings of Daubigny and Millet'.[18] The most direct reference is an engraving by Millet showing a field invaded by crows, of which Van Gogh had made a painting in January 1890 **(163)**.

The second canvas is *Wheatfield under Thunderclouds* **(136)**, which has the same simple composition in two broad, straight bands. This is the most austere of the double squares and the only one giving a predominant role to the sky, which is enlivened with heavy impasto and broad, lush brushstrokes. It contrasts with the previous work with its apparent calm and chromatic unity, although here too the space is compressed by the lines of the fields receding to the right and the trail of clouds building up on the left, further accentuating the elongation of the landscape, an effect enhanced by the long bands of the foreground.

The third canvas, *Daubigny's Garden* **(139)**, is characterized by a frontality defined by the lines of the buildings. It is, says Van Gogh, 'a painting I'd been *thinking* about ever since I've been here'[19] and which he had been talking about since mid-June: 'I have an idea for doing a more important canvas of Daubigny's house and garden, of which I already have a small study.'[20] He made two versions, the sole case in this group of thirteen double squares. The second version **(140)**, executed two weeks later, which he described as 'one of my most *deliberate* canvases'[21] is explained by Van Gogh's desire to give it to Daubigny's widow, who had welcomed him into her house. The first version is titled on the canvas – a unique occurrence in his works from Auvers – a sign of his intention to exhibit the work and to pay tribute to a painter he admired. The two canvases are in fact the most complex of the series in their synthesis of very different motifs and raised and receding planes accentuated with oblique lines that tilt the space of the garden, while adhering to a 'calm' structure of small brushstrokes.

The study of the painting mentioned by Van Gogh, executed in a more subdued Impressionist style, is a square painted on a household cloth **(141)**, of which a sketch in the Auvers notebook gives the general idea of two intersecting diagonals.[22] To these three canvases should be added the *Garden in Auvers-sur-Oise* **(142)**, whose central rose bed is unmistakably the same one as in the two elongated canvases. Van Gogh uses close-up to depict a concentrated space, animated by an interplay of curves and masses with clearly defined contours, and by the effervescence of a distinctly dotted brushstroke, reminiscent of his Neo-Impressionist experiments.

Together, these four paintings make us aware of the spatial distortions imposed by Van Gogh, even in the case of a supposedly recognizable, well-identified place. As Pickvance points out, the actual viewpoint cannot offer a view of the façade and the church together, a church without a transept, which

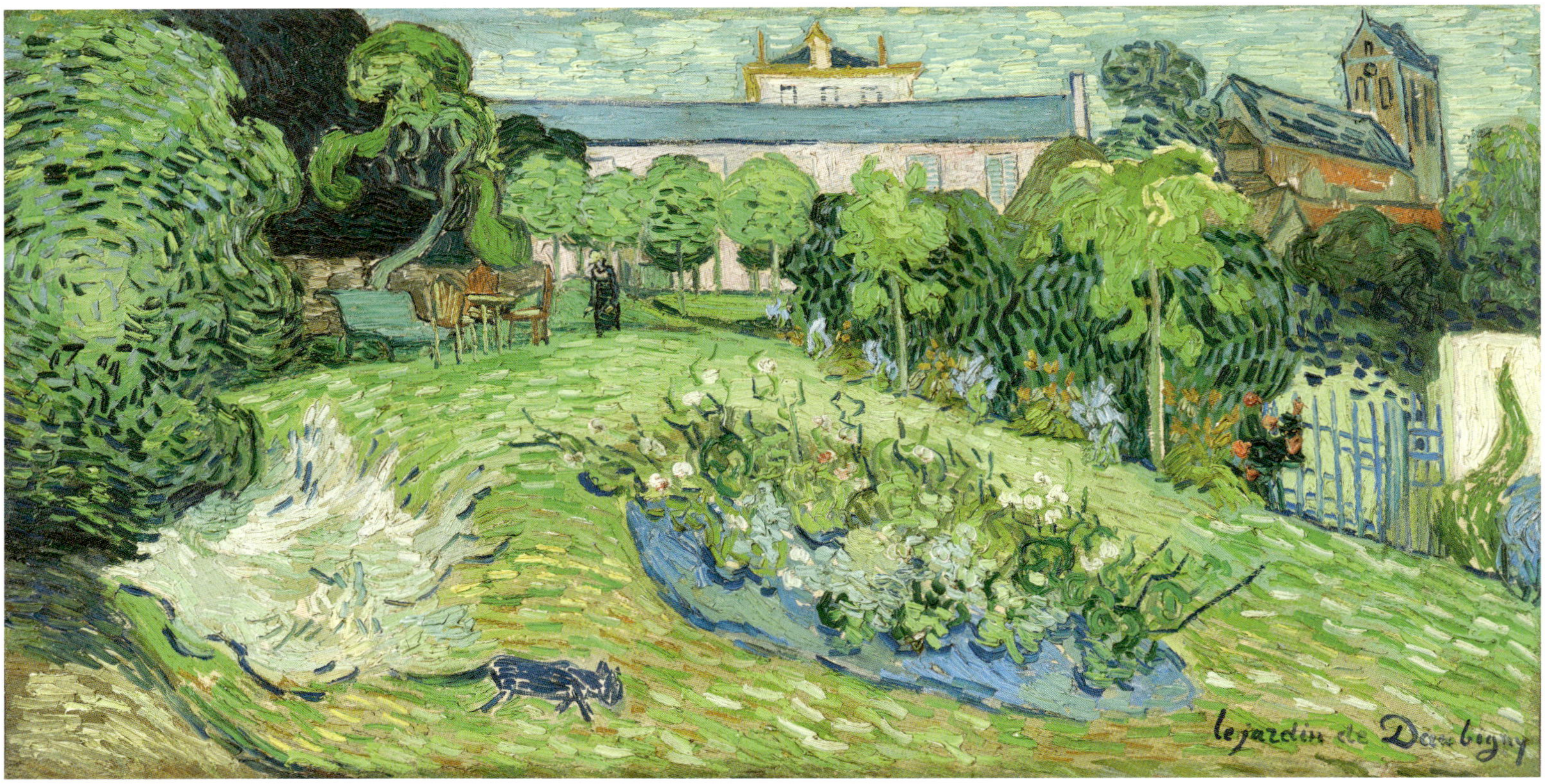

139 (#62)
Vincent van Gogh
Daubigny's Garden, 1890
Oil on canvas, 56 × 101.5 cm
Rudolf Staechelin Collection

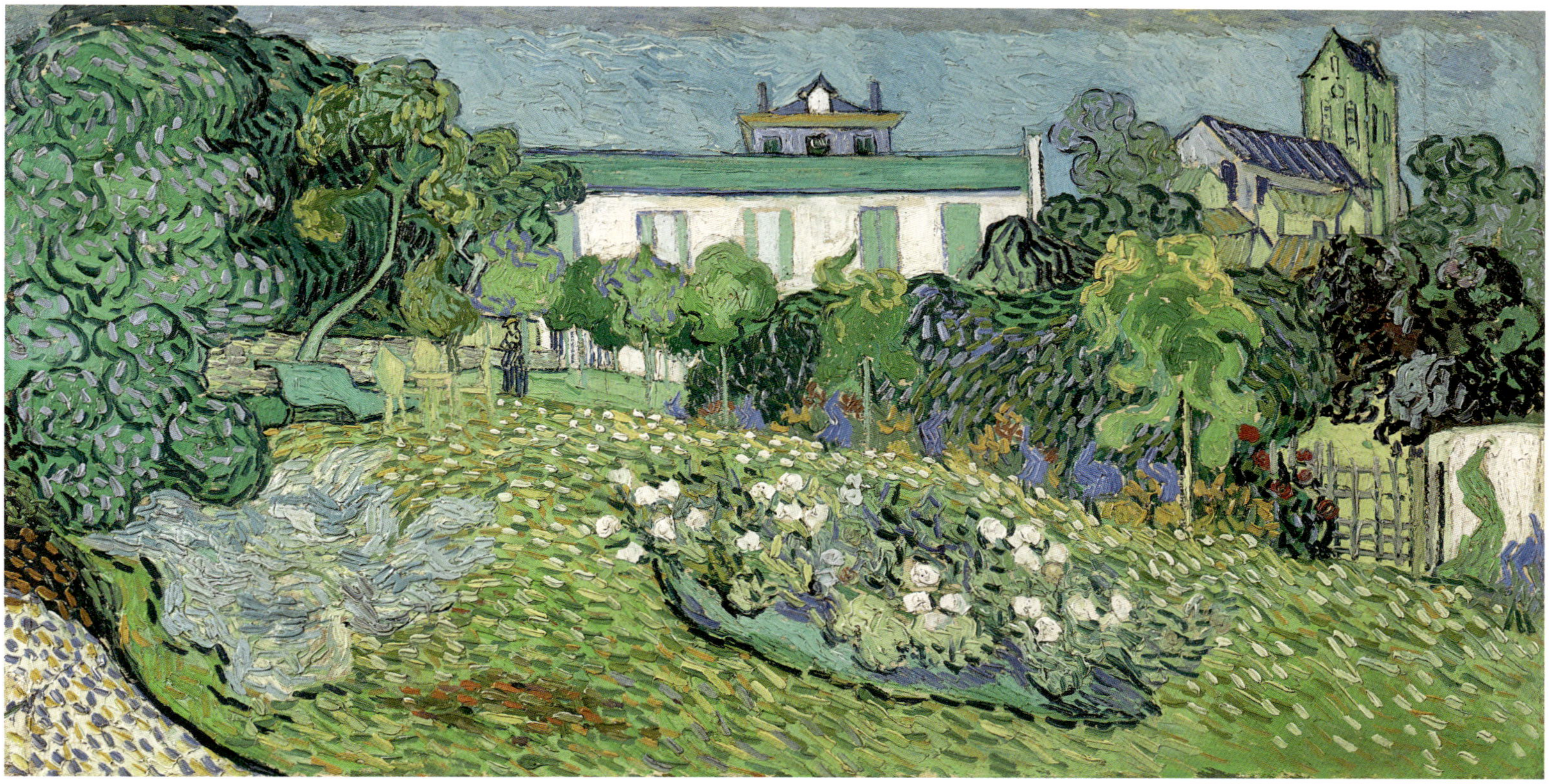

140 (#72)
Vincent van Gogh
Daubigny's Garden, 1890
Oil on canvas, 53.2 × 103.5 cm
Hiroshima Museum of Art

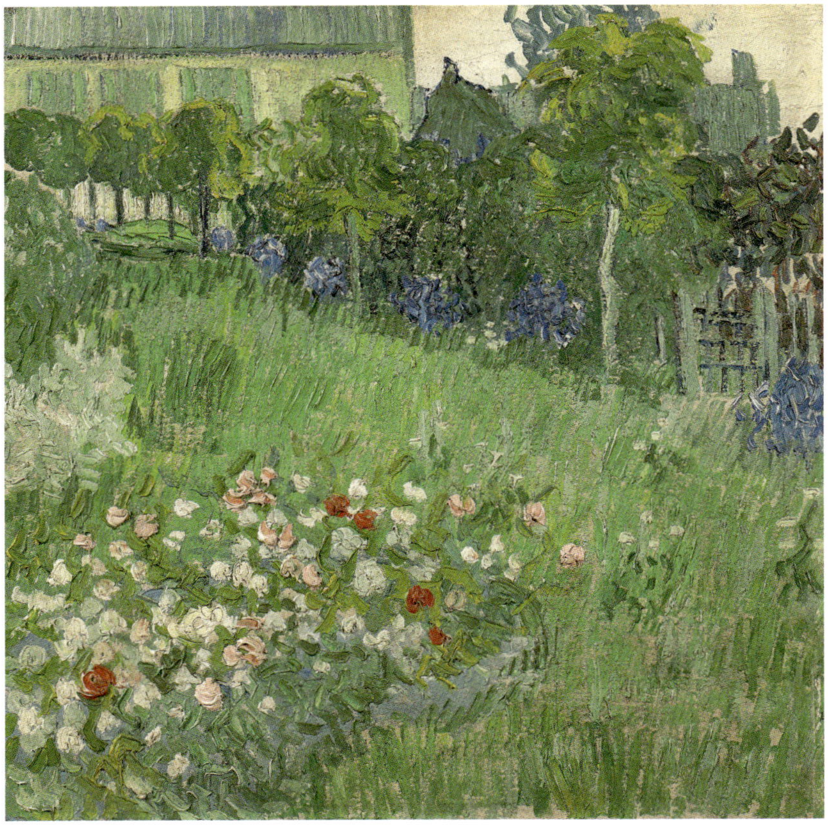

141 (#37)
Vincent van Gogh
Daubigny's Garden, 1890
Oil on *torchon*, 51 × 51.2 cm
Van Gogh Museum, Amsterdam

seems to be there to symbolically locate the place.[23] The difference in the proportions of the façade in the two versions shows the artist's casual attitude towards the real. For him, the essence lies elsewhere, in the freedom to recompose reality, right up to the provocative simplification of the black cat in the first version of *Daubigny's Garden* **(139)**, portrayed 'primitively' as in a child's drawing.

Sheaves of Wheat **(146)** is not mentioned in the correspondence and must date from mid-July, the harvest being done. As in *Undergrowth with Two Figures*, the horizonless space is defined by the close-up effect and a rising valley, punctuated by the repeated, crossed diagonals motif. The comparison with a large drawing on the same subject **(111)**, viewed at eye level, clearly shows the distortion caused by an artificially heightened viewpoint, which makes it possible to delimit the space and focus on the contrast between the yellow and the violet (turned blue through the fading of the red) of the straw and its shadow, just as it accounts for the markedly graphic style, with its regular, cross-hatched, pencil-like brushstrokes. The sweeping, light blue-violet shadows, applied with no optical logic, refute any illusionistic play of light.

Through its subject, this painting enters into a dialogue with a number 30 canvas, *Wheatfields with Reaper, Auvers-sur-Oise* **(14)**, which may have been made earlier, since the wheat is still being harvested, but in an unrealistic way, as large sheaves are already piled up. The bird's-eye view is imaginary, allowing Van Gogh to spread a wide expanse of yellow below, as in some of the paintings he made from the window of his upstairs room at the asylum in Saint-Rémy.

Field with Haystacks **(143)** can only be related to the drawing *Haystacks* (Whitworth Art Gallery, Manchester) that probably shows the same two haystacks from another viewpoint crossed by a rising diagonal, a method used for *Wheatfield with Cornflowers* **(144)** and especially *Green Wheatfields* **(11)**, which play on the folded-down plan by distinguishing clearly demarcated areas of colour. Here the elongated format merges these areas by compressing them, but they are rendered extraordinarily vivid by very varied brush- work, in horseshoe-shaped or straight strokes, ranging from green to yellow, with dark and light values equally present in the sky and in the landscape itself.

This work is perhaps reminiscent of Delacroix's Rubens-style landscapes, such as the one in the

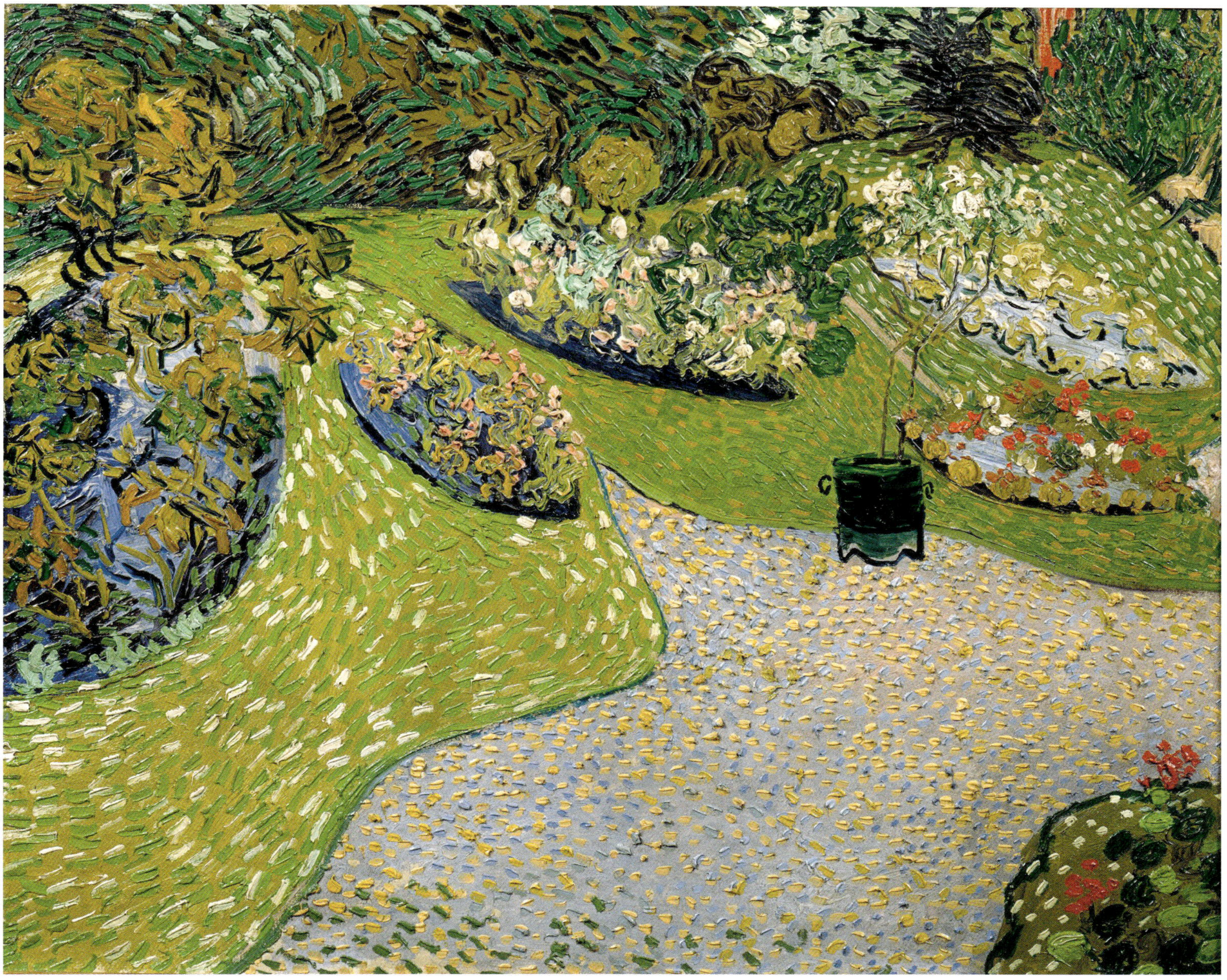

142 (#42)
Vincent van Gogh
Garden in Auvers-sur-Oise, 1890
Oil on canvas, 64 × 80 cm
Private collection

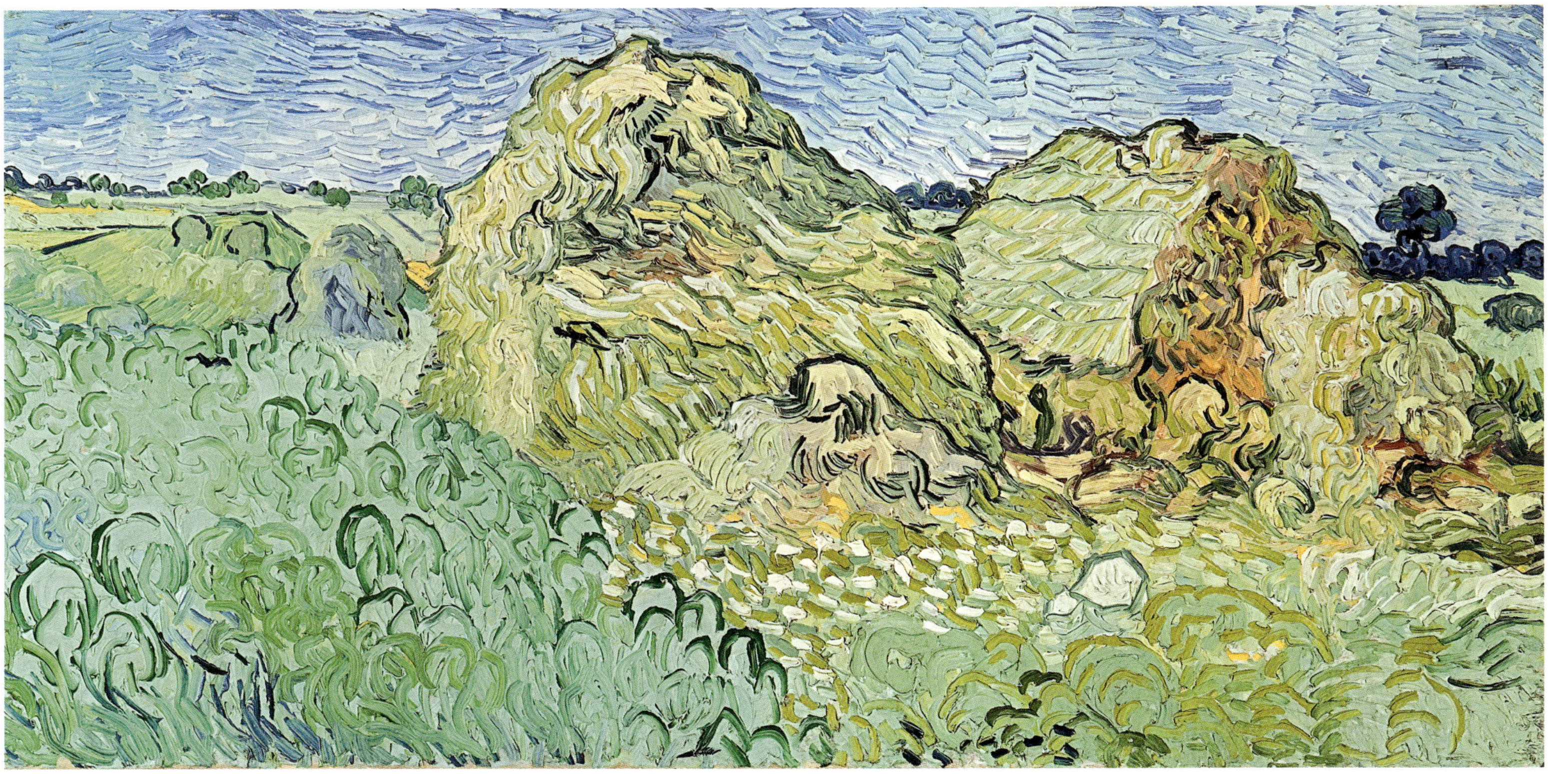

143 (#64)
Vincent van Gogh
Field with Haystacks, 1890
Oil on canvas, 50 × 100 cm
Fondation Beyeler, Riehen/Basel, Beyeler Collection

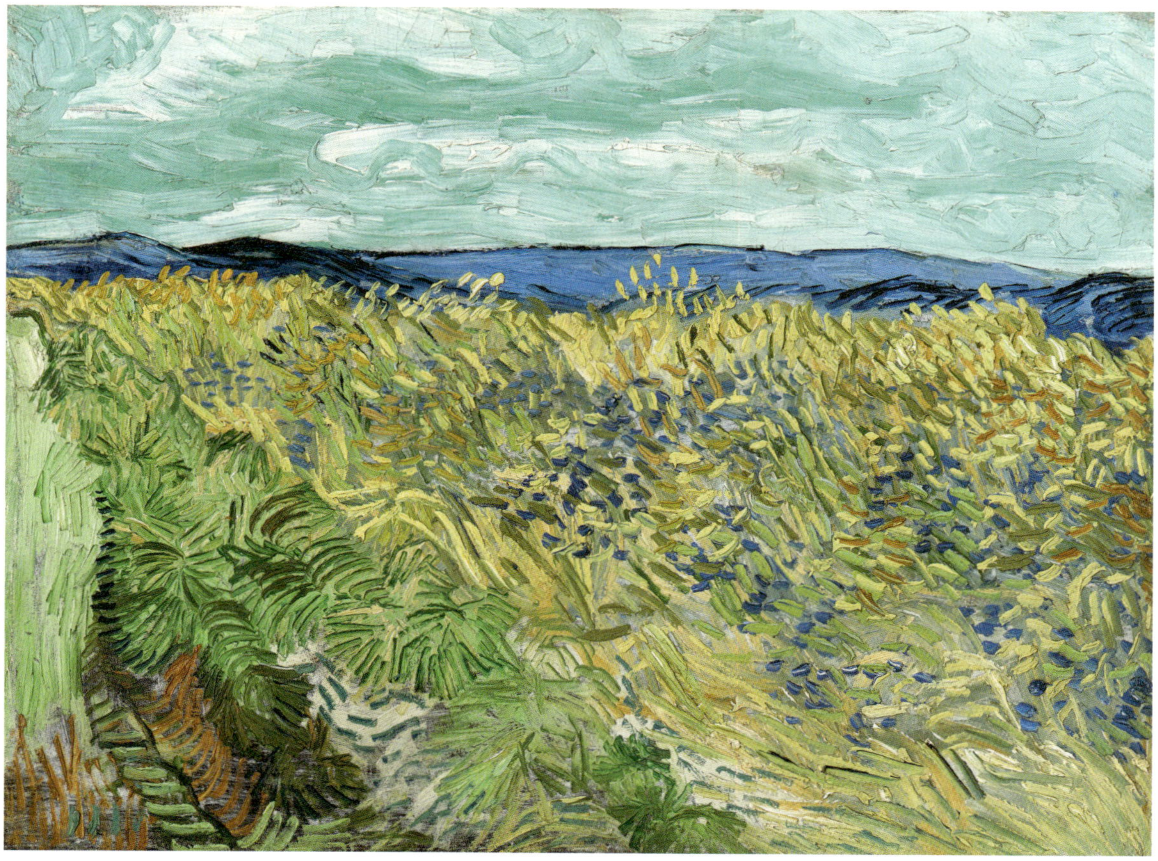

144 (#33)
Vincent van Gogh
Wheatfield with Cornflowers, 1890
Oil on canvas, 60 × 81 cm
Fondation Beyeler, Riehen/Basel, Beyeler Collection

background of *Jacob Wrestling with the Angel* (Church of Saint-Sulpice in Paris), admired and described by Van Gogh in wonderfully evocative terms: 'I dare urge you to believe that in landscapes one will continue to mass things by means of a drawing style that seeks to express the entanglement of the masses. Thus, do you remember Delacroix's landscape, Jacob's struggle with the angel?'[24]

This compositional principle can also be found in *Rain – Auvers-sur-Oise* **(145)**, here dated 18 July, with a shape in the left foreground that makes it similarly difficult to read the space: a mound or a flat area of farmland? Another view from above with a very high horizon, its colours reduced to just blue and yellow and the graphic effect created by the long streaks of rain lend the work the simplicity of a Japanese print. For Van Gogh, these prints evoked the motif of rain, which he had already depicted in *Bridge in the Rain (after Hiroshige)* (Van Gogh Museum, Amsterdam) and 'southernized' in Saint-Rémy in November 1889 in *Rain* (Philadelphia Museum of Art).

Rain – Auvers-sur-Oise also enters into a dialogue with a number 30 canvas, *Plain near Auvers-sur-Oise* **(68)**, probably painted at the same time, with the same bluish hue of rainy weather, and a contrast between a blue-green area in the foreground and the fields in the background.

Farms near Auvers-sur-Oise **(147)**, probably painted near Cordeville, is dated to the very end of the period, around 25–26 July, because of the clearly unfinished nature of the work and a note by Andries Bonger in 1891 referring to it as the 'last sketch'.[25] It is the only work in the series of which two small painted studies exist **(43, 44)**; they show, as confirmed by period photographs **(42)**, that Van Gogh started from real motifs. For the large format, he recomposed the whole by placing it in an open landscape and adding buildings in the background. With their completely separate perspective the latter do not fit well with the whole, while the building at the back right with the too-high roof blends strangely into the fields. The often sketchy brushstrokes, the unusually flat areas and the unworked sky indicate, among other things, that Van Gogh did not finish the landscape. Nevertheless, the painting remains fascinating because of the conversion of the studies, the attempt to compose a landscape with exaggerated relief, and the surprising blue-violet accent in the façades, which is typical of his use of colour in that period.

We now know from an account by Bonger published in 1893 that 'the morning before his death [his suicide attempt], [Vincent] had painted an undergrowth, full of sun and life'. This relates to his last painting, *Tree Roots* **(157)**, which he made on 27 July.[26] This interlacing of bare roots on a hillside, powerfully outlined in deep dark blue, standing out in blue against the yellowish background of the earth and tightly framed like a photographer's close-up, adds up to an almost indecipherable composition, so nearly abstract that one struggles to recognize any natural motifs. For the last time, and more than elsewhere, Van Gogh energized a tangled space by chromatically contrasting violet (now turned blue) and yellow, light and dark tones, continuous contours and short brushstrokes. Paradoxically, it is also the image that can be most directly associated with a real location, recently identified by Wouter van der Veen from old postcards **(19)**.[27]

Women Crossing the Fields **(127)**, a work in oil on paper, can be added to the group of thirteen canvases due to its elongated format of 30 × 60 cm. It is possibly a study for an unrealized painting, prepared in no fewer than three canvases: two with figures **(122, 125)** and a landscape **(54)**. This would have been the sole instance in the Auvers series of a landscape with figures in the foreground, a combination that was never very easy for Van Gogh, which perhaps explains the absence of a finished version. Even so, it shows that the artist was ready to take new directions.

WHERE SOURCES INTERSECT

There are a few rare examples of extended formats in Van Gogh's oeuvre, but never of exactly this size. The longest ones are six paintings on the seasons and peasant life finished in September 1884, related to the decoration project for the goldsmith and amateur painter Antoon Hermans in Eindhoven; these constituted Van Gogh's only completed commission. These canvases are 67 × 126 cm, 66 × 150 cm and 70 × 170 cm.[28] In terms of size, only *Autumn Landscape at Dusk* (c. 53 × 93 cm), which Van Gogh painted in Nuenen in October 1885 **(148)**, comes close, although it does not have the exact format, of which *Landscape at Twilight* **(138)** seems reminiscent.

During his stay in The Hague in 1883, Van Gogh made drawings that he hoped to offer to the English designer and art dealer Daniel Cottier as decoration for the panelling of a chimney piece. He executed at least two large drawings of 'about 1 metre by 1/2 metre',[29] the size of the Auvers double squares, on popular subjects including figures of men and women at work, rag pickers, manure collectors and peat cutters. He reproduced some of them scaled down for his uncle Cor **(150)**, and sent a sketch of them in a letter to his brother, where the format dictates the elongation of its subject.[30]

But what were Van Gogh's sources of inspiration for using such a format?

The first major example is certainly Charles-François Daubigny, who used it frequently, large and small, without any decorative concern for a particular placement in an interior – but never, to our knowledge, in the exact size of 50 × 100 cm.[31] It so happens that Daubigny had lived and worked in Auvers, and his widow was still living there in 1890, and it is not inconceivable that the recollection of his works triggered in Van Gogh an urge to experiment with this kind of format, initially as a tribute to an artist he admired. The two views of Daubigny's garden in the Auvers ensemble, one with his name on the canvas, which Van Gogh had 'meditated on' since his arrival, alongside two other canvases, amply demonstrates how important the work of the Oise painter was to his inspiration in Auvers.

Of Daubigny's double squares, Van Gogh could have seen *The Great Valley of Optevoz*[32] or *Spring* **(149)** in the Louvre – the latter also in an engraving by Daubigny – but it is difficult to ascertain whether he ever got to see *Snow*,[33] exhibited several times in the 1870s, whose expressive desolation and crows are reminiscent of *Wheatfield with Crows*. However, the Mesdag collection, from which Van Gogh saw paintings at the exhibition in The Hague in 1882, also included several landscapes by Daubigny and Corot in this format.[34]

This influence may have crystallized with visual memories of the work of Dutch contemporaries who used the format, such as Hendrik Willem Mesdag himself, Jozef Israëls, Jacob Maris and especially his friend Anthon van Rappard, who painted subjects close to Van Gogh's drawings for Cottier. But we do not know exactly which paintings Van Gogh saw, apart from Van Rappard's *Tile Painters* **(151)**.[35]

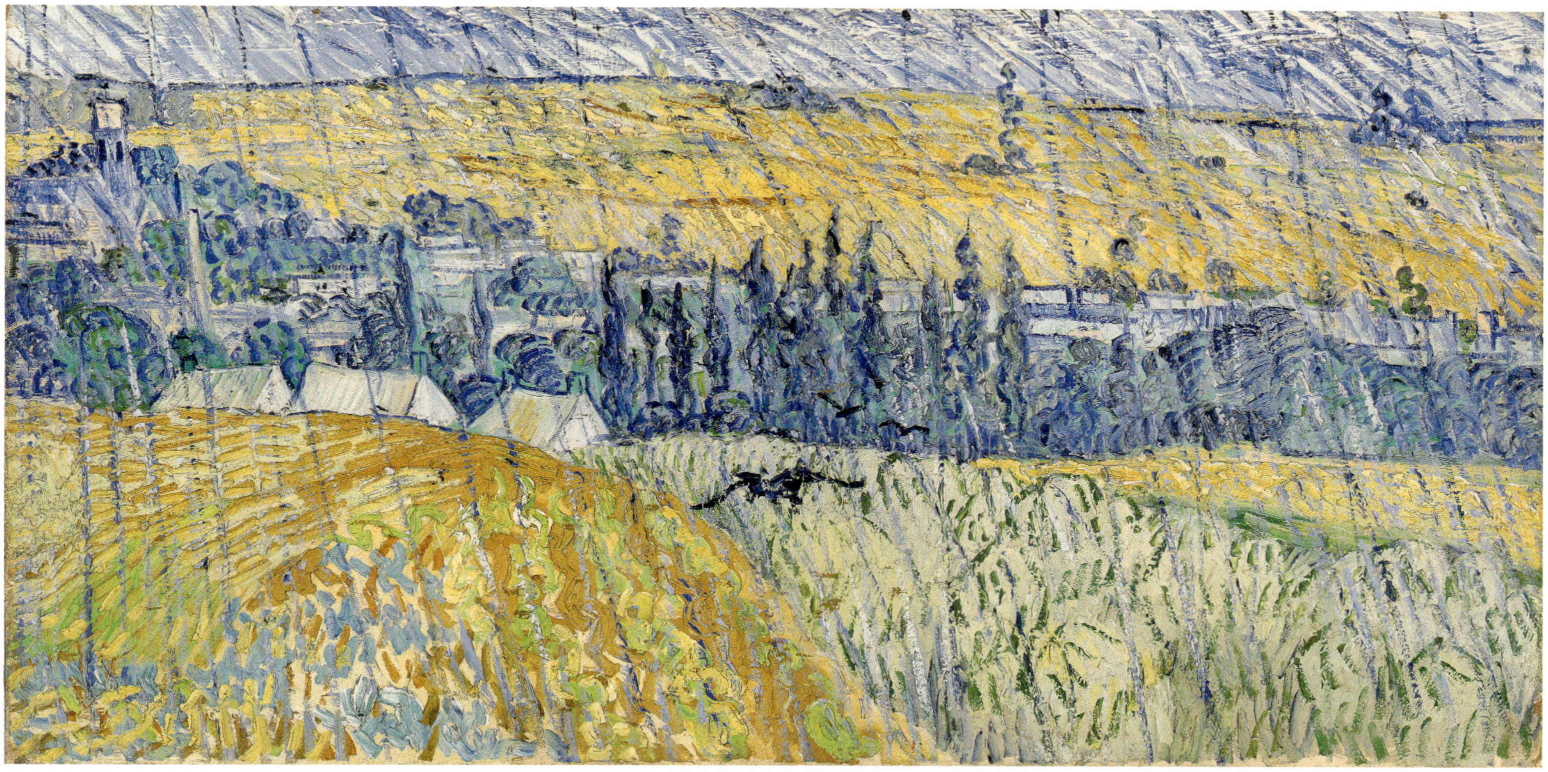

145 (#68)
Vincent van Gogh
Rain – Auvers-sur-Oise, 1890
Oil on canvas, 50.3 × 100.2 cm
Amgueddfa Cymru — National Museum Wales, Cardiff,
bequeathed by Gwendoline Davies, 1951

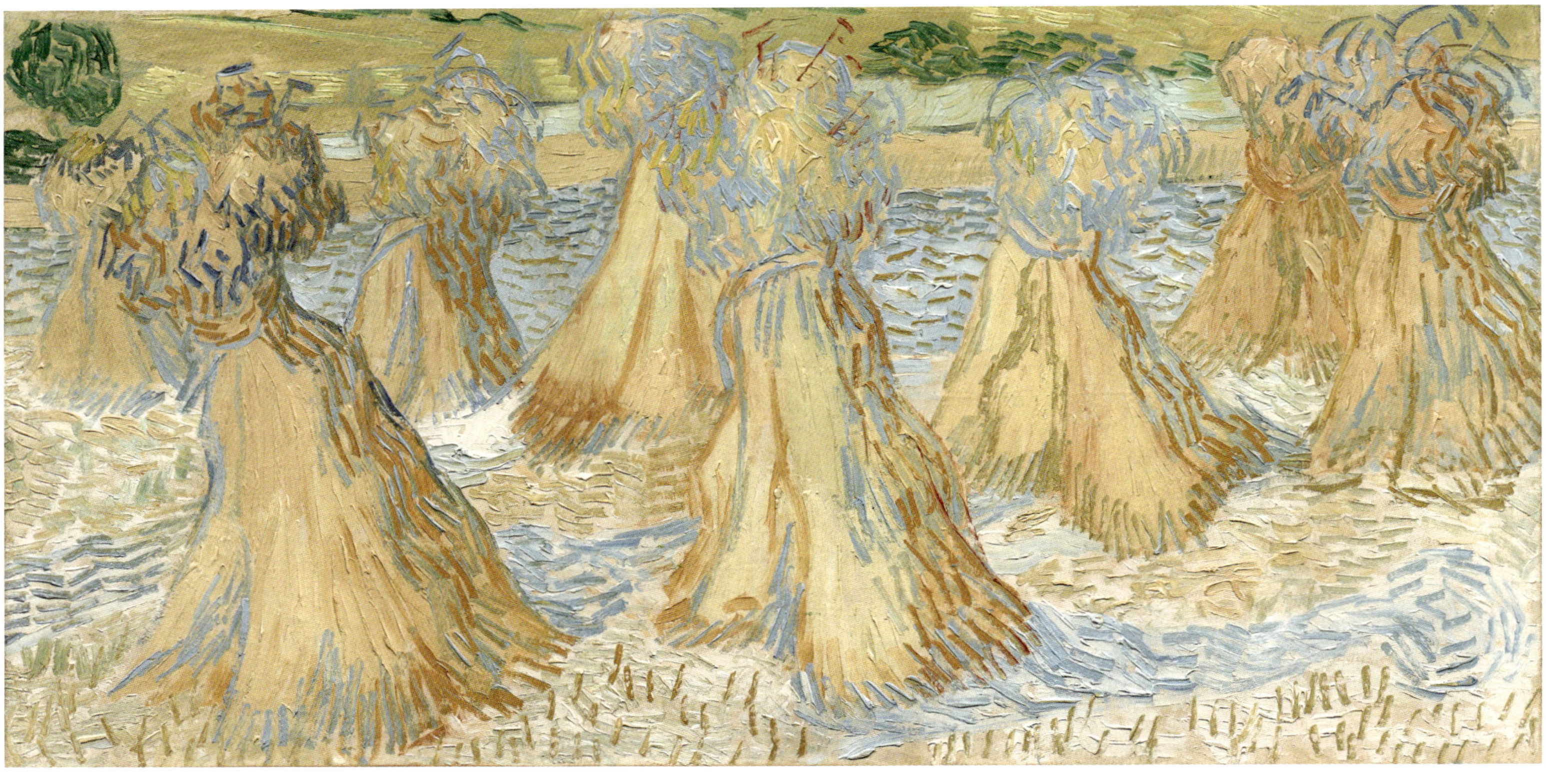

146 (#67)
Vincent van Gogh
Sheaves of Wheat, 1890
Oil on canvas, 50.8 × 101.6 cm
Dallas Museum of Art, The Wendy and Emery Reves Collection

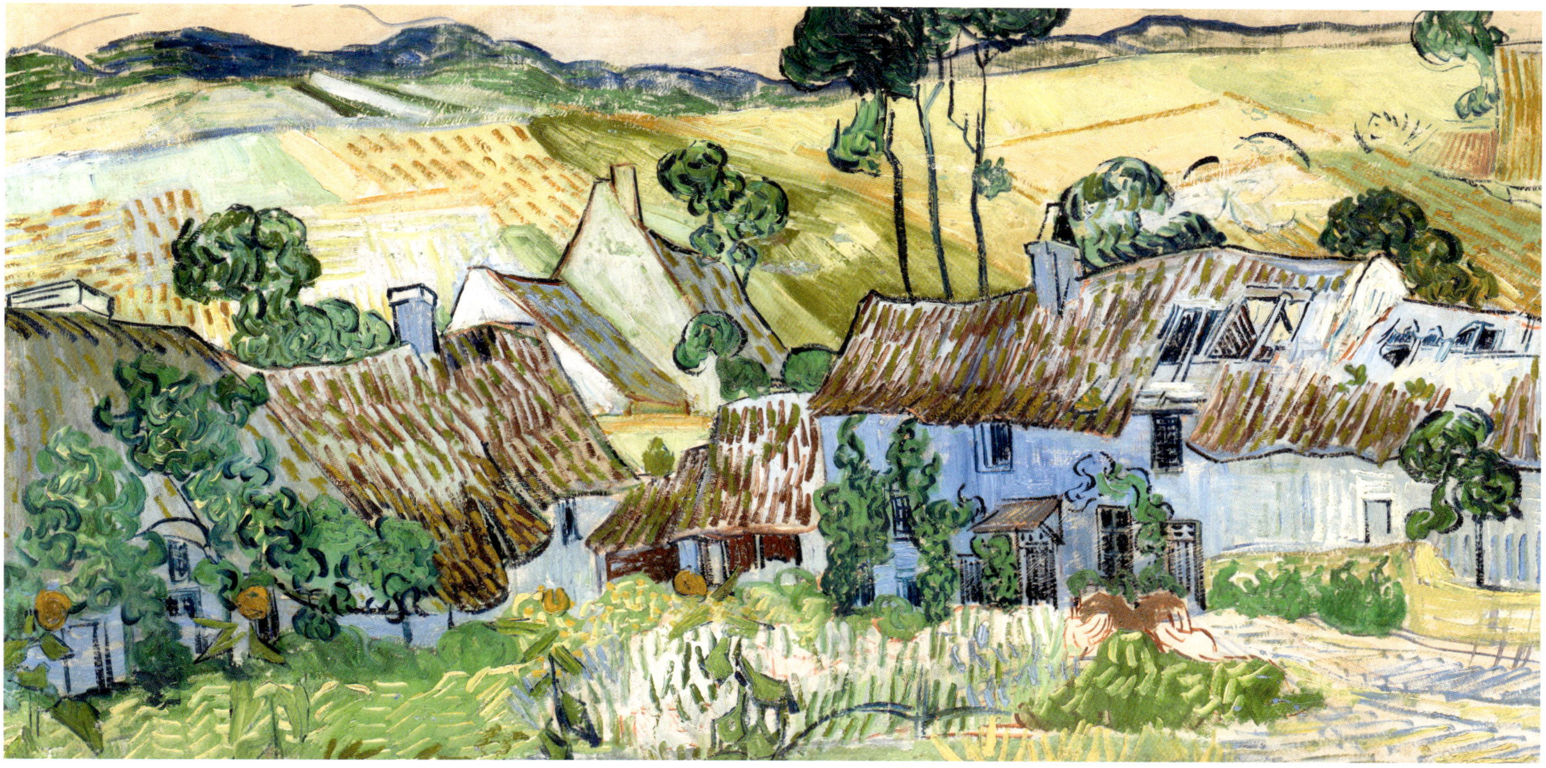

147 (#73)
Vincent van Gogh
Farms near Auvers-sur-Oise, 1890
Oil on canvas, 50.2 × 100.3 cm
Tate, London, bequeathed by C. Frank Stoop, 1933

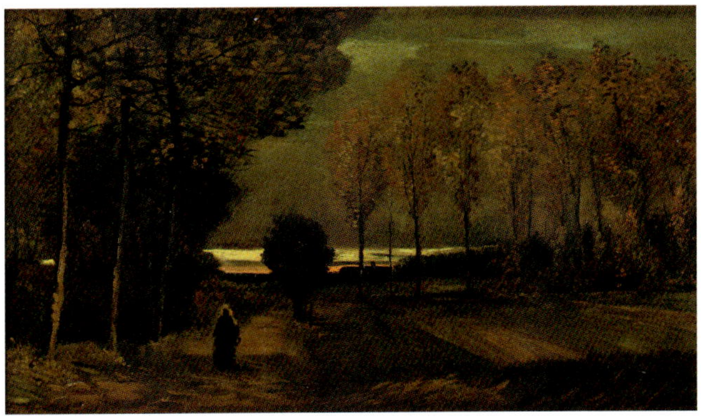

148
Vincent van Gogh
Autumn Landscape at Dusk, 1885
Oil on canvas, 53.3 × 92.6 cm
Centraal Museum, Utrecht, gift, 1936

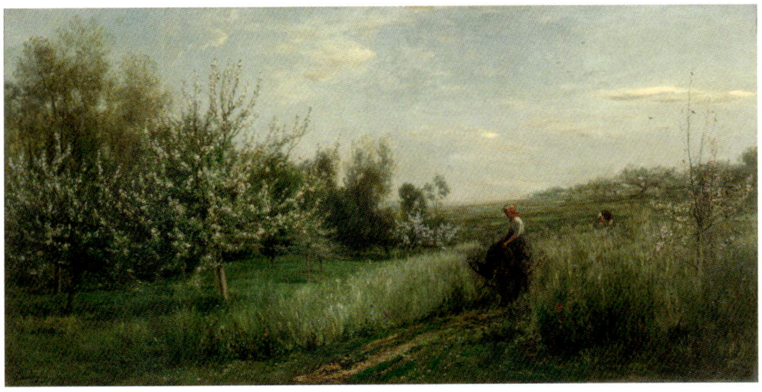

149
Charles-François Daubigny
Spring, 1857
Oil on canvas, 96 × 193 cm
Musée d'Orsay, Paris

Looking back to an earlier generation, Van Gogh mentioned Georges Michel in connection with *Fields near Auvers-sur-Oise* **(135)**: 'Then the horizontal landscape with the fields, a subject like one of Michel's.'[36] In March 1876, at Durand-Ruel, Van Gogh saw six paintings by this artist, nicknamed 'the Ruisdael of Montmartre',[37] who represented a link between the seventeenth-century Dutch landscape tradition and the modern generation. Michel, however, usually favoured more compact formats that allowed space for large, moving skies, and it is instructive that Van Gogh should think of a landscape painter so unattracted to the elongated format in connection with the motif of one of his own double squares. What he was seeking is the suggestion of a vast, deep space, in the seventeenth-century Dutch tradition, of those great national figures to whom he repeatedly referred throughout his correspondence: Jacob van Ruisdael, Philips Koninck, Meindert Hobbema, Isaac van Ostade and Jan van Goyen. For example, he spoke of the elevated view from his room in Saint-Rémy as 'a perspective in the manner of Van Goyen', or a view of a widened space like the seascapes with a low horizon by the Dutch painter.[38]

This is because the long landscape has its roots in the tradition of the panorama, which is regarded as the widest and most complete representation of a real landscape.[39] Some critics have detected the idea of a panorama in Van Gogh's series,[40] recalling his knowledge of the famous Mesdag Panorama, which he saw and admired in 1881,[41] and his plan in Arles to produce one based on his drawings from the hill of Montmajour, as he wrote to Theo: 'What I'd like to do is the panorama of which you have the first drawings – it's so *wide*'.[42]

But the panorama, whether large or small, is based on a topographical and mimetic approach that is totally foreign to Van Gogh's pictures. He did not try to reproduce the spectacle of nature, nor even, primarily, its vastness, but strove to express the human side of nature, shaped by the peasants who are its inhabitants and its voice. Thus Jules Breton, along with Millet, was 'the voice of the wheat'.[43]

Of Breton's work, he had seen the famous elongated *Blessing of the Wheat in Artois* **(152)** at the Palais du Luxembourg in Paris, with its dense procession of figures moving obliquely across the fields as crows fly overhead. Even more so than Daubigny or other landscape painters, Van Gogh's main sources in this expressive elongation of the format were the great figure paintings, especially those of the painter who, in his view, most fully embodied that genre at the time and for whom he had a renewed and intense interest: Puvis de Chavannes.

In May 1890, following his visit to the Salon de la Société Nationale des Beaux-Arts, at the Palais du

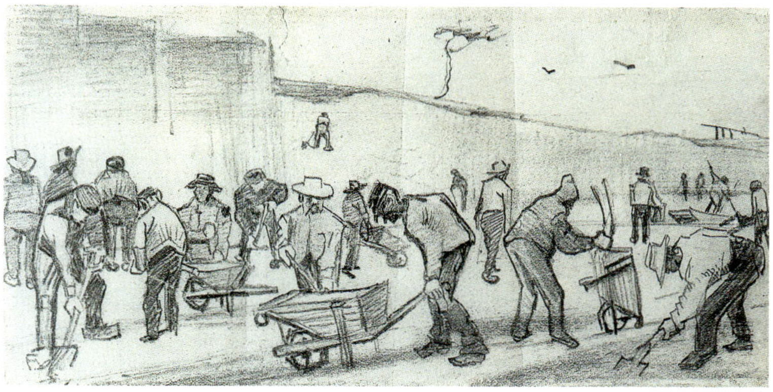

150
Vincent van Gogh
Sand Diggers in Dekkersduin near The Hague, 1883
Pencil, 10 × 20.5 cm
Present whereabouts unknown

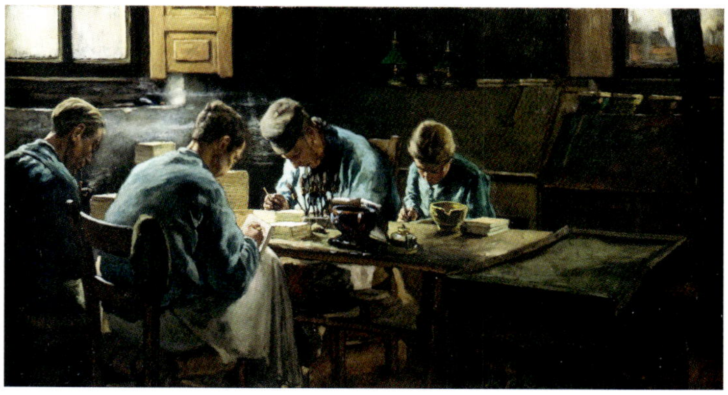

151
Anthon van Rappard
Tile Painters, 1884
Oil on canvas, 65.5 × 120.5 cm
Zeeuws Museum, Middelburg

Champ de Mars, Van Gogh only remembered Puvis and his single, large painting, the programmatically titled (as Vincent saw it), *Inter artes et naturam (Between Art and Nature)* **(153)**. He made a sketch of the painting for his sister Willemien at the beginning of June **(155)**[44] and mentioned it in several letters.

Van Gogh was well-acquainted with Puvis's work, having seen a monographic exhibition at Durand-Ruel in 1887. He particularly admired *Pleasant Land*, a decoration for Bonnat measuring 230 × 430 cm (almost a double square), and must have been struck by its blue-yellow harmony and the compositional simplicity of its large diagonal masses. Theo, who was doing business with Puvis in April 1890, probably had drawings by him[45] and the two brothers will certainly have spoken about the famous older painter.

When Van Gogh arrived in Auvers he compared the countryside to what he had seen in Daubigny's paintings, but he saw the village through Puvis's eyes – 'I see or *think* I see a calm there à la Puvis de Chavannes, no factories, but beautiful greenery in abundance and in good order'[46] – and particularly through the long painting that had impressed him: 'I even think that often in nature there is currently all the grace of Puvis's painting, Between art and nature'.[47] Puvis gave him a guide to the programme he had already set himself on 25 May, with 'a continuation of interesting *researches* into colour and modern sentiment, *parallel*, equivalent to those of Delacroix, Puvis de Chavannes', as he wrote to the Dutch artist and critic Joseph Jacob Isaäcson.[48]

In this search for form, with a simplification full of contrasts, another possible influence, that of Japan, should not go unmentioned.[49] The triptychs of *oban* prints, of which Vincent had incomplete examples in his collection,[50] have the same ratio of 1:2 – just like tatamis.

HIGH AND WIDE: LONGER MEANS BIGGER

But while all these examples may have fuelled Van Gogh's research into the use of such a format, they cannot account for his original impulse to use it.

Worth noting here is his strong inclination to extend his compositions in the sketches of paintings he drew in his letters. This is the case even with double squares, particularly the sketches of the *Fields near Auvers-sur-Oise* **(129)** and *Daubigny's Garden* **(18)**, which have a ratio of 1:3, or of the *Undergrowth with Two Figures* **(124)** (1:2.5), but also of several number 30 canvases, such as *Tree Trunks in the Grass* **(154)**, which becomes a double square in Vincent's sketch.[51]

Some of the older letters bear visual notations, without any painted equivalent, of a 1:2 or 1:3 format, such as the two drawings in letter 397, to Theo, of 16 October 1883. The same applies to Vincent's copies

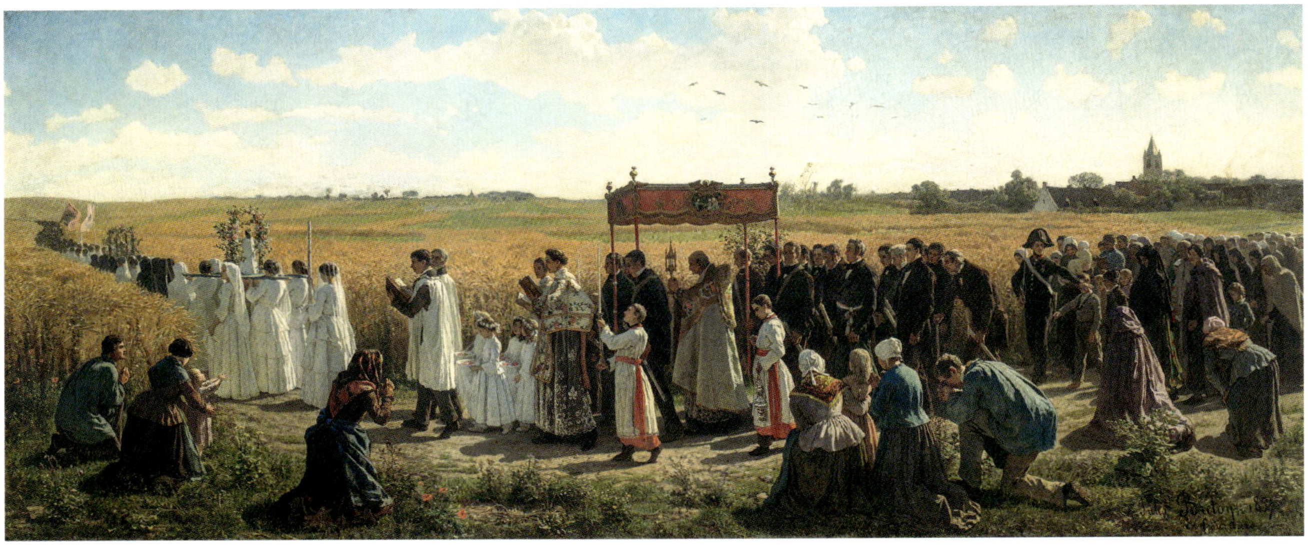

152
Jules Breton
The Blessing of the Wheat in Artois, 1857
Oil on canvas, 128.5 × 320 cm
Musée d'Orsay, on loan to the Musée des Beaux-Arts d'Arras

of works by other artists, such as Bernard's *Madeleine in the Bois d'Amour*, an almost square painting, of which he makes a double square according to the description provided by Paul Gauguin.[52] His own drawing of a perspective frame, made for Theo in 1882, is likewise disproportionately elongated, perhaps as a result of the writing, which stretches the image with the line, but also as a result of the synthetic vision produced by the artist's memory, which seems to have led to an enlargement.[53]

In July 1887, he spoke to Theo about 'big, long canvases' that are 'hard to sell' referring to his largest canvases, a metre or more wide,[54] but at just under a metre high not actually very elongated. What is significant, however, is that the artist adds 'long' to 'big' in order to characterize by this notation a state that is more a matter of size than of format.

This enlargement also seems to be linked to a concern for the 'large', a term that Van Gogh uses in various registers, from the most practical to the most spiritual. In relation to his paintings, 'large' describes not so much the actual size of the works (never more than number 30, and sometimes less), but rather their ambitiousness, effect of monumentality or generation of a feeling of satisfaction. Thus he may speak of '6 *very large* canvases [...] especially the *huge* bouquets of sunflowers', which are at most number 30 canvases, or emphasize the effect of size: 'as it's much bigger, this one creates quite an unusual effect'.[55]

Van Gogh had long cherished the ambition of a large format by which he would *surpass* the greats of the past: 'And yet, after Millet and Lhermitte what remains to be done is... the sower, with colour and in a large format'.[56] But he never dared to use the true large format, even though he claimed to be striving for it, as in this surprisingly ambivalent sentence of 15 or 16 June 1888: 'They're the rather large sizes, 30, 25, 20, 15, all square. It seems to me that the large sizes (after all, it's not very large) suit me better'.[57]

More than a question of size, for him *greatness* was an aspiration, an ambition, the very goal of style – 'colour has to do the job here, and through its being simplified by giving a *grander* style to things'[58] – and the inherent mark, 'the greatness of a masterpiece'.[59] Such greatness is achieved through ambition and hard work – 'I wouldn't be able to explain to you how pleased I am to find a *big*, serious job this way. Because I hope it'll be a true decoration that I'm going to undertake there'[60] – and therefore, by the accumulation of paintings: 'we're free to consider the 9 canvases as the initial idea for a much *larger*, definitive decoration'.[61]

However, perhaps prompted by his excellent command of English, Van Gogh also uses the French

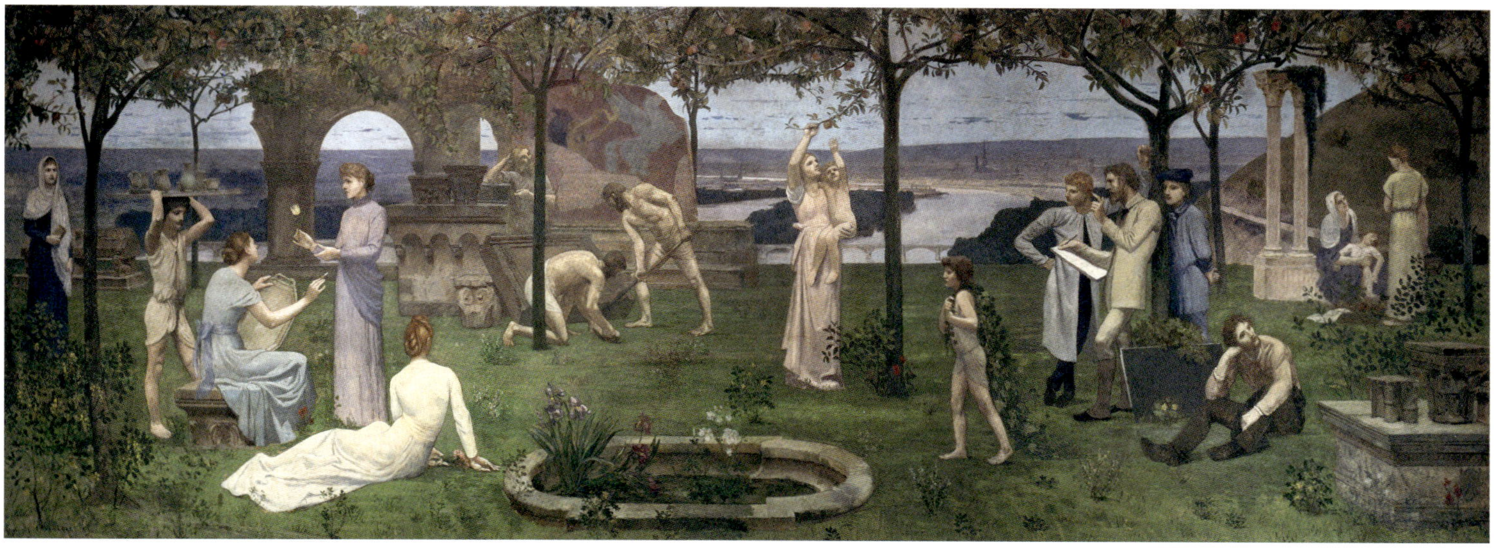

153
Pierre Puvis de Chavannes
Inter artes et naturam (Between Art and Nature), 1888–90
Oil and wax on canvas, 295 × 830 cm
Musée des Beaux-Arts, Rouen

large ('broad') both concretely and figuratively in the English sense of 'big': in 'this work on a broader scale' ('plus large')[62] the word refers to the decoration of his house in Arles, while elsewhere it is associated with notions such as 'beautiful' or 'solid'.[63] Aspiration and utilization merge.

In Auvers, Van Gogh strove more than ever for the great, the vastness of an open field, as he told his mother and sister on 14 July: 'For my part, I'm wholly absorbed in the *vast expanse* of wheatfields against the hills, *large* as a sea'.[64] By switching from views of village houses to views of fields, he shows himself in search of the greatness of infinity, *as if* facing an ocean horizon. Van Gogh logically sought to transcribe this aspiration in the large, elongated landscape format that was aptly called *marine* in French, and in the multiplication of these canvases.

But the elongation created by the double square is also *flattening*: these canvases are slightly wider than the number 30 (73 × 92 cm), the largest format Van Gogh usually used, but above all they are much less high.[65] In fact, in their closure of space the compositions have a claustrophobic dimension, a kind of anguished constriction. Van Gogh expressed this apparent contradiction with the aspiration to infinity by speaking of his desire to express the sadness that this countryside inspired in him, but also what he found 'healthy and fortifying' about it.[66]

This ambivalence, not to say psychological duality, that was so characteristic of Van Gogh, seems to be embodied in this format with its aspirations to the broad and the large, while entailing being flattened: 'Only', he says regretfully, '50 centimetres high'. It also has a moral and biblical origin, a deep historical link to the landscapes of the old Dutch masters: 'Whenever I look at a painting by Ruisdael, Van Goyen, Bosboom and so many others, I always think of the words "as sorrowful, yet always rejoicing"'.[67]

PURPOSE: AN IMPOSSIBLE SELF-EXHIBITION?

The connections Van Gogh made between the first paintings in landscape format point to various possible hanging combinations. His hesitations indicate that we should not see in them a predetermined vision, but rather an afterthought. In letters 891 and 893 the *Fields near Auvers-sur-Oise* is seen, respectively, as a counterpart to *Undergrowth with Two Figures* and to the portrait of Marguerite Gachet, 'which looks very good with [it]' based on the colours: 'one canvas being vertical and pink, the other pale green and green-yellow, complementing the pink'.

What is often overlooked[68] is that the presence of a few square canvases in the Auvers oeuvre – a rare

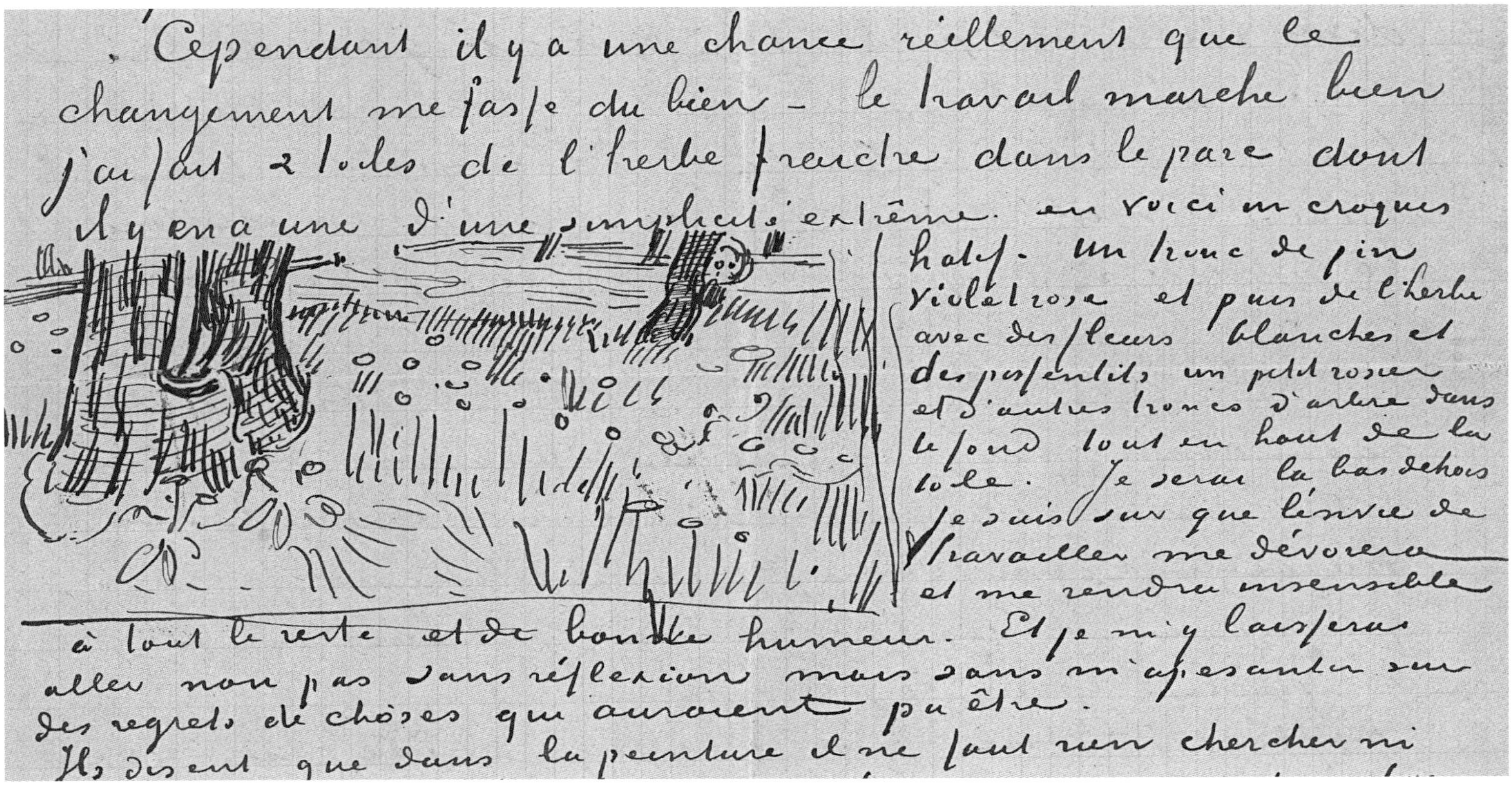

Cependant il y a une chance réellement que le changement me fasse du bien – le travail marche bien j'ai fait 2 toiles de l'herbe fraîche dans le parc dont il y en a une d'une simplicité extrême. en voici un croquis hatif. Un tronc de pin violet rose et puis de l'herbe avec des fleurs blanches et des pissenlits un petit rosier et d'autres troncs d'arbre dans le fond tout en haut de la toile. Je serai là bas dehors je suis sûr que l'envie de travailler me dévorera et me rendra insensible à tout le reste et de bonne humeur. Et je m'y laisserai aller non pas sans réflexion mais sans m'appesantir sur des regrets de choses qui auraient pu être.
Ils disent que dans la peinture il ne faut rien chercher ni

154
Letter from Vincent to Theo with sketch of *Tree Trunks in the Grass*, 4 May 1890

Pen on paper
Van Gogh Museum, Amsterdam

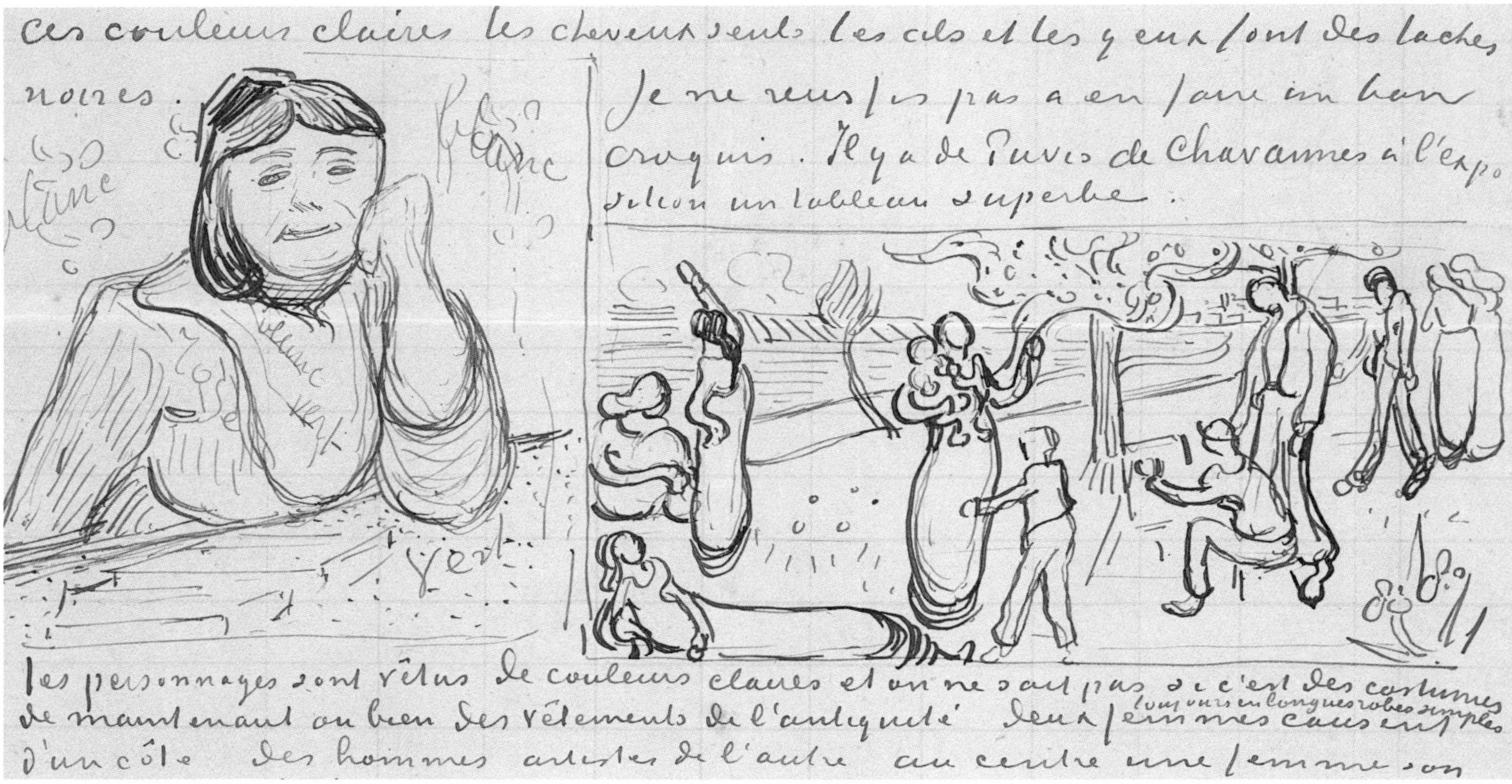

ces couleurs claires les cheveux seuls les cils et les yeux sont des taches noires.

Je ne réussis pas à en faire un bon croquis. Il y a de Puvis de Chavannes à l'exposition un tableau superbe.

les personnages sont vêtus de couleurs claires et on ne sait pas si c'est des costumes de maintenant ou bien des vêtements de l'antiquité deux femmes causent toujours en longues robes simples d'un côté des hommes artistes de l'autre au centre une femme son

155
Letter from Vincent to Willemien with sketches of his *Arlésienne* and *Inter artes et naturam*, after Pierre Puvis de Chavannes, 5 June 1890

Van Gogh Museum, Amsterdam

format in general, and one Van Gogh had never previously used[69] – must be related to the double squares, especially since their side measurement is 50 centimetres corresponding to the short side of the double squares. This emphasizes the artist's interest in new formats, just as it points out that the 'long' landscapes are double squares, rather than simply elongated formats. This exploratory aspect is expressed by the different genres to which these squares belong: four portraits **(120, 121, 132, 133, 134)**, one of which is repeated, two landscapes **(50, 141)** and a still life **(77)**.

The square format was no more available from commercial suppliers than the double square, which meant Van Gogh had to make them himself. In addition to the squares, it should be noted that five other canvases have a height of 50 cm, which does not correspond to any standard format at the time **(5, 17, 54, 61, #3)**. It seems that the artist resolutely opted for that height, but why?

Taken together, all these paintings could feasibly form a frieze, alternating portraits and landscapes, as Van Gogh himself suggests in his combination of the portrait of Marguerite Gachet with another painting **(135)**. However, it would be hasty to see this as a decorative project.[70] Nothing in the correspondence alludes to this – and what venue could have accommodated such a long series of canvases, thirteen to sixteen metres side by side?

It is striking to note that Van Gogh, more than any of his contemporaries, wanted to group his works in one way or another: to give them coherence by bringing them together, as if each work had no inherent meaning in isolation. More than just an artistic concern, this is a deep-seated psychological trait – a fear of loneliness and isolation – evidenced by his constant yearning, still very much alive in Auvers, to create a community of painters, or at the very least, to paint with other artists.[71]

And so the vocabulary used by Van Gogh to describe the groups of works he is referring to – that lexicon of shifting meanings – must be handled cautiously. For example, he reserves the word *series* for paintings of the same subject (which may have different intentions), while *ensemble* is a notion whose conceptual vagueness responds to the pragmatic requirement of an association that works,[72] that 'holds together' visually. He also speaks, from time to time, of a 'suite' or a 'group'.

This semantic vacillation seems to derive from an ambiguity regarding the purpose of these groupings. Thus, decoration can mutate into exhibition: 'Then next year I'd give them the decoration of the house to exhibit, when there would be an ensemble'.[73]

Van Gogh's aspiration to exhibit had been a constant since his group exhibition at the Restaurant du Chalet in Paris in the winter of 1887. While in Arles, his ambition was a solo exhibition of about thirty paintings in Theo's apartment.[74] In Saint-Rémy, in June 1889, he began to dream of an exhibition space – the asylum, for example: 'What a pity that one can't move the building here. It would be magnificent to hold an exhibition there, all the empty rooms, the big corridors.'[75] In fact, in the winter and spring of 1890, Van Gogh successfully exhibited at the Brussels artists' association Les Vingts and at the Salon des Indépendants.

Shortly after his arrival in Auvers, he once again raised the idea of a monographic exhibition: 'One day or another I believe I'll find a way to do an exhibition of myself in a café.'[76] A solitary project that he immediately tempered with a possible association with Jules Chéret, in a way that was characteristic of his ambivalence towards the recognition which he both sought and avoided.[77]

To exhibit was first of all to legitimize himself in the eyes of his brother,[78] then of his peers, as a professional painter, capable of earning a living. But it also meant taking the risk of showing a perpetually evolving body of work, with which he was always dissatisfied. Since the time in Saint-Rémy he had recoiled from fame, become afraid of being talked about, and taken refuge in painting alone.

PAINTING AS ROOTEDNESS

When he arrived in Auvers, Van Gogh was a man broken by his various crises and his sense of failure, and a harsh judge of his work and career. This is summed up, for example, in the unsent letter of 24 May, to Theo and Jo: 'I feel – a failure – that's it as regards me – I feel that that's the fate I'm accepting. And which won't change any more', and in another to Isaäcson of 25 May: 'I am <u>decidedly</u> certain that I shall never do important things', also unsent.[79]

Nonetheless in Auvers Van Gogh, always combative by temperament, set out to repair himself and to repair his past by returning to what were sometimes significant motifs, from before his arrival in France. Auvers thus marked a 'return to the north'. In Saint-Rémy, contrary to his habit, he had already made three paintings 'from memory' as 'reminiscences of the north', and conceived the idea of redoing the paintings of peasants from his early days in Nuenen.[80] It was as if his journey south had only served to open his eyes to the north and that this return was the culmination of his entire southern enterprise.[81] Solana has rightly emphasized that subjects from the north reappear in the works from Auvers, with its thatched roofs and its church, as seen in the Nuenen view of a garden (*The Parsonage Garden at Nuenen in Spring*, Groninger Museum). And as we have seen, the initial idea of the double squares, half a square metre in size, was partly inspired by the memory of some large drawings he had made in The Hague.

But on returning to Paris on his way to Auvers, Van Gogh was confronted with his entire oeuvre. He saw his paintings back at Theo's, and went to see those stored at Tanguy's, and it was a shock: 'It was odd to see all my canvases from the beginning again, from the time I left.'[82] This return gave him the feeling that they were not yet complete: 'They still need a great deal of retouching.'[83]

He conceived the plan to make a synthesis of his work from Provence in the form of a collection of etchings, which would be 'an ensemble, a rather deliberate and studied *summary*'.[84] In his paintings, and especially in the double squares, as mentioned above, he then entered into dialogue with many of his admired figures.

Repairing the past means re-establishing its connection with the present – to reconcile the two. This is why Van Gogh was so sensitive to the 'strange and happy meeting of the very distant days of antiquity with raw modernity'[85] in the large elongated painting by Puvis de Chavannes, whose 'figures are dressed in bright colours and one doesn't know if they're costumes from now or clothes from antiquity.' He notes, 'One feels [...] present at a *continuation* of all things, an inevitable but benevolent *rebirth*.'[86]

The village of Auvers itself offered him this link between past and present: 'I find the modern villas and the middle-class country houses almost as pretty as the old thatched cottages that are falling into ruin.'[87]

But, as he confided to his mother in the middle of his stay in Auvers, this link – that of the continuity of life – is organically rooted in an existential feeling of artistic creation, in his eyes a form of procreation. This is why painting can be capable of such a reparation: 'Last year I read somewhere that writing a book or making a painting was the same as having a child. [...] that work [...] is *the only tie that links the past and the present* for me.'[88]

Bringing back the past is one way to fill the void of an empty present. Another is to work feverishly to fight the passing of time. In his letter to Willemien of 13 June 1890, Van Gogh explains that he is working 'a lot and quickly' to 'express the *desperately swift* passage of things in modern life.'[89]

In Auvers, painting became a feverish and *desperate* attempt to put down roots in the present, to halt the dissolution of existence. It is therefore very significant that Van Gogh's last painting at Auvers, a double square, depicts tree roots.

For the painter, the root is the vital point, the connection with life. In March 1889, in a moment of creative exaltation, Van Gogh declared, 'from time to time in life one feels amazed, as if one was taking root in the ground'.[90] But in Auvers, two weeks before his suicide, he used the same image to express his despair: 'my life, too, is attacked at the very root'.[91]

With this final motif of roots, with which he deliberately concluded his work at Auvers, and the elongated formats in particular, Van Gogh seems to be defying the passage of time by seeking to anchor it in the painting with brushwork more mobile and overtly energetic than ever, but at the same time thick, heavily impastoed, generative, earthy, lumpy, sinuous and knotted like a root: brushwork that retains the memory of the painterly gesture and reconstructs the motif in full.

It must be emphasized that Van Gogh's quasi-systematic exploration of the elongated double-square format sprang mainly from the shock of seeing Puvis's *Between Art and Nature*. In his programmatic letter to Isaäcson, Van Gogh strikingly declares, 'I am increasingly beginning to feel that one may consider [that] Puvis de Chavannes [...] has equal worth with

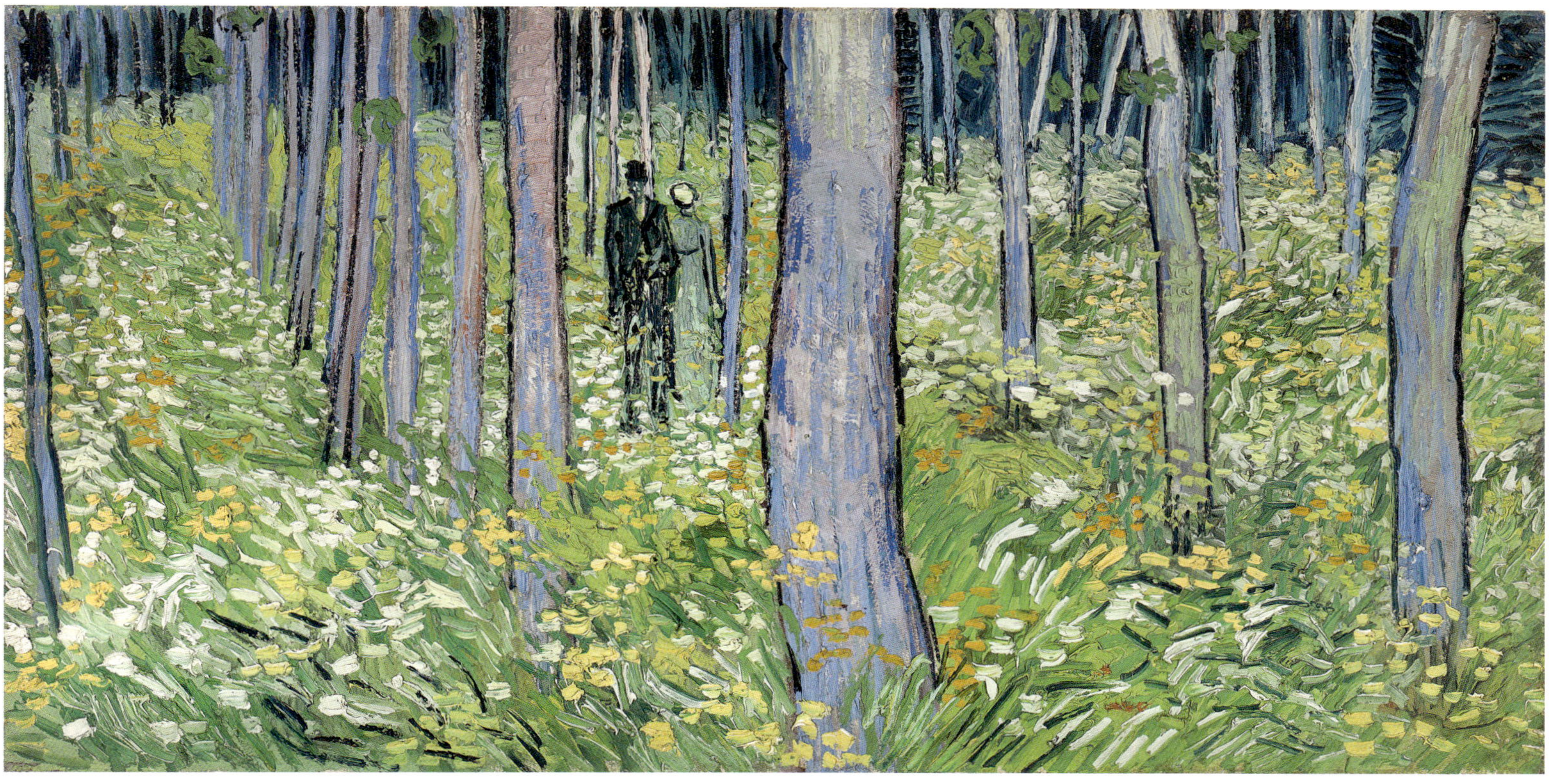

156 (#46)
Vincent van Gogh
Undergrowth with Two Figures, 1890
Oil on canvas, 49.5 × 99.7 cm
Cincinnati Art Museum, Bequest of Mary E. Johnston

the people whose genius *attains a thus-far-and-no-further, forever consoling*'.[92]

To achieve a 'thus-far-and-no-further' is to create a consummated oeuvre, the synthesis of a past that goes back to Giotto, mentioned in the same letter. An oeuvre that stops at the threshold of a radical change by which painting would become *something else*, a threshold from which the future can only be glimpsed. Van Gogh calls Puvis a 'seer' and attributes a 'prophetic' quality to his last paintings. For he was well aware of 'the possibility that a generation later we would still be continuing interesting research into colour and modern feeling', and concluded: 'I can see the possibility of a new painting from afar'.

Van Gogh's set of double squares is defined precisely by a visual characteristic – an original format of an identically repeated size – and not by subject matter: the only such group in Van Gogh's entire output. It is driven by an urge to innovate of a completely new order.

As Anthea Callen has rightly pointed out, by shattering the illusion formulated by Leon Battista Alberti of the painting as a window onto the world, and thus the illusionism of the post-Renaissance tradition, the square and the double square make visible the construction of the composition and allow us to see a painting as an object, rather than as a representation of the world.[93]

Because this format emphasizes the spatial form of the painting it allowed Van Gogh to fully liberate his brushstroke and confirm his style, something that Theo had reproached him for the previous winter: 'For despite what you say in your previous letter, that the search for style often harms other qualities, the fact is that I feel myself greatly driven to seek style, if you like, but I mean by that a more manly and more deliberate drawing'.[94] With the double square, he could afford not to be afraid of expressing sadness and loneliness.[95]

To render this hatched brushstroke, this overt and unrestrained graphic style, acceptable and artistically permissible, Van Gogh had to strive for a decorative effect, of which the quick brushstroke and simple structure were considered prerequisites – a decorative character to which the formats of squares and double squares also contributed by their very nature.[96] His remark, justifying the sketchy brushstroke by the enlargement of the size, takes on its full meaning: 'as the size gets *bigger*, the summary execution gets *its raison d'être*'.[97]

Van Gogh once referred to his art as 'painting in its rough state'[98] because of 'my rough and unskilful execution'.[99] In the series of squares and double squares from Auvers, this summary construction is both elevated and thwarted – and legitimized – by the geometric rigour of this unusual and assertive format.

Elongated format, expressiveness of the brushstroke, geometric compositions, the use of non-realistic colour: all these characteristics contribute to a demonstration of style, which leads to the primacy of style, that is to say the expressive feeling of the creator about the subject. Van Gogh knew that the future of painting lay in style. Between art and nature, to use Puvis's programmatic title, he resolutely – and for him, frighteningly – opted for art.[100]

For he no longer felt the driving force of such a future, which belonged to another 'generation', to the 'St John the Baptist of the painting of the future', which Gauguin was still talking about in June 1890.[101] Van Gogh gave up trying to go any further: he had reached his 'thus-far-and-no-further'. The artist may be buried, but his work, rooted in the expression of feeling, is 'forever consoling'.[102]

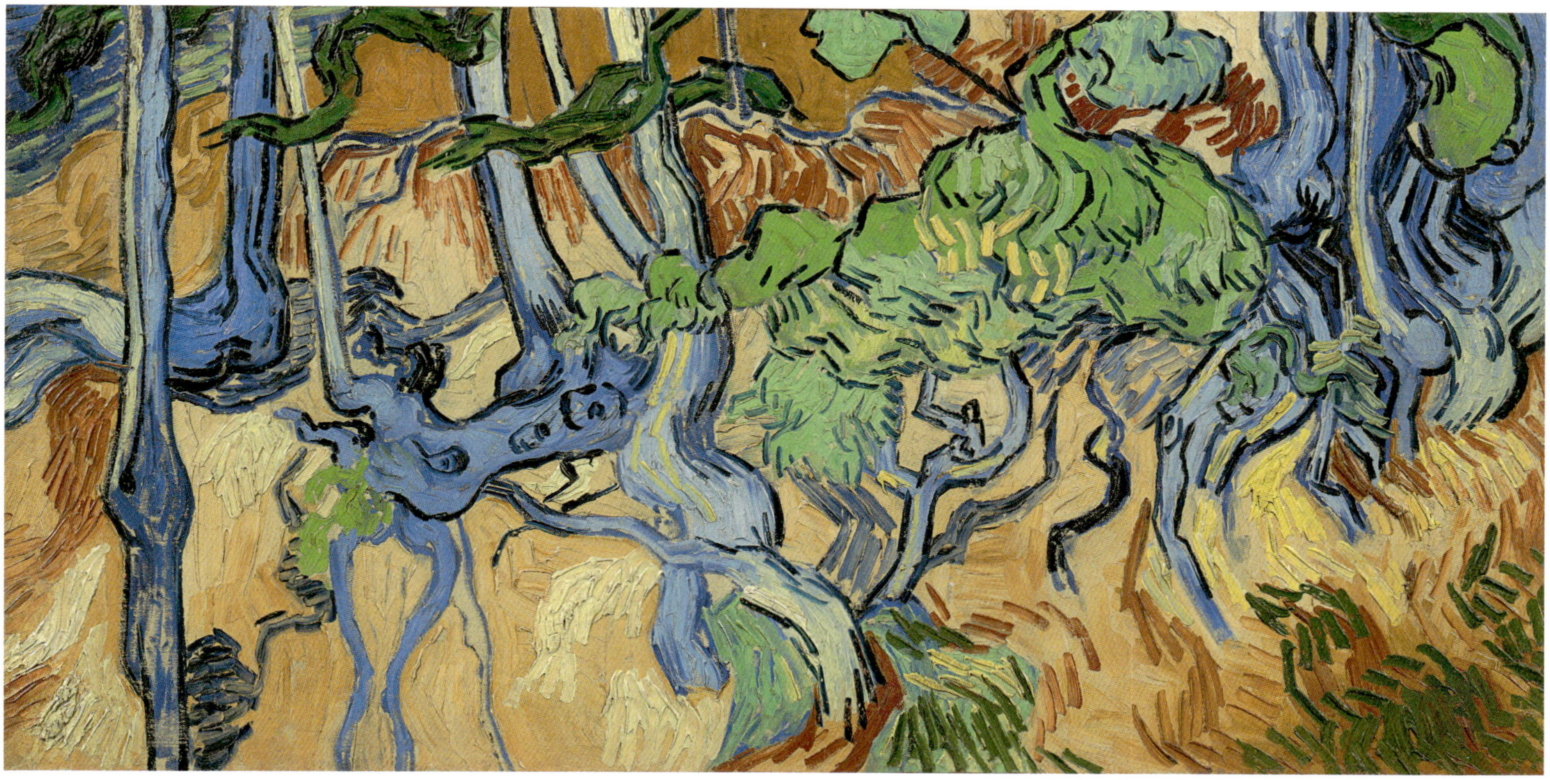

157 (#74)
Vincent van Gogh
Tree Roots, 1890
Oil on canvas, 50.3 × 100.1 cm
Van Gogh Museum, Amsterdam

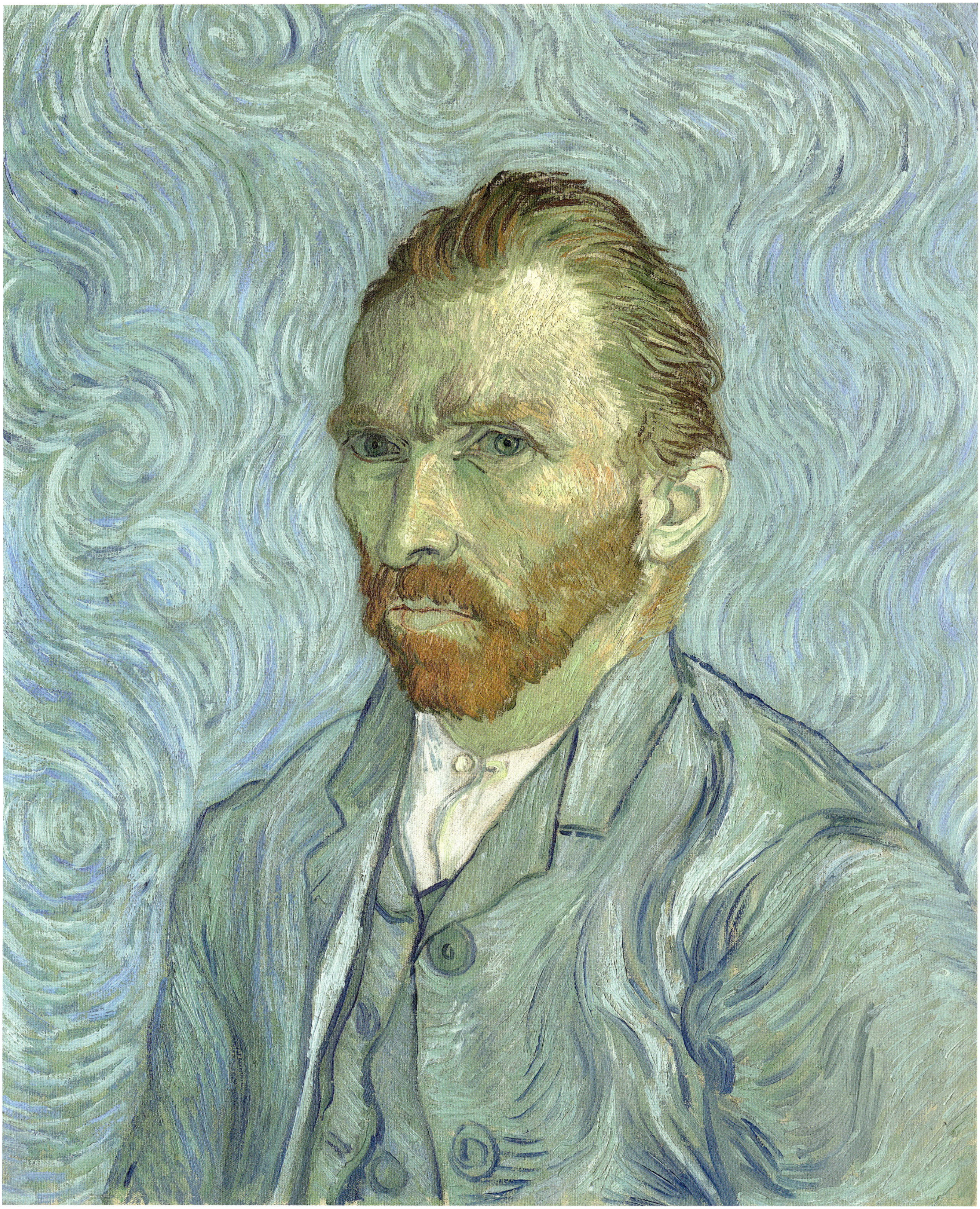

A SHORT BIOGRAPHY OF UNBEARABLE SUFFERING

VAN GOGH'S SELF-CHOSEN END

LOUIS VAN TILBORGH

It is doubtful whether Van Gogh's tragic death can be explained in terms that we can fully understand or with which we can truly empathize. All the same, there is more to be said about the downward momentum of his emotions and thoughts in the final year and a half of his life than his biographers have done so far.[1] Suicidal behaviour, psychiatrists tell us, is the result of a prolonged and highly individual process, consisting of multiple, cumulative phases, in which the person's state of mind fluctuates until the end. During the final, 'volitional' phase, in which suicidal thoughts take on concrete form, existential despair can suddenly be triggered by even seemingly insignificant things. So that the act can come unexpectedly to those nearest the victim.[2]

While every suicide has its own, individual lead-up, the underlying psychological processes are generally almost identical in nature. There is a sense of despair, of feeling trapped. The future fades from view, and suicide seems to hold out the possibility of escaping the crisis. Simply knowing that such a solution is available can be reassuring in itself, but so too is the idea of actually going through with it. Suicidal behaviour appears to be less a 'cry for help', in other words, than a 'cry of pain'. It is triggered by the feeling of hopeless suffering, and only in the second instance an attempt to communicate that pain to others.[3]

Van Gogh's suicide too seems to have been the result of depressive despair and was unanticipated by those around him. When he was discharged from the Saint-Paul-de-Mausole institution in Saint-Rémy-de-Provence on 16 May 1890, no one suspected that just over two months later he would attempt 'in complete lucidity' to take his own life.[4] A greater understanding of what motivated his tragic act can only be achieved when the process leading up to it is mapped out. While it would take a hefty biography to do the issue full justice, a first tentative attempt is made in what follows. Without such an analysis, interpreting Van Gogh's work and life in his final months remains somewhat arbitrary, and would amount to nothing less than a biographical misstep.

There are three parts to this essay. It begins with an overview of Van Gogh's history from the moment he expressed his desire to leave the asylum, focusing on what he communicated regarding his mental problems and the impression he gave the people around him. This is followed by a 'psychological autopsy', albeit a rather free one: a reconstruction of

158
Vincent van Gogh
Self-Portrait, 1889
Oil on canvas, 65 × 54 cm
Musée d'Orsay, Paris

changes in Van Gogh's life and conduct that might explain the origins of his suicidal behaviour. In his own opinion, as stated in early May 1890, these changes left him with 'wrinkles that won't be rubbed off in a hurry'.[5] With this in mind, the third section looks at the portrait of Paul Gachet, his physician in Auvers, which he painted in early June 1890 **(112, 159)**. What made him paint his doctor, and what did he intend the portrait to convey?

VAN GOGH'S MEDICAL HISTORY

At the time Van Gogh was discharged from the clinic in Saint-Rémy, Théophile Peyron, the asylum's director, pronounced him 'guéri' (cured).[6] According to Peyron's final report, the patient had been suffering from 'terrifying fears' that 'on several occasions' had led him 'to poison himself'.[7] In between times, however, Van Gogh appeared 'perfectly calm and lucid' and was also in that condition at the moment of discharge.

In the course of the previous year and a half, Van Gogh had lost his senses seven or eight times, and so there was no reason to suppose that further episodes would not occur. But this is not something Peyron raised in his report,[8] in which he pronounced the artist 'cured'. This was, after all, the only legitimate reason for allowing him to travel to Auvers-sur-Oise, where the patient wished to be independent again – albeit with the possibility of drawing on the services and hospitality of the aforementioned Gachet, who lived in Auvers but had his practice in Paris. Somewhat surprisingly, Gachet had informed Theo that he believed he could restore his brother to 'his normal condition' ('son état normal').[9]

It is not known whether Peyron had the same opinion and whether he felt Van Gogh's return to society was medically justified. 'Mr Peyron says vague things, to free himself from responsibility he says', Van Gogh wrote to Theo regarding his desire to leave the asylum.[10] The medical director had reservations, prompted by Vincent's most recent and quite severe crisis.[11] It lasted as long as two months, from late February to late April 1890, and was characterized by 'melancholy spells'.[12] During a brief respite in mid-March, Van Gogh wrote that 'my mind has been so affected – without pain, it's true – but totally stupefied'.[13] He felt utterly dejected, following which Peyron predicted in early April that the current crisis 'will leave its mark on his constitution'.[14]

His depression was, indeed, still reverberating in Van Gogh's mind as he picked himself up again in late April. 'What can I tell you of these two last months?' he wrote to Theo on the twenty-ninth. 'Things aren't going well at all, I'm more sad and bored than I could tell you, and I no longer know what point I'm at.'[15] But he lacked the mental strength to face a longer stay: 'My patience is at an end [...] I can't go on, I must move, even if as a stopgap.'[16] He did not want to end up like his fellow patients, who spent their days in total idleness. 'I've had too hard a life to kick the bucket as a result, or to lose the power to work.'[17]

Peyron felt that Van Gogh ought to allow himself more time to recover,[18] but eventually gave permission for him to leave. The fact that he did not object probably reflected his patient's understandable desire to live closer to his brother, but also Vincent's powers of persuasion and his rapid physical recovery. The heavy and prolonged crisis had 'disappeared like a thunderstorm' and if his 'clarity for work' were to be regained with similar speed, the doctor was presumably disinclined to stand in the way.[19] While his discharge seemed like a leap in the dark, the hope of departing provided Van Gogh with some respite and he thought – whether or not against his better judgement – that leaving both Provence and the asylum would protect him for a while from a fresh crisis. 'I'm almost sure that I'll soon get better in the north, at least for quite a long time, while still apprehensive of a relapse in a few years' time – but not immediately.'[20]

When Van Gogh arrived in Paris on 17 May, neither his demeanour nor his good physical appearance suggested that there might have been something more going on in his head than the hope for recovery. Theo's wife Jo met him for the first time and, to her surprise, was not presented with a someone 'sick', but with a 'sturdy, broad-shouldered man, with a healthy colour, a smile on his face, and a very resolute appearance'.[21] Jo remembered Vincent as 'lively and cheerful all the time' and that 'St Remy was not mentioned'. Her brother Andries thought 'it's good for him to be out of that asylum',

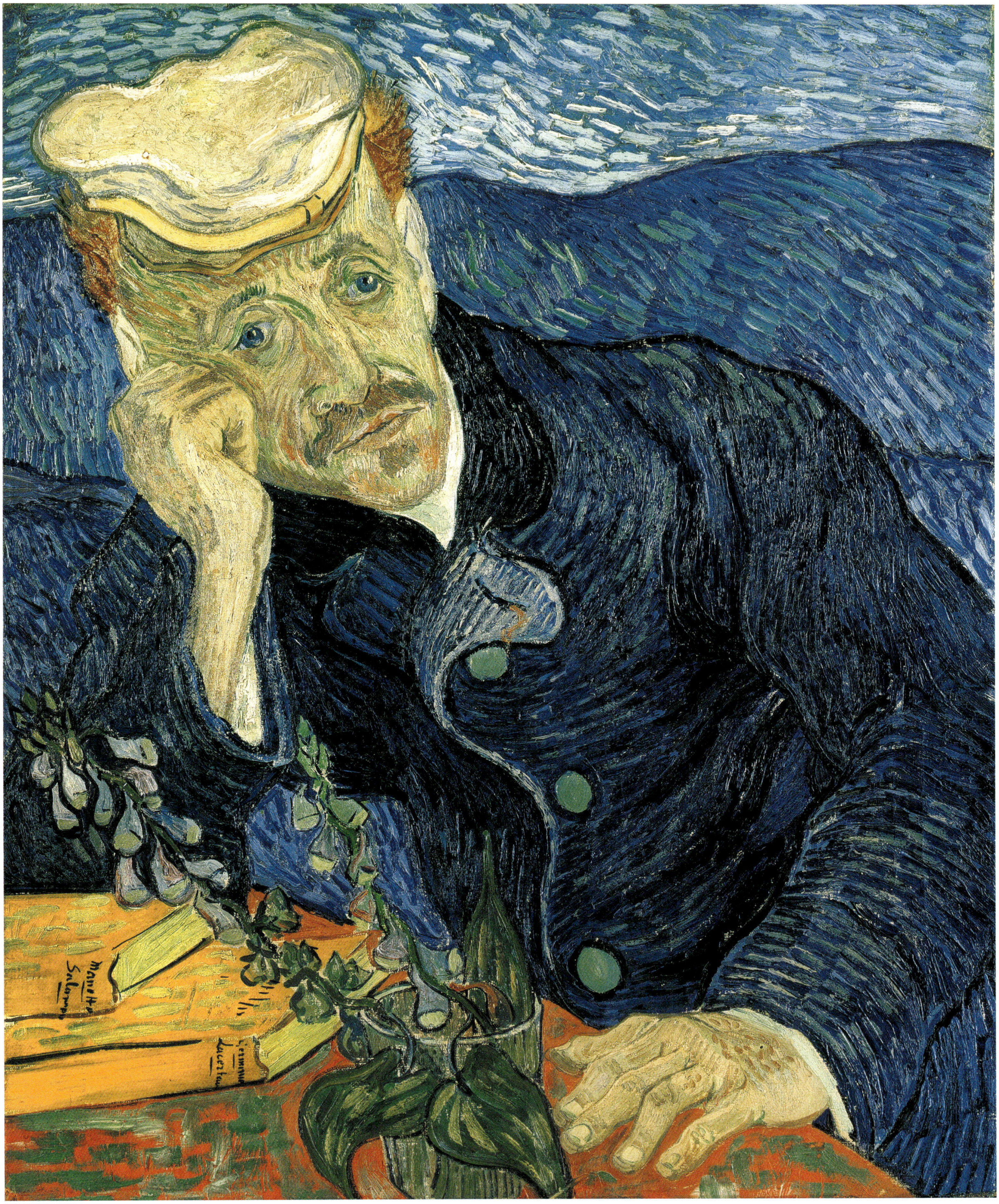

159 (#20)
Vincent van Gogh
Doctor Paul Gachet, 1890
Oil on canvas, 66 × 57 cm
Private collection

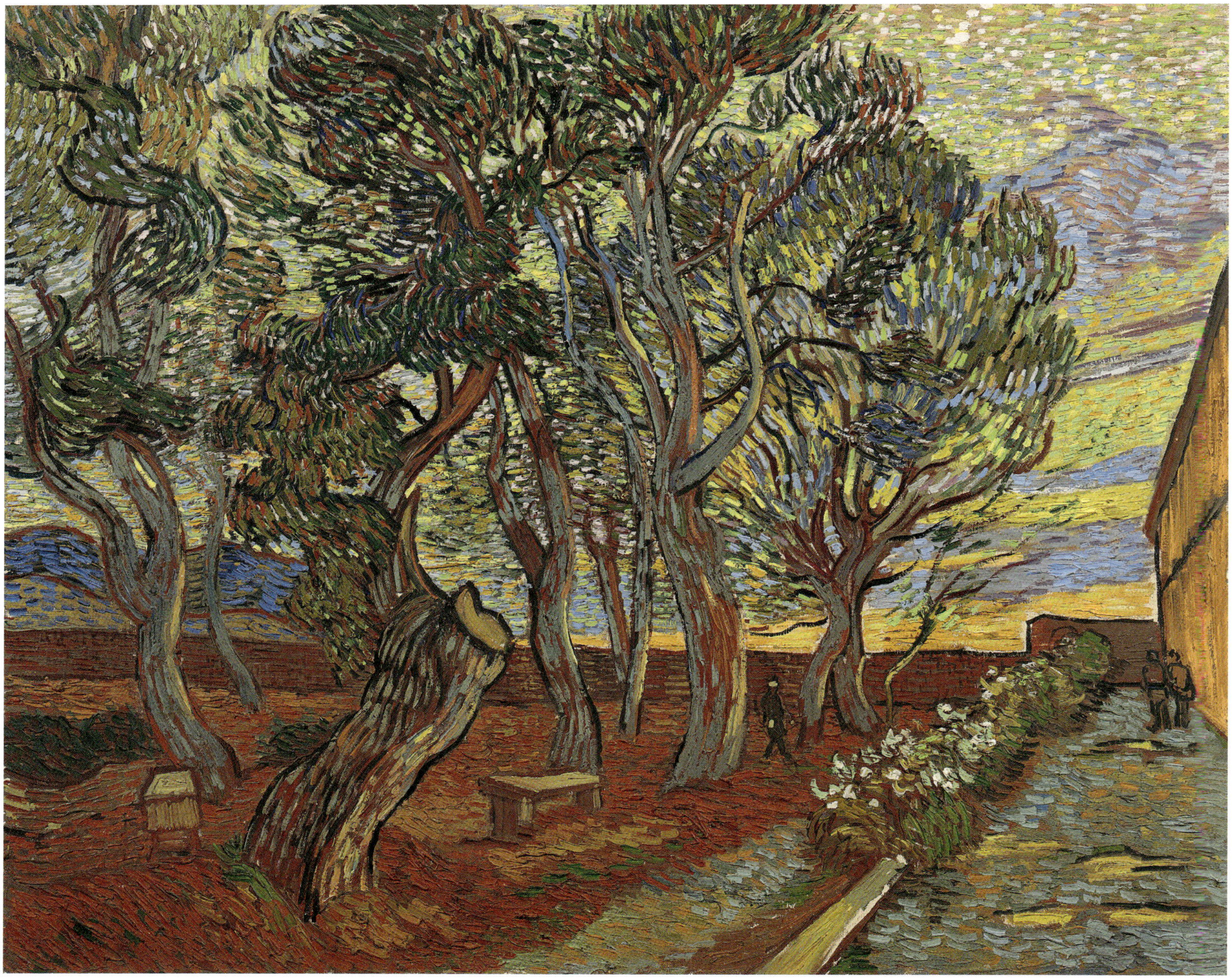

160
Vincent van Gogh
The Garden at the Asylum, 1889
Oil on canvas, 72 × 91 cm
Van Gogh Museum, Amsterdam

while Theo confirmed to his sister Willemien that their brother 'has never looked as healthy as he does now, and [...] also talks quite normally', although he felt compelled to add: 'he feels that the attacks could come back, and is afraid of that'.[22]

Van Gogh had to accustom himself to his new social environment and he struggled with the bustle of the city. Three days later, he hurried off to the much quieter Auvers-sur-Oise, where he met Gachet, who urged him to 'work a great deal, boldly' and 'not think at all about what I've had'.[23] The impossibility of the latter is already evident from his first, somewhat longer letter to Theo and Jo, which reveals that his self-confidence was not very high. He was sorry about his poor interaction with other people, described his painting as 'the least bad that I can do' and apologized that 'I can do nothing about my illness', adding that 'I'm suffering a little these days – it's just that after this long seclusion the days seem like weeks to me'.[24]

Yet no matter how hard it was for him, Van Gogh did not elaborate any further and stated that 'I don't regret coming back here'. 'Serenity' was in reach if he could get going with his work. 'I still believe that it's above all an illness of the south that I caught, and that the return here will be enough to dispel all that', he wrote four days later.[25] In the meantime, Gachet had offered him tranquillizers if 'melancholy or something else were to become too strong for me to bear', but he did not feel these were necessary for the time being. Shortly afterwards, he reported to Theo and Jo that the nightmares he had suffered frequently in Saint-Rémy, had dissipated.[26]

After Gachet had medically examined the artist on arrival and got to know him better, Vincent was actually able to reassure his brother on 3 June that the doctor felt it 'highly improbable' that the episodes would return.[27] Two days later, he likewise notified his mother that 'the symptoms of the malady [...] have disappeared altogether recently', although he qualified this by adding that 'I've learned that one may not make too much of that'.[28] The value of this new, unofficial declaration of health hinges on the sixty-two-year-old Gachet's status as an expert on psychiatric disorders. Yet even though, as he had throughout the past year, Theo urged his brother above all not to overstretch himself, he was basically convinced that Vincent was not at any significant risk while he was under Gachet's care.

Contrary to what Vincent had been expecting, contact with his brother remained limited. Theo was busy and visited Auvers with Jo and their four-month-old son just once on 8 June, at Gachet's invitation. Vincent later asked very tentatively for another visit. 'In this way we really feel that we're not so far from one another, and I hope that we'll see each other again often.'[29] Van Gogh was now living at an inn and discussed the possibility of renting a house. If that were to happen, he would appreciate it if his brother and sister-in-law would also use his 'pied-à-terre' as a country house. He also thought of 'an exhibition of myself in a café', which also persuaded his brother that things were going in the right direction. 'I'm really pleased that the news you give us remains good, and that the courage for work is far from abandoning you', he wrote on 15 June.[30]

So confident, indeed, had Theo become about Vincent's condition that he did not beat around the bush on 28 June when he complained to his brother of how unhappy he had become at Boussod, Valadon & Cie. He had toyed for years with the idea of setting up as an independent art dealer and was now keen to follow through. One implication would be a less certain future, but Vincent would not suffer, since he had now found his way again: 'your carriage is already sturdy and strong'.[31] If he were to go ahead, he hoped he could count on his older brother's support and understanding. Vincent certainly understood, but the thought of the future caused him to shrivel: 'I fear, rather, that towards let's say the age of forty – but let's not say anything – I declare that I know nothing, absolutely nothing, of what turn it may yet take.'[32] He was unwilling, unable even, to look beyond what life had to offer at that moment, and did not believe he was capable of living up to any expectations. 'I, too, am trying to do as well as I can, I don't hide from you that I scarcely dare count on always having the necessary health.'

Van Gogh paid Theo and Jo a visit on 6 July to talk through his brother's plan. It was a confusing encounter, which left Vincent feeling like a millstone around the couple's neck, as is clear from his letter of 10 July.[33] He conflated Jo and Theo's unclear future with his own, as it were, leaving him deeply troubled:

'my life, too, is attacked at the very root, my step also is faltering. I feared – not completely – but a little nonetheless – that I was a danger to you, living at your expense – but Jo's letter clearly proves to me that you really feel that for my part I am working and suffering like you.' Just how much it all affected him is evident in the landscapes he painted of wheatfields and stormy skies after the visit – works that he described as expressions of 'sadness, extreme loneliness'.[34]

In the reply he sent on 14 July, Theo did not dwell on what he plainly considered to have been a misunderstanding: 'the danger isn't as grave as you believed'.[35] He and Jo travelled to the Netherlands the next day for his annual visit to his mother, and he only began to suspect that something was wrong after he returned. Vincent's most recent letter has not survived, but Theo clearly found it incomprehensible and feared that a fresh crisis was brewing. In a letter to his wife dated 20 July, he wrote: 'As long as he's not melancholic & heading for another crisis, it was all going so well.'[36] He wrote to Vincent: 'I'm a little afraid that there's something that's bothering you or that isn't going right. In that case, do go and see Dr Gachet, he'll perhaps give you something that will buck you up again.'[37] Although he meant this well, in retrospect he completely misjudged Vincent's mood and seemed unaware of his brother's diminished relationship with Gachet, whom he had visited just once since the end of June.[38]

Vincent replied straight away, with a tone of utter resignation: 'I'd perhaps like to write to you about many things, but first the desire has passed to such a degree, then I sense the pointlessness of it.'[39] Theo did not respond immediately. Four days later, on 27 July, Vincent shot himself in the chest in an attempt to take his own life, causing his shocked brother to rush to Auvers the following morning. He found Van Gogh with a serious wound but entirely in his right mind. There was no evidence of a fresh breakdown and his brother was able to express what had driven him to this act. Theo tentatively wrote to his wife that when it came to Vincent's life, 'sometimes it was more than he could bear'.[40] His brother 'no long harbours any illusions.' He lacked 'faith in life' and 'he was lonely'. Were he to survive, he would seek to end his life again, so unbearable had it become for him.[41] Vincent died the next morning.

A PSYCHOLOGICAL AUTOPSY

Peyron already had his concerns, but Van Gogh's discharge from the clinic in Saint-Rémy was a far greater risk than could have been suspected at the time. Statistical studies show that at least ninety per cent of all suicides (or suicide attempts) today are linked to psychiatric disorders[42] and that the chance of a suicide attempt is exceptionally high in the first months after discharge from a clinic.[43]

In Van Gogh's case, the focus of the doctors at the time was not so much on the risk of suicide, but on a potential recurrence of the artist's seizures. Peyron did inform Theo that the initial crises had been accompanied by 'ideas of suicide', but he also reported that these had dissipated after recovery.[44] It was probably based on this knowledge that Jo suggested in 1914 that Vincent's decision to end his life had stemmed from 'fear of the renewed threat of illness or the crisis itself'.[45] As already stated, her brother-in-law did not suffer an attack at the end of July, nor is there any evidence that Van Gogh was so fearful of such episodes that he would have attempted to end his life to avoid them.

Recent research, however, suggests that having suffered a number of episodes, patients often achieve a certain equilibrium in dealing with their fear of new attacks. Although Vincent was still plainly afraid of the horrors of a fresh crisis, it does indeed appear that this fear had abated somewhat since the most recent one.[46] Where he had previously thought that 'a more violent crisis may destroy my ability to paint forever', this did not occur to him any longer.[47] He also refused to be accompanied on the train journey to Paris: Van Gogh did not want to be treated like 'a dangerous animal' and there was no need to 'fear accidents so much', he assured Theo.[48] It was better 'to try and take misfortune into account', and his 'distress' also seemed greater than the likelihood of 'madness'.

This feeling of immense sadness seems rather at odds with his doctors' opinion that Van Gogh was entirely calm and lucid between attacks. We know that he was tormented during these periods by nocturnal manias, 'terrible fits of anxiety [...] or then again a feeling of emptiness and fatigue in the mind', 'fits of melancholy, atrocious remorse', as he wrote in late April 1889.[49] In the wake of his first attack at the asylum, he reported that 'the feeling of loneliness takes hold of me in the fields in such a fearsome way that I hesitate to go out'.[50] Although his mood fluctuated, this severely undermined his self-confidence: 'as a painter, I'll never signify anything important, I sense it absolutely', he wrote to Theo in early May 1889.[51]

Van Gogh's suicide ultimately flowed from this pattern of melancholic feelings and thoughts, which intensified with more or less each successive crisis, just as the attacks grew more depressive in nature over time.[52] The best way to put it, perhaps, would be that the feelings of psychotic depression and anxiety he suffered during his crises persisted into his lucid periods, making them steadily more real to him. So firmly did this negative self-image settle in Van Gogh's consciousness, in fact, that it eventually took on a distinctly painful character. In this way, the future faded from view. The despair of the moment swallowed up all his energy, and while it is hard to determine when the thought of suicide first arose during this process, we do know that he was already alluding to it in the spring of 1889, even before he was admitted to the asylum in Saint-Rémy.[53]

The likelihood of suicidal behaviour increases, psychiatric research shows, the more profound the negative self-image and lack of future perspective.[54] Broadly speaking, several stages can be distinguished, from dejection to the idea of being trapped, and from that sense of feeling stuck to volitional behaviour. Van Gogh went through these stages in the course of about eighteen months, but it is very much open to question whether those around him were fully aware of it.[55] Peyron – and Theo too – following Vincent's crisis in the spring of 1890, seem to have recognized that the painter's resilience was declining rapidly, but apparently neither linked this to an increased risk of suicide.

Early detection also appears to be extremely difficult, since it is a gradual process accompanied by constantly fluctuating moods. Van Gogh had, moreover, long since suffered from a negative self-image. He was by nature a nervous personality, prone to gloom and melancholy – traits which were intensified during his time in Paris, when he succumbed to alcohol abuse. Van Gogh was bitterly aware at that time that, as a young, innovative artist, he was numbered among the artistic outcasts, besieged by 'failure that will last *the whole of our life*'.[56]

His pugnaciousness in the face of adversity meant that these bleak prospects did not initially blow him off course. This would change, however, from the end of 1888. His abortive and highly stressful collaboration with Paul Gauguin in December left him with the previously mentioned 'wrinkles that won't be rubbed off in a hurry': self-mutilation, three or four psychotic attacks; involuntary solitary confinement; eviction from his house in Arles in response to local protests; and, in the background, the constant threat of relapse into a harried lifestyle with an overdependence on alcohol.[57] All this explains his voluntary admission to the asylum in Saint-Rémy.

Although Van Gogh chiefly felt defeated and that his admission was a moral failure, he nevertheless hoped to be cured at the asylum. This prospect evaporated in the wake of his first, acute attack between mid-July and late August 1889, just as he was 'beginning to hope that it wouldn't recur'.[58] His earlier dejection now turned to despair. 'I'm perhaps exaggerating in the sadness I feel at being knocked down by illness again – but I feel a kind of fear.'[59] He also grew afraid for the first time that a fresh crisis 'may destroy my ability to paint forever'. Peyron 'doesn't give me much hope for the future, [...] he makes me really feel that *everything* is doubtful'.[60]

So far, working had always been a way for Van Gogh to arm himself against the horrors of life. But that now seemed to be in jeopardy too. Henceforward, the thought of failing in this regard began to torment him. He also obsessed about living at Theo's expense without being able to do anything in return, talking himself into a massive sense of guilt: 'the more my health returns to normal the more my mind is capable of reasoning very coldly, the more to do painting that costs us so much and doesn't bring in anything, not even the cost of producing them, seems madness to me, a thing completely against reason.'[61] Every setback seemed to confirm his incompetence, also causing him to dwell more and more on all the things his own failure had denied him: a wife, children and the security of a family life.

At times, his self-esteem dropped to zero following that severe attack. 'To succeed, to have lasting prosperity, one must have a temperament different from mine, I'll never do what I could have and ought to have wanted and pursued.'[62] His emotions fluctuated,

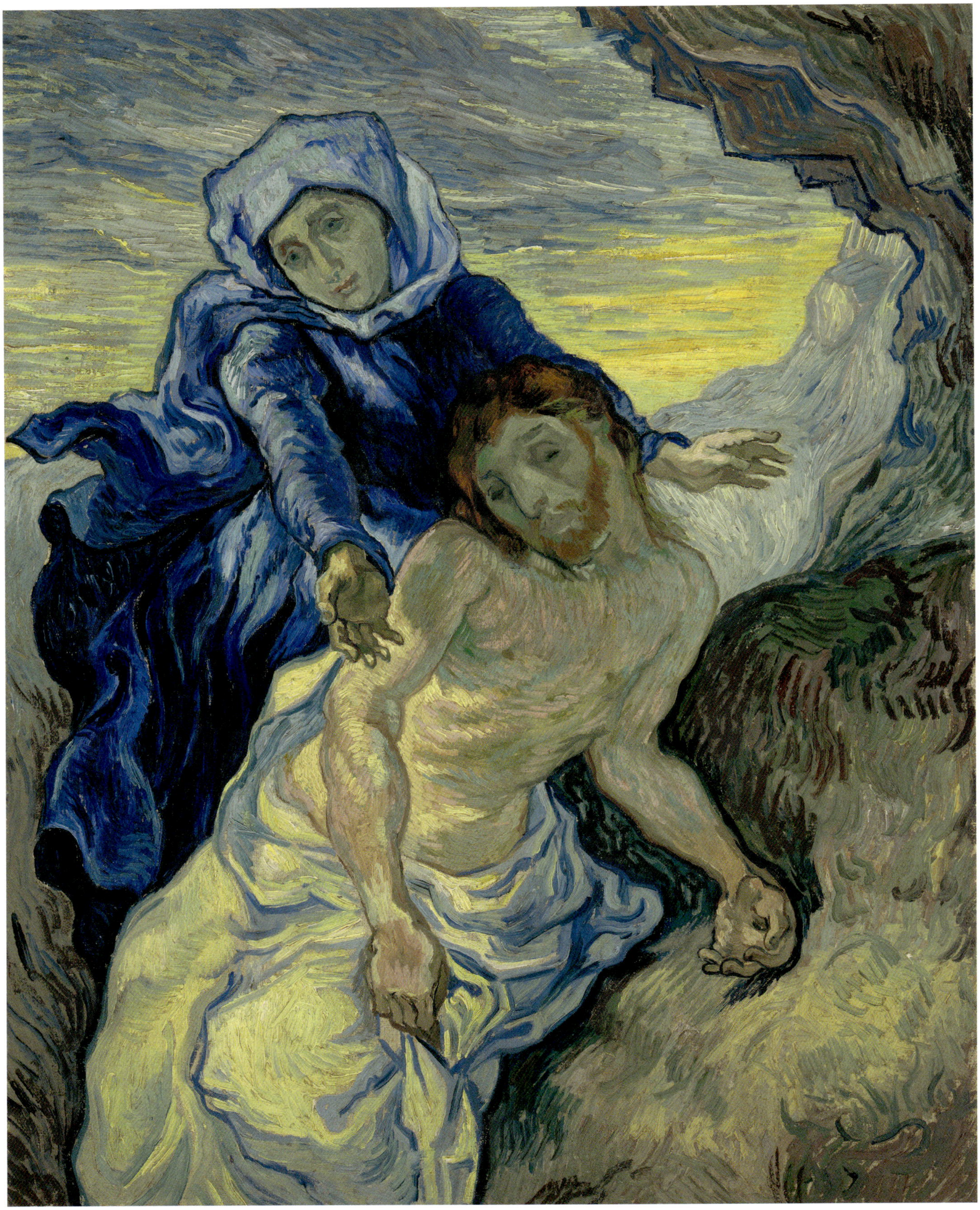

161
Vincent van Gogh
Pietà (after Delacroix), 1889
Oil on canvas, 73 × 60.5 cm
Van Gogh Museum, Amsterdam

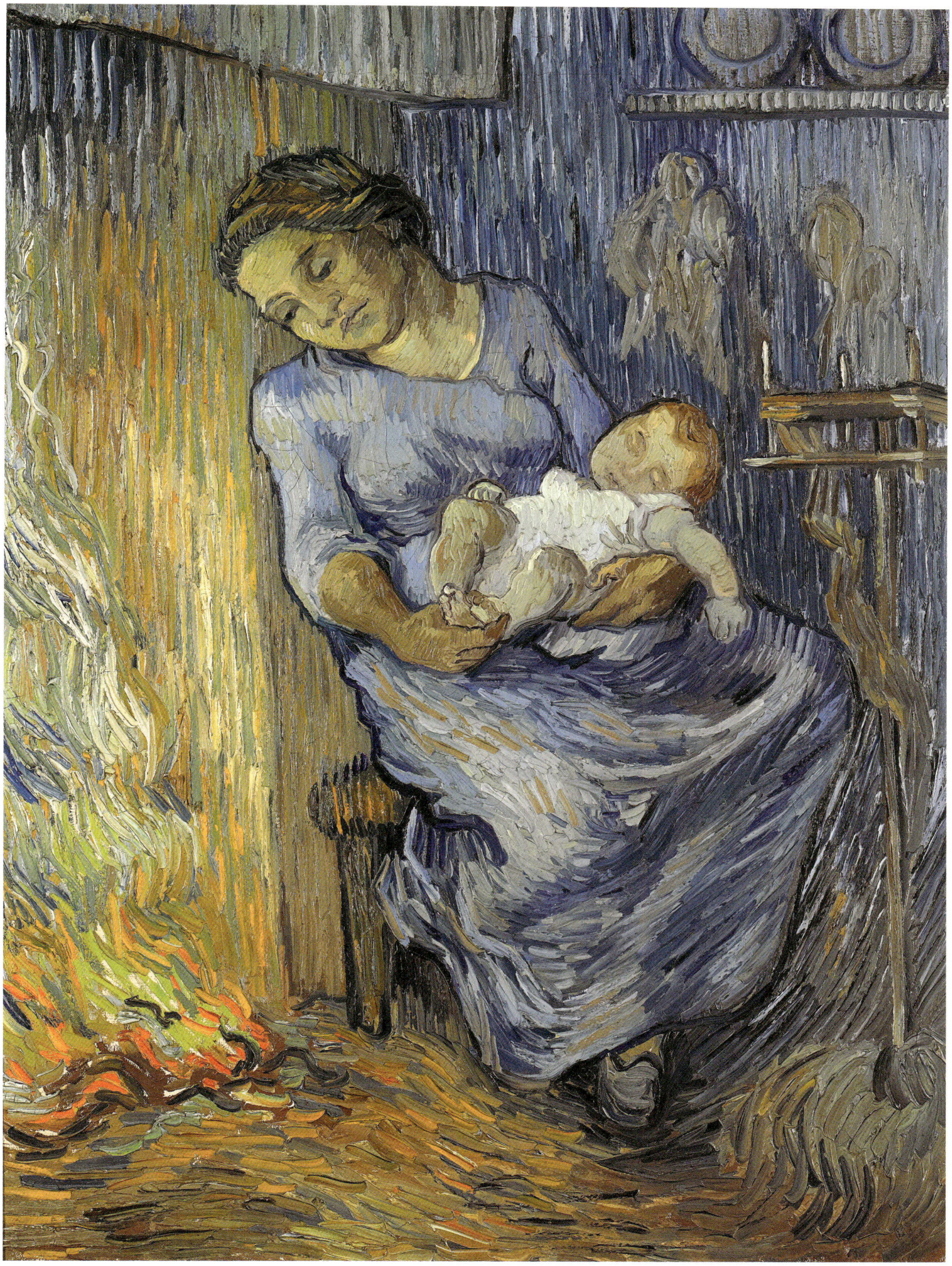

162
Vincent van Gogh
The Man is at Sea
(after Demont-Breton), 1889
Oil on canvas, 66 × 51 cm
Private collection, Larry Ellison

but he now felt that any great artistic ambitious were futile: 'as I have dizzy spells so often, I can only live in a situation of the fourth or fifth rank'. While he was led by chance to copy the works of earlier masters whom he admired **(161, 163)**, the underlying motivation was to 'have a basis in these artists, and then produce *the little I'm capable of in the same direction*' (my italics).

Just how much Van Gogh himself realized that he had changed is evident from his self-portraits at the time, in which he sought to present a slightly less dejected identity without unduly distorting the reality. He succeeded on his third attempt **(158)**. This portrait shows him with an expression almost as tranquil as the figures in 'the calm ancient portraits' of the seventeenth-century Dutch masters he so admired, such as Frans Hals and Carel Fabritius. However, the fact that he placed himself so serenely against a turbulent, almost swirling background clearly indicates that he was aiming to achieve an entirely different expression.[63] Serenity is linked here with turmoil, visually suggesting the metaphor of a rock buffeted by the waves. He has suffered but is *unbroken*, the portrait seems to say. Extremely fragile yet unyielding – this was the most that could be hoped for at that point. 'If I think rationally at present about my condition then certainly I tell myself that I mustn't have the *idée fixe* of being ill. [...] To remain for good in an asylum from now on would probably be exaggerating things.'[64]

A characteristic aspect of this period is the way Van Gogh relied far more on his painting than he had previously to shield him from such feelings of depression. It led him to paint his *Pietà*, for instance, from a reproduction of Eugène Delacroix's work around 1850 of the same name **(161)**. The theme of the painting was one of distress and grief, but even more so of maternal compassion, bestowed in the face of immense suffering and, in this instance, even after death. The effect was comforting.

Van Gogh's copy after Virginie Demont-Breton's *The Man is at Sea* **(162)**, which had caused a furore at the recent World Exhibition in Paris, falls into the same category. It is a tranquil image of a woman who has fallen asleep with her child. As she dozes, she dreams of 'the speedy return of the one she is waiting for' – this according to the commentary accompanying the reproduction on which Van Gogh based his own version. She is thus bolstered by a 'hope, which, heaven permitting, shall not be disappointed'.[65] Not only will the subject matter have resonated with Van Gogh's yearning for a secure and intimate family life, the work will also have appealed to him because of its maker, the daughter of the painter Jules Breton, of whom he was a great admirer. He had made a pilgrimage to Breton's home town in northern France in 1880.

While paintings like this were intended to be consoling, in his highly vulnerable state they ultimately failed to protect him from the torments of his life at the time. Something was *painfully* lacking; and where genuine security and compassion cannot be found, any such lack will eventually resurface. By the end of October, he had slipped back into downright depression. He felt 'utterly sad' and wrote that 'melancholy very often overtakes me with great force', prompting him to focus on the motif of solitary walkers in the asylum garden, beneath giant conifers with dark foliage.[66]

When a storm lashed the local landscape in early November, Van Gogh developed the motif, with a receding storm in the background, in a drawing and a large first version, and then an ambitious work **(160)**, in which he made use 'of red ochre, of green saddened with grey, of black lines that define the outlines'. In doing so, he explained to his artist friend Emile Bernard, he wanted to evoke in colour something of the 'anxiety' of his fellow patients.[67] This meaning was heightened by the large tree in the foreground, which had been struck by lightning in a storm and had been severely amputated, a 'dark giant – like a proud man brought low'. A painter did not have to depict the biblical episode directly in order to evoke Christ's agony in the Garden of Gethsemane, he continued, revealing the true subject of his picture. Like the Son of God, the patients at the asylum had to contend with an onerous destiny that they had to bear in utter solitude. And he too was one of them.

Peyron had instructed Van Gogh to 'react against the melancholy as much as I can', and it seems that after *The Garden at the Asylum* **(160)** he sought to do so as strictly as possible.[68] In the course of November and December, at least, he arrived at a remarkable new landscape idyll, depicting the local olive groves

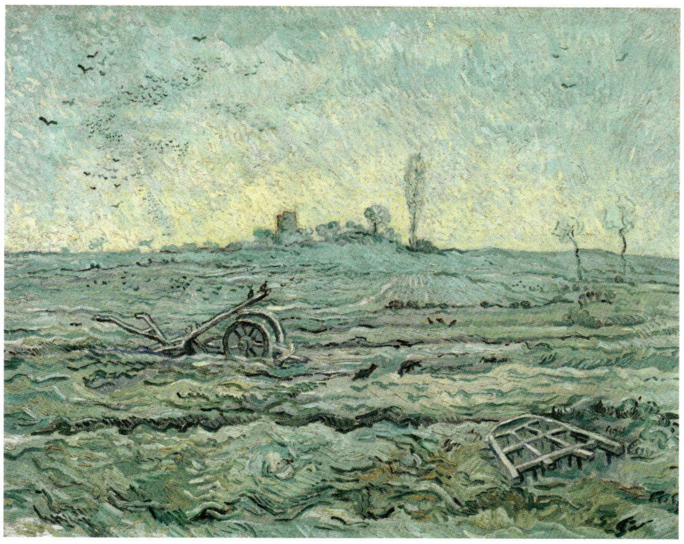

163
Vincent van Gogh
Snow-Covered Field with a Harrow (after Millet), 1890
Oil on canvas, 72.1 × 92 cm
Van Gogh Museum, Amsterdam

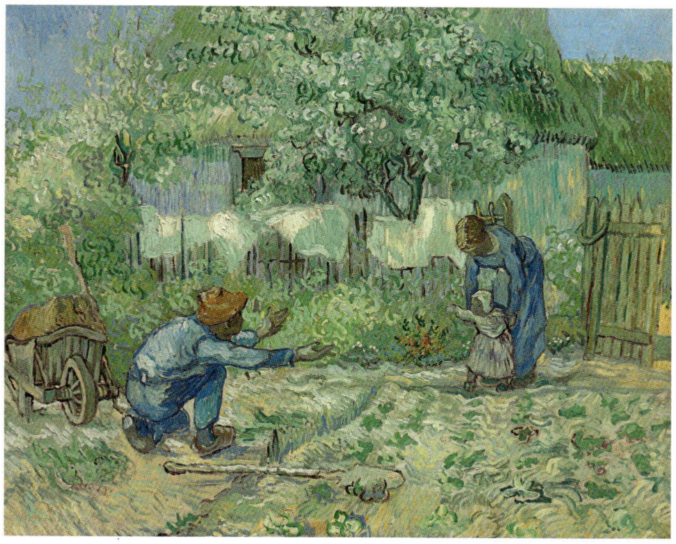

164
Vincent van Gogh
First Steps (after Millet), 1890
Oil on canvas, 72.4 × 91.2 cm
The Metropolitan Museum of Art, New York, Gift of George N. and Helen M. Richard, 1964

with the intention of turning them into *sunny* Gethsemanes, even though this was a contradiction in terms. The scenes could be related to the biblical Garden of Olives, but unlike *The Garden at the Asylum*, they do not evoke a dramatic, profoundly dark message in terms of their formal language **(12, 103)**.[69]

Yet it was to no avail: Van Gogh's morale plummeted further during the winter. He now felt like 'a most degenerate child' and wrote beautifully but heartbreakingly about his longing 'to remake myself and try to have myself forgiven for the fact that my paintings are [...] almost a cry of anguish'.[70] He might have had *The Garden at the Asylum* in mind, but his words seem to refer more to the copy he had recently completed in January of Jean-François Millet's *Winter: The Plain of Chailly* **(163)**, which depicts a desolate, wintry landscape with crows and, in the foreground, abandoned tools: a plough and a harrow. The painting formed a pair with his *First Steps* – also made after Millet **(164)**, which stood for everything that awaited his brother – married and soon to become a father – but that was denied to him. Picking a wintry scene like this suggests that he felt just as abandoned and side-lined as the tools left out in the cold. Nor will it have been a coincidence that he now interpreted *Gauguin's Chair*, painted in 1888 (Van Gogh Museum, Amsterdam), as showing 'the empty place' of his former companion.[71] His intention to copy Félix Régamey's series of prints of an American penal colony in colour **(166)** is further evidence of how disconnected he felt from the world.[72] In the end, he did not go through with it, limiting himself instead to 'translating' into colour a reproduction of Gustave Doré's *Exercise Yard at Newgate*, in which inmates of the London prison trudge aimlessly in circles as two butterflies flit around, reminding them of life outside **(165)**.

Van Gogh still managed to produce a life-affirming painting of spring in February 1890 **(70)**, but it comes as no surprise that he suffered a new and severe crisis at the end of that month. He recovered somewhat by the end of April, but the feelings of helplessness triggered by the episode remained so real and so onerous that the only option remaining to him was, he felt, to leave at once. He did not want to end up like his fellow patients. His 'capacity for work and what remains to me of common sense' were at stake, and while such a conclusion might appear understandable and reasonable, it sprang in reality from feelings that were compulsive and repetitive.[73]

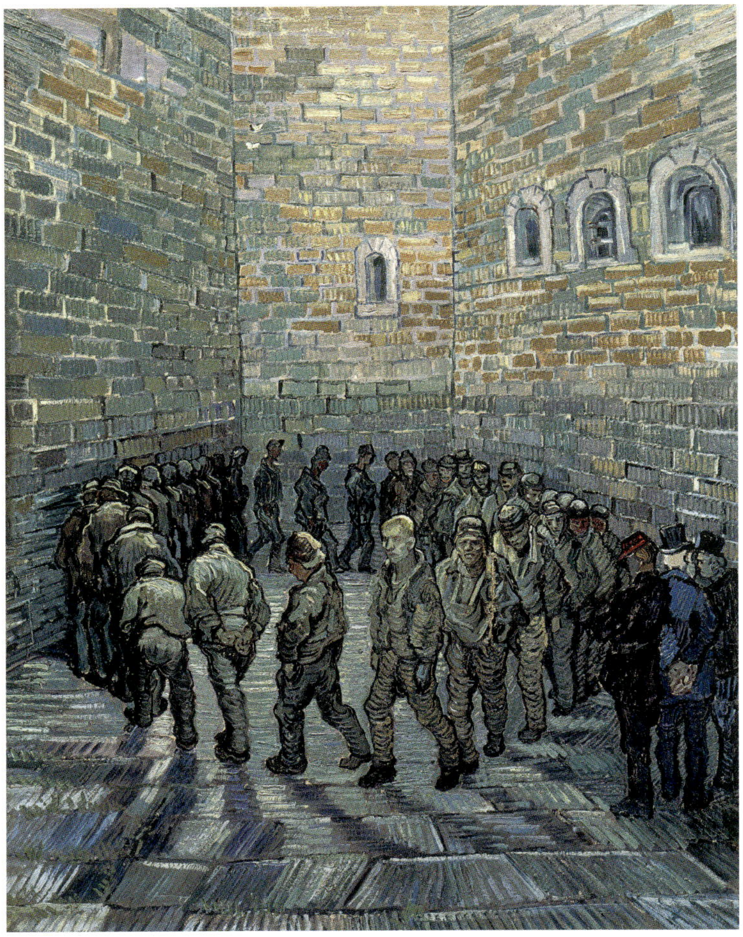

165
Vincent van Gogh
Penitentiary (after Doré), 1890
Oil on canvas, 80 × 64 cm
The Pushkin State Museum of Fine Arts, Moscow

166
Félix Régamey
Returning from Work, from the series 'American Sketches, Prison Life on Blackwell's Island', *The Illustrated London News*, February 1876
Wood engraving, 23.6 × 33.6 cm
Van Gogh Museum, Amsterdam

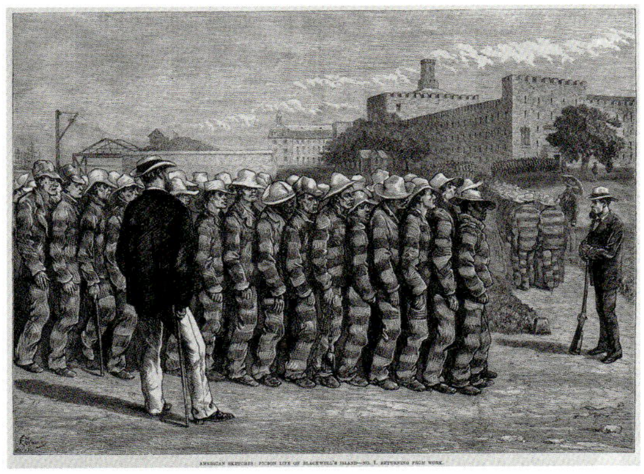

It goes without saying that life in the asylum was incredibly hard for him. All the same, there is a difference between an understandable sadness about what life is doing to you and a depressive hopelessness, in which the ability to think clearly is so compromised that one's morale reaches an absolute trough. This degree of decline distorted Van Gogh's perception of reality. He accused Peyron, for instance, of failing to pay him any attention during the crisis, 'leaving me to vegetate with the rest, who were profoundly corrupted'.[74] In reality, the doctor actually gave him permission to paint and draw during his attack. Having staged a recovery, Van Gogh also immediately disproved his own claim that the idleness of his fellow patients would have a disastrous effect on his skills. On the contrary, he painted the sublime works *Tree Trunks in the Grass* (Kröller-Müller Museum, Otterlo) and *Long Grass with Butterflies* (National Gallery, London).

While the idea of leaving somewhat alleviated his sense of depressive despair, he remained prey to what his own mind continued to tell him, namely that he was fundamentally weak and a failure. The intense fear that his life would not improve was undiminished. Van Gogh's last (or possibly second-to-last) painting at Saint-Rémy was *Sorrowing Old Man ('At Eternity's Gate')*, a free reworking in colour of his 1882 lithograph, which Theo had sent to him, for which he also used the title *Worn Out* and for which Andries Bonger came up with *Méditation tristesse* later in 1890 **(167)**.[75] It was 'with his head in his hands' just like this that Van Gogh had gone through the depression that afflicted him from February.[76] The work thus shows that he was still trapped by the same sinking feelings and thoughts he had hoped to leave behind him to as great an extent as possible.

The persistent fragility of his condition is also apparent from a letter he composed to Theo and Jo in the early days of his time in Auvers: 'I feel – a failure – that's it as regards me – I feel that that's the fate I'm accepting. And which won't change any more. But one more reason, *setting aside all ambition*, we can live together for years without ruining ourselves on either side. [...] That, though, is the absolute truth, it's difficult to acquire a certain facility of production, and by ceasing to work I would lose it much more quickly, more easily than it cost me in troubles to acquire it. And the prospect darkens, I don't see a happy future at all.'[77]

He never sent the letter, though. Van Gogh had suggested that things would improve for him after

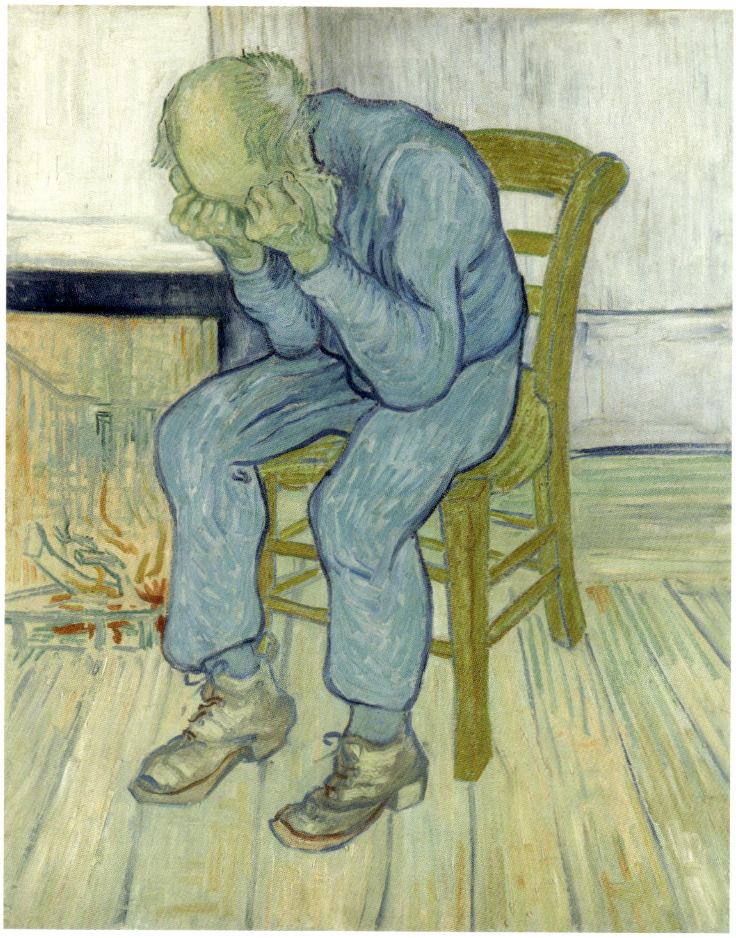

167
Vincent van Gogh
Sorrowing Old Man
('At Eternity's Gate'), 1890
Oil on canvas, 81.8 × 65.5 cm
Kröller-Müller Museum, Otterlo

he left, and it seems very much as though he was now too ashamed to show his brother the true, so very vulnerable side of his current personality. This was even more difficult for him than before, because even then he had been holding back. In the spring of 1889, for instance, it was not Theo to whom he sent his most candid letter about his depression, but his sister Willemien, who was also the only one he told after his severe crisis in the autumn of 1889 that his paintings were 'almost a cry of anguish'.[78] Theo likewise remained unaware that *The Garden at the Asylum* was not a picturesque and innocent view, but an expression of existential suffering, if not mortal anguish.[79]

It is further evident from his own correspondence that his personality had genuinely altered. Where his ardent pleas in Saint-Rémy to be allowed to leave still displayed something of 'that fighting, struggling, fervent, sombre Vincent, so often volatile and so impassioned', he increasingly effaced himself in his letters from Auvers, which were shorter and more business-like than before.[80] He even stated on one occasion that he had nothing to say, which seems highly revealing given his previous urge to talk at length in his letters.[81] At the same time, he became increasingly pliant, not wishing to be seen as demanding and avoiding having his weaknesses exposed. Although he had sought from the outset to persuade his brother to bring his wife and child to visit him in the countryside, when Theo informed him on 2 June that he would not have time for that until the beginning of August, he responded surprisingly meekly: 'I have hopes that it won't be disagreeable to be together again after a long absence.'[82]

In this way, Van Gogh side-lined himself in Auvers. Struggling against his sense of failure, he sought a new role in his relationship with his brother, but his depressive, black-and-white thinking limited his options: he was either a *help* to Theo (and his wife) or a *burden*, there was nothing in between.[83] He sought in his first month to settle into that initial role, to legitimize his own existence, as it were. But when his brother informed him at the end of June about his plans for the future, he was stricken with anxiety and the idea took shape that he was a millstone around their necks, as his letter of around 10 July shows.[84]

Whatever Van Gogh intended to convey through this letter, it ought to be read in the first place as an expression of a person who had become tangled up in his own feelings of depression.[85] While he himself connected them to the recent conversation in Paris, they were nevertheless the outcome of the mental process described above. Trivial matters had functioned as a catalyst, leaving him beset with existential angst, immense sadness and extreme loneliness on his return to Auvers. Although he suggested that Jo's letter had reassured him, we know from the subsequent course of events that Van Gogh's belief in his own ability and that of the people around him to restore his prospects for the future had dipped to an all-time low. His resilience was exhausted. 'I'd perhaps like to write to you about many things', he told Theo in his previously quoted final letter, 'but first the desire has passed to such a degree, then I sense the pointlessness of it.'[86] The despair and the pain had defeated him.

THE PORTRAIT OF DR GACHET

While it is clear from the above just how fragile Van Gogh's mental equilibrium was from day one in Auvers, he is still likely to have arrived in the village genuinely believing that Gachet would be able to help him. It seems significant at any rate that he brought several paintings with him from Paris, the choice of which can only be interpreted as providing the doctor with a thorough primer on his mental problems. All the works in question dated from the period after his first attack, when the sense of being trapped took firm hold of him: *Self-Portrait* **(158)**, *Pietà (after Delacroix)* **(161)**, *Marie Ginoux ('L'Arlésienne')* **(168)**, several of his *Olive Trees* **(103)**, *The Garden at the Asylum* **(160)**, *The Man is at Sea (after Demont-Breton)* **(162)** and *Penitentiary (after Doré)* **(165)**.[87]

Yet Van Gogh gave up on the idea that Gachet could help him straight after their first meeting. The doctor was, he wrote, a widower with a 'grief-stiffened face', which supposedly betrayed 'the nervous ailment from which it seems to me he's certainly suffering at least as seriously as I am'.[88] In his gloomy, unsent letter of late May, the artist went so far as to suggest that it was doing him no good to deal with a physician who could plunge him even deeper into despair.[89] He changed his mind, however, and began to work not long afterwards on a portrait of Gachet, in which he depicted the physician as a melancholic figure, echoing the portrait he had brought with him of Madame Ginoux, albeit to a much greater extent than he had done with his acquaintance from Arles.[90] To Van Gogh's mind, both of these sitters were as highly strung as himself, which he considered to be the worst illness of the modern era. By depicting Ginoux with copies of Charles Dickens's *Christmas Tales* and Harriet Beecher Stowe's *Uncle Tom's Cabin*, he was suggesting what seemed to him the only effective remedy, namely human compassion.[91]

It is significant that it was his sister Willemien rather than his brother Theo whom Van Gogh informed – and at some length – about what he meant to say with Gachet's portrait. 'I've done the portrait of Mr Gachet with an expression of melancholy which might often appear to be a grimace to those looking at the canvas', before continuing: 'And yet that's what should be painted, because then one can realize, compared to the calm ancient portraits, how much expression there is in our present-day heads, and passion and something like waiting and a shout. Sad but gentle but clear and intelligent.'[92] Van Gogh was referring here to existential suffering, which he made clear to his sister by basing his description of the intended expression on the example of Jesus, who, according to the Bible, patiently waited and meekly endured his death on the cross, yet when the end came, concluded his suffering with a wordless but all the more eloquent cry of anguish.[93]

In Van Gogh's view, the neurotic era in which he lived had primarily to struggle with the question of how to endure human suffering.[94] And it was to that struggle that not only the portraits of Gachet, himself and Madame Ginoux testified, but also the other works he brought with him. In his copy after Delacroix's *Pietà*, he continued to draw on the imagery of traditional painting, whereas in *The Garden at the Asylum*, the olive groves he brought with him, *The Man is at Sea* and *Penitentiary*, he chiefly sought to convey his own era.

Gachet's portrait, which Van Gogh painted for himself, was nothing other than an attempt after his departure from the asylum to capture the suffering of the age once more and in as sensitive a manner as possible. Healing was impossible, the picture seems to say, but the downcast physician, sitting at the table in his own garden, nonetheless offered

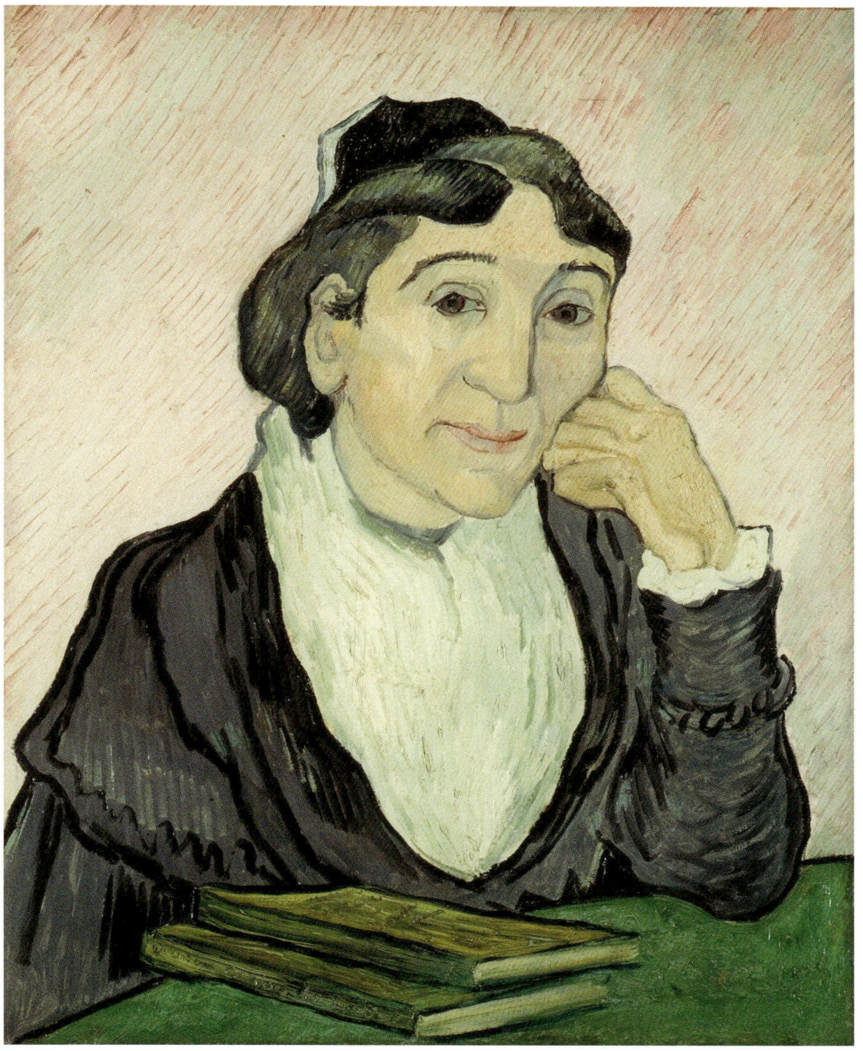

168
Vincent van Gogh
Marie Ginoux ('L'Arlésienne'), 1890
Oil on canvas, 63 × 47 cm
Galleria Nazionale d'Arte Moderna
e Contemporanea, Rome

his patients – above all the artists among them – compassion in the shape of a listening ear. And that meant a lot in itself. Fellow victims know better than anyone else what a person is going through, especially when that victim is a stricken, deeply melancholic doctor. This is how Van Gogh hoped to be comforted. Whether Gachet lived up to this ideal image, we do not know. But it is precisely what the artist was unable to ask so openly of his brother in the very last months of his life, for fear of seeming too vulnerable, weak or burdensome to him.

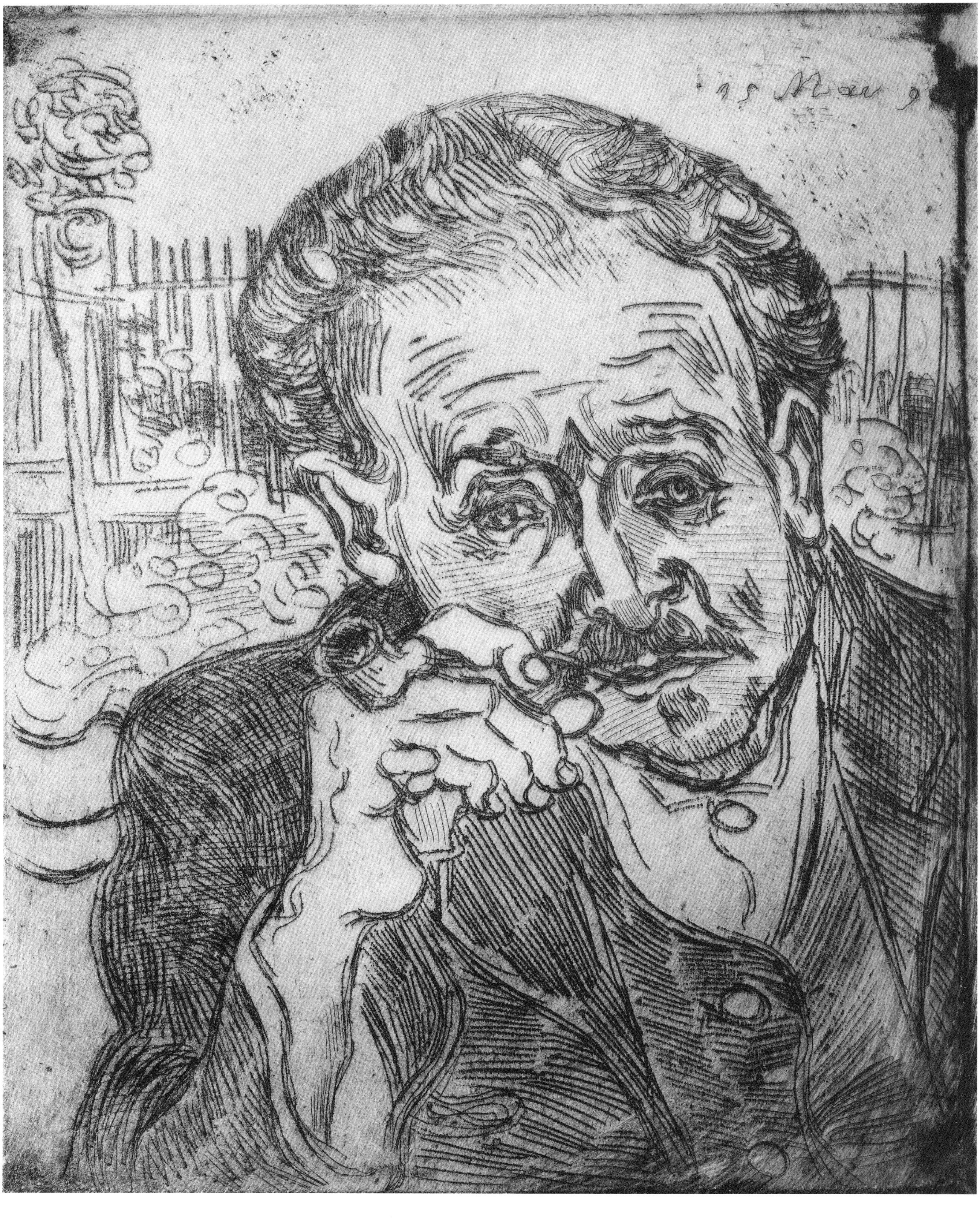

THE FIRST SIGNS OF RECOGNITION

BREGJE GERRITSE
AND SARA TAS

When the thirty-seven-year-old Vincent van Gogh arrived in Auvers-sur-Oise on 20 May 1890, it seemed to him that as a painter he was 'a failure [...] I feel that that's the fate I'm accepting. And which won't change any more.'[1] The onset of his psychiatric illness and the year that he had just spent at the asylum in Saint-Rémy had only worsened his negative self-image.[2] His deeply felt pessimism is understandable, yet it did not quite reflect reality. It simply took time to build a reputation and he had only been trying to carve out a place for himself among the Parisian avant-garde since the winter of 1886–87.

Fellow artists like Emile Bernard and Paul Gauguin had certainly recognized his talent at an early stage, but while this led to the mutual exchange and gifting of works, more was needed to build on this fledgling reputation.[3] Prior to 1888, Van Gogh's art could be seen at his brother Theo's Paris apartment and at the shop run by the paint seller Julien 'Père' Tanguy. When he exhibited a number of works at that year's Salon des Indépendants, established as an alternative to the official Salon, it immediately caught the eye of like-minded painters and commentators. The critic Gustave Kahn, for instance, wrote that 'Mr Van Gogh paints large landscapes, vigorously and with little concern for the value or precision of his tones.'[4] Van Gogh also took part in the 1889 and 1890 exhibitions of this Neo-Impressionist artists' association, drawing by far the most press coverage of any of the foreign exhibitors.[5]

An article by the journalist and artist Joseph Jacob Isaäcson, a friend of Theo's, was published in the Dutch press in August 1889 at the time of the Paris World Exhibition. Isaäcson was the first to mention Van Gogh's importance as 'a solitary pioneer; he struggles alone in the great night, his name, Vincent, is for posterity', and announced that he would soon be writing more on the subject.[6] Driven by his negative self-image, Van Gogh felt that his work was not yet worthy of such attention and asked Isaäcson not to publish anything about him for the time being.[7]

The breakthrough in the French press came in January 1890 when the poet and critic Albert Aurier made the case for his painting in the article 'Les isolés: Vincent van Gogh'. Aurier certainly touched a nerve. Van Gogh, he wrote, was a 'great painter' and a 'terrible and desperate genius', but 'he will only ever be fully understood by his brothers, the most artistic of artists... and by a few fortunate members of the common people'.[8] Part of Van Gogh was flattered – 'I rediscover my canvases in your

169
Vincent van Gogh
Portrait of Doctor Paul Gachet, 1890
Etching on paper, 18.3 × 15.1 cm
Van Gogh Museum, Amsterdam

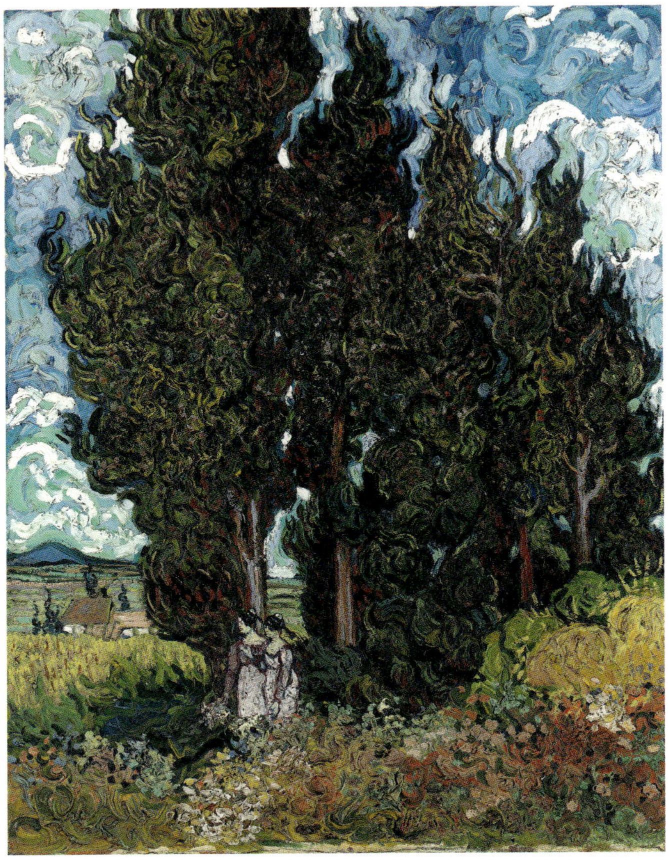

170
Vincent van Gogh
Cypresses with Two Figures, 1889–90
Oil on canvas, 91.6 × 72.4 cm
Kröller-Müller Museum, Otterlo

article, but better than they really are – richer, more significant', he wrote in his letter of thanks, but once again he found it hard to cope with praise.[9] He was uncomfortable, he told the critic, 'when I reflect that what you say should be applied to others rather than to me', and praised extensively other artists 'to whom I owe a great deal,' most notably Adolphe Monticelli and Gauguin. Aware at the same time of the opportunity that now arose, he presented Aurier with his *Cypresses with Two Figures* **(170)** as a token of gratitude. He also suggested to Theo that he send the article to three art dealers.[10]

That same month, Van Gogh took part in the annual exhibition of the artists' association Les Vingt, the Brussels equivalent to the Indépendants. The exhibition and Van Gogh's contribution in particular elicited a scathing review in his native Netherlands, but they did result in the first substantial sale of his work.[11] The Belgian painter Anna Boch purchased his *Red Vineyard* at Les Vingt for no less than 400 francs **(171)**.[12]

As far as others were concerned, therefore, Van Gogh was by no means a 'failure'. Several critics had already spotted him as an exceptional artist with an entirely personal style. His reputation was growing within a small yet important circle, and not only in France.

THE BOND WITH GACHET

In the meantime, Vincent was making plans with Theo to leave the asylum in Provence and move closer to Paris. Theo met Dr Paul Ferdinand Gachet towards the end of March 1890. Gachet, who was specialized in the phenomenon of 'melancholia', spent a large part of his week in Auvers, while also running a practice in Paris. He enjoyed the company of artists, collected art and painted in his spare time himself, using the pseudonym Paul van Ryssel. Theo was optimistic that the doctor would understand Vincent and be able to do a great deal for his mental health.[13] Vincent gratefully accepted Theo's suggestion to move to Auvers. 'I think that it'll be best for me to go myself to see this doctor in the country as soon as possible.'[14] The physician swiftly became an admirer of Vincent's work, and would eventually come to own many of his paintings, particularly ones produced in Auvers.

Van Gogh made the acquaintance of 'this doctor' on the very day of his arrival in Auvers, 20 May 1890. He thought Gachet 'an odd fellow' but that 'the impression he made on me isn't unfavourable'. He concluded, 'I really think that I'll stay friends with him'. The grief at the loss of his wife fifteen years earlier was imprinted on Gachet's face and Van Gogh knew straight away that he wanted to do his

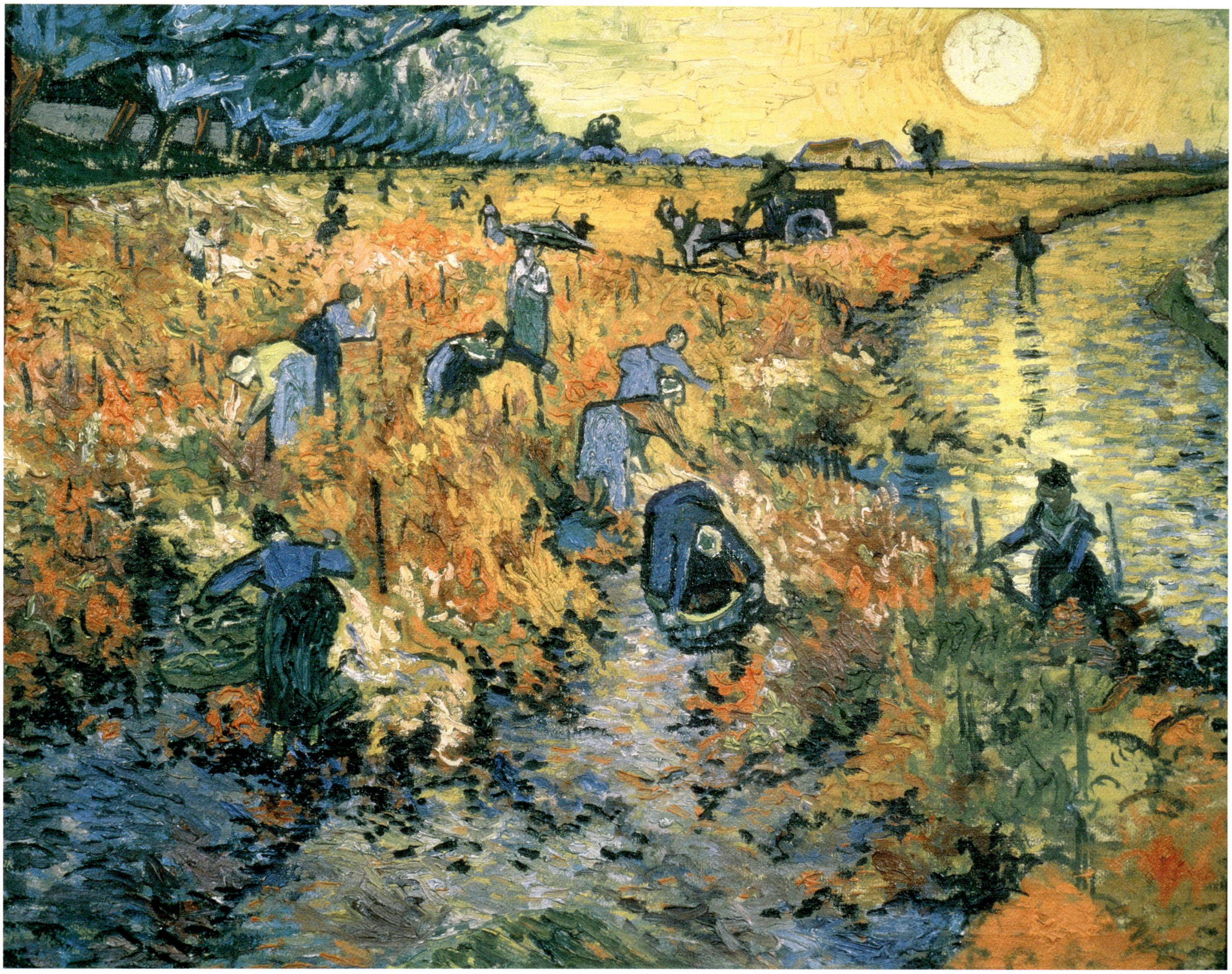

171
Vincent van Gogh
Red Vineyard, 1888
Oil on canvas, 75 × 93 cm
The Pushkin State Museum of Fine Arts, Moscow

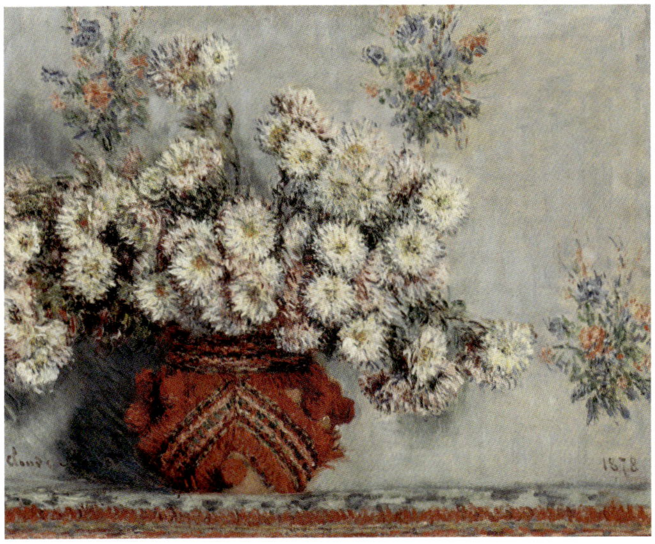

172
Claude Monet
Chrysanthemums, 1878
Oil on canvas, 54.3 × 65.2 cm
Musée d'Orsay, Paris

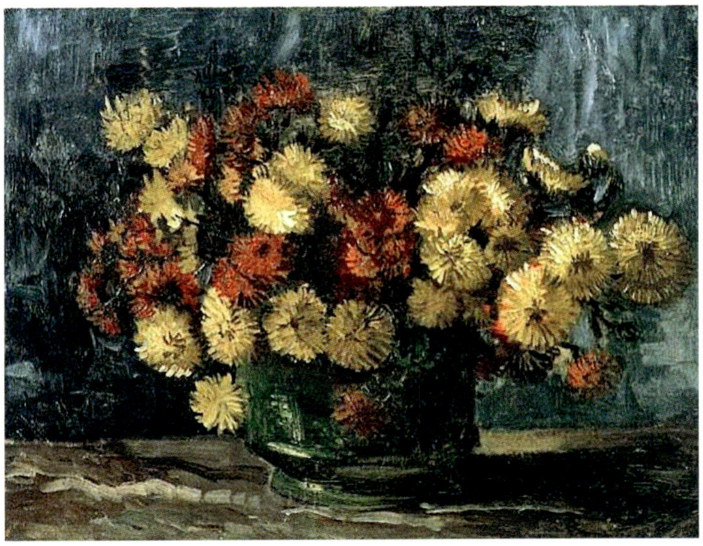

173
Vincent van Gogh
Chrysanthemums, 1886
Oil on canvas, 46 × 61 cm
Private collection

portrait.[15] Gachet in turn encouraged Vincent to paint as much as possible and gave him the idea of making his first and only etching **(115, 116, 169)**.[16]

His house was 'full of old things, dark, dark, dark', although it also contained several interesting Impressionist paintings, including floral still lifes by Paul Cézanne and Claude Monet, painters whom Van Gogh also admired.[17] Perhaps he saw an opportunity to position his own work among them, which might explain why two of his Paris flower paintings **(173, 175)**, which display certain similarities with Monet's *Chrysanthemums* and Cézanne's *Dahlias* **(172, 174)** found their way into Gachet's collection. Van Gogh may have brought flower still lifes with him as gifts when he arrived in Auvers and have given these two to Gachet because they fitted so well into his collection.[18]

THE FINAL DAYS

Gachet might have been an ally of Van Gogh's artistically and 'a ready-made friend [...] so much do we resemble each other physically, and morally too', but as a doctor he proved unable to play a significant role in alleviating his mental problems.[19] 'I think that we must IN NO WAY count on Dr Gachet. In the first place he's iller than I am, it seemed to me, or let's say just as much.'[20] Although Van Gogh tentatively suggested in Auvers at one point that he might 'do an exhibition of myself in a café', the extent to which he was still thinking about raising his profile on the art market is open to question.[21] This no doubt reflected his sense of failure. Van Gogh's mental health deteriorated in July. He hardly visited Gachet again, and tragedy struck at the end of the month.

On Sunday 27 July, he shot himself in the chest with a revolver in an attempt to end his life. Vincent did not want Theo to be informed, but Gachet immediately dispatched a letter urging him to come as quickly as possible to the Café de la Mairie, the inn where Vincent was staying. The letter was hand-delivered to Theo early the next morning by Anton Hirschig, a Dutch painter who was lodging at the same place.[22] Theo rushed to Auvers and never left Vincent's side until the end.[23] Van Gogh succumbed to his injury at one thirty in the morning of 29 July, barely ten weeks after arriving in Auvers-sur-Oise. Gachet was a great support in those dark days, Theo wrote to his wife Jo, who was in the Netherlands at the time: 'Dr Gachet had summoned the village doctor [Joseph Jean-Baptiste Mazery] as he did not trust himself, but it was nevertheless he in fact who did everything. Later, he did not leave me alone for a second, and was so very kind.'[24]

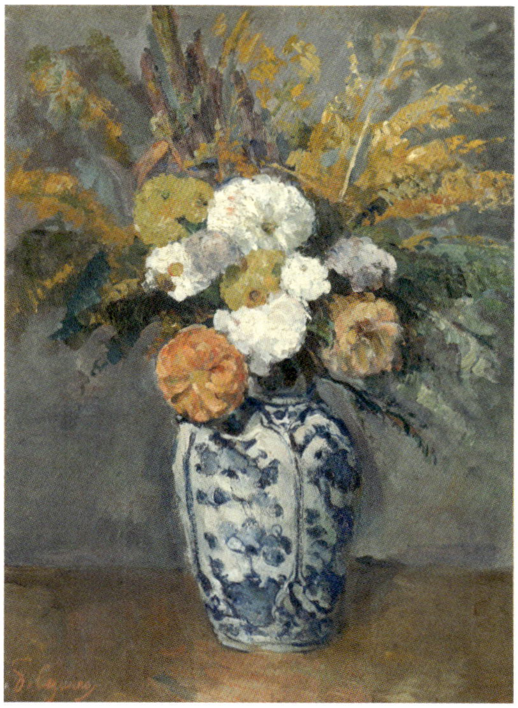

174
Paul Cézanne
Dahlias in Delft Blue Vase, c. 1873
Oil on canvas, 73 × 54 cm
Musée d'Orsay, Paris

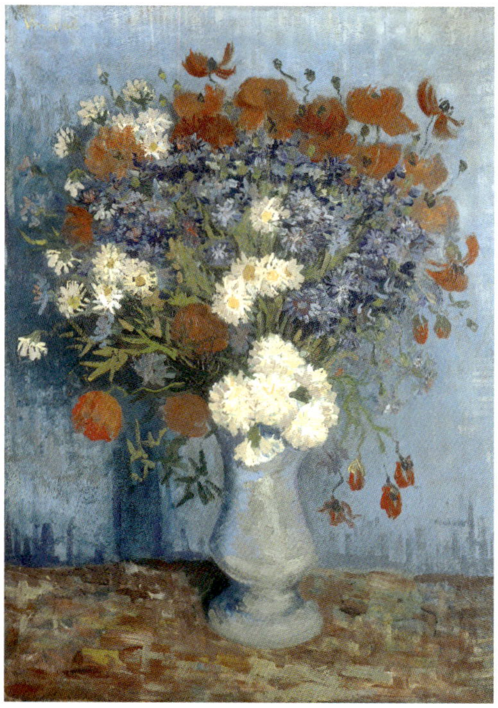

175
Vincent van Gogh
Vase with Cornflowers and Poppies, 1887
Oil on canvas, 80 × 67 cm
Private collection

Theo was stricken with grief – 'I miss him, everything seems to remind me of him'[25] – and Gachet was deeply affected too: although they had not spent a great deal of time together, Vincent had become precious to him as a person and as an artist. Gachet was the first to place 'a magnificent bouquet of sunflowers' by the coffin and made two sketches of Vincent on his deathbed **(177, 178)**.[26] He kept one of them for himself and gave the other to Theo, with the dedication 'à mon ami Theo van Gogh le 29 juillet. Dr P. Gachet'.[27]

THE FUNERAL

The funeral was held on Wednesday afternoon, 30 July **(176)**. Several acquaintances from artistic circles in Paris had hurried to Auvers that morning: the paint seller Père Tanguy, the artists Emile Bernard, Charles Laval and Auguste Lauzet, and the Dutch painter Maurits van der Valk with his fiancée Baukje van Mesdag. Lucien Pissarro, Camille's son, had travelled from Eragny. They had received news of the tragic death of their close friend just in time. Also present were Theo's brother-in-law Andries Bonger and, of course, Gachet, Hirschig and Arthur Ravoux, landlord of the Café de la Mairie. It was not possible for Jo or for the rest of the Van Gogh family to get to Auvers from the Netherlands in time.[28]

Bernard sent a letter to Aurier two days later with a detailed account, no doubt hoping that the art critic would publish something about the event and endorse Van Gogh's importance. Vincent was placed in the back room of the café in a closed coffin covered with a white cloth topped with yellow flowers, including 'the sunflowers he loved so much'. On the walls around the coffin, 'all his last canvases were hung making a sort of halo for him and the brilliance of the genius that radiated from them made this death even more painful for us artists.'[29] They included many canvases from Auvers: 'one with fields vanishing undulatingly towards the horizon', *The Church at Auvers-sur-Oise* **(1)**, *Auvers-sur-Oise Town Hall on 14 July 1890* **(63)**, *Child with Orange* **(132)**, one of the portraits of Adeline Ravoux **(118, 119)** and a version of *Daubigny's Garden*. The displayed works also included paintings from Saint-Rémy that Van Gogh had brought with him because they were of special personal significance, including 'the one with the sun right in the middle', his *Pietà (after Delacroix)* **(161)** and *Penitentiary (after Doré)* **(165)**.[30] The coffin was taken to the little cemetery at the top of the hill at three o'clock in the afternoon. Gachet delivered the eulogy. The doctor was so overcome by tears that his farewell was stammered, yet no less moving for all that.

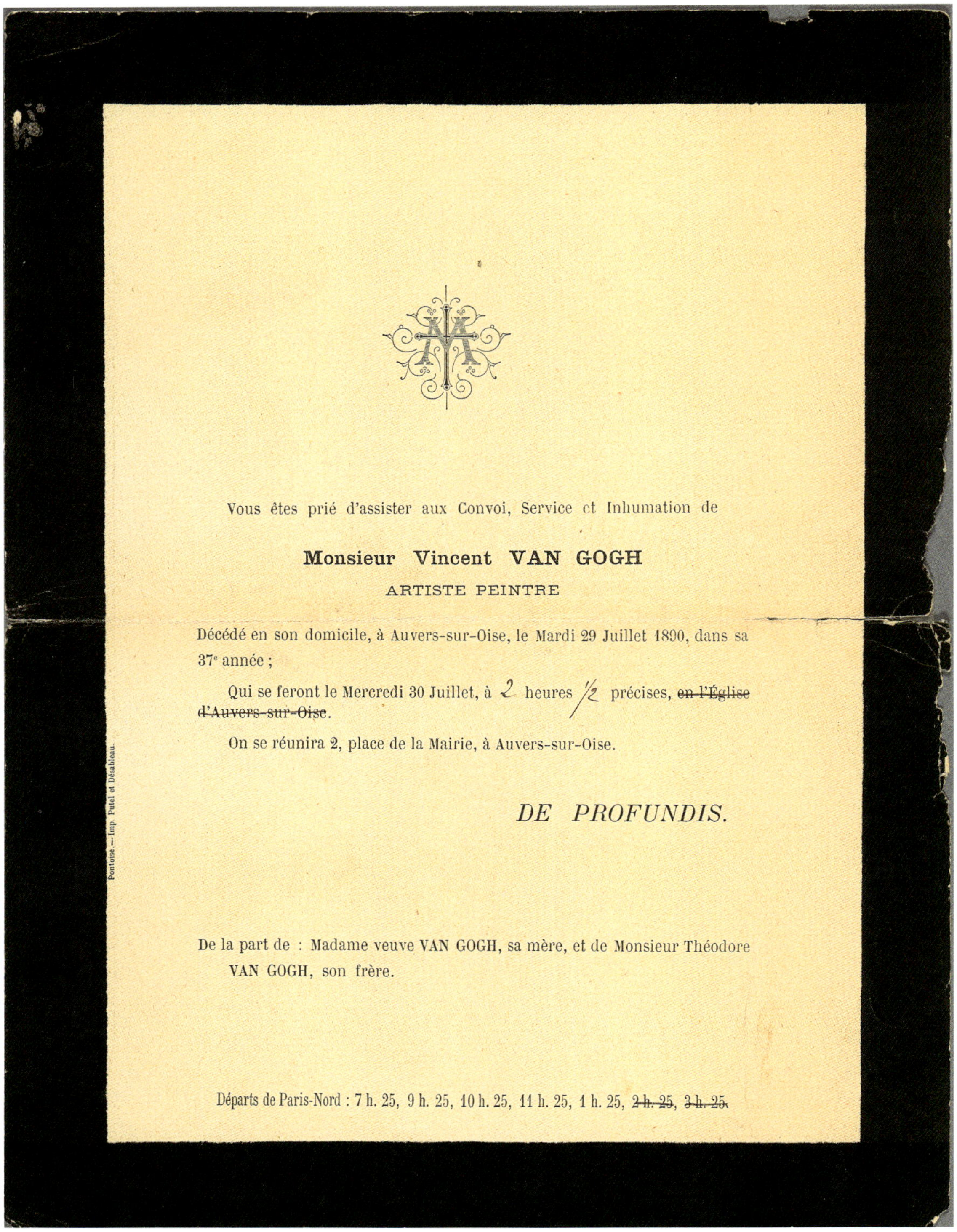

Vous êtes prié d'assister aux Convoi, Service et Inhumation de

Monsieur Vincent VAN GOGH

ARTISTE PEINTRE

Décédé en son domicile, à Auvers-sur-Oise, le Mardi 29 Juillet 1890, dans sa 37e année ;

Qui se feront le Mercredi 30 Juillet, à 2 heures 1/2 précises, ~~en l'Église d'Auvers-sur-Oise~~.

On se réunira 2, place de la Mairie, à Auvers-sur-Oise.

DE PROFUNDIS.

De la part de : Madame veuve VAN GOGH, sa mère, et de Monsieur Théodore VAN GOGH, son frère.

Départs de Paris-Nord : 7 h. 25, 9 h. 25, 10 h. 25, 11 h. 25, 1 h. 25, ~~2 h. 25~~, ~~3 h. 25~~.

Pontoise. — Imp. Putel et Désableau.

176
Mourning card, invitation to the funeral of Vincent van Gogh, 1890
Van Gogh Museum, Amsterdam

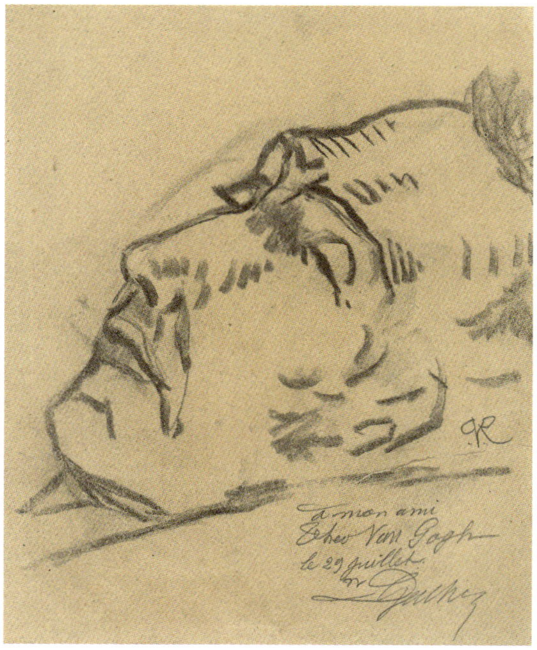

177
Paul van Ryssel (Paul Ferdinand Gachet)
Vincent van Gogh on his Deathbed, 1890
Charcoal on paper, 27.2 × 22.7 cm
Van Gogh Museum, Amsterdam

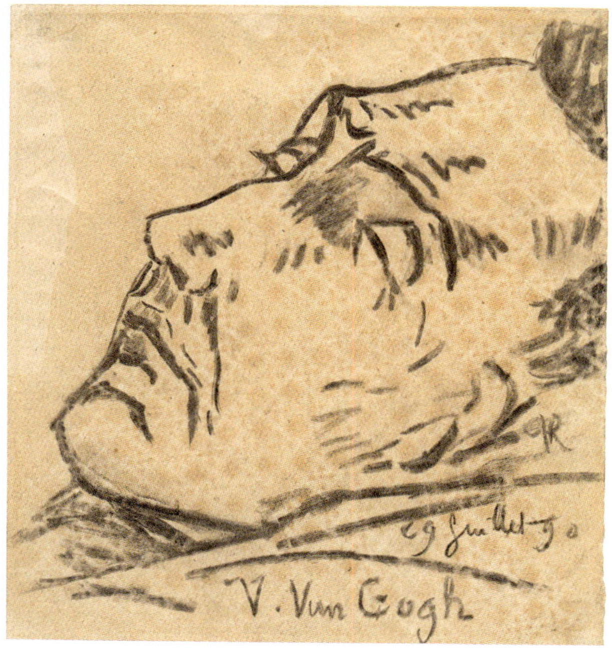

178
Paul van Ryssel (Paul Ferdinand Gachet)
Vincent van Gogh on his Deathbed, 1890
Charcoal on paper, 48 × 41 cm
Musée d'Orsay, Paris

He gave 'a short description of Vincent's struggles and achievements, stating how sublime his goal was and how great an admiration he felt for him [...] It was art that he prized above everything and which will make his name live...'[31] Besides his closest friends, all sorts of people from Auvers came to pay their respects, including artists,[32] and also, according to Adeline Ravoux, several neighbours, who until recently had observed Vincent setting off each morning to paint. Adeline, the daughter of the Café de la Mairie's landlord, was twelve at the time. She described the events, which made a deep impression on her and her family, several decades later. Her father had accompanied Theo when he visited the town hall that morning to report Van Gogh's death. She recalled that the coffin had been made by a neighbour, a carpenter called Vincent Levert, who also lent the trestles on which the casket was supported.[33]

After the funeral, Theo, Gachet, his son Paul Jr, Arthur Ravoux and Hirschig returned to the room where the coffin had been set up. To thank them for the solicitude they had showed his brother, Theo invited them to select works in Vincent's memory. Ravoux and his daughter Adeline had already received works from Vincent **(63, 119)** and the innkeeper declined this kind offer.[34] Gachet, however, chose many pieces, as a result of which he ended up with the largest Van Gogh collection in France – twenty-seven paintings in all, fourteen of which were works from Auvers.[35] This is also likely to have been the point at which the village doctor Mazery received two paintings from Auvers and that Vincent's close friend Bernard was given *Farmhouse and Vineyard* **(#3)**.[36] The remaining works were sent shortly afterwards to Theo and Jo's apartment in Paris, with the exception of the works made in Auvers, for which there was no further space. These were stored in Tanguy's paint shop, where part of Van Gogh's oeuvre was already located.[37]

Theo departed the following Sunday for the Netherlands, where he was now able to share his immense grief with Jo and his family.[38] It must have been an emotional reunion. He took with him the little sketch that Gachet had made of Vincent on his deathbed, later writing to the doctor that his mother was very grateful to him for this and for all the care he had offered Vincent **(177)**. 'My mother has particularly asked me to tell you of her deep gratitude [...] for all that you have done for her poor son whom you have shown as much devotion and affection as if you were a member of the family.'[39]

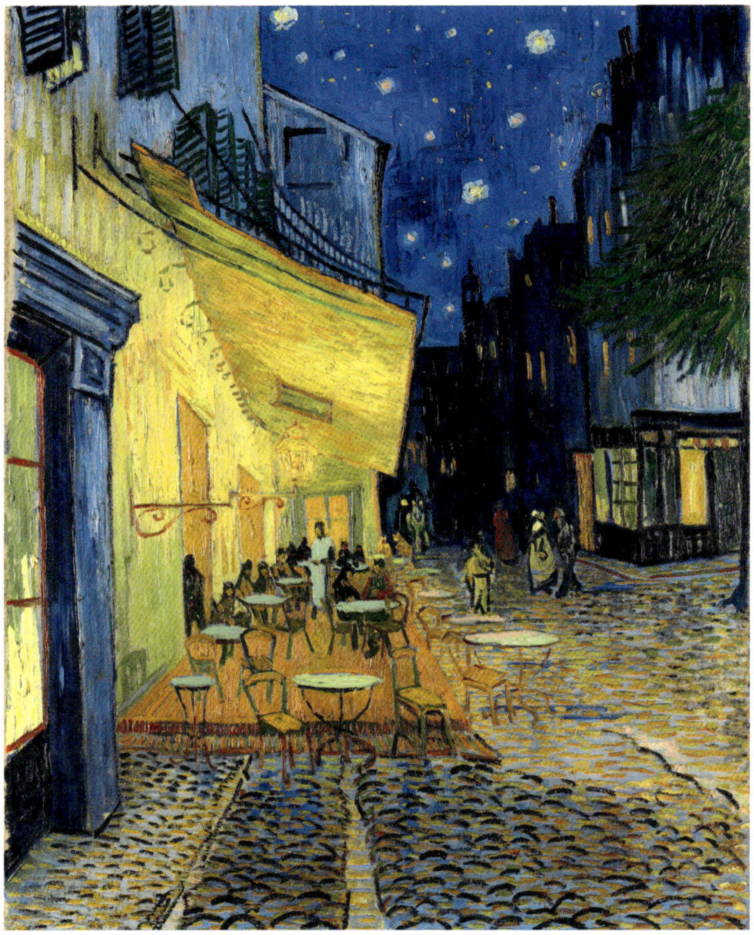

179
Vincent van Gogh
Terrace of a Café at Night (Place du Forum), 1888
Oil on canvas, 80.7 × 65.3 cm
Kröller-Müller Museum, Otterlo

TRIBUTES

In the weeks that followed, Theo and his family received no fewer than fifty letters of condolence from artists, critics and collectors in France and the Netherlands, many of them affirming the extent to which Vincent's talent had already been recognized by colleagues.[40] Paul Gauguin wrote that he was a true artist, 'a rare thing in our epoch'. Meijer de Haan called him 'an extremely important Artist'.[41] Van Gogh's early artist friend Anthon van Rappard wistfully recalled 'that fighting, struggling, fervent, sombre, Vincent, so often volatile and so impassioned, yet, for his noble mind, and artistic qualities, always worthy of friendship and admiration'.[42] A number of people, including artists Armand Guillaumin, Camille Pissarro, Henri de Toulouse-Lautrec, Eugène Carrière, Victor Vignon and the dealer Pierre-Firmin Martin, expressed their regret at having been unable to attend the funeral. Others, such as Claude Monet, Ernest Quost and Isaac Israëls, who did not know Vincent personally, wrote because of their connection with Theo.

Van Gogh's death did not go unnoticed by the press either. Six short articles on the subject were published in regional and Paris newspapers.[43] The widely read *La Petite Presse* wrote, somewhat sensationally: 'Van Gogh, highly nervous and sensitive by nature, was soon in a state of extraordinary excitement, drew his revolver from his pocket and fired a round into his head [*sic*]', but also praised him as 'one of the most interesting of our Impressionist painters'.[44] These words of appreciation demonstrated once again that Van Gogh already enjoyed a small but secure reputation in artistic circles at the time, and that his death acted as a catalyst.

THEO'S PLANS

Theo, like Gachet, was undoubtedly left with an enormous sense of guilt. Stricken with grief at Vincent's death, he resolved to redouble his efforts to bring his late brother's work to the attention of dealers and art critics and steadily to build his reputation. A few days after the funeral, he wrote to his sister Elisabeth (Lies): 'People should know that he was a great Artist, which often goes hand in hand with being a great Human Being. Time will bring recognition, and many will regret his having passed away so soon.'[45]

He began making plans that same week for an 'Exposition Vincent' – a large-scale exhibition in a rented space, where people would be able to see numerous works together in order to attract the attention of the press.[46] Theo approached Paul Durand-Ruel to explore the possibilities for an event of this kind at his gallery on rue Laffitte.[47] The dealer came to Theo's home in the week of 19 August to view Vincent's work, but hesitated, saying that he would first visit the paint seller Tanguy to view the paintings from Auvers that were stored there.[48]

There was no question in Gachet's mind either that Vincent's work needed to be better known. He informed Theo in a letter two weeks or so after the funeral that he was planning to write 'not a catalogue but a complete biography – for a man who was so exceptional something commonplace would be inappropriate...'[49] On 21 August, he had dinner with Theo and Jo. 'Theo was insistent that he should be received very well, because he has been so kind to Vincent and to Theo', Jo wrote to her parents the next day. 'It is remarkable how strongly *he* has been affected by Vincent's death – he says that he has felt nothing so keenly since the death of his wife (twenty [*sic*] years ago). He is working on a biography and talks and thinks about nothing except Vincent. He stayed until 12 o'clock.'[50]

Theo also invited Aurier to come and dine with him and Jo at the beginning of September, on which occasion they discussed the possibility of Aurier writing a biography too. Unlike Gachet, he was an art critic, after all, and so a book by him would do more for Van Gogh's reputation than the account that the doctor presumably had in mind. Aurier had got to know Van Gogh's work through Bernard and, when preparing for his article in early 1890, he had not only viewed paintings held by Tanguy and Theo, but had also read Van Gogh's letters to Bernard.[51] Theo thus decided to lend his brother's letters from Saint-Rémy to the writer.[52] This will also have been the moment, no doubt, when Aurier acquired most of his collection of Van Gogh paintings. He owned twelve of them, representing a cross-section of the artist's oeuvre, including peasant studies from Nuenen, still lifes from Paris and the masterpieces *Terrace of a Café at Night (Place du Forum)* **(179)** and *L'Arlésienne (Portrait of Madame Ginoux)* (Kröller-Müller Museum, Otterlo) from the south of France. It is highly plausible that he received many of these works from Theo in preparation for his biography, as an advance or as a thank you for his assistance.[53]

Around the same time, the critic Julien Leclercq published a brief obituary of Van Gogh in the *Mercure de France*: 'He will, perhaps, have his due hour of fame – posthumously alas! – before being ranked among the rare bold and personal artists of this *fin-de-siècle*.'[54] Leclercq also announced in his article that there was to be an 'exhibition of the painter's most important works', though without mentioning a location, indicating that he was aware of Theo's plans.[55] In the end, Durand-Ruel – who made a name for himself as a dealer selling works by the Barbizon painters and the Impressionists – did not go ahead with a solo exhibition for the avant-garde artist,[56] so Theo decided to set up his own new apartment, still vacant, at 6 cité Pigalle as an exhibition space from 22 September. The young family had started to move their belongings into the more spacious flat on 14 September, but the rent at the old address at 8 cité Pigalle was still running.[57] The walls were hung so full of paintings that according to Bernard, the various rooms looked like the galleries in an art museum. Bernard helped install the works, as he had done on the day of the funeral in Auvers. Vincent's ideas about exhibiting art were respected, with paintings displayed alongside others that intensified their colours.[58]

The exhibition quickly enjoyed a certain success. Theo managed to sell two works 'to an artist with whom they will be seen a great deal'[59] – undoubtedly Emile Schuffenecker, a close acquaintance of Vincent and Theo, who began to collect the work of fellow artists around 1880.[60] Attention was clearly growing, as Tanguy too sold two paintings a few months later. Works by Van Gogh were on constant display in his modest paint shop at the time, as Aurier repeatedly pointed out to readers of his 'Choses d'art' column in the *Mercure de France*.[61]

FATEFUL TURN OF EVENTS

In the meantime, Theo continued to search for an official venue for the 'Exposition Vincent' and made plans to visit Gachet. 'My doors and my arms are wide open!' the doctor wrote warmly on 4 October.[62] But it was on that same day that Theo himself showed the first signs of a severe nervous breakdown. He collapsed on 9 October and was hospitalized.[63] Jo and her brother Andries urged Gachet to visit Theo as soon as possible[64] and the doctor duly went to the clinic on 15 October with Hermanus Tersteeg, Theo's former boss from The Hague, but he was not able to speak to the patient.[65] The gravity of the situation soon became apparent. Aurier wrote to Gachet on 22 October: 'The misfortune you predicted has come to pass and all that now remains is to do our duty as friends.'[66] On 17 November, a now entirely unresponsive Theo was transferred to a clinic in Utrecht.[67]

Bernard did not give up, even though the most important representative of Vincent's artistic legacy was now absent. In December 1890, he arranged for three Van Goghs from Aurier's collection to be included in the group exhibition *Peintres impressionnistes et symbolistes* at Le Barc de Boutteville art gallery.[68] The presentation at Theo and Jo's apartment also seems to have continued until at least the end of the year. The Dutch newspaper the *Algemeen Handelsblad* reported visiting it on 28 December: '[...] some Dutchmen assembled in the sombre little rooms of a temporarily uninhabited apartment in Montmartre, and there they admired a few hundred paintings. Sad emotions interfered with their enthusiasm; the art treasures, which lay and stood together here in the cheerless, cold room were the legacy of an artist, dead too early, whose younger brother, in consequence of that loss, was himself by now seriously ill and, transported to his fatherland in hopes of recovery [...].'[69]

Theo died on 25 January 1891, six months after his brother. Not only was Jo now a single parent responsible for a child less than a year old, she also had to take charge of Theo's own collection and of Vincent's paintings. She swiftly understood that this was not merely a physical legacy, but required her to continue the brothers' shared mission to build Vincent's reputation as a painter. From that moment on, Jo's life would revolve around the brother-in-law whom she had only met in the flesh a few times. After Theo's funeral, she moved to Bussum in the Netherlands to be closer to friends and family, but the artworks initially remained in the Paris apartment.[70]

BERNARD'S EFFORTS

Having failed to get Aurier to write about Van Gogh, Bernard himself published two texts about his friend in 1891, in *Les Hommes d'aujourd'hui* and *La Plume*.[71] At the beginning of March that year, he and a group of friends continued the effort to get the 'Exposition Vincent' off the ground: 'All the friends will get to work – Schuffenecker, Fauché, Daniel, Denis, Tanguy, Redon and I. In the press it will be Huysmans – Mirbeau.'[72] He asked Jo to leave Van Gogh's works in Paris for a while longer and not to lend them to another – in his view, rival – exhibition.[73] Unfortunately, he too was unable to find a venue and Jo, contrary to his request, submitted ten works to the Salon des Indépendants, which opened on 20 March.[74] It turned out to be a sound strategic move. Van Gogh's work was mentioned in at least seven articles, including an extensive piece on the front page of *L'Echo de Paris*: 'it is immensely sad to think that this painter, so magnificently talented, that this artist, so thrilling, so instinctive, so visionary, is no more'.[75] Gachet showed his own work at the exhibition for the first time. He took the opportunity to testify publicly to the special bond he had enjoyed with Vincent by showing the sketch of him on his deathbed, which was then reproduced in a review in *Le Magazine français illustré*.[76]

The collection of paintings in the apartment in Paris was relocated to Jo's Bussum address in April, with the assistance of Andries and Bernard.[77] Plans for a major retrospective in Paris were now shelved for the time being. While four exhibitions were devoted to Van Gogh in the Netherlands in the course of the following year, Bernard finally managed to organize a modest solo presentation in Paris of works still in France: a few paintings in storage at Tanguy's and those that Van Gogh had given to or exchanged with acquaintances and artist friends. Sixteen works were exhibited at Le Barc de Boutteville gallery in April 1892 **(180)**, including a version of *La Berceuse*, which belonged to Bernard. The critic at *La Vie moderne* was enthusiastic: Van Gogh was 'inspired', he wrote, and praised not only

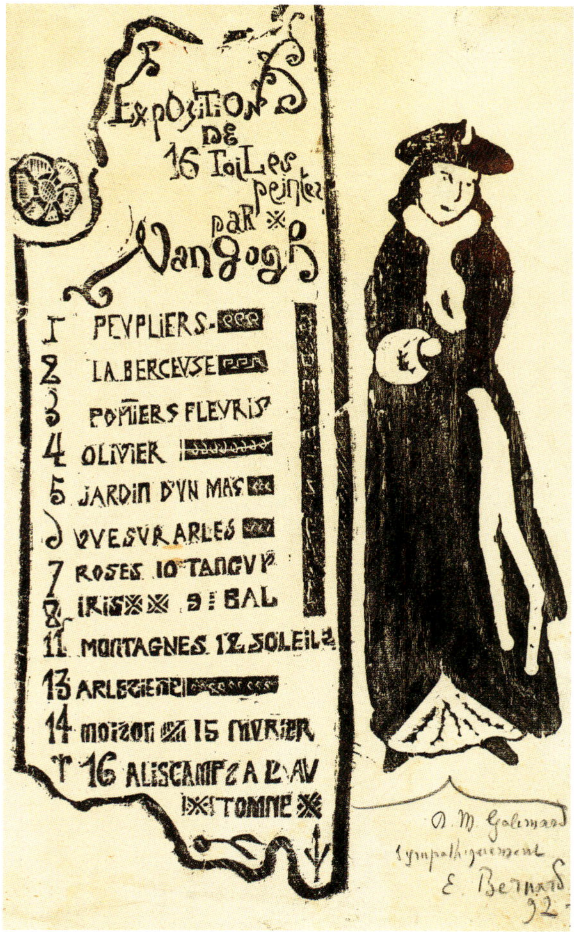

180
Emile Bernard
Catalogue for the Van Gogh exhibition at Le Barc de Boutteville gallery, 1892
Woodcut on paper, 43.8 × 27.2 cm
Van Gogh Museum, Amsterdam

the paintings but the drawings too: 'Let anyone who mocks him go to Le Barc. They will be forced to admit that many serious "artists" would be incapable of producing in pen and ink landscapes like the ones exhibited there.'[78]

Aurier died suddenly in October from an infection. While he had studied Van Gogh and seemed the ideal person to write his biography, the publication never got off the ground. All the same, his article on the painter in January 1890 had set the tone. It was frequently quoted in the year that followed and the press described Van Gogh on several occasions in terms similar to those in the article, that is to say as a fevered and temperamental genius, who produced strange yet powerful paintings.[79]

Bernard had meanwhile conceived the idea of publishing Van Gogh's letters. In early 1893, he persuaded Alfred Vallette, publisher of the *Mercure de France*, to present a series of them in the literary magazine, complete with illustrations, including reproductions of letter sketches and a self-portrait of Van Gogh in Andries Bonger's possession.[80] Bonger paid for the reproductions and Bernard wrote an article to introduce the letters.[81] Bernard departed a few months later for Istanbul, Jerusalem and finally Egypt, where he remained until 1896. He took the letters with him, however, so that the series could continue. The final one was published in August 1897. For the time being, there were no further initiatives. Bernard gradually began to sell the substantial collection of Van Goghs that had come into his possession through exchanges with Vincent, no doubt reflecting a lack of cash on his part but probably also a waning interest, since his own art had taken a different turn in the meantime.[82]

As far as we are aware no Van Gogh exhibitions were held in Paris in 1893. Only at Le Barc de Bouteville was a work of his on display, namely the *Self-Portrait with Bandaged Ear*, which was included in the exhibition *Les portraits du prochain siècle* (Portraits of the Next Century), which ran at the gallery from July to September. The work was borrowed from Schuffenecker.[83]

When Tanguy died in 1894 after a short illness, the location in Paris where Van Gogh's work had been continuously displayed also disappeared. The art critic Octave Mirbeau began his obituary on the front page of *L'Echo de Paris* with a quote from Tanguy: 'Ah! Poor Vincent!... What a terrible thing, Mr Mirbeau!... What a terrible thing!... Such a genius!...

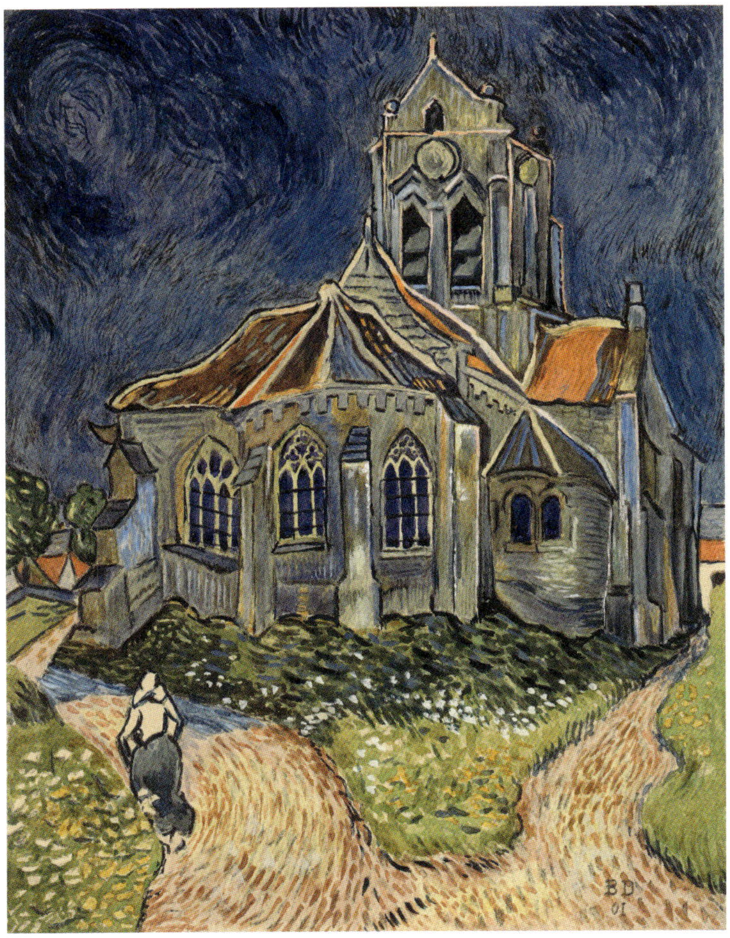

181
Blanche Derousse
Copy after the painting
The Church at Auvers-sur-Oise, 1901
Drypoint and watercolour on paper, 20.9 × 16.2 cm
Van Gogh Museum, Amsterdam

And such a good lad!... Wait, let me show you some more of his masterpieces!... Because that's what they are, *n'est-ce pas*?... They are masterpieces!...'[84] These opening words were not only a tribute to the special bond between the paint seller and the painter, they also indicate the extent to which a knowledge of Van Gogh was already assumed on the public's part.[85]

Following Tanguy's death, the art dealer Ambroise Vollard picked up the baton, organizing his first Van Gogh exhibition in 1895. While this did not result in any sales, it did elicit a ringing endorsement on 15 June 1895 in *La Revue blanche*, which cited 'those famous sunflowers, so colourful and genuine'.[86] From that moment on until the early twentieth century, Vollard became the leading dealer for Van Gogh's work in Paris.

GACHET REMAINS SILENT, HIS COLLECTION HIDDEN FROM VIEW

Contact between Jo and Gachet fell away after Theo's death. Her brother, Andries Bonger, paid a visit to Auvers with his wife in the summer of 1891,[87] but remarkably enough, there appears to have been no further contact between the Van Gogh family and Gachet for the next twelve years. The doctor probably saw no reason to correspond with Jo, while she did not seek to contact him either.[88]

Gachet continued to prepare his biography and catalogue of Van Gogh's work – a venture that assumed steadily grander form. It was now to be an artistic edition, with a handwritten text in different colours of ink on parchment, a personal tribute that would, perhaps, also highlight his own role in the artist's life. The illustrations would be at least as important as the text. Gachet planned to make etchings that he would print himself, but nothing came of this. Only around 1901, he had his pupil Blanche Derousse make a series of coloured etchings after works in his collection, which could serve as illustrations **(181)**.[89] In the end, however, the entire project came to nothing. According to Gachet's son, the doctor had taken the project so very seriously that it was obvious from the start that it could never be accomplished. So great was his admiration for the deceased artist that he set too high a bar for himself.

An equal silence had grown up in the meantime around the works that Gachet had received from Vincent and, after the painter's death, from Theo.[90] They ran to a total of twenty-seven paintings, twenty drawings – mostly double-sided sketches – and three prints, which remained hidden from public view for the first fifteen years after the funeral. Bernard must have been aware of the significant collection of Van Goghs in Gachet's possession, but the doctor did not lend the paintings for the exhibitions that were organized; he most likely wanted to keep them for himself until he had completed his publication.[91] Very few people got to see the impressive collection, among them the artist Joseph Delattre in 1894 and the dealer Théodore Duret in 1900.[92] There is nothing to suggest, moreover, that Gachet allowed visitors. Only when the critic Julius Meier-Graefe contacted him in 1903 did the hidden existence of the collection come to an end: Meier-Graefe published his art-historical survey *Entwicklungsgeschichte der modernen Kunst* (History of the Development of Modern Art) a year later, in which he also listed Gachet's Van Goghs.[93]

Gachet asked Meier-Graefe for Jo's address and contacted her again.[94] The main reason was that the burial rights for Vincent's grave, which had been purchased for fifteen years in 1890, were due to expire.[95] Gachet had tended to the grave throughout that period. There is no evidence that Jo or other members of the family went to the cemetery in the years in question, although some visitors to Auvers did go to the grave and Jo was informed that it was being kept nicely.[96] At Gachet's suggestion, Vincent was reinterred in a more beautiful, spacious plot in the same graveyard in 1905, and it was on that occasion that Jo, accompanied by her son, visited the village for the first time since 1890. Henceforward, cordial relations between the two families were restored and the two sons would also remain on friendly terms.[97]

'UN GÉANT'

Van Gogh died at the very moment that after ten years as an artist, interest in his work had started to grow and he was beginning to receive recognition in artistic circles. Theo doggedly committed himself to building his reputation further. As fate would have it, though, he and several other of Vincent's champions would all die in the space of a few years, while for certain others the task would prove too onerous. Yet despite all these setbacks, Van Gogh's reputation was swiftly burnished in the first years after his death. Bernard and, above all, Jo saw to it that his paintings were shown at various exhibitions, which meant that the painter was still written about from time to time. Gachet, who had been one of the first to recognize the quality and genius of Van Gogh's work – 'The more I think of it, the more I regard Vincent as *un géant* [a giant]', he had written to Theo – ultimately contributed little to Van Gogh's reputation in those early years.[98] He had, by contrast, been invaluable to the artist's productivity in the final months of his life and an important ally. When Jo published the letters in 1914, she wrote in her introduction that none of his contemporaries had understood Vincent better than Gachet.[99]

In 1905, Gachet agreed for the first and last time to lend some of his Van Goghs for exhibitions, beginning with three works for a special *Exposition rétrospective Vincent van Gogh* in March–April at the Salon des Indépendants. A few months later, he also loaned works to the large-scale retrospective that Jo organized at the Stedelijk Museum in Amsterdam. After this, the biggest Van Gogh exhibition ever, the reputation of an artist who had considered himself a failure steadily grew to unprecedented heights in the course of the twentieth century.

Following Gachet's death in 1909, his son sought to complete his father's life's work, but he too failed to finish the manuscript on Van Gogh.[100] Gachet Jr's most important legacy was to donate iconic works from his father's collection to the French state in the 1950s. This ensured a strong and permanent representation of Van Gogh, and the Auvers period in particular, in the French national collection.[101]

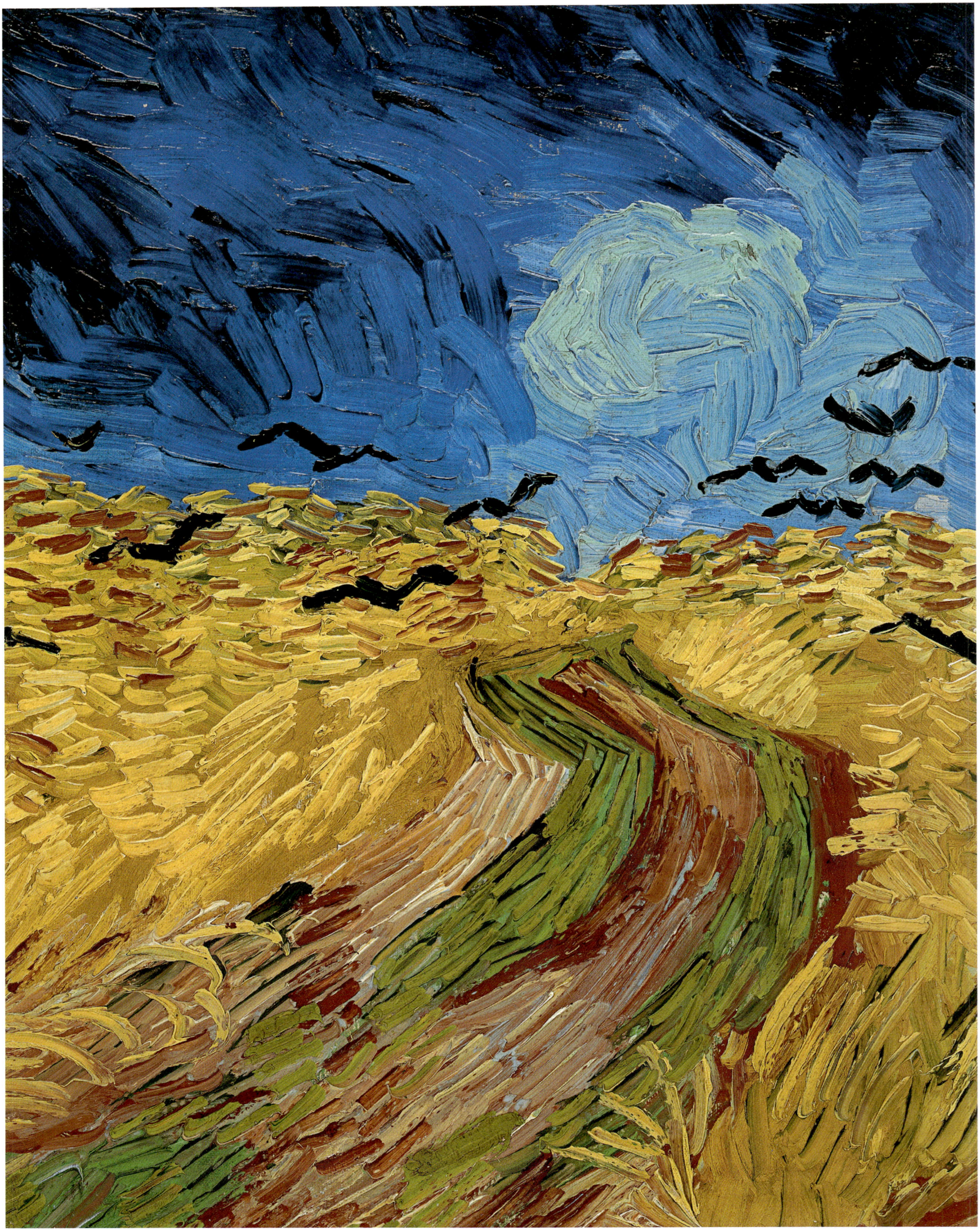

CHRONOLOGY

VINCENT VAN GOGH'S FINAL MONTHS

WOUTER VAN DER VEEN

This chronology is based chiefly on two groups of sources enabling us to track Vincent van Gogh's stay in Auvers-sur-Oise. The principal source is Vincent and Theo's correspondence; these letters contain the most precise and most detailed information. The second group comprises the testimony – provided shortly or long afterwards – of individuals who were present at the events described. The most important of these are the various interviews with Adeline Ravoux in the 1950s, together with several texts, published or unpublished, by Paul Louis Gachet, son of Dr Gachet. This second group needs to be treated with caution, however, as both Adeline Ravoux's and Paul Louis Gachet's testimony show wide variations.

Information for which Gachet – who was inaccurate at times – is the sole source is shown in grey.

The numbers in square brackets refer to Van Gogh's correspondence (Jansen, Luijten and Bakker 2009) and other letters kept at the Van Gogh Museum, Amsterdam.

1889

MID-NOVEMBER

Van Gogh, who has been admitted to the Saint-Paul-de-Mausole psychiatric clinic in Saint-Rémy-de-Provence, expresses the desire to move back north, closer to his brother Theo. Theo suggests that there is a doctor called Paul Ferdinand Gachet living in Auvers-sur-Oise, whom Camille Pissarro has recommended to him and who might be prepared to take Vincent under his wing when he settles in the village.

AROUND TUESDAY 19 NOVEMBER

Van Gogh writes to Theo that he thinks he will no longer require medical assistance if he changes his surroundings. But he would prefer to wait a little longer, to be sure he does not suffer an attack that would hinder his plans to return north [820].

AROUND TUESDAY 24 DECEMBER

Van Gogh suffers a fresh attack, during which he tries to poison himself by swallowing his paints.

1890

22 FEBRUARY

Van Gogh's decision to return north is now a firm one and he travels unaccompanied to Arles to say goodbye to his friends Marie and Joseph Ginoux.

Vincent van Gogh
Wheatfield with Crows, 1890
Detail of 137 (#60)

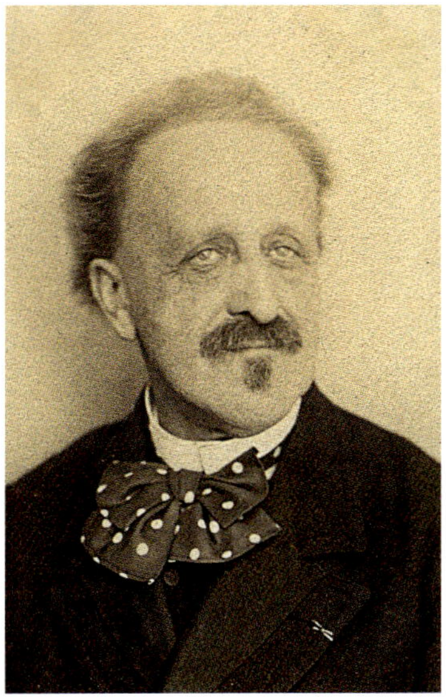
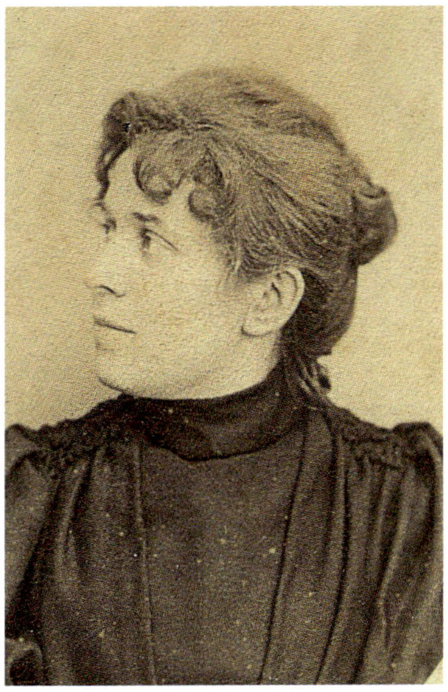
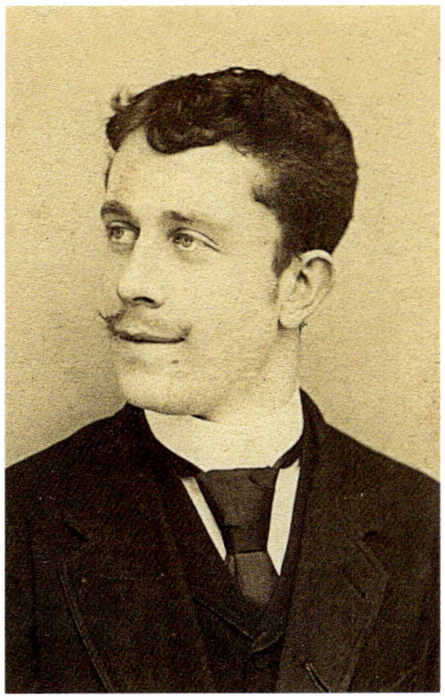

182–84
(left to right)
Paul Ferdinand Gachet, 1894
Marguerite Gachet, 1894
Paul Louis Gachet, undated
From: family album of Paul Ferdinand Gachet
Wildenstein Plattner Institute, New York

While there, he has another episode, following which he is taken back to the asylum. This latest crisis, which leaves him virtually unable to work, read or write, lasts for about two months.

SATURDAY 29 MARCH

Theo writes to Vincent after meeting Paul Gachet. Based on what Theo has told him, the doctor thinks he can cure Vincent. To be more certain, though, he will need to see and speak to him in person [860].

FRIDAY 9 MAY

Theo writes to Dr Gachet to ask if he will receive his brother in Auvers-sur-Oise, find him somewhere to stay and support him [b2014].

AROUND MONDAY 12 MAY

Vincent writes to Joseph Ginoux, asking him to have some of the furniture in his former house in Arles sent to Paris: the mirror he used for his self-portraits and two beds [871]. The items are intended for a house he plans to furnish in Auvers-sur-Oise.

TUESDAY 13 MAY

Following a final consultation with Dr Peyron, director of the institution, Vincent informs Theo that he is leaving Saint-Rémy and expects to arrive in Paris the following Friday or Saturday. He mentions that he will bring his easel and a few picture frames and stretching frames so that he can get back to work as soon as possible.

FRIDAY 16 MAY

Dr Peyron declares Van Gogh cured and he leaves the asylum.

SATURDAY 17 MAY

Vincent arrives in Paris, where Theo is waiting to meet him at the Gare de Lyon. The brothers take a carriage across Paris to Theo's home. Vincent meets his sister-in-law Jo and his nephew, godson and namesake, Vincent Willem, who is four months old. He insists on speaking French to his Dutch relatives, which Jo finds ridiculous.

SUNDAY 18 – MONDAY 19 MAY

Van Gogh meets a number of friends and acquaintances, possibly Albert Aurier, Henri de Toulouse-Lautrec and Jo's brother, Andries Bonger. He is reunited with his paintings at Theo's place and in an attic room he describes as a 'bedbug-infested hole' [RM20], which Theo had rented from the paint seller Julien Tanguy. Vincent visits the exhibition of the Société Nationale des Beaux-Arts on the Champ de Mars – where he is particularly struck by Pierre Puvis de Chavannes's *Inter artes et naturam (Between Art and Nature)* **(153)** – and the exhibition of Japanese prints at the Ecole Nationale des Beaux-Arts.

TUESDAY 20 MAY

Van Gogh arrives in Auvers-sur-Oise and meets Dr Gachet **(182)** for the first time, who performs a discreet medical examination and diagnoses an 'unfounded syphilomania'. He also performs an optical examination, which shows excellent vision

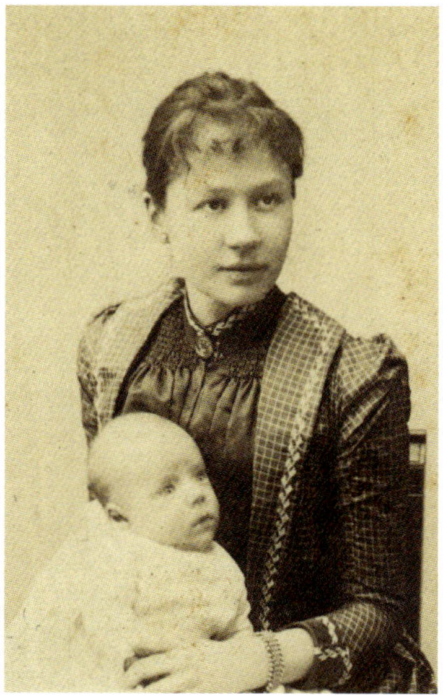

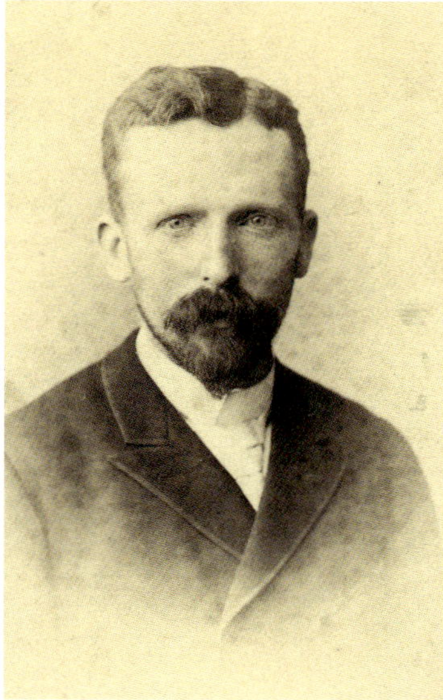

185–86
Jo van Gogh-Bonger and
Vincent Willem van Gogh (left), 1890
Theo van Gogh (right), c. 1889
Van Gogh Museum, Amsterdam

and correct colour perception. Gachet is of the opinion, moreover, that the painter's self-inflicted turpentine poisoning has not been properly treated. Van Gogh moves into the Café de la Mairie, run by Arthur Ravoux. He immediately writes to Theo and Jo to report his first impressions of Auvers: 'it's gravely beautiful, it's the heart of the countryside, distinctive and picturesque'. He hopes that 'Jo will permit me [...] to write in French' [873].

WEDNESDAY 21 MAY

Writes again to Theo and Jo that 'Auvers is decidedly very beautiful' and mentions having made a first study **(33)**. Asks for money, ten metres of canvas, twenty sheets of Ingres paper and Charles Bargue's drawing course *Exercices au fusain* [874].

THURSDAY 22 MAY

Pays a visit to Dr Gachet who is not at home.

FRIDAY 23 MAY

Dr Gachet visits Theo at Boussod, Valadon & Cie, boulevard Montmartre. Gachet no longer thinks Vincent can be cured, but assures Theo of his interest and sympathy for his brother.

SATURDAY 24 MAY

In a very sombre letter to Theo that he will not send, Vincent asks for more clarity regarding his financial situation. He feels 'a failure' and does not 'see a happy future at all' [RM20].

SUNDAY 25 MAY

Vincent receives a letter (since lost) and fifty francs from Theo, which reassures him [875]. Visits Dr Gachet and plans to go there again on Tuesday 27 May to paint. Tries to persuade Theo of the benefits of raising his son in the countryside; he fears the city's harmful effect on baby Vincent's fragile health.

TUESDAY 27 MAY

The Jean-François Raffaëlli exhibition opens at Theo's firm on boulevard Montmartre. Organizing and overseeing the event demands all his attention. Vincent arrives early at Gachet's to work. He paints *Doctor Gachet's Garden* **(34)** in three hours. In the afternoon, the doctor and his son accompany Vincent to the Café de la Mairie and see his *Pietà (after Delacroix)* **(161)**, his *Blossoming Chestnut Branches* **(71)**, a *Self-Portrait* **(158)** and an *Arlésienne* **(168)**.

SUNDAY 1 JUNE

Vincent visits Dr Gachet again. Has lunch there for the third time. Paints *Marguerite Gachet in the Garden* **(35)**.

MONDAY 2 JUNE

Theo writes that it would indeed do him and his family good to spend some time in the countryside. He reveals that he is planning to come to Auvers for part of his holiday, probably in August [876].

TUESDAY 3 JUNE

Vincent visits Dr Gachet again. Views his collection, including a self-portrait and a nude by Armand Guillaumin. Does not like the fact that the last work is not framed. Paints the *Portrait of Doctor Gachet* **(159)** in five hours. Writes to Theo, reassuring him about his health and expressing the hope that he will 'continue to feel much surer of my brush than before I went to Arles' [877]. Makes plans to paint portraits and hopes Gachet will help him find models.

WEDNESDAY 4 JUNE

Gachet visits Theo in Paris in the evening and invites him to spend Sunday 8 June in Auvers with Jo and little Vincent. Van Gogh paints *The Church at Auvers-sur-Oise* **(1)**.

THURSDAY 5 JUNE

Van Gogh writes to his mother and his sister Willemien [878, 879]. He reassures them about himself, but expresses concern about Theo's health.

SATURDAY 7 JUNE

Vincent visits Gachet again. He completes his second version of the doctor's portrait on the spot **(112)**.

SUNDAY 8 JUNE

Theo, Jo and baby Vincent arrive in Auvers by train. Lunch is in Gachet's garden. The mood is excellent, Vincent pays great attention to his nephew. Also present are Marguerite, Paul Louis and Madame Chevalier, the governess, who serves the guests. Around six o'clock in the evening, the Van Goghs are escorted back to the station after taking a final walk.

TUESDAY 10 JUNE

Vincent writes an optimistic letter to Theo, marvelling 'that the nightmare should have ceased to such an extent here'. He thinks that 'one day or another [...] I'll find a way to do an exhibition of myself in a café' [881]. Receives a letter from Mr and Mrs Ginoux: they will send his furniture soon [882]. It is intended for a three-room house that Vincent plans to rent in Auvers as somewhere to live, set up a studio, store the canvases left in Paris, and provide a pied-à-terre in the countryside for Theo and his family [881].

THURSDAY 12 JUNE

Paints *Landscape with Carriage and Train* **(29)** from a vantage point close to Dr Gachet's house.

FRIDAY 13 JUNE

Receives a letter from Paul Gauguin, informing him of his plan to establish an artists' colony in Madagascar [884]. Writes a letter to his mother in which he talks of his feelings of loneliness [885]. Also writes to Willemien, explaining that he is working 'a lot and quickly' to express 'the desperately swift passage of things in modern life' [886].

SATURDAY 14 JUNE

Writes to Theo that he is working on a new study, *Poppy Field* **(13)**, and asks him to send paint and canvas [887]. Auguste Lauzet visits Theo, cité Pigalle, to view Vincent's paintings. Lauzet is planning to make lithographs after the paintings.

SUNDAY 15 JUNE

Theo informs his brother that the Dutch painter Anton Hirschig is coming to Auvers soon [888]. He suggests that when his furniture has arrived from Arles, Vincent might be able to live with another artist. Vincent lunches at Gachet's, where he makes the etching *Portrait of Doctor Paul Gachet* **(169)**. Gachet gives him two photographs of portraits he had drawn of the artist Charles Méryon.

MONDAY 16 JUNE

Anton Hirschig arrives in Auvers. The young painter, whose talent does not impress Van Gogh much, moves into the room next door at the Café de la Mairie.

TUESDAY 17 JUNE

Letter to Theo confirming receipt of the canvases and paints he had ordered the previous Saturday [889]. Plans to go to Brittany to join Gauguin and Meijer de Haan, and hopes to make etchings of some of the works he created in Provence. Around this time he paints *Vase with Wild Flowers* **(82)** and *White House at Night with Star* **(31)**. During an impromptu visit to Gachet, he makes half a dozen prints of his etching in colour **(116)**. Gives *Cows* **(7)** to the doctor.

SATURDAY 21 JUNE

Paints *Landscape at Twilight* **(138)**, one of his first three works measuring 50 × 100 cm. The other two are *Undergrowth with Two Figures* **(156)** and *Fields near Auvers-sur-Oise* **(135)**.

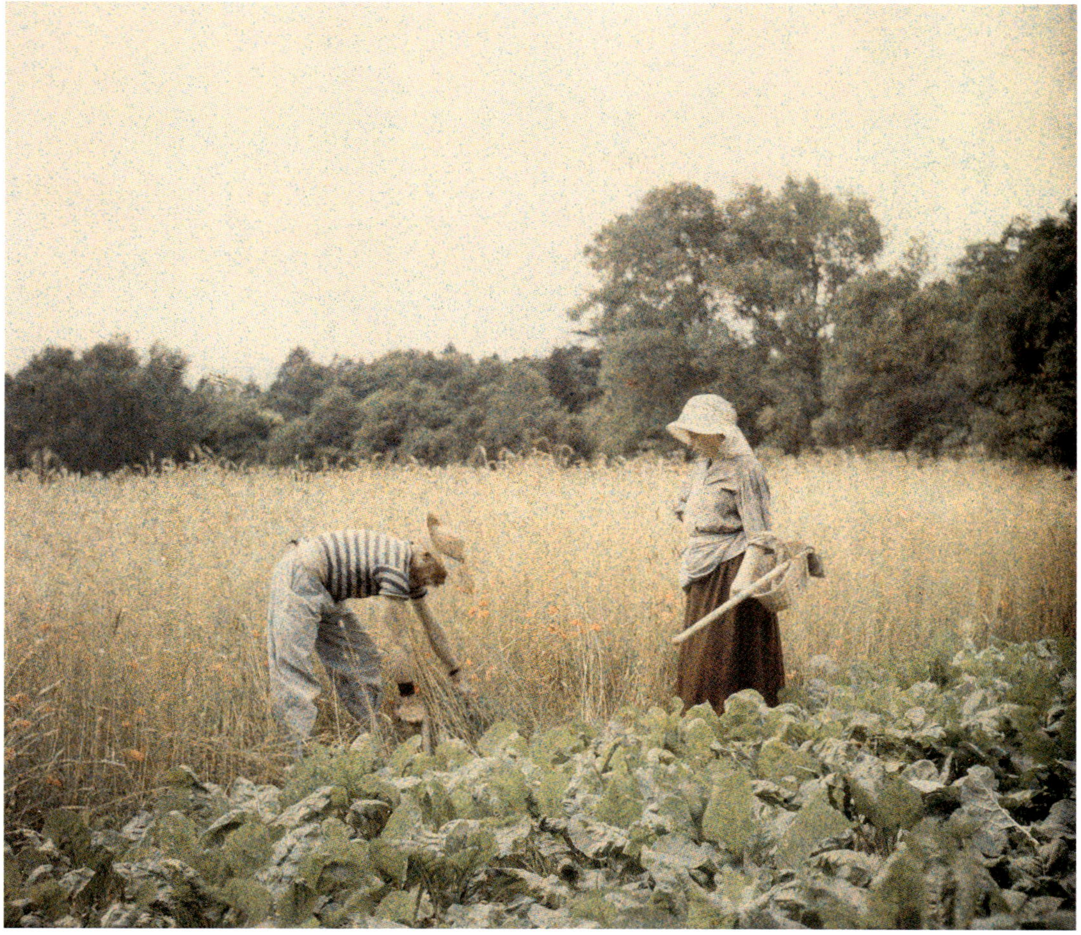

187
Antonin Personnaz
Man and Woman Working in the Fields, between 1907 and 1914
Autochrome, 8 × 9 cm
Société française de photographie, Paris

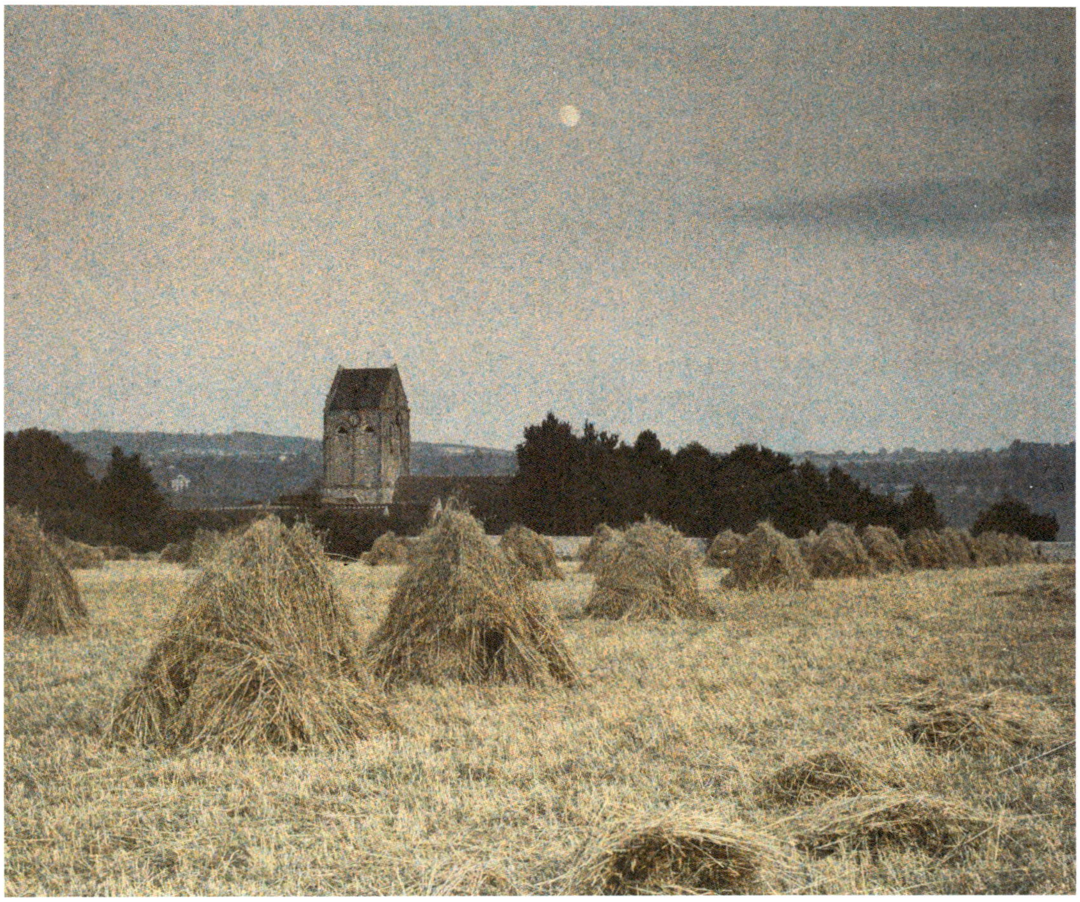

188
Antonin Personnaz
Wheatsheaves, Auvers-sur-Oise, between 1907 and 1914
Autochrome, 9 × 12 cm
Société française de photographie, Paris

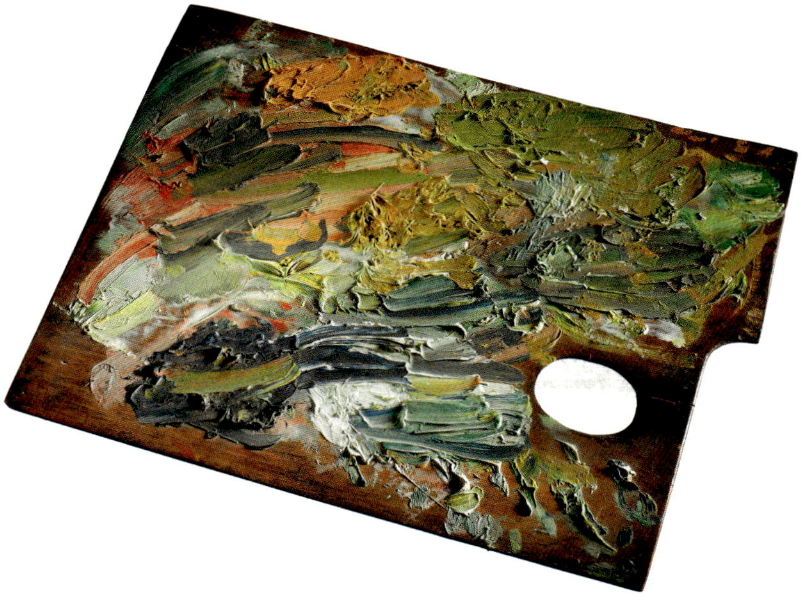

189
Palette used by Vincent van Gogh for *Marguerite Gachet at the Piano*, 1890
Wood, 27 × 35 cm
Musée d'Orsay, Paris

SUNDAY 22 JUNE

In the morning, Theo visits the Salon in Paris with the artist Eugène Boch. In the afternoon, they dine at Theo's home, where Boch views Vincent's paintings. There is an exchange of studies [890]. Vincent has lunch at Gachet's. Celebrates the birthdays of Marguerite and Paul Louis, who are twenty-one and seventeen respectively; both were born on 21 June.

MONDAY 23 JUNE

Letter from Theo expressing how much he likes Vincent's etching *Portrait of Doctor Gachet* and mentioning that the Raffaëlli exhibition has finished [890]. He will finally have more time. Vincent paints the portrait of Adeline Ravoux, the daughter of the Café de la Mairie's landlord **(119)**.

TUESDAY 24 JUNE

Van Gogh takes delivery of works that had been left at Saint-Rémy. He has worked 'this week' on Adeline Ravoux's portrait and made a second version of it for his brother **(118, 119)** [891]. Gachet visits the Café de la Mairie to see the canvases from Provence. Vincent is invited to dinner at Gachet's, where he discovers that Guillaumin's *Nude* has still not been framed.

THURSDAY 26 AND FRIDAY 27 JUNE

Paints *Marguerite Gachet at the Piano* **(130)** at Gachet's home.

SUNDAY 29 JUNE

Lunch at Gachet's.

MONDAY 30 JUNE – TUESDAY 1 JULY

Theo writes to Vincent in a fit of emotion: baby Vincent, now five months old, has been seriously ill [894]. The young parents feared they might lose him. Theo expresses his dissatisfaction with his pay and working conditions. He firmly intends, he writes, to threaten to resign and go into business for himself if his employers do not respond to his demands. He also expresses his gratitude at having a wife like Jo: 'you will have one day, I hope with all my heart, a wife'.

TUESDAY 1 JULY

Visit to Gachet. Vincent sees the paintings again that he gave him and criticizes *Doctor Gachet's Garden* **(34)**, which he wants to redo. The doctor notices that he is nervous and restless.

WEDNESDAY 2 JULY

Letter to Theo in which Vincent expresses concern about his nephew's health [896]. Would like to help, but fears that by coming to Paris he would only add to the confusion. Insists that Theo should settle at least temporarily in the countryside with his family. He does not encourage Theo to leave Boussod, Valadon & Cie, but does not seek to dissuade him either, 'what will be, will be' [896]. As for ever having a wife of his own, 'I don't believe in it very strongly'. He describes several canvases including a new painting, *Country Girl with Straw Hat* **(125)** and realizes that he is unable to influence the course of events.

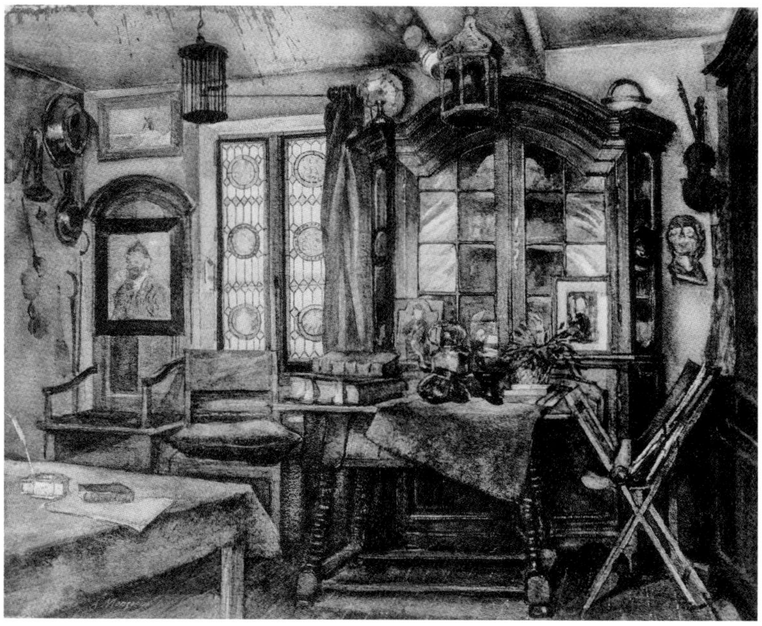

190
Léopold Robin
The Sitting Room in Auvers-sur-Oise during the Lifetime of Doctor Paul Gachet
Watercolour, 1903
From: 'Le Dr Gachet par l'image', Paul Ferdinand Gachet and Paul Louis Gachet Papers
Wildenstein Plattner Institute, New York

SATURDAY 5 JULY

Reassuring letter from Theo: baby Vincent is doing better [897]. He invites his brother to Paris the next day. Theo's business is up and down: he is having little success with the expensive paintings but has managed to sell two works by Gauguin.

SUNDAY 6 JULY

Takes the first train to Paris and arrives at his brother's around eight o'clock. Goes to Julien Tanguy's paint shop to see his stored works. While there he meets Edmund Walpole Brooke, whom he had previously encountered in Auvers; Albert Aurier, who is keen to view the paintings with Vincent present; Henri de Toulouse-Lautrec; the sculptor Sara de Swart and Andries Bonger. In a fractious atmosphere, Vincent, Theo and Jo discuss a number of issues such as Theo's plan to quit Boussod, Valadon & Cie and set up in business with Andries; whether it is appropriate to raise baby Vincent in the city; using French in their conversations; and the young family's holiday destination. Vincent thinks that a trip to the Netherlands will be too much of an ordeal and insists that Auvers is a better alternative. Theo and Jo argue in front of Vincent; Andries and his wife Annie might be involved too.

MONDAY 7 JULY

Writes a letter to Theo and Jo, which he will not send. Fears that he is the reason for the discord and tension between 'you all' [RM24].

MONDAY 7 – THURSDAY 10 JULY

Paints 'immense stretches of wheatfields' in which he expresses 'sadness, extreme loneliness' **(136, 137)** [898]. Also paints *Daubigny's Garden* **(139)**. Theo issues Boussod and Valadon with an ultimatum. He threatens to leave the company and set up his own business if they refuse to increase his pay.

WEDNESDAY 9 JULY

Vincent goes to see Dr Gachet, but does not find him at home.

THURSDAY 10 JULY

Vincent replies to a letter (since lost) from Jo – 'like a gospel for me, a deliverance from anguish' – which has reassured him about 'the rather difficult and laborious hours' he had shared with them on Sunday 6 July [898]. Describes the threat that he shares with Theo: their state of health. No longer questions the journey that Theo and his family are to make to the Netherlands and ends on a positive note.

MONDAY 14 JULY

French national day. Paints *Auvers-sur-Oise Town Hall on 14 July 1890* **(63)**.

TUESDAY 15 JULY

Receives a letter from Theo with fifty francs and confirmation that his brother is setting off that day with Jo and baby Vincent for Leiden to visit their mother [900]. He discovers that Andries has refused to commit to Theo's project for his own art dealership and that Boussod and Valadon have not responded to his ultimatum.

Vincent visits Gachet in the afternoon and tells him he is worried. He views his brother's trip to the Netherlands as an abandonment. Vincent sees Guillaumin's *Nude* and finds that it is still unframed, which makes him angry. He calms down, but he does not return to the doctor's house.

WEDNESDAY 16 – SATURDAY 19 JULY

Dr Gachet is in Paris. Theo is travelling in the Netherlands and Belgium.

SUNDAY 20 JULY

Theo writes from Paris to Jo, who remains in the Netherlands [b2058]. His employers have still failed to respond to his ultimatum. He is less confident than before about setting up on his own and now fears for his job. Mentions receiving a letter from Vincent, in which the latter referred to 'intense domestic quarrels' during his visit to Paris on 6 July (the letter itself has not been preserved). He fears that Vincent is about to suffer another attack. Van Gogh explores the east of the village, towards Cordeville, and probably paints *Wheatfields with Reaper, Auvers-sur-Oise* **(14)**.

MONDAY 21 JULY

Theo writes again to Jo [b2061]. He has withdrawn his ultimatum and hopes to continue his cooperation with Boussod, Valadon & Cie.

TUESDAY 22 JULY

Letter from Theo to Vincent [901]. He tries to discover which domestic quarrels Vincent was referring to. Does not, however, mention his decision to stick with Boussod, Valadon & Cie. Theo is concerned about Vincent's health and advises him to go and see Gachet. Vincent has ceased to visit the doctor, despite two written invitations that have gone unanswered. According to a discreet informant, who is a regular at Ravoux's, Gachet knows that he is, however, continuing to work hard.

WEDNESDAY 23 JULY

Vincent writes his final letter, addressed to Theo [902]. It is a sombre and pessimistic text suggesting a feeling of resignation. Confirms that he did see tensions in the couple. A first, even more pessimistic draft of the letter, which he did not finish, refers to his own end: 'I risk my life for my own work and my reason has half foundered in it' [RM25]. He encloses several sketches of paintings he has made in the past few days **(18, 30, 67, 68, 140)**.

FRIDAY 25 JULY

In a letter to Jo, Theo expresses his concern at Vincent's latest communication, which he finds incomprehensible [b2063].

FRIDAY 25 – SATURDAY 26 JULY

Dr Joseph Jean-Baptiste Mazery moves into Auvers-sur-Oise. Van Gogh's suicide attempt the following Sunday will be his first emergency call.

SUNDAY 27 JULY

Vincent works until sometime in the afternoon on his last painting: *Tree Roots* **(157)**. Around 7.30–8 pm, on the plain behind the park of the chateau, Vincent shoots himself in the area of his heart with a revolver. He returns to the inn and retreats to his room. At 9 pm, someone comes from Ravoux's to fetch Dr Gachet, for whom Vincent has been asking. The doctor and his son prepare to leave, while his colleague Mazery, who has also been alerted by Ravoux and who lives much nearer, examines the patient. After Gachet arrives, they start again and attempt to calculate the path traced internally by the bullet. A dark red opening, surrounded by a double purple-and-brownish circle, about three to four centimetres below the left nipple, shows where the bullet entered. There is no further external bleeding and no vital organs have been hit. Removing the bullet is not an option and transporting the wounded man poses too many risks. Gachet still has some faint hope that Vincent will survive. The doctor is keen to notify Theo, but Vincent refuses to provide his address. Ravoux, his wife and his daughter Adeline are all present, as is Hirschig. The night continues without incident. Vincent smokes two more pipes without complaining.

MONDAY 28 JULY

Hirschig travels to Paris and delivers a note from Gachet to Theo at Boussod, Valadon & Cie around 9.30 am, reporting the bad news and asking him to come to Auvers as soon as possible [b3265]. They get there by noon. Theo writes to Jo, cautiously

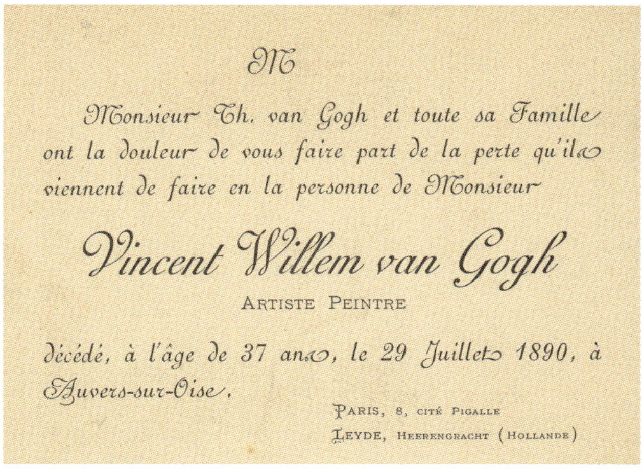
M

Monsieur Th. van Gogh et toute sa Famille ont la douleur de vous faire part de la perte qu'ils viennent de faire en la personne de Monsieur

Vincent Willem van Gogh

ARTISTE PEINTRE

décédé, à l'âge de 37 ans, le 29 Juillet 1890, à Auvers-sur-Oise.

PARIS, 8, CITÉ PIGALLE
LEYDE, HEERENGRACHT (HOLLANDE)

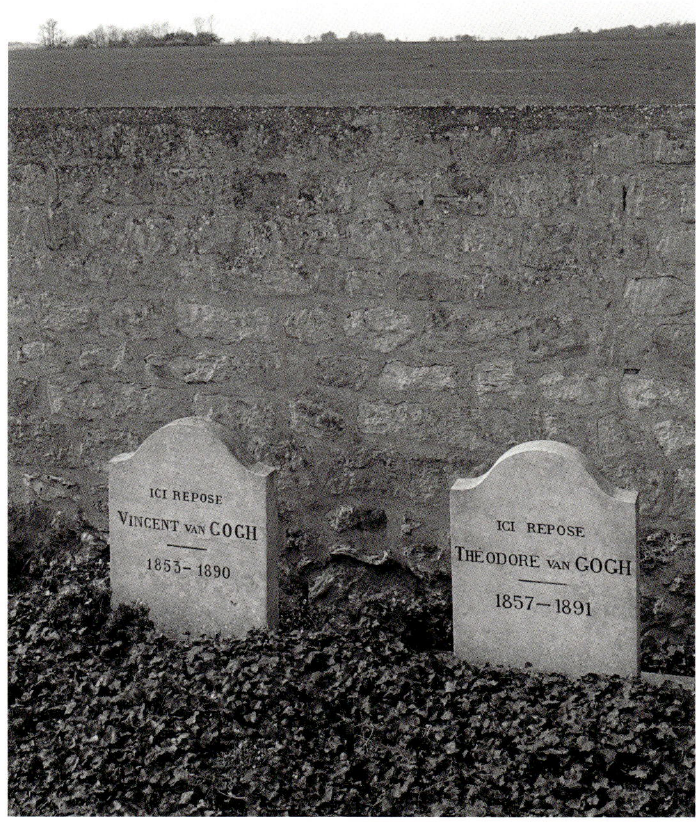

191
Mourning card for Vincent van Gogh, 1890
Van Gogh Museum, Amsterdam

192
The graves of Vincent and Theo van Gogh in Auvers-sur-Oise
Van Gogh Museum, Amsterdam

explaining to her what has happened [b2066]; Dr Gachet advises him to spare her feelings while she is nursing baby Vincent.

TUESDAY 29 JULY

Vincent dies around 1.30 am. At ten o'clock the following morning, Theo goes to the town hall with Ravoux to report his brother's death. Abbé Tessier, the parish priest in Auvers, refuses to lend the parish hearse so Hirschig fetches the one from Méry-sur-Oise instead. The funeral is scheduled for the following afternoon at three o'clock. Gachet draws the dead Vincent's portrait **(177, 178)**. Theo finds the draft version of Vincent's last letter, which the painter had on him when he died [RM25].

WEDNESDAY 30 JULY

Theo, Paul Gachet and his son, Arthur Ravoux, Andries Bonger, Emile Bernard, Charles Laval, Auguste Lauzet, Julien Tanguy, Lucien Pissarro, Anton Hirschig, Nicolas Martinez de Valdivielso and several acquaintances attend Vincent's funeral. The dining room at the Café de la Mairie is turned into a temporary chapel of rest, decorated with yellow flowers and the painter's canvases. At the cemetery, Theo is only able to speak a few words. Dr Gachet delivers a short eulogy.

THURSDAY 7 AUGUST

L'Echo Pontoisien publishes the following terse report: 'Sunday 27 July, a person named Van Gogh, age thirty-seven, [...] Dutch citizen, painter by profession, living temporarily in Auvers, shot himself with a revolver in the fields and, being only wounded, returned to his room, where he died two days later.'

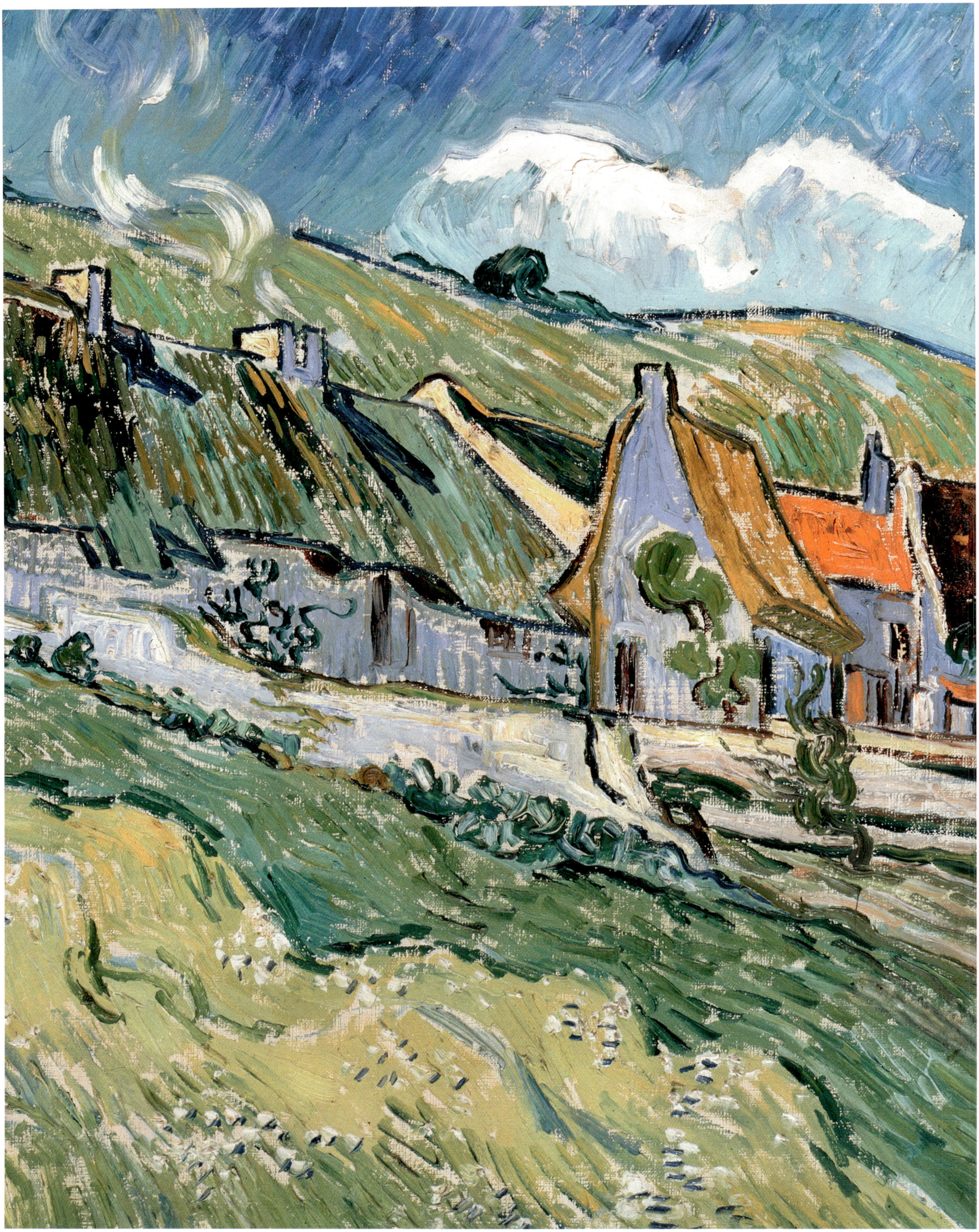

CATALOGUE OF PAINTINGS FROM AUVERS-SUR-OISE

LOUIS VAN TILBORGH
AND TEIO MEEDENDORP

To the best of our knowledge, Vincent van Gogh produced seventy-four paintings in Auvers-sur-Oise: forty-nine landscapes and village views; thirteen portraits; eleven still lifes; and one animal painting.[1] We have attempted to arrange these works chronologically in this catalogue, where we also explain how we arrived at this sequence. Roughly half of the paintings can be dated with some precision based on written sources. There is less clarity, however, when it comes to dating the remaining items. Their position in the chronology thus relies on a more interpretative approach, as will become apparent.

WRITTEN SOURCES

Van Gogh referred to a total of thirty-three works in his letters: three still lifes, five portraits and twenty-five landscapes. In all but perhaps two of these instances **(#27, #28)** the paintings can be firmly identified, providing us with secure dates. Moreover, in the case of four works in this group – all of them portraits **(#20, #48, #49, #53)** – there are also surviving preliminary studies, second versions and one related figure piece **(#22, #50, #51, #54, #55)**. Since Van Gogh generally produced variants like this one after the other, we have been able to identify the date of their creation based on the related painting as referred to in the letter.

Vincent mentioned a considerable number of paintings, therefore, in his letters from Auvers, yet his correspondence with his brother Theo was shorter and less frequent there compared to that from Saint-Rémy, and he was less forthcoming about his activities than he had been in the past. The letters offer especially little guidance as to his artistic output in the periods 25–31 May, 22 June–7 July and between 10 July and his suicide attempt on 27 July.[2] It is nevertheless possible to add to the thirty-eight paintings that can be dated with a fair degree of precision. Additional information can be found in sources published after Van Gogh's death. For instance, Andries Bonger, Theo's brother-in-law, designated two paintings as Van Gogh's very last works in 1891 and 1893 respectively, and while the value of his information was disregarded for over a century, it is now believed that the works in question were indeed painted just before Vincent's self-inflicted death **(#73, #74)**.[3]

While Van Gogh's letters have always been the most important source of dates for the compilers of his catalogues raisonnés, knowledge of his Auvers-sur-Oise paintings has also drawn since

Vincent van Gogh
Thatched Cottages, 1890
Detail of 33 (#1)

1994 on a manuscript by Paul Gachet Jr, published posthumously in that year and dealing with Vincent's life and work in Auvers.[4] Gachet had completed the text in 1959 and, like the compilers of Van Gogh's 1928, 1970 and 1996 catalogues raisonnés, he occasionally drew on dates for letters that have since been adjusted and on a number of incorrect identifications.[5] Because of this, his recollections do not always appear reliable. In some instances, however, they are so specific and detailed that we have adopted his dating of the works in question – a scene with flowering acacias and a free copy of an etching after Jacob Jordaens **(#23, #36)**.[6]

SUBJECT MATTER

Where the forty-two paintings referred to above were dated on the basis of written sources, the remaining works had to be ordered entirely differently. Many paintings reveal their date of creation by what they depict: the flags and lanterns in the view of the village with the town hall were part of the *quatorze juillet* (Bastille Day) celebrations to mark the national day of France **(#65)**, while two landscapes include the wheat harvest, which traditionally occurred in mid-July **(#66, #67)**.[7] One of Van Gogh's village scenes shows blossoming acacias **(#7)**, the season for which is May–mid-June, indicating that the work must have been made in that period. Cornflowers, poppies, corn marigolds, buttercups, carnations and similar flowers, by contrast, bloom throughout the summer, and so their inclusion by Van Gogh does not offer a narrower timespan for their creation. Young green wheat, by contrast, suggests an early date – before July **(#26)**[8] – while a field full of large cabbages tells us that the painting in question was done in July **(#64)**.

Meteorological reports proved helpful when it came to dating landscapes with rain or ominously dark skies not mentioned in the letters **(#5, #63, #68)**.[9] They also helped refine the creation dates of five works with similar content that *did* appear in Van Gogh's correspondence, including two vistas 'after the rain', mentioned in his very last letter **(#4, #60, #61, #69, #70)**.[10] A storm during the weekend of 24–25 May leads us to believe that he painted his large still life with broken-off chestnut branches in the days that followed **(#6)**.[11] The violence of the summer wind was evidently too much for the chestnut trees that were in full blossom at the time, giving the artist an opportunity to capture the season in this unconventional way. In another nice turn, the same reports proved helpful in dating the four remaining portraits **(#56, #57, #58, #59)**. These were added to Van Gogh's output during the rainy week from 29 June to 5 July, and we already know that he had thrown himself into the genre only the week before, whether or not obliged by the inclement weather **(#48, #49, #51, #52, #53, #54)**.

The unmentioned works also include six still lifes **(#18, #19, #24, #25, #34, #39)**, and it seems plausible that these, along with the three paintings in the same genre that are referred to in Van Gogh's correspondence **(#17, #38, #40)** and the small painting of acacias **(#23)** alluded to above, were painted at Gachet Sr's home. This means that they too can be dated, albeit only approximately compared to the other works. Van Gogh was basically free to paint at the doctor's home on Saturdays, Sundays, Mondays and possibly Tuesdays. He appears to have started on 27 May and then to have taken advantage of Gachet's hospitality again the following weekend – a pattern that, with a few exceptions, then repeated itself each week until July.[12]

REMAINING WORKS

This left twelve paintings to be dated **(#9, #10, #11, #12, #13, #14, #15, #33, #35, #42, #43, #44)**, to which end several rules of thumb were applied, based on Van Gogh's working methods. These include his smallest paintings of village views and cottages **(#9, #10, #11, #12, #13)** which, given his customary practice, are likely to have been done while he was getting his bearings in his new surroundings, that is to say at the beginning of his stay. The same group also includes four works with the ambitious standard size 30 (92 × 73 cm; **#14, #15, #43, #44**), and since it is odd that Van Gogh did not mention them in his letters, we have sought to date them in such a way as to render this omission understandable.[13] Account was also taken here of what we already knew about his production in a given period from the aforementioned reconstruction: where were any 'gaps' to be found? After all, in the space of seventy-two days, he produced seventy-four paintings, and we know there were certain moments when he did not work.[14]

We therefore placed two of these works **(#14, #15)** in the second week of his stay when, in our view as stated above, he might have produced small, exploratory studies of his surroundings but, in keeping with his customary practice, will also have been turning his mind to more ambitious works, for which space was available in our reconstruction. We know, moreover, that he did not write during this time, but was waiting instead for a letter from Theo.[15] By the time his brother had got round to writing to him, he had thrown himself into his portrait of Gachet **(#20)**, and since this work was more important to him, Vincent's next letter mentions its execution alone and ignores the landscapes.[16] We were also able in this way to date the other two size 30 paintings **(#43, #44)** more precisely, to just before the creation of his first 50 × 100 cm works around 20–22 June **(#45, #46, #47)**. Vincent had written to Theo on 17 June 1890, but when he did so again on the 24th, the two preceding size 30 landscapes were no longer so important, with the result – so the reasoning goes – that he only mentioned those ambitious, much more spatial, metre-wide paintings along with two of his recent portraits **(#48, #49)**.[17]

That leaves three paintings **(#33, #35, #42)**, one of which – *Garden in Auvers-sur-Oise* **(#42)** – is rather stylized and dovetails well in our opinion with Van Gogh's equally fanciful *White House at Night with Star* **(#41)**, which he described in his letter of 17 June 1889. The work can be linked, moreover, to a clear shift in his use of canvas, as revealed by the Automated Canvas Analysis Project.[18] Fifty-two of his Auvers works had their canvas type examined as part of that initiative, the results of which contributed to the sequencing and dating effort. Van Gogh initially used canvas from Saint-Rémy, for instance, both unprepared and commercially prepared.[19] He might also have picked up some canvas in Paris and/or replenished his stock locally, but by the middle of June he had used it all up. For paintings **#34**, **#37**, **#38**, **#40**, **#41**, which have already been dated above, he then went on to use *torchon* and otherwise anomalous painting canvas, and since the as yet undated **#33** and **#35** belonged to the same category, this provided us with a fairly precise date of creation. A consignment of primed canvas arrived from Paris on 17 June and all the subsequently created works appear to have been painted on it, beginning with *Garden in Auvers-sur-Oise* **(#42)**.[20]

The latter example indicates that in some cases, several arguments have been used to assign a particular date to a painting, including a corresponding style or similarities in working processes, but it would be going too far to list all the subtleties here; specific dating is explained as fully as possible in the previous essays. We would also like to emphasize that our sequence is a reconstruction, the result of both certainties and uncertainties. The ranking suggests that one work was actually made after or before another, and while we believe that the order we have set out is close to the historical truth, we recognize that the suggestions made about their sequencing are not always equally firm. The reader can, however, identify those works to which this applies by the somewhat wider date range that has been retained. Ultimately, dating and ordering are a matter of interpretation and there will always be somewhat greater uncertainty in one instance than in another.

Where the identified locations are specified in the catalogue, the current addresses have been used rather than the historical ones. Chaponval and Cordeville are hamlets belonging to Auvers-sur-Oise and are located to the west and east of the village respectively; Les Vessenots is the neighbourhood in which Dr Gachet lived.

The stated date of creation does not take account of instances where Van Gogh subsequently revisited a more or less finished painting. To evaluate the dating information contained in the letters as effectively as possible, we have assumed that he wrote them in the evenings, as Adeline Ravoux suggested in her reminiscences of Van Gogh.[21]

An asterisk placed after the technique and dimensions of the work indicates that the canvas was analysed as part of the Automated Canvas Analysis Project (see Note to the Reader on p. 11). *Torchon* refers to a type of household cloth that was common at the time, which Van Gogh used in Auvers when he ran out of professional painting canvas.

The provenance of all paintings draws on Stolwijk and Veenenbos 2002 and on Feilchenfeldt 2013, from which we have not deviated unless our own research produced different results. Only the first two owners are listed, as we wished to keep the early distribution of the works as clear as possible. Where Paul Gachet Sr is listed as the first owner without any further explanation, the painting in question was among those given to him by Theo van Gogh after Vincent's funeral.

'Inv. 1890' refers to the inventory that Andries Bonger compiled in late 1890 of the paintings in Theo van Gogh's collection, which Jo van Gogh-Bonger later supplemented; we have adopted the title of the work from this inventory, as well as the standard format, which was frequently appended to the title in brackets. 'List 1896' refers to the list that Jo van Gogh-Bonger drew up of works that she sent to the art dealer Ambroise Vollard in Paris that year. Both documents are in the Van Gogh Museum.

The provenance of all the works in the Van Gogh Museum is as follows: Theo van Gogh; after having been inherited by Jo van Gogh-Bonger and Vincent Willem van Gogh in 1891, transferred to the Vincent van Gogh Foundation in 1962; on loan to the Van Gogh Museum, Amsterdam, since 1973. The provenance of the paintings from the Gachet collection at the Musée d'Orsay is as follows: donated to (or, in the case of **#21**, acquired by) the Musée du Louvre between 1948 and 1954, placed in the Musée du Jeu de Paume, and from 1986 in the Musée d'Orsay.

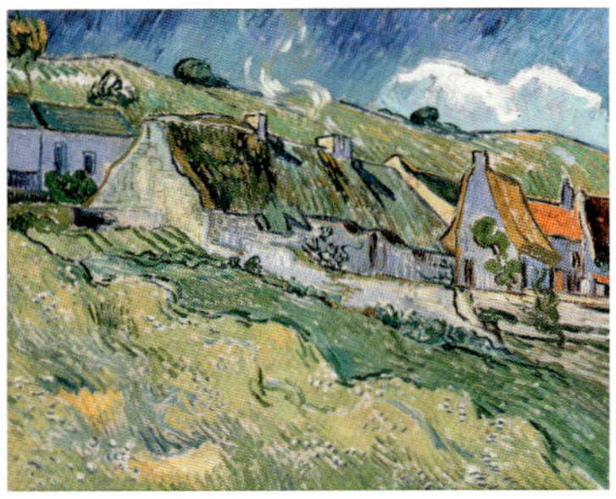

1 | *Thatched Cottages*

Rue du Gré, Chaponval
Wednesday 21 May 1890
Oil on canvas, 59 × 72 cm

The State Hermitage Museum, Saint Petersburg

F750 JH1984; letters 874 (21 May 1890), RM20 (24 May 1890)

Theo van Gogh, inv. 1890, no. 291: 'Hameau près d'Auvers (20)'; sold by Jo van Gogh-Bonger to Maurice Fabre, Paris, around 1901, possibly through Julien Leclercq.

[ill. 33]

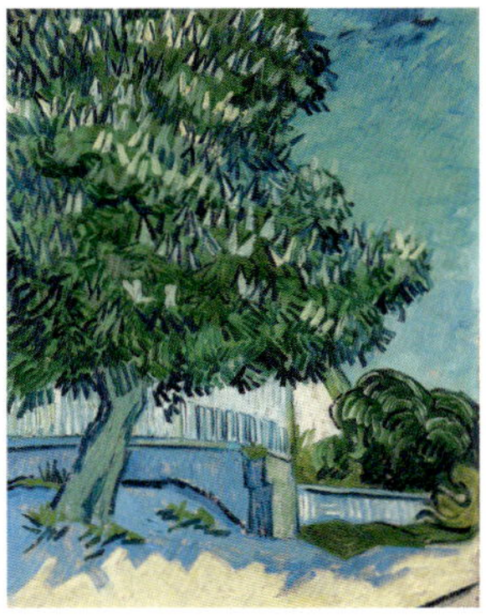

2 | *Blossoming Chestnut Trees*

Near 25 rue du Général de Gaulle
Around Thursday 22 May 1890
Oil on canvas, 63.3 × 49.8 cm*

Kröller-Müller Museum, Otterlo

F752 JH1991; letters RM20 (24 May 1890), 875 (25 May 1890)

Theo van Gogh; sold by Jo van Gogh-Bonger to Carl and Thea Sternheim, Munich, 1909, through C.M. van Gogh art dealers, Amsterdam.

[ill. 58]

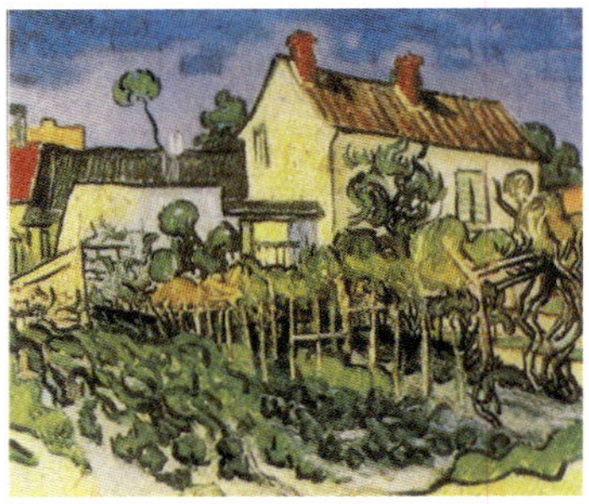

3 | *Farmhouse and Vineyard*

20 rue Carnot, home of the Romaru family
Around Friday 23 May 1890
Oil on canvas, 51 × 58 cm

Private collection

F794 JH2002; letter RM20 (24 May 1890)

Given by Theo van Gogh to Emile Bernard, Paris; sold to Galerie Vollard, Paris, c. 1899.

[not illustrated elsewhere in this book]

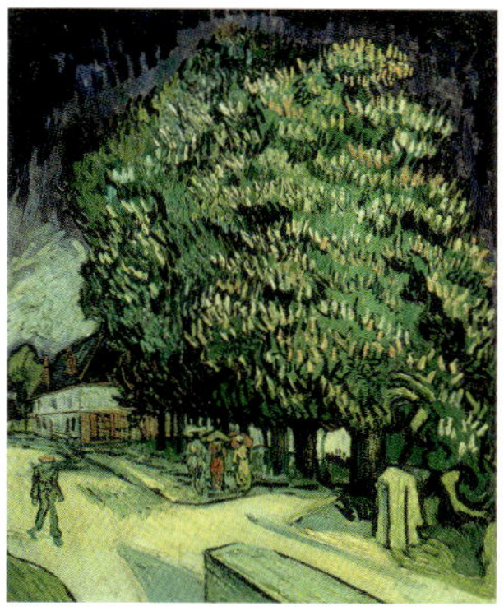

4 | *Blossoming Chestnut Trees*

21 rue du Général de Gaulle
Saturday 24 May 1890
Oil on canvas, 70 × 58 cm

Private collection

F751 JH1992; letters RM20 (24 May 1890), 875 (25 May 1890)

Theo van Gogh, list 1896, no. 317: 'Maronnier [*sic*] en fleurs'; sold by Jo van Gogh-Bonger to Paul Cassirer art dealers, Berlin, 1905.

[ill. 59]

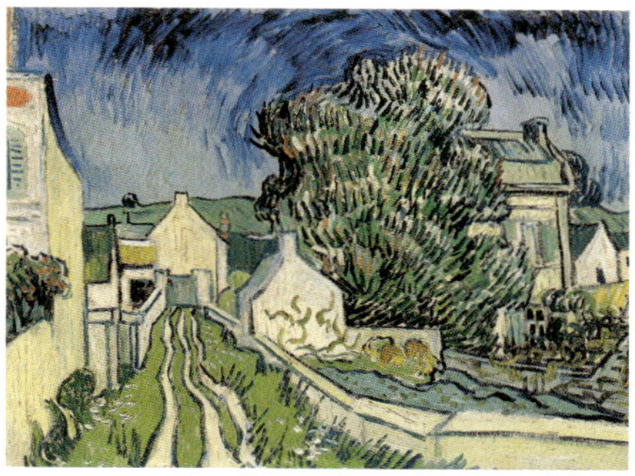

5 | *The House of Père Pilon*

18 rue François Villon
Sunday–Monday 25–26 May 1890
Oil on canvas, 49 × 70 cm

Private collection

F791 JH1995

Theo van Gogh, inv. 1890, no. 290: 'Maisons avec jardin (20)'; sold by Jo van Gogh-Bonger to Alexej von Jawlensky, Munich, 1908, through Moderne Kunsthandlung, Munich.

[ill. 61]

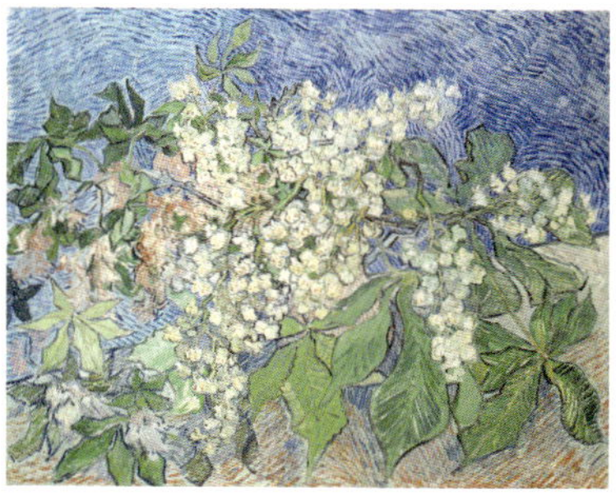

6 | *Blossoming Chestnut Branches*

Monday 26 or Tuesday 27 May 1890
Oil on canvas, 73 × 92 cm*

Emil Bührle Collection, on long-term loan to Kunsthaus Zürich

F820 JH2010

Paul Gachet Sr; sold by Paul Gachet Jr to Galerie Bernheim Jeune & Cie, Paris, 1912.

[ill. 71]

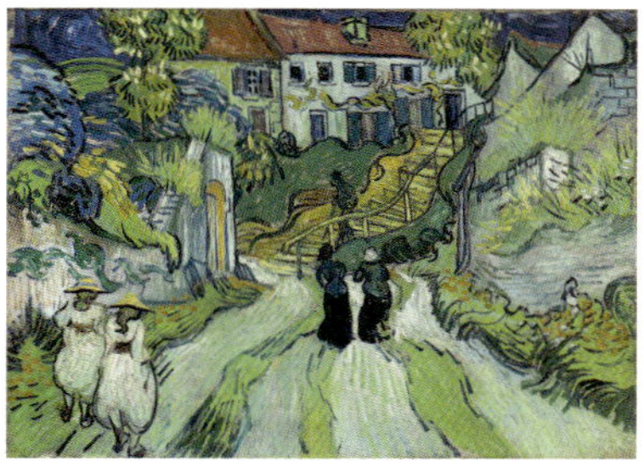

7 | *Stairway at Auvers-sur-Oise*

Rue de la Sansonne
Late May–mid-June 1890
Oil on canvas, 50 × 70.5 cm*

Saint Louis Art Museum, purchased 1935

F795 JH2111

Theo van Gogh, inv. 1890, no. 278: 'Village'; sold by Jo van Gogh-Bonger to Galerie Bernheim Jeune & Cie, Paris, 1909.

[ill. 5]

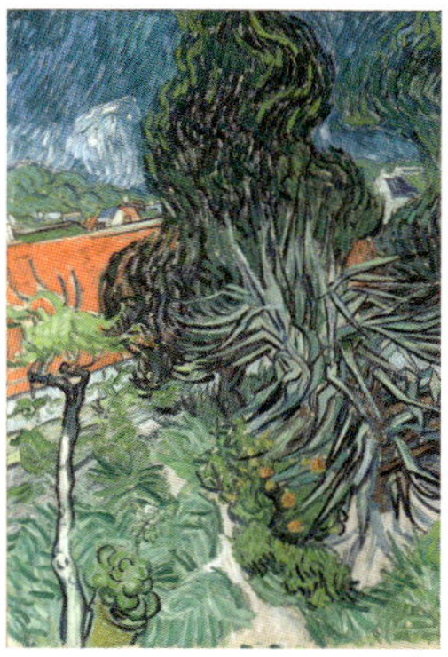

8 | *Doctor Gachet's Garden*

78 rue Gachet
Tuesday 27 May 1890
Oil on canvas, 73 × 52 cm*

Musée d'Orsay, Paris

F755 JH1999; letters 877 (3 June 1890), 879 (5 June 1890)

Given by Vincent to Paul Gachet Sr; donated by Paul Gachet Jr to Musée du Louvre, Paris, 1954.

[ill. 34]

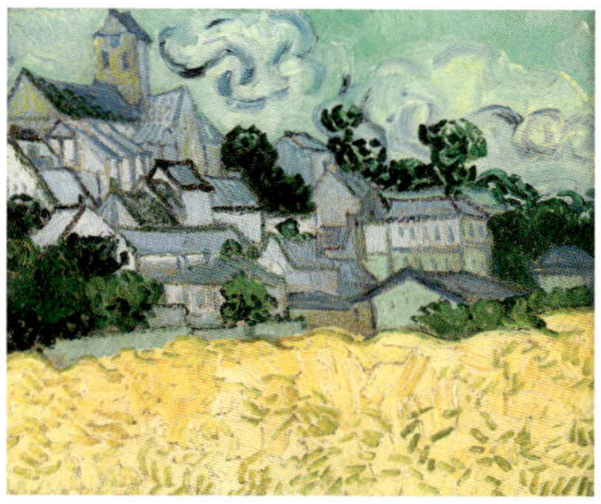

9 | *View of Auvers-sur-Oise*

Near the railway station
Late May–June 1890
Oil on canvas, 34 × 42.1 cm*

Museum of Art, Rhode Island School of Design, Providence, given in memory of Miss Dorothy Sturges by a friend

F800 JH2122

First owner unknown; sold by Galerie Vollard, Paris to Maurice Fabre, Paris, before 1904.

[ill. 52]

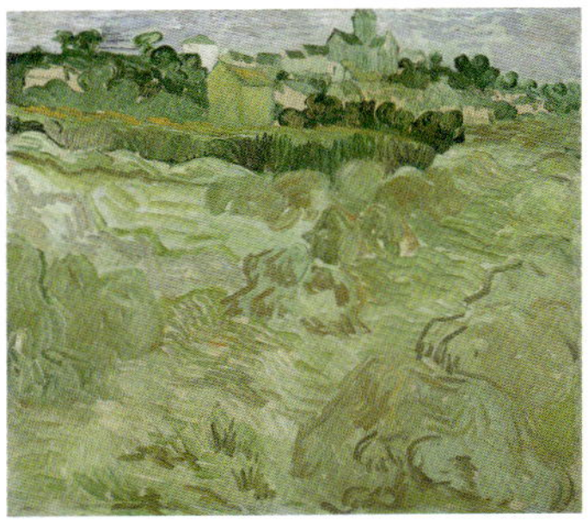

10 | *Field near Auvers-sur-Oise*

Near rue de la Bourgogne
Late May–mid-June 1890
Oil on canvas, 44 × 51.5 cm

Musée d'art et d'histoire, Geneva,
former loan of the Fondation Garengo, 1990

F801 JH2123

Theo van Gogh; given by Jo van Gogh-Bonger to Isaac Israëls, The Hague, after 1914.

[ill. 53]

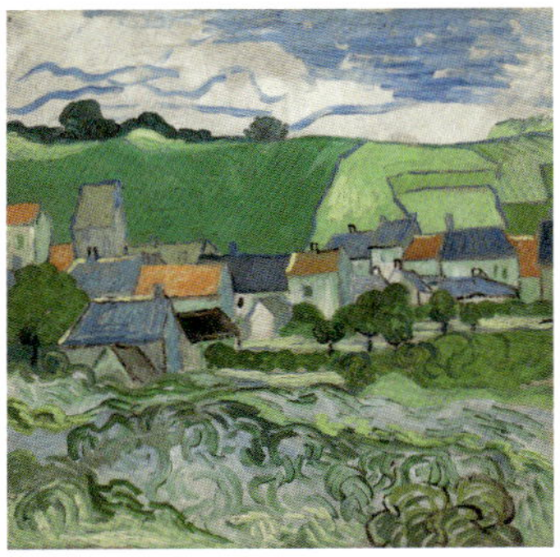

11 | *View of Auvers-sur-Oise*

Probable view of Les Vessenots
Late May–mid-June 1890
Oil on canvas, 50.2 × 52.5 cm*

Van Gogh Museum, Amsterdam
(Vincent van Gogh Foundation)

F799 JH2004

Theo van Gogh, inv. 1890, no. 302: 'Vue d'Auvers (carré) (champs) 8'.

[ill. 50]

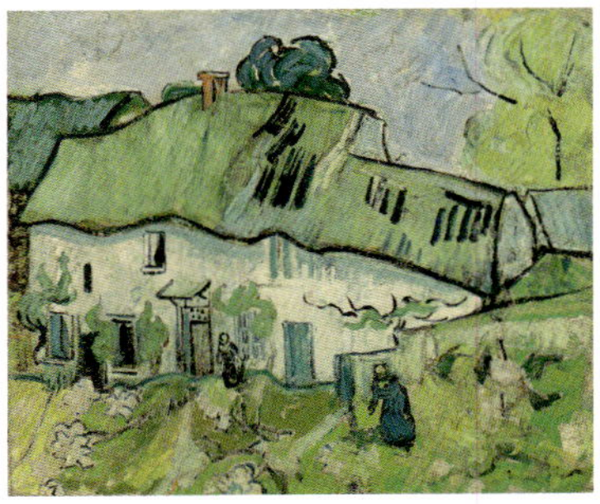

12 | *Farmhouse*

24 rue Rajon, Cordeville
Late May–mid-June 1890
Oil on canvas, 38.9 × 46.4 cm*

Van Gogh Museum, Amsterdam
(Vincent van Gogh Foundation)

F806 JH2017

Theo van Gogh.

[ill. 43]

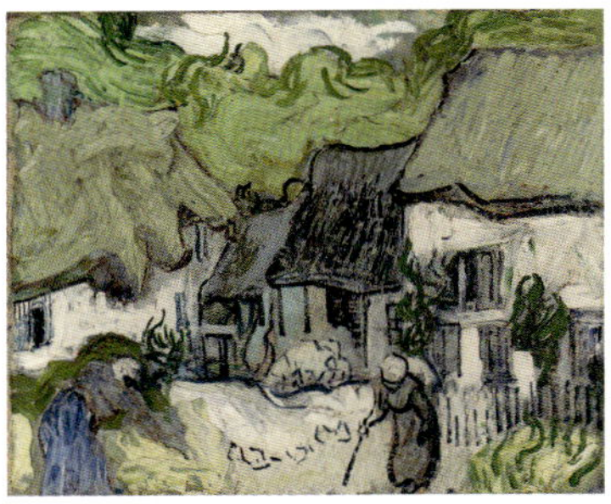

13 | *Thatched Cottages*

24 rue Rajon, Cordeville
Late May–mid-June 1890
Oil on canvas, 33 × 40.5 cm*

West Coast Masters

F758 JH2016

Paul Gachet Sr; sold by Paul Gachet Jr to Wildenstein, Paris/New York, before 1951.

[ill. 44]

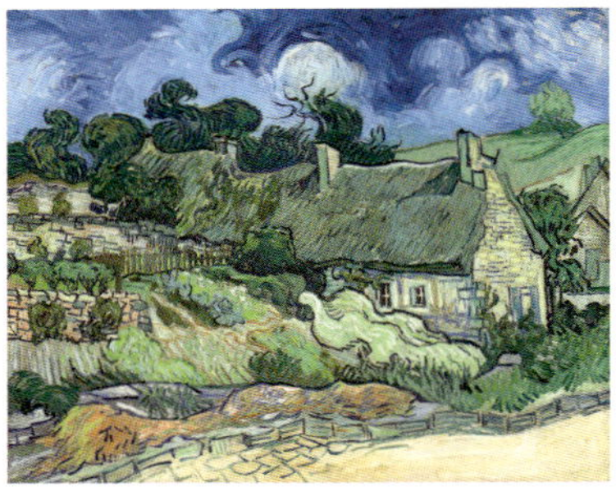

14 | *Thatched Cottages in Cordeville, Auvers-sur-Oise*

24 rue Rajon, Cordeville
Late May–early June 1890
Oil on canvas, 73 × 92 cm*

Musée d'Orsay, Paris

F792 JH1987

Paul Gachet Sr; donated by Paul Gachet Jr to Musée du Louvre, Paris, 1954.

[ill. 41]

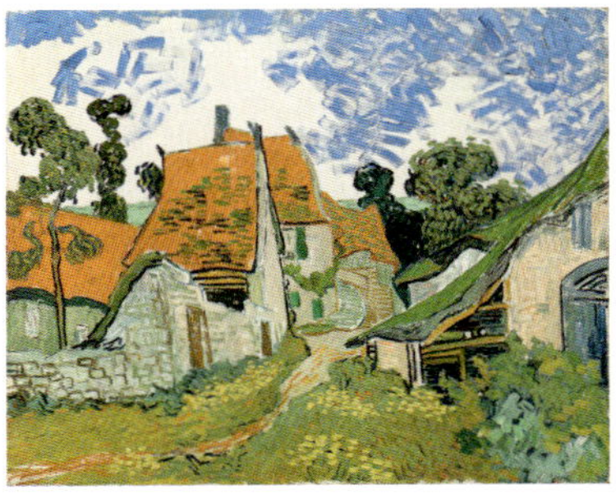

15 | *Farmhouses in Auvers-sur-Oise*

Near 67 rue Daubigny
Late May–early June 1890
Oil on canvas, 73.5 × 92.5 cm*

Finnish National Gallery, Ateneum Art Museum, Helsinki, Antell Collections

F802 JH2001

Theo van Gogh; sold by Jo van Gogh-Bonger to Julien Leclercq, Paris, 1900.

[ill. 46]

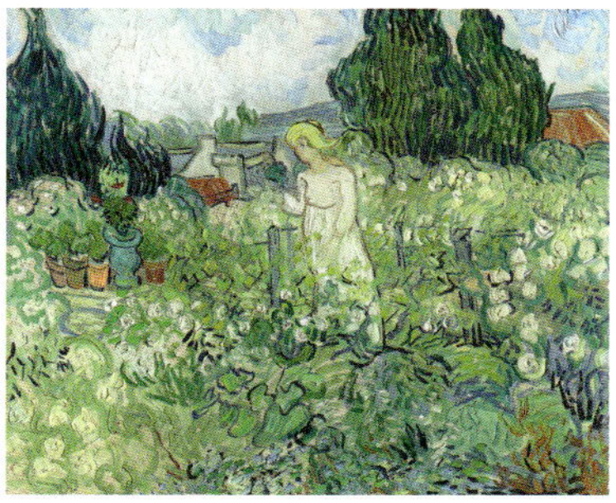

16 | *Marguerite Gachet in the Garden*

78 rue Gachet
Saturday 31 May or Sunday 1 June 1890
Oil on canvas, 46 × 55.5 cm*

Musée d'Orsay, Paris

F756 JH2005; letter 877 (3 June 1890)

Given by Vincent to Paul Gachet Sr; donated by Paul Gachet Jr to Musée du Louvre, Paris, 1954.

[ill. 35]

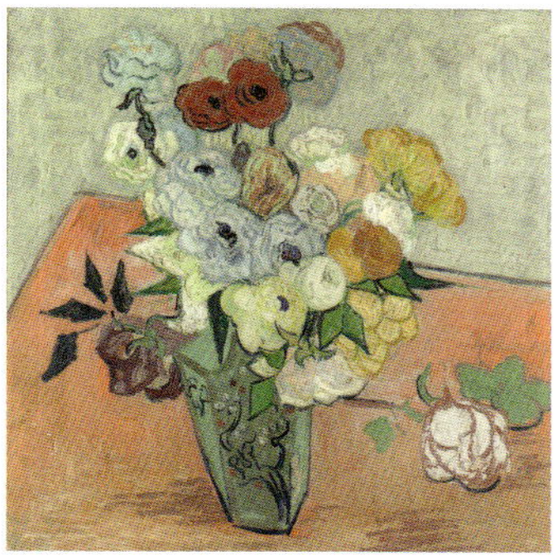

17 | *Roses and Turban Buttercups*

Sunday 1–Tuesday 3 June 1890
Oil on canvas, 51.7 × 52 cm*

Musée d'Orsay, Paris

F764 JH2045; letter 879 (5 June 1890)

Given by Theo van Gogh to Paul Gachet Jr; donated to Musée du Louvre, Paris, 1954.

[ill. 77]

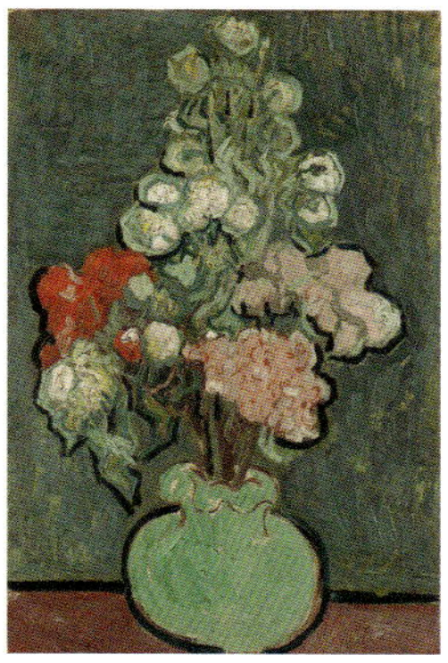

18 | *Vase of Flowers*

First half of June 1890
Oil on canvas, 42.2 × 29 cm*

Van Gogh Museum, Amsterdam (Vincent van Gogh Foundation)

F764a JH2046

Theo van Gogh, inv. 1890, no. 201: 'Fleurs dans un petit pot'.

[ill. 76]

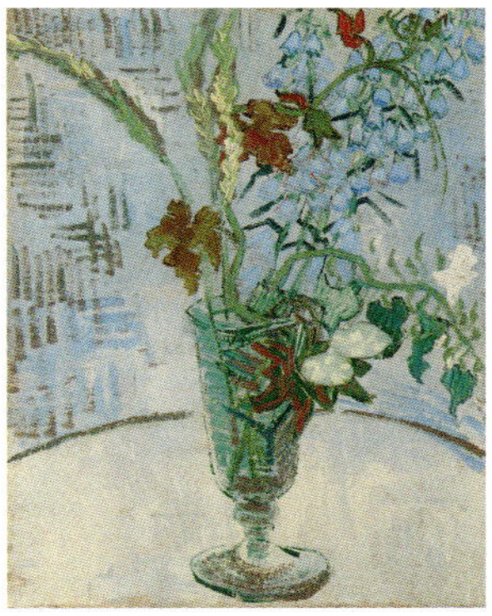

19 | *Absinthe Glass with Wild Flowers*

First half of June 1890
Oil on canvas, 41.3 × 33.3 cm*

Private collection

F589 JH2033

First owner unknown; Galerie Vollard, Paris, before or in 1908.

[ill. 79]

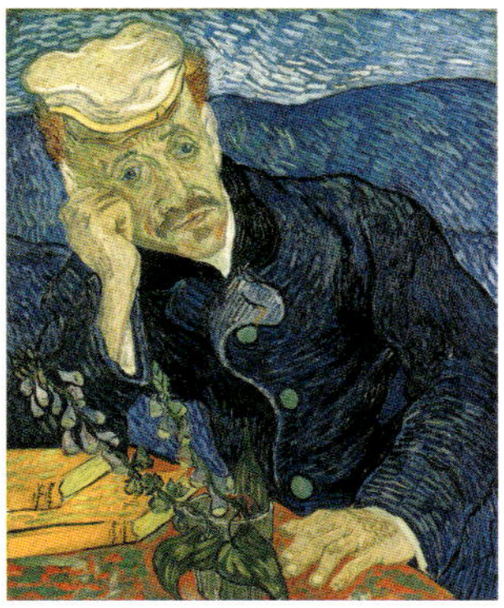

20 | *Doctor Paul Gachet*

Tuesday 3–Wednesday 4 June 1890
Oil on canvas, 66 × 57 cm*

Private collection

F753 JH2007; letters 877 (3 June 1890), 879 (5 June 1890), 886 (13 June 1890), RM23 (around 17 June 1890)

Theo van Gogh, inv. 1890, no. 251: 'Portrait du Dr. Gachet (25)'; sold by Jo van Gogh-Bonger to Alice Ruben-Faber, Copenhagen, 1897, through Galerie Vollard, Paris.

[ill. 159]

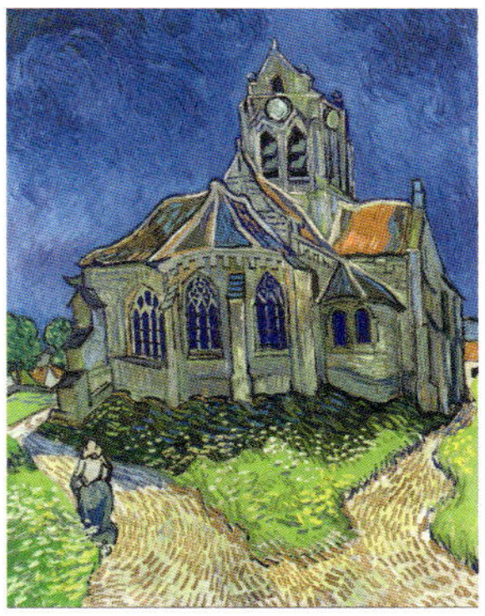

21 | *The Church at Auvers-sur-Oise*

Rue Ferdinand Mesny
Wednesday 4–Thursday 5 June 1890
Oil on canvas, 93 × 74.5 cm*

Musée d'Orsay, Paris

F789 JH2006; letter 879 (5 June 1890)

Paul Gachet Sr; acquired by Musée du Louvre, Paris, 1952, with the assistance of Paul Gachet Jr and an anonymous Canadian donation.

[ill. 1]

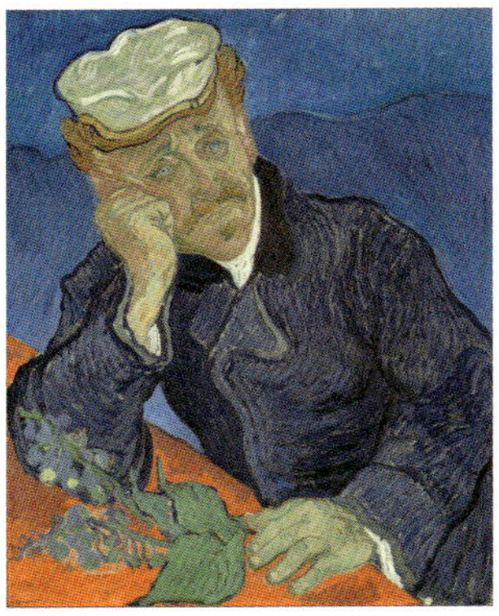

22 | *Doctor Paul Gachet*

Friday 6 and Saturday 7 June 1890
Oil on canvas, 68.2 × 57 cm*

Musée d'Orsay, Paris

F754 JH2014

Given by Vincent to Paul Gachet Sr; donated by Paul Gachet Jr and Marguerite Gachet to Musée du Louvre, Paris, 1949.

[ill. 112]

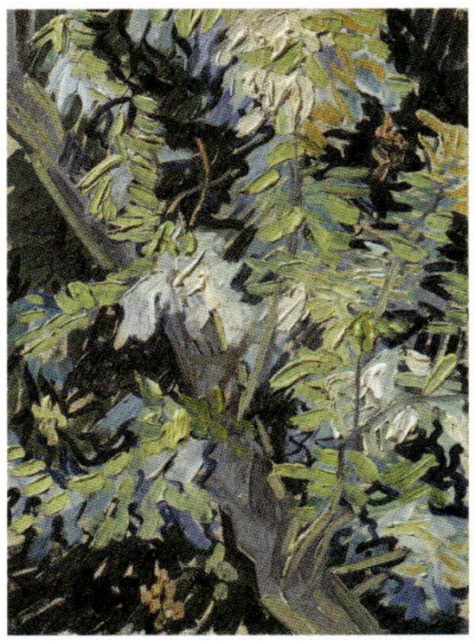

23 | *Blossoming Acacia*

Saturday 7 June 1890
Oil on canvas, 33 × 24 cm*

Nationalmuseum, Stockholm

F821 JH2015

Probably given by Vincent to Paul Gachet Sr; sold by Paul Gachet Jr to Victor Doiteau, Péronne, 1941.

[ill. 83]

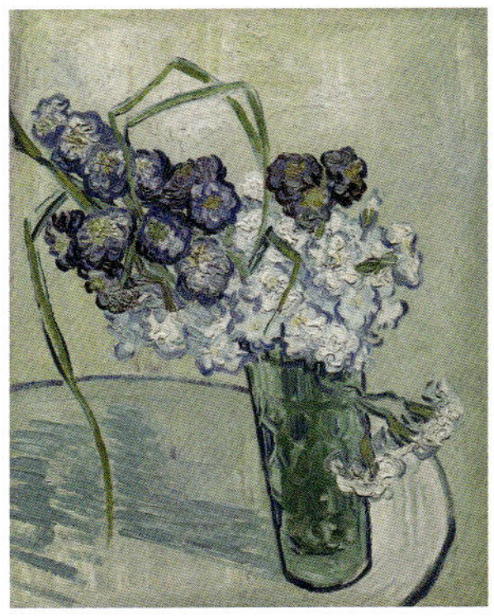

24 | *Glass with Carnations*

First half of June 1890
Oil on canvas, 41 × 32 cm

Private collection

F598 JH1890

Theo van Gogh, inv. 1890, no. 300: 'Verre rempli de fleurs (6)'; sold by Jo van Gogh-Bonger to Georg Schwarz, Berlin, 1905, through Paul Cassirer art dealers, Berlin.

[ill. 69]

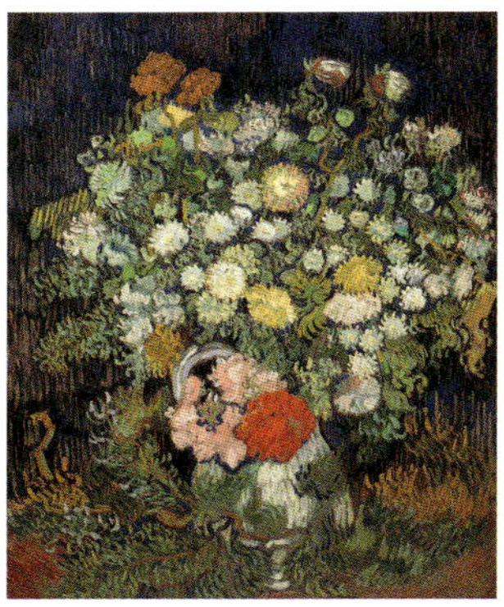

25 | *Bouquet of Flowers in a Vase*

First half of June 1890
Oil on canvas, 65.1 × 54 cm*

The Metropolitan Museum of Art, New York, The Walter H. and Leonore Annenberg Collection, Gift of Walter H. and Leonore Annenberg, 1993, bequest of Walter H. Annenberg, 2002

F588 JH1335

First owner unknown; Gyula Andorkó, Budapest/Paris, before 1908.

[ill. 84]

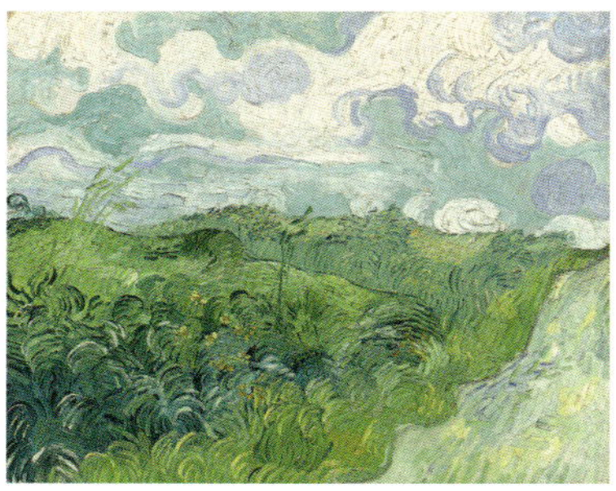

26 | *Green Wheatfields*

The plain above Auvers
First half of June 1890
Oil on canvas, 72.4 × 91.4 cm*

National Gallery of Art, Washington, Collection of Mr. and Mrs. Paul Mellon

F807 JH1980

Theo van Gogh; sold by Jo van Gogh-Bonger to Curt Herrmann, Berlin, 1906, through Paul Cassirer art dealers, Berlin.

[ill. 11]

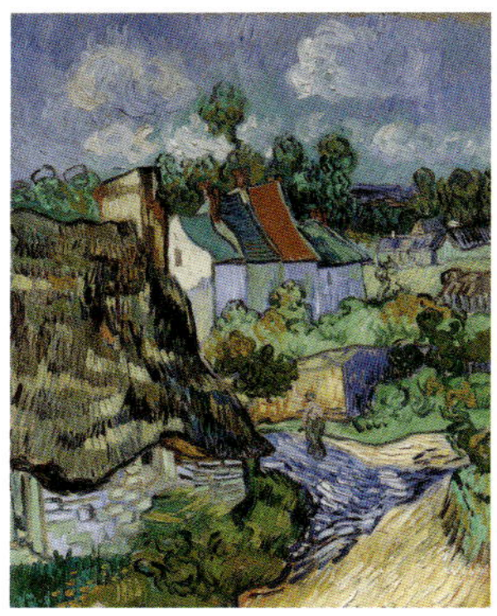

27 | *Houses at Auvers-sur-Oise*

Rue du Four
Monday 9 or Tuesday 10 June 1890
Oil on canvas, 75.6 × 61.9 cm*

Museum of Fine Arts, Boston, bequest of John T. Spaulding

F805 JH1989; letter 881 (10 June 1890)

Theo van Gogh; sold by Jo van Gogh-Bonger to Moderne Kunsthandlung, Munich, 1908.

[ill. 4]

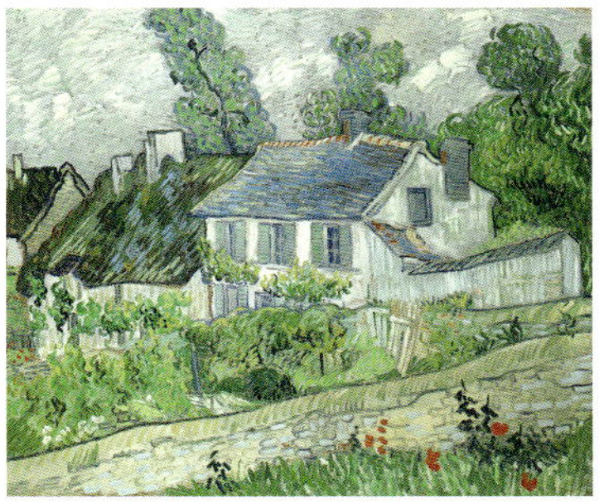

28 | *Houses at Auvers-sur-Oise*

Rue du Gré, Chaponval
Monday 9 or Tuesday 10 June 1890
Oil on canvas, 60 × 73 cm

Toledo Museum of Art, purchased with funds from the Libbey Endowment, Gift of Edward Drummond Libbey

F759 JH1988; letter 881 (10 June 1890)

Theo van Gogh; given by Jo van Gogh-Bonger to Andries Bonger, Hilversum/Amsterdam, probably before 1905.

[ill. 40]

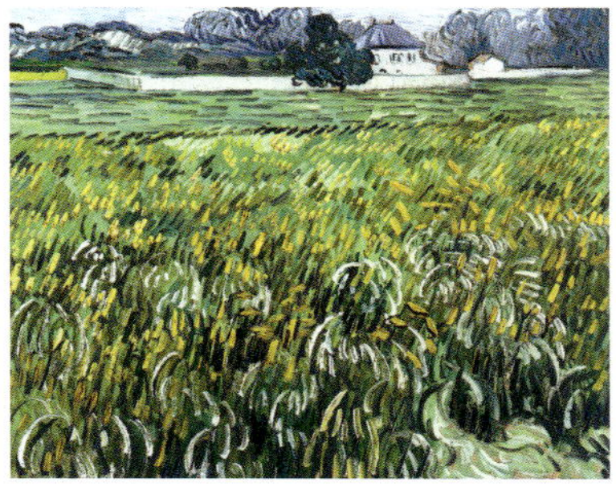

29 | *House at Auvers-sur-Oise*

Location undetermined
Around Wednesday 11 June 1890
Oil on canvas, 48.6 × 62.9 cm*

The Phillips Collection, Washington, acquired 1952

F804 JH2018; letter 886 (13 June 1890)

Theo van Gogh; sold by Jo van Gogh-Bonger to Paul Cassirer art dealers, Berlin, 1907.

[ill. 54]

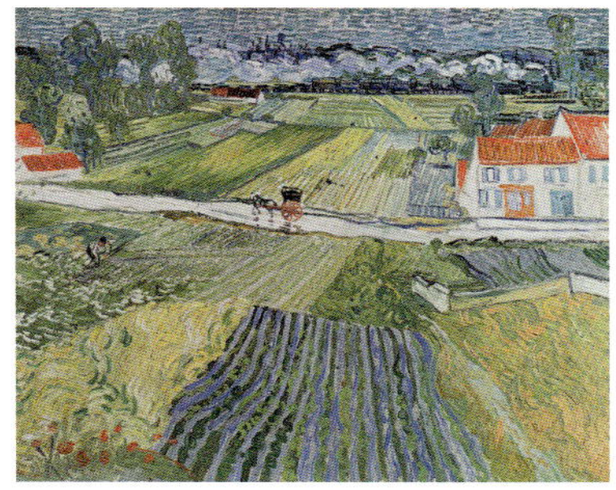

30 | *Landscape with Carriage and Train*

View of rue François Villon
(right nos. 53 and 55), from rue Gachet
Thursday 12 June 1890
Oil on canvas, 72 × 90 cm

The Pushkin State Museum of Fine Arts, Moscow

F760 JH2019; letter 886 (13 June 1890)

Theo van Gogh, list 1896, no. 312: 'Paysage (Auvers)'; sold by Jo van Gogh-Bonger to Alexandre Berthier, Prince de Wagram, Bêziers, 1906, through Paul Cassirer art dealers, Berlin.

[ill. 29]

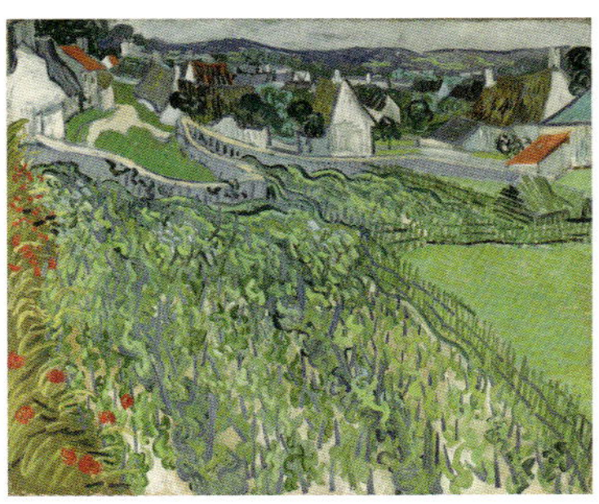

31 | *Vineyards at Auvers-sur-Oise*

Rue des Meulières, Chaponval
Around Thursday 12 June 1890
Oil on canvas, 65.1 × 80.3 cm*

Saint Louis Art Museum, Funds given by Mrs. Mark C. Steinberg

F762 JH2020; letters 886 (13 June 1890), 887 (14 June 1890)

Theo van Gogh; sold by Jo van Gogh-Bonger to Paul Cassirer art dealers, Berlin, 1905.

[ill. 55]

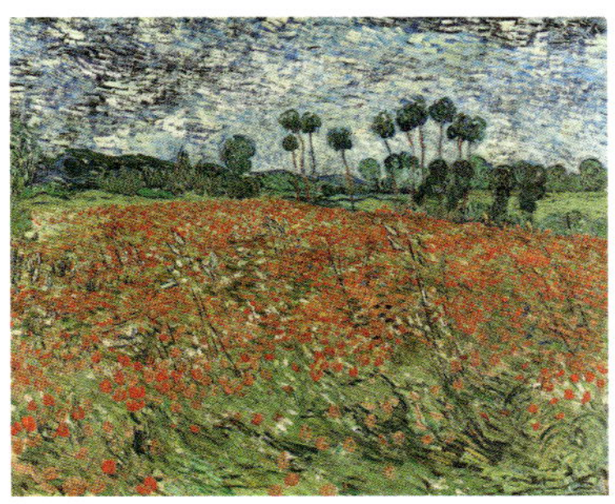

32 | *Poppy Field*

Location undetermined
Saturday 14 June 1890
Oil on canvas, 73 × 91.5 cm*

Kunstmuseum Den Haag, long-term loan Cultural Heritage Agency of the Netherlands

F636 JH2027; letter 887 (14 June 1890)

Theo van Gogh, inv. 1890, no. 297: 'Champs de coquelicots (30)'; sold by Jo van Gogh-Bonger to Wilhelmina Haakma van Royen, Utrecht, 1898, through Arts and Crafts art dealers, The Hague.

[ill. 13]

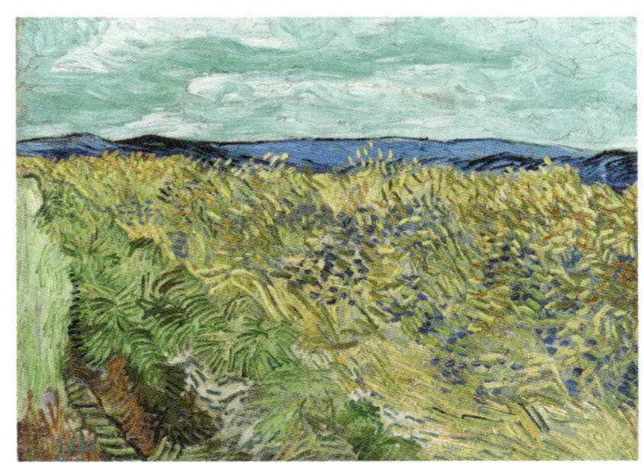

33 | *Wheatfield with Cornflowers*

The plain above Auvers
Mid-June 1890
Oil on canvas, 60 × 81 cm*

Fondation Beyeler, Riehen/Basel, Beyeler Collection

F808 JH2118

Theo van Gogh; sold by Jo van Gogh-Bonger to Max Liebermann, Berlin, 1907, through Paul Cassirer art dealers, Berlin.

[ill. 144]

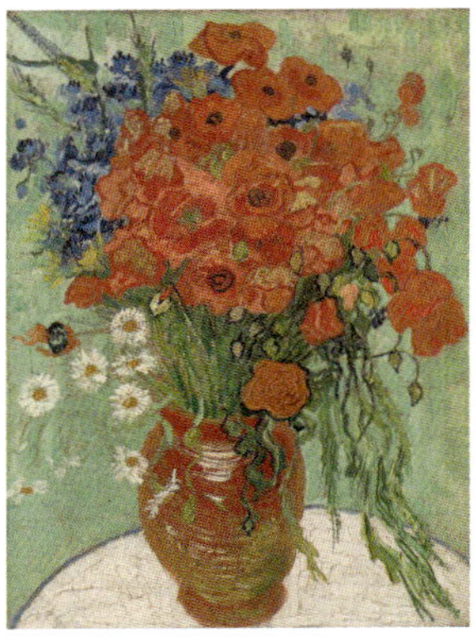

34 | *Vase with Red Poppies, Cornflowers and Daisies*

Mid-June 1890
Oil on *torchon*, 65 × 50 cm

Private collection

F280 JH2032

First owner unknown; Gaston A. Camentron, Paris, before 1911.

[ill. 81]

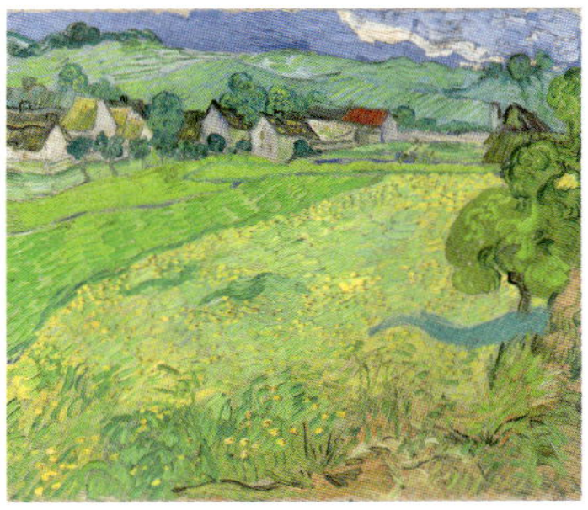

35 | *Les Vessenots in Auvers-sur-Oise*

Location undetermined (possibly Les Vessenots)
Mid-June 1890
Oil on canvas, 55 × 65 cm*

Museo Nacional Thyssen-Bornemisza, Madrid

F797 JH2003

Paul Gachet Sr; sold by Paul Gachet Jr to Paul Rosenberg, Paris, 1909.

[ill. 66]

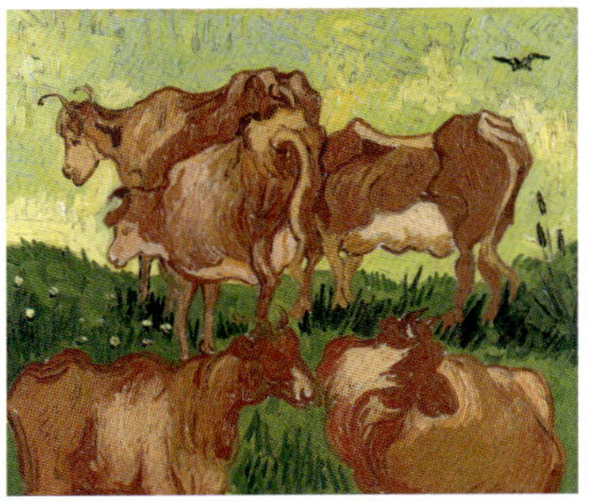

36 | *Cows (after Gachet Sr, after Jordaens)*

Monday 16 June 1890
Oil on canvas, 55 × 65 cm*

Palais des Beaux-Arts, Lille

F822 JH2095

Given by Vincent to Paul Gachet Sr; donated by Paul Gachet Jr to Musée des Beaux-Arts, Lille, 1950.

[ill. 7]

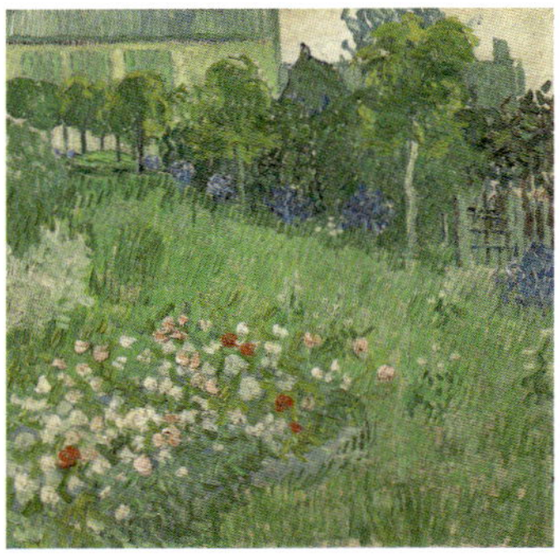

37 | *Daubigny's Garden*

24 rue du Général de Gaulle
Around Monday 16 June 1890
Oil on *torchon*, 51 × 51.2 cm*

Van Gogh Museum, Amsterdam (Vincent van Gogh Foundation)

F765 JH2029; letter 889 (17 June 1890)

Theo van Gogh, inv. 1890, no. 271: 'Jardin à Daubigny (10)'.

[ill. 141]

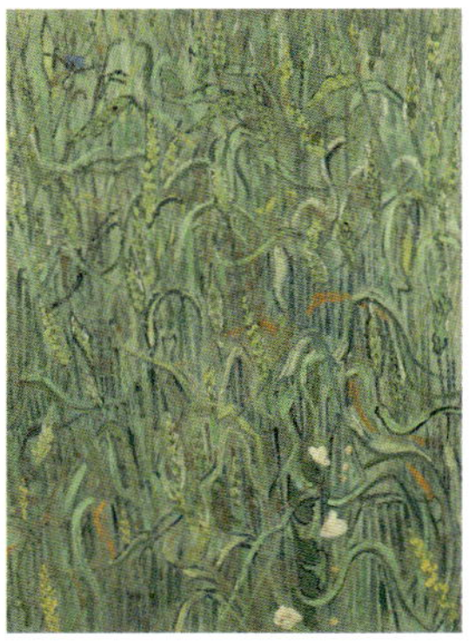

38 | *Ears of Wheat*

Around Tuesday 17 June 1890
Oil on *torchon*, 64 × 48 cm*

Van Gogh Museum, Amsterdam (Vincent van Gogh Foundation)

F767 JH2034; letter RM23 (around 17 June 1890)

Theo van Gogh, inv. 1890, no. 295: 'Epis de blé (12)'.

[ill. 123]

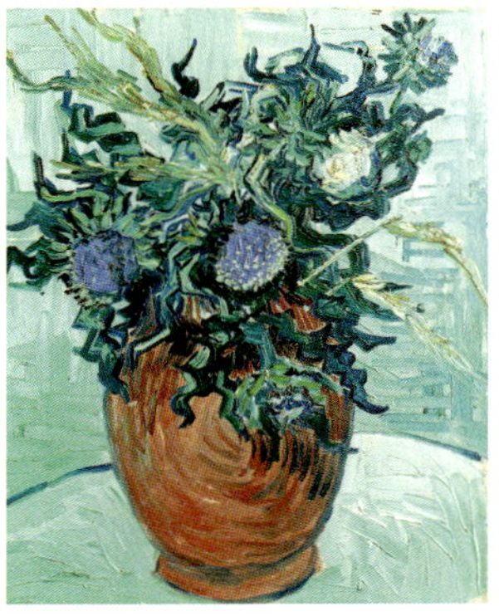

39 | *Vase with Thistles*

First half of June 1890
Oil on canvas, 40.8 × 33.6 cm

Pola Museum of Art, Hakone

F599 JH2044

First owner unknown; Alphonse Kann, Saint-Germaine-en-Laye, before 1917.

[ill. 80]

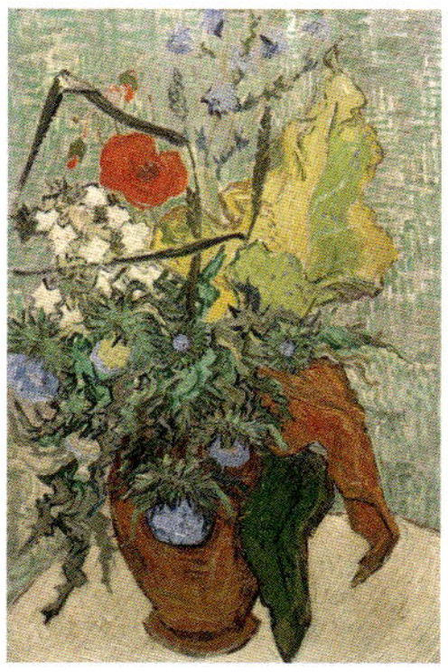

40 | *Vase with Wild Flowers*

Around Tuesday 17 June 1890
Oil on *torchon*, 66 × 45 cm

Private collection

F763 JH2030; letter 889 (17 June 1890)

Paul Gachet Sr; sold by Paul Gachet Jr to Paul Rosenberg, Paris, before 1928.

[ill. 82]

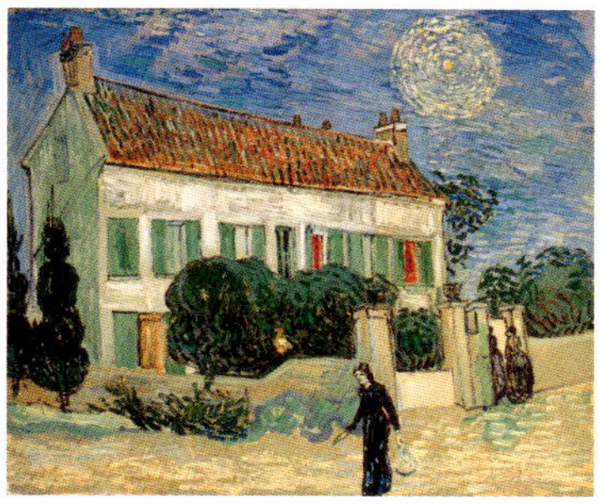

41 | *White House at Night with Star*

25 rue du Général de Gaulle
Around Tuesday 17 June 1890
Oil on canvas, 59 × 72.5 cm

The State Hermitage Museum, Saint Petersburg

F766 JH2031; letter 889 (17 June 1890)

Theo van Gogh; sold by Jo van Gogh-Bonger to Fritz Meyer-Fierz, Zurich, 1908, through C.M. van Gogh art dealers, Amsterdam.

[ill. 31]

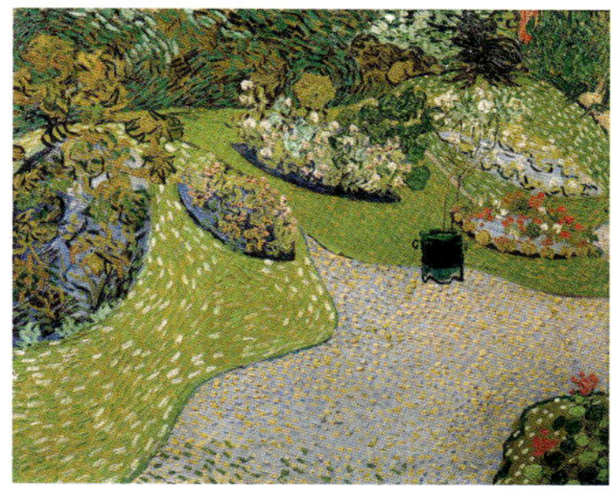

42 | *Garden in Auvers-sur-Oise*

Between Wednesday 18 and Friday 20 June 1890
Oil on canvas, 64 × 80 cm*

Private collection

F814 JH2107

Theo van Gogh, inv. 1890, no. 394: 'Jardin'; sold by Jo van Gogh-Bonger to Paul Cassirer art dealers, Berlin, 1908.

[ill. 142]

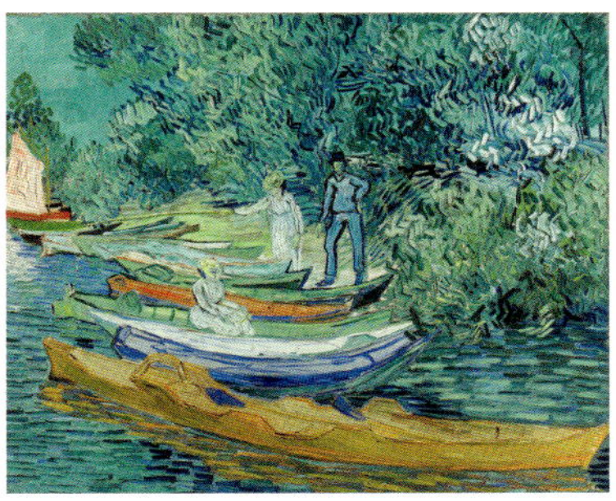

43 | *Bank of the Oise at Auvers*

Location undetermined (possibly Chaponval)
Second half of June 1890, after the 17th
Oil on canvas, 71.1 × 93.7 cm*

Detroit Institute of Arts, bequest of Robert H. Tannahill

F798 JH2021

Theo van Gogh; sold by Jo van Gogh-Bonger to Carl Reininghaus, Vienna, 1905, through Paul Cassirer art dealers, Berlin.

[ill. 57]

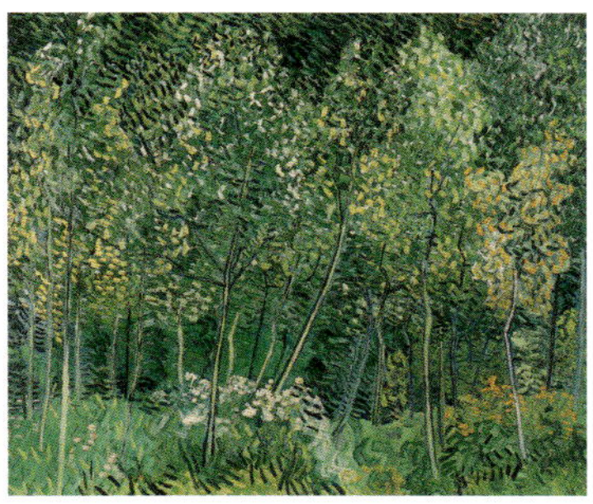

44 | *Undergrowth*

Location undetermined
Second half of June 1890
Oil on canvas, 73 × 90 cm

Private collection

F817 JH1319

Theo van Gogh, inv. 1890, no. 283: 'Sous-bois (Auvers) 30'; sold by Jo van Gogh-Bonger to Galerie Bernheim Jeune & Cie, Paris, 1909.

[ill. 2]

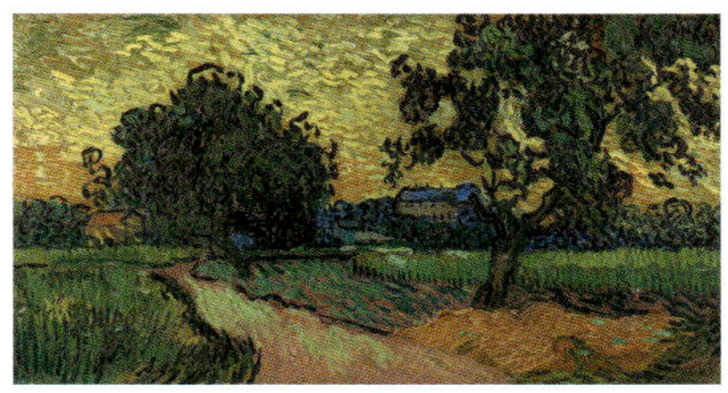

45 | *Landscape at Twilight*

Near rue Vincent van Gogh
Around Friday 20–Sunday 22 June 1890
Oil on canvas, 50.2 × 101 cm*

Van Gogh Museum, Amsterdam (Vincent van Gogh Foundation)

F770 JH2040; letter 891 (24 June 1890)

Theo van Gogh, inv. 1890, no. 259: 'Soleil couchant (30 en longueur)'.

[ill. 138]

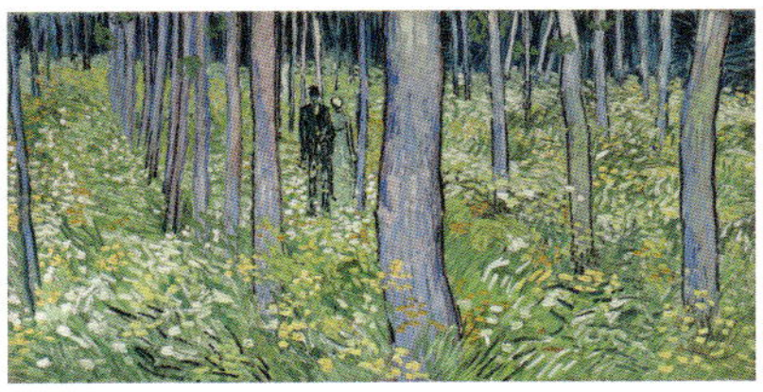

46 | *Undergrowth with Two Figures*

Location undetermined
Around Friday 20–Sunday 22 June 1890
Oil on canvas, 49.5 × 99.7 cm

Cincinnati Art Museum, bequest of Mary E. Johnston

F773 JH204; letters 891 (24 June 1890), 896 (2 July 1890)

Theo van Gogh, inv. 1890, no. 286: 'forêt (40 en longeur)'; sold by Vincent Willem van Gogh to Leicester Galleries, London, 1927.

[ill. 156]

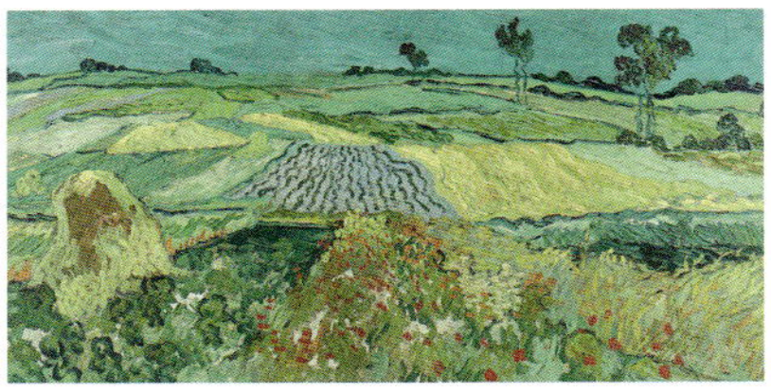

47 | *Fields near Auvers-sur-Oise*

The plain above Auvers
Around Friday 20–Sunday 22 June 1890
Oil on canvas, 50 × 101 cm*

Belvedere Museum, Vienna

F775 JH2038; letters 891 (24 June 1890), 893 (28 June 1890), 894 (30 June and 1 July 1890), 896 (2 July 1890), 897 (5 July 1890)

Theo van Gogh, inv. 1890, no. 257: 'Les champs (30 en longueur)'; sold by Jo van Gogh-Bonger to the Moderne Galerie, Vienna, 1903, via the Vienna Secession.

[ill. 135]

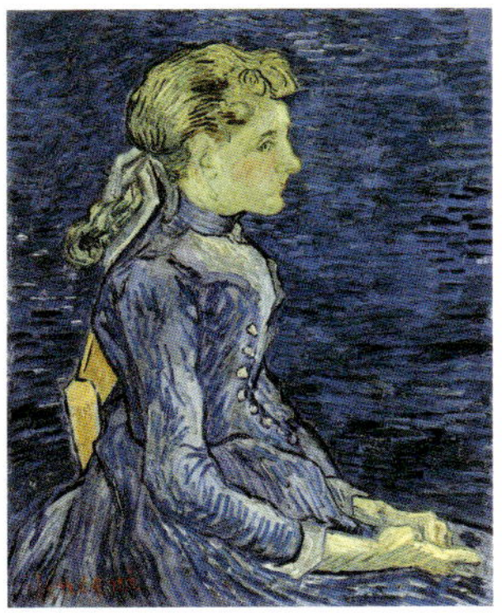

48 | *Adeline Ravoux*

Around Sunday 22 June 1890
Oil on canvas, 67 × 55 cm

Private collection – courtesy of HomeArt

F768 JH2035; letter 891 (24 June 1890)

Given by Vincent to Adeline Ravoux; sold by Arthur Ravoux, Meulan-en-Yvelines to Walter Bondy, Paris, 1908.

[ill. 119]

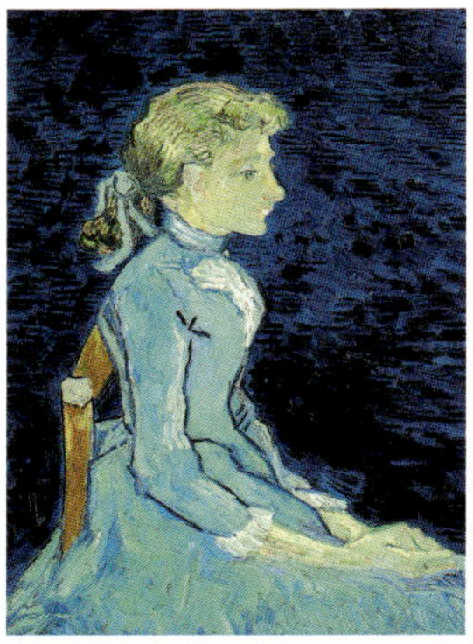

49 | *Adeline Ravoux*

Around Monday 23 June 1890
Oil on canvas, 71.5 × 53 cm

Private collection

F769 JH2037; letter 891 (24 June 1890)

Theo van Gogh, inv. 1890, no. 262: 'Portrait de jeune fille (gamme bleue) (25)'; sold by Jo van Gogh-Bonger to Theodore Pitcairn, New York, 1921, through Montross Gallery, New York.

[ill. 118]

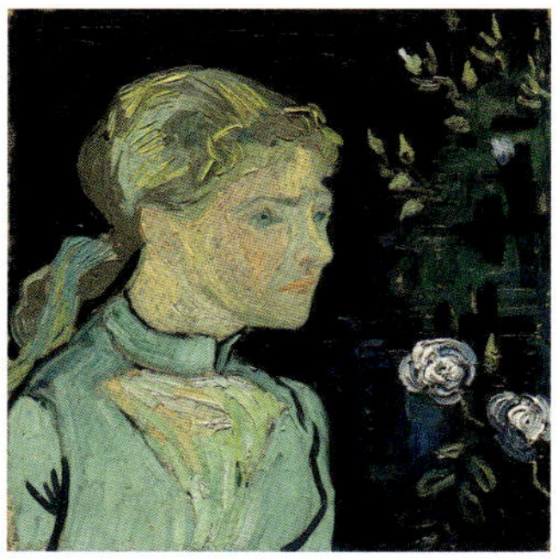

50 | *Adeline Ravoux*

Between Tuesday 24 and Sunday 29 June 1890
Oil on canvas, 50.2 × 50.5 cm*

The Cleveland Museum of Art, bequest of Leonard C. Hanna, Jr. 1958

F786 JH2036

Theo van Gogh, inv. 1890, no. 267: 'Jeune fille (sur fond noir) 10'; sold by Jo van Gogh-Bonger to Katherine S. Dreier, New York, 1912, through C.M. van Gogh art dealers, Amsterdam.

[ill. 120]

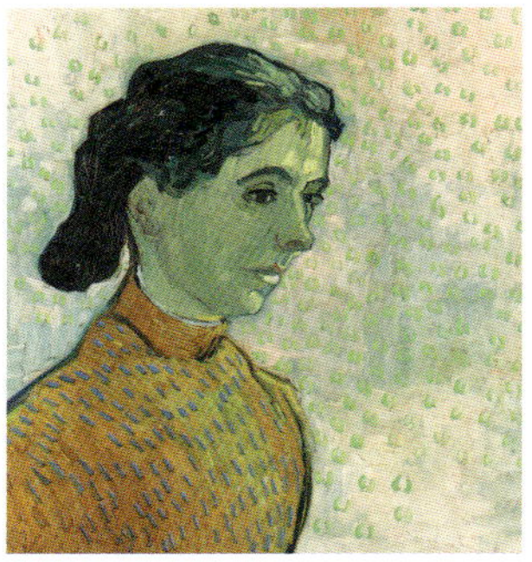

51 | *Portrait of a Young Woman*

Between Tuesday 24 and Sunday 29 June 1890
Oil on canvas, 51 × 49.5 cm*

Kröller-Müller Museum, Otterlo

F518 JH2056

Theo van Gogh, inv. 1890, no. 301: 'Portrait de jeune fille (10)'; sold by Jo van Gogh-Bonger to Carl and Thea Sternheim, Munich, 1909, through C.M. van Gogh art dealers, Amsterdam.

[ill. 121]

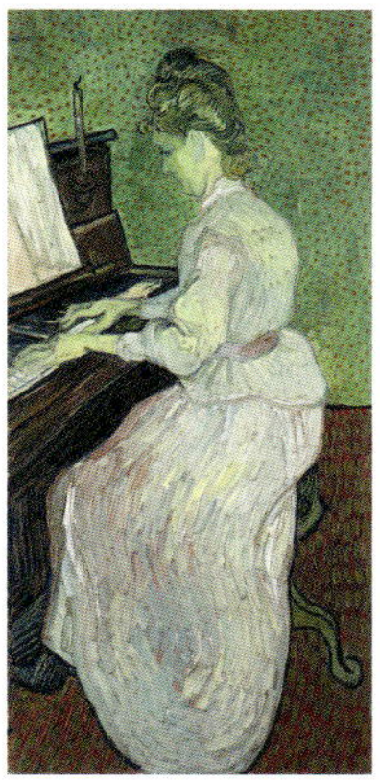

52 | *Marguerite Gachet at the Piano*

Thursday 26 and Friday 27 June 1890
Oil on canvas, 102.5 × 50 cm*

Kunstmuseum Basel

F772 JH2048; letter 893 (28 June 1890)

Given by Vincent to Marguerite Gachet; sold to the Kunstmuseum Basel, 1934.

[ill. 130]

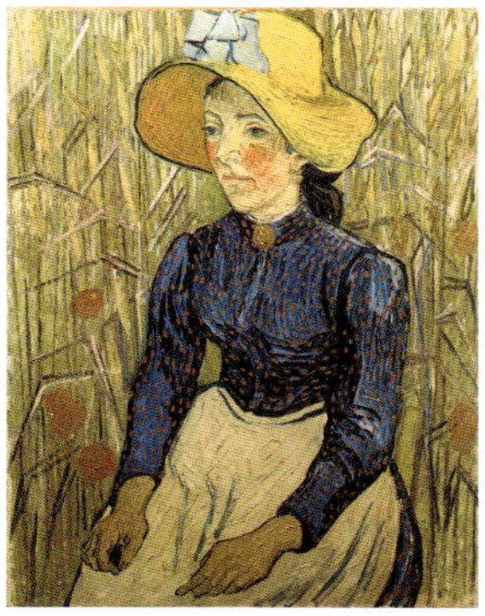

53 | *Country Girl with Straw Hat*

Around Monday 30 June 1890
Oil on canvas, 92 × 73 cm

Private collection

F774 JH2053; letters 896 (2 July 1890), 897 (5 July 1890)

Theo van Gogh, inv. 1890, no. 274: 'Portrait de femme (30) gamme jaune, épis de blé'; sold by Jo van Gogh-Bonger to W.M.A. Müller-Abeken, Scheveningen, 1912, through C.M. van Gogh art dealers, Amsterdam.

[ill. 125]

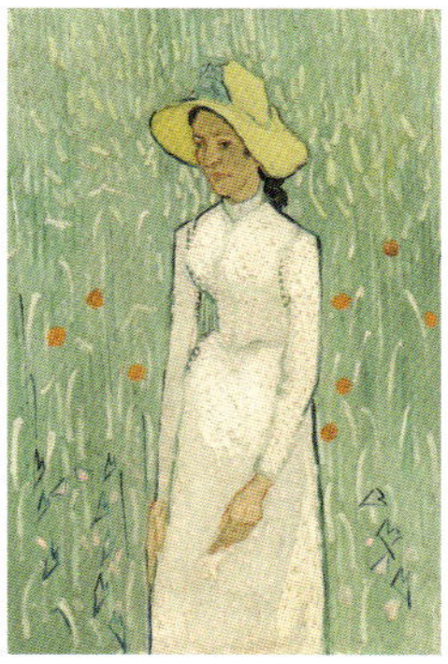

54 | *Girl in White*

Around Tuesday 1 July 1890
Oil on canvas, 66.7 × 45.8 cm*

National Gallery of Art, Washington, Chester Dale Collection

F788 JH2055

Theo van Gogh, inv. 1890, no. 255: 'Jeune fille en blanc (12)'; sold by Jo van Gogh-Bonger to Richard Kisling, Zurich, 1908, through C.M. van Gogh art dealers, Amsterdam.

[ill. 122]

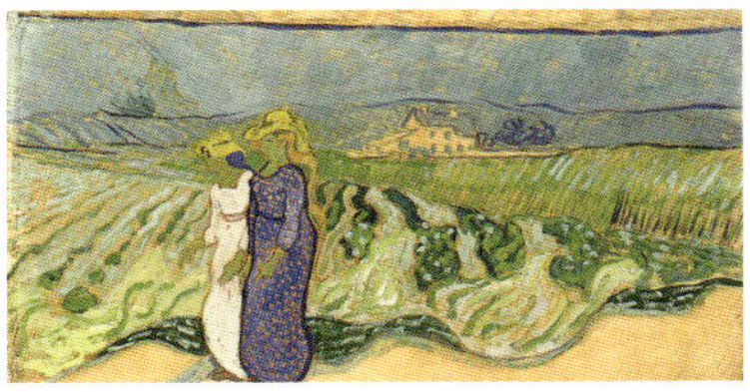

55 | *Women Crossing the Fields*

Around Tuesday 1 July 1890
Oil on paper, 30.3 × 59.7 cm

McNay Art Museum, San Antonio, bequest of Marion Koogler McNay

F819 JH2112

Theo van Gogh, inv. 1890, no. 272: 'Femmes en promenade (10 en longueur)'; sold by Vincent Willem van Gogh to Leicester Galleries, London, 1927.

[ill. 127]

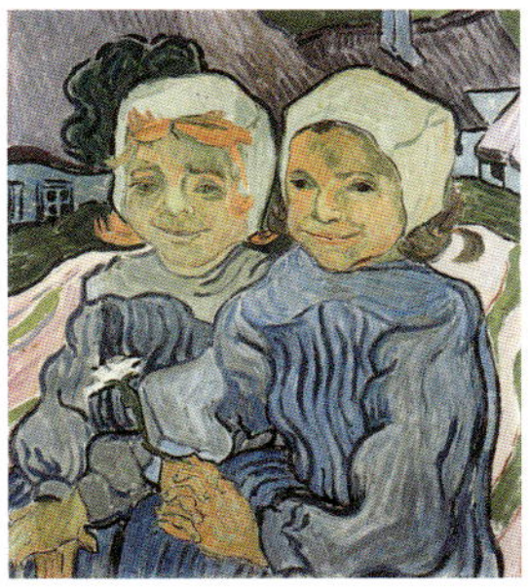

56 | *Two Girls*

June–early July 1890
Oil on canvas, 51.5 × 46.5 cm

Private collection

F784 JH2052

Theo van Gogh, inv. 1890, no. 250: 'Portrait de deux petites filles (12)'; sold by Jo van Gogh-Bonger to Richard Kisling, Zurich, 1907, through C.M. van Gogh art dealers, Amsterdam.

[ill. 133]

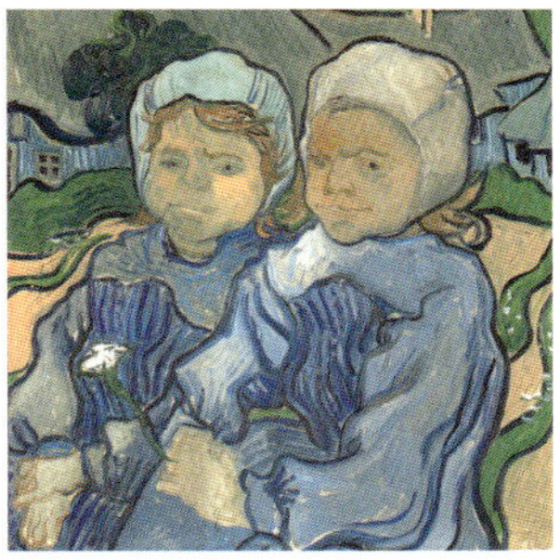

57 | *Two Girls*

June–early July 1890
Oil on canvas, 51.2 × 51 cm*

Musée d'Orsay, Paris

F783 JH2051

Paul Gachet Sr; donated by Paul Gachet Jr to Musée du Louvre, Paris, 1954.

[ill. 134]

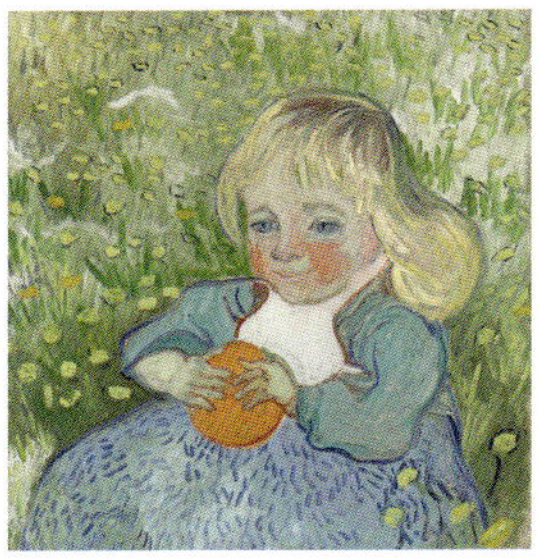

58 | *Child with Orange*

June–early July 1890
Oil on canvas, 50 × 51 cm

Private collection

F785 JH2057

Theo van Gogh, inv. 1890, no. 273: 'Bébé à l'orange (10)'; sold by Jo van Gogh-Bonger to Fritz Meyer Fierz, Zurich, 1908, through C.M. van Gogh art dealers, Amsterdam.

[ill. 132]

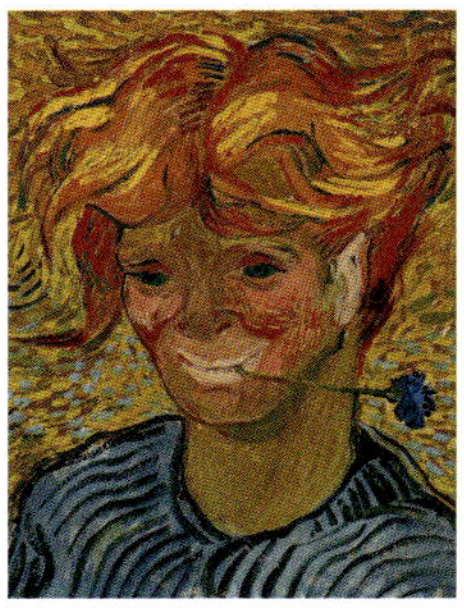

59 | *Young Man with Cornflower*

June–early July 1890
Oil on canvas, 39 × 30.5 cm*

Private collection

F787 JH2050

Theo van Gogh, inv. 1890, no. 269: 'Tête de jeune paysan (6)'; sold by Jo van Gogh-Bonger to Paul von Mendelssohn-Bartholdy, Berlin, 1909, through Galerie Bernheim Jeune & Cie, Paris.

[ill. 131]

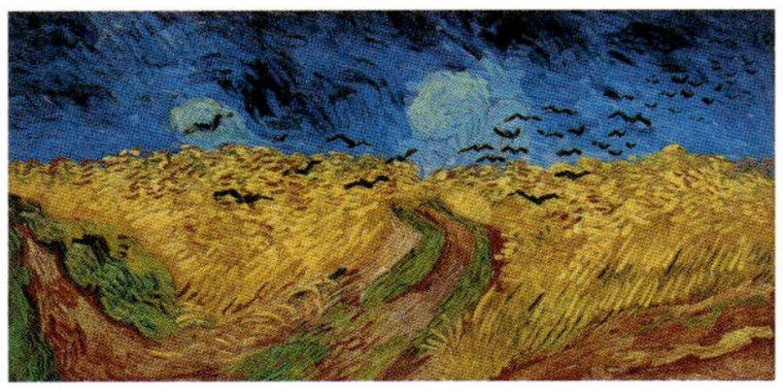

60 | *Wheatfield with Crows*

The plain above Auvers
Tuesday 8 July 1890
Oil on canvas, 50.5 × 103 cm*

Van Gogh Museum, Amsterdam
(Vincent van Gogh Foundation)

F779 JH2117; letter 898 (around 10 July 1890)

Theo van Gogh, inv. 1890, no. 261: 'effet d'orage (champs de blé) 30'.

[ill. 137]

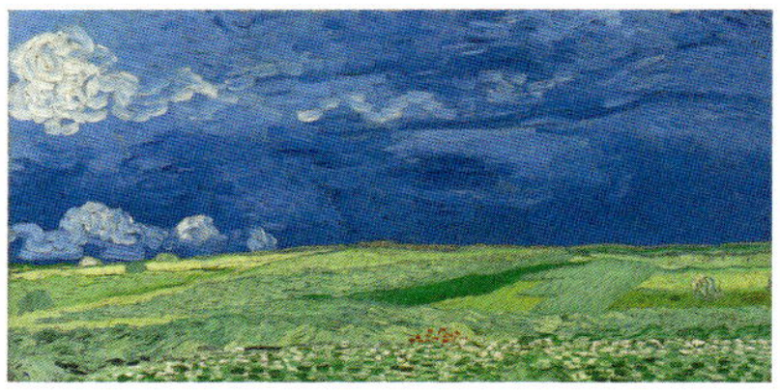

61 | *Wheatfield under Thunderclouds*

The plain above Auvers
Wednesday 9 July 1890
Oil on canvas, 50.4 × 101.3 cm*

Van Gogh Museum, Amsterdam
(Vincent van Gogh Foundation)

F778 JH2097; letter 898 (around 10 July 1890)

Theo van Gogh, inv. 1890, no. 289: 'Champs (temps d'orage) (40 en longueur)'.

[ill. 136]

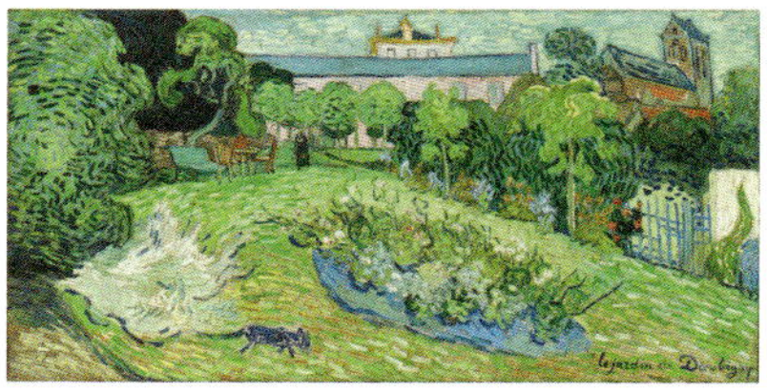

62 | *Daubigny's Garden*

24 rue du Général de Gaulle
Around Thursday 10 July 1890
Oil on canvas, 56 × 101.5 cm*

Rudolf Staechelin Collection

F777 JH2105; letter 898 (around 10 July 1890)

Theo van Gogh, inv. 1890, no. 285: 'Jardin de Daubigny (40 en long)'; sold by Jo van Gogh-Bonger to Amédée Schuffenecker, Paris, 1894.

[ill. 139]

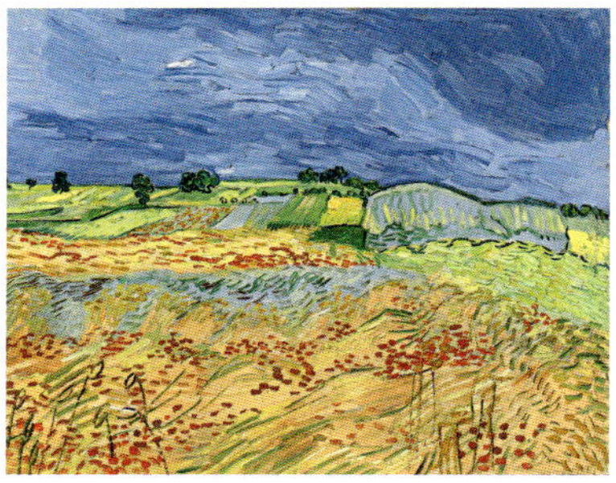

63 | *The Fields*

The plain above Auvers
Friday 11 July 1890
Oil on canvas, 50 × 65 cm*

Private collection

F761 JH2120

Theo van Gogh, inv. 1890, no. 268: 'Champs ensoleilés [sic] (15)'; sold by Jo van Gogh-Bonger to Hermann Freudenberg, Berlin, 1907, through Paul Cassirer art dealers, Berlin.

[ill. 17]

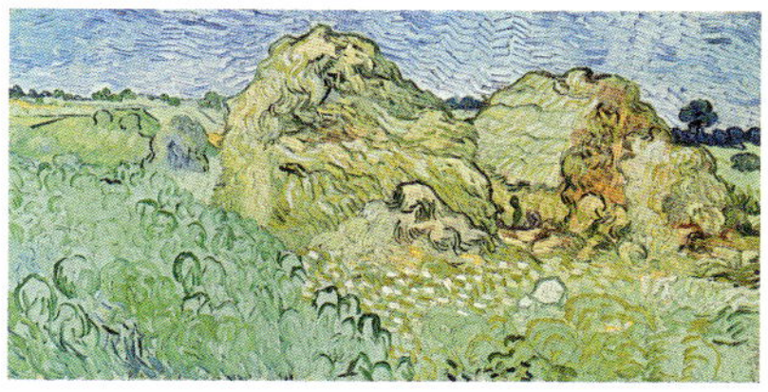

64 | *Field with Haystacks*

The plain above Auvers
July 1890
Oil on canvas, 50 × 100 cm*

Fondation Beyeler, Riehen/Basel, Beyeler Collection

F809 JH2098

Theo van Gogh, inv. 1890, no. 288: 'Meules de foin (40 en longueur)'; sold by Jo van Gogh-Bonger to Galerie Paul Vallotton, Lausanne, 1909, through Galerie Bernheim Jeune & Cie, Paris.

[ill. 143]

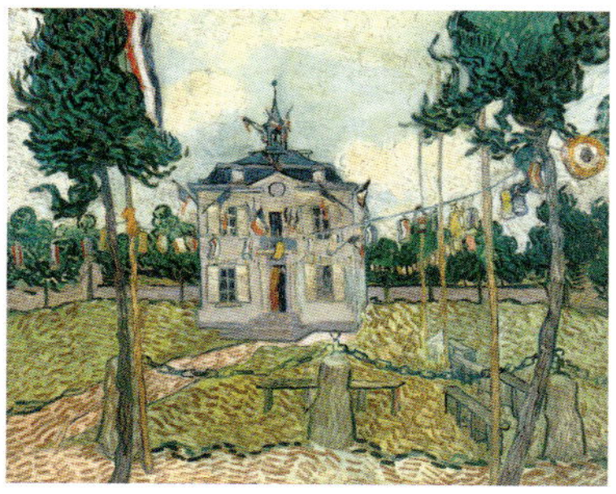

65 | *Auvers-sur-Oise Town Hall on 14 July 1890*

Place de la Mairie
Monday 14 July 1890
Oil on canvas, 72 × 93 cm

Private collection

F790 JH2108

Given by Vincent to Arthur Ravoux; sold by Arthur Ravoux, Meulan-en-Yvelines, to Walter Bondy, Paris, 1908.

[ill. 63]

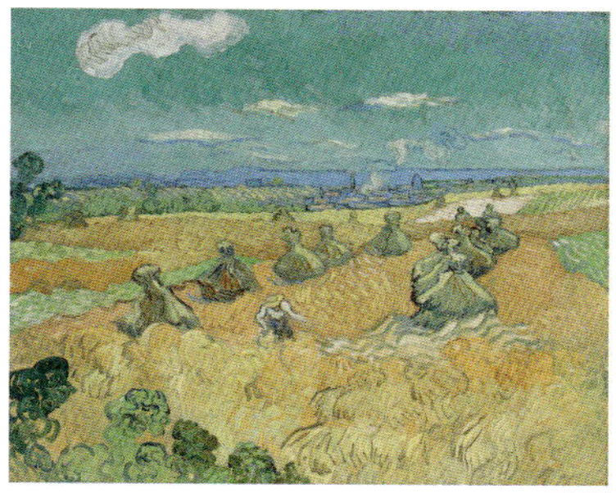

66 | *Wheatfields with Reaper, Auvers-sur-Oise*

The plain above Cordeville
with Auvers in the background
Mid-July 1890
Oil on canvas, 73.6 × 93 cm*

Toledo Museum of Art, purchased with funds from the Libbey Endowment, Gift of Edward Drummond Libbey

F559 JH1479

Theo van Gogh, inv. 1890, no. 282: 'Champs de blé (moisson) 30'; sold by Jo van Gogh-Bonger to Claude-Emile Schuffenecker, Paris, 1901, through Julien Leclercq.

[ill. 14]

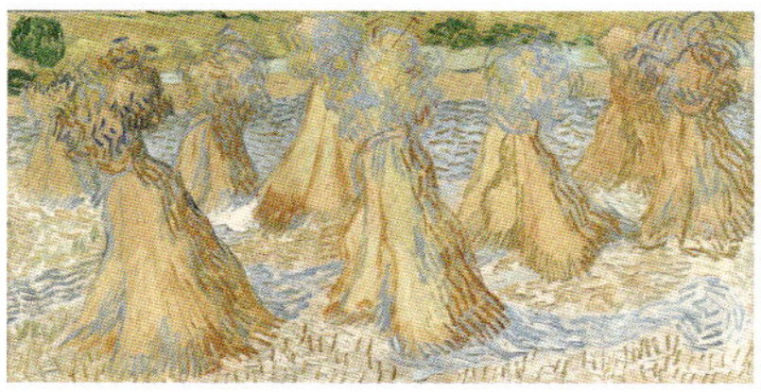

67 | *Sheaves of Wheat*

The plain above Auvers
Mid-July 1890
Oil on canvas, 50.8 × 101.6 cm*

Dallas Museum of Art, The Wendy and Emery Reves Collection

F771 JH2125

Theo van Gogh, inv. 1890, no. 260: 'Gerbes de blé (Indépendants, 19 Mars 1891)'; sold by Vincent Willem van Gogh to Leicester Galleries, London, 1927.

[ill. 146]

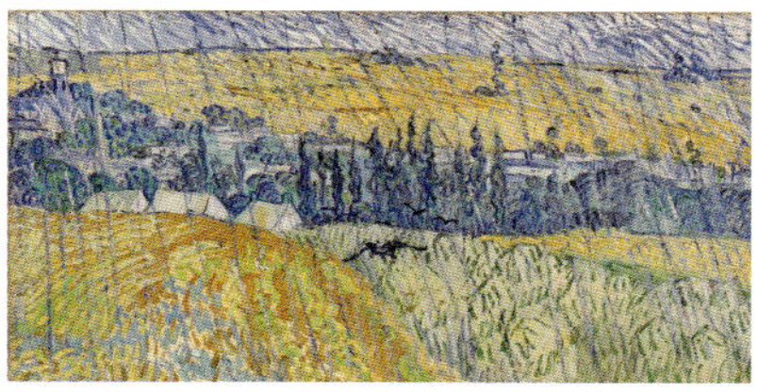

68 | *Rain – Auvers-sur-Oise*

Between rue Thérèse Lethias and rue de Pontoise, Méry-sur-Oise, with Auvers in the background
Friday 18 July 1890
Oil on canvas, 50.3 × 100.2 cm*

Amgueddfa Cymru – National Museum Wales, Cardiff, bequeathed by Gwendoline Davies, 1951

F811 JH2096

Theo van Gogh, inv. 1890, no. 258: 'La pluie (30 en longueur)'; sold by Jo van Gogh-Bonger to Gwendoline E. Davies, London, 1909, through Galerie Bernheim Jeune & Cie, Paris.

[ill. 145]

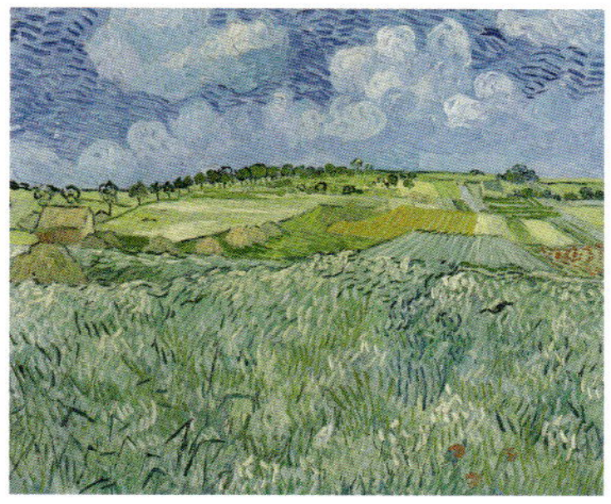

69 | *Plain near Auvers-sur-Oise*

The plain above Auvers, possibly with the long road with trees to Hérouville on the left
Friday 18 July 1890 (or Tuesday 22 July)
Oil on canvas, 73.5 × 92 cm

Bayerische Staatsgemäldesammlungen – Neue Pinakothek, Munich

F782 JH2099; letter 902 (23 July 1890)

Theo van Gogh, inv. 1890, no. 281: 'Champs à Auvers (30)'; sold by Jo van Gogh-Bonger to Hugo von Tschudi, Berlin, 1905, through Paul Cassirer art dealers, Berlin.

[ill. 68]

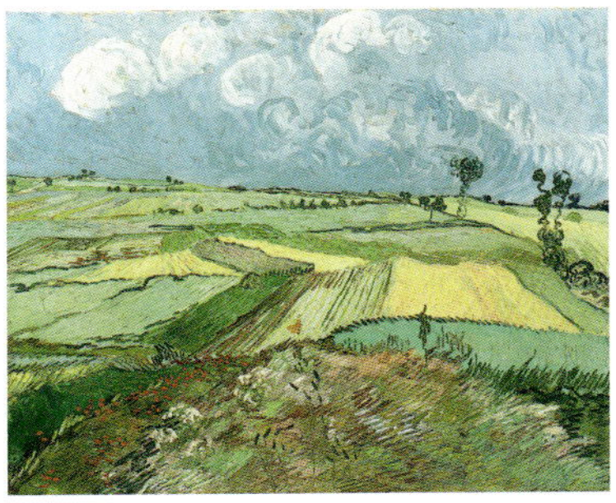

70 | *Wheatfields after the Rain (The Plain of Auvers-sur-Oise)*

The plain above Auvers
Tuesday 22 July 1890 (or Friday 18 July)
Oil on canvas, 73.3 × 92.4 cm

Carnegie Museum of Art, Pittsburgh, acquired through the generosity of the Sarah Mellon Scaife family

F781 JH2102; letter 902 (23 July 1890)

Theo van Gogh, inv. 1890, no. 284: 'Champs (30)'; sold by Jo van Gogh-Bonger to Harry Kessler, Weimar, before 1901.

[ill. 67]

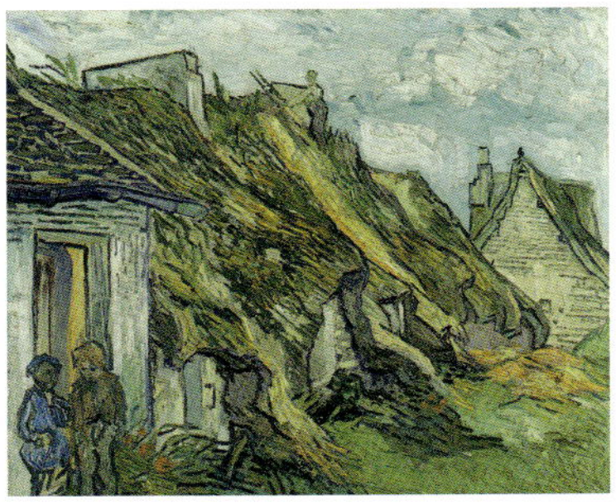

71 | *Cottages in Chaponval*

Rue du Gré, Chaponval
Between Saturday 19 and Wednesday 23 July 1890
Oil on canvas, 65 × 81 cm*

Kunsthaus Zürich, bequest Hans Schüler, 1920

F780 JH2115; letter 902 (23 July 1890)

Theo van Gogh, inv. 1890, no. 299: 'Chaumières à Auvers (25)'; sold by Jo van Gogh-Bonger to Hans Schuler, Zurich, 1908, through C.M. van Gogh art dealers, Berlin.

[ill. 30]

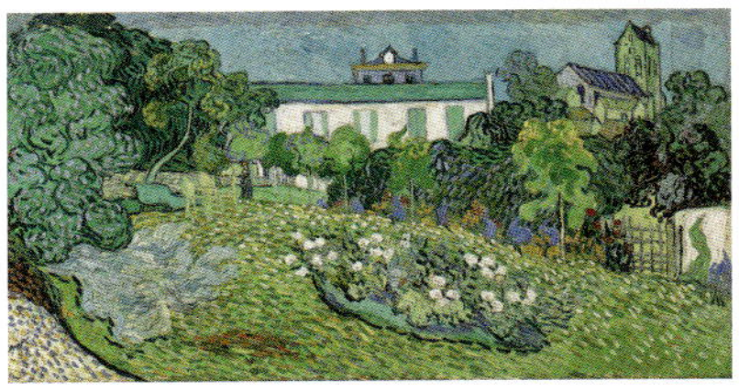

72 | *Daubigny's Garden*

24 rue du Général de Gaulle
Between Saturday 19 and Wednesday 23 July 1890
Oil on canvas, 53.2 × 103.5 cm*

Hiroshima Museum of Art

F776 JH2104; letter 902 (23 July 1890)

Given by Theo van Gogh to the widow of François Daubigny; Galerie Vollard, Paris, 1898.

[ill. 140]

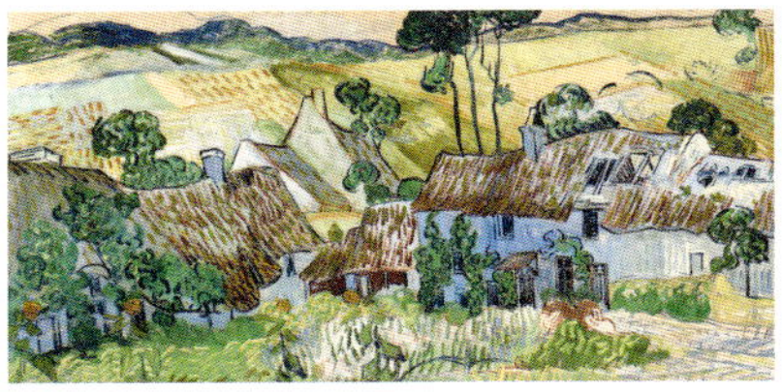

73 | *Farms near Auvers-sur-Oise*

24 rue Rajon, Cordeville
Friday 25 or Saturday 26 July 1890
Oil on canvas, 50.2 × 100.3 cm*

Tate, London, bequeathed by C. Frank Stoop, 1933

F793 JH2114

Theo van Gogh, inv. 1890, no. 287: 'Village (40 en longueur)'; sold by Jo van Gogh-Bonger to A.W. von Heymel, Bremen, 1907, through Galerie Bernheim Jeune & Cie, Paris.

[ill. 147]

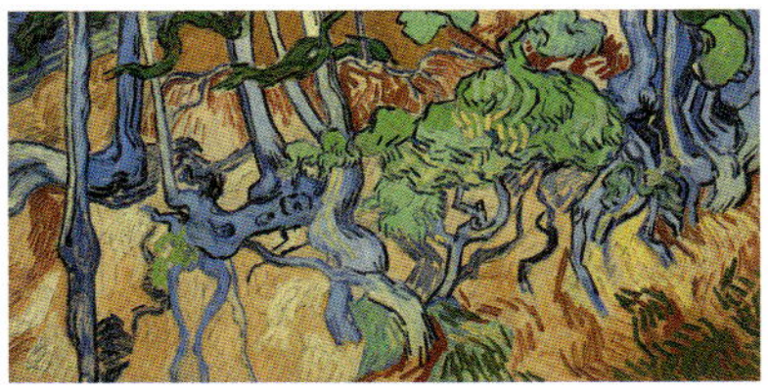

74 | *Tree Roots*

Rue Daubigny, near the Manoir de Colombières
Sunday 27 July 1890
Oil on canvas, 50.3 × 100.1 cm*

Van Gogh Museum, Amsterdam (Vincent van Gogh Foundation)

F816 JH2113

Theo van Gogh.

[ill. 157]

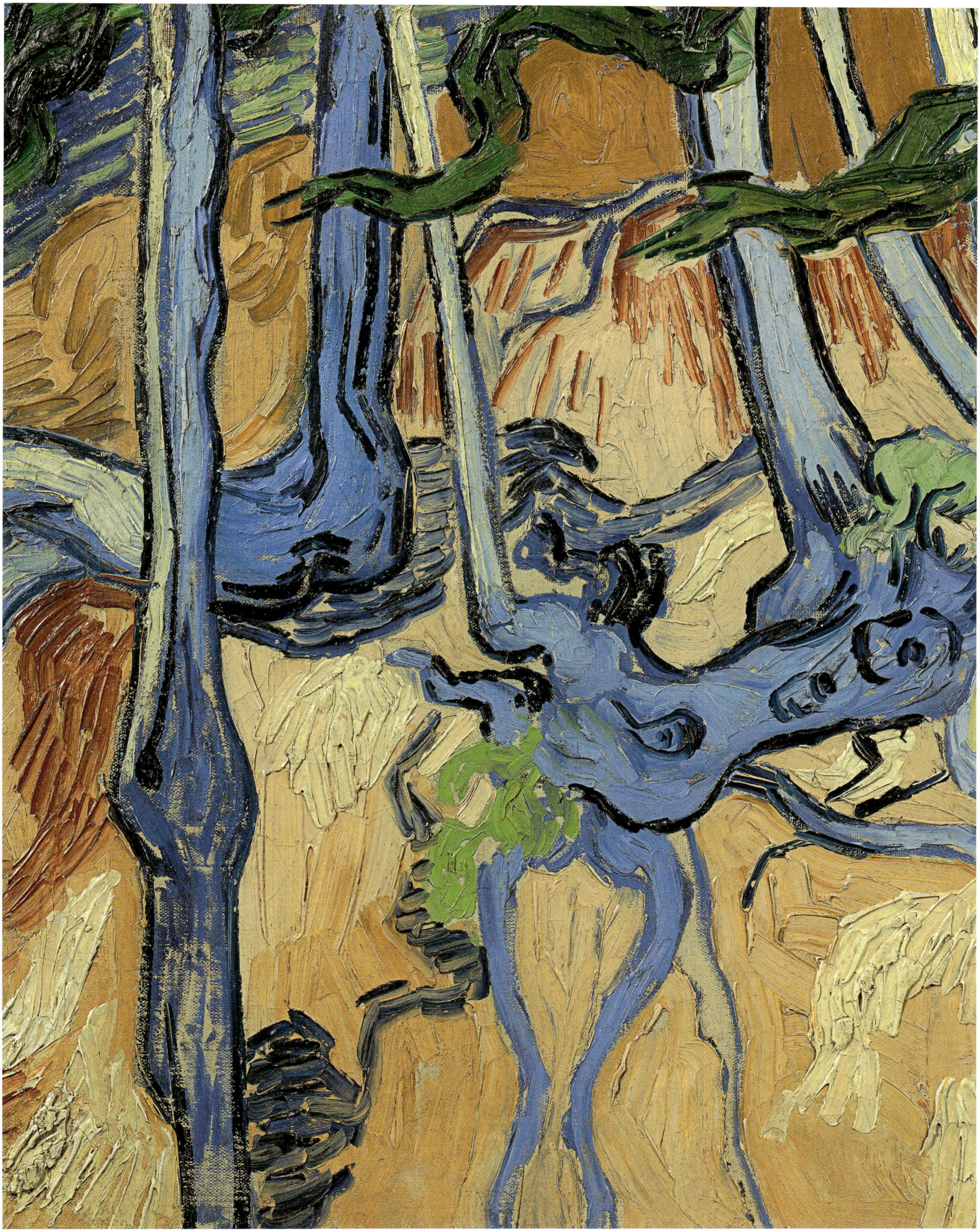

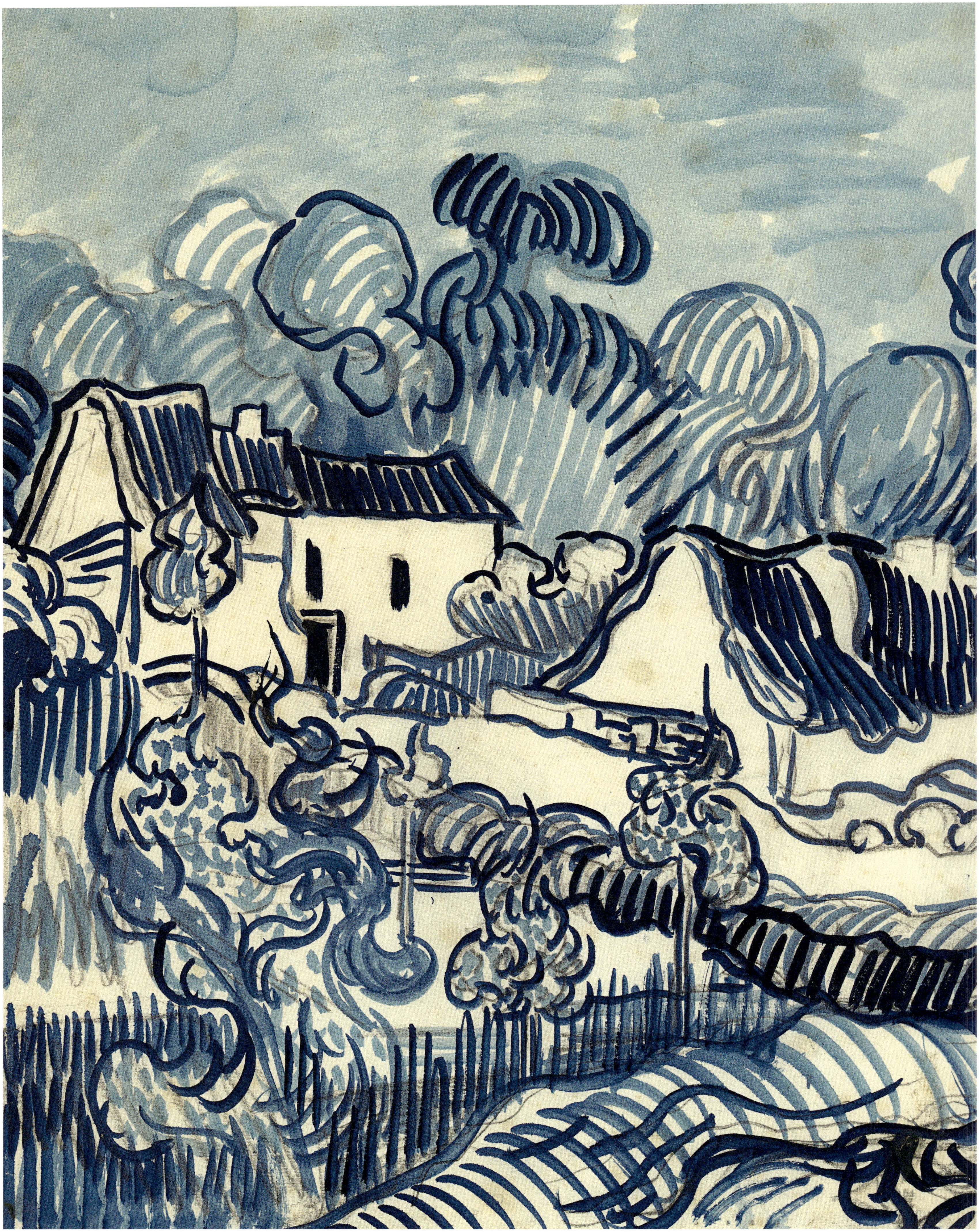

NOTES

Preface

pp. 12–13

1 Gombrich 1972, p. 58.

2 Letter 698, to Emile Bernard, around 5 October 1888.

3 See, in this regard, note 1 in Louis van Tilborgh's essay, pp. 162–77.

Vincent van Gogh's Final Months

Louis van Tilborgh
pp. 14–33

1 Held 1987, p. 127.

2 See Blotkamp 2019 in this regard.

3 This so-called *Altersstil* is discussed in ibid., pp. 17–21, and Held 1987.

4 Letter 371, to Theo, around 7 August 1883.

5 Letter 572, to Theo, between around 23 and around 25 July 1887.

6 For the origins of this conception of art, see Heumakers 2015.

7 Letter 678, to Willemien, 9 and around 14 September 1888.

8 Letter 841, to Willemien, 20 January 1890.

9 See my essay on Van Gogh's self-chosen death on pp. 162–77, for the thinking with regard to his mental problems.

10 See the *Catalogue of Paintings* on pp. 202–19.

11 See **#8, #16, #22, #23, #36, #48, #52, #65** in the *Catalogue of Paintings*.

12 Letter from Paul Gachet Jr to Jo van Gogh-Bonger, around 19 February 1912 (b3398). The very last, not yet fully dried works were most likely in the 'painting room' at the inn.

13 Van Gogh's wider reputation is discussed in Bregje Gerritse's and Sara Tas's essay on pp. 178–91.

14 Regarding the paintings that Vincent had already given away, see note 11 above, and for the ones Theo gave to Gachet, see Stein 1999, nos. P.G. 13–26, and the *Catalogue of Paintings*.

15 Van Eeden 1890, p. 268.

16 Beaubourg 1890, p. 401.

17 Van Eeden 1890, p. 268.

18 De Meester 1890.

19 De Meester 1891, p. 319.

20 Bonger 1893, and see also Maes and Van Tilborgh 2012, pp. 67–68.

21 De Meester 1891, p. 319.

22 See Bregje Gerritse's and Sara Tas's essay on pp. 178–91.

23 For this and other details in this paragraph, see Feilchenfeldt 2013 and the *Catalogue of Paintings*.

24 Cohen Gosschalk 1905, p. 14.

25 Kōdera 1996.

26 Luijten 2022, pp. 346, 477, note 119.

27 Jaspers 1926, p. 131.

28 Elgar 1958, pp. 251, 253.

29 Pickvance 1986, p. 15. For criticism of this, see Sund 1988, p. 674, note 75.

30 Pickvance 1984, p. 11.

31 Fuchs 2002, p. 40.

32 Ibid., p. 45.

33 Letter 800, to Theo, 5 and 6 September 1889.

34 Ibid., and for his admiration of the preface, see RM08 (unsent) and letter 93.

35 Quotes from the first edition, pp. 7, 8; see also letter 93, to Theo, 7 and 8 October 1876.

36 See my essay on pp. 162–77 in this regard.

37 Letter 533, to Theo, 4 October 1885, and for *La foi du charbonnier* letters 286, 358, 368, 396, 397, 403, 404.

38 Letter 879, to Willemien, 5 June 1890.

39 See Teio Meedendorp's essay on pp. 58–79 in this regard.

40 Letter 898, to Theo and Jo, around 10 July 1890, and letter 902, to Theo, 23 July 1890.

41 See Nienke Bakker's essay on pp. 80–95.

42 Van Gogh's admiration of Jordaens is mentioned in letter 551, to Theo, around 2 January 1886.

43 The relevant work of 1872 is at the Musée d'Orsay in Paris.

44 Letter 575, to Emile Bernard, about December 1887.

45 See in this regard Van Tilborgh 2021b, p. 55.

46 Letter 823, to Theo, 26 November 1889.

47 See also Teio Meedendorp's essay on pp. 58–79.

48 See in this regard Van Tilborgh 2021b, pp. 52–58.

49 Letter 396, to Theo, around 15 October 1883.

50 See Emmanuel Coquery's essay on pp. 134–61.

51 Fromentin 1876, pp. 256–57. Ruisdael's reputation in the nineteenth century is discussed in Walford 1991, pp. 192–96. The translation is taken from the English edition, Fromentin 1981, pp. 144–45.

52 Fromentin 1876, p. 248. For the translation, see Fromentin 1981, p. 139.

53 See Nienke Bakker's essay on pp. 116–33 for more on these portraits.

54 See my essay on pp. 162–77 in this regard.

55 Letter 868, to Theo, 4 May 1890.

56 Gachet 1994, p. 254.

57 Letter 400, to Theo, 28 October 1883, and Zeldin 1979, pp. 292–93.

58 Merchant 1983, pp. 2–9; for Michelet's attitudes and the criticism they attracted, see Zeldin 1979, pp. 292–93.

59 Letter 893, to Theo, 28 June 1890. It does not strike me as a coincidence that one of the landscapes features a couple surrounded by a large number of trees **(156)**.

60 See for this visit my essay on pp. 162–77, as well as the Chronology on p. 199.

61 Letter 898, to Theo and Jo, around 10 July 1890.

62 Letter 381, to Theo, around 5 September 1883. By 'paradou', Van Gogh was referring to the paradisical garden in Emile Zola's 1875 novel *La faute de l'abbé Mouret*; 'Gethsemane' is the historical garden at the foot of the Mount of Olives in Jerusalem, where, according to the New Testament, Christ was overwhelmed by grief and fear before his crucifixion.

63 Sensier 1873, p. 93. Regarding Michel, also see Briat-Philippe and Luijten 2017, and Taws 2021.

64 Letter 898.

65 See, in this regard, my essay on pp. 162–77.

66 Letter 899, to his mother and Willemien, between around 10 and 14 July 1890.

67 Letter 800, to Theo, 5 and 6 September 1889. For this symbolism see Sund 1988, pp. 674–76.

68 Letter 222, to Theo, 1 May 1882.

69 Fromentin 1876, p. 258 The translation is taken from Fromentin 1981, p. 145.

70 All this is dealt with in Van Tilborgh and Van Uitert 2012, pp. 15–18.

71 Beaubourg 1890, p. 397.

72 I am indebted to Kitty Caiden (Senior Painting Conservator, Amgueddfa Cymru – National Museum Wales), who informed me that the painting was probably executed in two sessions. The rain was added over dry paint, making the flow finer and sharper than would have been possible painting wet-on-wet.

Exploring Auvers-sur-Oise: People and Places

Wouter van der Veen
pp. 34–57

* The topographical research underlying this essay was conducted in the archives and in situ, in close collaboration with Teio Meedendorp.

1 Trublot 1887. This article was cited copiously by Ronald Pickvance in the introduction to his chapter on Auvers-sur-Oise in Pickvance 1986 (p. 195), with some questionable translations, including the term 'pécores', which is rendered as 'stupid creatures'.

2 Letter 873, to Theo and Jo, 20 May 1890.

3 Letter 874, to Theo and Jo, around 21 May 1890.

4 Letter 875, to Theo and Jo, 25 May 1890 and letter 886, to Willemien, 13 June 1890.

5 Among others, see Doiteau 1923–24 and Distel and Stein 1999.

6 Letter 872, to Theo, 13 May 1890.

7 The interest in the centennial of Van Gogh's birth in March 1953 translated into several articles in the press. In that context, journalists Georges Charensol and Maximilien Gauthier came across Adeline Carrié-Ravoux. She was the daughter of the innkeeper of the Café de la Mairie, where Van Gogh stayed in Auvers, and had vivid memories of the artist, including that she – aged twelve – had posed for him. Charensol and Gauthier interviewed her several times; the first version, recorded and broadcast on 4 April 1953, is preserved in the Institut National de l'Audiovisuel (INA), collection RDF/RTF/Autres (1949–1963), *L'art et la vie, Vincent van Gogh*. In August 1954, she wrote a letter to Gauthier giving her latest version of the facts she remembered. Her recollections vary and are sometimes contradictory or fabricated. See also Van der Veen 2020, pp. 115–24.

8 Doiteau 1957.

9 Paul Louis Gachet set about compiling a catalogue of Van Gogh's work in Auvers, which, however, he never completed. The unedited material from that project formed the basis for his (posthumous) publication *Les 70 jours de Van Gogh à Auvers*, Editions du Valhermeil, 1994, richly annotated by Alain Mothe. Earlier, Gachet Jr published *Souvenirs de Van Gogh et de Cézanne* (1928) and *Lettres impressionnistes au Dr Gachet et à Murer* (1957), with his father's role as one of the main themes. Gachet Jr was a privileged witness to Van Gogh's final months, but the accuracy of his recollections is questionable. He is mistaken, contradicts himself and gradually assigns increasing importance to his own relationship with Van Gogh. For example, in a 1912 letter to Jo van Gogh-Bonger (b3398) he describes how his father watched over the painter during the night of 27–28 July after his suicide attempt, but from 1928 he attributes that watching to himself (Gachet 1953b).

10 Mothe 2003; Millon 2002.

11 The train from Paris also stopped at Chaponval, at the level crossing, closer to Dr Gachet's house. However, that simple stop did not offer the same service as the station at Auvers-sur-Oise, which Van Gogh needed due to the volume of his luggage. With thanks to the Cercle Historique du Rail Français and Secretary General Daniel Vauvillier for this clarification.

12 Gachet 1994, p. 41.

13 Letter 877, to Theo, 3 June 1890.

14 Letter 875, to Theo and Jo, 25 May 1890.

15 Gachet 1994, p. 43; Coquiot 1923, p. 244.

16 In his first letter from Auvers-sur-Oise (letter 873, to Theo and Jo, 20 May 1890) Van Gogh mentions a conversation with Gachet about his choice of the Café de la Mairie: 'I told Dr Gachet that I would find the inn he suggested preferable at 4 francs a day, but that 6 francs was 2 francs too dear for the expenses I'm having. It's alright for him to say that I'll be quieter there, enough is enough.'

17 Van Heugten and Pabst 1995. The title 'L'Homme à la pipe' comes from Gachet Jr (in Gachet 1994, among others).

18 *Cahiers de dénombrement avec liste nominative des habitants d'Auvers-sur-Oise en 1891*, Archives Départementales du Val-d'Oise, Pontoise.

19 The locations of *Farmhouse* **(43)**, *Thatched Cottages* **(44)** and *Farms near Auvers-sur-Oise* **(147)** in Valhermeil, assumed by Alain Mothe (Mothe 2003, pp. 165–68), do not correspond to the cadaster of the hamlet.

20 A highly complete picture of the economic and social particularities of Auvers-sur-Oise at

the end of the nineteenth century is provided by the *Monographie communale d'Auvers-sur-Oise*, compiled in 1899 by the educator Samson Cazier, preserved in the Archives Départementales du Val-d'Oise, Pontoise (1 T 146 – Auvers-sur-Oise 1899).

21 Letter 879, to Willemien, 5 June 1890.

22 Letter 877, to Theo, 3 June 1890.

23 Letter 891, to Theo, 24 June 1890.

24 The existence of Louise ('Lisette') Joséphine Elisa Chevalier was revealed in 2002 by Claude Millon (Millon 2002, pp. 204–08); Paul Louis Gachet was completely silent on this subject in his publications. Millon suggests that Lisette's biological father was Dr Gachet; her mother, the governess Louise Anne Virginie Chevalier, was, according to Millon, the doctor's mistress before, after and perhaps also during his marriage to Elisa Angélique ('Blanche') Castets. Millon's findings are supported by letters from Paul Alexis, Emile Bernard and Norbert Goeneutte to the doctor (Correspondence, c. 1816–1953; Paul Ferdinand Gachet and Paul Louis Gachet Papers [6t4hso8t], The Wildenstein Plattner Institute, Inc. – hereafter: Gachet Papers). They repeatedly convey their greetings to young Lisette, and also to her mother, which seems unusual given her position as governess in the house. Moreover, Alexis writes in his article published in *Le Cri du peuple* (see note 1 above) that in 1887 Gachet had three children to raise: 'Monsieur Coco' (nickname of Paul Louis Gachet) and 'the two know-it-alls'. The composition of this particular household, an open secret, seems compatible with the doctor's nonconformist ideas, set forth by his niece Marguerite Poradowska, née Gachet, in the short story 'Le Vase d'Urbino, Ultimes souvenirs d'Auvers', 1891 (Gachet Papers). The doctor's misogyny exposed by Poradowska may explain the extremely discreet role assigned to the women of the Gachet family – a peculiarity which his son adopted and which is confirmed in Millon 2002, pp. 155–59, and Golbéry 1990, pp. 83–108.

25 Trublot 1887. A postcard addressed to Dr Gachet dated 1 January 1889 reinforces the impression of an established household: 'Mr and Mrs Paul Alexis & Ms Paule send their best regards to Dr Gachet and his charming family – send polite greetings to Ms Chevallier [*sic*] and Ms Lisette – ... When will that dear doctor make Mr Coco and the know-it-alls climb the hill ...' (Gachet Papers [6jc96m3m]).

26 Letter 874, to Theo and Jo, around 21 May 1890.

27 Marianne Reiley Burt claims in Reiley Burt 1975, p. 61, that Eugène Murer (whose real name was Hyacinthe-Eugène Meunier) and Van Gogh saw each other occasionally. She relied on a notebook by Murer that was in her possession. In that notebook, Murer allegedly jotted down some of the words Van Gogh would have addressed to him: '"You are meagre", he says to me bluntly. "And your painting is meagre. It is too dry. It should be fatter." It was a pointed observation.' We were unable to trace the author or the notebook.

28 Ravoux 1953.

29 Gachet 1994, p. 52.

30 This location is confirmed by the discovery of a 1903 photograph of the same place in an unidentified photo album by a native of Auvers-sur-Oise, Mr Daniel Vauvillier. The spelling of Vallembourg, like that of Valhermeil, Montcel and many other toponyms, has strong variations depending on the sources – and sometimes even within the same source.

31 Letter 889, to Theo, 17 June 1890.

32 Ravoux 1953.

33 See Teio Meedendorp's essay on pp. 96–115.

34 Doiteau 1957. The words recorded show mainly what charmed a young man on the threshold of adulthood: sex, drunkenness and firearms; it is a pity that the eldest, Gaston, an artist in the making and more mature, never said anything about his impressions of contact with the painter.

35 See Teio Meedendorp's essay on pp. 96–115.

36 The location of the main motif, the farmhouse with the long gable, has caused some confusion in the past. The painting was exhibited in 1905 under the title *Chaumières au Montcel* at the exhibition of the Société des Artistes Indépendants. Paul Gachet Jr, the owner of the work, changed the title at some point (it is not known when) to *Chaumières à Cordeville*. In fact, the plot on which the farmhouse stands is on the border of the two hamlets. In Mothe 2003 (p. 72), the motif is located approximately in the correct place, but the viewpoint indicated is erroneous.

37 Cazier 1899.

38 The schematic-looking background of *Two Girls* may indicate that Van Gogh was depicting something he had not observed but reused for the composition of this double portrait: it is not at all certain whether the girls were part of the family living in the farmhouse depicted, or even whether they both belonged to the same family. The 1891 census of Auvers-sur-Oise, held in the Archives Départementales du Val-d'Oise, Pontoise, does not allow us to identify them with sufficient probability.

39 Letter 898, to Theo and Jo, around 10 July 1890.

40 Mothe 2003, p. 172.

41 Van der Veen 2020.

42 Letter 650, to Theo, 29 July 1888.

43 Ravoux 1953.

44 Gachet 1994, p. 247.

45 Louis van Ryssel (pseudonym of Paul Louis Gachet), *De l'endroit où Van Gogh s'est suicidé*, 1904, oil on canvas, 26 × 33.5 cm, Musée Tavet-Delacour (musée Camille Pissarro), Pontoise.

46 Ravoux 1953.

47 See also Rohan 2012, pp. 106–12.

48 Letter from Emile Bernard to Albert Aurier, 31 July 1890, in Bakker, Van Tilborgh and Prins 2016, pp. 160–64.

A Rural Village in all its Aspects

Teio Meedendorp
pp. 58–79

1 Letter 873, to Theo and Jo, 20 May 1890.

2 Letter 874, to Theo and Jo, around 21 May 1890.

3 The church tower does crop up regularly, however, in the background of landscapes and village scenes. The town hall dates from 1867.

4 Joanne 1856, p. XIII. The journalist Adolphe Joanne wrote a whole series of guidebooks. The *Guides de voyages Joanne*, continued in the twentieth century as the famous *Guides bleus*. Joanne himself drew inspiration from Claude-François Denecourt, who had written guides to Fontainebleau and its surroundings, see Jones et al. 2008, p. 15.

5 Joanne 1856, pp. 469–70, illustration on p. 471. Second and third editions of the guide followed in 1872 and 1878.

6 Artists' interest in Barbizon, located to the south of Paris, and the forest near Fontainebleau actually dated back to the 1820s, well before the railway arrived there. But when stations opened at Fontainebleau and Chailly in 1849, the region began to experience a steady influx of day-trippers, tourists and artists. There was, incidentally, a sophisticated campaign behind it all: see Jones et al. 2008, pp. 13–21.

7 A statue of Van Gogh was unveiled in Auvers in 1956; Daubigny's was installed in 1907, and the village high street was renamed rue Daubigny.

8 Now the museum Maison-Atelier Daubigny. Artists who settled in the countryside often kept up their studios in Paris, where they generally worked during the winter. Van Gogh was no stranger to Daubigny's Paris studio on the Ile Saint-Louis, 13 quai d'Anjou: he paid a visit there in 1887 to Guillaumin, who had moved into the studio after Daubigny's death; see letter 575, to Emile Bernard, around December 1887.

9 'What Auvers meant to Daubigny was first and foremost the Oise', Van Ryssel, Bazin and Chatelet 1954, p. 21.

10 Letter 246, to Theo, 15 and 16 July 1882. The whereabouts of the work in question, *Village in France (Street in Auvers-sur-Oise)*, is not known. The only evidence of it is a photograph; see ibid., note 16.

11 The population of Auvers grew considerably in the second half of the nineteenth century. There were 1,500 residents in 1850, an increase of 100 since 1800. By 1896, the figure was 2,259, see Cazier 1899, pp. 3, 6.

12 Berthe Morisot, who knew Corot and was taught by Achille Oudinot – the architect and painter who designed Daubigny's house in Auvers – also worked in the area in the 1860s and visited Daubigny in the village.

13 Letter 801, to Theo, 10 September 1889. Vignon was staying in Nesles-le-Vallée at the time, a little to the north of Auvers.

14 Duvivier et al. 2003, p. 54. Daubigny's fellow artist, Jules Dupré, had already settled in the slightly more distant Isle-Adam in 1850.

15 Barron 1886, p. 582.

16 Letter 885, to his mother, 13 June 1890.

17 Pearce (1851–1914) lived in Auvers from 1886 until his death in 1914 and was buried there. Barlow (1861–1917) spent the period 1889–92 in the village and Wickenden (1861–1931) worked there in the summers of 1887–90, before living there all year round from 1892 to 1900. The American journalist Sheridan Ford (1860–1922), a close acquaintance of James Abbott McNeill Whistler and a friend of Wickenden, also lived in Auvers at the time.

18 Wickenden undated, p. 60. Alfred Wickenden was only four years old in 1890 and admitted recalling little from the early days. But what lends credibility to his memory of the visit paid by Van Gogh, whose 'sombre, brooding appearance' scared him, is that he especially remembered a certain 'Hirschwick', whom he found genuinely frightening. This is plainly a reference to Anton Hirschig, who occupied the small room next to Van Gogh's at the Café de la Mairie from the middle of June 1890, before leaving shortly after his companion's death.

19 Wickenden rented it from the widow of Karl Daubigny, the artist-son of Charles-François, who had died in 1886, eight years after his father: see Gustavison 1989, p. 21. The American befriended her as early as 1887 and Wickenden went on to play a significant role in the sale of both Charles-François's and Karl's paintings and prints to American collectors, ibid., chapter 2, *passim*.

20 Wickenden rented the studio from July to September, having previously stayed at an old farmhouse in the same area: see Gustavison 1989, p. 24, and Wickenden undated, p. 29. Van Gogh himself might well have been in contact with Karl Daubigny's widow – who managed the family's affairs – when he was seeking to paint the garden of Daubigny's other house in Auvers, diagonally opposite the station.

21 For an impression, see http://www.atelier-daubigny.com/laMaison.htm.

22 Letter 877, to Theo, 3 June 1890.

23 Letter 881, to Theo and Jo, 10 June 1890.

24 See Emmanuel Coquery's essay on pp. 134–61.

25 Rudi Fuchs specifically referred to 'fragmentering' in relation to this painting. He considered it a highly original step in Van Gogh's development: see Fuchs 2002, and Louis van Tilborgh's essay on pp. 14–33.

26 See, among others, Chatelet 1978 and Mothe 1987, p. 174.

27 See also Kilpinen 1995.

28 The land between the Oise and the village was chiefly used for horticulture and growing vegetables (peas, beans, asparagus, artichokes and cabbages, among others). Most of the produce was sent to the market of Les Halles in Paris, see Cazier 1899, p. 22.

29 See the Note on the Catalogue in the *Catalogue of Paintings* on p. 206.

30 The buildings were originally more blue-purple, see Van Tilborgh and Van Maanen 2015.

31 Purple tones show through in various places, as well as greyish tints that were also more purple at one time.

32 See Louis van Tilborgh's essay on pp. 14–33.

33 Letter 886, to his sister Willemien, 13 June 1890.

34 The sketches in question are F1627, F1629, F1628 and F1578, all Van Gogh Museum, Amsterdam.

35 Dr Gachet, for example, was a keen angler: when he was called to Van Gogh's bedside on the night of 27 July after the painter shot himself, he was found along the Oise, where he was fishing with his son; see letter from Paul Gachet Jr to Jo van Gogh-Bonger, 19 February 1912, b3398.

36 A sheet with three pencil sketches of boats on the Oise, F1646 verso, has also survived.

37 Monet and Renoir mostly did so along the Seine closer to Paris, see Herbert 1988, pp. 210–19.

38 There were several boat-hire firms along the Oise between Auvers and Chaponval. This is probably the one on the Ile de Vaux, the vegetation of which can be made out in the left background. The island was a popular spot for rowing and fishing.

39 See Nienke Bakker's essay on pp. 116–33, my essay on pp. 96–115, and, with specific regard to Van Gogh's views on women and marriage, Louis van Tilborgh's essay on pp. 14–33.

40 On one occasion, they set up their easels at precisely the same spot, right next to the Café de la Mairie in rue de la Sansonne **(5)**. The painting by Bourges (1838–1909), oil on panel, 26 × 37 cm, is at the Musée Daubigny in Auvers-sur-Oise, see http://www.van-gogh.fr/leonide-bourges.php.

41 See, regarding the constellation, Olson and Doescher 2001.

42 RM23, to Gauguin, around 17 June 1890 (unsent). Van Gogh was referring to *Country Road in Provence by Night* (F683).

43 Shortly afterwards, he also painted a still life with blossoming chestnut branches **(71)**.

44 Letter 875, to Theo and Jo, 25 May 1890.

45 Gachet 1994, pp. 61–62. This was also adopted in 1928 by De la Faille; the title in the Bonger list was the neutral 'Maisons et jardins', see the *Catalogue of Paintings*, **#5**. 'Père Pilon' was not, incidentally, the glass painter and amateur artist Pierre Pilon, to whom Gachet Jr devoted a separate publication, *Un peintre méconnu, Pierre Pilon (1824–1912)*, Paris 1953. Gachet Jr did not identify the other Pilon.

46 Cazier 1899, p. 21.

47 Ravoux 1957, p. 10.

48 Chatelet 1978, p. 441.

49 The drawing shows the town hall from the same angle – not exactly from the front, but slightly from the side, so that a foreshortened right-hand wall can be made out.

50 Cazier 1899, p. 74.

51 Letter 900, Theo to Vincent, 14 July 1890.

52 Mothe 1987, p. 150, was the first to identify this as a quarry dwelling.

53 Cazier 1899, p. 35. The 'Guide Joanne' of 1856 (Joanne 1856, p. 470), still describes quarrying as 'la principale industrie'.

54 This is also clearly visible in *Fields near*

Auvers-sur-Oise **(135)**, *Wheatfield under Thunderclouds* **(136)**, *The Fields* **(17)** and *Wheatfields with Reaper, Auvers-sur-Oise* **(14)**.

55 A three-yearly cycle was followed on the plain: the first year was devoted to a 'hoe crop' of root vegetables ('plante sarclée') such as beets or potatoes, followed by a year of cereals and a third year with an intermediate crop such as alfalfa and clover, which also served as cattle feed. The fields were not left fallow, see Cazier 1899, pp. 22–23.

56 I am grateful to Hans den Nijs for the botanical information. This flower, *Lilium bulbiferum*, can grow to around 75 cm in height.

Charmed by Flowers

Nienke Bakker
pp. 80–95

1 Letter 875, to Theo and Jo, 25 May 1890.

2 The paintings of acacia branches **(83)** and ears of wheat **(123)** are not included in the total of nine. I am indebted to Hans den Nijs for his help in identifying the varieties of flower in the still lifes.

3 The reasons for dating the floral still lifes to this short period are explained later in this essay and in the *Catalogue of Paintings* on p. 204.

4 The sunflower still lifes from January 1889 are F455 (Philadelphia Museum of Art) and F458 (Van Gogh Museum, Amsterdam).

5 Letter 870, to Theo, 11 May 1890. The four paintings are **72**, F678, F680 and F682. The only other floral still life that Van Gogh painted in Saint-Rémy was a small study of a geranium, mentioned in letter 836, to Theo, 4 January 1890, but which has not been identified.

6 The idea of floral still lifes for sale dates back to Van Gogh's time in Paris; see Hendriks and Van Tilborgh 2011, pp. 236, 240.

7 Aurier 1890, p. 28. The sunflower still lifes F454 and F456 were shown at the exhibitions of Les Vingt in Brussels (January–February 1890) and Les Indépendants in Paris (March–April 1890). Theo informed Vincent that in Monet's opinion his paintings were the best things there (letter 862, 23 April 1890). Gauguin's admiration for Van Gogh's sunflowers is discussed by Bakker and Riopelle 2019.

8 RM19, to Willemien, around 21 May 1890 (unsent).

9 Letter 870, to Theo, 11 May 1890. The sketchbook that Van Gogh used in Paris and Auvers contains sketches of his *Irises* and *Sunflowers*, which might be linked to his idea in Auvers of making etchings after his best pieces from Provence. Cf. letter 889, to Theo, 17 June 1890.

10 Letter 866, to Theo, around 2 May 1890: '*père* Quost must have a darned good painting in the Salon.' The work featured in the Salon des Artistes français, which opened at the Palais des Champs-Elysées on 1 May. Van Gogh read about it in *Le Figaro* of 30 April: 'Monsieur Quost brilliantly paints flowers in the open air, in the full light, full green and full yellow.'

11 Theo did not visit the Salon until June, writing to Vincent afterwards: 'You, though, judged well as regards the Quost. If I had to choose one that's the one I'd take' (letter 890, 23 June 1890). Theo suggested visiting Quost together (letter 890), but nothing came of it. The painter had a flower garden in Montmartre, which Van Gogh must have known, as he had noted the address in his Paris sketchbook (Hendriks and Van Tilborgh 2011, p. 236, note 2).

12 Georges Jeannin, *Vase with Flowers* and *Vase with Peonies*, both c. 1856–91, Van Gogh Museum, Amsterdam. Jeannin's *Le Centenaire* and *Camelias et tulipes* were shown at the Salon. Van Gogh related his achievement as a flower painter to that of Quost and Jeannin: 'if Jeannin has the peony, Quost the hollyhock, I indeed, before others, have taken the sunflower.' Letter 739, to Gauguin, 21 January 1889.

13 Adolphe Monticelli, *Vase with Flowers*, c. 1875, Van Gogh Museum, Amsterdam.

14 Van Gogh must have taken two of these Parisian floral still lifes with him to Auvers; see below. Letter 792, Theo to Vincent, 16 July 1889, letter 771, Jo to Vincent, 8 May 1889, and letter 879, to Willemien, 5 June 1890.

15 Van Gogh mentioned the storm and rain in letter 875 of 25 May, by which time he had already completed two paintings of chestnut trees in blossom **(58, 59)**; he included a dark, stormy sky in the latter painting (see Teio Meedendorp's essay on pp. 58–79). He had brought the canvas on which he painted *Blossoming Chestnut Branches* with him from Saint-Rémy. New supplies arrived shortly after 25 May; see letter 875.

16 Theo had written to him that the exhibition was 'superb' (letter 869, 10 May 1890). Vincent replied that he would love to go (letter 870) and is sure to have done so. It included two series of colour woodcuts of flowers by the Japanese artist Hokusai, whom he admired. Soda 2017, cats. 481–86, 507.

17 Ravoux 1957, p. 11, and Wouter van der Veen's essay on pp. 34–57.

18 Letter 875, to Theo, 25 May, and Gachet 1994, p. 63.

19 Letter 877, to Theo, 3 June 1890.

20 He continued to use the format for landscapes and on one occasion for a figure painting **(125)**.

21 Letter 877, to Theo, 3 June 1890.

22 Letter 879, to Willemien, 5 June 1890, and letter 889, to Theo, 17 June 1890.

23 Two floral still lifes from Van Gogh's Paris period came into Dr Gachet's possession, *Chrysanthemums*, 1886 **(173)** and *Cornflowers and Poppies*, 1887 **(175)**. Vincent most likely brought these works with him from Paris; see note 87 on p. 232.

24 See note 6 above.

25 Letter 878, to his mother, 5 June 1890. See Bregje Gerritse's and Sara Tas's essay on pp. 178–91 for the works that came into Gachet's possession. He gave two paintings to Arthur Ravoux, the landlord of the café. Ravoux 1957, p. 10.

26 Letter 877, to Theo, 3 June 1890.

27 Letter 879, to Willemien, 5 June 1890. Van Gogh mentions the still life immediately after the two paintings he had done of Gachet's garden. They will have been painted in that order, followed by the portrait of Gachet he had done 'the other day'. See also Gachet 1994, pp. 93–94.

28 There were several surimonos at the exhibition of Japanese prints, most of them still lifes. Soda 2017, cats. 581, 583. Van Gogh went on to paint *Daubigny's Garden* on a square canvas as well as five portraits. See my essay on pp. 116–33.

29 Gachet 1994, p. 94.

30 Van Dongen 2022, p. 192.

31 Letter 879, to Willemien, 5 June 1890.

32 Letter 873, to Theo and Jo, 20 May 1890.

33 Gachet 1953b.

34 Letter 589, to Theo, around 25 March 1888. The link with this flower painting by Monticelli (*Vase with Flowers*, c. 1875, Van Gogh Museum, Amsterdam) was made in Stein and Miller 2009, pp. 234–35.

35 Letter 889, to Theo, 17 June 1890.

36 The new canvas arrived while he was working on *Vase with Wild Flowers* **(82)** (letter 889), but he did not use any of it for floral still lifes.

37 Letter 887, to Theo, 14 June 1890.

38 Tralbaut 1969, pp. 90–91.

39 See Bregje Gerritse's and Sara Tas's essay on pp. 178–91.

40 Gachet 1994, p. 94. Gachet Jr wrote in a letter to Jo van Gogh-Bonger dated around 19 February 1912 (b3398) that he had spent the night watching over Vincent, together with his father, Theo and the Dutch artist Anton Hirschig.

Drawing in Auvers-sur-Oise

Teio Meedendorp
pp. 96–115

1 This includes two drawings found on the endpapers of a sketchbook that was otherwise filled in Saint-Rémy: see Vellekoop and Zwikker 2007, pp. 413–15. Van Gogh took it with him to Auvers and several sheets from the sketchbook wound up in Dr Gachet's collection (F1618, F1620rv, F1645rv, F1647rv, F1648rv, F1649rv, F1651rv). A number of drawings and sketches were undoubtedly lost too, as can be inferred in part from F1634rv, which Van Gogh drew on a piece of blue paper watermarked ED&Cie. He divided a large sheet into quarters to this end, but the other three quarters, which will have contained the countermark PL BAS, have not survived, see ibid., p. 500.

2 Of the 142 pages in this book, 84 were drawn on: see Van der Wolk 1986, pp. 212–72 and Vellekoop and Suijver 2013, pp. 19–22, 56–68.

3 For the drawings in the Van Gogh Museum, see Vellekoop and Zwikker 2007, pp. 27–29, 36, 41–42, 413–514.

4 The double-sided drawings that he sold and the sketchbook sheet he gave away were later acquired by the Van Gogh Museum. See Distel and Stein 1999, pp. 224–28 for the Auvers drawings in the Gachet collection. Gachet also owned several drawings from Saint-Rémy, and father and son alike were responsible for distributing the various editions of the etching, see Van Heugten and Pabst 1995, pp. 79–86, 99–106.

5 The fourth drawing, *Evening Landscape with Two Peasants* **(109)** has remained in private hands throughout.

6 Letter 874, to Theo and Jo, around 21 May 1890. As far as his drawing is concerned, Van Gogh had actually paused more or less entirely since the summer of 1889 in Saint-Rémy.

7 By far the most informative source is Vellekoop and Zwikker 2007, pp. 27–42, 413–514; see also, among others, Van der Wolk, Pickvance and Pey 1990, pp. 317–29.

8 Wadley 1991, p. 278.

9 Letter 874, to Theo and Jo, around 21 May 1890. 'Ingres' is a laid paper, chiefly intended for drawing with dry materials, although Van Gogh generally took little notice of such things.

10 In letter 875 of 25 May 1890 to Theo and Jo, Van Gogh thanks his brother in advance for sending the canvas and paper he had requested in his earlier letter.

11 RM20, to Theo and Jo, 24 May 1890 (unsent). He wrote letter 875 the next day. His reference there to the drawing is the only time he mentioned a work of this kind in his letters from Auvers.

12 There were originally purple tones too, which faded over time to a grey-blue: see Vellekoop and Zwikker 2007, p. 423. Van Gogh seems to have used a large piece of thick cardboard as a drawing board for these works, see ibid., pp. 522–23.

13 Van Tilborgh 2018, pp. 87–88. See Soda 2017 for the content of the exhibition. Working with a single colour was something new in his drawing. In oils, he had mainly done so with dominant yellow tones (a still life with quinces in Paris, F383 and later, of course, his sunflowers F454 and variants F457 and F458 in Arles).

14 Letter 874, to Theo and Jo, around 21 May 1890.

15 Letter 873, to Theo and Jo, 20 May 1890.

16 Local rural wine was known as 'jinglet' according to Gachet 1994, p. 61. The area allotted to vineyards in Auvers declined steadily throughout the nineteenth century. Of the fifty hectares recorded in 1850, only two remained in 1890; see Lachiver 1982, p. 832.

17 Letter 875, to Theo and Jo, 25 May 1890. The standard *figure* 30 format, Van Gogh's favourite large size, measures 92 × 73 cm; *Farmhouse and Vineyard* **(#3)** is roughly a standard *figure* 12 format.

18 See my essay on pp. 58–79.

19 He had previously used coarse watercolour paper (*torchon* type) by the same papermaker from Hallines for numerous figure and head studies during this time in The Hague (1882–83). A sheet of *carré* measures 45 × 56 cm; the sheets later sent to Van Gogh were of the slightly larger *cavalier* and *petit-raisin* formats, measuring 46 × 62 cm and 49 × 64 cm respectively.

20 Letter 877, to Theo, 3 June 1890. Charles Bargue, *Exercises au fusain pour préparer à l'étude de l'académie d'apès nature*, vol. III of the *Cours de dessin*, Paris 1871. He had also asked for it in letter 874, to Theo and Jo, 21 May 1890.

21 Gachet told him he might be able to provide sitters, including his daughter Marguerite. See letter 877, to Theo, 3 June 1890, which is also where he repeated his request for the Bargues. In the absence of models, he had worked in Saint-Rémy after prints of figure pieces by Millet and others to keep his hand in, but later on he mostly drew endless figures from memory.

22 Three sketches after plate 1 (sitting model), and one each of plates 2 and 5 (standing models).

23 One after plate 1 and one after plate 5, along with two after plates 2 and 4 (standing model). No copy has survived of plate 3.

24 See, for instance, **59**, **31**, **119** and particularly the second version **118**, and also **122**, **125** and **127**.

25 On the back of *Landscape with Houses*, there is a rough, less literal pencil-and-chalk sketch of a house behind a row of chestnut trees, which can be linked to the painting **(58)**. All we know of otherwise from Auvers is a study drawing for *Marguerite Gachet at the Piano* **(128, 130)**.

26 Gachet 1994, p. 98. Paul Cézanne included the same glass in a still life: see, for instance, Distel and Stein 1999, pp. 64, 204.

27 The postcard shows that a large new building has been erected in the foreground. However, part of the house furthest to the right on the left-hand side of the street is still there.

28 Gachet 1994, p. 68. The height of the chimney is mentioned in a document of the Val-d'Oise departmental archives in Pontoise, inv. 2511 W 468 – Ancienne féculerie, aux Vesserot [*sic*]. See also Mataigne 1901, p. 35. The chimney can also be seen in the right background of *The House of Doctor Gachet in Auvers-sur-Oise* by Paul Cézanne (1872–73, Musée d'Orsay, Paris). The starch factory was demolished around 1900 to make way for a new road, rue Central (now rue Louis Ganne).

29 Van Gogh did not make any large, stand-alone drawings in this period, only studies and sketches, although the somewhat more careful elaboration of one of them, *Figures by the Fireplace* (F1608r), might be considered a more serious composition. See Vellekoop and Zwikker 2007, pp. 388–91.

30 See F1603v, F1608r, F1651v.

31 He appears to refer in the sketches mentioned in the previous note to both Madame Roulin and baby Marcelle, whom he painted in Arles (F490, F491), and to the print *The Man is at Sea* by Virginie Demont-Breton, which he copied in Saint-Rémy; he took that copy with him to Auvers **(162)**. See also

Vellekoop and Zwikker 2007, p. 390.

32 Letter 885, to his mother, 13 June 1890.

33 Ibid.

34 See Andrew Pattle and Wayne Mann, *Mr Otto's 'Bicycle': A Brief History of the Otto Dicycle and Its Link with Ipswich*, Ipswich 2015, and https://www.vintag.es/2018/10/otto-dicycle.html.

35 On the bottom leaf he also sketched a few fish, including an eel. It is not clear, though, whether he did so from his imagination or after decorative examples somewhere in the area.

36 He might have brought some of the pink with him from Saint-Rémy. The watermarks differ and we also know of the pink paper watermarked AL – PL BAS (a paper mill in Plancher Bas) from Saint-Rémy. Blue paper with the watermark MBM MBM (from the Arches paper mill in the Vosges) is only found in Auvers. He also had white paper of that brand in Auvers.

37 See Vellekoop and Zwikker 2007, pp. 41–42, regarding the self-made sketchbooks. These have not, incidentally, survived in that form, only as loose sheets.

38 Gachet 1994, p. 67. The fact that it was Père Eloi's farm also comes from Gachet. Mothe 1987, p. 163, thought that the Ferme du Four, located further to the east, was the one depicted, but this is not correct.

39 Letter from Paul Louis Gachet to Jo van Gogh-Bonger, mid-December 1909, Van Gogh Museum, Amsterdam, inv. b3396V/1984. The apartment was on rue du Faubourg-Saint-Denis in Paris, where Dr Gachet used to hold consultations.

40 The sketchbook he assembled with the pink paper does contain a few riverbank studies (F1578, F1627, F1628, F1629), and there are also several sketches of figures in boats on the water (F1646v). The Oise otherwise appears in just one painting, *Bank of the Oise* **(57)**, although most of the space is commanded by the boat hire firm and the river is of only secondary importance; see my essay on pp. 58–79.

41 Townsend and Freemantle 2023.

42 Letter RM19, to Willemien, around 21 May 1890 (unsent).

43 According to Millon 2002, p. 201, the villa was built around 1870 and occupied by a wealthy cattle trader.

44 The head has a pharaonic headdress, the *nemes*, but it lacks the customary *uraeus* (cobra), allowing it to be identified as a sphinx. This is also suggested by the slight smile, although this is barely visible any more due to damage, see Verweij 2022, pp. 20–21. France was seized by Egyptomania in the wake of Napoleon's campaigns in the late eighteenth century. The Louvre opened four rooms of Egyptian objects in 1820 and in 1852 the museum received six sphinxes donated by the amateur Egyptologist Auguste Mariette, who also helped design the Egyptian Pavilion at the Paris World Exhibition in 1867, ibid., pp. 3–4.

45 The stripes that Van Gogh drew on the headdress seem originally to have been present: traces of notched lines can be seen at the top of the sculpture, suggesting their edges: see Verweij 2022, p. 21.

46 Letter 779, to Theo, 9 June 1889.

47 A reference to 2 Corinthians 6:10. See, for example, letter 35, to Theo, 19 June 1875. Two other heads (F1520r and F1521v), are slightly more neutral.

48 The child in **132** also displays similarities with the drawings in terms of the smile and, once again, the nose and eyes.

49 For a long time, *Evening Landscape with Two Peasants* was dated to Saint-Rémy (De la Faille 1928/1970 and Hulsker 1996a), obscuring the connection between the works. Heenk 1995, pp. 198–99, 202, 271, was the first to identify the similarity of the drawing materials and to place the evening landscape in Auvers. See also note 52 below.

50 This is quite exceptional in his oeuvre: Van Gogh generally drew in ink over pencil sketches without going back over them in pencil at any great length.

51 'Automatic writing', as championed by André Breton and the Surrealist movement.

52 The drawing underwent detailed examination at the Van Gogh Museum in 2019. Although traditionally described as a landscape with moon (see De la Faille 1928, p. 163), the faded ink led it to be interpreted in later years as a daytime scene with a brightly shining sun: see De la Faille 1970, p. 534 and Hulsker 1996a, p. 439.

53 It is entirely possible that Van Gogh observed the motif somewhere on the border between the hillside and the fields above Auvers during the day and then reworked it into an evening landscape from memory.

54 The quotation is from letter 800, to Theo, 5 and 6 September 1889, and relates to *Wheatfield with a Reaper* (F617).

55 See letters 36 and 128 to Theo in 1873 and 1877. Van Gogh refers in the latter to his father, who used the print for a funeral service he delivered as minister.

56 'Even in Arcadia, there am I [death]'; for this seventeenth-century view, see Panofsky 1970.

Timeless Portraits: On Melancholy and Youth

Nienke Bakker
pp. 116–33

1 Letter 652, to Theo, 31 July 1888.

2 Letter 673, to Theo, 3 September 1888.

3 Ibid. See also Van Tilborgh 2022, pp. 37–42.

4 Letter 875, to Theo and Jo, 25 May 1890.

5 Letter 658, to Theo, 9 August 1888, and Van Tilborgh 2022, pp. 42–46, 51–59.

6 The other two self-portraits are F528 (Nasjonalgalleriet, Oslo) and F626 (National Gallery of Art, Washington).

7 Letter 856, to Willemien, 19 February 1890.

8 See Louis van Tilborgh's essay on pp. 162–77.

9 Letter 879, to Willemien, 5 June 1890, and letter 873, to Theo and Jo, 20 May 1890.

10 Letter 877, to Theo, 3 June 1890, and letter 879. Gachet came to see the *Self-Portrait* and the *Arlésienne* on 27 May; Gachet 1994, p. 63.

11 Gachet 1994, pp. 102–05, 114. Van Gogh painted the second version at Ravoux's, where he was lodging, on 6 June, taking the first portrait as his basis, and returned to Gachet's the following day to put the finishing touches to it with his model present.

12 Doiteau 1923–24, p. 216. Paul Louis Gachet donated the cap to the Louvre (now in the Musée d'Orsay) in 1954.

13 Pierre-Auguste Renoir made a portrait of the Auvers-based artist and collector Eugène Murer in the same pose in 1877. See Stein and Miller 2009, pp. 108–13. Van Gogh is unlikely to have seen Murer's collection.

14 According to Doiteau, the flower was included on Gachet's suggestion, see Doiteau 1923–24, p. 254. See also Pickvance 1986, p. 232.

15 Letter 655, to Emile Bernard, around 5 August 1888.

16 Gachet 1994, p. 95.

17 Letter 877.

18 Letter 879.

19 Letter 877.

20 Letter 879.

21 RM23, to Gauguin, around 17 June 1890 (incomplete, unsent).

22 Letter 886, to Willemien, 13 June 1890.

23 Letter 829, to Theo, around 19 December 1889.

24 It is hard to tell whether the date in the upper left of the etching is 15 or 25 May 1890, which has led to differing interpretations. We concur with

Van Heugten and Pabst's reasoning that it must have been done on 15 June; Heugten and Pabst 1995.

25 Paul Cézanne also produced his only ever etching at Gachet's, and Camille Pissarro and Armand Guillaumin made etchings there too.

26 Gachet 1994, p. 55; Distel and Stein 1999, p. 100.

27 Letter 877. Bracquemond's etching is *Auguste Comte (after Guichard)*, 1851. Guillaumin's *Self-Portrait with Palette* (1878) and *Nude Woman on a Bed* (c. 1877) are in the Musée d'Orsay.

28 Letter 874, to Theo and Jo, around 21 May 1890, and letter 877. Regarding the drawings after Bargue, see Teio Meedendorp's essay on pp. 96–115.

29 Letter 877.

30 See Teio Meedendorp's essay on pp. 96–115.

31 Letter 884, Gauguin to Van Gogh, around 13 June 1890. According to Gauguin, who called the canvas 'very fine and very curious', Van Gogh had 'never worked with so much *balance* while conserving the sensation and the interior warmth needed for a *work of art*'.

32 Letter 891, to Theo, 24 June 1890. A standard size '15 portrait' canvas is 65 × 54 cm. Both portraits of Adeline Ravoux roughly share those dimensions, although the second is slightly taller at 71.5 × 53 cm.

33 Drawings F833 and F847 **(117)** of 1880–81. He had also drawn his girlfriend Sien's ten-year-old daughter in The Hague in this pose, including *Girl with Shawl*, 1882–83 (F1008, Van Gogh Museum).

34 Ravoux 1957, p. 9. Regarding Hokusai's *aizuri-e*, see Van Tilborgh 2018, pp. 87–88.

35 Ravoux 1953.

36 On one occasion, for instance, she talks about 'a posing session', while elsewhere, she stated that 'I only posed for five or six sessions'. Ravoux 1953; Ravoux 1957, p. 9.

37 He had painted a flower still life **(77)** in this format in early June and *Daubigny's Garden* **(141)** around the sixteenth of that month.

38 The first three landscapes mentioned in letter 891 of 24 June are **135, 138** and **156**. See Emmanuel Coquery's essay on pp. 134–61.

39 In the letter in which he described Adeline's portrait (891, 24 June), he mentioned that 'a country girl' might come and sit for him. This was probably the young woman in the work mentioned here, who can be recognized in two other works, which must also have been made in late June–early July **(122, 125)**.

40 *Head of a Woman*, black chalk, in the Paris-Auvers-sur-Oise sketchbook, 1890, Van Gogh Museum, Amsterdam.

41 Letter 896, to Theo and Jo, 2 July 1890. She is unlikely to have been Lisette Chevalier, the governess' daughter who lived with the Gachet family, since Gachet Jr referred to her as an unknown Auversoise: 'She definitely lived in Auvers, but we don't know who the girl was. [...] The model, a girl aged about seventeen – unknown.' Gachet 1994, p. 158.

42 Letter 893, to Theo, 28 June 1890. Van Gogh was mistaken, the engraving was not reproduced in *L'Illustration*, but in *La Vie moderne* (10 June 1882, p. 358) and *L'Univers illustré* (9 August 1884, p. 504, and 4 April 1885, p. 213).

43 Paul Gachet recalled seeing the portrait of Adeline in Vincent's room. Letter from Gachet to Jo van Gogh-Bonger, around 19 February 1912 (b3398).

44 Letter 858, Theo to Vincent, 19 March 1890. It is *Mademoiselle Dihau au piano*, 1890, Musée Toulouse-Lautrec, Albi.

45 Letter 893.

46 Gachet 1953a. A kakemono is a vertical scroll painting or a print in vertical format, mostly consisting of two sheets that together form a work measuring approximately 75 × 25.5 cm.

47 Ibid.

48 Gachet 1994, p. 163.

49 Letter 893.

50 Gachet 1953a He states in Gachet 1994, p. 166, that after completing the portrait, Van Gogh 'asked the doctor's permission to give it to Miss Gachet. What an extraordinary gift! [...] Father and daughter, were moved, taken aback one might say, and thanked him warmly.'

51 Distel and Stein 1999, p. 168. It was previously thought that the two prints had been lost, but these are the two separate female figures that Van Gogh hung on either side of his bed and which Gachet Jr later had framed together **(126)**.

52 Letter 893.

53 Ibid.

54 Letter 896, to Theo and Jo, 2 July 1890.

55 RM23.

56 See Teio Meedendorp's essay on pp. 96–115.

57 Letters 877 and 896.

58 Ravoux 1957, p. 15. According to Adeline, the little boy, whose name was Raoul, can be seen next to her in the photograph of the Ravoux family in front of the inn **(38)**. The child in question has very short hair, however, while that of the boy in Van Gogh's portrait is long. So either Adeline was mistaken or Van Gogh gave the child longer hair than he had in reality.

59 Coquiot 1923, p. 253. Coquiot must have been told this by Gachet Jr, but surprisingly, the latter did not write about it himself. See also Distel and Stein 1999, pp. 86–88.

60 Letter from Joseph Delattre to Charles Angrand, 14 December 1894, quoted in Montaigne 2010, p. 125.

61 Letter 885, to his mother, 13 June 1890.

62 Letter 898, to Theo and Jo, around 10 July 1890.

On the Threshold of a 'New Painting': The Double-Square Works

Emmanuel Coquery
pp. 134–61

1 Letters 891 and 893, to Theo, 24 and 28 June 1890.

2 Hendriks et al. 2013.

3 I cannot go into further detail here regarding Van Gogh's bibliography, which is made up of often divergent interpretations. About this group, the bibliography mainly comprises Pickvance 1986, pp. 258–60; Zemel 1997, pp. 207–45; Dorn 2002, pp. 47–50; Solana 2007, pp. 162–63; Schröder et al. 2008, pp. 424–37; Zimmer 2009, pp. 111–13.

4 Letter 875, to Theo and Jo, 25 May 1890.

5 Letter 873, to Theo and Jo, 20 May 1890.

6 Letter 698, to Emile Bernard, around 5 October 1888: 'I don't invent the whole of the painting; on the contrary, I find it ready-made – but to be *untangled* – in the real world', and letter 809, to Emile Bernard, around 8 October 1889: 'Everything's hard to do here, to *disentangle* its intimate character, and so that it's not something vaguely true'. In Van Gogh's letters quoted in this article, the italics are those of the author rather than of Van Gogh himself. The words sometimes emphasized by Van Gogh are underlined.

7 Letter 850, to Theo, 1 February 1890.

8 Letter 896, to Theo and Jo, 2 July 1890.

9 Letter 891.

10 Homburg et al. 2016.

11 Letter 891.

12 Letter 822, to Emile Bernard, around 26 November 1889.

13 Letter 891.

14 See *Wheatfield with Reaper and Sun* (F617), *Pine Trees at Sunset* (F652) or the *Olive Trees* (F710), which carry, to varying degrees, a funereal allusion.

15 Letter 893.

16 Letter 858, Theo to Vincent, 19 March 1890: 'De Lautrec has an excellent portrait of a woman at the piano, and a large painting which holds its own very well'.

17 Letter 898, to Theo and Jo, around 10 July 1890.

18 Letter 158, to Theo, 24 September 1880.

19 Letter 898.

20 Letter 889, to Theo, 17 June 1890.

21 Letter 902, to Theo, 23 July 1890.

22 Van Gogh Museum, Amsterdam, inv. d0414-057V1962.

23 Pickvance 1986, p. 236.

24 Letter 816, to Theo, around 3 November 1889.

25 Maes and Van Tilborgh 2012, p. 68. The authors assume that Theo van Gogh's brother-in-law, who was present at the funeral, will have repeated something he heard, but Bonger may have referred to it as the last sketch *because of* its unfinished nature.

26 Maes and Van Tilborgh 2012.

27 Van der Veen 2020.

28 These are F41, F42, F43, F172, respectively.

29 Letter 347, to Theo, around 30 May 1883. The corresponding sketch (F1028) bears an annotation: '1 metre × ½ metre'.

30 F1028, F1029, F1030 and F1031. Letter 350, to Theo, around 5 June 1883. The whereabouts of the drawings are no longer known, except in reproductions by J.-B. de la Faille. They measure approximately 10 × 20 cm.

31 See Bakker 2016b and, for the catalogue raisonné of the artist, Hellebranth 1976.

32 1857, 97 × 193 cm, Musée de Compiègne.

33 1873, 100 × 200 cm, Musée d'Orsay.

34 See letter 246, to Theo, 15 and 16 July 1882. The exhibition showed five landscapes by Daubigny, including *Moonlight, Champigny* (22 × 45 cm), and by Corot, *Meadow by the Water* (22 × 46 cm), and *Château des Papes, Villeneuve-les-Avignon* (37 × 74 cm), as well as a Théodore Rousseau, *Undergrowth* (23 × 41 cm).

35 Letter 331, to Theo, around 21 March 1883: 'Rappard wants to send a large painting to the Amsterdam exhibition. It shows 4 tile painters around a table'.

36 Letter 896.

37 One of his rare long formats is a copy after Jacob van Ruisdael. *View of Naarden*, private collection, 37 × 68 cm, see Briat-Philippe and Luijten 2017, no. 11. For an example of a double square, see Blanc 2017, p. 386, fig. 351.

38 Letter 776, to Theo, around 23 May 1889.

39 On the panorama in the nineteenth century, see Madeleine and Bouiller 2015.

40 Zimmer 2009, p. 113.

41 Letter 171, to Theo, 26 August 1881.

42 Letter 615, to Theo, 28 May 1888.

43 RM21, to Joseph Jacob Isaäcson, 25 May 1890 (unsent).

44 Letter 879, to Willemien, 5 June 1890.

45 Wattenmaker 1981, p. 65.

46 Letter 875.

47 Letter 893.

48 RM21.

49 See for example, letter 678, to Willemien, 9 and about 14 September 1888: 'You know that the Japanese instinctively look for contrasts, and eat sweetened peppers, salty sweets, and fried ices and frozen fried dishes.'

50 See Uhlenbeck 2018.

51 Letter 868, to Theo, 4 May 1890.

52 Letter 822.

53 Letter 254, to Theo, 5 or 6 August 1882.

54 Letter 572, to Theo, between about 23 and about 25 July 1887. These are probably F316 and F350, which are 81 × 100 cm and 96 × 120 cm.

55 Letter 678, and letter 668, to Theo, 23 or 24 August 1888.

56 Letter 629, to Theo, 21 June 1888.

57 Letter 625, to Theo, around 15–16 June 1888.

58 Letter 705, to Theo, 16 October 1888.

59 Letter 673, to Theo, 3 September 1888.

60 Letter 677, to Theo, 9 September 1888.

61 Letter 597, to Theo, around 13 April 1888.

62 Letter 704, to Theo, 15 October 1888.

63 Letter 714, to Theo, 27 or 28 October 1888: 'Of course, everything there is better, bigger [*plus large*], more beautiful than here'; letter 694, to Theo, 3 October 1888: 'But the broader and more substantial character that I'd wish to give the thing would nevertheless demand it.'

64 Letter 899, to his mother and Willemien, between about 10 and 14 July 1890. Wouter van der Veen has drawn my attention to the original Dutch term, *onafzienbaar*, which literally means 'the end of which cannot be *seen*', 'as far as the eye can see'.

65 It should be noted that a number 30 canvas is significantly larger in reality than the double square (about 6,700 cm², as opposed to 5,000), which corresponds in area to a number 25.

66 Letter 898.

67 An allusion to 2 Corinthians 6:10; letter 114, to Theo, 19 May 1877.

68 Only Dorn 2002, pp. 46–47, makes the connection.

69 One exception is *Pollard Willows at Sunset* (F572), from March 1888 (32 × 34 cm).

70 On the notion of decoration in Van Gogh's oeuvre, see Dorn 1990.

71 See RM23, to Paul Gauguin, around 17 June 1890 (unsent).

72 Letter 703, to Theo, 13 October 1888.

73 Letter 677, to Theo, 9 September 1888.

74 Letter 722, to Theo, around 21 November 1888.

75 Letter 783, to Theo, 25 June 1889.

76 Letter 881, to Theo and Jo, 10 June 1890.

77 See his reaction to Aurier's article, just before he came to Auvers (letter 863, to Theo, 29 April 1890): 'Please ask Mr Aurier not to write any more articles about my painting, tell him earnestly that first he is wrong about me, then that really I feel too damaged by grief to be able to face up to publicity. Making paintings distracts me – but if I hear talk of them that pains me more than he knows'.

78 Letter 687, to Theo, 25 September 1888: 'I'm not keen on it, but what I'm certainly keen on is to show you something that isn't entirely bad'.

79 RM20, to Theo and Jo, 24 May 1890, and RM21 (both unsent).

80 F673, F674 and F675. Letter 863: 'While I was ill I nevertheless still did a few small canvases from memory which you'll see later, reminiscences of the north [...] Please send me what you can find of *figures* among my old drawings, I'm thinking of redoing the painting of the peasants eating supper, lamplight effect'.

81 Letter 874, to Theo and Jo, around 21 May 1890: 'It did me good to go into the south the better to see the north'.

82 RM19, to Willemien, around 21 May 1890 (unsent).

83 Letter 877, to Theo, 3 June 1890.

84 RM23.

85 Letter 879.

86 RM21.

87 Letter 874.

88 Letter 885, to his mother, 13 June 1890.

89 Letter 886, to Willemien, 13 June 1890.

90 Letter 753, to Theo, 29 March 1889.

91 Letter 898.

92 RM21.

93 Callen 2000, pp. 21–25. A good illustration of contemporary opinion regarding the difficulty of the square format and the experiments that could be associated with it, is given by Jean-François Raffaelli, whose last exhibition Van Gogh, who was in Auvers at the time, regretted having missed. 'It is curious to observe how certain absolute forms are disapproved of more than ever today by our innate taste. [...] This can lead to the conclusion that the cube, the square, the round, the oval, the sphere, are not aesthetic forms; [...] Driven by a somewhat violent temperament, I have often tried to enclose my pictorial compositions in a square frame. I have often, I say, chosen a square frame for my canvases, and I have, in this square, established as best I could very authoritarian, very deliberate compositions of lines; – lines ordered, moreover, by the very shape chosen for my canvas, and in which each line had to stand, as a sort of will and affirmation'. Raffaelli 1888, pp. 175–77.

94 Letter 816.

95 Letter 898.

96 Monet executed his first decorative commission *Turkeys* (for Ernest Hoschedé, in Montgeron) on a large square format: 172 × 172 cm. The work was shown at the Impressionist exhibition of 1877. He would use this format more and more in his later period in Giverny, as well as the very elongated formats that would lead to his famous Water Lilies cycle in the Musée de l'Orangerie, Paris.

97 Letter 776.

98 Letter 662, to Theo, 15 August 1888.

99 Letter 695, to Paul Gauguin, 3 October 1888.

100 See in particular the ideas on abstraction advocated by Gauguin, in letter 822, to Emile Bernard, around 26 November 1889.

101 Letter 884, Paul Gauguin to Vincent, around 13 June 1890.

102 This text owes much to the amiably vigilant reading of Nienke Bakker, Louis van Tilborgh, Teio Meedendorp and Wouter van der Veen. I would like to thank them warmly for their help.

A Short Biography of Unbearable Suffering: Van Gogh's Self-Chosen End

Louis van Tilborgh
pp. 162–77

1 Writing in *Van Gogh: The Life* (2011), Steven Naifeh and Gregory White Smith argued that the artist did not take his own life but was most likely shot by the sixteen-year-old René Secrétan and his brother Gaston, nineteen, whether or not accidentally (Naifeh and Smith 2011, pp. 869–85). Van Gogh, they suggested, misled everyone by failing to admit what had happened. To protect the two youths, he supposedly framed his injuries as resulting from an attempted suicide. As tends to be the case with conspiracy theories, the reasoning behind the American biographers' arguments in defence of their thesis was rather inconsistent. The fallacies underpinning them were pointed out by Nickell 2012 and by Van Tilborgh and Meedendorp 2013. Naifeh and Smith responded in 2014, but rather than engaging with the criticism, they shifted the debate to the question of whether the gunshot wound was consistent with suicide. The forensic specialist they consulted, Vincent Di Maio, did not believe it was, but his findings were ably rebutted by Joe Nickell, a researcher affiliated with the Committee for Skeptical Inquiry. He exhorted Naifeh and Smith 'to give up their conspiratorial theories and their half-baked and unnecessarily complicated scenarios, and stop misleading themselves and others' (Nickell 2014a; see also Nickell 2014b for his final conclusion), yet his critique too was ignored. Fresh publications on the subject followed, including Kaufman Arenberg's *Killing Vincent: The Man, the Myth, and the Murder* in 2018. This argued that Van Gogh was probably not shot by the Secrétan brothers, but by Dr Paul Gachet, possibly in collusion with his son. The supposed motive was Van Gogh's alleged affair with Gachet's daughter Marguerite and the couple's prospective marriage. It is a characteristic of the genre that one conspiracy theory tends to trigger another – one more reason we do not engage here any further with the discussion that began in 2011.

2 This article draws on Williams 2001, Joiner 2007, the individual articles in Van Heeringen et al. 2019, De Beurs 2020, and O'Connor and Portzky 2018. Regarding the three phases (pre-motivational, motivational and volitional) see Kerkhof, De Beurs and Portzky 2019, pp. 62–69. I use many terms in my essay to describe Van Gogh's state of mind, but without seeking to conform to their clinical, medical definition. I am also grateful to Jan Swinkels, who kindly read and critiqued my text.

3 Regarding the 'cry of pain', see Williams 2001, pp. 136–54.

4 Letter from Emile Bernard to Albert Aurier, 31 July 1890 (Bakker, Van Tilborgh and Prins 2016, pp. 160–61 and b3052).

5 Letter 868, to Theo, 4 May 1890.

6 For Peyron's report, see Bakker, Van Tilborgh and Prins 2016, pp. 157–59.

7 We know from Peyron's letters to Theo and from his final report (see previous note) that the doctor believed Van Gogh had attempted to poison himself during his attacks by eating paint and drinking turpentine and paraffin used for lamps (Bakker, Van Tilborgh and Prins 2016, p. 157). He first reported this behaviour following Vincent's first crisis at the asylum (in a letter that has not been preserved, see Bakker 2016a, p. 66). After Van Gogh's recovery, the doctor reported in early September 1889: 'His ideas of suicide have disappeared; there remain only his bad dreams, which are tending to disappear, and are of lesser intensity' (added by Peyron to letter 798 from Vincent to Theo, around 2 September 1889; see also letter 797, note 6 and, regarding later incidents, letter 833, note 2, letter 835, note 3, letter 838). Peyron might have considered these incidents to be examples of suicidal behaviour, but Van Gogh barely recalled them, leaving the question of whether or not we ought to see them as such. He had been told that he picked up 'filthy things' from the ground and ate them (letter 797, to Theo, 22 August 1889).

8 Regarding the history and nature of the attacks, see Prins 2016, pp. 100–18, and Nolen et al. 2020.

9 Letter from Theo to Paul Gachet, 9 May 1890, b2104.

10 Letter 868.

11 Regarding Peyron's objections, see letter 867, Theo to Vincent, around 2 May 1890, note 1. Peyron had noted in February that 'the crises are recurring more frequently and come after each journey he makes outside this home' (letter, Peyron to Theo, 24 February 1890, b1062), possibly worrying him that Van Gogh's move would swiftly trigger a fresh attack. Theo shared this view, as indicated by his letter of 15 April to his mother and sister Willemien (b928): 'having him come here would be irresponsible unless one were sure that there is not one moment of danger that the crisis will return during the journey or while here.'

12 Letter from Theo to his mother, 3 May 1890 (b929), in which he summed up Peyron's letter.

13 Letter 857, to Theo, around 17 March 1890.

14 See note 12 above, and letter from Theo to his mother and Willemien, 15 April 1890, b928.

15 Letter 863, to Theo, 29 April 1890, and 870, to Theo, 11 May 1890.

16 Letter 868.

17 Letter 865, to Theo, around 1 May 1890.

18 See note 12 above.

19 Letter 865 and letter 870, to Theo, 11 May 1890.

20 Letter 865.

21 Van Gogh-Bonger 1914, pp. LX–LXI.

22 Theo to Willemien, letter dated 2 June 1890 (b931). For Andries's comments see the letter to his parents of around 21 May 1890, b1852.

23 Letter 873, to Theo and Jo, 20 May 1890.

24 Letter 874, to Theo and Jo, on or about 21 May 1890.

25 Letter 875, to Theo and Jo, 25 May 1890.

26 Letter 881, to Theo and Jo, 10 June 1890.

27 Letter 877, to Theo, 3 June 1890. According to Gachet 1994, p. 43, the medical examination took place straight away on 20 May.

28 Letter 878, to his mother, 5 June 1890. Gachet also informed Theo of his opinion in person (letter 880, Theo to Vincent, 5 June 1890). Peyron inquired about Vincent's health sometime later (letter 891, to Theo, 24 June 1890), which means he too was aware of the news. In a warm letter to Vincent on 1 July 1890, the asylum director wrote: 'I see with pleasure that your health continues to be satisfactory, and that your life in the midst of this world of artists is spent more pleasantly than here' (letter 895).

29 Letter 881.

30 Letter 888, Theo to Vincent, 15 June 1890. Theo suggested that it would make sense for Vincent to move in with another artist, as he had done in Arles. The subject of taking a home of his own was not raised again.

31 Letter 894, Theo to Vincent, 30 June and 1 July 1890.

32 Letter 896, to Theo and Jo, 2 July 1890.

33 Letter 898, to Theo and Jo, around 10 July 1890. Jo's letter has been lost (see Hulsker 1996b regarding the issue of lost letters from this period); for her recollection of that day, see Luijten 2022, pp. 104–11.

34 See, in this regard, my essay on pp. 14–33.

35 Letter 900, Theo to Vincent, 14 July 1890.

36 Letter from Theo to Jo, 20 July 1890 (Van Crimpen 1999, p. 250).

37 Letter 901, Theo to Vincent, 22 July 1890.

38 According to Gachet 1994, p. 220, Van Gogh visited the doctor only on 15 July to tell him about the meeting in Paris on the 6th.

39 Letter 902, to Theo, 23 July 1890.

40 Letter from Theo to Jo, 28 July 1890 (Van Crimpen 1999, p. 271). Theo made no reference to a suicide attempt in this letter, merely stating that Vincent's 'life could be in danger'.

41 Theo did not state this, but it is revealed in Bernard's letter to Aurier (see note 4 above).

42 Van Heeringen and Kerkhof 2019, p. 336.

43 See, in this regard, Williams 2001, pp. 184–85.

44 See notes 6 and 7 above.

45 Van Gogh-Bonger 1914, p. LXIII.

46 Van Heeringen et al. 2019, pp. 345–46.

47 Letter 801, to Theo, 10 September 1889.

48 Letter 868.

49 Letter 764, to Willemien, between around 28 April and 2 May 1889.

50 Letter 804, to Willemien, 19 September 1889.

51 Letter 768, to Theo, 3 May 1889.

52 See note 8 above regarding his attacks.

53 Letter 765, to Theo, 30 April 1889. But this was still at the motivational phase: it did not become volitional until after 6 July 1890.

54 See the literature cited in note 2 above for the following passages.

55 Van Gogh was given bromide and cinchona wine after his first attack in Arles to combat the after-effects. He stuffed his mattress and pillows with camphor for the same reason and was also prescribed long walks by his doctors. But this is as far as the intervention of the relevant doctors went (Prins 2016, p. 103). The artist was even deprived of tranquillizers at the asylum and it was considered, in keeping with medical thinking at the time, that 'absolute sobriety in eating, drinking, smoking, with two two-hour baths a week' would have a similar effect on him as on his fellow inmates (letter 782, to Theo, 18 June 1889). There seem to have been virtually no talking sessions other – probably – than with Gachet, but those would not have been about what was on his patient's mind. Gachet also offered Van Gogh sedatives in the event the melancholy became too onerous (see letter 875).

56 Letter 660, to Theo, around 13 August 1888.

57 Letter 868.

58 Letter 797, to Theo, 22 August 1889.

59 Letter 798, to Theo, around 2 September 1889.

60 Letter 801, to Theo, 10 September 1889.

61 Letter 815, to Theo, around 25 October 1889.

62 Letter 801.

63 For this interpretation, see Van Tilborgh 2022, pp. 56–57.

64 Letter 800, to Theo, 5 and 6 September 1889.

65 See letter 800 for Van Gogh's knowledge of the work, and *Le Monde illustré* (6 July 1889), no. 33, where the commentary can be found on p. 7 and the reproduction on p. 9.

66 The quoted words come from letter 815.

67 Letter 822, to Emile Bernard, around 26 November 1889.

68 Letter 839, to Theo, around 13 January 1889.

69 See Van Tilborgh 2021b for this question and interpretation.

70 Letter 856, to Willemien, 19 February 1890.

71 Letter 853, to Albert Aurier, 9 or 10 February 1890. For the shifting significance of this work, see Van Tilborgh 2022, pp. 334–41, esp. 337–38.

72 See letter 839.

73 Letter 878, to his mother, 5 June 1890.

74 RM20, to Theo and Jo, 24 May 1890 (unsent).

75 For the subject and the lithograph, see Meedendorp 2021; for the title *Méditation tristesse*, see Bonger 1890, no. 279. The other painting was F683. We know that both this work and *Sorrowing Old Man ('At Eternity's Gate')* **(167)** were the two last paintings from Saint-Rémy thanks to the Automated Canvas Analysis Project. Both works were done on the canvas type that Vincent received on 11 May (letter 870, to Theo, 11 May 1890).

76 According to Peyron, Van Gogh generally sat during this period 'with his head in his hands and if someone speaks to him, it is as though it hurts him, and he gestures for them to leave him alone'. This letter is lost, but Theo summarized it in his letter of 15 April 1890 to his mother and Willemien (b928).

77 RM20, to Theo and Jo, 24 May 1890 (unsent). Van Gogh sent another missive instead (letter 874), in which he substituted his morbid vision of the future with the blander 'I'm suffering a little these days'.

78 Letters 764 and 856.

79 Van Gogh only confided this to Emile Bernard (letter 822), and even then played it down.

80 This is how his former friend Anthon van Rappard described Van Gogh after his death; see Pickvance 1992, p. 102.

81 Letter 887, to Theo, 14 June 1890.

82 Letter 877, to Theo, 3 June 1890.

83 See Williams 2001, p. 144 for this psychological response.

84 Letter 898.

85 For a further interpretation of the letter, see my essay on pp. 14–33.

86 Letter 902.

87 We know from letter 877, to Theo, 3 June 1890, and letter RM19, to Willemien, around 21 May 1890 (unsent), that Van Gogh had included his *Self-Portrait*, *Pietà*, the portrait of Madame Ginoux and several paintings of olive groves. Just like the *Pietà*, and possibly the *Reaper* (F617 or F618; see note 30 on p. 233), *Penitentiary*, was among the paintings placed as decoration around his coffin at the inn (see Bregje Gerritse's and Sara Tas's essay on pp. 178–91), so we can assume that it too was among the works Van Gogh had brought with him at the end of May. There is no reason to suppose, at any rate, that Van Gogh had this work – or any others – sent to him from Paris in the meantime, or that Theo would have given *The Garden at the Asylum* or *The Man is at Sea* to Gachet in August–October 1890, well after Vincent's death. There are few plausible explanations as to how the latter works also ended up in Gachet's possession (see Stein 1999, pp. 212–30, regarding his collection), other than to assume that Vincent himself also brought them from Paris at the end of May, and that Theo then gave them to Gachet immediately after the funeral, along with the *Self-Portrait* and many of the paintings from Auvers. Gachet also owned two Paris still lifes by Van Gogh **(173, 175)** which, citing the same arguments again, will also have been among the works brought at the end of May. Flower still lifes were a popular genre and the artist will have picked them out as a gift to Gachet as soon as he arrived, in return for the doctor's kind offer of medical support during his stay. *Self-Portrait*, *The Garden at the Asylum*, *The Man is at Sea* and the two still lifes remained with Gachet, but Theo took *Pietà*, *Penitentiary* and the portrait of Ginoux back to Paris. The doctor and his housekeeper Madame Chevalier each owned another canvas from Saint-Rémy – F674 **(6)** and F673 respectively – but these paintings are likely to have been among the works left behind at the asylum, which were then sent on to Van Gogh in Auvers in late June (see letter 891, Vincent to Theo, 24 June 1890).

88 Letter 873.

89 RM20.

90 Letter 873, and see for both this portrait and its second version, Nienke Bakker's essay on pp. 116–33.

91 For this portrait, see Van Tilborgh, Meedendorp and Pilz 2020, p. 101.

92 Letter 886, to Willemien, 13 June 1890.

93 The cry is mentioned in Mark 15:37.

94 Regarding this struggle in his portraits and self-portraits, see Van Tilborgh 2022, pp. 44–46, 53–58.

The First Signs of Recognition

Bregje Gerritse and Sara Tas
pp. 178–91

1 RM20, to Theo and Jo, 24 May 1890 (unsent).

2 See Louis van Tilborgh's essay on pp. 162–77.

3 Van Gogh also exchanged works with other artists. See Bowness 1989, pp. 7, 11, 16, 21, on the subject of peer recognition.

4 Gustave Kahn, 'Peinture, Exposition des indépendants', *La Revue indépendante* (18 April 1888), p. 163.

5 Van Dijk 2017, pp. 22, 136–37. Van Gogh exhibited at the Salon des Indépendants in 1888, 1889 and 1890, and posthumously in 1891 and 1905. Besides the Indépendants, he considered taking part at the 'Volpini' exhibition of the Groupe impressionniste et synthétiste, headed by Paul Gauguin, during the 1889 World Exhibition in Paris, but he and Theo decided against it. He also hoped to show his work in the offices of *La Revue indépendante*, although he later changed his mind: letter 590, to Willemien, around 30 March 1888; letter 677, to Theo, 9 September 1888, note 16; letter 718, to Theo, 10 November 1888, note 2.

6 Isaäcson 1889. Partially in Stein 1986, p. 178.

7 Letter 815, to Theo, around 25 October 1889: 'No need to tell you that I find what he says about me in a note extremely exaggerated, and one more reason why I prefer him not to say anything about me', and RM21, to Joseph Jacob Isaäcson, 25 May 1890 (unsent). Isaäcson respected Van Gogh's request and did not write about him more extensively until after his death.

8 Aurier 1890, pp. 26, 28, 29.

9 Letter 853, to Albert Aurier, 9 or 10 February 1890.

10 In letter 854, to Theo, 12 February 1890: 'Would it not be a good idea to send Reid, and perhaps also Tersteeg, or rather C.M., a copy of Aurier's article?' Alexander Reid was a Scottish art dealer and friend, Hermanus Tersteeg was the head of the Hague branch of the Goupil firm and Cornelis Marinus van Gogh, Theo and Vincent's uncle, was an art dealer in Amsterdam.

11 R. 'Belgische brieven', *Het Vaderland* (28 January 1890), no. 23, p. 1.

12 Anna Boch was the sister of the Belgian artist Eugène Boch, who had met Van Gogh in Arles. The following year, she bought another work, *Peach Trees in Blossom* (1889, The Courtauld Gallery), see Feilchenfeldt 2013, p. 178.

13 Letter 860, Theo to Vincent, 29 March 1890, and letter from Theo to Paul Gachet, 8 May 1890, b2014.

14 Letter 866, to Theo, around 2 May 1890.

15 Letter 873, to Theo and Jo, 20 May 1890.

16 Letter 889, to Theo, 17 June 1890.

17 Letter 873, to Theo and Jo, 20 May 1890.

18 See also Nienke Bakker's essay on pp. 80–95.

19 Letter 879, to Willemien, 5 June 1890. Regarding Van Gogh's illness, see also Bakker, Van Tilborgh and Prins 2016.

20 RM20, to Theo and Jo, 24 May 1890 (unsent).

21 Letter 881, to Theo and Jo, 10 June 1890.

22 Letter from Paul Gachet to Theo, 27 July 1890, b3265 (Pickvance 1992, p. 27).

23 Letter from Theo to Jo, 28 July 1890, b2066 (Van Crimpen 1999, p. 271).

24 Letter from Theo to Jo, 1 August 1890, b2076 (Pickvance 1992, pp. 39–40).

25 Ibid.

26 Ibid.

27 The version kept by Gachet himself was later donated to the Louvre.

28 Auguste Lauzet was a lithographer who knew Theo well. Theo had shown him pen drawings and paintings by Vincent in January 1890. Letter from Theo to Jo, 1 August 1890, b2067 (Van Crimpen 1999, p. 281); Pickvance 1992, p. 34, note 13. Given the short time frame in which all this took place, not only Jo and the Van Gogh family were absent, but several other important people too; see Luijten 2022, pp. 107–10 and Pickvance 1992, pp. 32, 109, 111, 114, 115, 118, 127; Andries Bonger mentioned 'Bauk and Valk' in a letter to Gustave Coquiot, 23 July 1922, b899.

29 Letter from Emile Bernard to Albert Aurier, 31 July 1890, b3052 (Bakker, Van Tilborgh and Prins 2016, pp. 160–61; Pickvance 1992, p. 35). Theo mentioned 'eight friends' in his letter to Jo on 1 August 1890, b2067; Pickvance 1992, p. 39, note 4, identified seven of them: Bernard, Lauzet, Tanguy, Gachet, Hirschig, L. Pissarro and Laval. The eighth was Andries Bonger, Theo's brother-in-law.

30 Regarding the personal significance of these works, see Louis van Tilborgh's essay on pp. 162–77 and Nienke Bakker's essay on pp. 80–95. Letter from Anton Hirschig to Albert Plasschaert, 8 September 1911, b3023. According to Hirschig, the following works were displayed: 'There was the one with fields vanishing undulatingly towards the horizon, the one with the sun right in the middle, the one with the Mairie decorated with flags and Chinese lanterns, the portrait of the girl in blue with blue background, and still so many others.' The first two works have not yet been identified, but are thought to be one of his many undulating, larger landscapes from Auvers and F618 or F617 from Saint-Rémy; see further Van Crimpen 1988, p. 87; Ravoux 1957, p. 15.

31 See note 29 above.

32 Ibid. and letter from Theo to Jo, 1 August 1890, b2067 (Van Crimpen 1999, p. 281).

33 Ravoux 1957, pp. 7–17.

34 Ibid., p. 15.

35 Paul Gachet owned the following twenty-seven paintings: Paris: F217, F324; Saint-Rémy: F580, F627 **(158)**, F595, F624, F659 **(160)**, F674, F673, F726, F727, F728, F740; Auvers: **1, 7, 34, 35, 41, 44, 66, 69, 71, 82, 83, 112, 130, 134**. Stein 1999, pp. 212–30.

36 Alain Mothe, 'Extraits de lettres de Paul Gachet à Gustave Coquiot', p. 185 (Van Gogh Museum Archives). It is not known which two works went to Dr Mazery. There are four possibilities among the Auvers paintings, the first owner of which has not been identified **(52, 79, 80, 84)**.

37 Letter from Theo to his mother and his sister Willemien, 24 August 1890, b936.

38 Letter from Theo to his mother, 1 August 1890, b934 (Pickvance 1992, p. 56).

39 Letter from Theo to Paul Gachet, 12 August 1890 (Pickvance 1992, p. 143).

40 Pickvance 1992, pp. 12, pp. 81–103, 105–06. French acquaintances who wrote letters of condolence or otherwise expressed their sympathy included Claude Monet, Albert Aurier, Félix Fénéon, the collector Comte Armand Doria, Henri Rouart, Léo Gausson, Ernest Quost, Louis Hayet, Emile Bernard, Georges Seurat, Paul Signac, Georges-Charles Lecomte, the critic Maurice Beaubourg (who wrote an obituary in September for *La Revue indépendante*), and the critic Mario Varvara, who is not mentioned in Pickvance 1992, b1204.

41 Letter from Paul Gauguin to Theo, 2 August 1890, b1481 (Pickvance 1992, p. 133) and letter from Meijer de Haan to Theo, 2 August 1890, b1481 (Pickvance 1992, p. 83).

42 Letter from Anthon van Rappard to Van Gogh's mother, undated (Pickvance 1992, p. 102).

43 *L'Echo Pontoisien*, 7 August 1890 (in Stein 1986, p. 219); *Le Petit Parisien*, 2 August 1890; *Le Petit Moniteur Universel*, 3 August 1890; *L'Avenir de Pontoise*, 3 August 1890; *Le Régional*, 7 August 1880; 'Vincent van Gogh', *La Petite Presse*, 18 August 1890 (in Bailey 2021, p. 139).

44 'Vincent van Gogh', *La Petite Presse*, 18 August 1890 (in Bailey 2021, p. 139).

45 Letter from Theo to Lies, 5 August 1890 (Pickvance 1992, p. 73).

46 'I intend to try and arrange an exhibition of his work in Paris in a few months' time. [...] one should see lots of pieces side by side, the better to understand them. He will also be written about. The exhibition will take place in the month of October or at the beginning of November if I can get a venue; that's when Parisians are in town [...]. He will certainly not be forgotten.' Letter from Theo to Lies, 5 August 1890 (Pickvance 1992, p. 73).

47 Letter from Theo to Paul Gachet, 12 August 1890 (Pickvance 1992, pp. 142–43).

48 Letter from Theo to his mother and his sister Willemien, 24 August 1890, b936.

49 Letter from Paul Gachet to Theo, 15 August 1890, b3266 (Pickvance 1992, p. 144). Theo also wrote to Gachet (12 September 1890, b2015) that he had arranged for the doctor to publish an article in the journal *Art et critique*, but this did not materialize.

50 Letter from Jo to her parents, 22 August 1890, b4307.

51 In a short article of April 1889, he already described some of the paintings by Van Gogh he had seen at Tanguy's, and he visited Theo at his apartment later that year to view more works. Letter 825, Theo to Vincent, 8 December 1889: 'That friend of Bernard's called Aurier also came to my place, the one who came to rue Lepic once. He's very interested in what you're doing and showed me a little journal he ran in which he talked about Tanguy's shop, and in which he also mentions your paintings.' Aurier 1889: 'Do you know Tanguy? Yes or no? 14 rue Clauzel; an ugly-looking shop, and so small! [...] Go in and you'll see treasures out of the Arabian Nights... This *père* Tanguy, what an astute spotter of masterpieces! How good he's been at discovering today's unknowns, tomorrow's masters! [...] here are some canvases by Vincent, extraordinarily fiery, intense, sunny.' Letter from Bernard to Aurier, undated [September 1889] (McWilliam 2012, pp. 100–01); Emile Bernard, 'Impressionnistes. Vincent Van Ghogh' [*sic*], unpublished article, sent to Albert Aurier for *Le Moderniste*, July or August 1889, New York, Thaw Collection, The Morgan Library & Museum (MA 4148). See also Jansen, Luijten and Bakker 2007, pp. 361–63.

52 Letter from Theo to his mother, 8 September 1890, b937; letter from Jo to Albert Aurier, 27 March 1892, b1510.

53 The works from Nuenen were F85, F112, F154 and F160a; those from Paris F323, F332a, F583; from Arles **(179)**; and from Saint-Rémy F563, F541, F742 and *Cypresses with Two Figures* **(170)**, which Van Gogh had given to Aurier. After Aurier's death, these works came into the possession of his sister Suzanne Williame-Aurier. She might have bought the floral still life F323 from Paris herself, but this cannot be stated with any certainty. Her husband sold ten of the twelve works to the Kröller-Müllers through H.P. Bremmer in 1914. Meedendorp 2003b, pp. 406–10.

54 Leclercq 1890, p. 330. Lerclerq did not address how Van Gogh had died; he had first met the artist at Aurier's home in May 1890, see Stein 1986, p. 241.

55 Ibid.

56 Letter from Theo to Willemien, 27 September 1890, b947.

57 Theo evidently continued to seek an official venue until the last minute. Letter from Bernard to Theo, 18 September 1890, b1154:'I have not given up on finding a venue for the Vincent Exhibition, either at the Théâtre Libre or the Théâtre d'Application – we are discussing it.' (McWilliam 2012, p. 122); letter from Theo to his mother, 16 September 1890, b938.

58 Bernard 1911, pp. 2–3; De Meester 1890, in Stein 1986, p. 246.

59 Letter from Theo to Willemien, 27 September 1890, b947; letter from Andries Bonger to Jo, 8 January 1891, b1868. Theo sold the two works for a combined total of 300 francs.

60 Meedendorp 2003a, pp. 411–12.

61 Tanguy sold 'one landscape from Arles, while the other might be from Auvers, but that is unlikely', for 400–500 francs to a lawyer from Copenhagen, thought to be Hans Christian Christensen. Letter from Andries Bonger to Jo, 8 January 1891 (b1868). Albert Aurier, 'Choses d'art', *Mercure de France* (1890), no. 8, p. 303; no. 9, p. 333; no. 12, p. 447; (1891), no. 13, p. 62; no. 18, p. 374; no. 20, p. 126; (1892), no. 27, p. 284.

62 Letter from Paul Gachet to Theo, 4 October 1890, b3267.

63 Luijten 2022, p. 112.

64 Letter from Andries Bonger to Paul Gachet, 10 October 1890, Paul Ferdinand Gachet and Paul Louis Gachet Papers [wzheafwo], The Wildenstein Plattner Institute, Inc. (hereafter: Gachet Papers), and letter from Andries Bonger to Paul Gachet, 16 October 1890, b887.

65 Letter from Andries Bonger to his parents, 16 October 1890, b1860.

66 Letter from Albert Aurier to Paul Gachet, 22 October 1890, b888.

67 The diagnosis was 'acute maniacal agitation with megalomania and progressive generalized paralysis'. This might indicate the final stage of syphilis infection, although it is not clear whether this was stated explicitly at the time. Luijten 2022, p. 115.

68 Thirty-five artists took part in the exhibition. Gaston Lesaulx, *Peintres impressionnistes et symbolistes*, Paris 1890, p. 20. Van Gogh's paintings have been identified as **179**, **170** and F563.

69 De Meester 1890, in Stein 1986, pp. 246–57.

70 Luijten 2022, pp. 127–30.

71 Bernard 1891a; Bernard 1891b.

72 Letter from Emile Bernard to Eugène Boch, 1 March and 3 March 1891 (McWilliam 2012, pp. 134–37); letter from Emile Bernard to Jo, 8 March 1891, b1089 (McWilliam 2012, pp. 137–38). Gauguin did not help, having previously told Bernard that he was not in favour of the exhibition: 'I begin my letter because I have received one from Sérusier, who tells me that you are organizing an exhibition on Vincent. How inconsiderate! You know that I love Vincent's art. But given the stupidity of the public, it is entirely the wrong moment to draw attention to Vincent and his madness at the very time his brother Theo is in the same condition. Lots of people say that our painting is madness! This would hurt us without doing any good to Vincent, etc. So go ahead by all means! But it is idiotic.' Letter from Gauguin to Bernard, undated, before 25 January 1891 (McWilliam 2012, p. 137).

73 Letter from Emile Bernard to Jo, 8 March 1891, b1089 (McWilliam 2012, pp. 137–38).

74 Letter from Emile Bernard to Jo, 7 April 1891, b1090 (McWilliam 2012, pp. 141–42).

75 Mirbeau 1891, p. 1; Eugène Tardieu, 'Le Salon des Indépendants', *Le Magazine français illustré* (25 April 1891); Julien Leclercq, 'Aux Indépendants', *Mercure de France* (May 1891), no. 17, pp. 298–99; Jules Antoine, 'Exposition des artistes Indépendants', *La Plume* (1 May 1891), p. 157; Emile Verhaeren, 'Le Salon des Indépendants', *L'Art Moderne* (5 April 1891), no. 14, pp. 111–12; Georges Lecomte, 'Salon des Indépendants', *L'art dans les deux mondes* (28 March 1891), no. 19, p. 225; Albert Aurier, 'Ratiocinations familières à propos des trois Salons de 1891', *Mercure de France* (July 1891), no. 19, pp. 30–39.

76 Gachet exhibited ten works under his Paul van Ryssel pseudonym, including 'Le peintre Vincent Van Gogh sur son lit de mort. Fusain d'après nature', Lobstein 2003, vol. 2, p. 705; Eugène Tardieu, 'Salon des Indépendants', *Le Magazine français illustré* (25 April 1891), p. 535.

77 Luijten 2022, pp. 118, 127–30.

78 Francis 1892.

79 Julien Leclercq, 'Beaux-arts. Aux Indépendants', *Mercure de France* (1890), no. 5, pp. 174–76; De Meester 1890, in Stein 1986, p. 246.

80 Vincent van Gogh, 'Extraits de lettres de Vincent Gogh [*sic*] à E. Bernard (1887-1888-1889-1890)', *Mercure de France* (1893), no. 40, pp. 333–39. Letters were also published that year in *Mercure de France* nos. 44–47, in 1894 in nos. 49, 51, 55, 57, in 1895 in no. 63, and in 1897 in no. 92; McWilliam 2012, pp. 204, 210–11, 220; Leeman 2013, pp. 224–25. The portrait in Bonger's possession was F295.

81 Bernard 1893.

82 Leeman 2013, pp. 217, 220, 224–25. Examples of works that Bernard sold to Ambroise Vollard include F328, F526, F502, F540, F667, F654; McWilliam 2012, pp. 325, 463.

83 Private collection, F529. Paul-Napoléon Roinard, 'Revue artistique. Les Portraits du vingtième siècle', *Revue Encyclopédique* (1893), no. 71, p. 644.

84 Octave Mirbeau, 'Le Père Tanguy', *L'Echo de Paris* 1 (13 February 1894), no. 3550, p. 1.

85 Delporte, Blandin and Robinet 2016, p. 16. See also 'Les principaux quotidiens', Bibliothèque Nationale de France, https://gallica.bnf.fr/html/und/presse-et-revues/les-principaux-quotidiens?mode=desktop [28-07-2022].

86 Natanson 1895.

87 Letter Andries Bonger to Paul Gachet, 26 August 1891, Gachet Papers [ptffseuv].

88 Luijten 2022, pp. 120–21. The visit paid by her overbearing brother might also have hindered further contact. Andries Bonger showed little respect in this period for his sister's efforts with respect to Vincent's legacy: see a letter from Andries to Jo, 8 January 1891, b1868.

89 Golbéry 1990, p. 41.

90 See note 35 above.

91 He turned down a request from Leclercq to this effect. Letter from Julien Leclercq to Paul Gachet, 15 February 1901, Gachet Papers [dnsk56y4].

92 See pp. 132, 228 (note 60) and letter from Théodore Duret to Paul Gachet, 4 April 1900, Gachet Papers [szxcwm55].

93 Meier-Graefe 1904, pp. 119–20.

94 Letter from Julius Meier-Graefe to Paul Gachet, 21 July 1903, Gachet Papers [aqskvlig] (Distel 1999, p. 22).

95 Letter from Paul Gachet Jr to Jo, 25 November 1904, b3411.

96 'As you know, Valk and Bauk live in Auvers-sur-O. They also visited Vincent's grave and it looked so simply neat.' Letter from Sara de Swart to Jo, summer 1892, b3576. 'Bauk' was Baukje van Mesdag (1853–c. 1920). Together with her later husband Maurits van der Valk she attended Van Gogh's funeral, see note 28 above.

97 See, among others, letter from Paul Gachet Jr to Jo, 15 July 1905, b1974; letter from Paul Gachet Sr to Johan Cohen Gosschalk, 7 November 1905, b3153; letter from Paul Gachet Sr to Jo, 18 August 1907, b2170; letter from Jo to Clementine and Paul Gachet Jr, 13 January 1909, Gachet Papers [8ic8tk13]. Later, Vincent van Gogh Jr developed a certain antipathy towards Gachet Jr, see Hendriks and Van Tilborgh 2001, pp. 145–49.

98 Letter from Paul Gachet to Theo, 15 August 1890, b3266 (Pickvance 1992, p. 144).

99 Van Gogh-Bonger 1914, p. LXII.

100 He did, however, publish several other books about his father and the artists in his collection, including Gachet 1953a, Gachet 1953b, Gachet 1954a, Gachet 1956 and Gachet 1957. His most ambitious publication, devoted to 'Van Gogh's Seventy Days in Auvers', was finished by Alain Mothe and only published in 1994.

101 Today, the Gachet Collection is part of the collection of the Musée d'Orsay in Paris.

Catalogue of Paintings from Auvers-sur-Oise

Louis van Tilborgh and Teio Meedendorp
pp. 202–19

1 For the sake of convenience, we have included Van Gogh's village and garden views in the landscape category. His flowering acacia and painting of ears of wheat have been counted as still lifes **(#23, #38)**. All the works were painted on canvas, apart from one made on paper **(#55)**. De la Faille 1970, Hulsker 1996a, Feilchenfeldt 2013 and Van der Veen and Knapp 2010 list additional works which, in our view, were not painted in Auvers-sur-Oise. Some of these were misattributions (F796, F812, F815), while others are now situated almost unanimously during his stay in Saint-Rémy (F563, F595, F597, F740, F749, F748, F757, F803, F818). One painting was done during his time in Paris (F810). René Secrétan claimed in 1957, moreover, that when he was sixteen, he and his brother Gaston had been given six paintings by Van Gogh (Doiteau 1957, pp. 42–43), which were later lost. This is entirely implausible, however. See Van Tilborgh and Meedendorp 2013, pp. 457–62 for more on this boastful personality.

2 We only know the contents of one letter sent in the latter period, namely the one dated 23 July to Theo, in which Van Gogh described and sketched four works (letter 902 and **#69**, **#70**, **#71**, **#72**).

3 See Maes and Van Tilborgh 2012, pp. 67–68 in this regard; for the sources: Bonger 1893, Paris 1891, no. 1204.

4 Gachet 1994, cited by both Van der Veen and Knapp 2010 and Feilchenfeldt 2013.

5 De la Faille 1928, De la Faille 1970, and Hulsker 1996a.

6 See Nienke Bakker's essay on pp. 80–95 in this regard.

7 According to Gachet 1994, p. 229, Vincent was in the Cordeville area on 20 July, and so it is possible that **#66** was done on that date.

8 **#9** is an exception in this regard: see Wouter van der Veen's essay on pp. 34–57.

9 Mascart 1892, vol. 3, pp. 94, 116, 138.

10 Letter 902, to Theo, 23 July 1890.

11 See Nienke Bakker's essay on pp. 80–95 in this regard.

12 Gachet Sr spent his other days in Paris, where he had his medical practice. For a full list of Van Gogh's visits, see the Chronology pp. 192–201.

13 Another size 30 work, also not mentioned in the letters, which had already been broadly dated in the manner described above **(#26)**, could be situated more precisely using the same approach. Vincent visited Theo and Jo in Paris on 6 June and the painting was probably done shortly before that date, so there was no need for him to mention it in his next letter.

14 These occasions include at least 20 May (first day), 8 June (visit of Theo and Jo) and 6 July (visit to Paris), while we could already see from our provisional dating that Van Gogh had produced fewer works in July than in the preceding period, which is entirely understandable from a psychological point of view: see Louis van Tilborgh's essay on pp. 162–77.

15 The urge to make larger paintings was already there; see RM20, to Theo and Jo, 24 May 1890 (unsent). See letter 875, to Theo and Jo, regarding Vincent waiting for a response from Theo.

16 Letter 876, Theo to Vincent, 2 June 1890, and letter 877, to Theo, 3 June 1890.

17 Letters 889 and 891. **#43** also includes a woman fishing, and since the fishing season opened on 16 June, this provides a *post quem* date (see the Chronology on pp. 192–201).

18 See for this project Note to the Reader on p. 11.

19 He used the latter for **#6** and **#32**.

20 Letter 889, to Theo, 17 June 1890. Van Gogh produced thirty-three paintings in the subsequent period, eight of which have not been analysed **(#44, #48, #53, #56, #58, #65, #69, #70)**; the remaining canvases all have the same thread density. The new stock probably consisted of two rolls with the same weaving pattern but differently primed (the authors are grateful for this information to Muriel Geldof, specialist in material-technical aspects of painting at the Rijksdienst voor Cultureel Erfgoed, Amsterdam). Hendriks et al. 2013, p. 178, states that Vincent had also used canvas from Saint-Rémy for his so-called double squares – his 50 × 100 cm paintings – but this is not correct.

21 Ravoux 1957, p. 12.

BIBLIOGRAPHY

Ambrosini, Fowle and Van Dijk 2016
Lynne Ambrosini, Frances Fowle and Maite van Dijk (eds.), *Daubigny, Monet, Van Gogh: Impressions of Landscape*, exh. cat., Cincinnati (Taft Museum of Art), Edinburgh (National Gallery of Scotland), Amsterdam (Van Gogh Museum) 2016–17

Amiel 2009
Alain Amiel, *Vincent van Gogh à Auvers-sur-Oise*, Nice 2009 (vangoghaventure.com)

Arenberg, Di Maio and Baden 2020
I. Kaufman Arenberg, Vincent Di Maio and Michael Baden, 'A Reevaluation of the Death of Vincent van Gogh: Suicide or Murder? The Need for a Definitive Autopsy', *American Journal of Forensic Medicine and Pathology* 41 (December 2020), no. 4, pp. 291–98

Aurier 1889
Luc le Flâneur (pseudonym for Gabriel-Albert Aurier), 'En quête de choses d'art', *Le Moderniste illustré* (13 April 1889), no. 2, p. 14

Aurier 1890
Gabriel-Albert Aurier, 'Les isolés: Vincent van Gogh', *Mercure de France* (1 January 1890), no. 1, pp. 24–29

D'Auvers 1973
Yves d'Auvers, *Les impressionnistes d'Auvers-sur-Oise: 1er exposition-rétrospective de 1856 à 1907 – autour du Dr Gachet*, Auvers-sur-Oise, s.a. [1973]

Bailey 2021
Martin Bailey, *Van Gogh's Finale: Auvers and the Artist's Rise to Fame*, London 2021

Bakker 2016a
Nienke Bakker, 'Van Gogh's Illness: The Witnesses Recall', in Bakker, Van Tilborgh and Prins 2016, pp. 29–86

Bakker 2016b
Nienke Bakker, 'In Daubigny's Footsteps: Vincent van Gogh', in Ambrosini, Fowle and Van Dijk 2016, pp. 105–29

Bakker, Van Tilborgh and Prins 2016
Nienke Bakker, Louis van Tilborgh and Laura Prins, *On the Verge of Insanity: Van Gogh and his Illness*, exh. cat., Amsterdam (Van Gogh Museum) 2016

Bakker and Myers 2021
Nienke Bakker and Nicole R. Myers (eds.), *Van Gogh and the Olive Groves*, exh. cat., Dallas (Dallas Museum of Art), Amsterdam (Van Gogh Museum) 2021

Bakker and Riopelle 2019
Nienke Bakker and Christopher Riopelle, 'The *Sunflowers* in Perspective', in Hendriks and Vellekoop 2019, pp. 21–47

Barron 1886
Louis Barron, *Les Environs de Paris*, Paris 1886

Beaubourg 1890
Maurice Beaubourg, 'La Mort de Dubois-Pillet et de Vincent van Gogh', *La Revue indépendante* 16 (September 1890), no. 47, pp. 391–402

Ten Berge et al. 2003
Jos ten Berge, Teio Meedendorp, Aukje Vergeest and Robert Verhoogt, *The Paintings of Vincent van Gogh in the Collection of the Kröller-Müller Museum*, Otterlo 2003

Bernard 1891a
Emile Bernard, 'Vincent van Gogh', *Les Hommes d'aujourd'hui* 8 (1891), no. 390

Bernard 1891b
Emile Bernard, 'Néo-traditionnistes [...] Vincent van Gogh', *La Plume* (1 September 1891), no. 57, pp. 300–01

Bernard 1893
Emile Bernard, 'Vincent van Gogh', *Mercure de France* (April 1893), no. 40, pp. 324–30

Bernard 1911
Emile Bernard, 'Avant-propos', in *Lettres de Vincent van Gogh à Emile Bernard*, Paris 1911, pp. 59–63

Bernard 1994
Emile Bernard, *Propos sur l'art*, 2 vols., Paris 1994

Béthencourt-Devaux 1972
Robert Béthencourt-Devaux, *Montmartre, Auvers-sur-Oise et Van Gogh*, Paris 1972

De Beurs 2020
Derek de Beurs, *Mythen over zelfmoord*, Amsterdam 2020

Blanc 2017
Jan Blanc, *Van Gogh: ni dieu ni maitre*, Paris 2017

Blotkamp 2019
Carel Blotkamp, *The End: Artists' Late and Last Works*, London 2019

Bonger 1890
Andries Bonger, *Catalogue des œuvres de Vincent van Gogh*, manuscript, Van Gogh Museum, Amsterdam 1890

Bonger 1893
[Andries Bonger], 'Vincent', *Nieuwe Rotterdamsche Courant*, 5 September 1893

Bonis, Jourdheuil and Perrault 2021
Armelle Bonis, Michel Jourdheuil and Elodie Perrault, *Le Docteur Gachet, médecin, collectioneur et artiste amateur*, Veux-sur-Mer 2021

Bowness 1989
Alan Bowness, *The Conditions of Success: How the Modern Artist Rises to Fame*, London 1989

Bredius 1934
Abraham Bredius, 'Herinneringen aan Vincent van Gogh', *Oud Holland* 51 (1934), no. 1, p. 44

Briat-Philippe and Luijten 2017
Magali Briat-Philippe and Ger Luijten (eds.), *Georges Michel 1763–1843. Le paysage sublime*, exh. cat., Bourge-en-Bresse (Monastère royal de Brou), Paris (Fondation Custodia) 2017–18

Brimo 1990
Albert Brimo, *Auvers-sur-Oise. Mémoire d'un village. C.-F. Daubigny, Cézanne, Pissarro, Van Gogh, Zadkine et les autres...*, Paris 1990

Brown Price 1975
Aimée Brown Price, 'Two Portraits by Vincent van Gogh and Two Portraits by Pierre Puvis de Chavannes', *The Burlington Magazine* 117 (November 1975), no. 872, pp. 714–18

Buckman 1955
Eduard Buckman, 'An American Finds the Real Van Gogh at Auvers-sur-Oise', *De Tafelronde. Algemeen cultureel tijdschrift* 2 (1955), no. 8–9, pp. 46–53

Callen 2000
Anthea Callen, *The Art of Impressionism: Painting, Technique and the Making of Modernity*, New Haven/London 2000

Cazier 1899
Samson Cazier (teacher), *Monographie Communale d'Auvers-sur-Oise*, September 1899, manuscript, archives départementales du Val-d'Oise (https://archives.valdoise.fr/archives/archives/fonds/FRAD095_00023/open:all/view:all/page:1?pagination=10)

Chatelet 1978
Albert Chatelet, 'Le dernier tableau de Van Gogh', *Archives de l'art français* (1978), no. 25, pp. 439–42

Cohen Gosschalk 1905
Johan Cohen Gosschalk, 'Vincent van Gogh', in *Tentoonstelling Vincent van Gogh*, exh. cat., Amsterdam (Stedelijk Museum) 1905, pp. 3–14

Cooper 1955
Douglas Cooper, 'The Painters of Auvers-sur-Oise', *The Burlington Magazine* 97 (April 1955), no. 625, pp. 100–06

Coquiot 1923
Gustave Coquiot, *Vincent van Gogh*, Paris 1923

Van Crimpen 1988
Han van Crimpen, 'Friends Remember Vincent in 1912', in Takashina, Pickvance and Arikawa 1988, pp. 73–90

Van Crimpen 1999
Han van Crimpen (ed.), *Brief Happiness: The Correspondence of Theo van Gogh and Jo Bonger* (Cahier Vincent 7), Amsterdam/Zwolle 1999

Van Crimpen and Berends-Albert 1990
Han van Crimpen and Monique Berends-Albert (eds.), *De brieven van Vincent Van Gogh*, 4 vols., The Hague 1990

Delporte, Blandin and Robinet 2016
Christian Delporte, Claire Blandin and François Robinet, *Histoire de la presse en France XXe–XXIe siècles*, Paris 2016

Demory 1985
Evelyne Demory, *Entre coteau et rivière. Auvers en 1900*, Paris 1985

Van Dijk 2017
Maite van Dijk, *Foreign Artists versus French Critics: Exhibition Strategies and Critical Reception at the Salon des Indépendants in Paris (1884–1914)*, dissertation, University of Amsterdam, 2017

Distel 1999
Anne Distel, 'Gachet, Father and Son', in Distel and Stein 1999, pp. 3–25

Distel and Stein 1999
Anne Distel and Susan Alyson Stein (eds.), *Cézanne to Van Gogh: The Collection of Doctor Gachet*, exh. cat., Paris (Grand Palais), New York (Metropolitan Museum of Art), Amsterdam (Van Gogh Museum) 1999

Doiteau 1923–24
Victor Doiteau, 'La curieuse figure du docteur Gachet, un ami et un amateur de la première heure de Cézanne, Renoir, Pissarro, Van Gogh', *Aesculape* (August 1923), pp. 169–73; (September 1923), pp. 211–16; (November 1923) pp. 250–54; (December 1923), pp. 278–83; (January 1924), pp. 7–11

Doiteau 1957
Victor Doiteau, 'Deux "copains" de Van Gogh, inconnus, les frères Gaston et René Secrétan, Vincent, tel qu'ils l'ont vu', *Aesculape* (March 1957), pp. 38–58

Van Dongen 2022
Alexandra van Dongen, *Dichter bij Vincent. Alledaagse voorwerpen in het werk van Vincent van Gogh*, Gorredijk 2022

Dorn 1990
Roland Dorn, *Décoration. Vincent van Goghs Werkreihe für das Gelbe Haus in Arles*, Hildesheim/Zurich/New York 1990

Dorn 2002
Roland Dorn (interview by Dorothee Hansen), 'Van Gogh's Fields', in Herzogenrath and Hansen 2002, pp. 32–51

Dorn et al. 2000
Roland Dorn, George S. Keyes, Joseph J. Rishel et al., *Van Gogh. Face to Face: The Portraits*, exh. cat., Detroit (Detroit Institute of Arts), Boston (Museum of Fine Arts), Philadelphia (Philadelphia Museum of Art) 2000–01

Dumas et al. 2010
Ann Dumas, Leo Jansen, Hans Luijten and Nienke Bakker, *The Real Van Gogh: The Artist and His Letters*, exh. cat., London (Royal Academy of Arts) 2010

Duvivier et al. 2003
Christophe Duvivier, Eva-Marina Froitzheim, Wolf Eiermann, Claire Durand-Ruel Snollaerts and Janine Bailly-Herzberg, *Entre ciel et terre. Camille Pissarro et les peintres de la vallée de l'Oise*, exh. cat., Böblingen (Städtische Galerie), Pontoise (Musée Tavet-Delacour) 2003

Van Eeden 1890
Frederik van Eeden, 'Vincent van Gogh', *De Nieuwe Gids* 6 (December 1890), no. 2, pp. 263–70

Elgar 1958
Frank Elgar, *Van Gogh: A Study of his Life and Work*, New York 1958

De la Faille 1928
J.-B. de la Faille, *L'Oeuvre de Vincent van Gogh. Catalogue raisonné*, 4 vols., Paris/Brussels 1928

De la Faille 1939
J.-B. de la Faille, *Vincent van Gogh*, Paris 1939

De la Faille 1970
J.-B. de la Faille, *The Works of Vincent van Gogh: His Paintings and Drawings*, Amsterdam 1970

Feilchenfeldt 2013
Walter Feilchenfeldt, *Vincent van Gogh: The Years in France. Complete Paintings 1886–1890*, London 2013

Fieberg et al. 2017
Jeffrey E. Fieberg, Per Knutas, Kurt Hostettler and Gregory D. Smith, 'Paintings Fade Like Flowers: Pigment Analysis and Digital Reconstruction of a Faded Pink Lake Pigment in Vincent van Gogh's *Undergrowth with Two Figures*', *Applied Spectroscopy* 71 (2017), no. 5, pp. 794–808

Florisoone and Huyghe 1952
Michel Florisoone and René Huyghe, *Van Gogh und die Maler von Auvers bei Dr. Gachet*, Paris/Lucerne 1952

Fowle 2016
Francis Fowle, 'Auvers-sur-Oise as an Artists' Colony: from Daubigny to Van Gogh', in Ambrosini, Fowle and Van Dijk 2016, pp. 93–103

Francis 1892
Francis, 'Exposition Van Gogh', *La Vie moderne* 14 (24 April 1892), no. 17, pp. 1–2

Fromentin 1876
Eugène Fromentin, *Les Maîtres d'autrefois. Belgique – Hollande*, Paris 1876

Fromentin 1981
Eugène Fromentin, *The Masters of Past Time: Dutch and Flemish Painting from Van Eyck to Rembrandt*, ed. H. Gerson, trans. A. Boyle, Oxford 1981

Fuchs 2002
Rudi Fuchs, 'Ontsnapt aan de eeuw: Vincent van Gogh', in ibid., *Tussen kunstenaars: een romance*, Amsterdam 2002, pp. 39–46 (originally published in *NRC Handelsblad*, 6 April 1990)

Furutani 2010
Yoshiyuki Furutani (ed.), *'Daubigny's Garden' 1890 by Vincent van Gogh*, Hiroshima 2010

Gachet 1953a
Paul Gachet, *Van Gogh à Auvers: Histoire d'un tableau: Un modèle de Vincent van Gogh et le tableau qu'il en fit, Mademoiselle Gachet au piano*, Paris 1953

Gachet 1953b
Paul Gachet, *Souvenirs de Cézanne et de Van Gogh à Auvers* [1928], Paris 1953

Gachet 1954a
Paul Gachet, *Vincent à Auvers. 'Les Vaches' de J. Jordaens*, Paris 1954

Gachet 1954b
Paul Gachet, *Paul van Ryssel: le docteur Gachet, graveur*, Paris 1954

Gachet 1956
Paul Gachet, *Deux amis des impressionnistes : le Dr Gachet et Murer*, Paris 1956

Gachet 1957
Paul Gachet, *Lettres impressionnistes au Dr Gachet et à Murer*, Paris 1957

Gachet 1994
Paul Gachet, *Les 70 jours de Van Gogh à Auvers. Essai d'éphéméride dans le décor de l'époque (20 mai–30 juillet 1890) d'après les lettres, documents, souvenirs et déductions (Auvers-sur-Oise, 1959)*, ed. Alain Mothe, Paris 1994

Garnier 1959
Christine Garnier, 'Auvers-sur-Oise et Van Gogh', *Revue des Deux Mondes*, 1 January 1959, pp. 40–50

Garnier 1960
Christine Garnier, *Auvers-sur-Oise*, Paris 1960

Garnier 1962
Christine Garnier, *Aux Américains. La maison du mystère? Auvers-sur-Oise: Christine Garnier chez le Dr. Gachet.*, [s.l., s.a.]

Gauthier 1953
Maximilien Gauthier, 'La femme en bleu nous parle de l'homme à l'oreille coupée', *Les Nouvelles littéraires, artistiques et scientifiques*, 16 April 1953, pp. 1–6

Gauthier 1954a
Maximilien Gauthier, 'La femme en bleu revient à Auvers', *Les Nouvelles littéraires, artistiques et scientifiques*, 12 August 1954, p. 8

Gauthier 1954b
Maximilien Gauthier, 'Van Gogh à Auvers: autour d'une exposition', *Les Nouvelles littéraires, artistiques et scientifiques*, 25 November 1954

Geskó 2006
Judith Geskó (ed.), *Van Gogh in Budapest*, exh. cat., Budapest (Szépművészeti Múzeum) 2006–07

Van Gogh-Bonger 1914
Johanna van Gogh-Bonger, 'Inleiding', in ibid (ed.), *Vincent van Gogh. Brieven aan zijn broeder*, 3 vols., Amsterdam 1914, vol. 1, pp. XI–LXIV

Golbéry 1990
Roger Golbéry, *Mon oncle, Paul Gachet. Souvenirs d'Auvers-sur-Oise 1940–1960. Suivi de deux nouvelles inédites de Paul Gachet*, Paris 1990

Golbéry 1992
[Roger Golbéry], 'Marguerite Gachet énigmatique et silencieuse: en marge du film *Vincent van Gogh* de Maurice Pialat', *Vivre en Val-d'Oise* (January 1992), no. 11, pp. 71–75

Gombrich 1972
Ernst Hans Gombrich, *Art and Illusion: A Study in the Psychology of Pictorial Representation*, London 1972

Gotsch 1954
Friedrich Karl Gotsch, 'Van Gogh's Tod', *Schri Kunst Schri. Ein Almanach alter und neuer Kunst*, Baden Baden 1954, pp. 60–62

Gustavison 1989
Susan J. Gustavison, *Robert J. Wickenden (1861–1931) and the Late Nineteenth-Century Print Revival*, dissertation, Concordia University, Montreal 1989 (https://static.s123-cdn-static-d.com/uploads/2198716/normal_5cfaef7c209c9.pdf)

Heenk 1995
Liesbeth Heenk, *Vincent van Gogh's Drawings: An Analysis of their Production and Uses*, unpublished PhD dissertation, Courtauld Institute of Art, University of London, 1995

Van Heeringen et al. 2019
Kees van Heeringen, Gwendolyn Portzky, Derek de Beurs and Ad Kerkhof (eds.), *Handboek suïcidaal gedrag*, Amsterdam 2019

Van Heeringen and Kerkhof 2019
Kees van Heeringen and Ad Kerkhof, 'Verklaringsmodellen', in Van Heeringen et al. 2019, pp. 99–107

Held 1987
Julius S. Held, 'Commentary [on "Old-Age Style"]', *Art Journal* 46 (1987), no. 2, pp. 127–33

Hellebranth 1976
Robert Hellebranth, *Charles-François Daubigny 1817–1878*, Morges 1976

Hendriks et al. 2013
Ella Hendriks, C. Richard Johnson Jr, Don. H. Johnson and Muriel Geldof, 'Automated Thread Counting and the Studio Practice Project', in Vellekoop et al. 2013, pp. 156–81

Hendriks and Van Tilborgh 2001
Ella Hendriks and Louis van Tilborgh, 'Van Gogh's "Garden of the Asylum": genuine or fake?', *The Burlington Magazine* 143 (March 2001), no. 1176, pp. 145–56

Hendriks and Van Tilborgh 2011
Ella Hendriks and Louis van Tilborgh, *Vincent van Gogh Paintings, Volume 2. Antwerp and Paris 1885–1888*, Van Gogh Museum, Amsterdam 2011

Hendriks and Vellekoop 2019
Ella Hendriks and Marije Vellekoop (eds.), *Van Gogh's Sunflowers Illuminated: Art Meets Science* (Van Gogh Museum Studies 1), Amsterdam 2019

Herbert 1988
Robert L. Herbert, *Impressionism. Art, Leisure, and Parisian Society*, New Haven/London 1988

Herzogenrath and Hansen 2002
Wulf Herzogenrath and Dorothee Hansen (eds.), *Van Gogh: Fields. The Field with Poppies and the Artists' Dispute*, exh. cat., Bremen (Kunsthalle Bremen) 2002–03

Van Heugten and Pabst 1995
Sjraar van Heugten and Fieke Pabst, *The Graphic Work of Vincent van Gogh* (Cahier Vincent 6), Amsterdam 1995

Heumakers 2015
Arnold Heumakers, *De esthetische revolutie. Hoe verlichting en romantiek de kunst uitvonden*, Amsterdam 2015

Homburg 2012
Cornelia Homburg (ed.), *Van Gogh: Up Close*, exh. cat., Ottawa (National Gallery of Canada), Philadelphia (Philadelphia Museum of Art) 2012

Homburg et al. 2016
Cornelia Homburg, Simon Kelly, Laura Prins and Jenny Reynaerts, *Van Gogh: Into the Undergrowth*, exh. cat., Cincinnati (Cincinnati Art Museum) 2016–17

House 1987
John House, 'The Final Year [review of Pickvance 1986]', *Times Literary Supplement*, 6–12 November 1987

Hulsker 1985
Jan Hulsker, *Lotgenoten. Het leven van Vincent en Theo van Gogh*, Weesp 1985

Hulsker 1988
Jan Hulsker, 'Review of *Van Gogh à Paris* by B. Welsh-Ovcharov; *Van Gogh in Arles* by R. Pickvance; *Van Gogh in Saint-Rémy and Auvers* by R. Pickvance; *Vincent van Gogh à Auvers-sur-Oise* by A. Mothe', *Simiolus: Netherlands Quarterly for the History of Art* 18 (1988), no. 3, pp. 177–92

Hulsker 1990
Jan Hulsker, *Vincent and Theo van Gogh: A Dual Biography*, Ann Arbor 1990

Hulsker 1996a
Jan Hulsker, *The New Complete Van Gogh: Paintings, Drawings, Sketches*, Amsterdam/Philadelphia 1996

Hulsker 1996b
Jan Hulsker, 'De Van Goghs en de Bongers', *Jong Holland* 12 (1996), no. 2, pp. 44–53

Ikegami 1988
Chūji Ikegami, 'Two Portraits of Dr Gachet by Vincent van Gogh', in Takashina, Pickvance and Arikawa 1988, pp. 255–65

Isaäcson 1889
Joseph Jacob Isaäcson, 'Parijsche Brieven III. Gevoelens over de Nederlandsche kunst op de Parijsche Wereld-tentoonstelling', *De Portefeuille* 11 (17 August 1889), no. 20, pp. 248–9

Ives et al. 2005
Colta Ives, Susan Alyson Stein, Sjraar van Heugten and Marije Vellekoop, *Vincent van Gogh: The Drawings*, exh. cat., Amsterdam (Van Gogh Museum), New York (Metropolitan Museum of Art) 2005

Jansen, Luijten and Bakker 2007
Leo Jansen, Hans Luijten and Nienke Bakker (eds.), *Vincent van Gogh, Painted with Words: The Letters to Emile Bernard*, exh. cat., New York (Morgan Library and Museum), Amsterdam (Van Gogh Museum) 2007–08

Jansen, Luijten, and Bakker 2009
Leo Jansen, Hans Luijten, and Nienke Bakker (eds.), *Vincent van Gogh: The Letters. The Complete, Illustrated and Annotated Edition*, Amsterdam/The Hague/Brussels 2009 (www.vangoghletters.org)

Jaspers 1926
Karl Jaspers, *Strindberg und Van Gogh. Versuch einer pathographischen Analyse unter vergleichender Heranziehung von Swedenborg und Hölderlin*, Berlin 1926

Joanne 1856
Adolphe Joanne, *Les Environs de Paris illustré. Itinéraire descriptif et historique*, Paris 1856

Joiner 2007
Thomas Joiner, *Why People Die by Suicide*, Cambridge, MA 2007

Jones et al. 2008
Kimberly A. Jones, Simon Kelly, Sarah Kennel and Helga K. Aurisch, *In the Forest of Fontainebleau: Painters and Photographers from Corot to Monet*, exh. cat., Washington (National Gallery of Art), Houston (Museum of Fine Arts) 2008

Kerkhof, De Beurs and Portzky 2019
Ad Kerkhof, Derek de Beurs and Gwendolyn Portzky, 'Psychologische processen', in Van Heeringen et al. 2019, pp. 62–69

Kilpinen 1995
Tuulikki Kilpinen, 'Beneath the Surface: Study and Conservation of Vincent van Gogh's Painting *Street in Auvers-sur-Oise*', *Ateneum: The Finnish National Gallery Bulletin* (1995), pp. 43–69

Kōdera 1996
Tsukasa Kōdera, *Van Gogh's 'Wheatfield with Crows': The 'Last Work' as Narrative Closure*, manuscript, Van Gogh Museum Library, Amsterdam 1996

Kōdera et al. 2017
Tsukasa Kōdera, Tatsuya Saito, Megumi Soda and Geneviève Aitken, 'Reconstructing Bing's Legendary 1890 Exhibition of Japanese Prints at the Ecole des Beaux-Arts', *Journal of Japonisme* 2 (January 2017), no. 1, pp. 1–37

Kōdera and Rosenberg 1993
Tsukasa Kōdera and Yvette Rosenberg (eds.), *The Mythology of Vincent van Gogh*, Amsterdam/Philadelphia 1993

Lachiver 1982
Marcel Lachiver, *Vin, vigne et vignerons en région parisienne du XVIIe au XIXe siècle*, Pontoise 1982

Leclercq 1890
Julien Leclercq, 'Vincent van Gogh', *Mercure de France* 1 (September 1890), no. 9, p. 330

Leeman 2013
Fred Leeman, *Emile Bernard (1868–1941)*, Paris 2013

Lesaulx 1890
Gaston Lesaulx, *Peintres impressionnistes et symbolistes*, Paris 1890

Lobstein 2003
Dominique Lobstein, *Dictionnaire des indépendants, 1884–1914*, 3 vols., Dijon 2003

Ludovici 1913
Anthony M. Ludovici, 'Introductory Essay on Van Gogh and his Art', in Vincent van Gogh, *The Letters of a Post-Impressionist: Being the Familiar Correspondence of Vincent Van Gogh*, Boston/New York 1913, pp. v–xlvi

Luijten 2022
Hans Luijten, *Jo van Gogh-Bonger: The Woman Who Made Van Gogh Famous*, trans. Lynne Richards, London 2022

Madeline and Bouiller 2015
Laurence Madeline and Jean-Roch Bouiller (eds.), *J'aime les panoramas. S'approprier le monde*, exh. cat., Geneva (Musée Rath), Marseilles (MuCEM) 2015–16

Maes and Van Tilborgh 2012
Bert Maes and Louis van Tilborgh, 'Van Gogh's *Tree Roots* Up Close', in Van Tilborgh 2012, pp. 55–71

Malraux 1952
André Malraux, *Van Gogh et les peintres d'Auvers chez le docteur Gachet*, Paris 1952

Mascart 1892
Eleuthère Mascart, *Annales du Bureau central météorologique de France, année 1890*, Paris 1892

Masheck 1996
Joseph D. Masheck (ed.), *Van Gogh 100*, Westport 1996

Mataigne 1885
Henri Mataigne, *Notes historiques et géographiques sur Auvers-sur-Oise*, Pontoise 1885

Mataigne 1901
Henri Mataigne, *Histoire de la commune d'Auvers-sur-Oise depuis les origines jusqu'à nos jours*, Pontoise 1901

Mathey 1956
François Mathey, *Van Gogh: Auvers-sur-Oise*, New York 1956

McWilliam 2012
Neil McWilliam (ed.), *Emile Bernard. Les lettres d'un artiste (1884–1941)*, Dijon 2012

Meedendorp 2003a
Teio Meedendorp, 'Paintings from the Aurier Collection', in Ten Berge et al. 2003, pp. 406–10

Meedendorp 2003b
Teio Meedendorp, 'The Schuffenecker Brothers and the Prince of Wagram', in Ten Berge et al. 2003, pp. 411–19

Meedendorp 2021
Teio Meedendorp, 'Study for *Worn Out*: A Newly Discovered Van Gogh Drawing', *The Burlington Magazine* 163 (October 2021), no. 1423, pp. 916–23

De Meester 1890
Johan de Meester, 'Vincent van Gogh', *Algemeen Handelsblad*, 31 December 1890

De Meester 1891
Johan de Meester, 'Vincent van Gogh', *Nederland* (March 1891), no. 1, pp. 312–19

Meier-Graefe 1904
Julius Meier-Graefe, *Entwicklungsgeschichte der modernen Kunst. Vergleichende Betrachtung der bildenden Künste, als Beitrag zu einer neuen Aesthetik*, 3 vols., Stuttgart 1904

Merchant 1983
Carolyn Merchant, *The Death of Nature: Women, Ecology, and the Scientific Revolution*, San Francisco 1983

Millon 1990
Claude Millon, *Vincent van Gogh et Auvers-sur-Oise*, Pontoise 1990

Millon 2002
Claude Millon, *Vincent van Gogh in Auvers*, Paris 2002

Milner 1988
John Milner, *The Studios of Paris: The Capital of Art in the Late Nineteenth Century*, New Haven/London 1988

Mirbeau 1891
Octave Mirbeau, 'Vincent van Gogh', *L'Echo de Paris* (31 March 1891), no. 2507, p. 1

Montaigne 2010
Jean-Marc Montaigne, *Eugène Murer, un ami oublié des impressionnistes. Paris, Auvers-sur-Oise, Rouen*, Rouen 2010

Moon and Taws 2021
Iris Moon and Richard Taws (eds.), *Time, Media, and Visuality in Post-Revolutionary France*, London 2021

Mothe 1987
Alain Mothe, *Vincent van Gogh à Auvers-sur-Oise*, Paris 1987

Mothe 2003
Alain Mothe, *Vincent van Gogh à Auvers*, Paris 2003

Naifeh and Smith 2011
Steven Naifeh and Gregory White Smith, *Vincent van Gogh: The Life*, London 2011

Naifeh and Smith 2014
Steven Naifeh and Gregory White Smith, 'NCIS: Provence: The Van Gogh Mystery', *Vanity Fair*, December 2014 (https://www.vanityfair.com/culture/2014/12/vincent-van-gogh-murder-mystery)

Natanson 1895
Thadée Natanson, 'Jean Carriès, Vincent van Gogh', *La Revue blanche* (15 June 1895), pp. 572–73

Nickell 2012
Joe Nickell, 'The "Murder" of Vincent van Gogh', *Skeptical Inquirer* 36 (September–October 2012), no. 5, pp. 14–17

Nickell 2014a
Joe Nickell, 'Van Gogh "Murdered"– Again', *Center for Inquiry*, 25 November 2014 (https://centerforinquiry.org/blog/van_gogh_murderedagain/)

Nickell 2014b
Joe Nickell, 'Van Gogh Still Being Murdered', *Center for Inquiry*, 2 December 2014 (https://nickell56.rssing.com/chan-13844733/article85-live.html)

Nolen et al. 2020
Willem A. Nolen, Erwin van Meekeren, Piet Voskuil and Willem van Tilburg, 'New Vision on the Mental Problems of Vincent van Gogh. Results from a Bottom-up Approach Using (Semi-)structured Diagnostic Interviews', *International Journal of Bipolar Disorders* 8 (2020), no. 30 (https://journalbipolardisorders.springeropen.com/articles/10.1186/s40345-020-00196-z)

Obst 2010
Andreas Obst, *Records and Deliberations about Vincent van Gogh's First Grave in Auvers-sur-Oise*, Lauenau 2010

O'Connor and Portzky 2018
Rory C. O'Connor and Gwendolyn Portzky, 'The Relationship between Entrapment and Suicidal Behavior through the Lens of the Integrated Motivational-Volitional Model of Suicidal Behavior', *Current Opinion in Psychology* (2018), no. 22, pp. 12–17

Olson and Doescher 2001
Donald W. Olson and Russell L. Doescher, 'Identifying the "Star" in a Long-Lost Van Gogh', *Sky & Telescope* 101 (April 2001), no. 4, pp. 34–39

Outhwaite 1969
David Outhwaite, *Vincent van Gogh at Auvers-sur-Oise*, Master's thesis, Courtauld Institute of Art, University of London 1969

Panofsky 1970
Erwin Panofsky, '*Et in Arcadia Ego*: Poussin and the Elegiac Tradition', in ibid., *Meaning in the Visual Arts*, Harmondsworth 1970, pp. 295–320

Paris 1891
7e exposition de la Société des artistes indépendants, exh. cat., Paris (Pavillon de la Ville de Paris) 1891

Pickvance 1984
Ronald Pickvance, *Van Gogh in Arles*, exh. cat., New York (Metropolitan Museum of Art) 1984

Pickvance 1986
Ronald Pickvance, *Van Gogh in Saint-Rémy and Auvers*, exh. cat., New York (Metropolitan Museum of Art) 1986–87

Pickvance 1992
Ronald Pickvance, *'A Great Artist is Dead': Letters of Condolence on Vincent Van Gogh's Death*, ed. Sjraar van Heugten and Fieke Pabst, Zwolle 1992

Pickvance 2000
Ronald Pickvance, *Van Gogh*, exh. cat., Martigny (Fondation Pierre-Gianadda) 2000

Prins 2016
Laura Prins, 'Van Gogh's Physical and Mental Health: A Chronology', in Bakker, Van Tilborgh and Prins 2016, pp. 89–118

Raffaëlli 1888
Jean-François Raffaëlli, 'Caractère des lignes', *La Revue indépendante* 6 (February 1888), no. 16, pp. 175–81

Rathbone and Robinson 2013
Eliza E. Rathbone and William H. Robinson (eds.), *Van Gogh's Repetitions*, exh. cat., Washington (Philips Collection), Cleveland (The Cleveland Museum of Art) 2013–14

Ravoux 1953
Interview with Adeline Carrié (née Ravoux) and Germaine Guilloux (née Ravoux) by Georges Charensol, broadcast on 2 April 1953 on the show 'L'art et la vie', Institut National de l'Audiovisuel (INA), published in Van der Veen 2020, pp. 113–22

Ravoux 1957
Adeline Ravoux [interview by Louis Anfray], 'Souvenirs sur le séjour de Vincent van Gogh à Auvers-sur-Oise', *Les Cahiers de Van Gogh* 1 (1957), pp. 7–17

Reiley Burt 1975
Marianne Reiley Burt, 'Le pâtissier Murer: un ami des impressionnistes', *L'Œil: Revue d'art* (December 1975), no. 245, pp. 54–61, 92

Rewald 1952
John Rewald, 'Gachet's Unknown Gems Emerge', *Art News* 51 (March 1952), no. 1, pp. 10–13

Rohan 2012
Alain Rohan, *Vincent van Gogh. Aurait-on retrouvé l'arme du suicide?*, Paris 2012

Roskill 1966
Mark Roskill, 'Van Gogh's 'Blue Cart' and His Creative Process', *Oud Holland* 81 (1966), no. 1, pp. 3–19

Roskill 1990
Mark Wentworth Roskill, 'Van Gogh at Auvers: The Majesty of Nature', in Masheck 1996, pp. 322–34

Van Ryssel, Bazin and Chatelet 1954
L. van Ryssel [Paul Gachet Jr], Germain Bazin and Albert Chatelet, *Van Gogh et les peintres d'Auvers-sur-Oise*, exh. cat., Paris (Orangerie des Tuileries) 1954–55

Saltzman 1999
Cynthia Saltzman, *'Portrait of Dr. Gachet': The Story of a Van Gogh Masterpiece: Modernism, Money, Politics, Collectors, Dealers, Taste, Greed, and Loss*, New York 1999

Schapiro 1978
Meyer Schapiro, 'On a Painting of Van Gogh', in ibid., *Modern Art: 19th and 20th Centuries. Selected Papers*, New York 1978, pp. 87–99 (originally published in *View* 1 (Fall 1946), pp. 8–13)

Schröder et al. 2008
Klaus Albrecht Schröder, Heinz Widauer, Sjraar van Heugten and Marije Vellekoop (eds.), *Van Gogh: Heartfelt Lines*, exh. cat., Vienna (Albertina) 2008

Sensier 1873
Alfred Sensier, *Etude sur Georges Michel*, Paris 1873

Serres 2022
Karen Serres (ed.), *Van Gogh Self-Portraits*, exh. cat., London (Courtauld Gallery) 2022

Soda 2017
Megumi Soda, 'Exposition de la gravure japonaise, 1890: The Complete List of Identified Works with Full Illustrations and Notes', *Journal of Japonisme* 2 (January 2017), no. 1, pp. 1–56 (https://brill.figshare.com/articles/journal_contribution/Exposition_de_la_gravure_japonaise_1890_-_The_complete_list/4509251/2)

Solana 2007
Guillermo Solana, *Van Gogh. Los últimos paisajes : Auvers-sur-Oise, 20 de mayo – 29 de julio 1890*, exh. cat., Madrid (Museo Thyssen-Bornemisza) 2007

Standring and Van Tilborgh 2012
Timothy Standring and Louis van Tilborgh (eds.), *Becoming Van Gogh*, exh. cat., Denver (Denver Art Museum) 2012

Stein 1986
Susan Alyson Stein (ed.), *Van Gogh: A Retrospective*, New York 1986

Stein 1999
Susan Alyson Stein, 'Summary Catalogue of Works by Major Artists', in Distel and Stein 1999, pp. 185–241

Stein and Miller 2009
Susan Alyson Stein and Asher Ethan Miller (eds.), *The Annenberg Collection: Masterpieces of Impressionism and Post-Impressionism*, New Haven/London 2009

Stolwijk and Veenenbos 2002
Chris Stolwijk and Han Veenenbos, *The Account Book of Theo van Gogh and Jo van Gogh-Bonger*, Amsterdam/Leiden 2002

Sund 1988
Judy Sund, 'The Sower and the Sheaf: Biblical Metaphor in the Art of Vincent van Gogh', *The Art Bulletin* 70 (December 1988), no. 4, pp. 660–76

Sund 2000
Judy Sund, 'Famine to Feast: Portrait Making at St.-Remy and Auvers', in Dorn et al. 2000, pp. 182–227

Supinen 1995
Marja Supinen, 'Vincent van Gogh, *Street in Auvers-sur-Oise*: An Acquisition for the Antell Collection, 1903', *Ateneum: The Finnish National Gallery Bulletin* (1995), pp. 32–41

Takashina, Pickvance and Arikawa 1988
Shūji Takashina, Ronald Pickvance and Haruo Arikawa (eds.), *Vincent van Gogh. International Symposium Tokyo, 17–19 October 1985*, Tokyo 1988

Taws 2021
Richard Taws, 'A Storm is Coming: Georges Michel in the Wind', in Moon and Taws 2021, pp. 221–46

Van Tilborgh 2012
Louis van Tilborgh (ed.), *Van Gogh: New Findings* (Van Gogh Studies 4), Zwolle/Amsterdam 2012

Van Tilborgh 2018
Louis van Tilborgh, 'In the Light of Japan: Van Gogh's Quest for Happiness and a Modern Identity', in Van Tilborgh and Bakker 2018, pp. 41–91

Van Tilborgh 2021a
Louis van Tilborgh, 'Van Gogh, Gauguin, and Rembrandt: On Chairs, Portraits and Poetry', *Simiolus. Netherlands Quarterly for the History of Art* 43 (2021), no. 4, pp. 331–52

Van Tilborgh 2021b
Louis van Tilborgh, 'Van Gogh, Olive Trees, and His Search for What Turned Out to Be a Modern Pastoral', in Bakker and Myers 2021, pp. 49–59

Van Tilborgh 2022
Louis van Tilborgh, 'Van Gogh's Self-Portraits: Reaching for the Infinite', in Serres 2022, pp. 37–61

Van Tilborgh and Bakker 2018
Louis van Tilborgh and Nienke Bakker (eds.), *Van Gogh & Japan*, exh. cat., Sapporo (Hokkaidō Museum of Modern Art), Tokyo (Tokyo Metropolitan Art Museum), Kyoto (The National Museum of Modern Art), Amsterdam (Van Gogh Museum) 2018

Van Tilborgh and Van Maanen 2015
Louis van Tilborgh and Oda van Maanen, 'Dominant Blues and Disappearing Violets: Van Gogh's *View of Auvers-sur-Oise* Revisited', *RISD Manual: A Journal about Art and its Making* (Spring 2015), no. 4, pp. 23–34

Van Tilborgh and Meedendorp 2013
Louis van Tilborgh and Teio Meedendorp, 'The Life and Death of Vincent van Gogh', *The Burlington Magazine* 155 (July 2013), no. 1324, pp. 456–62

Van Tilborgh, Meedendorp and Pilz 2020
Louis van Tilborgh, Teio Meedendorp and Kathrin Pilz, 'Van Gogh as Mentally Ill: His Contested Oslo Self-Portrait', *The Burlington Magazine* 162 (February 2020), no. 1403, pp. 88–101

Van Tilborgh and Van Uitert 2012
Louis van Tilborgh and Evert van Uitert, 'In Search of his Own Voice', in Standring and Van Tilborgh 2012, pp. 15–43

Townsend and Freemantle 2023
Joyce H. Townsend and Rosie Freemantle, 'Three Works on Paper by Vincent Van Gogh: Technical Study, Display Considerations and a Conjectural Colour Reconstruction', *Journal of the Institute for Conservation* 46 (2023), no. 1, pp. 3–22

Tralbaut 1969
Marc Edo Tralbaut, *Van Gogh*, New York 1969

Trublot 1887
Trublot [Paul Alexis], 'Auvers-sur-Oise', *Le Cri du peuple*, 15 August 1887

Uhlenbeck 2018
Chris Uhlenbeck, 'Van Gogh's Japanese Prints: From Dealer's Stock to Artist's Collection', in Van Tilborgh and Bakker 2018, pp. 147–60

Van Uitert, Van Tilborgh and Van Heugten 1990
Evert van Uitert, Louis van Tilborgh and Sjraar van Heugten, *Vincent van Gogh. Schilderijen*, exh. cat., Amsterdam (Van Gogh Museum) 1990

Van der Veen 2020
Wouter van der Veen, *Attacked at the Very Root: An Investigation into Van Gogh's Last Days*, Strasbourg 2020 (https://arthenon.com/wp-content/uploads/2021/07/20210715_Racinesebook-en_01.pdf)

Van der Veen and Knapp 2010
Wouter van der Veen and Peter Knapp, *Van Gogh in Auvers: His Last Days*, New York 2010

Vellekoop et al.
Marije Vellekoop, Muriel Geldof, Ella Hendriks, Leo Jansen and Alberto de Tagle (eds.), *Van Gogh's Studio Practice*, Amsterdam/Brussels 2013

Vellekoop and Suijver 2013
Marije Vellekoop and Renske Suijver, *Vincent van Gogh: The Sketchbooks*, Amsterdam/London 2013

Vellekoop and Zwikker 2007
Marije Vellekoop and Roelie Zwikker, *Vincent van Gogh. Drawings: Volume 4. Arles, Saint-Rémy & Auvers-sur-Oise 1888–1890. Van Gogh Museum*, 2 vols., Zwolle/Amsterdam 2007

Verweij 2022
Emma Verweij, *De Zon Aanbiddende Landbouwers. Vincent van Gogh en zijn perceptie van het Oude Egypte*, tutorial paper, Department of Art History, University of Amsterdam, 2022

De Vries 1927
R.W.P. de Vries Jr, 'M.W. van der Valk', *Elseviers Magazijn* 74 (1927), no. 12, pp. 369–75

Wadley 1991
Nicholas Wadley, *Impressionist and Post-Impressionist Drawing*, London 1991

Walford 1991
E. John Walford, *Jacob van Ruisdael and the Perception of Landscape*, New Haven/London 1991

Wattenmaker 1981
Richard Wattenmaker, 'Vincent van Gogh et Puvis de Chavannes', *Vie des arts*, 26 (Autumn 1981), no. 104, pp. 62–97

Wickenden s.a.
Alfred Ahier Wickenden, *Castle in Bohemia: Memoirs of Robert John Wickenden, Artist, of his Wife Ada Louise Ahier, and their Family, to 1900*, s.a. (https://www.thomas-r-wickenden-families.com/wickendens-around-the-world/usa-france-robert-john-wickenden-brother-of-thomas-rogers-wickenden-and-james-william-wickenden)

Williams 2001
Mark Williams, *Suicide and Attempted Suicide: Understanding the Cry of Pain*, London 2001

Wilson and Young 1995
Carol Wilson and Catherine Young, 'Deux tableaux de Vincent van Gogh identifies à Auvers sur Oise', *Vivre en Val-d'Oise* (November 1995), no. 34, pp. 62–65

Van der Wolk 1986
Johannes van der Wolk, *The Seven Sketchbooks of Vincent van Gogh*, trans. Claudia Swan, New York/Amsterdam 1986

Van der Wolk, Pickvance and Pey 1990
Johannes van der Wolk, Ronald Pickvance and E.B.F. Pey, *Vincent van Gogh. Drawings*, exh. cat., Otterlo (Kröller-Müller Museum) 1990

Zeldin 1979
Theodore Zeldin, *France 1848–1945: Ambition and Love*, Oxford 1979

Zemel 1980
Carol M. Zemel, *The Formation of a Legend: Van Gogh Criticism 1890–1920*, Ann Arbor 1980

Zemel 1997
Carol Zemel, *Van Gogh's Progress: Utopia, Modernity, and Late-Nineteenth-Century Art*, Berkeley, CA 1997

Zimmer 2009
Nina Zimmer, 'Serial Van Gogh: Cycles, Groups, Triptychs', in Zimmer and Werthemann 2009, pp. 96–117

Zimmer and Werthemann 2009
Nina Zimmer and Seraina Werthemann (eds.), *Vincent van Gogh: Between Earth and Heaven. The Landscapes*, exh. cat., Basel (Kunstmuseum Basel) 2009

LIST OF EXHIBITED WORKS

[A]: Amsterdam only
[P]: Paris only

PAINTINGS BY VINCENT VAN GOGH

Self-Portrait, 1889
Oil on canvas, 65 × 54 cm
Musée d'Orsay, Paris
[158]

Pietà (after Delacroix), 1889
Oil on canvas, 73 × 60.5 cm
Van Gogh Museum, Amsterdam
[161]

The Man is at Sea (after Demont-Breton), 1889
Oil on canvas, 66 × 51 cm
Private collection, Larry Ellison
[A] [162]

The Garden at the Asylum, 1889
Oil on canvas, 72 × 91 cm
Van Gogh Museum, Amsterdam
[A] [160]

Blossoming Chestnut Trees, 1890
Oil on canvas, 63.3 × 49.8 cm
Kröller-Müller Museum, Otterlo
[58]

The House of Père Pilon, 1890
Oil on canvas, 49 × 70 cm
Private collection
[61]

Blossoming Chestnut Branches, 1890
Oil on canvas, 73 × 92 cm
Emile Bührle Collection, on long-term loan to Kunsthaus Zürich
[A] [71]

Stairway at Auvers-sur-Oise, 1890
Oil on canvas, 50 × 70.5 cm
Saint Louis Art Museum, purchased 1935
[5]

Doctor Gachet's Garden, 1890
Oil on canvas, 73 × 52 cm
Musée d'Orsay, Paris
[34]

View of Auvers-sur-Oise, 1890
Oil on canvas, 34 × 42.1 cm
Museum of Art, Rhode Island School of Design, Providence, given in memory of Miss Dorothy Sturges by a friend, 35.770
[52]

Field near Auvers-sur-Oise, 1890
Oil on canvas, 44 × 51.5 cm
Musée d'art et d'histoire, Geneva, former loan of the Fondation Garengo, 1990
[53]

View of Auvers-sur-Oise, 1890
Oil on canvas, 50.2 × 52.5 cm
Van Gogh Museum, Amsterdam
[50]

Farmhouse, 1890
Oil on canvas, 38.9 × 46.4 cm
Van Gogh Museum, Amsterdam
[43]

Thatched Cottages in Cordeville, Auvers-sur-Oise, 1890
Oil on canvas, 73 × 92 cm
Musée d'Orsay, Paris
[41]

Farmhouses in Auvers-sur-Oise, 1890
Oil on canvas, 73.5 × 92.5 cm
Finnish National Gallery, Ateneum Art Museum, Helsinki, Antell Collections
[46]

Marguerite Gachet in the Garden, 1890
Oil on canvas, 46 × 55.5 cm
Musée d'Orsay, Paris
[35]

Roses and Turban Buttercups, 1890
Oil on canvas, 51.7 × 52 cm
Musée d'Orsay, Paris
[77]

Vase of Flowers, 1890
Oil on canvas, 42.2 × 29 cm
Van Gogh Museum, Amsterdam
[76]

The Church at Auvers-sur-Oise, 1890
Oil on canvas, 93 × 74.5 cm
Musée d'Orsay, Paris
[1]

Doctor Paul Gachet, 1890
Oil on canvas, 68.2 × 57 cm
Musée d'Orsay, Paris
[112]

Blossoming Acacia, 1890
Oil on canvas, 33 × 24 cm
Nationalmuseum, Stockholm
[83]

Glass with Carnations, 1890
Oil on canvas, 41 × 32 cm
Private collection
[69]

Houses at Auvers-sur-Oise, 1890
Oil on canvas, 75.6 × 61.9 cm
Museum of Fine Arts, Boston, bequest of John T. Spaulding
[4]

Houses at Auvers-sur-Oise, 1890
Oil on canvas, 60 × 73 cm
Toledo Museum of Art, purchased with funds from the Libbey Endowment, Gift of Edward Drummond Libbey, 1935.5
[40]

House at Auvers-sur-Oise, 1890
Oil on canvas, 48.6 × 62.9 cm
The Phillips Collection, Washington, acquired 1952
[54]

Vineyards at Auvers-sur-Oise, 1890
Oil on canvas, 65.1 × 80.3 cm
Saint Louis Art Museum, Funds given by Mrs. Mark C. Steinberg
[55]

Poppy Field, 1890
Oil on canvas, 73 × 91.5 cm
Kunstmuseum Den Haag, long-term loan Cultural Heritage Agency of the Netherlands
[13]

Wheatfield with Cornflowers, 1890
Oil on canvas, 60 × 81 cm
Fondation Beyeler, Riehen/Basel, Beyeler Collection
[144]

Vase with Red Poppies, Cornflowers and Daisies, 1890
Oil on *torchon*, 65 × 50 cm
Private collection
[81]

Cows (after Gachet, after Jordaens), 1890
Oil on canvas, 55 × 65 cm
Palais des Beaux-Arts, Lille
[7]

Daubigny's Garden, 1890
Oil on *torchon*, 51 × 51.2 cm
Van Gogh Museum, Amsterdam
[A] [141]

Ears of Wheat, 1890
Oil on *torchon*, 64 × 48 cm
Van Gogh Museum, Amsterdam
[123]

Garden in Auvers-sur-Oise, 1890
Oil on canvas, 64 × 80 cm
Private collection
[142]

Bank of the Oise at Auvers, 1890
Oil on canvas, 71.1 × 93.7 cm
Detroit Institute of Arts, bequest of Robert H. Tannahill
[57]

Landscape at Twilight, 1890
Oil on canvas, 50.2 × 101 cm
Van Gogh Museum, Amsterdam
[138]

Undergrowth with Two Figures, 1890
Oil on canvas, 49.5 × 99.7 cm
Cincinnati Art Museum, bequest of Mary E. Johnston, 1967.1430
[156]

Fields near Auvers-sur-Oise, 1890
Oil on canvas, 50 × 101 cm
Belvedere Museum, Vienna
[135]

Adeline Ravoux, 1890
Oil on canvas, 67 × 55 cm
Private collection – courtesy of HomeArt
[119]

Adeline Ravoux, 1890
Oil on canvas, 50.2 × 50.5 cm
The Cleveland Museum of Art, bequest of Leonard C. Hanna, Jr. 1958
[120]

Portrait of a Young Woman, 1890
Oil on canvas, 51 × 49.5 cm
Kröller-Müller Museum, Otterlo
[121]

Women Crossing the Fields, 1890
Oil on paper, 30.3 × 59.7 cm
McNay Art Museum, San Antonio, bequest of Marion Koogler McNay, 1950.49
[127]

Two Girls, 1890
Oil on canvas, 51.2 × 51 cm
Musée d'Orsay, Paris
[134]

Wheatfield with Crows, 1890
Oil on canvas, 50.5 × 103 cm
Van Gogh Museum, Amsterdam
[137]

Wheatfield under Thunderclouds, 1890
Oil on canvas, 50.4 × 101.3 cm
Van Gogh Museum, Amsterdam
[136]

Daubigny's Garden, 1890
Oil on canvas, 56 × 101.5 cm
Rudolf Staechelin Collection
[139]

The Fields, 1890
Oil on canvas, 50 × 65 cm
Private collection
[P] [17]

Field with Haystacks, 1890
Oil on canvas, 50 × 100 cm
Fondation Beyeler, Riehen/Basel, Beyeler Collection
[143]

Wheatfields with Reaper, Auvers-sur-Oise, 1890
Oil on canvas, 73.6 × 93 cm
Toledo Museum of Art, purchased with funds from the Libbey Endowment, Gift of Edward Drummond Libbey, 1935.4
[14]

Sheaves of Wheat, 1890
Oil on canvas, 50.8 × 101.6 cm
Dallas Museum of Art, The Wendy and Emery Reves Collection, 1985.R.80
[P] [146]

Rain – Auvers-sur-Oise, 1890
Oil on canvas, 50.3 × 100.2 cm
Amgueddfa Cymru – National Museum Wales, Cardiff, bequeathed by Gwendoline Davies, 1951
[145]

Farms near Auvers-sur-Oise, 1890
Oil on canvas, 50.2 × 100.3 cm
Tate, London, bequeathed by C. Frank Stoop, 1933
[147]

Tree Roots, 1890
Oil on canvas, 50.3 × 100.1 cm
Van Gogh Museum, Amsterdam
[157]

WORKS ON PAPER BY VINCENT VAN GOGH

Old Vineyard with Peasant Woman, 1890
Pencil, brush and oil paint and watercolour, on laid paper, 44.3 × 54 cm
Van Gogh Museum, Amsterdam
[A] [85]

Landscape with Houses (recto) and *Blossoming Chestnut Trees by a House* (verso), 1890
Pencil, brush and oil paint and watercolour, on laid paper, 44 × 54.4 cm
Van Gogh Museum, Amsterdam
[P] [32]

Dead-End Street with Houses, 1890
Pencil, pen and ink, on laid paper, 45 × 55.6 cm
Van Gogh Museum, Amsterdam
[60]

Village Street, 1890
Pencil on laid paper, 44.5 × 27.5 cm
Van Gogh Museum, Amsterdam
[90]

Glass, Pewter Jug, Arum Lily and other Sketches, 1890
Pencil on laid paper, 44.5 × 27.4 cm
The Levett Collection
[88]

Sitting and Standing Male Nude (after Bargue, Cours de dessin, vol. III, plates 1 and 5), 1890
Pencil on laid paper, 44.6 × 54.6 cm
Van Gogh Museum, Amsterdam
[A] [89]

Standing Male Nude and *Sitting Figure (after Bargue, Cours de dessin, vol. III, plates 1 and 2)* (recto) and *Interior with Tables and Chairs, and a Sketch of 'The Bedroom'* (verso), 1890
Pencil on paper, 44.3 × 27.3 cm
Van Gogh Museum, Amsterdam
[P]

Portrait of Doctor Paul Gachet, 1890
Etching on paper, 31.6 × 23.4 cm (sheet), 18.3 × 15.1 cm (image)
Van Gogh Museum, Amsterdam
[169]

Portrait of Doctor Paul Gachet, 1890
Colour etching on paper, 30.7 × 23.6 cm (sheet), 18.3 × 15.1 cm (image)
Van Gogh Museum, Amsterdam
[116]

Portrait of Doctor Paul Gachet, 1890
Lithograph, 54.2 × 41.8 cm (sheet), 18.1 × 15.1 cm (image)
Bibliothèque Nationale de France, Département des Estampes et de la Photographie, Paris
[P]

Horse and Carriage, 1890
Pencil on laid paper, 26.9 × 43.7 cm
Van Gogh Museum, Amsterdam
[A]

Marguerite Gachet at the Piano (recto) and *Study of a Tree* (verso), 1890
Chalk on laid paper, 30.5 × 23.8 cm
Van Gogh Museum, Amsterdam
[128]

Egyptian Head and *Figure Study* (recto) and *Stooping Man* (verso), 1890
Chalk on blue-grey laid paper, 31.4 × 23.9 cm
Van Gogh Museum, Amsterdam
[A] [106]

Egyptian Head (recto) and *Peasant with a Scythe* (verso), 1890
Chalk on blue-grey laid paper, 31.4 × 23.8 cm
Van Gogh Museum, Amsterdam
[P] [107]

Auvers Town Hall and Head of a Man (recto) and *Landscapes with Houses* (verso), 1890
Chalk on laid paper, 48.4 × 31.2 cm
Van Gogh Museum, Amsterdam
[A] [65]

Sketches of Horse with Covered Wagon and Baby in a Pram (recto) and *Sketch of Women Working* (verso), 1890
Pencil on pink laid paper, 21.3 × 47.3 cm
Van Gogh Museum, Amsterdam
[A] [98]

Sketches of Animals and Children (recto) and *Sketches of Women Doing the Washing* (verso), 1890
Pencil on pink laid paper, 20.8 × 47.3 cm
Van Gogh Museum, Amsterdam
[P]

Peasant Woman Working the Land (recto) and *Two Peasant Women in a Field* (verso), 1890
Chalk on pink laid paper, 30.5 × 23.9 cm
Van Gogh Museum, Amsterdam

Landscape with Peasants Reaping (recto) and *Landscape with Peasant Women Harvesting* (verso), 1890
Chalk on laid paper, 23.8 × 31.2 cm
Van Gogh Museum, Amsterdam
[P]

Sketchbook Paris-Auvers-sur-Oise, 1890
142 pages, 84 of which contain sketches, notes, smudges or rub-offs, 13.5 × 8.5 cm Van Gogh Museum, Amsterdam
[100]

Woman in Striped Skirt (recto) and *Woman Seen from the Back* (verso), from sketchbook Paris-Auvers-sur-Oise, 1890
Pencil on paper, 12.5 × 8 cm
Musée d'Orsay, Paris

Rear of a Horse (recto) and *Boy with Hat* (verso), from sketchbook Paris-Auvers-sur-Oise, 1890
Pencil on paper, 12 × 8.7 cm
Musée d'Orsay, Paris

Couple with Child, from sketchbook Paris-Auvers-sur-Oise, 1890
Chalk on paper, 13.2 × 8.4 cm
Musée d'Orsay, Paris
[95]

Sitting Woman with Child, from sketchbook Paris-Auvers-sur-Oise, 1890
Chalk on paper, 13.2 × 8.3 cm
Musée d'Orsay, Paris
[94]

Père Eloi's Farm, 1890
Pencil, reed pen and brush in ink, on faded pink laid paper, 48 × 61.7 cm
Musée d'Orsay, Paris
[101]

The Oise at Auvers, 1890
Pencil, pen and ink, watercolour and oil paint, on pink laid paper, 47.3 × 62.9 cm
Tate, London, bequeathed by C. Frank Stoop, 1933
[105]

Cottages with a Woman Working in the Middle Ground, 1890
Black and white chalk, blue pastel, reed pen and brush in ink, on faded blue-grey laid paper, 47 × 62.5 cm
The Art Institute of Chicago, Bequest of Kate L. Brewster
[102]

Field with Sheaves of Wheat, 1890
Black chalk and brush in ink, on blue-grey laid paper, 47.5 × 62.8 cm
Van Gogh Museum, Amsterdam
[P] [111]

WORKS ON PAPER BY OTHER ARTISTS

Emile Bernard
Poster for 'Exposition de 16 toiles par Van Gogh', 1892
Lithograph, 40.2 × 31 cm
Bibliothèque Nationale de France, Département des Estampes et de la Photographie, Paris
[P]

Blanche Derousse, after Vincent van Gogh
Portrait of Mlle Gachet at the Piano, 1901
Watercolour, 22 × 11 cm
Musée d'Orsay, Paris
[P]

Blanche Derousse, after Vincent van Gogh
The Church at Auvers-sur-Oise, 1901
Watercolour, 28 × 22 cm
Musée d'Orsay, Paris
[P]

Paul van Ryssel (Paul Ferdinand Gachet)
Woman in a Straitjacket and Cap, in sketchbook 'Croquis de folles (Salpêtrière)', 1854
Sketchbook with 25 pages, 35.1 × 26.3 cm
Musée d'art et d'histoire de l'hôpital Saint-Anne, Paris
[P]

Paul van Ryssel (Paul Ferdinand Gachet)
Stooping Woman Seen from Behind, in sketchbook 'Croquis de folles (Salpêtrière)', 1854
Sketchbook with 25 pages, 35.1 × 26.3 cm
Musée d'art et d'histoire de l'hôpital Saint-Anne, Paris
[P]

Paul van Ryssel (Paul Ferdinand Gachet)
Cows, after Jordaens, in *Recueil. Œuvre. Tome 1*, 1873
Etchings, 13.9 × 18 cm
Bibliothèque Nationale de France, Département des Estampes et de la Photographie, Paris
[P]

Paul van Ryssel (Paul Ferdinand Gachet)
Mme Gachet at the Piano, first state (worked up with watercolour), in *Recueil. Œuvre. Tome 1*, 1873
Etching, 18.1 × 14.6 cm
Bibliothèque Nationale de France, Département des Estampes et de la Photographie, Paris
[P]

Paul van Ryssel (Paul Ferdinand Gachet)
Sunken Lane in Auvers (The Hanged Man's House), in *Recueil. Œuvre. Tome 1*, 1873
Etching, 50 × 35 cm (folio)
Bibliothèque Nationale de France, Département des Estampes et de la Photographie, Paris
[P]

Paul van Ryssel (Paul Ferdinand Gachet)
Cows (after Jordaens), 1873
Etching and roulette on paper, 22.5 × 27.7 cm
Van Gogh Museum, Amsterdam
[A] [8]

Paul van Ryssel (Paul Ferdinand Gachet)
Swallow, in *Recueil. Œuvre. Tome 1*, 1886
Lithograph, 11.1 × 13 cm
Bibliothèque Nationale de France, Département des Estampes et de la Photographie, Paris
[P]

Paul van Ryssel (Paul Ferdinand Gachet)
Vincent van Gogh on his Deathbed, 1890
Charcoal on paper, 27.2 × 22.7 cm
Van Gogh Museum, Amsterdam
[A] [177]

Paul van Ryssel (Paul Ferdinand Gachet)
Vincent van Gogh on his Deathbed, 1890
Charcoal on paper, 48 × 41 cm
Musée d'Orsay, Paris
[178]

Paul van Ryssel
(Paul Ferdinand Gachet)
Vincent van Gogh on his Deathbed, first state, ninth state, in *Recueil. Œuvre. Tome 2*, 1890

Lithograph, 50 × 35 cm (folio)
Bibliothèque nationale de France, Département des Estampes et de la Photographie, Paris
[P]

Paul van Ryssel
(Paul Ferdinand Gachet)
Monticelli pictor. 1824–1888, in *Recueil. Œuvre. Tome 2*, 1892

Etching, 18.8 × 15.2 cm
Bibliothèque Nationale de France, Département des Estampes et de la Photographie, Paris
[P]

Paul van Ryssel
(Paul Ferdinand Gachet)
Collapsed House (Auvers-sur-Oise), in *Recueil. Œuvre. Tome 2*, 1894

Etchings, 12.5 × 17.2 cm and 12.2 × 17.3 cm
Bibliothèque Nationale de France, Département des Estampes et de la Photographie, Paris
[P]

LETTERS AND DOCUMENTS

Letter from Vincent van Gogh to Theo van Gogh with sketch of *Portrait of Doctor Gachet*, 3 June 1890

Van Gogh Museum, Amsterdam
[P] [114]

Letter from Vincent van Gogh to Willemien van Gogh with sketch of *Arlésienne* and Puvis de Chavannes's *Inter artes et naturam*, 5 June 1890

Van Gogh Museum, Amsterdam
[P] [155]

Letter from Vincent van Gogh to Theo van Gogh and Jo van Gogh-Bonger with sketches of *Country Girl with Straw Hat*, *Undergrowth with Two Figures* and *Fields near Auvers-sur-Oise*, 2 July 1890

Van Gogh Museum, Amsterdam
[A] [124]

Letter from Vincent van Gogh to Theo van Gogh with sketches of *Daubigny's Garden*, *Wheatfields* and *Cottages in Chaponval*, 23 July 1890

Pen and ink on paper, 17 × 21.7 cm
Van Gogh Museum, Amsterdam
[A] [18]

Letter from Paul Ferdinand Gachet to Theo van Gogh, 27 July 1890, and envelope

Van Gogh Museum, Amsterdam

Mourning card, invitation to the funeral of Vincent van Gogh, 1890

Van Gogh Museum, Amsterdam
[176]

Mourning card for Vincent van Gogh, 1890

Van Gogh Museum, Amsterdam
[191]

Register with Vincent van Gogh's death certificate of 29 July 1890

Archives départementales du Val-d'Oise, Pontoise

Letter from Eugène Carrière to Theo van Gogh, 30 July 1890

Van Gogh Museum, Amsterdam
[P]

Letter from Camille Pissarro to Theo van Gogh, 30 July 1890

Van Gogh Museum, Amsterdam
[P]

Letter from Félix Fénéon to Theo van Gogh, 31 July 1890

Van Gogh Museum, Amsterdam
[P]

Letter from Emile Bernard to Albert Aurier, 31 July 1890

Van Gogh Museum, Amsterdam

Letter from Anna van Gogh-Carbentus and Willemien van Gogh to Theo van Gogh, 31 July 1890

Van Gogh Museum, Amsterdam
[A]

Letter from Henri de Toulouse-Lautrec to Theo van Gogh, 31 July 1890

Van Gogh Museum, Amsterdam
[P]

Letter from Theo van Gogh to Jo van Gogh-Bonger, 1 August 1890

Van Gogh Museum, Amsterdam
[A]

Letter from Theo van Gogh to Anna van Gogh-Carbentus, 1 August 1890

Van Gogh Museum, Amsterdam
[A]

Letter from Albert Aurier to Theo van Gogh, 1 August 1890

Van Gogh Museum, Amsterdam

Letter from Paul Gauguin and Meijer de Haan to Theo van Gogh, 2 August 1890

Van Gogh Museum, Amsterdam

Letter from Eugène Boch to Theo van Gogh, 4 August 1890

Van Gogh Museum, Amsterdam
[A]

Letter from Paul Gachet to Theo van Gogh, c. 15 August 1890

Van Gogh Museum, Amsterdam

Letter from Claude Monet to Theo van Gogh, 15 August 1890

Van Gogh Museum, Amsterdam

Letter from John Russell to Theo van Gogh, August 1890

Van Gogh Museum, Amsterdam
[A]

Postcards of Auvers-sur-Oise, early twentieth century

Private collection

OBJECTS

Vincent van Gogh's palette, 1890
Wood, 27 × 35 cm
Musée d'Orsay, Paris
[89]

Paint tubes belonging to Vincent van Gogh, 1890
Musée d'Orsay, Paris

Vincent van Gogh
Portrait of Doctor Paul Gachet (The Man with the Pipe), 1890
Etched copper plate, 18.5 × 15.1 cm
Musée d'Orsay, Paris
[115]

Medicine kit belonging to Paul Ferdinand Gachet
Musée d'Histoire de la Médecine, Paris
[A]

Photo album belonging to Paul Ferdinand Gachet, c. 1865–95
Collection David and Heidi Freilich
[A]

BOOKS AND ARTICLES

Cent tableaux de Vincent van Gogh, Galerie Bernheim Jeune, Paris 1908
Musée d'Orsay, Paris
[P]

Cinquante tableaux de Vincent van Gogh, Galerie E. Druet, Paris 1909
Musée d'Orsay, Paris
[P]

Exposition d'oeuvres de Vincent van Gogh, Galerie Bernheim Jeune, Paris 1901
Musée d'Orsay, Paris
[P]

Lettres de Vincent van Gogh à Emile Bernard, publiées par Ambroise Vollard, Paris 1911
Musée d'Orsay, Paris
[P]

Albert Aurier
'Les isolés: Vincent van Gogh', *Mercure de France*, 1 January 1890, pp. 24–29
Bibliothèque Nationale de France – bibliothèque de l'Arsenal, Paris
[P]

Charles Bargue and Jean-Léon Gérôme
Cours de dessin. Exercices au fusain pour préparer à l'étude de l'académie d'après nature, plate 2, [Paris] 1870
Bibliothèque Nationale de France, Département des Estampes et de la Photographie, Paris
[P]

Emile Bernard
'Néo-traditionnistes [...] Vincent van Gogh', *La Plume*, 1 September 1891, pp. 300–01
Bibliothèque Nationale de France – bibliothèque de l'Arsenal, Paris
[P]

Emile Bernard
'Vincent van Gogh', *Mercure de France*, 1 April 1893, pp. 324–30
Bibliothèque Nationale de France – bibliothèque de l'Arsenal, Paris
[P]

Emile Bernard
'Lettres de Vincent van Gogh à son frère Théodore (Arles, 1887-88-89-90-91)', *Mercure de France*, 1 August 1893, pp. 303–15
Bibliothèque Nationale de France – bibliothèque de l'Arsenal, Paris
[P]

Francis
'Exposition Van Gogh', *La Vie moderne*, 24 April 1892, pp. 1–2
Bibliothèque Nationale de France – bibliothèque du musée de l'Opéra, Paris
[P]

Paul Ferdinand Gachet
Etude sur la mélancolie, degree thesis (Medicine), 1858
Bibliothèque Nationale de France, Paris
[P]

Octave Mirbeau
'Vincent van Gogh', *L'Echo de Paris*, 31 March 1891, p. 1
Bibliothèque Nationale de France – bibliothèque de l'Arsenal, Paris
[P]

Johanna van Gogh-Bonger
Vincent van Gogh. Brieven aan zijn broeder, 3 vol.
Maatschappij voor Goede en Goedkoope Lectuur, Amsterdam, 1914
Van Gogh Museum, Amsterdam
[P]

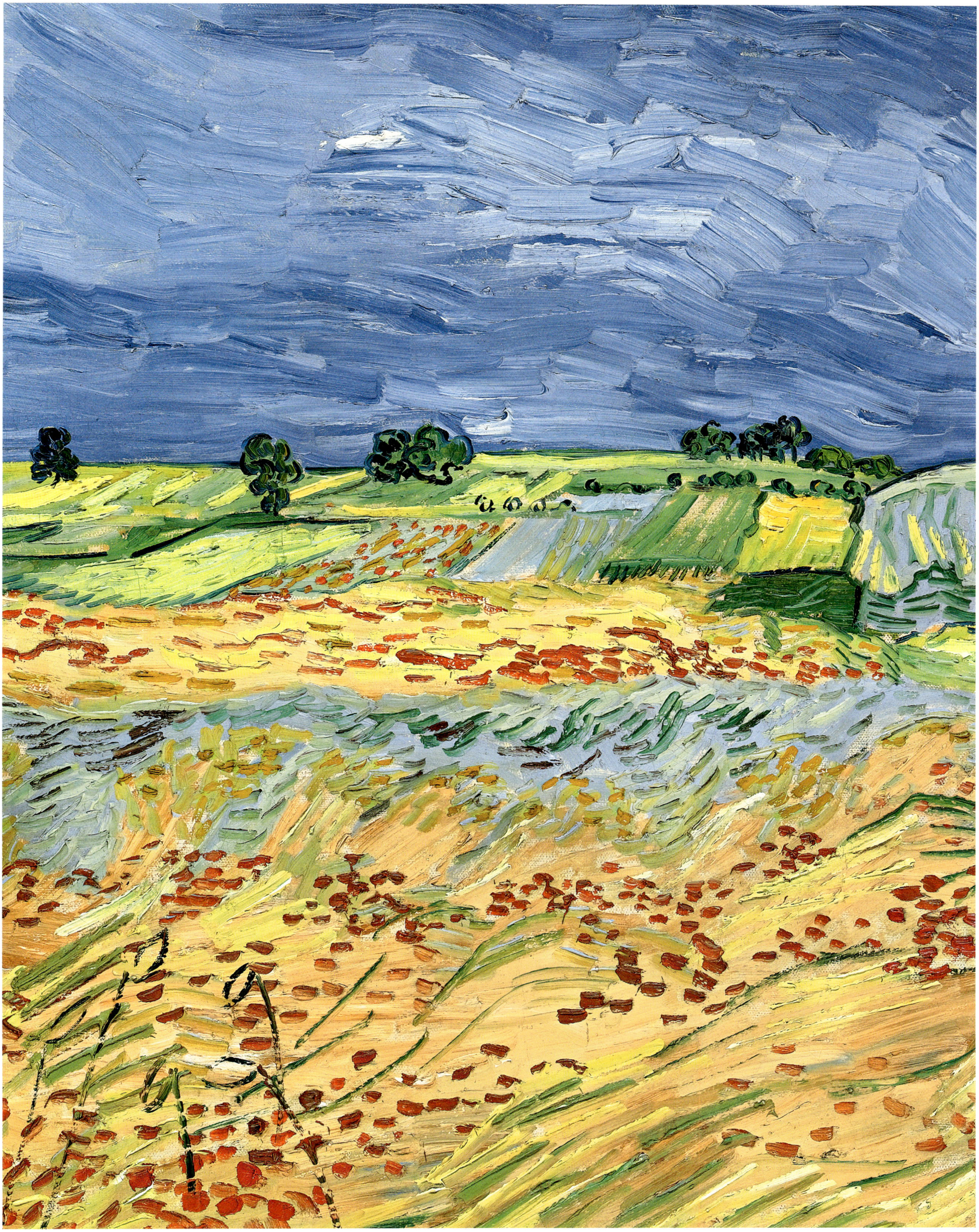

INDEX

Page numbers in *italic* refer to images; page numbers followed by an n refer to endnotes.

ABOUT THE AUTHORS

NIENKE BAKKER is the Van Gogh Museum's Senior Curator of Paintings. She was part of the editorial team behind the online version of Van Gogh's complete correspondence (www.vangoghletters.org) and the six-volume publication *Vincent van Gogh: The Letters* (2009). She has contributed to many exhibitions and publications on Vincent van Gogh and late nineteenth-century art, including *Van Gogh at Work* (Amsterdam, 2013), *Félix Vallotton* (Paris, Amsterdam and Tokyo, 2013–14), *Splendours & Miseries: Images of Prostitution in France, 1850–1910* (Paris and Amsterdam, 2015–16), *On the Verge of Insanity: Van Gogh and his Illness* (Amsterdam, 2016), *Van Gogh & Japan* (Sapporo, Tokyo, Kyoto and Amsterdam, 2017–18) and *Van Gogh and the Olive Groves* (Dallas and Amsterdam, 2021–22).

EMMANUEL COQUERY is Senior Curator at the Musée d'Orsay in Paris, in charge of the Centre de Ressources et de Recherches – Daniel Marchesseau, and curator of Van Gogh's paintings. He has published widely on painting and decorative arts of the seventeenth century and late nineteenth to early twentieth centuries.

BREGJE GERRITSE is a Researcher at the Van Gogh Museum. She curated the exhibitions *The Potato Eaters: Mistake or Masterpiece?* (Amsterdam, 2021–22) and *Van Gogh and the Avant-Garde: Along the Seine* (Chicago and Amsterdam, 2023–24), and contributed to the exhibition and publication *On the Verge of Insanity: Van Gogh and his Illness* (Amsterdam, 2016). She is currently a PhD candidate at the University of Amsterdam; her research topic is *The Reception of Vincent van Gogh in Paris, 1886–1914*.

TEIO MEEDENDORP is a Senior Researcher at the Van Gogh Museum. He is interested in authenticity issues and everything connected to the places where Van Gogh lived and worked. He wrote the catalogue of Van Gogh's drawings in the collection of the Kröller-Müller Museum, Otterlo, and has contributed to various publications on Van Gogh, including *Van Gogh's Studio Practice* (2013), *The Vincent van Gogh Atlas* (2015) and the exhibition catalogue *Van Gogh and the Olive Groves* (Dallas and Amsterdam, 2021–22).

SARA TAS is an Associate Curator at the Van Gogh Museum, where she curated the exhibition *Etel Adnan: Colour as Language* (Amsterdam, 2022). She is currently engaged on a long-term research project into Dr Paul Gachet. As part of this work, she presented the small exhibition *Dr Gachet & Van Gogh: Experiments in Etching* (Amsterdam, 2023). She is also working on the online catalogue of paintings and drawings by Van Gogh's contemporaries in the Van Gogh Museum. From 2013 to 2019 she was a Curator at the Jewish Museum in Amsterdam.

LOUIS VAN TILBORGH is a Senior Researcher at the Van Gogh Museum and Emeritus Professor of Art History, specializing in Van Gogh, at the University of Amsterdam. He has published widely on Van Gogh and was jointly responsible for several exhibitions on the artist, including *Van Gogh & Millet* (Amsterdam, 1988–89 and Paris, 1998–99), the major survey of Van Gogh's paintings at the Van Gogh Museum (1990), *On the Verge of Insanity: Van Gogh and his Illness* (Amsterdam, 2016), *Van Gogh & Japan* (Sapporo, Tokyo, Kyoto and Amsterdam, 2017–18) and *Van Gogh and the Olive Groves* (Dallas and Amsterdam, 2021–22).

WOUTER VAN DER VEEN is a researcher specializing in Van Gogh and Auvers-sur-Oise, CEO of Boussod, Valadon & Cie, and Associate Researcher at the University of Strasbourg. He received his doctorate from the University of Utrecht in 2007 with the dissertation *Van Gogh: A Literary Mind* (published 2009). His other publications include *Van Gogh in Auvers: His Last Days* (2010), *Le Capital de Van Gogh* (2018) and *Attacked at the Very Root: An Investigation into Van Gogh's Last Days* (2020) – reporting on his discovery of the location where Van Gogh painted his last masterpiece.

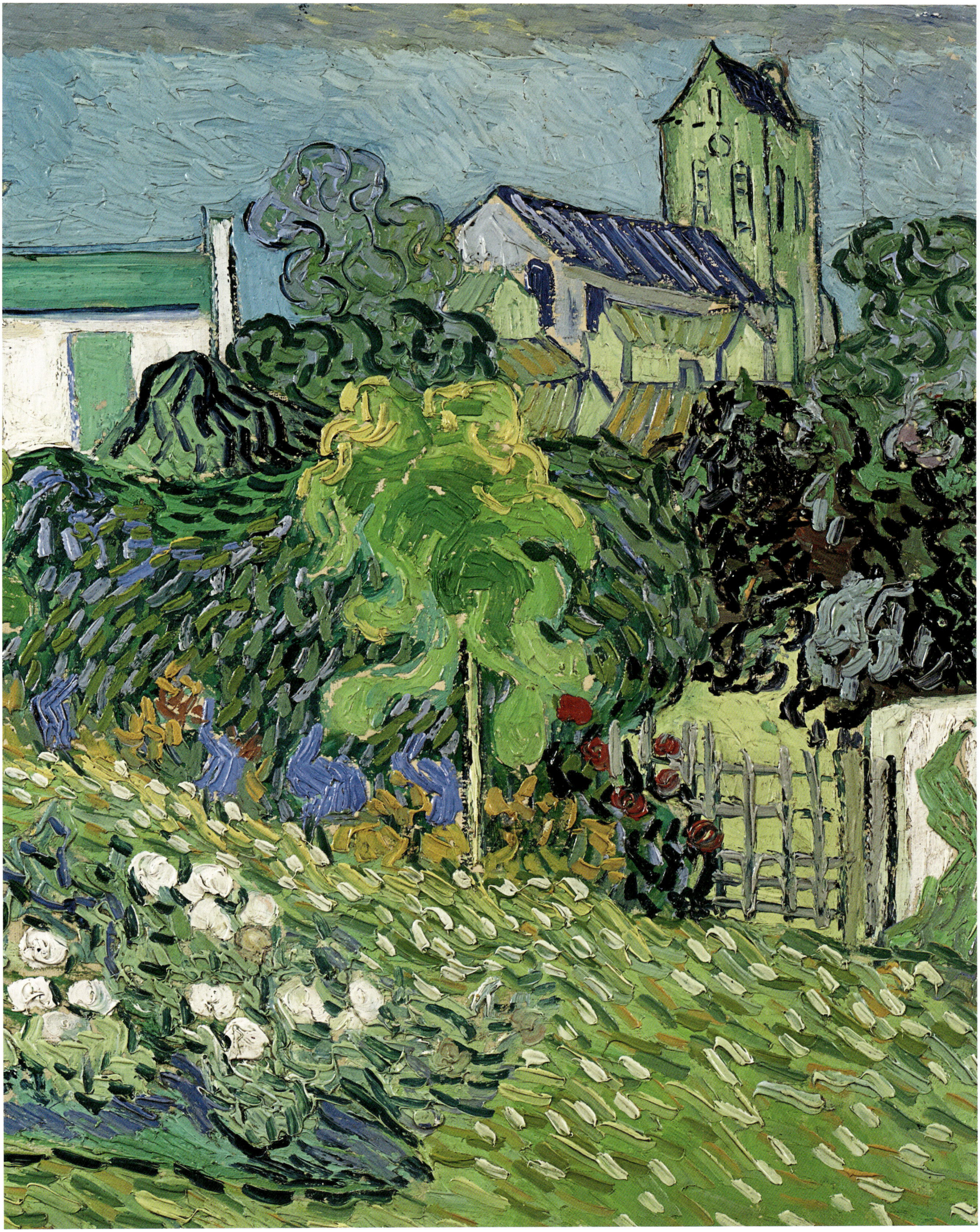

Van Gogh in Auvers-sur-Oise. His Final Months would not have been possible without the support and assistance we have received from numerous individuals over the years. First and foremost, we are grateful to our directors, Emilie Gordenker and Christophe Leribault, for their support and dedication to our project. We would also like to sincerely thank their predecessors, Axel Rüger and Laurence des Cars, and the Musée d'Orsay's former Head of Collections Sylvie Patry, for their encouragement in the initial stages of developing the exhibition. A special word of thanks should go to our fellow authors Bregje Gerritse, Sara Tas and Wouter van der Veen for their essential contribution to this publication and their enthusiasm and commitment to the project.

Furthermore, we are profoundly thankful to our colleagues at the many museums and institutions that generously lent works of art to the exhibition:

David Anderson and Kath Davies, Amgueddfa Cymru – National Museum Wales; James Rondeau, Jay Clarke and Gloria Groom, The Art Institute of Chicago; Marie-Hélène Peltier, Archives départementales du Val-d'Oise, Pontoise; Marja Sakari and Anna-Maria von Bonsdorff, Finnish National Gallery, Ateneum Art Museum, Helsinki; Stella Rollig and Markus Fellinger, Belvedere Museum, Vienna; Laurence Engel, Bibliothèque Nationale de France, Paris; Cameron Kitchin and Peter Bell, Cincinnati Art Museum; William Griswold and Heather Lemonedes Brown, The Cleveland Museum of Art; Agustín Arteaga and Nicole Myers, Dallas Museum of Art; Salvador Salort-Pons and Jill Shaw, Detroit Institute of Arts; Sam Keller and Ulf Küster, Fondation Beyeler, Riehen/Basel; Rosaline Wong, HomeArt; Lisette Pelsers and Renske Cohen Tervaert, Kröller-Müller Museum, Otterlo; Benno Tempel, Doede Hardeman and Frouke van Dijke, Kunstmuseum Den Haag; The Levett Collection; Leisa Paoli; Richard Aste, Liz Paris and Lyle Williams, McNay Art Museum, San Antonio; Anne-Marie Dubois, Musée d'art et d'histoire de l'Hôpital Sainte-Anne, Paris; Andréa Barbe-Hulmann, Musée d'histoire de la médecine, Paris; Marc-Olivier Wahler, Lada Umstätter and Victor Lopes, Musées d'art et d'histoire, Geneva; Sarah Ganz Blythe and Maureen O'Brien, Museum of Art, Rhode Island School of Design, Providence; Matthew Teitelbaum, Frederick Ilchman and Katie Hanson, Museum of Fine Arts, Boston; Susanna Pettersson and Magnus Olausson, Nationalmuseum, Stockholm; Bruno Girveau, Palais des Beaux-Arts, Lille; Dorothy Kosinski and Jonathan P. Binstock, The Phillips Collection, Washington; Rudolf Staechelin Collection; Brent Benjamin and Simon Kelly, Saint Louis Art Museum; Lukas Gloor, Stiftung Sammlung E.G. Bührle, Zurich; Maria Balshaw and Alex Farquharson, Tate, London; Adam Levine and Robert Schindler, Toledo Museum of Art; The Vincent van Gogh Foundation; and the private collectors who prefer to remain anonymous.

We also wish to thank those who have supported our project by helping locate works of art, facilitating loan requests, sharing research, or providing assistance and advice in numerous other ways:

Alexander Apsis, Magalie Bouchet, Laurent Bourcellier, Rupert Burgess, Philippe Büttner, Kitty Caiden, Marie-Christine Cavecchi, Nathalie Crinière, Fabrice Dassé, Ann Demeester, Walter Feilchenfeldt, Maciej Fiszer and his team, Manuel Fontán del Junco, Matthi Forrer, David and Heidi Freilich, Rudi Fuchs, Bruno Gaudichon, Rob Groenman, Ina Hindle, IJsbrand Hummelen, Dominique Janssens, Julian Kleyn, Stefan Koldehoff, Kerstin Kracht, Teresa Krasny, Michelle Kwok, Elisa Laristan, Hélène Lecarpentier, Jean-Yves Le Caz, Isabelle Lhomel, Jan Gorm Madsen, Isabelle Mézières, Hans den Nijs, Christophe Nobile, David Oakey, Devi Ormond, Petra Pearman, Elodie Perrault, Stéphanie Piard, Laura Prins, Thomas Reveau, Geneviève Roche-Bernard, Almudena Ros, Catherine Roth, Hélène Serlinger, Jean-François Serlinger, Leah Sheehan, Willemijn Somers, Susan Alyson Stein, Jan Swinkels, Adèle Taillefait, Lauren Tan, Joyce Townsend, Bénédicte Tremolières, Chelsea Troper, Daniel Vauvilliers, Emma Verweij, Ken Watson, and all the inhabitants of Auvers-sur-Oise.

Our thanks are also due to the past and present colleagues who contributed to the development of the exhibition and the production of this publication.

At the Van Gogh Museum, we would like to thank in particular Ann Blokland, Suzanne Bogman, Annemieke Bouma-Bouwmans, Geeta Bruin, Domenico Casillo, Sarah Dekker, Hannie Diependaal, Merel Dijkhuizen, Heleen van Driel, Sonia Gunning, Ronald van den Haak, Monique Hageman, Ruth Hoppe, Alain van der Horst, Edwin Kolster, Charlotte Kösters, Nico Lingbeek, Oda van Maanen, Babette Meerdink-Schenau, Anniek Meinders, Frederieke Melsen, Saskia van Oudheusden, Kathrin Pilz, Gideon Querido van Frank, Jolande Roest, Fleur Roos Rosa de Carvalho, Marvin Rot, Esther Roth, Edith Schreurs, Sarah Sprenger, Anne Steegstra, Marije Vellekoop, Josine Vermei and Saskia Wurpel.

At the Musée d'Orsay, our sincere thanks go especially to Marie-Caroline Dufayet and Marie Leimbacher, at the Publishing department, Clémence Maillard, Cristina Barroqueiro, Delphine Dupuy and Hélène Flon, at the Exhibition department, Béatrice Remoissenet, Candice Brunerie, Fanny Matz, at the Collections department, Guillaume Roux at the PR & sponsorship department, for their decisive involvement, and to many other colleagues from other teams at the museum, for their contribution to the project: Agnès Abastado, Mélinée Audiard, Saskia Bakhuys, Tommaso Benelli, Sandra Bernhard, Guillaume Blanc, Martine Bozon, Lionel Britten, Myriam Bru, Cécile Castagnola, Renaud Cesson, Michael Chkroun, Caroline Corbeau-Parsons , Sophie Crépy, Silvia Cristini, Milan Dargent and Sonia Hamza and their team, Jonathan Deledicq, Rodolphe Doucet, Mathilde Feugère, Didier Frémond, Antonine Fulla, Françoise Fur, Marion Guillaud, Clémence Guyomard-Deimat, Major Pascal Haffner, Amélie Hardivillier, Laurence Imbert, Éric Jouvenaux, Camille Kenarlikdjian, Jean-Claude Lalumière, Cyrille Lebrun, Ludovic Le Goff, Élise Lopez, Agnès Marconnet, Constance de Marliave, Claire Mayeux, Céline Meler, Nathalie Mengelle, Anat Meruk, Odile Michel, Florence Midy, Coline Monduc, Marie Ormevil, Paul Perrin, Romuald Picard, Thomas Porreca, Anne-Fleur Pouyat, Maud Ramier, Océane Régnier, Béatrice Remoissenet, Scarlett Reliquet and Hugo Valette.